Poland under Commu

This is the first English-language history of Poland from the Second World War until the fall of Communism. Using a wide range of Polish archives and unpublished sources in Moscow and Washington, Anthony Kemp-Welch integrates the Cold War history of diplomacy and inter-state relations with the study of domestic opposition and social movements. His key themes encompass political, social and economic history; the Communist movement and its relations with the Soviet Union; and the broader East–West context with particular attention to US policies. The book concludes with a first-hand account of how Solidarity formed the world's first post-Communist government in 1989 as the Polish people demonstrated what can be achieved by civic courage against apparently insuperable geo-strategic obstacles. This compelling new account will be essential reading for anyone interested in Polish history, the Communist movement and the course of the Cold War.

Anthony Kemp-Welch is Senior Lecturer at the School of History, University of East Anglia. His previous publications include *The Birth of Solidarity* (second edition, 1991) and, as co-author and editor, *Stalinism in Poland* (1999).

Poland under Communism

A Cold War History

A. Kemp-Welch

University of East Anglia

CAMBRIDGE UNIVERSITY PRESS
Cambridge, New York, Melbourne, Madrid, Cape Town, Singapore, São Paulo, Delhi

Cambridge University Press
The Edinburgh Building, Cambridge CB2 8RU, UK

Published in the United States of America by Cambridge University Press, New York

www.cambridge.org
Information on this title: www.cambridge.org/9780521711173

First published 2008

Printed in the United Kingdom at the University Press, Cambridge

A catalogue record for this publication is available from the British Library

Library of Congress Cataloguing in Publication data

ISBN 978-0-521-88440-2 hardback
ISBN 978-0-521-71117-3 paperback

To Klara, Hannah, Maia and Nadia

Contents

Preface

In 1989, Poland became the first country to leave communism peacefully. Its ruling generals invited leaders of the outlawed Solidarity to a Round Table on the future of communist power. Expecting to co-opt the opposition, they were swept away by an electoral avalanche and resigned. Solidarity then formed the world's first post-communist government. Within a few months, the Polish paradigm was emulated across all of Eastern Europe.

Afterwards, many actors claimed the credit. Soviet leaders from the Gorbachev era state that they took power in 1985 determined to withdraw from the region. They argue that their message was misunderstood by their East European counterparts, or simply disbelieved. Western officials are no more reticent in attributing to their own actions – whether CIA funding at critical junctures or the quiet word in the oppositional ear prior to the Round Table – the decisive tilting of the balance towards freedom. Some Catholic publicists – though not the Vatican – report that the Pope, in private audience with General Jaruzelski, put Poland on the path to power-sharing. Finally, Polish communists themselves declare that they always wished to liberate their country and had done so the moment geopolitics permitted. We are invited to believe that 1989 was the consummation of 'revisionism' they had espoused since 1956.

This book will take account of these prominent players. But it will also include the unsung heroes, easily overlooked by historians, and less able to claim their place in history. Politics also took place on the shop floor where grievances were discussed and strike posters sometimes put up. It occurred covertly in fields and forests at dead of night when farmers and their families planned to protect their property from seizure by the state. Local priests were political too, permitting uncensored publishing in their crypts, and steering their congregations from the pulpit to vote (or to abstain) in mono-Party elections. Thousands of young people jeopardised their future by joining the political opposition and the Solidarity underground.

Such activities by ordinary citizens, muted voices from the chorus, do eventually achieve legal expression. In this sense the Polish experience under communism holds wider lessons. The Polish success owed nothing to the threat of military force. It showed what could be achieved by civic courage against apparently insuperable geo-strategic obstacles. Refusing to be victims, they too helped to end the Cold War.

When I first visited (in 1971) Poland was opening to the West for capital and technology and communism was placating society with popular measures such as rebuilding Warsaw's Royal Castle, dynamited by the Nazis. Though writing a thesis on Stalinism in the 1930s, I became an increasingly engaged spectator of contemporary Poland. Under the pen-name 'Joseph Kay', I was able to record the origins of political opposition. During Solidarity's sixteen months of legality I was fortunate to attend its meetings at every level, including the Gdańsk Congress in 1981. These experiences informed my first book, *The Birth of Solidarity*.

After the fall, the British Academy enabled me to visit the post-communist historians assembling at the Polish Academy's new Institute of Political Studies. There was an immediate meeting of minds. The important works of its founder members Andrzej Paczkowski, Paweł Machcewicz and Andrzej Friszke have been seminal for mine. We jointly convened panels at the 1995 World Congress of Central and East European Studies (in Warsaw) which became *Stalinism in Poland, 1944–1956* (1999). Its Russian contributor, Sergei Kudryashov, has always been an indispensable guide to Moscow archives. Vital too are the findings and analyses of Mark Kramer (Harvard).

Poland under Communism was largely written during a Leverhulme Trust Research Fellowship and Study Leave extension funding from the British Arts and Humanities Research Council. The author gratefully acknowledges their generous assistance. He has also learned much from the other seventy-four contributors to the forthcoming three-volume *Cambridge History of the Cold War* being edited by Mel Leffler (Virginia) and Arne Westad (LSE).

Amongst many colleagues, Zbigniew Pełczyński (Oxford) has been encouraging throughout the project. The School of History at UEA has proved a happy home. Thanks are due to Michael Watson, my commissioning editor at CUP, and all his staff, especially Leigh Mueller. Quiet places to write were provided by Selima Hill in Lyme Regis, and by Joyce Divers and Willy Bulow in north Norwich. Thanks also to founder members of the Friday Club: Dave Corker, Ali Harvey, Ken Kennard and Andy Patmore. My main debts are to Alice and the dedicatees.

Abbreviations

AAN	Archive of Modern Acts
AFL/CIO	American Federation of Labor / Congress of Industrial Organisations
AK	Home Army
CC	Soviet Central Committee
COMECON	Council for Mutual Economic Assistance
CPSU	Soviet Communist Party
CRZZ	Central Council of Trade Unions
CSCE	Conference on Security and Cooperation in Europe
DDR	German Democratic Republic
DiP	'Experience and the Future' (Discussion Club)
FNU	Front of National Unity
IMF	International Monetary Fund
KBW	Polish Internal Security Corps
KIK	Clubs of Catholic Intelligentsia
KKP	National Coordinating Commission (of Solidarity)
KKW	National Executive Committee (of Solidarity)
KOK	National Defence Committee
KOR	Committee for the Defence of Workers
KPN	Confederation of Independent Poland
KPP	Poland's Communist Party (pre-war)
KSS	Social Self-Defence Committee (KOR)
KUL	Catholic University of Lublin
MKS	Interfactory Strike Committee
MKZ	Interfactory Founding Committee
MSW	Ministry of Internal Affairs
NIK	Supreme Control Commission
NKVD	Soviet secret police
NSA	National Security Archive
NSC	National Security Council
NSZZ	Independent self-governing trade union (Solidarity)
NZS	Independent students union

OPZZ	Official trade unions
ORMO	Voluntary reserve of the civic militia
PAP	Polish Press Agency
POP	Basic party organisation
PPN	Polish League for Independence
PPR	Polish Workers' Party
PPS	Polish Socialist Party
PRON	Patriotic Movement for National Rebirth
PSL	Peasants' Party
PZPR	Polish United Workers' Party
RAPP	Russian Association of Proletarian Writers
RFE	Radio Free Europe
ROPCiO	Movement for the Defence of Human and Civic Rights
RSFSR	Russian Soviet Federal Socialist Republic
SB	Security Service
SDKPiL	Social-Democratic Party of the Congress Kingdom of Poland and Lithuania
SKS	Students' Solidarity Committee
TRS	Provisional Council of Solidarity
UB	Secret police
UNRRA	UN Relief and Rehabilitation Administration
WRN	Provincial People's Council
ZiSPO	Stalin Factory in Poznán
ZLP	Polish Writers' Union
ZMP	Polish Youth Union
ZMS	Communist Youth Organisation
ZOMO	Motorised Units of Civil Militia (riot police)
ZSL	United Peasants' Party

1 Prelude

At the Tehran Conference of the 'Big Three' (Stalin, Churchill and Roosevelt), Churchill proposed that the future Polish state should lie between the 'Curzon Line' and the 'line of the Oder River, including within Poland East Prussia and Pomerania'. The official transcript does not record the American view. However, Roosevelt had a private meeting with Stalin during the proceedings (1 December 1943) at which he accepted the Soviet version of future Polish frontiers.[1] In return, he asked for no publicity for this endorsement. As an additional precaution, he did not inform his own State Department of the arrangement.[2] There were six or seven million US citizens of Polish origin, mainly Democrats, and he did not want to jeopardise their votes. He would seek an unprecedented fourth term in 1944. Polish-Americans were well organised and expected to hold the balance in key states such as New York, Illinois, Ohio and Pennsylvania. Stalin graciously concurred with these democratic niceties, noting that Soviet foreign policy did not suffer from such impediments. In fact, he was more than satisfied with their 'secret agreement'. He asked US envoy Harriman to confirm it in June 1944 and received a 'positive reply'.[3]

In the same month, the Prime Minister of the Polish government in exile visited the USA. Mikołajczyk was assured that the USA was opposed to any agreements of frontier changes in Europe – or elsewhere – prior to the end of the war. The Polish leader was promised a rich package of territorial advances, including oil fields in Eastern Galicia, all totally at variance with the Allied understandings at Tehran. The diplomatic historian Jan Karski, normally forthright in his analyses, merely notes

[1] W. Franklin (ed.), *The Conferences at Cairo and Tehran, 1943* (Washington, 1961), pp. 867–68.

[2] Mary E. Glantz, *FDR and the Soviet Union: The President's Battles over Foreign Policy* (Lawrence, Kans., 2005).

[3] S. Kudryashov, 'Diplomatic Prelude' in A. Kemp-Welch (ed.), *Stalinism in Poland, 1944–1956.* (New York, 1999), p. 36.

that the President 'misled' Mikołajczyk.[4] Roosevelt's own view was evidently that there was no way to prevent Moscow taking control of Poland, should it so desire, and he tried to bring the State Department round to this way of thinking.[5] His main attention was elsewhere, primarily on developing and achieving his conception of a new post-war order.

The Atlantic Charter (August 1941) had mentioned the need for a revived League of Nations. But for fear of antagonising US opinion – Congress refused to ratify the League Covenant in 1921 – its last Article referred to the essential need for disarmament 'pending the establishment of a wider and more permanent system of general security'. The President proposed a new United Nations to keep the peace. The new body would be truly inclusive. To ensure that the great powers of the day would join – to avoid a boycott like that of the League – they would be given a veto, which would enable them to block any operation mounted against them. In a structural innovation, the UN Charter talked about 'the Organisation and its Members', granting significant institutional authority to the former. In due course, the Secretary-General would emerge as a genuine international actor. Finally, the issue of sovereignty was side-stepped. Thus the Charter talked about the 'sovereign equality' of all its members (a hybrid jurists found puzzling). After Stalin demanded that the USSR, being a federal state, receive a seat each for its sixteen republics, to which the USA replied that it had even more constituent states, the super-powers signed up. The existence of Permanent Members of the Security Council meant that some were more equal than others.

At his first meeting with Molotov, Roosevelt expounded his conception of the Four Policemen. Thus the USA, UK, USSR and China would have the most significant military establishments in the post-war world, and between them would enforce world peace.[6] Molotov did not respond, though he commented in retirement that 'it was to our advantage to preserve the alliance with America. That was important.'[7] Stalin, however, saw the point at once, cabling his reaction to Molotov: 'Roosevelt is absolutely correct. Without creation of an association of the armed forces of England, the USA and the USSR able to forestall aggression, it will not

[4] Jan Karski, *The Great Powers and Poland, 1919–1945, from Versailles to Yalta* (London, 1985), p. 517.
[5] G. Lundestad, *The American Non-Policy towards Eastern Europe* (Tromso, 1978), p. 188.
[6] *Foreign Relations of the United States* (hereafter FRUS): *1942*, vol. III, pp. 568–9.
[7] *Sto sorok besed c Molotovym. Iz dnevnika F. Chueva* (Moscow, 1991), p. 76.

be possible to preserve peace in future.'[8] His omission of China was not accidental.

As Krystyna Kersten remarks, 'FDR thought issues such as Poland and Romania would be resolved within the UNO.'[9] As her magnificent study shows, Soviet policies towards Poland were advancing rapidly. In addition to the Ministry of Foreign Affairs, Red Army and other public bodies of the Soviet state, Comintern's successor played a crucial role in preparing the post-war order. Thus its formal dissolution (May 1943) was a deception. Its functions were taken over and expanded by the innocently entitled Department of International Information. This carried out a so-called 'national front' strategy for the post-war control of (communist) Eastern Europe. Re-named 'the strategy of Popular Democracy' after the war, it was also designed to minimise Western objections to the steady establishment of governments loyal to Moscow.[10]

In early 1944, senior Soviet diplomats prepared position papers on the post-war order. Thus Ivan Maisky, long-serving Soviet Ambassador in London, sent Molotov a *tour d'horizon* 'on desirable bases for the future world'. After a general overview, he turned to particular, problem countries. On Poland he declared:

> The purpose of the USSR must be *the creation of an independent and viable Poland; however we are not interested in the appearance of too big and too strong a Poland.* In the past, Poland was almost always Russia's enemy and no-one can be sure that the future Poland would become a genuine friend of the USSR (at least during the lifetime of the rising generation). Many doubt it, and it is fair to say there are serious grounds to harbour such doubts [emphasis in original].[11]

Consequently, he recommended that Poland be restricted to 'minimal size', according to ethnographic boundaries. Lwów and Wilno should become Soviet cities. At the same time, a different gloss was being put on statements for Allied consumption.

Stalin's response to Churchill's questions about post-war Poland were models of urbanity. 'Uncle J replied that of course Poland would be free and independent and he would not attempt to influence the kind of government they cared to set up after the war ... Of course the Polish Government (in exile) would be allowed to go back and to establish the

[8] E. Mark, *Revolution by Degrees. Stalin's National-Front Strategy for Europe, 1941–1947*, Cold War International History Project (hereafter CWIHP) Working paper no. 31 (Washington, 2001), p. 11.

[9] K. Kersten, *The Establishment of Communist Rule in Poland, 1943–1948* (Berkeley, Calif., 1991), p. 120.

[10] Mark, 'Revolution by Degrees', pp. 6–7.

[11] T. V. Volokitina (chief ed.), *Sovetskii faktor v vostochnoi Evrope, 1944–1953*, vol. I. *1944–1948 Dokumenty* (Moscow, 1999), pp. 29–30.

broad-based kind of government they had in mind. Poland was their country and they were free to return to it.' If Poland sought guarantees for their future security, then the Soviet Union would provide them. Reporting this to Roosevelt, Churchill added his understanding that the USA was unable to join in any guarantee 'other than those general arrangements for maintaining world peace which we have to make at the end of the war'.[12]

Roosevelt responded to Churchill that being too wedded to the 'present personalities of the Polish Government-in-exile' might give Stalin the erroneous impression of 'a design on your part to see established along the borders of the Soviet Union a government which rightly or wrongly they regard as containing elements irrevocably hostile to the Soviet Union'. He realised this was not the intent, since Churchill sought rather to preserve the right of countries to choose their government without outside interference 'and specifically to avoid the creation by the Soviet Government of a rival Polish government'. To Stalin, Roosevelt expressed confidence that 'a solution can be found which would fully protect the interests of Russia and satisfy your desire to see a friendly, independent Poland, and at the same time not adversely affect the cooperation so splendidly established at Moscow and Tehran.' He earnestly hoped that while this 'special question' remained unresolved, there would be no hasty or unilateral action that 'adversely affected the larger issues of international collaboration'.[13]

There is a premonition here that the balance of forces within the Grand Alliance was changing. The previously cosy Anglo-American 'special relationship' was becoming a less comfortable *ménage à trois*. Stalin must have been delighted, if not necessarily surprised, to see that an essential issue for him – the future of Poland – had become a bone of contention between the capitalist powers – the more so since the Soviet Union had as yet done rather little to impose its own solution.

The decisive moves took place in July 1944. On 22 July, the Soviet Union announced the formation of a Committee of National Liberation in Poland (the Lublin Committee). In response, Mikołajczyk sent Churchill and the US administration a strongly worded declaration, stating that the Soviet Union clearly intended 'to impose on Poland an illegal administration that has nothing in common with the will of the nation. All this is happening contrary to the repeated assurances of Marshal Stalin that he desires the restoration of an independent

[12] *Roosevelt and Churchill. Their Secret Wartime Correspondence* (New York, 1975), pp. 428–9 (5 February 1944).

[13] S. Butler (ed.), *My Dear Mr. Stalin. The Complete Correspondence of Franklin D. Roosevelt and Joseph V. Stalin* (New Haven, 2005), pp. 201–2.

Poland.'[14] A public statement by the government in exile on 25 July called the Lublin Committee 'an attempt by a handful of usurpers to impose on the Polish nation a political leadership which is at variance with the overwhelming majority'.[15] A week later, the Warsaw Uprising against the Germans began.

Stalin fully understood the intention of the Polish government in exile to liberate their capital before the Red Army arrived. He had not been consulted during its military preparations. He also had a personal score to settle, having been part of the Soviet offensive of 1920 when the Red Army was miraculously defeated outside Warsaw. Without logistical support, which Stalin withheld, even to the extent of denying Soviet facilities for Western air-drops until 9 September when they were too late, the Uprising was doomed. Some 200,000 Poles perished in the Uprising, after which the city was systematically destroyed. It is worth adding, however, that the Red Army did not remain idle outside Warsaw. It faced fierce attacks from the German defences, and suffered 23,483 fatalities in August alone. As Kudryashov comments, such 'objective factors' on the Warsaw front provided a good pretext for non-intervention.[16]

Once re-elected, Roosevelt felt freer to make representations to Stalin on the future Polish government. Roosevelt emphasised that these were not driven by any particular preference for the London government. But there was a growing recognition in Washington that the Lublin Committee represented only a small proportion of the Polish population. This intervention was unavailing. Moscow entered into diplomatic relations with the Lublin government on 5 January 1945.

On 3 February 1945, Roosevelt and Churchill flew in separate planes to the Crimea and were then conveyed by mountain roads to the Livadia Palace, outside Yalta. It was a gruelling journey, particularly for an ailing President. Next morning, Stalin arrived – overland – from Moscow. The three Allies, whose armies were now victorious on all fronts, agreed a settlement for Germany. The country was to be divided into three zones of occupation, with France later acquiring a fourth, on British insistence. Germany would be jointly administered by an Allied Council and an economic settlement would be agreed later. Meantime, Stalin's bill for $20 billion reparations was noted. Poland's eastern border would be the 'Curzon Line', with minor modifications, thus granting the Soviet Union large new areas. Poland was to be compensated by 'substantial

[14] *Documents on Polish–Soviet Relations, 1939–1945* (London, 1961), vol. II, no. 164.
[15] *Idem* no. 165.
[16] 'Diplomatic Prelude' in A. Kemp-Welch (ed.), *Stalinism in Poland*, pp. 38–9.

accessions of territory in the north and west'. This would be finalised at a later peace conference.

The future of formerly Nazi-occupied areas, and above all the shape of the government of Poland, proved more contentious. Underlying discussion was the fact of the Red Army's presence in both the Balkans and substantial areas of Eastern and Central Europe. The conference began with Soviet armies seventy miles from Berlin. Given that Sovietisation was also being imposed in these areas, to question their future governance seemed somewhat artificial. Nonetheless a statement of democratic intent was made. Roosevelt proposed a 'Declaration on Liberated Europe', which reaffirmed the Atlantic Charter's principle of 'the right of all peoples to choose the form of government under which they will live'. The Declaration, to which Stalin solemnly subscribed, called for the formation of 'interim governmental authorities broadly representative of all domestic elements in the population and pledged to the earliest possible establishment through free elections of government responsive to the will of the people'. No mechanisms for monitoring the conduct of such elections were put in place, nor did Roosevelt press the State Department's advice that a European High Commission should supervise implementation of the Declaration. This was particularly a problem for Poland.

Churchill reminded Stalin that his country had gone to war for Poland. 'Honour' demanded that the 150,000 Poles who had fought with the Allies should not be abandoned and their government could not just be disowned.[17] Roosevelt, though speaking as a 'visitor from another hemisphere', acknowledged that some gesture was needed for the six million Poles in his country, 'indicating that the United States was in some way involved with the question of freedom of elections'. After an extensive exchange of views, it was agreed that a new Polish coalition should be formed, to include members of both the government in exile and the Lublin Committee. In another verbal commitment that did not achieve reality, the new interim government was 'to hold free and unfettered elections as soon as possible'.

Roosevelt gave an upbeat report of Yalta on 1 March 1945. 'I am confident that the Congress and the American people will accept the results of this conference as the beginnings of a permanent structure of peace.'[18] But within weeks, the emptiness of the Polish settlement became apparent. As Churchill complained to Roosevelt: 'After a fairly

[17] J. Charmley, *Churchill's Grand Alliance. The Anglo-American Special Relationship, 1940–1957* (London, 1995), p. 141.

[18] *Public Papers and Addresses of Franklin D. Roosevelt*, vol. 13 (New York, 1950) (1 March 1945).

promising start, Molotov is now refusing to accept any interpretation of the Crimea proposals except his own extremely rigid one. He is attempting to bar practically all our candidates from the consultations (for the Polish government), is taking the line that he must base himself on the views of Berut [*sic*] and his gang, and has withdrawn from his offer that we should send observers to Poland.' Churchill saw Poland as a 'test case between us and the Russians of the meaning which is to be attached to such terms as democracy, sovereignty, independence, representative government, and free and unfettered elections'.[19] The President discouraged a message to Stalin in these terms, preferring a lower-level, ambassadorial approach. Churchill replied: 'Poland has lost her frontier. Is she now to lose her freedom?'[20]

Roosevelt's plans for a new world body, which Stalin seemed to regard as a somewhat marginal initiative, gave Moscow a lever with Washington. In return for participation in the putative United Nations, and also for complying with American wishes that the Soviet Union, on the completion of war with Germany, should join that against Japan, Moscow sought concessions. They were principally on the Polish issue.[21]

Ambiguous drafting at Yalta had attempted to gloss over the likelihood that the Lublin Government and Moscow would prevail. The key sentence in the Yalta Protocol stated, 'The Provisional Government which is now functioning in Poland should ... be reorganised on a broader democratic basis with the inclusion of democratic leaders from Poland itself and from abroad.' Roosevelt admitted later, 'as clearly shown in the agreement, somewhat more emphasis is placed on the Lublin Poles than on the other two groups from whom the new Government is to be drawn'.[22]

In one of his last messages to Stalin, Roosevelt put the position squarely: 'I must make it clear to you that any such solution which would result in a thinly disguised continuance of the present Warsaw regime would be unacceptable and would cause the people of the United States to regard the Yalta agreements as having failed.'[23] He stated that representation of non-Warsaw elements should be substantial. Stalin replied that it was Roosevelt who was derogating from the Yalta Agreement and proposed a formula under which non-Lublin Poles would be given one fifth of the Cabinet posts, without specifying their comparative importance.[24]

[19] *Roosevelt and Churchill*, pp. 662–4 (8 March 1945). [20] *Idem* p. 671 (13 March 1945).
[21] G. Lundestad, *The American Non-Policy towards Eastern Europe*, p. 194.
[22] FRUS: 1945, vol. V, p. 189. [23] Butler (ed.), *My Dear Mr. Stalin*, p. 311.
[24] *Ibid.* pp. 318–20.

On 12 April, the new US President Truman announced a policy of continuity. Roosevelt's own ambiguities, and the usual complications of policy-making in Washington, made that easier to declare than to define. But the imperatives were clear: to end the war with Japan and to find an effective way to deal with Stalin's Russia. The latter led to a division of opinion. Some sought a tough approach to the Soviets, particularly against their imposition of communist or pro-communist governments in Soviet-occupied Eastern Europe. A milder approach encouraged Truman to address Stalin's own security imperatives and reach accommodations with them where possible. That in turn meant achieving some consensus with the Soviets on the nature of the post-war order.[25]

The first days of the Truman Administration were coterminous with signature of a treaty of mutual assistance between the Soviet Union and the Warsaw Government (21 April), and the Soviet insistence that it be the sole Polish representative at the inauguration of the United Nations in San Francisco and other international forums. At his first meeting with Molotov (23 April) President Truman told the Soviets bluntly to stick to the Yalta Agreement on Poland. He made clear that American economic assistance, essential to Russia's post-war recovery, would depend upon compliance. The intention was not nit-picking over the words of an international agreement but to stand up to the Russians. This was given urgency by the arrest of sixteen Poles prominent in the anti-Nazi underground, and their imprisonment in the Lubyanka. They were brought to trial in Moscow in June 1945.

Talks between Harry Hopkins and Stalin did not make progress on future elections or political freedom in Poland. However, the American envoy conceded that the present Warsaw government would constitute 'a majority' of the new Polish provisional government. It was sanctified at Potsdam.

The successful testing of the atomic bomb (July 1945) gave new impetus to the incipient Cold War. Truman told Stalin about it during the Potsdam Conference. The newly styled 'Generalissimo' affected surprise about a development he had known about through espionage almost from its inception. Its first usages a few weeks later were intended, *inter alia*, to forestall Soviet involvement in the Far East, as promised at Yalta. In October, Truman called the atomic bomb a 'sacred trust' for all mankind, while remaining vague about placing it under some international supervision.

[25] M. Leffler, *A Preponderance of Power: National Security, the Truman Administration and the Cold War* (Stanford, 1992).

Truman used his Navy Day address (27 October) to outline a new agenda. American power would be used to promote self-determination and national sovereignty. Territorial changes should not be imposed upon peoples without their will. The United States would not recognise governments created by fait accomplis.[26] This policy of non-recognition was accompanied by non-intervention in the sphere already under Soviet hegemony.

Poland henceforth occupies a much smaller part in super-power relations. As Walt Rostow puts it, 'after Potsdam, the question of the fate of democracy in Poland virtually disappeared from Truman's and [his new Secretary of State] Byrnes' agenda.'[27] Thereafter, American leverage over the course of events in Poland was largely economic. A significant package was ready by mid-1945, including UNRRA supplies, and export credits. A six-point plan was presented to the Warsaw Government in early 1946. It included most-favoured nation status, compensation for nationalisation of American property and a commitment to free trade. The only overtly political condition was point 6: Polish adherence to the Potsdam declaration on free elections. But the weakness of this leverage was demonstrated by Poland's referendum.

Instead of the promised 'free election', three issues were brought before the public. (1) Abolition of the Senate. No replacement was named, leaving open the (theoretical) possibility for representatives of self-governing organisations; (2) land reform and nationalisation; (3) Poland's Western borders. The poll was held on 30 June 1946. The turnout was impressive: almost 12 million or 85% of those eligible to vote. An official declaration on 12 July stating that 68.2% had voted 'yes' for abolition contrasted with the 83.3% 'no' vote claimed by Mikołajczyk, who had urged a 'no' vote against. Though neither figure seems reliable, the true one will probably never be known.[28] Issues 2 and 3 were answered with massive affirmatives, again on the official figures. On 19 August 1946, the British and American governments formally protested to Moscow about electoral irregularities. They were told not to interfere in Polish sovereign affairs.

The locus of East–West confrontation in Europe shifted to Germany. Yet Poland remained a key issue in this regard, and would remain so throughout the Cold War. An independent Poland would not threaten the Soviet Union in narrow military terms, as the subsequent neutralisation of Austria and Finland showed. But it would make it mightily

[26] *Public Papers of the Presidents: Harry S. Truman, 1945* (Washington, 1961), pp. 431–8.
[27] W. W. Rostow, *The Division of Europe after World War II, 1946* (Austin, 1981), p. 18.
[28] Kersten, *The Establishment of Communist Rule*, pp. 280–3.

difficult for Moscow to maintain security and supply routes between its home base and East Germany where twenty divisions were stationed. A democratic Poland would also reduce Soviet-controlled Eastern Germany to the status of a pawn in some future power-play, a bargaining counter with the West to assure reparations or tool to prevent German reunification.[29] Worst of all for the Soviet Union, a reunited Germany might opt for neutrality, or even join the Western bloc. But that was unthinkable whilst a Cold War continued.

As 1946 proceeded, it became more generally accepted that world politics and economics were splitting into two camps. On 9 February, Stalin attributed this to the 'development of world economic and political forces on the basis of modern monopoly capitalism'. The Western counterpart was Churchill's 'Sinews of Peace' speech in Fulton, Missouri on 5 March. It has lodged in historical memory for the famous sentence,

> From Stettin [*sic*] in the Baltic to Trieste in the Adriatic, an iron curtain has descended across the Continent. Behind that line lie all the capitals of the ancient states of Central and Eastern Europe. Warsaw, Berlin, Prague, Vienna, Budapest, Belgrade, Bucharest and Sofia, all the famous cities and the populations around them lie in what I must call the Soviet sphere, and all are subject in one form or another, not only to Soviet influence but to a very high, and in some cases, increasing, measure of control from Moscow.[30]

The old doctrine of the balance of power was thus unsound. Not only were communist parties and their lackeys imposing their regimes across eastern Europe, those beyond the reach of Soviet armies were still plotting to seize power in southern and western Europe. Less well-remembered, though more controversial at the time, was his continued championing of the Anglo-American special relationship.[31] He argued that Anglo-Saxons needed to unite to withstand the new totalitarianism. The ensuing controversy did not help Truman's cause.

In November 1946, the Republicans won a crushing victory in the congressional elections. Though fought on bread and butter issues, work stoppages, high taxation and inflation, the result had important international implications. To address these issues at home, Truman needed tax cuts and a smaller government. At the same time, a deteriorating international outlook argued for greater foreign aid and increased military capabilities. Not for the last time, rhetoric came to the rescue. 'At the present moment in world history nearly every nation must choose

[29] Rostow, *The Division of Europe*, p. 15.

[30] R. R. James (ed.), *Churchill Speaks. Winston S. Churchill in Peace and War. Collected Speeches, 1897–1963* (New York, 1981), p. 881.

[31] See Charmley, *Churchill's Grand Alliance*, Chapter 18.

between alternate ways of life. The choice is too often not a free one ... Collapse of free institutions and loss of independence would be disastrous not only for them but for the world ... Should we fail to aid Greece and Turkey in this fateful hour, the effect will be far-reaching.'[32]

The 'Truman Doctrine' was indeed far-reaching. Initially asking Congress for $400 million for the Eastern Mediterranean, it implied additional funds might be requested for other areas of the globe threatened with subversion or aggression. Without supporting freedom 'wherever it was threatened', the US's own security would be endangered. His memoirs recall a global scenario. 'If we were to turn our back on the world, areas such as Greece, weakened and divided as a result of the war, would fall into the Soviet orbit without much effort on the part of the Russians. The success of Russia in such areas and our avowed lack of interest would lead to the growth of domestic communist parties in European countries such as France and Italy, where there were already significant threats.' American inaction 'could only result in handing to the Russians vast areas of the globe now denied to them'.[33] Truman appointed General Marshall as Secretary of State and he in turn set up a Policy Planning Staff under George Kennan. 'Together they formulated a strategy not simply for containing Soviet power, but eventually for winning the Cold War.'[34]

American Cold War objectives may be summarised under three headings. Firstly, the USA should move from unilateral 'isolationism' to a forward strategy of global defence. This meant bases abroad during peace-time. The 'heartlands' of Asia and Europe were deemed areas of essential US national interest, to be denied to any potential aggressor. Second, there should be a policy of military strength, including retaining a monopoly over the atomic bomb, at least for the foreseeable future. Finally, the world economy should be directed towards liberalisation, utilising the Bretton Woods Agreement and bodies such as the International Monetary Fund and World Bank to promote 'peace and prosperity'. These objectives overlapped and were thought to be self-reinforcing.

Washington analysts saw no immediate danger on the Asian continent. Japan was firmly held by US occupation authorities under General Douglas MacArthur. Its new constitution precluded a revival of militarism, even for minimal defensive purposes. Attention thus fell on Western Europe. Nothing would damage US interests more than 'the conquest

32 *Public Papers of the Presidents. Harry S. Truman, 1947* (Washington, 1963), pp. 176–80.

33 H. Truman, *Memoirs: Years of Trial and Hope* (New York, 1965), pp. 123–8.

34 M. Leffler, 'Truman, Grand Strategy, and the Cold War, 1945–1952', in M. Leffler and O. Westad (eds.), *Cambridge History of the Cold War*, vol. II (forthcoming).

or communisation' of Britain and France. To avert that eventuality, the economic resurgence of Germany was essential: German coal, for instance, was essential to industrial recovery in France. More generally, German resources would be the 'motor' driving European economic recovery. An underlying concern, not always made public, was that more prosperous Western European states would become politically more stable and less prone to communism.

Stalin took the opposite view: Germany had caused the war and should pay for it. Moscow thus treated its zone as an area for exploitation. Germany should not be allowed to recover: its size of population, strategic position and economic potential made it too dangerous for the rest of Europe. A demilitarised and agricultural, even pastoral, Germany would be preferable. In a somewhat inconsistent addition, Moscow demanded $20 billion as reparations for war-damage, without explaining how Germany might be able to pay.

The Potsdam Conference had agreed to treat Germany as a single economic unit. A general reparations plan was to be negotiated within six months. Given the Soviet policy of dismantling factory equipment in its zone – and in much of Eastern Europe and Manchuria – the American negotiators concentrated on preventing the same happening in the Western zones. Potsdam envisaged a four-Power settlement, through the Council of Foreign Ministers, leading towards an eventually reunited Germany. Afterwards, the search for cooperative solutions was abandoned and unilateral action by each side became the norm.

On 5 June 1947, General Marshall gave his Harvard commencement address. He announced substantial US funding for a European Recovery Programme. The generous and somewhat vaguely worded nature of this announcement gave Moscow pause, as intended. There was some risk that the Soviet Union might participate. But as Acheson noted, 'If the Russians came in the whole project would probably be unworkable because the amount of money involved in restoring both eastern and western Europe would be so colossal it could never be got from Congress, especially in view of the strong and growing reaction against the Soviet Union.'[35] As the small-print emerged, however, Moscow came to see the Marshall Plan as subversion, potential or actual, of its new allies in Eastern Europe. At its starkest, the Plan could be seen as an attempt to wean them away from the Soviet sphere and integrate them in a capitalist West.

An influential study by the Soviet economist Evgenii Varga in 1946 had suggested that a limited form of planning could be introduced in Western

[35] Quoted by J. M. Jones, *The Fifteen Weeks (February 21–June 5, 1947)* (New York, 1955), pp. 252–63.

Europe, thus helping it to avoid a return to the crises of the Great Depression. This implied both that Western European economies had the capacity to stabilise themselves – contrary to the analysis in Washington – and that a constructive Soviet policy of cooperation with them could pay dividends. Varga was forced to recant his views as soon as the Plan had been rejected.[36] Before that, Molotov asked him for an economist's assessment of US motivations.

Varga reported that the US economy needed to increase exports to avert depression. Since the Europeans could not afford to pay, they would receive massive credit under the Plan. The plan was a way to fill the 'dollar gap' – the huge import–export imbalance – between Europe and the United States. He might have added that the credits would allow Germany to pay its French and British reparations, who could thus repay their wartime US borrowings, thus adding to the multiplier effect. Going beyond economics, Varga suggested that Marshall's demand for an all-European response, if met, would be followed by an American demand for the economic unification of Germany and possibly the removal of the 'iron curtain' as preconditions. There seemed scope for negotiation here.

Molotov agreed to attend the Paris Conference to discuss Marshall's Plan. He also suggested the Polish, Czechoslovak and Yugoslav governments attend the meeting. But there soon came a change of mind. One suspicion, from the Soviet Ambassador in Washington, was that the Marshall Plan represented little more than the Truman Doctrine in disguise. It was a somewhat more subtle means of involving Western European governments in policies against the Soviet Union. Hence, the call for a European 'initiative' was the prelude to enlisting their support for American policies directed against the Soviet Union. He advised Soviet attendance as a precaution to sound out the Plan, proposing a country-based response. If it condemned eastern Europe to supplying raw materials to the more developed West, it could be rejected.

Polish officials expressed keen interest in the Plan. Their Washington Ambassador thought that negative commentary appearing in the Soviet press did not exclude the possibility of Soviet participation.[37] Such prospects lingered on a little longer. The Polish Foreign Minister, Zygmunt Modzelewski, told the US Ambassador that he felt certain that his country would attend.[38] Possibly, this interest from its allies fed Soviet

[36] S. Parrish, *New Evidence on the Soviet Rejection of the Marshall Plan, 1947*, CWIHP Working Paper no. 9 (Washington, 1994), p. 10.

[37] *FRUS: 1947*, vol. III, p. 261. [38] *Ibid.* p. 313.

suspicions that the whole Plan was designed not simply to stabilise the West but also to turn eastern Europe into an American dependency.[39] Even after Molotov had withdrawn from the Paris Conference, he recommended the Czechoslovak delegation should attend the next meeting, even though the main instruction was to disrupt it by walking out with 'as many delegates of other countries as possible'.

But a Czechoslovak government delegation was abruptly summoned to Moscow. Its senior communist Gottwald was received by Stalin first, then the full delegation was called to the Kremlin. Stalin stated that Moscow had concluded, on the basis of diplomatic advice, that in the guise of an offer of financial assistance to Europe, the Plan was intended to create a 'western bloc against the Soviet Union'. Czechoslovakia should not assist this effort to isolate the Soviet Union. The Czech Jan Masaryk explained that his country's industry was reliant on Western assistance. He mentioned that a Polish delegation, led by the economist Hilary Minc, had been in Prague to affirm the same need. Molotov replied by asking whether he wanted to take part in a meeting 'against the Soviet Union'.[40] Masaryk commented afterwards, 'I went to Moscow as a Foreign Minister of an independent sovereign state; I came back as a lackey of the Soviet government.'[41]

The Polish government was also forced to withdraw. Early on 9 July, Polish leader Bierut had told the US Ambassador that no decision had been taken. He was summoned back to the Foreign Ministry that evening to hear that Poland would not be attending.[42] Thus, whatever its original intentions, the Marshall Plan confirmed the division of Europe. Economic development in each half would diverge thereafter.

Soviet policy shifts during the summer of 1947. Up to that point, the door was left open to the West in the sense that financial assistance for Soviet recovery could be acceptable, if there were no strings. Now the Soviet Union sought recognition as a responsible great power. No longer a pariah in international relations, it was an important war victor and sought to have its new-found status recognised in world affairs. There was fresh determination to assert authority in its own 'sphere'.

A few days before the Marshall Plan was announced, Stalin proposed that the Polish leader Gomułka convene a 'Special Information Conference' in Poland, with attendance restricted to nine European

[39] Molotov thought so in retirement: *Sto sorok besed*, pp. 88–9.

[40] G. P. Murashko *et al.* (eds.), *Vostochnaia Evropa v dokumentakh rossiiskikh arkhivov, 1944–1953*, vol. I (Moscow, 1997), p. 673.

[41] R. Bruce-Lockhart, *My Europe* (London, 1952), p. 125.

[42] *FRUS: 1947*, vol. III, pp. 320–2.

communist parties. Stalin's initial agenda was modest: to exchange information 'on the situation in each country'. They would launch a new journal on 'questions of the workers' movement in the individual countries', but no other organisations would be set up. When invitations were sent out, the scope had widened considerably. 'A representative of the Soviet Communist Party' would deliver an expert report on the international situation, and the meeting would elaborate a 'common point of view' on its main themes. These would include the 'duty of democratic organizations to struggle against the attempts by American imperialism to enslave the countries of Europe economically ("Marshall Plan")'.[43]

At the founding conference, Zhdanov condemned 'the crusade against Communism proclaimed by America's ruling circle with the backing of the capitalist monopolies'. American grand strategy envisaged creating a vast network of overseas bases: 'America has built, or is building, air and naval bases in Alaska, Japan, Italy, South Korea, China, Egypt, Iran, Turkey, Greece, Austria and Western Germany. There are American military missions in Afghanistan and even in Nepal. Feverish preparations are being made to use the Arctic for purposes of military aggression.' A second and important supplement to this strategy was economic. 'American imperialism' was endeavouring to turn the post-war shortages in European countries to its own advantage. An extortionate credit system was being put in place to open up Europe to US capital and marketing; its proposed 'economic assistance' had the intention of enslavement. Finally, a huge cultural campaign – through cinema, radio, the Church and the press – was designed to promote anti-Soviet and anti-communist propaganda. In consequence, the world had split into 'two camps (*lageria*)'.

Robert Tucker sees this as a defining moment in Soviet official thinking.[44] After a period of post-war ambiguity, the division of the world into 'two camps' was now complete. It was therefore necessary to create an 'anti-imperialist democratic camp' controlled from Moscow. The implications were extensive. Expectations of future divisions within the 'imperialist camp', in particular the long-predicted Anglo-American dispute over the British Empire, were jettisoned. The utility of collaboration between communist and non-communist parties was questioned; broad anti-fascist fronts and the notion of a 'parliamentary road' to socialism were abandoned. The Soviet experience, with its distinctive 'model' of development, gained centrality.

At the founding conference of Cominform, the Soviet delegation took the lead. But the original agenda provided for individual reports from the

[43] A. di Biagio, 'The Establishment of the Cominform' in G. Procacci (ed.), *The Cominform, Minutes of Three Conferences 1947/1948/1949* (Milan, 1994), pp. 11–13.

[44] Robert C. Tucker, *The Soviet Political Mind* (New York, 1973), pp. 222–8.

nine participating parties. Welcoming delegates, Gomułka took care to stress the informality of the occasion. 'A need to exchange views' had arisen amongst the nine parties present (including the French and Italian). It confirmed the correctness of Engels' prediction some seventy years earlier that proletarian solidarity could be asserted 'even without the bond of a formal association'. Communist solidarity was contrasted with Lenin's prophecy that 'harmonious and proportionate development' was impossible amongst capitalists.[45] Poland had taken a negative attitude towards the 'so-called Marshall Plan'. Whilst not ruling out the use of American credits, the Plan was not a 'raft of salvation'. On the contrary, 'we see it as a form of expansion which threatens the sovereignty of the European state and dooms the countries of Europe to the role of America's semi-colonies'.

The East European parties were surprised to hear a sharp critique of the policies of their Western European counterparts – French and Italian. Moreover, the Soviet delegation – in constant touch with Stalin by ciphered telegrams – brushed aside objections to making Cominform public. Gomułka in particular had raised doubts about the constitution of a 'legal Informburo'.[46] He held a well-founded fear that this would be seen in the West as a resurrection of the Comintern.

The 'two camps' theory, by now official policy of the Comintern, brought with it a dual notion of sovereignty. West European countries were to be sovereign in the traditional sense: their national independence should be protected against the rapacity of American imperialism. It was pointed out, by Gomułka amongst others, that East European states, relying 'on their forces alone', would be unable to block the expansionist plans of the USA.[47] But East European sovereignty was now limited in a new sense. Its own domestic opponents were henceforth dupes or lackeys of external enemies, 'reactionaries' or 'agents of British and American imperialism'.

American thinking about international affairs reached a similar *impasse*. Morgenthau's classic text argued in the Machiavellian tradition that all politics, including international politics, is concerned with power.[48] Consequently law and morality have little place in the political arena. A state's primary motive is 'national interest' and is achieved through power. The consequences for the growing Cold War were fateful. All states now had a permanent 'security dilemma', expressed in arms-racing and alliances, which led to huge standing armies in peace-time. Since the existence of 'conflict' was given, no analysis of root causes was undertaken. The prophecy became self-fulfilling.

45 *The Cominform*, pp. 36–9. 46 Di Biagio, 'The Establishment of the Cominform', p. 28.
47 *The Cominform*, p. 339. 48 H. Morgenthau, *Politics Among Nations* (Chicago, 1948).

2 Stalinism

> Stalinism did not fall from the skies: It was eagerly created by thousands of supporters.
>
> Nadezhda Mandel'stam, 1970

The Stalinism of the Soviet Union and that of Poland had many commonalities. The theory arrives in Poland fully formed along with the Red Army – the economist Włodzimierz Brus calls it 'ready-to-wear' – but implementation proceeded more slowly. Brus argues that a 'third stage' can be squeezed in between the liberation from Nazism and full Stalinism three years later. He refers to this as an acceptance of socialist goals but reluctance to impose them in a Stalinist manner.[1] There was also a difference of duration. Soviet Stalinism endured for a quarter of a century. In Poland it lasted less than half this time. Even from 1948, though confronted and transformed, Polish society is not crushed as an independent force. As Krystyna Kersten notes, historical and cultural roots made Polish society more immune to forcible transformation than many of its neighbours. It was more able to retain the 'green shoots of recovery'.[2]

Stalin had always recognised that Polish communists would face a cultural challenge. In a hand-written note of 1 September 1945 to Roman Zambrowski (head of the Polish Party's organisation and personnel department) he called for co-ordination of plans with the CPSU (Soviet Communist Party) for political literature and cinema.[3] Underlying his correspondence was the fear, which Lenin had expressed soon after the Russian Revolution, that a politically vanquished population might yet impose its culture on the conquerors.[4]

[1] W. Brus, 'Stalinism and the "People's Democracies"' in Robert C. Tucker (ed.), *Stalinism: Essays in Historical Interpretation* (New York, 1977).

[2] K. Kersten, '1956 – Punkt zwrotny', *Krytyka* 1993 (40).

[3] Archiwum Akt Nowych (hereafter AAN) Oddział VI, teczka (p.) 112, tom (t.) 25, p. 19.

[4] Lenin's 'On Co-operation' (1922) is discussed in M. Lewin, *Lenin's Last Struggle* (London, 1975), pp. 113–14.

Poland's pre-war Communist Party (KPP) had been dissolved by the Comintern in 1938, and many of its leaders executed. The resolution explained that 'agents of Polish fascism had managed to gain positions in its leadership'. When its resurrection was being considered in autumn 1941, the word 'communist' was dropped for pragmatic reasons:

1. So our enemies cannot use the 'bogey' of communism
2. Many elements, even in the working-class, remain distrustful of the communists because of their previous mistakes. [This referred above all to the 'anti-nation' stance it had adopted, as part of communist internationalism]
3. After all that has happened, as Comrade Dimitrov [Secretary of Comintern] has explained, before we can call ourselves communist, we must, by our deeds, earn the right to this term
4. It is essential that the masses see in our party an organisation closely linked to the Polish nation, and its most vital interests, and that our enemies will not be able to refer to us as agents of a foreign power
5. *It will be easier if we use a new name to unite around ourselves the broad mass of workers, peasants and intelligentsia and organise under our direction a united national front to struggle with the German fascist occupation.*[5]

The name chosen was 'Polish Workers' Party' (PPR). This had been approved by Stalin: 'It would be better to create a workers' party of Poland with a Communist programme. The Communist party frightens off not only alien elements but some of our own as well.'[6]

The first contingent was sent to Poland to found the new PPR two days later. Dimitrov noted: 'Formation of a workers' party (with Communist programme). Not formally linked with the Comintern'.[7] But this did not prevent precise political directives being sent to the Polish avant-garde. They were initially instructed: 'As for the party, do not go after sheer quantity of organisations and members, but try instead to form strong, proven and battle-worthy organisations in the major localities.' They should watch out for provocateurs: 'As regards admitting PPS [Polish Socialist Party] members, maintain the strictest vigilance. A united front with PPS organisations is not the same as admitting them into the Workers' (Communist) Party.'[8]

In spring 1943, Moscow sent encoded instructions on wartime objectives: 'In your telegram to Stalin you speak of "establishing worker and peasant power in Poland". At the present juncture this is politically

[5] A. Polonsky and B. Drukier, *The Beginnings of Communist Rule in Poland* (London, 1980), pp. 128–9.
[6] I. Banac (ed.), *The Diary of Georgi Dimitrov 1933–1949* (New Haven, 2003), p. 191 (meeting with Stalin, 27 August 1941).
[7] *Ibid.* p. 192 (29 August 1941). [8] *Ibid.* p. 232 (17 July 1942).

incorrect. Avoid such formulations in your political campaign.' The preferred slogans were: (1) expulsion of the occupiers from Poland; (2) winning national freedom; (3) establishing people's democratic power (not worker and peasant power!).[9] The messages from Moscow, intercepted by British intelligence, reproved the Polish avant-garde for their too radical intent. They should not echo the Soviet (1936) Constitution but rather stress 'the consolidation of the liberty and independence of POLAND, the swift restoration of the country, the assurance [to all?] of freedom, bread, work, a roof overhead and peace'. Of course, they should add that the attainment of such goals required 'a sincere alliance with the USSR'.[10]

A further instruction insisted they should not 'create a false impression that the PPR is carrying out a course of Sovietization in POLAND'. The correct policy was one of national fronts. Within countries, such as 'France, Czechoslovakia, Italy, Yugoslavia etc.', this would split the domestic oppositions without fundamentally altering the communist aims. It would serve the further purpose of not threatening the Grand Alliance. The plan was to muster sufficient forces within each country to overthrow the reactionaries, whilst avoiding a seizure of power which would 'make Poland a bone of contention between the Tehran powers'.[11]

Shortly before the war in Europe had ended, Gomułka told a PPR Central Committee Plenum that 'with the capitulation of Germany the contradictions between the worlds of capitalism and socialism are coming to the surface. The Polish question is an expression of these contradictions.' The pace and direction of socio-political change in post-war Poland would depend on the international situation, primarily the Peace Conference and the Conference on Collective Security. Whilst class struggle would continue, Soviet military power would facilitate a non-violent transition to a new social system. Soviet power would ensure that reactionary elements would be held at bay and then pushed aside.

Despite this optimism, he saw dangers in growing anti-Sovietism: 'A nation's past lives on. The frontier changes increase suspicion. We are Marxists, so we understand certain things, but the average Pole simply sees that Russia has deprived Poland of no small amount of territory. Deportations and mistakes that the Soviet organs have made in dealing with the Poles have also influenced views.' He added that 'terror has been intensified. The population's favourable and enthusiastic attitude to the Soviet Union is falling off rapidly. There is a danger that we may come to

[9] Banac (ed.), *The Diary of Georgi Dimitrov*, p. 263.
[10] Mark, *Revolution by Degrees*, p. 20. [11] *Ibid.* pp. 21–2 (February 1944).

be seen as Soviet agents. The masses should see us as a Polish party. Let them attack us as Polish communists, not agents.'[12]

Gomułka raised bi-lateral matters at frequent meetings with Stalin. In addition to the conduct of Soviet security organs on Polish territory, he raised economic issues: reparations, the removal of raw materials eastwards and the dismantling of industry. He commented later: 'In fact throughout 1945 I had difficult disputes with Stalin over Poland.' His obstinacy earned him the ire of Vyshinsky, chief prosecutor in the Moscow Trials of the late thirties and now a foreign minister: 'You are no better than Sikorski.'[13]

A particular bone of contention was agriculture. Stalin had expressed the view in the autumn of 1944 that the slow pace of land reform was giving opponents time to organise. He took the view that 'Resistance is growing. The abolition of a whole class (rich landowners) is not a reform but a revolution and cannot be carried out with the full majesty of law.' Stalin sought a class-based solution: 'Create a mass movement.' It was a mistake to be soft: he wanted to know why not a single landowner had been arrested.[14]

The PPR Central Committee held a variety of views. Ochab, who had spent the war in the USSR, noted: 'Before we returned to Poland we thought the peasants themselves would take the land.' But no such movement had arisen. Kasman, another wartime exile, stated: 'Our Party has caught the parliamentary disease. It is in power and has not used terrorist tactics on the reactionaries. Workers' brigades should be sent to the countryside.' The most interesting analysis came from the chief economist Hilary Minc. He argued that, unlike the USSR, Poland had a shortage of land. Even the division of large estates would lead to disputes between existing small-holders and the landless. Polish land reform had not been a spontaneous movement: 'It has been imposed from above.'[15]

Polish leaders expressed society's fears: 'the population was terrified by the spectre of Soviet-type collective farms'. When summoned to meetings for the formation of farming 'collectives', peasants asked Party agitators prescient questions:

- Will they be run by bureaucrats? Under the Soviet regime, they were all run by commands from above. Everyone was told to do the threshing when it was time to dig potatoes. So they rotted.

[12] Polonsky and Drukier, *The Beginnings of Communist Rule*, pp. 425–6.
[13] J. Ptasiński, *Pierwszy z trzech zwrotów, czyli rzecz o Gomułce* (Warsaw, 1983), pp. 115–16.
[14] Polonsky and Drukier, *The Beginnings of Communist Rule*, pp. 299–300.
[15] *Ibid.* pp. 301–2.

- If cooperatives are as good as you say, how can we explain the sorrow and tears of Russian soldiers (in 1944–45) who deplored the poverty of Russian *kolkhozes* and so envied the prosperity of peasants in Poland?
- If a young couple get married and want to build a house, who will give them a plot of land if their parents have none?
- What will happen to large orchards?
- May we borrow a horse to drive to church? If so, how often?[16]

At a May 1945 Central Committee meeting, Zambrowski saw shortcomings of Party (PPR) work in every field. A pro-communist Peasants' Self-Help Organisation (*Samopomoc Chłopska)* had been created amongst poor farmers at the end of 1944, to encourage a new cooperative movement: 'In that body there are 400,000 peasants, but so far co-operativism has been unsuccessful. Ochab's slogan of a "co-operative republic" is incorrect. We need different slogans, not a socialisation but the polonisation of the Western territories and the philosophy of co-management. We are a poor country.' It had been left to Red Army soldiers 'to agitate in favour of *kolkhozes*'.[17]

Rebuilding

Whoever had taken power in 1945 would have faced the same tasks: clearing away the rubble, restoring essential services, rationing and rebuilding. This needed a state authority and it could call on the powerful motive of patriotism. This was far more promising for the new authorities than any attraction to 'Soviet power'. As Kersten puts it, 'For most Poles, Soviet rule was primarily a symbol of satrapy and oppression.'[18] They primarily remembered the violence and repression of the 1939–40 deportations to the GULag[19] and Katyń, and Soviet passivity during the Warsaw Uprising. Moscow tried to improve its image accordingly.

Khrushchev wrote to Bierut on 7 March 1945 offering assistance in rebuilding the capital. He proposed to send to Warsaw a group of specialists to help rebuild the city: planners, engineers and experts in public utilities, housing and transportation. A six-page itemisation followed (17 March 1945) on the order of the 'President of the State Committee of Defence,

16 D. Jarosz, 'Polish Peasants versus Stalinism' in *Stalinism in Poland*, ed. Kemp-Welch, pp. 60–2.

17 Polonsky and Drukier, *The Beginnings of Communist Rule*, p. 432.

18 K. Kersten's preface to Robert Kupiecki, *'Natchnienie milionów': kult Józefa Stalina w Polsce, 1945–1956* (Warsaw, 1993).

19 Jan T. Gross, *Revolution from Abroad. The Soviet Conquest of Poland's Western Ukraine and Western Byelorussia* (Princeton, N.J., 1988).

I Stalin'.[20] A year later Bierut wrote to Soviet leaders requesting the return of the Ossolineum Library from Lwów, founded in 1817. It contained important manuscripts of 'Mickiewicz, Słowacki and many other poets and writers, whose return would be greatly esteemed by the entire Polish intelligentsia'.[21] The transfer, to Wrocław, took place later in 1946.

The Nazi occupation of Poland not only had dissolved many assumptions inherited from the pre-war order, it had challenged the notion of 'order' itself.[22] Cicero used to end his speeches with 'Carthage must be destroyed.' A similar precept governed the German retreat from Poland. The capital was razed to the ground. Wandering through its ruins in mid-1945, the poet Miłosz recalled the occupation. Warsaw's streets were littered with broken glass, and papers marked 'Confidential' or 'Top Secret' fluttered in the wind. Family homes were cut open to public view. Theft had ceased to be culpable: how else could one survive? Under occupation, even 'The killing of a man presents no great moral problem.'[23]

Nazi occupation offered the population no prospect other than subjugation or extermination. Of all occupied Europe, Poland arguably engaged in the least collaboration. Alternative forms of collective life emerged under German rule: a vast network of informal social institutions, a parallel society, including an extensive clandestine press.[24]

Kazimierz Wyka noted that Poles behaved, as far as possible, 'as if' there were no Germans present in daily life. A split reality was created in which the occupiers were circumvented and ignored, treated as inanimate objects or a natural calamity, instead of being a part of the social system.[25] The economy was 'excluded' from any form of creative purpose. To survive at all, citizens had to exclude 'the most important processes of social life from responsibility and active participation necessarily provoked a profound moral corruption. A corruption generally not intentional, but resulting from the very necessity of surviving within a system based on falsehoods that served those in power, on injustice as a principle.'[26]

The further consequence of wartime and the post-war settlement was demographic. At the first post-war census (February 1946), some

[20] AAN 295 (PPR: Polish Workers' Party) /VII/260.
[21] AAN 295/VII/266 (22 June 1946).
[22] J. Gross, 'War as Revolution' in N. Naimark and L. Gibianskii (eds.), *The Establishment of Communist Regimes in Eastern Europe, 1944–1949* (Westview, 1997), pp. 17–40.
[23] C. Miłosz, *The Captive Mind* (1953; rpt London, 1985), pp. 24–6.
[24] J. Gross, *Polish Society Under German Occupation: The Generalgouvernement, 1939–1944* (Princeton, N.J., 1979), p. xi.
[25] K. Wyka, *Życie na niby: pamiętnik po klęsce* (Warsaw, 1959; rpt 1984).
[26] K. Wyka, 'The Excluded Economy' (1945) in J. Wedel (ed.), *The Unplanned Society* (New York, 1992), pp. 54–5.

20.5 million people described themselves as Poles. This was an increase of 1.5 million since May 1945. The returnees were predominantly from Germany, with 22,000 from the USSR and some 141,800 from other European countries. There was also emigration, illegal – by members of the non-communist underground faced with arrest – and legal – by people principally of Jewish or Polish Jewish descent, in a flow that was permitted until 1948.[27]

Even more dramatic was the troubled process of resettlement of the Poles displaced from lands in the east given to the USSR, in the Western Recovered Territories, the name given to land previously German. The process of uprooting such people continued for more than a decade. As with the occupation, such mass movement of peoples broke traditional structures and social patterns. This transformation was 'an important cause of weakening of resistance to the Communist authorities'. Migration fostered social disintegration and people who had settled in areas that had until recently been part of another state 'quite naturally grew ties to the new authorities. They had some grounds for asserting that the western territories "bind the nation to the system".'[28]

A much smaller category of migrants came home with the Red Army. They belonged to the pro-Soviet Polish army formed in the USSR, and supervised by the NKVD (the Soviet secret police). This was a return in triumph. Miłosz records their progress sardonically:

> This was the reward for those who knew how to think correctly, who understood the logic of History, who did not surrender to senseless sentimentality. It was they, not those tearful fools from London, who were bringing Poland liberation from the Germans. The nation would, of course, have to undergo a major operation: Gamma felt the excitement of a good surgeon in the operating theatre.[29]

A prime target in the operation was the Home Army (AK).

As the Red Army advanced, it assisted and promoted the arrest and deportation of Home Army leaders. Its official disbandment in January 1945, in order to protect its members, did nothing to halt the flow. Even after the ending of the war with Germany, resistance and repression continued for three more years. As John Micgiel notes, 'some scholars consider this period to be one of civil war, claiming as many as 30,000 people perished in the struggle'.[30] He notes that anti-communist resistance also continued elsewhere, against Tito in the Yugoslav mountains,

[27] Kersten, *The Establishment of Communist Rule*, pp. 163–4.

[28] *Ibid.* p. 165. [29] Miłosz, *The Captive Mind*, p. 158.

[30] J. Micgiel, ' "Bandits and Reactionaries": The Suppression of the Opposition in Poland, 1944–1946' in Naimark and Gibianskii (eds.), *The Establishment of Communist Regimes*, pp. 93–110.

and against Soviet and Romanian communist rule in Transylvania. The London government in exile received a graphic account of the Soviet operation in the Lublin and Warsaw provinces, dated 26 April 1945: 'The Soviet Army surrounds the villages and transports all the men, other than youngsters and the elderly, eastwards. Arrests, numbering between ten and twenty thousand have provoked a mass exodus to the forests and the formation of irregular armed units, which nevertheless adopt a passive attitude, only defending themselves when attacked. The Soviet Air Force bombed the Czermiernickie forests.'[31]

Stalinism tried to subjugate Polish society by rupturing its natural pattern of relationships. The aim was to atomise individuals by closing down contexts for free association. The communist state proclaimed the 'revolutionary march' of an abstraction: a mass society without personal contacts or human bonds. 'Working class' and 'the collective' became empty formulae. Inter-generational conflict was fomented. Young people, members of a 'new era', were encouraged to treat their elders as 'reactionary remnants' or even as 'enemies of the revolution'.

When Soviet armies were approaching Łódź in early 1945, local workers 'asserted their Polishness' by reclaiming factories and expelling German (state, private or military) management. As the Red Army arrived, this action became forcible resistance to the liberators' looting and attempted confiscations.[32] Kenney sees such resistance as crucial to the post-war reformation of working-class identity. By acting this way, the workers evoked wartime resistance, during which industrial sabotage had been 'the only means of anti-Nazi resistance'. Such actions were not directed 'from above'. They offered the ordinary worker an individual means with which to oppose the enemy. Consequently, they posed a threat to the new state.

Across the country, workers took the communist slogan of nationalisation at face value, understanding that they were now the masters and could organise production in their own way. Kenney shows how metalworkers took the communist slogan of 'self-management' literally. They formed factory committees with directly elected directors and heads of department. Such spontaneity, a blend of nationalism and anarcho-syndicalism, was seen as a direct challenge by the new authorities. Party officials deplored a condition in which enterprise directors could be dismissed by a mass meeting. The workforce tended to react negatively to the replacement of their own chosen director by a ministerial appointee.

[31] Cited by Polonsky and Drukier, *The Beginnings of Communist Rule*, p. 109.
[32] P. Kenney, *Rebuilding Poland. Workers and Communists, 1945–1950* (Ithaca, N.Y., 1997), pp. 78–81.

A report from the Łódź Party Committee for April–May 1945 detailed the 'strong feeling of tension' in the region's factories. There had been a dozen brief strikes in recent days which the Party's local cells had been quite impotent in dealing with. At stormy shop-floor meetings, 'the workers and especially working women heckle the speakers. They shouted "Fine democracy when we have nothing to eat". "The parasites stuff themselves and the workers starve".'[33] The report concluded that strikes were clearly caused by reactionaries.

Communism steadily eliminated the last vestiges of working-class autonomy in the workers' state. To go on strike was now declared logically impossible. As co-owners of the means of production, workers could not strike 'against themselves'. Even so, strikes continued. When the fall in real wages, as the result of price increases, in early 1947 led to social protests, the official response was unrelenting: 'no concessions whatsoever'. Party leader Gomułka portrayed the protests as the last throw of 'reactionary ideology', making a vain attempt to counteract its 'rapid disintegration in the consciousness of the working-class'.[34] In September that year, cotton workers in Łódź began a week-long strike, which spread to the rest of the city's cotton industry and led to a major rethinking of the Party's industrial policy.

The September 1947 strike began with a conflict over work-space. Under a new scheme, selected 'volunteers' undertook to increase output in the spinning mills. They were given improved machinery and extra, well-lit space in which to meet their new norms. The remainder of the workforce feared they would be given new norms – extra output targets for the same wages – without the special facilities in which to meet them. There was outrage when the Party Secretary switched on a set of forty looms in an effort to coax weavers back to work. This was treated as usurpation of the principle that each weaver was responsible for 'their own' machine, even when it was not running. The largely female workforce could not stay overnight in an occupation strike, and management responded with a lock-out. Crowds gathered before the gates and the strike spread across the city. In response, ten 'ring-leaders' were dismissed. Party members were collected from their homes to start the first shift. Popular opinion interpreted the round-up as the start of mass arrests. The rumour-mill soon asserted that a pregnant women had been kicked and several murdered by the management. Secret Police Colonel Julia Brystygierowa stated, without evidence, that 'clergy are

[33] Polonsky and Drukier, *The Beginnings of Communist Rule*, p. 101.
[34] Kersten, *The Establishment of Communist Rule*, p. 362.

the source of ferment (in the factories) and it cannot be precluded that the clergy was the inspiration and organizer of the strike'.[35]

Opening the Cominform conference, Gomułka gave a full and rather frank account of the problems being encountered on the 'Polish road to socialism'. It had not been necessary to destroy the old state machine as this had been done by the German occupation. Rather, a new state had to be constructed. The prime mover was the PPR which had grown since liberation from 20,000-strong to a Party of 800,000 members. He noted that 'if the Polish road is to be applied in another country', the Marxist Party must master the state machine from top to bottom. It was essential to break the resistance of reactionaries 'in accordance with the so-called peaceful road to socialism, whether this is a Polish, Yugoslav or Bulgarian road'.[36] In the Polish case, the current line was to curb – rather than eradicate – capitalist elements. The low level of agricultural output and industrial production necessitated 'the development, within definite conditions and limits, of *kulak* farms in the countryside and of artisan and private industrial enterprises in the towns'. The liquidation of retail trade could not be contemplated, though the black market and foreign currency speculation would be combated.

Turning to politics, he noted the continued strength of the PPS, which had successfully played the nationalist card in times when the former KPP had been against it. The 'harmful traditions of anti-sovietism and social-democratism' were being overcome. There was also a policy to neutralise the Church: 'International reaction, using the clergy, is trying to create a reactionary Catholic party in Poland. We shall not allow this.' An essential element was to reassure the private peasantry: 'Our enemies frighten the rural population with talk of collective farms.' But, he noted, 'Our party has, for a long period, renounced the organizing of collective farms.'[37] Yet, within a year, all these policies had been reversed. The prospect of a 'Polish road' was removed. Its replacement was a Stalinist model in which one Party ruled autonomously over all sections of society.

Soviet bloc

Pre-war Poland had pluralist traditions. No less than twenty-eight political parties had contested the 1928 elections.[38] Now it was to have a

[35] Kenney, *Rebuilding Poland*, pp. 122–34; L. Kamiński, *Strajki robotnicze w Polsce w latach 1945–1948* (Wrocław, 1999), pp. 95–106.

[36] Procacci (ed.), *The Cominform*, pp. 40–1. [37] *Ibid.* pp. 54–9.

[38] A. Polonsky, *Politics in Independent Poland 1921–1939. The Crisis of Constitutional Government* (Oxford, 1972), pp. 234–51.

political monopoly. Economic monopoly soon followed. A Commission to combat 'Corruption and Economic Sabotage' spear-headed the infamous 'battle for trade'.[39] By eliminating the 'third tier' of cooperative associations, existing between the private sector and the state, it firmly installed 'socialist construction'.[40] Western historians had always expected this outcome: the Red Army occupied Eastern and Central Europe; the Soviet political and economic system would follow.

Churchill thought he had solved the problem with his 'percentage agreement' in the Kremlin in October 1944. Under his proposed spheres of interest in the post-war Balkans and Central Europe, Russia was to have interests in Romania (90%) and Bulgaria (75%), Greece (Britain 90%) and Yugoslavia and Hungary would be 50%–50% with Britain. His memoirs recall that Stalin put a tick in the margin of this 'naughty piece of paper' and passed it back to the British side.[41] The partitioning of Europe had taken a few moments. But subsequent Russian research indicates a longer negotiation. At a meeting between Foreign Ministers (Eden and Molotov) the next day, the Soviet side sought to increase its share in Hungary to 75% and Bulgaria to 90%. A figure of 80% was agreed in both cases.[42] It is worth noting that countries north of Hungary were excluded from this understanding.

There is a divergent pattern of communist take-overs in Eastern Europe, but the outcome is always the same. The most developed strategies were in Poland and Romania, the least active in Czechoslovakia, the final country in the region to become communist, only after a seizure of power in February 1948. However, rumours of a similar *coup* in Finland, or even Norway – the two remaining non-communist countries on Soviet Western borders – proved false. There was no further Soviet expansion after this point. Instead, the emphasis shifted to consolidation, and pressure from Moscow for each country to follow the 'Soviet model'. Stalin abandoned the patient approach.

His primary consideration was Germany. The 'Big Three' at Yalta 'each believed that their designs for Germany would secure him the greatest possible room for manoeuvre in attaining his subsequent objective'.[43] The initial objective had been to dismember Germany: the state would cease to exist and, until the succession had been determined,

[39] D. Jarosz and T. Wolska, *Komisja specjalna do walki z nadużyciami i szkodnictwem gospodarczym 1945–1956. Wybór dokumentów* (Warsaw, 1995).
[40] T. Kowalik, *Spory o ustrój społeczno-gospodarczy Polski 1944–48* (Warsaw, 1980).
[41] W. Churchill, *The Second World War*, vol. VI (London, 1954), p. 198.
[42] O. A. Rzheshevskii, cited by M. Ellman, 'Churchill on Stalin: A Note', *Europe–Asia Studies* 2006 (58.6).
[43] P. Windsor, *City on Leave. A History of Berlin, 1945–1962* (London, 1963), pp. 11–12.

the 'Big Three' (later Four) would administer part of its territory. Meanwhile, the threat of eventual reunification would hold the Three together. But within a few months, this prospect vanished. The occupying powers did not dismember Germany by mutual agreement but shared it out between them.

To Churchill, the prospects of communist advance looked ominous. By the time of Potsdam, he saw Soviet domination of Poland and the possible strike of the Red Army across North Germany into Scandinavia, and Tito's expansion in the Balkans, as confirming his worst fears. He commented: 'I hardly like to consider dismembering Germany until my doubts about Russia's intentions have cleared away.' But German unification would require agreement on both common economic policies and a central administrative authority. In autumn 1945, US Secretary of State James Byrnes offered the Soviets a comprehensive settlement under which Stalin would accept domestic self-determination for the states of Eastern Europe in exchange for a treaty demilitarising Germany, and strict enforcement procedures to prevent any remilitarisation.[44] The one option not openly stated thus far was permanent division of Germany. That applied particularly to the most decisive prize, and the biggest test for Soviet intentions: Berlin.

Stalin's German policy was predicated on a rapid withdrawal of Western, and especially American, troops from their zones of occupation. Meanwhile, the Soviet zone could be consolidated and promoted as a magnet to its Western counterparts. The endgame would be a unified 'friendly' Germany, inclined towards the USSR.[45] But this prospect was undermined by the Soviet Union's own behaviour. A range of issues, such as Red Army misconduct, reparations and dismantlings, undermined the possibility of trust in Soviet hegemony.[46] The plight of 6 million German refugees from territories acquired by Poland heightened the tensions. As America's European policy developed, it was the Western zones that proved the more magnetic. And that revived the spectre of Bismarck: a divided Germany might be re-unified in future by military means and for expansion.

Stalin did not proceed at once to the Sovietisation of the Soviet zone. He calculated that would make reunification more difficult. But in late 1947, the Western powers agreed to proceed with the founding of a

[44] Mark, *Revolution by Degrees*, p. 44.

[45] V. Zubok and C. Pleshakov, *Inside the Kremlin's Cold War: From Stalin to Khrushchev* (Cambridge, Mass., 1966), p. 48.

[46] N. Naimark, *The Russians in Germany. A History of the Soviet Zone of Occupation, 1945–1949* (Cambridge, Mass., 1995), esp. pp. 74–7, 166–83.

German state on the basis of their occupational zones. Stalin responded by a series of measures, and half-measures, to squeeze them out of Berlin, by a selective blockade of their three sectors. In June 1948, President Truman responded with a US Air Force operation to supply West Berlin. At the same time, the Soviet blockade was presented as further evidence of the brutality and inhumanity of the Soviet regime.[47] A climate was thus fostered in which a majority of Western countries would turn to the USA for military protection against the 'red menace'. The formation of NATO followed a few months later.

Fear of Soviet intentions proved a stronger motive than was suggested by the ideologically based assumption in Moscow that intra-capitalist 'contradictions' would prevent the consolidation of an anti-Soviet camp. Stalin proceeded rapidly during 1948 towards a 'Soviet Bloc'. But no sooner had the 'bloc' been constituted, than it was threatened by a new heresy.

Titoism

Tito's partisans had assumed control in Yugoslavia after a brief coalition with royalists, and declared a Federal People's Republic in January 1946. At the outset, there were good relations with the Soviet Union. A one-Party system was imposed and its state management of the economy followed the Soviet 'model'. Soviet leaders always singled out Yugoslavia as the most 'revolutionary' of the new communist states and when naming its best-known leaders invariably placed Tito first.[48] Nonetheless, Soviet leaders were not satisfied that Tito's partisans were totally subordinate to the USSR.

Rumblings over the post-war status of Trieste and its environs had found Soviet policy at odds with Yugoslav territorial ambitions. Prior to the first meeting of Cominform, Tito had expressed enthusiasm for the new organisation. He did not know that the first draft of Zhdanov's address was designed to strike against the 'leftist mistakes' of the Yugoslav leadership, as a counterpart to the 'rightist mistakes' of the Czechoslovak, French and Italian comrades. It was dropped, perhaps in response to Tito's vigorous rejection of the Marshall Plan. But the Kremlin had yet to deal with reports it was receiving from diplomats in Belgrade claiming that the Yugoslav leaders considered the Soviet Union was more concerned with cultivating imperialist powers than with protecting the

[47] *Ibid.* p. 52.
[48] Gibianskii, 'The Beginning of the Conflict' in Procacci (ed.), *The Cominform*, pp. 466–7.

smaller socialist states.[49] It was, however, noted that Yugoslavia appeared to harbour ambitions of its own.

More worrying than the perception of the Cominform as a vehicle for promoting its own notion of socialism, there had been diplomatic moves in the Balkans without prior Soviet consent. On 30 July 1947, Tito met Dimitrov in Sofia. They declared their intention to sign a Yugoslav–Bulgarian Treaty of Friendship, Cooperation and Mutual Assistance. On hearing of it, Stalin cabled that this was a mistake. It was likely to be used by 'reactionary Anglo-American elements' to expand their military interventions from Greece and Turkey to Bulgaria and Yugoslavia.[50] This was smoothed over and Yugoslavia agreed that future bi-lateral treaties, with Romania and Hungary, would be cleared with Moscow beforehand. Less readily resolved were Yugoslav–Albanian relations. Here Belgrade played with Tirana, through military advisers and economic assistance, much the same role that Moscow played with Belgrade.

Stalin appeared to accept this but advised Yugoslavia not to rush into a formal unification with Albania. Tito should delay a federation until the moment was more opportune. The issue of Soviet or Yugoslav primacy over Albania was put on hold. But a secret memorandum in the Soviet archives, from autumn 1947, noted that 'when deciding questions connected with the application of foreign policy, certain leaders of the Yugoslav CP sometimes display national narrowness, failing to take into account the interests of other countries and of fraternal CPs'. Moreover, the memo detected a tendency of Yugoslav leaders to present themselves as a form of 'leading Party' in the Balkans.[51]

Further premonitions of a change came from the Cominform journal now established under its chief editor Pavel Yudin, first noted as an enthusiastic young Stalinist in 1928.[52] In November 1947, he sent out plans for future issues, soliciting ideas and contributions. The next number would lead its theoretical section with an article on 'The Role of Comrade Stalin in Organising the Victory of the Soviet People over Germany'. It would mark the fifth anniversary of the battle of Stalingrad. But secret information conveyed back to Warsaw indicated a more controversial agenda. Yudin had told the editorial board that Stalin had personally authorised key ideological themes for the new journal, including 'the changing form of class struggle, especially in the People's democracies, and the Marxist–Leninist basis of Party-building in conditions of intensified class struggle'. It was essential to eliminate

[49] Zubok and Pleshakov, *Inside the Kremlin's Cold War*, pp. 134–5. [50] *Ibid.* pp. 128–9.

[51] Gibianskii, 'The Beginning of the Conflict' in Procacci (ed.), *The Cominform*, pp. 471–2.

[52] A. Kemp-Welch, *Stalin and the Literary Intelligentsia, 1928–1939* (London, 1991), p. 74.

deviations in the workers' movement. Yudin singled out the 'so-called theory of "autonomous development" propounded by Milovan Djilas [a Yugoslav leader and theoretician]' for particular critique.[53] The Yugoslav board member did not respond, merely saying he would refer the issue to his party's Politburo. However, it was stated that Zhdanov would attack Yugoslavia in the next number, though not by name.

On the surface, Soviet–Yugoslav relations remained cordial. At a nocturnal banquet on 17 January 1948, Stalin, on hearing that socialism was now being achieved 'in ways different from those of the past', remarked, perhaps jocularly, that 'today socialism is possible even under the English monarchy'. Djilas volunteered the view that 'in Yugoslavia the government was essentially of the Soviet type; the Communist Party held all the key positions and there was no serious opposition party'. Stalin replied, 'No, your government is not Soviet – you have something between De Gaulle's France and the Soviet Union.' He added the classic *dictum*: 'War is not as in the past; whoever occupies a territory also imposes on it his own social system. Everyone imposes his own system as far as his army has power to do so. It cannot be otherwise.' He further predicted a rapid German resurgence, based on its high level of industrial development and ample, skilled workforce: 'Give them twelve to fifteen years and they'll be on their feet again.'[54]

Two days later, Tito proposed to the Albanian communist leader Enver Hoxha the provision of a base for Yugoslav forces in southern Albania. Its ostensible purpose was to head off an imminent invasion by 'Greek monarch–fascists backed by the Anglo-Americans'. Hoxha agreed the next day. But Molotov protested to Tito that such a procedure was 'abnormal' and a fait accompli. He noted serious differences between their countries, not only on foreign policy but on 'the conception of relations between our two countries'. As relations deteriorated still further, to the point where it was claimed that Yugoslavia was withholding economic statistics from the Soviet trade representative, Moscow recalled its military and civilian advisers. The same day, Moscow's main ideologist, Suslov, received a memorandum from the CC (Soviet Central Committee) Foreign Policy department on the 'anti-Marxist positions of the Communist Party of Yugoslavia on questions of foreign and domestic policy'. In addition to attempting an anti-Tito revolt in Belgrade, which failed, Moscow brought Cominform into play.

Several of the East European leaders did not take Soviet claims at face value. Gomułka in particular failed to endorse the allegation that Tito and

[53] AAN 295/V/247. [54] M. Djilas, *Conversations with Stalin* (London, 1963), pp. 89–91.

his associates had abandoned Marxism–Leninism and betrayed the socialist camp.[55] Gomułka is sometimes said to have attempted to mediate in the dispute, but archives found by Leonid Gibiański show only that he urged Tito to attend the second conference of Cominform, in the interest of solidarity with the 'world revolutionary movement'. He volunteered to visit Belgrade, but the offer was declined. Following this intervention, Moscow prevailed. All other members of Cominform agreed to attend its second session, in Romania from 19 to 23 June 1948, to discuss 'Soviet–Yugoslav differences'.

Prior to this meeting, Moscow began preparations that went beyond the 'Yugoslav case'. On 5 April 1948, the Foreign Policy department presented Suslov with a long paper, 'On the Anti-Marxist Ideological Positions of the Leaders of the Polish Workers' Party'. Here Gomułka, like Tito, was accused of a litany of departures from Marxist–Leninism

Gomułka was ignoring the Soviet experience, sliding into nationalism, wrongly contrasting Poland's 'peaceful path' to socialism with the Soviet Union's 'bloody revolution'. The Polish leadership was denying the importance of the 'dictatorship of the proletariat' on the road to communism, and had preserved a separation of legislative and executive functions, and parliamentary democracy. Whilst necessary in the initial post-war period, for tactical purposes, such tenets now constituted opposition to the Soviet experience. Both Poles and Yugoslavs were accused of minimising the Soviet role in their liberation. Finally, both rejected collectivisation, which was to be a special priority of the Cominform meeting.[56] The charges against Gomułka were held back for some months, however, whilst attention focussed on Tito and his team.

Moscow particularly objected to the claims in Belgrade that the Soviet Union had become 'degenerate' (a term from Trotsky), and that 'great-power chauvinism is rampant in the USSR' (later a Chinese epithet). Stalin expected self-criticism in the communist tradition. Instead, Tito answered back. He stated that his League of Communists looked to the Soviet system as an example, 'but we are developing socialism in our country in somewhat different forms, forced on us by the specific conditions in our country'.[57] Moscow retorted that this was a failure to take criticism 'in a Marxist manner'. When Yugoslav self-criticism was not forthcoming, they were expelled from the bloc.

[55] J. Ptasiński, *Pierwszy z trzech zwrotów, czyli rzecz o Gomułce* (Warsaw, 1983), p. 111.

[56] Gibianskii, 'The Beginning of the Conflicts' in Procacci (ed.), *The Cominform*, pp. 655–6. The next target was the Czechoslovak communist leadership (*ibid.* p. 657).

[57] *Soviet–Yugoslav Dispute. Text of the Published Correspondence* (London, 1948).

Moscow's indictment stated that the Yugoslav government had regularly violated its bi-lateral agreement to consult with the Soviet Union 'on the more important questions of international relations'. Yugoslavia had sent a military division into Albania, which the 'Anglo-Americans' might have made the pretext for launching a general war in the Balkans. The Soviet government had learned about this grave step from newspapers. During the chorus of disapproval, Cominform heard from a new Polish delegate, Jakub Berman: 'The example of Yugoslavia shows what pernicious consequences result from an ideological degeneration which has assumed the characteristic features of Trotskyist adventurism and bourgeois nationalism. We must sharpen our vigilance against this kind of danger.'[58]

Expulsion from the bloc took Tito's leadership by surprise. The first response was 'how could we, good Stalinists, have gone wrong?', and continuation of orthodox policies. However, a hasty survey of other sources – the young Marx, early Lenin and G. D. H. Cole – provided bases for a 'model' of their own. This rehabilitated the doctrine of the 'withering away of the state', long-rejected under Stalinism, and proposed an ideological innovation with little precedent except the Paris Commune: workers' councils. The idea was to avoid both the reversion to private property and the command economy (with its parasitic bureaucracy) through a syndicalist solution. The new programme, summarised by Tito's slogan 'Factories to the Workers' (1950), was enshrined in a self-management system.

Self-management was from the outset an ambivalent expression. It combined interests that had hitherto been considered mutually incompatible. Thus the ruling elite would be masked by a newly democratic slogan 'proletarian power', whilst keeping power in its own hands. To critical intellectuals, it became essentially an aspiration, encouraging further research into the gulf between hope and reality. To workers themselves, it seemed, for a moment, to present a chance to exercise more control over their own affairs. The outcome, studied by Neca Jovanov, is focussed on the right to strike.

Although legally a last resort where the processes of self-management had broken down, strikes tended to happen when the system was working. Shop-floor decision-making was constantly thwarted by the misuse of professional skills. Workers would be presented with a file of 50 or 100 pages in preparation for a meeting. They took the simplest way out:

[58] Procacci (ed.), *The Cominform*, p. 545.

voting for the plans and later organising strikes against them. In short, workers rebelled 'against a society governed by the working class'.[59] Despite this, Yugoslavia presented an attractive 'model' for socialists within the Soviet bloc. As we shall see, it became more visible to other Eastern Europeans during the post-Stalin thaw.

After action against Yugoslavia, attention turned to Poland. A Polish Politburo resolution criticised a speech by Gomułka to the previous (3 June) Plenum as 'one-sided, since it only looked at past political parties from the aspect of national independence. Hence he had collated the Luxemburgist SDKPiL [Social-Democratic Party of the Congress Kingdom of Poland and Lithuania] and the PPS, that is conflated reformists with socialist revolutionaries.' As Stalin had done in the 'great turn',[60] a seemingly marginal point of Party history was taken as emblematic of a new campaign. Despite its apparently Aesopian language, the debate went to the heart of current politics. Though none of the participants would say so openly, the main point at issue was Warsaw's relationship with Moscow.

According to the resolution, Gomułka was mistaken in referring to the PPS programme as 'realistic'. It was realistic only in the sense that it reflected a 'chauvinistic-bourgeois' notion of independence, linked in turn to Austro-German imperialism. But Polish independence was regained in 1918 'not as the result of the victory of one of the Partitioning powers, but in consequence of the victorious revolution in Russia and the revolutionary movements that brought about in Central Europe'. The PPS' aim was a bourgeois notion of independence instead of a joint movement of revolutionary workers in Poland and Russia.[61]

Gomułka sent the Politburo a letter excusing himself from attending the next Party plenum on health grounds.[62] His removal for 'Right-National Deviation' was now only a matter of time.

Preparing to drop him, his wartime colleagues engaged in self-criticism. Zenon Kliszko made a craven apology for being seduced by 'the right-nationalist deviation in our Party leadership'. Zawadzki sought reinstatement in Party work. After a severe talking-to by Comrade Baryła, he had abandoned his earlier false beliefs and understood that 'the march to socialism is being delayed by the spread of anti-Russian sentiments and ill-feelings towards the USSR'. They were in fact close to war. Though the Red Army was far from the Atlantic, the situation in the USA was very

[59] N. Jovanovic, *Radnički štrajkowi u SFRJ, od 1958. do 1969. godire* (Belgrade, 1979).
[60] J. Barber, *Soviet Historians in Crisis, 1928–1932* (London, 1981), Ch. 10.
[61] AAN 295/VII/248. [62] AAN 295/VII/248 (26 June 1948).

uncertain.[63] A Ministry of Security official, Mieczysław Moczar, noted that Gomułka's non-participation in the Plenum had played badly with the country: 'not strengthening our Party, quite the reverse'. His own loyalty was unequivocal. The Soviet Union was not only an ally, but essential to the nation: 'For us, the Soviet Union is our Fatherland. Our borders cannot be defined: today beyond Berlin and tomorrow at Gibraltar.'[64]

Social life

The new drive for uniformity had profound implications for ordinary life in all countries concerned. We begin with the official beneficiaries of the new order: the role of workers in the 'workers' state'.

In 1949, Polish trade unions were amalgamated into a single Federation. Non-affiliated bodies had no legal right to exist. The purpose of this new organ was declared to be 'transmitting directives to the masses'.[65] At the same time, the state introduced new management techniques for the workforce, such as 'shock-working' and 'socialist competition'. These split the working class into an aristocracy of labour, with well-publicised heroes, and an amorphous and impoverished majority.

A 1950 Law on Socialist Work imposed severe penalties for workers' ill-discipline and absenteeism, in effect classifying recalcitrant or slack workers as enemies of the state. Those going on strike were punished under this new legislation.[66] Forced labour camps were established in several regions.[67] Striking miners were denounced as 'Hitlerites and class enemies' and sometimes crushed by the military.[68] The result of such repression was a sharp fall in the number of reported strikes and a similar drop in their duration and support.

According to the Stalinist model, a social structure can be remoulded 'from above' by deliberate promotion out of previously excluded classes: workers and peasants. As Stalin announced in 1928, 'We need hundreds and thousands of new Bolshevik cadres capable of mastering the most diverse branches of knowledge.'[69] In the first stage of the Soviet cultural

63 AAN 295/VII/248 (24 August 1948). 64 AAN 295/VII/248 (28 August 1948).

65 Kersten, *The Establishment of Communist Rule*, p. 382.

66 B. Brzostek, *Robotnicy Warszawy. Konflikty codzienne (1950–1954)* (Warsaw, 2002), pp. 117–31.

67 B. Kopka, *Obozy pracy w Polsce 1944–1950* (Warsaw, 2002).

68 T. Grosse, 'Szarzy ludzie zaplątani w codzienności komunizmu', *Przegląd Historyczny* 1993 (3).

69 J.V. Stalin, *Sochineniya*, vol. XI (Moscow, 1949), pp. 70–4 (speech to the Eighth Congress of Komsomol, 16 May 1928).

offensive, young writers and critics of the Russian Association of Proletarian Writers (RAPP) were allowed to gain political 'hegemony'.[70] Their Polish counterparts were grouped around the periodical *Kuźnica*[71] whose manifesto of 1 June 1945 addressed Polish elites with stark challenges: 'Will the creators of national culture – from rural teachers, engineers, doctors, architects, university professors, to actors, writers and composers – remain in an atmosphere of eclectic marasmus, mysticism and pessimism, elitist escapism, turning their cowardly backs on reality, refusing to disclose their true attitudes?'[72] Activists were impatient with elite hesitations and pressed for political intervention.

The cultural spokesman, Jan Kott, complained: 'For the past three years, neither the Ministry of Culture and Art nor any political party, artistic union or educational institution has come forward with any plan for a cultural offensive to change the structure of cultural life in Poland.'[73] Another activist noted: 'the profound dissonance between the economic and social revolutions now taking place in Poland and the absence of any cultural revolution'.[74] The political authorities adopted their title 'cultural revolution'[75] and accepted the *Kuźnica* programme.

Its main aims were to reorder social life 'to accord with the ideals of progress and popular democracy' and to make 'past attainments and contemporary achievements of culture' accessible to workers and peasants.[76] According to the Polish–Russian Friendship Society, this process should involve 'much greater familiarity with Russian culture, through film, artistic enterprises and literature'. The Soviet Ambassador added: 'We must have a significant expansion of our cultural work in Poland. I think our work in this sphere must now become one of the top priorities of our Embassy.'[77]

A special Commission on Education and Culture was created.[78] A draft resolution on schools condemned 'the absence of a clearly formulated Party programme for education' and deplored the many 'anti-democratic – in many cases anti-state – views of a significant number of teachers in rural schools'. This had adverse political implications:

[70] S. Sheshukov, *Neistovye revniteli. Iz istorii literaturnoi bor'by 20-kh godov* (Moscow, 1970).
[71] Z. Żabicki, *'Kuźnica' i jej program literacki* (Krakow, 1966).
[72] *Kuźnica* 1945 (1). [73] J. Kott, 'Gorzkie obrachunki', *Kuźnica* 1947 (31/32).
[74] W. Sokorski, 'Zagadnienie walki o nową kulturę', *Odrodzenie* 10 August 1947 (32).
[75] The slogan first appears in L. Kruczkowski, 'Głos w dyskusji', *Nowe Drogi* 1947 (1); see J. Kądzielski, *0 problemie modelu rewolucji kulturalnej* (Łódź, 1964).
[76] On the equivalent stage in Soviet history, see Sheila Fitzpatrick (ed.), *Cultural Revolution in Russia, 1928–1931* (Bloomington, Ind., 1978).
[77] Cited in A. Korzoń, *Polsko-radzieckie kontakty kulturalne w latach 1944–1980* (Wrocław, 1982), p. 39.
[78] AAN 295 (Central Committee PPR) /XVII/43 (27 February 1947).

'Reactionary elements of the Peasant Party (PSL) remain passive and tolerant towards fascist agitation taking place among the young'; many teachers tried to conceal their attitude behind the mendacious slogan 'schools are apolitical'.[79]

Similar anxieties were expressed about the 'ideological front'. The high-priest of Polish Stalinism, Adam Schaff, complained that the main philosophical journal, *Myśl Współczesna* (Contemporary Thought), which intended to link 'respected socialist scholars [in the PPR and PPS] with democrats of the Kotarbiński and Chałasiński type', had a dearth of original Marxist articles. 'Even though the editorship rests in our hands', comrades were neglecting Marxism and some were even criticising it.[80] A list of remedial lecturers on 'contemporary socio-economic doctrines' was approved.[81] The Ministry of Culture and Art displayed 'excessive liberalism', had no programme and merely improvised. The Commission called for a 'broad ideological offensive', to attack 'individual creative work' as 'the anachronistic and misunderstood ideal of "artistic freedom" focussing culture solely on the satisfaction of personal wants to the total exclusion of social needs'.[82] The cultural unions should play a much greater role than before the war, and influence 'the whole cultural policy of the state'.[83]

The cultural offensive also aimed to eradicate illiteracy amongst the post-war population. This was estimated as 25 per cent total illiterates and a further 35 per cent semi-literates.[84] It launched a programme of 'mass enlightenment': a Bolshevik conception, using modern means of communication. As Bierut put it, opening the Wrocław radio station in autumn 1948: 'Good literature must be cheap and accessible to the widest readership. Theatre must have a high artistic level, at cheap prices, oriented towards the broad masses not the elite. The best musical performances must be heard by concert halls of peasants and workers. It is essential to plan a national network for radio and cinema.'[85]

Mobilisation of the intelligentsia was to begin with a conference of 'leading activists (*aktyw*)', followed by a Central Committee Plenum, national conferences, an *agitprop* campaign and the 'mobilisation of

[79] AAN 295/XVI/1143 (Marian Spychalski). [80] AAN 295/XVI/1143.
[81] Including Albrecht, Arnold, Bieńkowski and Bobińska: AAN 295/XVI/1143 (28 March 1947).
[82] AAN 295/XVI/1143 (9 May 1947).
[83] AAN 295/XVI/1143. For the Polish Writers' Union, see B. Fijalkowska, *Polityka i twórcy (1948–1959)* (Warsaw, 1985).
[84] For this estimate, AAN 295/XVI/4.
[85] B. Bierut, *0 upowszechnienie kultury* (Warsaw, 1948), pp. 20–1.

teachers for this work'.[86] As an appended 'discussion thesis' showed, the Party knew such procedures could be self-defeating. On the one hand, the policy meant increased state control (*etatyzacja*) and bureaucratic intervention, while, on the other, it depended for effectiveness on the increased spontaneity of society.[87]

The consequences for philosophy were reviewed by the outstanding sociologist Stanisław Ossowski in 1948: 'Marxism now takes on certain notions peculiar to religious systems: sectarianism, orthodoxy and heresy, for which are coined such terms as revisionism and deviation; from which arises the fear that violations of doctrine, particularly in the theoretical sphere, will devalue the organised workers' movement.'[88] Such developments, he predicted, would lead to expulsions for apostasy reminiscent of the Catholic Church. Marx and Engels had foreseen the danger and insisted that historical materialism was a method not a dogma. The Polish Party's insistence on unanimity of doctrine might be favourable in certain circumstances, but it would become harmful in the long run.[89] Marx's method must be applied to the history of Marxism itself. The dialectic is fruitful if not reduced to rote or attached to a petrified ideology. It was time to systematise the doctrine by separating out its a-priori assertions, laws and empirical generalisations and its historical hypothesis. The articles provoked a number of rejoinders which indicated that Marxism had become unfavourable territory for intellectual debate.[90] Senior ideologists had earlier complained that current discussion of Marxism was boring; when it became interesting, they closed it down.

Changes in the structure of higher learning were enacted to ensure that, as one critic from abroad put it, 'the teaching of all subjects conformed to the official doctrine of dialectical materialism, and included specific fallacious theories which enjoyed the support of the Communist Party'.[91] The right to teach was withdrawn from Ossowski, Maria Ossowska, and the eminent philosophers Ingarden and Tatarkiewicz. Former chairs of sociology and philosophy became chairs of logic and the history of social thought. Independent philosophical publications were closed down and replaced by *Myśl Filozoficzna*, whose inaugural editorial declared an ideological struggle on all fronts: from 'harmful philosophical schools

86 AAN 295/XVII (Education and Culture Department)/4. 87 *Ibid.* p. 67.

88 S. Ossowski, *Myśl Współczesna* 1948 (1) (marked by the editors 'for discussion').

89 S. Ossowski, *Myśl Współczesna* 1947 (12), pp. 501–13.

90 J. Hochfeld, '0 znaczeniu marksizmu', *Myśl Współczesna* 1948 (4), and A. Schaff, 'Marksizm i rozwój nauki', *Myśl Współczesna* 1948 (6–7). Ossowski replied in 'Na szlakach marksizmu', *Myśl Współczesna* 1948 (8–9).

91 Z. Jordan, *Philosophy and Ideology: The Development of Philosophy and Marxism–Leninism in Poland since the Second World War* (Dordrecht, 1963), p. 158.

including Thomist, Christian philosophy; phenomenology (idealist and reactionary), Husserl, Ingarden on the theory of literature and art' to Znaniecki's school of empirical sociology.[92]

Politicisation of historiography proceeded apace. The Central Committee set up a Department of Party History under the 'direct control of Party leader Bierut'.[93] The Politburo envisaged the construction in Warsaw of a Central Museum of the 'progressive-revolutionary tradition of the working class and Polish nation', which would illustrate its close links with 'the Russian revolutionary movement, the Party of Lenin–Stalin and the History of the CPSU'.[94] The First Congress of Polish Science heard that 'Marxist historical thought is guided by the genius of Lenin and Stalin, forging a methodological conception for all Polish Marxist historians, establishing the basis for a Marxist–Leninist contemporary history of Poland, and blazing the trail towards a truly Marxist–Leninist historical science in Poland.'[95]

Terror

Stalinism was driven by a dynamic ideology, which varied in intensity but contained one constant feature: the ever-expanding control by the authorities over the lives of society, social groups and private individuals. The main thrust of policy was to accelerate the process of subjugating Poland to the Soviet model.

From December 1948, political monopoly was established at the 'Unification Congress' between the PPR and PPS. Power was taken by the communists as the Polish United Workers' Party (PZPR), purportedly 'in coalition' with allied parties. Since it allowed no independent parties to compete for office, or even to exist, we will call it hereafter 'the Party'.

From that point, the essential elements of Polish Stalinism were put in place: the announcement of the six-year plan, collectivisation, the imposition of socialist realism and the unleashing of fresh terror against new targets. Its climax came in autumn 1953 (six months after Stalin's death), when the Primate of Poland, Cardinal Wyszyński, was arrested and an attempt was made to subordinate the Church, the last independent structure in Poland, to the communist state.

92 'Od Redakcji', *Myśl Filozoficzna* 1950 (1); see F. Znaniecki, *The Social Role of the Man of Knowledge* (New York, 1940).
93 AAN 237/XXI (Party History Department)/1. 94 AAN 237/XXI/25.
95 'Referat Podsekcji Historii', *Kwartalnik Historyczny* 1951 (3/4).

The assault was led by a new team, whose head was Bolesław Bierut. Second in command was Jakub Berman, with the economist Hilary Minc to complete the *troika*. The link with Moscow was essential to their rule. Through the efforts of the Polish journalist Teresa Torańska, we know more about their outlook.

Stalin was fundamental to their worldview. As Berman puts it: 'For me Stalin was victory incarnate. He bore upon his shoulders the whole burden of the war with Hitler and he was the hope for the changes in Poland of which we expected so much. For me he was a man whose name was on the lips of millions as they went into battle and died.'[96] After their annual holidays in the Crimea, Polish leaders would be entertained to a stag party in Moscow: 'It always started late in the evening and lasted until dawn. The food and drink were exquisite; I particularly remembered a delicious roast of bear. Bierut always sat next to Stalin, and I sat beside Bierut.' Stalin would propose toasts to each in turn and then came entertainment. Berman danced with Molotov, the latter leading, while Stalin wound the gramophone.[97]

In his interview, conducted during the Solidarity period, Berman characterises the post-war years as a 'civil war'. The communists were not recognised by the general public and had no authority. A little later, he modifies this thought: 'I'm not claiming there was a civil war in Poland, but there were certain elements of civil war. In a civil war either one side is right or the other is; never both.' Consequently, anti-communist partisans who took to the forest for resistance were a 'lost cause from the outset' because they had misunderstood history. For Berman, geopolitics was the key:

> The international situation – the Cold War and the conflict in Korea – created a pathological wartime mentality: pathological suspicion and the feeling of being hemmed in ... these were the results of a specific international situation, which was one of confrontation. The West was mobilising its resources and was firmly set on breaking us off from the Soviet Union, a situation repeated in 1980 and 1981.[98]

Enlarging the analogy, he shouts at his interviewer:

> Poland can only be pro-Soviet or pro-American; there's no other possibility. Poland can't be uprooted from the Soviet bloc. How? Uproot it and then where would you put it? On the moon? Poland lies on the road between the Soviet Union and Western Europe, and its position is clear: either/or. There are no half-shades because Poland can't float in the air.[99]

[96] T. Torańska, *Oni. Stalin's Polish Puppets* (London, 1987), p. 233.
[97] *Ibid.* p. 235. [98] *Ibid.* p. 309. [99] *Ibid.* p. 352.

Stalin had once declared 'cadres decide everything'. The policy of social mobility was now enacted in Poland. Thousands of people in their twenties were appointed to top jobs in the Party apparatus, state-run enterprises, engineering and journalism. The Polish intelligentsia numbered 862,000 by 1939. Despite the ravages of the Second World War, it now grew exponentially. Included in its ranks were intellectual elites; leaders of economic, political and cultural life; technical and other specialists (teachers, doctors, journalists); state officials; and numerous employees in services, trade and bureaucracy. Its growth accelerated particularly under the Stalinist programme of forced industrialisation, creating numerous positions in a new social hierarchy for those 'pushed up' through the Party and higher technical schooling.

Maria Hirszowicz has identified their common ethos: unreserved loyalty to, and faith in, the Party leadership; rejection of any personal or group loyalties that might conflict with the interests of the Party; readiness to adjust personal plans to the whim of the Party bosses; abdication of their critical faculties and humble submission to official ideology. As she notes, while these requirements ran counter to the traditional independence of the old intelligentsia, the new state provided the compensations of job security and personal rewards: 'There was the feeling of belonging to the elite, the taste of power, the joy of participation in a chosen group that was arbitrarily reshaping society, the privilege of prying into other people's lives, the exhilarating experience of acting beyond the law and beyond the social rules that limited the freedom of ordinary citizens.'[100]

The Party vetted all key posts to ensure its 'leading role' in society and the state.[101] Its appointments system (*nomenklatura*) grew exponentially from modest beginnings. By 1988, it was secretly admitted to be 270,000 strong.[102] Adding their dependants, we have about 1 million people, some 2–3 per cent of the population. They were well-privileged, protected from consumer shortages by special shops 'behind the yellow curtains', and had weekly packages delivered to their private apartments. Another privilege was political inclusion. The excluded public could see it meant 'negative selection': promotion for political loyalty rather than qualifications or ability.

100 M. Hirszowicz, *The Bureaucratic Leviathan: A Study in the Sociology of Communism* (Oxford, 1980), p. 182.

101 A. Paczkowski, 'System nomenklatury' in A. Paczkowski (ed.), *Centrum władzy w Polsce, 1948–1970* (Warsaw, 2003), pp. 115–39.

102 W. Jaruzelski in S. Perzkowski [A. Paczkowski] (ed.), *Tajne dokumenty Biura Politycznego i Sekretariatu KC. Ostatni rok władzy 1988–1989* (London, 1994), p. 43.

Stalinist terror from 1948 to 1953 was less violent in scale than in the immediately preceding years, though torture of political prisoners became more regular, even routine. Yet crimes commited during that period seem to last longer in the popular memory. It may be in the nature of resistance: at least some of those persecuted prior to 1948 were actual or potential opponents of communist rule. Thereafter, the victims are entire social categories: above all, private farmers or religious believers. Yet, as Kersten notes, terror is a crime against humanity, whomsoever it falls upon.[103] It also included a new target: communists themselves.

Following the expulsion of Yugoslavia, 'Titoists' were tracked down across the bloc. Later, the hunt was widened to international 'Trotskyite' and 'Zionist' agents allegedly lurking within communist ranks. The Ministry of Public Security cast a wide net, set out in a memo to Bierut on 2 March 1950. In accordance with the Stalinist notion of 'intensifying class struggle', which amounted to the absurd thesis that enemies of socialism grow stronger the more often they are defeated, the Ministry stated: 'The enemy will respond to our six-year plan with even greater hatred and even more underhand attacks.' The priority was 'uncovering and eliminating foreign agents and anti-Party groups intent on infiltrating the Party with spies and diversionists from hostile centres'.

Terror was coordinated by a Public Security Commission, established on 24 February 1949. It kept the files of the *nomenklatura* system for appointments at every level in public life. It oversaw the security and intelligence apparatus. Bierut chaired all its sessions. Soviet 'advisors' – some fifty in all – had free run of this Commission, gave orders and had complete access to all its information-gathering, which was coordinated with Soviet security agencies across the 'bloc'.

On the same day, General Tartar and Lieutenants Utnik and Nowicki were arrested and brought to a show trial before the Supreme Military Court. They were given long prison sentences for organising a 'diversionary espionage group within the Polish army' and conspiring to 'restore the rule of landowners and capitalists' in Poland. Gomułka was arrested on the first day of the trial and interned in a country house. Psychological pressures were put on him but physical torture was not used – unlike on his counterparts in the neighbouring states. It was hoped to destroy him by implication.

According to the defector 'Światło', an envoy from the Hungarian Politburo 'came to Warsaw and told Bierut about the uncovering of a widespread Titoist conspiracy. He gave Bierut a list of Polish communists

[103] K. Kersten, 'The Terror, 1949–1954' in Kemp-Welch (ed.), *Stalinism in Poland*, p. 79.

allegedly mixed up in the conspiracy.'[104] Bierut's speech, on the eve of the trial of László Rajk – Former Minister of the Interior – in Hungary, called for 'Revolutionary Vigilance in the Present Situation'. It stated that the Party still contained 'foreign agents' acting against the anti-imperialist camp. There were gangs of 'double-dealers' and provocateurs hiding inside the Party. He added that Gomułka had been responsible for the infiltration of foreign agents into the Party and had tolerated them after Liberation and had tacitly supported the Tito group in Yugoslavia. But, unlike his counterparts in the neighbouring states, Gomułka was not brought to trial.

Hanna Świda-Ziemba suggests that Stalinist terror was internalised. Since almost everyone was threatened with arrest, or even death, this was bound in time to create conformity.[105] Nazi terror, although even more violent, had not been internalised to the same degree. She agrees with the sociologist Kazimierz Wyka that it was an external imposition, not part of the social system. Stalinism also spread complicity. The state delegated the 'responsibility' of de-masking enemies to the public at large. Regular denunciation became a social duty. Accusers demanded recantations; those who obliged were required to confirm their sincerity by accusing others. You had to join the hunt to protect yourself from being 'unmasked' as a witch. What, indeed, could be more convincing proof of innocence than to denounce one's former friends? To remain neutral 'in conditions of capitalist encirclement' was tantamount to 'capitulation'.

The Great Leader was not held responsible for the terror. His official seventieth birthday (December 1949) prompted such slogans as:

- Long Live the Continuer of the Immortal Works of Marx, Engels, and Lenin – The Great Stalin!
- Long live the Organiser of the Victory over Fascism, Leader of the World Camp of Peace – Generalissimo Joseph Stalin!
- Long live the Great Friend of Poland – Joseph Stalin![106]

The Party despatched lecturers to big enterprises and 'intellectual circles' to explain Stalin's colossal contribution to knowledge in every sphere.[107] He was acclaimed 'Philologist of Genius', 'Life-Giving Genius', 'Genius Architect of Communism', 'Genius of Theoretical Thought', 'Greatest Genius of Our Epoch', (and finally) 'Greatest Man of All Times'. A Polish

[104] Z. Błażyński, *Mówi Józef Światło. Za kulisami bezpieki i partii 1940–1955*, 3rd edn (London, 1986), pp. 24–42.

[105] H. Świda-Ziemba, 'Stalinizm i społeczeństwo polskie' in J. Kurczewski (ed.), *Stalinizm* (Warsaw, 1989), pp. 15–95; 'Wróg Stalinizmu. Notatki z życia systemu', *Karta*, 1991(3).

[106] AAN 237/XVI/1190. [107] AAN 237/IV/41 (6 March 1951).

scholar found over 300 types of tribute in the Polish press alone.[108] It is difficult to tell how seriously such propaganda was taken by the public.[109]

The Church

Despite the ravages of Stalinism in Poland, important differences from the imported 'Soviet model' still prevailed. Above all, the Catholic Church survived persecution, perhaps thrived on it, and remained a powerful force independent of the state.[110] As always in Polish history, the Church served as a repository of national ideals and as a sanctuary in times of trouble.

Under partition it was a bastion of Polish Catholicism against Prussian Protestantism and Russian Orthodoxy. During the Russo-Polish war of 1920, Red Army troops occupied eastern Poland and reached the gates of Warsaw itself, where they were repelled by the defenders. This 'miracle on the Vistula' was popularly attributed to the 'Black Madonna of Częstochowa'. This referred back to another famous victory, against Swedish invaders. Following their siege of Jasna Góra, a monastery successfully defended by 150 noblemen and 70 monks, the King of Poland, Jan Kazimierz, vowed to entrust the country to the Madonna, recognising her as Queen of Poland. Annual pilgrimages to the shrine at Częstochowa were a major event, continuing throughout the communist period.

Polish Stalinists knew that disarming the Church would be essential to the consolidation of their rule. Berman had observed, in a secret note to Bierut:

> The Church is a great obstacle to us because in it are concentrated the philosophical bases of ideological reaction, which it ceaselessly relays to the masses. In the popular consciousness – above all amongst the humanist intelligentsia – it is the bulwark of Polish tradition and culture, the most complete expression of 'Polishness'. This traditional understanding of patriotism is the greatest strength of the Church, even stronger and more powerful than the magic of ritual. The Church is a natural source of opposition, both ideological and philosophical.[111]

In its first statements under communist rule, the Church hierarchy set out a dual policy towards the new regime. In a sermon in Poznań on 28 October 1945, the Primate of Poland, Cardinal August Hlond, noted

[108] Kupiecki, *'Natchnienie milionów'*, pp. 238–50.
[109] D. Jarosz and M. Pasztor, *W krzywym zwierciadle. Polityka władz komunistycznych w Polsce w świetle plotek i pogłosek z lat 1949–1956* (Warsaw, 1995).
[110] A. Dudek, *Państwo i Kościół w Polsce, 1945–1970* (Krakow, 1995).
[111] AAN Oddział VI [PZPR], p. 112, t. 26, pp. 213–20.

that 'Poland has been experiencing Christianity in its own way for ten centuries and has its own distinctive approach towards today's attitudes. Poland is moving towards rebirth on its own path.' The Church would never compromise its ethical principles with any materialistic ideology. At the same time, the Church did not identify with any oppositional groups. It was willing to cooperate with the secular authorities in 'building a system without privileges and injustice'.[112]

A pastoral letter read from all pulpits in March 1946 was equally uncompromising: 'Poland should be modern, just, successful, richer in knowledge, technology and culture, and well-organised. But Poland cannot be godless. Poland cannot be de-coupled from its membership in the Christian communion. Poland cannot betray its Christian spirit. Poland must not be communist. It must remain Catholic.'[113] When the pre-election campaign got under way in autumn 1946, the Episcopate made clear that all citizens had the right to vote but that Catholics could not support any organisation or party which stood against Christianity. They could support only those standing on the basis of Christian ethics. This meant not voting for 'candidates whose programmes, or methods of governing, are contrary to common-sense, to the good of the nation and state, to Christian morality and the Catholic worldview'.[114]

This general policy was maintained by Hlond's successor as Primate, from 1948, the Bishop of Lublin, Stefan Wyszyński. It rested on the assumption that communism would endure in Poland for a long time. Securing the widest possible scope for its activities required some degree of cooperation with the new authorities. This bore immediate fruit. Even before the war ended, the future Cardinal of Kraków, Adam Sapieha, arranged the launch of two independent periodicals: the popular newspaper *Tygodnik Powszechny* and the more intellectual monthly *Znak*. They sought to foster Polish Catholic opinion amongst followers from diverse political backgrounds, and to enter into some form of dialogue with the secular, communist state.

Tygodnik Powszechny's opening editorial began by acknowledging the need to grant to God what is God's and to Caesar what is Caesar's. Whilst passionately concerned with the human personality, and with expressing Catholic social attitudes, it rejected purely political activities. Its editor from October 1949 was the journalist Jerzy Turowicz, who held the post for fifty years, apart from a brief interval when he refused to publish an obituary of Stalin in March 1953. His editorial precepts were open-minded: to explain the Gospel's meaning in the social sphere; to develop

[112] *Listy Pasterskie Episkopatu Polski* (Paris, 1975), pp. 11–15.
[113] AAN 295/VII/243. [114] AAN 295/VII/243 (Jasna Góra, 10 September 1946).

an ecclesiology which recognised the links between the Church and the world; and to achieve a universalism that rejected provincialism or nationalism. *Znak* sought to enter into dialogue with the new authorities on the basis of 'unbiased opinions'. A Catholic–Marxist dialogue was sought. But there were many points of contention: anti-clericalism in the communist press, attacks on church schooling, military chaplains.

At the outset, the Party hid its counter-measures against the Church. From 1948, however, it increasingly used juridical and police methods to challenge the Church's huge influence. Some 400 priests were imprisoned on various pretexts in September 1948 alone.[115] An Episcopal Letter expressed extreme concern about the state's resort to force, fearing it would lead to violent resistance and tragedy, particularly in the countryside: 'Let us conscientiously perform the duties of our calling. Let farmers honestly sow the fields. Let noble work, which is humanity's vocation, hum in the steel-works, mines, workshops, offices and stores. Let the reconstruction of Polish life, in the capital, cities, farms and churches, grow from month to month.' No-one should be provoked into 'dissolute steps'. Life was sacred: 'Polish blood must not be squandered on an ill-advised pastime.'[116] But the blood-letting was only just beginning.

A Cominform conference in February 1949, presided over by Vishinsky, was devoted entirely to the struggle with religion. Berman insisted much later that Polish communists had retained autonomy over matters in which they considered it had to be retained: 'One example is the Catholic Church. We took a categorical decision not to interfere in its affairs. This was entirely contrary to what was going on in Russia on a vast scale.'[117] In fact, Bierut renewed the anti-clerical campaign in a speech on 'foreign agents' shortly afterwards. The 'reactionary part of the clergy' was drawing some of the faithful 'into the game which, under the mask of fine phrases such as the idea of Atlanticism, is steering down the road of Americanised Prussianism'. The time had come for the Church hierarchy to declare its loyalty: either to accept its obligations under the Polish government's policy on Church–State relations or to side with the 'anti-popular' and 'anti-national' forces linked to foreign powers and the underground.[118]

[115] Kersten, 'The Terror: 1949–1954' in Kemp-Welch (ed.), *Stalinism in Poland*, p. 84.
[116] *Listy Pasterskie Episkopatu Polski* (23 September 1948).
[117] T. Torańska, *Oni. Stalin's Polish Puppets*, pp. 302–3.
[118] *Nowe Drogi* 1949 (2), cited by Kersten, 'The Terror: 1949–1954' in Kemp-Welch (ed.), *Stalinism in Poland*, p. 85.

Church broadcasts were stopped and its publications were heavily censored or banned. As an opening shot, *Tygodnik Warszawski* was closed in August 1948. Its editor-in-chief was later tried *in camera* for allegedly attempting to construct 'a Catholic-national mass movement which, with the help of allied armies, aimed to overthrow the existing Polish system by force'. He died in prison. *Znak* was shut in 1949. Catholic youth organisations were closed down and charitable bodies, such as Caritas, were re-staffed by state appointees. Church hospitals were turned over to the state. On 6 March 1950, the greater part of Church land was expropriated.

Despite all this, a Church–State accord was abruptly announced on 16 April 1950. It was based on reciprocity. The Episcopate would be guided by the Polish *raison d'état* and would 'counteract activities hostile to Poland, especially anti-Polish and revisionist actions on the part of the German clergy'. This referred to the deeply contested question of the status of Poland's Recovered Territories, which the Vatican was reluctant to recognise. At home, the Church was to 'oppose the misuse of feelings for anti-state activity' and curb its clergy where guilty. In particular, 'the Episcopate will explain to the clergy that it should not oppose the development of cooperatives in rural areas because all cooperatives are essentially based on the ethical concept of human nature'.

In return, the government would restore many of the Church's recently abolished rights and privileges. Catholic associations (which Kersten numbers at almost 5,000)[119] were reinstated and the Catholic University of Lublin was allowed to continue to exist. Catholic press and publications were to receive equal treatment with others. Religious education would be permitted in schools and public worship freed from interference. The welfare organisation Caritas would return to Catholic control.[120] Thus the package set out conditions for more normal relations between Church and state, a form of co-habitation which respected separate spheres. The Episcopate urged its flock not to boycott the 1952 *Sejm* elections, reminding the faithful of the civic duty to vote. They even took a constructive approach to the promulgation of the new 'Stalin' Constitution in the same year.

Normality did not ensue. There were continuous arrests of priests and monks: 900 believers were in prison by the end of 1951. In the winter of 1952–3, a new campaign against the Church was prepared. The death of Stalin led to a thaw in many spheres, but for the Church it led to increased persecution. The authorities sought to crush any Church-inspired

[119] *The Establishment of Communist Rule*, p. 213.

[120] B. Szajkowski, *Next to God ... Poland. Politics and Religion in Contemporary Poland* (London, 1983), p. 14.

notions of liberalisation. The campaign's climax came in September 1953 when a show trial, of Bishop Kaczmarek of Kielce, was held. On the defendants' bench sat victims of lengthy and brutal interrogations. Convicted of 'weakening the defensive spirit of Polish society in the face of threatened Hitlerite aggression, disrupting the reconstruction of the country and planned economy, and of sabotage on Polish soil in the interests of American imperialism', Bishop Kaczmarek and other 'ring-leaders' received twelve-year sentences.

Anticipating public protests, the Ministry of Interior put all informants on immediate alert: 'They must report all inimical behaviour, intentions and events. Agents should give particular attention to the Bishop's Curia, to priests known to have hostile attitudes, to clerical circles and meetings, to bandits, supporters of émigré groups, revisionists and all those who listen to imperialist broadcasts.'[121] By the end of 1953, 8 bishops and 900 priests were imprisoned. The Primate of Poland was also detained.

During three years of confinement in remote monasteries, Cardinal Stefan Wyszyński chose modern martyrdom, 'the road of work, not of blood'. It was better to be a 'scorned priest than a praised Caesar'. He saw Marxism as a Western product transplanted to Orthodox soil. No accommodation was possible without an alteration in the authorities' attitudes. Implacable atheism was producing merely sterile orthodoxy, alienating even the more enlightened communists. Persecution could only strengthen its resolve.

Overtures were made to Wyszyński in April 1956.[122] But he refused a deal that would allow his return to Warsaw while other bishops remained outside their dioceses: 'I could return as the last but never as the first.'[123] His return was also predicated on repeal of a 1953 edict under which the government controlled Church appointments. Wyszyński's diaries for spring 1956 noted that those who had doubted the Stalin cult and suffered for it were now vindicated: 'Who should be going to prison today, when it turned out that non-communists were the better communists, who understood better the spirit of Marxism?' Such was the fate of gods wrought by human hands: 'a doctrine that condemns today what yesterday it raised to the altar'.[124]

121 Kersten, 'The Terror: 1949–1954' in Kemp-Welch (ed.), *Stalinism in Poland*, p. 88.

122 A. Paczkowski (ed.), *Tajne dokumenty Biura Politycznego. PRL–ZSRR 1956–1970* (London, 1998), pp. 13–15.

123 *A Freedom Within. The Prison Notes of Stefan, Cardinal Wyszyński* (London, 1985), pp. 246–7.

124 *Ibid.* pp. 234–5.

3 Thaw

President Truman 'was sure that the United States was God's own country, the city on the hill, the exemplar of a superior way of life based on personal freedoms, private property and entrepreneurial opportunity'.[1] All this had been endangered by German and Japanese militarism, against which inter-war isolationism had proved ineffective. He thus agreed with Roosevelt that the USA must practise collective security and join international organisations, and trade associations, dedicated to this end. Within a few years, such general notions had hardened into a formal alliance structure, whose main object was confrontation with the Soviet Union.

When the Soviet Union began a Berlin blockade in June 1948, the USA responded with an airlift of supplies. But US military assessment of Soviet potentialities was cautious: the Soviets were bluffing and their hand could and should be called. Specialists on the Soviet Union considered the USSR too weak to risk war, despite overwhelming conventional superiority in Europe – which continued until the end of the Cold War. They had little at sea or in the air. Their satellites were unreliable and they had lost face in Italy, France and Finland (where communists had left government).[2] Even so, the threat perception sharpened greatly following the Soviet detonation of an atomic bomb in August 1949. It now seemed to Washington that the Soviet leadership might go beyond bluff, particularly over Berlin. The possible addition of a hydrogen bomb, many hundred times more powerful than the weapons the USA possessed, was a further anxiety. It would give Stalin the option of nuclear 'blackmail'.

The President ordered a comprehensive reassessment of US policy towards Eastern Europe. 'The Strategy of Freedom', formally labelled 'NSC 68' and drafted by Paul Nitze, became emblematic of the Cold War. Though ostensibly intended to focus on one region of Europe, the

[1] M. Leffler, 'Truman, U.S. Grand Stategy and the Cold War, 1945–1952' in Leffler and O. A. Westad (eds.), *Cambridge History of the Cold War*, vol. II (forthcoming).
[2] *Ibid.*

opening pages present an apocalyptic struggle between American Good and Soviet Evil[3]: 'Unwillingly our free society finds itself mortally challenged by the Soviet system'; 'There is a basic conflict between the idea of freedom under government of laws and the idea of slavery under the grim oligarchy of the Kremlin.' Earlier aims of US policy were reiterated: 'To reduce the power and influence of the USSR to limits which no longer constitute a threat to the peace, national independence and stability of the world family of nations'. But they were extended to a more active policy: 'To bring about a basic change in the conduct of international relations by the government in power in Russia, to conform with the purposes and principles set forth in the UN Charter'.[4] These objectives were to be attained through methods 'short of war'.

As a key part of the strategy, the 'present perimeter areas around traditional Russian boundaries' should be retracted and the satellite countries encouraged to emerge as 'entities independent of the USSR'. National independence should be fostered 'to help modify current Soviet behaviour'. In particular, the USA should 'strengthen the orientation toward the United States of the non-Soviet nations; and help such of those nations as are able and willing to make an important contribution to US security, to increase their economic and political stability and their military capability'. The document concluded by advocating 'an affirmative program intended to wrest the initiative from the Soviet Union, confront it with convincing evidence of the determination and ability of the free world to frustrate the Kremlin design of a world dominated by its will'.[5]

Although Truman accepted this strategy, he was hesitant about its costs. The escalating Korean conflict was a constraining factor. Despite this, four US army divisions were deployed to Europe, giving military shape to NATO, under General Eisenhower. At the end of 1950, the President embarked on a massive security programme for the next eighteen months. During that time, the army was to increase to 1,353,000 troops (from 655,000), the navy to 397 major combat vessels (from 238) and the air force fleet to 95 (from 48). In his 'Farewell Address' (15 January 1953), he noted: 'history will remember my term in office as the years when the "cold war" began to overshadow our lives'. History would also record 'that in those 8 years we have set the course that we can win it'.[6] Six weeks later, the Soviet leader also left the stage.

3 S. Lucas, *Freedom's War. The US Crusade Against the Soviet Union, 1945–1956* (Manchester, 1999), p. 79.

4 E. May (ed.), *American Cold War Strategy: Interpreting NSC 68* (Boston, 1993), p. 78.

5 *Ibid.* pp. 78–81.

6 *Public Papers of the Presidents. Harry S. Truman 1952–1953* (Washington, 1963), p. 1199.

Death of a deity

Stalin had suffered his first stroke in October 1945. Stalin's daughter Svetlana notes that 'my father fell ill and was quite sick for some months'.[7] She was not allowed to visit him or even communicate by telephone, which led to the rumour that he had temporarily lost the power of speech. Thereafter, his Kremlin office hours were cut to a maximum of three, usually in the mid-evening, after which he was driven out to his favourite *dacha* at Kuntsevo, guarded by more than 100 Ministry of State Security officers. The domestic staff – cook, servants, cleaners and so on – were also all on the Ministerial payroll. Svetlana, who saw him there for the last time on 21 September 1952, noted a further change of health. He had given up smoking, the habit of a lifetime, and his normally pallid face – some called it yellowish – had turned red. She rightly assumed this was caused by high blood pressure. But he was not under medical supervision. His personal physician had been arrested and his entire medical staff was about to be purged as part of a 'Jewish Doctors' Plot'.

On 28 February 1953, Stalin invited his four closest colleagues to the usual nocturnal supper at his *dacha*. It ended at 5 a.m. Khrushchev noted that Stalin drank a lot and was in a good mood. But the next day, a Sunday, passed with no communication from the intercom in Stalin's quarters. However, his rooms were also equipped with special sensors telling his staff and guards exactly where Stalin was at any moment. Given an 'absence of movement', it seems likely that the chief of guards alerted the Kremlin to this fact and awaited their instructions. These were evidently to do nothing. No doctor was called until 7 a.m. on 2 March. There was thus a clear day in which Stalin's closest allies – Beria, Bulganin, Malenkov and Khrushchev – could collude. They all feared the 'spontaneous reaction that would both erupt in the country's leadership and the public at large' if news of Stalin's death leaked out before they had arranged the succession amongst themselves.[8]

One of their first decisions (1 March) was to discontinue investigation of the Doctors' Plot and release the intended victims. The propaganda campaign about a 'Zionist Plot' and a series of other 'show trials' fabricated on Stalin's orders were also cancelled. Molotov's wife, Zhemchuzhina, was released from the GULag and selective rehabilitations began. Over the spring and summer, the population of the GULag was halved by the release of prisoners convicted for non-political 'crimes', and many forced labour

[7] S. Alliluyeva, *Twenty Letters to a Friend* (New York, 1967), pp. 207–8.
[8] Z. A. Medvedev, 'Zagadka smerti Stalina', *Voprosy istorii* 2000 (10).

camps and enterprises were returned to civilian control.[9] Rules governing the internal passport, reintroduced by Stalin in 1931, were relaxed. Taken together, these measures resulted in significant movement of the population across the country, including former *zeks* (political prisoners) who returned home to confront their denouncers.

On 2 March the Politburo, recently abolished by Stalin, was restored under the new name of 'Presidium'. Meeting in Stalin's Kremlin office, leaving his chair empty, they decided to call a full meeting of the Central Committee 'as soon as possible'. That was the evening of 5 March. When it convened, the writer Simonov, a candidate (deputy) member, noted that only Molotov seemed perturbed by Stalin's imminent demise: his face was 'motionless, as if petrified'.[10] The rest were businesslike and energetic, acting as if a great burden had been lifted. Seventy minutes after they adjourned, the Great Leader of Mankind expired.

Since deities do not die, the Stalin myth might have ended in March 1953. But the unexpected announcement, taken with the recent hysterical press campaign against the 'Doctor's Plot', led to a widespread outpouring of emotions. A letter to Khrushchev from a rank-and-file communist declared that 90 per cent of Party members did not believe that Stalin had died naturally: 'this is the work of despicable killers who have done their wicked deed so skilfully that even medical experts could not discover anything'. He thought all Jews should be removed from the government forthwith.[11] Except perhaps in the Western Ukraine and Baltic republics, public mourning was widespread and seemingly sincere.[12] One citizen donated a month's pay towards the construction of a Stalin mausoleum. Resolutions poured into the Central Committee and other central bodies demanding the attachment of Stalin's name to factories and institutions (including Moscow University). Some suggested a Georgian Soviet Stalinist Republic and even the Union of Soviet Stalinist Republics. Several participants, including the young Yevtushenko, describe mass panic among crowds at the funeral.

Stalin's death was abruptly announced in Poland on 6 March 1953. Public opinion was shocked. 'What will happen now without Stalin?' In the Katowice province, '*Kulaks* [better-off farmers] stated that soon after

[9] Y. Gorlizki and O. Khlevniuk, *Cold Peace. Stalin and the Soviet Ruling Circle, 1945–1953* (Oxford, 2004), p. 167.

[10] K. Simonov, *Glazami cheloveka moego pokoleniia* (Moscow, 1988), p. 228.

[11] I. Aksiutin, 'Popular Responses to Khrushchev' in W. Taubman S. Khrushchev and A. Gleason (eds.), *Nikita Khrushchev and the Creation of a Superpower* (Yale, 2000), pp. 178–80.

[12] E. Zubkova, *Russia After the War. Hopes, Illusions, and Disappointments, 1945–1957* (New York, 1998), Chs. 17, 18.

the death of Piłsudski there was war and now after Stalin's death it may be the same.' In Kraków province they asked: 'Who is going to defend the peace now? There will surely be a war'; 'Now the Americans will feel strong. There may be war.'[13] Applications to join the Party rose – 320 new candidates in Gdańsk alone. Many workers made production pledges in Stalin's memory. Others stated that it was thanks to Stalin and the Red Army that Poland had regained its independence. But it was rumoured in the Kielce countryside that Stalin's death would mean an end to the attempt to collectivise.[14]

On the day of the funeral, 9 March, shops were shut. Sirens rang out in all factories. Church bells, however, rang less frequently. Some priests refused to toll them at all. One in Przemyśl remarked: 'Comrade Stalin was an unbeliever and we don't have to ring for him.'[15] Sometimes a compromise was reached with youth activists ringing the church bells. The weekly newsreel shows a candle-lit procession winding past the Central Committee headquarters in Warsaw. Red and black flags are ubiquitous and every shop displays a portrait of the late leader. In the early evening, snow fell on the statue of Stalin, giving an effect of socialist surrealism.

Marcin Zaremba records a variety of emotions: from genuine grief, through uncertainty and fear, to hope and joy. Some Poles held Stalin in high regard as an authority figure, guarantor of peace and security, a man who had modernised the country and fostered social advancement. Others saw Stalin as the incarnation of evil, responsible for the Katyń massacres and persecutor of the Church and peasantry, whose departure would make the world a better place.[16]

Bolshevism had no procedure for succession. Nor did Stalin groom a successor. The consequent inertia is well captured by Khrushchev: 'Our boat continued to float down the stream, along the same course that had been set by Stalin, even though we all sensed that things were not right.'[17] He also reflected on Soviet vulnerability, recalling Stalin's frequent admonition that, once he had gone, 'the imperialistic powers will ring your necks like chickens.'[18] This was Stalin's legacy. He left no obvious

[13] AAN 237/VII/1134–5 *Meldunki z terenu*, 6 March 1953.
[14] AAN 237/VII/1136–8 *Meldunki z terenu*, 7 March 1953.
[15] AAN 237/VII/1140–2 *Meldunki z terenu*, 9 March 1953.
[16] M. Zaremba,'Opinia publiczna w Polsce wobec choroby i śmierci Józefa Stalina' in A. Friszke (ed.), *Władza a społeczeństwo w PRL* (Warsaw, 2003), pp. 29–53.
[17] *Khrushchev Remembers: The Last Testament* (Boston, 1974), p. 220.
[18] *Khrushchev Remembers* (Boston, 1970), p. 392.

means to overcome it. As Zubok remarks, 'the tyrant deliberately maintained an analytical vacuum below him'.[19]

In Stalin's last years, the Presidium had met irregularly and did not discuss foreign policy questions. Instead, Stalin liked to arrange ad hoc panels of subordinates – *troiki* (trios) or *shestyorki* (sextets) – without regard to expertise, and gave them impossible agendas. Khrushchev describes the outcome in his memoirs.[20] Such deliberate chaos gave him a free hand to determine policy. Of the vast amount of material collected by foreign policy organs, a brief daily digest was prepared by Molotov's Secretariat. Molotov delivered it to Stalin at nocturnal briefing sessions. An exhausted Secretariat often worked past midnight and then had to remain at work to hear Stalin's orders for the next day.

A primary concern of the post-Stalin leadership was to head off disorder or panic, both at home and in Eastern Europe, not least because of the opportunities they would offer to the West. Soviet intelligence reported that 'ruling circles' within NATO 'assumed that the death of Stalin would trigger domestic unrest in the Soviet Union and would lead to a weakening of the USSR's international influence'. The West's 'reactionary press' was rife with speculation about a 'power struggle' in the Kremlin.[21] The new leadership also thought that paralysis or indecision in Moscow would be taken as a sign of weakness in the West, which would push for unilateral advantages. They might press the Soviet Union into concessions, particularly on the unresolved German question. To head off these dangers, a 'peace initiative' was announced on various fronts: from ending harassment of Western diplomats in Moscow, to restoring diplomatic relations with Greece and Israel. Private channels were used to press the Chinese and North Koreans towards an armistice, eventually declared in July 1953, leading to an end of the Korean War.

There were also the first attempts to remedy some of Stalin's blunders, notably the avoidable split with Yugoslavia. The police chief since 1938, Beria, appears to have been pioneering in this regard. It was alleged in July 1953 that Beria had approached Ranković, head of the Yugoslav secret police, for a top secret negotiation to restore relations between the two countries. Such talks, which might include Beria travelling to Tito, were to remain a secret from Soviet colleagues.[22] It was even rumoured later that Beria envisioned a more general retreat from empire,

[19] V. Zubok, *Soviet Intelligence and the Cold War: The 'Small' Committee of Information, 1952–53*, CWIHP Working Paper no.4 (Washington, 1992), p. 9.

[20] *Khrushchev Remembers*, p. 297.

[21] Zubok, *Soviet Intelligence*, pp. 14–15.

[22] J. Richter, *Re-examining Soviet Policy Towards Germany during the Beria Interregnum*, CWIHP Working Paper no. 3 (Washington, 1992), p. 21.

neutralising Germany and perhaps Eastern Europe, possibly the Baltic states and even the Ukraine, thus reconstituting the Soviet boundaries of Brest-Litovsk in 1918.[23] Given that Beria was arrested at this point and shot on the spot, or, according to the official record, executed after a military tribunal six months later, testimony is likely to be inconclusive.

Stalin had left an impasse in Eastern Europe. A 'buffer zone' had been built against the West, but was largely populated by reluctant allies, and the manner of its acquisition and retention had led to East–West confrontation. Could a means be found to retain the territory while reducing the risk of its causing a catastrophe? Much depended on the analysis of US intentions, over which Soviet interpretations were divided. One view recalled Eisenhower's electoral promise to end the war in Korea, if necessary by going there to achieve a peaceful settlement. This appeared to be confirmed by the President's 'Chance for Peace' speech of 16 April 1953.[24] He indicated to Soviet leaders that, given the costs and uncertainties of continuing the Cold War, accommodation could be reached given concessions on their side, such as free elections in Eastern Europe or an Austrian peace treaty. More sceptical Soviet analysts saw President Eisenhower's 'peace initiative' as a stalling measure, designed to make it harder for the Soviet Union to pursue a peace agenda of its own.

A third view saw the new Secretary of State Foster Dulles as the real author of a Cold War 'offensive' to 'roll back' Soviet influence, which demanded a total revision of Stalin's policies, above all in Eastern Europe. Dulles told the National Security Council (13 March 1953) that 'If we keep our pressures on, psychological and otherwise, we may either force a collapse of the Kremlin regime or else transform the Soviet orbit from a union of satellites dedicated to aggression, into a coalition for defence only.'[25] Soviet analysts believed Dulles had the backing of powerful forces in Washington, including the Defence department, CIA and senior Republicans in Senate.[26]

Not dissimilar polarities could be found amongst Stalin's successors. Scholars have sought evidence of policy debates within Stalin's post-war entourage and attempted to identify the sponsors of differing policies. A variety of views can be seen. Molotov remained an unreconstructed Stalinist to the end of his days. According to this outlook, capitalism and socialism were engaged in a permanent struggle, which would be

[23] J. Rainer, *The New Course in Hungary in 1953*, CWIHP Working Paper no. 38 (Washington, 2002), p. 9 note 22.
[24] *FRUS: 1952–54*, vol. II (Washington, 1984), pp. 1699–1706.
[25] Cited by C. Ostermann, *The United States, the East German Uprising of 1953, and the Limits of Rollback*, CWIHP Working Paper no.11 (Washington, 1994), p. 13.
[26] Zubok, *Soviet Intelligence*, pp. 12–16.

resolved by force. No concessions should be made to the 'imperialists' while socialism led all progressive peoples to their inevitable victory. By contrast, Malenkov was nuanced. He considered that Soviet nuclear weapons guaranteed protection against a direct attack and provided a position of advantage from which genuine concessions could be offered to the West. This would counteract American attempts to present the Soviet Union as an aggressive enemy and help to divide opinions within NATO as to the extent of a 'Soviet threat'. The key was to change the policy in East Germany.

In summer 1952, the East German leadership announced a crash programme of Sovietisation. Heavy industry was given absolute priority, forced collectivisation was accelerated, the Protestant Church was more heavily persecuted and travel between East and West Germany further restricted. The main results were consumer shortages, budgetary deficits and mass emigration. Stalin's successors wished to halt this policy and couple it with a conciliatory response to Eisenhower's speech. *Pravda* suggested on 25 April 1953 that German reunification might be possible prior to a peace treaty, thus obviating the obstacle of both Germanys having to take part in such a treaty. Soon afterwards, *Pravda* announced that reunification of Germany was at the centre of the Soviet Union's European policy and called for 'coordinated' action by the four powers to resolve the matter.[27]

Ulbricht's campaign was halted on 9 June. Consumers, farmers, would-be emigrants and religious believers were all given hope. But an internal report noted that the suddenness of this reversal had an adverse effect on many citizens: 'A broad segment of the population did not understand the Party's "New Course". They saw it as a sign of weakness or even as a victory by the Americans or the Church.'[28] Others thought it was the result of Western pressure: 'over there they finally forced a change of course here'. One official reported that villagers had congregated in the local bar to drink the health of the West German leader, Adenauer.[29]

But one crucial section of the population was excluded from the concessions of the 'New Course'. Higher work norms, arbitrarily imposed the previous month, remained in force. On 16 June, several hundred construction workers in East Berlin called for a general strike. Faced with this, the Party declared that the announced increased norms would now be 'voluntary'. It was too late to avert a tragedy. Next day, mass protests took place in most cities and towns throughout the DDR. Only the use

27 Richter, *Re-examining Soviet Policy*, pp. 13–14.
28 Ostermann, *The United States, the East German Uprising of 1953*, p. 8.
29 *Ibid.* p. 22.

of massive Soviet military force prevented the toppling of the East German regime.

The indirect role of the United States in this first post-Stalin crisis in Eastern Europe deserves further examination. It led to a serious reconsideration of 'roll-back' as a strategy towards Soviet power in Eastern Europe. While the USA had encouraged resistance in East Germany, and would again in Hungary in 1956 as we shall see, there proved to be little if any operational substance to its rhetorical appeal for 'liberation'.

Psychological warfare against Eastern Europe was aimed at weakening Soviet power in the region and undermining local communist regimes. A secret report by State Department consultants in 1950 suggested a range of overt and covert projects, from military demonstrations, sabotage, abductions and assassinations to a propaganda campaign, 'Operation Debunk,' to unmask Soviet mythologies. Focussing on East Germany as the most vulnerable state, the report suggested sponsoring a 'unified, strong, growing resistance movement within the Soviet zone'. By October 1952, this had been elaborated into a comprehensive psychological warfare plan (Psychological Strategy Board D-21) directed against East German communism. It was designed to maximise dissatisfaction and defections.[30]

A particularly potent instrument was thought to be the American radio station in West Berlin, which also started to transmit from Hof on the Bavarian – East German border. Up to 70 per cent of East Germans were reckoned to tune in on a regular basis. Though not instigating the June 1953 uprising, it played a significant part in reporting the nascent strikes (15 June) and broadcasting the initial demands. Going beyond the issue of high work norms and prices, these included 'We want free elections.' Though anxious not to act as the mere mouthpiece for the demonstrations, the radio did repeat the call for a general strike, which asked specifically (in a late-night news special at 11 p.m. on 16 June) for East Berliners to congregate for a demonstration at 7 a.m. next day. But when the CIA station chief in Berlin cabled Washington for permission to supply arms to the demonstrators in face of overwhelming Soviet firepower, he was told 'sympathy and asylum, but no arms'.[31]

There was an obvious disjunction between the American notion of 'liberation' and the paucity of response to the uprising. Many East Germans had taken their regime's abrupt reversal of policy as the result of Western pressure and anticipated active support. Even after its bloody

[30] *Ibid.* pp. 13–15.

[31] J. Hershberg, '"Explosion in the Offing". German Rearmament and American Diplomacy', *Diplomatic History* Autumn 1992 (16.4).

suppression, such expectations continued. Until late summer, most East Germans were convinced that the West would not ignore their outcry. This expectation was well recognised in Washington.

The National Security Council, the day after the uprising, called the event 'a sign of real promise', especially as CIA Director Allen Dulles stated that 'the United States had nothing whatsoever to do with inciting these riots'. But they also provided 'a very tough problem for the United States to know how to handle'.[32] The President made clear that, in order to show no semblance of approval for Soviet action, he would not attend a mooted four-power summit on Germany – a project of which the newly reinstated Prime Minister Churchill was particularly fond. As John Charmley puts it:

> the death of Stalin in March had given the old boy not just a fresh lease of life, but also a new purpose to his remaining in power. As the only surviving member of the 'Big Three', and with his faith in personal destiny undimmed, Churchill felt he had a perfect opportunity for trying to thaw out the Cold War.[33]

Churchill saw in Stalin's death a 'precious chance' and thought history would look ill upon the Western leaders if they failed to take it. He at once proposed to Eisenhower a summit meeting with the Russians. But Eisenhower replied: 'I feel we should not rush things too much with the Soviets. Premature action by us in that direction might have the effect of giving them an easy way out.' His primary concern was the consequences in the USA – with McCarthyism in full flight – of being seen to conciliate the Soviets. Undeterred, Churchill announced to the House of Commons (11 May) that he sought a 'conference at the highest level ... between leading powers without a long delay'. Even the suppression of the East German rising did not seem to Churchill to be sufficient grounds for postponement. In the event, nothing came of it for health reasons: the 78-year-old, burdened with carrying both the Premiership and the Foreign Office – in Eden's absence – had a major stroke on 23 June.

Instead of a summit, President Eisenhower asked the Psychological Strategy Board for a short-term contingency plan to cope with the crisis. Adopted by the National Security Council on 29 June (NSC-158), this set out new guidelines for US policy towards communist East Europe. The East German rising was seen in the context of potentially similar unrest in Czechoslovakia, Poland, Romania and Albania. Noting that the trigger was often economic deprivation, it stated that such issues were 'overshadowed by the clearly expressed political objectives of the German

[32] *FRUS: 1952–4*, vol. VII, p. 1587.
[33] Charmley, *Churchill's Grand Alliance*, pp. 263–4.

rebels'. The document saw the uprising as 'a kind of spontaneous direct-action plebiscite in which the East German masses voted with their feet for free elections, the reunification of Germany and the withdrawal of Soviet occupation forces'. It was the 'greatest opportunity for initiating effective policies to help roll back Soviet power that has yet come to light'.

The policy was dual-track. First, the USA would seize the chance to push for German reunification, based on free elections, and to promote the four-power talks as a matter of priority, to begin at Foreign Minister level in the autumn. That was expected to wrest the initiative from the Soviets on the German issue. Secondly, all measures of psychological warfare, open and covert, should be deployed 'to nourish resistance to Communist oppression throughout satellite Europe'. The complex aim would be to 'undermine satellite puppet authority' without compromising 'the spontaneous nature of future revolts'. Under NSC-158 there would also be consideration of 'large-scale systematic balloon propaganda operations to the satellites'. A State Department official proposed to encourage 'mass, passive resistance which would indicate to one and all under Soviet rule that they are not alone and which would demonstrate to the outside world the validity of their opposition'.[34]

But there were dissenting voices. It did not take the strategic wisdom of Clausewitz to see that stirring up resistance in Eastern Europe might have the opposite effect to the one intended. Incitements to revolt – 'keeping the pot virtually at boiling point' – might have the long-term effect of delaying Soviet troop withdrawals. Some US diplomats therefore argued that the approach should be reversed. The Soviet Union should be brought into a negotiation process whereby it could eventually make an honourable – and self-interested – departure from the region.[35] This meant a strategy of evolution, not revolution.

Strict realists regarded Central and East European societies as emasculated and absorbed. However, more liberal analysts came to see Soviet-type societies as permeable entities, where cultural dissent was rife and to be fostered.[36] There was every opportunity to expose weaknesses on the 'cultural front'. Broadcasting information that did not accord with censored sources could challenge what Gramsci called 'hegemony'. So began the cultural Cold War.

Radio Free Europe (RFE) was founded in 1949. The inspiration came from George Kennan who thought it would provide useful employment

34 Ostermann, *The United States, the East German Uprising of 1953*, pp. 24–6.
35 *FRUS: 1952–4*, vol. VII, p. 1598.
36 P. Coleman, *The Liberal Conspiracy: The Congress for Cultural Freedom and the Struggle for the Mind of Post-war Europe* (New York, 1989).

for anti-communist refugees, who could broadcast back to the region in their own languages, providing information and analyses about the outside world and events elsewhere in the Soviet bloc. The broadcasting station, which began transmission in 1951, was largely financed by the CIA.[37] It led to repression by the communist authorities. A minor Polish official, Jerzy Stepaczenko, turned on the late news broadcast from Radio Free Europe in the hearing of some thirty to forty people at the Białystok railway station. For disseminating 'false news harmful to the interests of the USSR, People's Democracies and Polish State', he was given eighteen months in a labour camp.[38]

After Stalin's death, Radio Liberty was created and the BBC World Service broadcast native-language programmes to countries east of the Iron Curtain. Finally, Voice of America formed the major channel for US criticism of Soviet policies, including their nuclear testing, with programmes in Russian, Ukrainian, Georgian and the Baltic languages, as well as English.[39] The utility of such broadcasting was long contested in Washington. Diplomats tended to the view that the broadcast of unsparing attacks on the policies of communist governments made establishment of good relations with them more difficult. It also ran the risk of encouraging East Europeans to believe that they would one day be freed – though no such Western project for their release existed. After Stalin's death, the question of political priorities became even more pressing. Should the cultural Cold War be confrontational – assailing the Soviet Union by every means available, short of warfare? Alternatively, should the West seek to offer cooperation and conciliatory agreements in the hope of achieving eventual liberalisation in the East?

The dilemma was well expressed by Jan Nowak, who headed the Polish desk at RFE from 1952 to 1976:

> In the years 1952–1956 I had major difficulty in interpreting and explaining to listeners the true meaning of the liberation policy launched by the Eisenhower-Dulles administration. It was not clear if by 'liberation' the United States meant a rollback of the Soviets by war or threat of war or if the Americans intended to encourage self-liberation by insurgency.[40]

Inventing resistance movements in Eastern Europe, or vastly exaggerating their strength, played into the hands of hard-line communists.

[37] C. Gati, *Failed Illusions. Moscow, Washington, Budapest and the 1956 Hungarian Revolt* (Stanford and Washington, 2006), p. 97.
[38] AAN *Komisja Specjalna do Walki 1952–3* (File no. 402).
[39] N. Cull, 'The Man Who Invented Truth' in R. Mitter and P. Major (eds.), *Across the Blocs: Cold War Cultural and Social History* (London, 2004), pp. 30–3.
[40] Cited by Gati, *Failed Illusions*, p. 101.

It enabled them to argue that the region was indeed threatened by internal forces egged on by 'imperialist' enemies, against whom utmost 'vigilance' must be maintained.[41]

Eisenhower inherited many elements of Truman's national security policy. He accepted that US security in the Cold War required a preponderance of American power across the Eurasian heartland. This included a vital stake in the integrated defence for Western Europe, as an essential barrier to further Soviet expansionism. He thought the burden of defence-sharing should fall more evenly, which meant in practice that the West Europeans should provide a greater proportion of ground forces thus enabling a measured US withdrawal. In view of Soviet conventional superiority, it was inevitable that deterrence would rest upon a willingness to use nuclear weapons, including first use should that become necessary. However, he agreed with the Soviet military consensus that no 'limited nuclear war' would be possible. Once such a conflict began – and Eisenhower threatened it several times, though never in the European theatre – there would be mutual destruction. In July 1954 he remarked 'Atomic War will destroy civilization. There will be millions of people dead . . . If the Kremlin and Washington ever lock up in a war, the results are too horrible to contemplate.'[42] He saw the Cold War as a long-term project in which time was on the West's side. Patient attrition would prevail.

Over the summer of 1953, Eisenhower concluded a series of in-house strategic seminars, known as 'Project Solarium', which reviewed three possible contingencies. Task Force A – headed by Kennan – reviewed the Truman policy of containment. Task Force B was instructed to identify areas in which Soviet policy could be confronted more directly, and Task Force C was to consider the possibility of 'rolling-back' Soviet power, as a part of a strategy to liberate Eastern Europe. This last option was made public in Dulles' 'massive retaliation' speech at the end of 1953.

Eisenhower considered that military expenditure – which had trebled the defence budget between 1950 and 1953 – had become disproportionate. The 'New Look' national security policy, adopted on 30 October 1953, tried to reduce the burden. A corollary of this was greater reliance on nuclear weapons: 'In the event of hostilities, the United States will consider nuclear weapons to be as available for use as other munitions.'[43] However, an imminent threat from the Soviet Union was not anticipated. It was also noted that stock-piling by both superpowers might result in a

[41] *Ibid.* [42] *FRUS: 1952–4*, vol. XV, pp. 1844–5.
[43] *Ibid.* vol. II, p. 593 (NSC-162/2).

stalemate in which neither side was willing to initiate a general war. It seems that this view was shared in Moscow. Molotov observed later that – though the Cold War involved pressure from both sides – 'of course, you have to know the limits'.[44]

Washington concluded that, despite the death of Stalin and protests in East Germany, Soviet rule was secure for the time being. Military force was enabling both effective control and resource exploitation in the region. The Yugoslavs had shown that the Kremlin could be defied successfully and proved 'there is a practical alternative for national Communist leaders to submission to Soviet control'. The long-run objective of US policy was to promote 'the eventual fulfilment of the rights of the peoples in the Soviet satellites to enjoy governments of their own choosing, free of Soviet domination'. But this was not a current possibility. Indeed, NATO should avoid incitement to 'premature revolt' and avoid 'commitments on the nature and timing of any U.S. action to bring about liberation'.[45]

Nuclear war could not be won and therefore should not be fought. However, a range of techniques could be used to seize the moral high ground in the Cold War, undercutting the Soviets and influencing world opinion, including amongst the non-aligned. Naturally, the Republican Right saw this preference for 'containment' rather than 'liberation' as a betrayal of electoral promises and evidence of the administration 'going soft on communism'. It is not known whether Moscow was apprised of Washington's overall conclusion, but Khrushchev's later policy towards the Third World is very similar.

De-Stalinisation

Poles soon heard the RFE revelations of Lieutenant-Colonel 'Józef Światło'. After defecting to West Berlin in December 1953, he was transferred to Frankfurt and Washington, where his de-briefing took nine months. His real name was Izaak Fleischfarb.[46] His reminiscences, broadcast back to Poland in more than 140 transmissions from autumn 1954, were a severe indictment of Polish communism.

According to 'Światło', the Tenth Department of the secret police (of which he had been Deputy Head) had become a state within a state. Established on 30 November 1951, to 'defend the workers' movement'

[44] *Sto sorok besed*, pp. 88–9. [45] *FRUS: 1952–4*, vol. II, pp. 435–40.
[46] Z. Błażyński, *Mówi Józef Światło. Za kulisami bezpieki i partii 1940–1955*, 3rd edn (London, 1986), p. 320.

from enemies within the Party, the Tenth Department held the personnel files on all top Party leaders except for Bierut (whose file was held in Moscow). Its subdivisions were responsible for: (1) 'all rightist, nationalist, and Trotskyite movements'; (2) members and officials of the Party who had any connection with the West, in whatever capacity; (3) uncovering informers and agents sent to Poland during or since the Second World War. A Fourth Department conducted 'investigations' on behalf of the other three. No means were forbidden. 'Światło' does not record his nickname: 'The Butcher'. Subdivision (1) conducted the investigation of Gomułka. 'Światło' had arrested him on 12 August 1951, along with many other leading figures. These included Cardinal Wyszyński on 26 September 1953, though, according to secret police protocol, 'Światło' refused to identify himself to the Primate by name.[47]

Listeners heard that Bierut wished to destroy Gomułka who was very popular in Party ranks. Moscow pressed for a trial and Bierut, in turn, pressed Interior Minister Radkiewicz to produce the proof. However, the trial was endlessly postponed. In explaining this, 'Światło' noted that Gomułka admitted nothing and was not 'worked over' to make a confession. Others under arrest did not incriminate him. Gomułka defended himself robustly during interrogation, accusing the Bierut clique of collaboration with the Nazi occupiers and of selling-out Polish communists arrested in the Soviet Union. Correspondence confiscated from Gomułka showed he had indeed traced and talked to the few freed from the Soviet Union. Moscow had ordered that the Church be neutralised to prevent its becoming a nucleus for anti-communist resistance. Other parties had been wiped out or absorbed. An electoral system had been introduced in which opposition votes did not count.[48]

Such adverse publicity led to significant concessions from the political authorities. Gomułka was released on 13 December 1954, though this was not made public. The Ministry of Public Security was abolished and its notorious Minister, Radkiewicz, was dismissed, together with three deputies. A Ministry of Interior was put in its place.[49] Particularly sadistic officials, including torturers named by 'Światło', were imprisoned. The most notorious were given 12–15-year sentences. But all were reprieved and released in October 1964.

A million copies of the 'Światło' revelations were printed abroad in an edited booklet of forty pages. 'The Inside Story of the *Bezpieka* [secret police] and the Party' began to be dropped over Poland by balloon from

[47] *A Freedom Within*, pp. 2–6. [48] Błażyński, *Mówi Józef Światło*.
[49] A. Paczkowski, *Aparat bezpieczeństwa w latach 1945–1956*, 2 vols. (Warsaw, 1994).

12 February 1955 as part of 'Operation Spotlight'. The method chosen was explained as a response to the 'abnormal conditions created by Communists in the subjugated countries'. In London you could buy current issues of *Pravda* or *Izvestiya* and books published in Poland. But the only window to the free world for people behind the Iron Curtain had until then been Western radio stations. Now, 'balloons provide one more effective way to pierce the Iron Curtain, and experiences in Czechoslovakia (Operation Veto) and Hungary (Operation Focus) prove that the enemy, faced with this new method, is entirely helpless'. Indeed, Polish peasants, many no doubt illiterate, were instructed to gather up these booklets – sent by plastic or rubber balloons which burst at high altitudes – and deliver them to local Party headquarters. The Operation's purpose was 'to weaken the Communist apparatus of control and, through detailed exposure of Communist methods, to better enable the Polish people to defend themselves'.[50]

But political changes soon petered out. The ruling Party had one, self-centred, concern: the fate of their predecessors in the KPP dissolved by Stalin before the war. In 1944, PPR leaders had asked him to review the question of their predecessors' arrests 'which must be settled properly because they infringe Polish sovereignty'.[51] Stalin said he would, but nothing happened.

Ten years later, the Poles requested rehabilitation of thirty members killed or executed in the Soviet Union and for a search for any surviving relatives in the GULag.[52] Khrushchev replied that the Polish communists had been arrested in 1937–8 'by the inimical leadership of the NKVD' and promised posthumous rehabilitation of the KPP.[53] The CPSU added later that the dissolution 'on the basis of falsified materials, unmasked subsequently as provocations' had been groundless. A proposed draft resolution described the former KPP as a 'militant, monolithic party' leading the struggle of Polish workers for socialist construction. An agreed formulation, endorsed by the other parties to the original Comintern resolution (Italian, Bulgarian and Finnish), was finally promulgated during the Twentieth Party Congress (1956).[54]

In the period between Stalin's death and his dethronement at the Twentieth Congress, his name largely disappeared from the public arena. Exceptions were made for the first anniversary of his death and his official

[50] *News from Behind the Iron Curtain* 1955 (6), pp. 37–8.
[51] Polonsky and Drukier, *The Beginnings of Communist Rule*, p. 268.
[52] AAN VI/ p. 112, t. 26, pp. 15–18. [53] AAN VI/ p. 112, t. 26, p. 67.
[54] *Trybuna Ludu* 19 February 1956; *Pravda* 21 February 1956.

birthday in December 1955. During this period of 'silent de-Stalinisation', rehabilitations took place without public announcement. Many were posthumous and referred to honest Stalinists who had perished 'unjustly' in the later thirties. In addition to being inspired 'from above', it seems that they were often the result of pressures on the Party leadership. These came from the relatives of victims, from Old Bolsheviks and historians, and from communist leaders – such as those in Poland – in East European countries. The main victims of the 1949 'show trials' in Hungary (László Rajk) and Bulgaria (Traicho Kostov) were rehabilitated. The Slansky Trial in Czechoslovakia was eventually annulled. It is worth noting that the new leaders of Poland and Hungary from autumn 1956, Gomułka and Kádár, were both former political prisoners.

The thaw was accelerated by the *entente* between Soviet and Yugoslav leaders, during which the accusation of 'Titoism' against defendants became void. But this raised many further questions for Polish Party lecturers on the international situation:

- Is Yugoslavia a People's Democracy?
- What are US relations with Yugoslavia?
- Is Titoism still espionage or just a deviation?
- What is the class structure of Yugoslavia?
- Why did Tito go to India?
- How is the Djilas affair going to turn out?[55]

They also asked whether the new attitude towards Tito would mean a similar change towards Gomułka.

The writers

Communist Party officials did not make cultural policy in a vacuum. Like all social engineers they needed to understand the society they governed in order to influence it. Therefore, alongside a censorship designed to silence dissident views,[56] they erected an equally elaborate apparatus of informants to discover what the public really thought and said. Groups to which the authorities paid particular attention included opinion-forming intellectual 'circles', existing more or less independently of the state. In a closed society, as Solzhenitsyn puts it, 'a writer is another government'. The authorities are highly sensitive to literary concerns. We will therefore take *belles-lettres* as an example.

[55] AAN 237/VII/1454–62, *Meldunki z terenu*, 22 January – 19 February 1955.
[56] For its origin, see D. Nałęcz (compiler), *Główny urząd kontroli prasy, 1945–1956* (Warsaw, 1994).

Harold Swayze notes that 'immediately after Stalin's death there was a noticeable quickening of the discussion of the situation in belles-lettres'.[57] The debate was still conducted within the Stalinist parameters of socialist realism. There were no direct attacks on 'Zhdanovshchina' (the policies of Stalin's cultural commissar Andrei Zhdanov) at this time. Even so, there was a new note of openness, in clear reaction to the sterility that the orthodoxy of socialist realism had imposed. In October 1953, the novelist Ilya Ehrenburg, who had survived the purges partly by the good fortune of journalistic postings abroad, insisted that writing was solely the business of writers. A writer could not operate on the basis of external orders. No-one had told Chekhov what to write or ordered Tolstoy to produce *Anna Karenina*. Books could not be planned, nor writers merely instructed by critics or censors. It was time to resurrect the forgotten words 'vocation and inspiration'.[58]

Ehrenburg's 'Thaw' gave its name to the era.[59] His novel shows a young painter, Pukhov, wasting his artistic personality on political opportunism and constant adjustment to the zigzags of official ideological requirements. He paints large canvasses (*Feast on a Collective Farm*) for the authorities. By contrast, the artist Saburov remains true to his vocation, despite neglect by the critics, poverty and hunger. Apparently cut off, he is the repository of the humanist values of generosity, tolerance and compassion. Critics at the time assailed Saburov as an escapist, divorced from his time and condemned to the ivory tower. But Part Two (after the Twentieth Congress) shows Saburov transformed. Far from remote, he is in touch with society and using his art to inspire the heroes of socialist construction. Recognition reaches him. By contrast, Pukhov fades away. Political tastes have changed: 'no-one will pay a kopeck for his portrait of a now-disgraced manager'. But there is an optimistic ending. Walking past young lovers in the park, he sees an assortment of natural miracles: the snow melts to reveal leaves and flowers. 'Never been so happy to see the spring', he resumes his childhood game of breaking the ice on puddles. The natural and emotional worlds thaw together.

The Polish thaw developed cautiously. In April 1954, the Minister of Culture, Włodzimierz Sokorski, made critical remarks about socialist realism. It should not be treated as a dogma, or as a directive mode for literature and the arts, he said. But his audience was not immediately receptive to these official changes of direction. As Gomori explains,

[57] H. Swayze, *Political Control of Literature in the USSR, 1946–1959* (Cambridge, Mass., 1962), p. 84.

[58] I. Ehrenburg, 'O rabote pisatelya', *Znamya* October 1953.

[59] 'Ottepel'', *Znamya* May 1954 (Part 1); April 1956 (Part 2).

'Many writers were still confused and, fearing a reversal of the trend, did not dare to exploit them.'[60] Yet there was the start of a tectonic shift. In Stalin's time, socialist realism was 'an artificial mixture of imitative styles, conceived in the spirit of Party-mindedness, a didactic yet superficial eclecticism'.[61] Now the old taboos were being questioned. But former socialist realists were not transformed overnight. The ice melted slowly, and there was always the prospect of another frost. To some extent, the interim saw a-political poetry, displaying the individual preferences and talents that Stalinist orthodoxy denied.

The interval may be characterised as a turning-point (*przełom*) in public life. A critique of certain aspects of cultural policy swelled into an attack on the Party's governance of culture as a whole. Years of official isolation from Western culture began to end. Orwell's *Nineteen Eighty-Four* was published in Polish, and copies of Miłosz's *Captive Mind* arrived unofficially from Paris. In addition to accounts of Soviet literary discussions, the first part of 'Thaw' was translated in March 1955.

The Party's Third Plenum (21–24 January 1955) heard by far the most forthright criticisms of Stalin's legacy so far. Central power had become burdened with bureaucracy and leaders had lost touch with ordinary people. Party Secretary Morawski stated that 'constitutional rights were violated by certain offices of the security services, innocent people were arrested and held in prison, and instead of aiming to establish the truth, false accusations were manufactured and inhuman methods used during interrogations'.[62] But political initiatives 'from above' again petered out, causing disquiet amongst the rank-and-file.

Party *aktyw* at Warsaw University wanted to know why the Third Plenum's procceedings had not been published. They sought more information about the now-disbanded Ministry of Security. The Central Committee Department for Party History was accused of unscientific methods, suppression of primary sources and publishing material with sections censored. The work of the Education Faculty at Warsaw University was criticised for 'varnishing' reality and not employing a single scholar in its ranks. Professors Zygmunt Bauman and Krysztof Pomian (both later *émigrés* to the West) deplored infringements of academic freedom.[63]

The Fifth World Festival of Youth and Students was due to be held in Warsaw in summer 1955. But the older generation of Poles was often

[60] G. Gomori, *Polish and Hungarian Poetry. 1945–1956* (Oxford, 1964), p. 219.
[61] *Ibid.* p. 126. [62] J. Morawski, *Nowe Drogi* February 1955.
[63] AAN 237/VII/1469 *Meldunki z terenu*, 15 March 1955.

resentful. Farmers in the Olsztyn region complained that young people were using it as an excuse for evading domestic duties and that many would be away in the capital at harvest time. Others thought the cost would be better put towards building hospitals and schools. Reports from many regions noted an 'activisation of clergy' who were busy arranging counter-attractions, such as cultural outings and excursions and sporting events, to deter young people from attending the Festival. In general, the rumour mill was trying to discredit the event by attributing all 'difficulties in supply' (shortages) to the coming Festival.[64]

There were significant stirrings amongst intellectuals. In August 1955, the Polish clamour for political change was expressed in the famous 'Poem for Grown-Ups' – 'there are Polish apples which Polish children cannot reach'. It caused a scandal.[65] A newly formed intelligentsia discussion group, 'The Club of the Crooked Circle', named after the street in Warsaw's old town where it met, sought official recognition. As state censorship lessened, radical young intellectuals transformed the journal *Po prostu* from a boring Youth Union (ZMP) rag into an important social institution.[66] However, the major impulse came from Moscow, where the dramatic dethronement of the erstwhile dictator opened up new possibilities for political change.

Secret speech

Khrushchev's 'secret speech' (25 February 1956) was very much a personal initiative.[67] None of his contemporaries had the courage to face the Party with so frank a catalogue – though far from complete – of Stalin's crimes. Some were aware of the need to say something: their view that the next Congress 'would be too late' was reflected in Malenkov's opening report.[68] But most members of the Presidium considered that Khrushchev's proposal to invite former *zeks* to address the Congress would 'let criminals judge us'.[69] A compromise was eventually worked out, allowing limited disclosure without recording, stenographers or discussion.[70]

64 AAN 237/VII/1500 *Meldunki z terenu*, 14 June 1955.
65 A. Ważyk, 'Poemat dla dorosłych', *Nowa Kultura* 19 August 1955.
66 B. Łopieńska and E. Szymańska, *Stare numery* (Warsaw, 1990), pp. 63–77.
67 F. Burlatskii, *Vozhdi i sovetniki. O Khrushcheve, Andropove i ne tol'ko o nikh* (Moscow, 1990), p. 85.
68 *XX S"ezd KPSS: stenograficheskii otchet*, vol. I (Moscow, 1956), pp. 302–25; *Khrushchev Remembers*, pp. 308–19.
69 R. Medvedev, *Khrushchev* (Oxford, 1982), pp. 85–7.
70 *The Anti-Stalin Campaign and International Communism. A Collection of Documents* (New York, 1956).

Khrushchev's harangue had been compiled at the last minute. Its basic source was the report of a Commission set up to investigate 'violations of socialist legality', chaired by Pospelov, a long-serving Stalinist who had edited both *Pravda* throughout the 1940s and the *Brief Biography* of Stalin, which appeared in 7 million copies in 1951 alone. Despite this pedigree, Pospelov painted a horrifying picture of mass terror unleashed on Stalin's personal orders.

Almost two million citizens had been arrested for 'anti-Soviet activity' between 1935 and 1940. One-third was executed and the rest dispatched to the GULag for a routine eight- or ten-year (i.e., death) sentence. A vast apparatus of torture had extracted false confessions, sometimes on Stalin's direct instructions. To Pospelov's summary was added material, now published from archives,[71] on the wartime and post-war periods, as well as Khrushchev's own dictations.[72] Other parts of the speech were off-the-cuff or simply improvisations. These included a matter of great concern to the military members of his audience: Stalin's handling of the attack by Nazi Germany on 22 June 1941, which led to five million Soviet soldiers being taken prisoner. Four million were never seen again.

Although the 'secret speech' offered the CPSU a partial explanation for its decimation in the later 1930s, it gave a far from complete assessment of Stalinist crimes. Little or nothing was said about the wider sufferings, especially to recent returnees from the GULag or surviving relatives of the millions who had perished there.[73] Consequently, a host of further questions followed from his selective disclosures.

Though delivered to an all-Soviet audience, Khrushchev's 'secret speech' had important international implications. Chinese leaders responded negatively and considered the dethronement a mistake. Mao later called the 'secret speech' a surprise attack and said he resented the lack of consultation beforehand. In his view, Stalin's work had been 70 per cent correct and only 30 per cent incorrect, with the achievements far outweighing the mistakes. The latter clearly included hitherto unacknowledged errors committed against China (and Mao personally). He evidently intended to use the campaign against Stalin's cult of personality to strengthen his own.[74]

[71] 'O kul'te lichnosti i ego posledstviyakh', *Istochnik* 2000 (6).

[72] W. Taubman, *Khrushchev. The Man and his Era* (New York, 2003), pp. 280–2.

[73] Albert P. van Goudoever, *The Limits of De-Stalinization in the Soviet Union: Political Rehabilitations in the Soviet Union since Stalin* (London, 1986), pp. 37–49.

[74] P. Vamos, *Evolution and Revolution: Sino-Hungarian Relations and the 1956 Revolution*, CWIHP Working Paper no. 54 (Washington, 2006), pp. 3–4.

Communism in Eastern Europe became multi-polar. Romanian communists came to consider they had more in common, in their treatment of the Stalin issue and de-Stalinisation, with Mao's China and Hoxha's Albania than with Poland. They regarded 'the disbandment of Stalin's myth as a major strategic and ideological blunder, a godsend for imperialist propaganda and a concession to Titoist "rotten revisionism" '.[75]

Bierut had difficulty coming to terms with Khrushchev's revelations.[76] His physical health also worsened and he did not travel back to Warsaw with other delegates. While news of his illness was kept secret from the Polish public, rumours about the 'secret speech' soon filtered out. Other senior politicians demanded a meeting with the Moscow delegation so they could explain the Congress and, more widely, defend the continuing legitimacy of the ruling *troika* (Bierut, Berman, Minc). Bierut himself kept in touch with Poland by phone and became daily more agitated by developments. The Party could hardly hold a formal Plenum in his absence, but nor could the political elite be held at bay much longer.

The outcome was an unofficial Plenum of the Central Committee (3–4 March 1956) at which Morawski reported back on Khrushchev's speech. He cited Khrushchev's statement, at a reception for foreign delegates, that the struggle with the 'cult of the individual' was by no means over but would continue until all remnants had been eradicated from social life, including science and education, art and literature. Morawski noted: 'Each of us speaks about this with bitterness. We developed this cult ourselves. Distortions to which it gave rise went deep into the life of the party and of the country.' Manifestations of the cult included 'stubborn, petrified bureaucracy', disregard for 'the needs and views of the population', servility, conformism and the absence of independent thought and initiative. The speech gave rise to 'thousands of questions and misgivings'. It provided a unique chance to revive Polish communism, picking up the threads that had been dropped after the Third Plenum. This was the moment to seize the popular initiative and launch a 'great offensive of our ideas'.[77]

The second speaker, Cyrankiewicz, echoed the idea that the 'cult of the individual' was not simply a matter of 'one person or style'. It had a social basis in 'the system of governing over all spheres of life'. The mode was 'domineering and intimidating, instead of using persuasion, and involved

[75] V. Tismaneanu, *Gheorghiu-Dej and the Romanian Workers Party: From De-Sovietization to the Emergence of National Communism*, CWIHP Working Paper no. 37 (Washington, 2002), pp. 13–14.

[76] J. Berman in Torańska, *Oni. Stalin's Polish Puppets*, p. 346.

[77] AAN 237/V/231.

disdaining the collective'. The task was to 're-educate the Dzierżymordas [repressors of culture]' who stifled initiative and criticism and were either unwilling or unable to change their political behaviour.[78]

First from the floor was the impassioned Warsaw Party Secretary Staszewski. In retirement, he contrasted his conduct favourably with that of Zambrowski who was 'constrained by limitations typical of communists, and couldn't cross the Rubicon and say to himself: I am no longer a communist – my programme, the one I believed in, has not and cannot now be realised'. He *had* crossed the Rubicon at about the time of the XXth Congress.[79]

Professor Schaff reported on ideological responses. Some of the Party's rank-and-file had disagreed with the negative appreciation of Stalin. But this approach was naive: 'It's not about assessing Stalin's activity, but a whole row of questions.' Many members simply did not know what the Leningrad Affair was, or 'the business with Yugoslavia and Tito'.[80]

For Albrecht, the XXth Congress meant there could be no way forward without a critical review of the past: 'The source of the cult and of our mistakes was a certain disdain for the masses, and underestimating their rationality, role and conscience. We should tell them the hard truth about the six-year plan (1950–55) and the tasks of the five-year plan. They will not believe us otherwise.'[81] An establishment author, Putrament, professed himself delighted with the 'entire theses' of Khrushchev's speech, but less so with those of Soviet writers. Surkov's Congress speech was pure generalisation, irrelevant to the actual state of Russian literature, with not a word about the Writers' Union. Sholokhov was 'a writer of genius, author of the best works of the twentieth century'. But what did he tell the Congress? 'He just said build writers nice *dachas* and all will be wonderful.'[82]

Thus far, the meeting had heard defensive manoeuvres from leading politicians. Now the storm broke. Successive speakers opened up new avenues of debate. The first noted that workers' *aktyw* 'make a close connection between the XXth Congress and Polish affairs, the life of our party, and their own in factories and in the basic party cells. Great hopes have arisen of an improvement at home.' He called for free debate.[83] Another regarded all Party members as products to some extent of the 'anti-humanistic relations prevalent' in the Stalinist period. Now, however, she considered debate within the Party to be the liveliest since the Second

[78] AAN 237/V/231 (Józef Cyrankiewicz: Prime Minister 1956–70).
[79] He liked to boast about his role: Torańska, *Oni. Stalin's Polish Puppets* (1987), pp. 162–3.
[80] AAN 237/V/231 (Adam Schaff). [81] AAN 237/V/231 (Jerzy Albrecht).
[82] AAN 237/V/231 (Jerzy Putrament). [83] AAN 237/V/233 (Romaniuk).

World War.[84] A third pointed out that Berman supported both the arrest of Gomułka as correct in its time and his release as correct for the present time – 'a terribly dogmatic approach to the problem'. Berman interpolated: 'I will explain the circumstances.' The speaker continued: 'I look for freely exchanging thoughts within the Party – within it, not outside.'[85] Baczko saw the Congress as sparking off an ideological revival, political and moral, personal and collective, against the prevalent cynicism of public life. Another speaker said such cynicism spread out from the *apparatus* to corrupt the whole social environment.[86] The lines were thus drawn up for a confrontation within the Party.

The meeting ended with some insubordinate complaints. The Poznań Party Secretary had received an arrogant telegram from Warsaw: 'We will send you three speakers, including one from the Central Committee. They will clear up all doubts about the Congress.' Another referred to the 'colossal disproportion' between currently existing lies and rights that were guaranteed in the constitution. Staszewski called for a full Plenum. But Zawadzki replied from the chair that this would require the presence of Bierut 'who is at present indisposed'.[87]

Bierut died on 12 March. The sudden announcement was met with widespread disbelief. Reports from Stalinogrod (the once and future Katowice) asked why there had been no bulletins on Bierut's illness, while there were regular communiqués about the illnesses of Eisenhower and Adenauer. Others were even more suspicious: 'Who knows whether there aren't still Beria supporters in the USSR who murder our leaders?'[88] Reports from Łódź asked: 'Why do activists always die in Moscow?' They named Gottwald and Dimitrov. Another declared that, had Bierut died in the USA, rather than the USSR, it would have been admitted that he was poisoned.[89] It was rumoured in the Szczecin Shipyard that the motive for murdering Bierut was his refusal to sign a decree in Moscow making Poland the seventeenth Soviet Republic. Reports from Rzeszów asserted that the XXth Congress had seen a show-down between supporters of Stalin and of Khrushchev, during which Bierut had a heart attack, or even committed suicide. Several attributed his death to Światło's activity in the West.[90]

The funeral began with a lying-in-state at the House of Soviets, followed by a motorcade to the airport. Moscow's broad boulevards

[84] AAN 237/V/233 (Zofia Zemankowa). [85] AAN 237/V/233 (Malewski).
[86] AAN 237/V/233 (Bronisław Baczko). [87] AAN 237/V/231 (Aleksander Zawadzki).
[88] AAN 237/VII (Central Committee Organisational Department) /2755.
[89] AAN 237/V11/2755. [90] AAN 237/VII/2755.

contrast starkly in the newsreel with Warsaw's war-ravaged streets.[91] The return of their late leader in an open coffin was a shock to many Poles. His cortège, made up of banners, military bands and numerous official delegations, including '100 well-known leading workers', took the body to Warsaw's military cemetery.[92] It was not buried in the Kraków Wawel, traditional resting-place of Polish monarchy, as proposed by the Bierut University (Wrocław) 'because comrade Bierut was as important to Poland as a king'. Also rejected was the proposed Mausoleum in Warsaw, and the re-naming of a major city (such as Łódź)[93] or a premier work-place (the Gdańsk Shipyard).[94]

Despite the public face of solemnity and sadness, the secret police reported many instances of 'hooligan' and anti-state activity. Party archives contain four top-secret reports concerning the burial, derived from informers and the militia, mainly through gossip in queues, bars and public transport (also telephone intercepts, including those of diplomats). They describe graffiti and insulting slogans, the removal or defacement of portraits, vulgar songs, nihilistic declarations and provocative pamphleteering. Several workers were sacked for proposing toasts ('initiating libations') such as 'the nation breathes more freely after the death of Bierut'. There were isolated acts of arson, with a burnt-out wagon proclaiming 'Bierut Be Praised'. One citizen declared: 'Bierut was not trusted, he made donations to the Church.'[95]

Political succession was complicated by the continuing stay of Khrushchev after the funeral. Ignoring hints from Staszewski and others, the Russian delegation showed no sign of going home. Despite public denials of any wish to interfere, it was keenly interested in the new leadership and freely available over four days to dispense fraternal advice. Khrushchev himself made a speech to PZPR *aktyw* on 20 March.

After a huge preamble on the dangers of nuclear weapons and NATO, and some broadsides against the 'backwardness' of Polish agriculture, he returned to the Stalin question. The years of repression in the USSR had ended and past wrongs were being put right. Some episodes, like the Kirov murder, remained 'mysterious', but most were straightforward. The 'Doctors' Plot' had been trumped up. Khrushchev had protested Dr Vinogradov's innocence to Stalin at the time, who replied ominously: 'What do you know about people?' Stalin regularly ignored his advice.

[91] *Polska Kronika Filmowa* 12 and 17 March 1956. [92] AAN 237/VII/2755.

[93] AAN 237/VII/3835, *Informacje* 24 March 1956 (23).

[94] AAN 237/VII/3835, *Informacje* 14 March 1956 (21).

[95] Commission for Public Security (13–15 March 1956). Copies held at AAN 237/VII/2755.

Stalin 'abused power and did completely intolerable things. You have read about it all in the speech.' Now, however, there had been a restoration of legality, beginning with the 'arrest' of Beria, 'who had blocked rehabilitation of the pre-war Polish Party'.[96]

The final agenda item was elections. Ochab was unanimously 'elected' First Secretary 'on the Politburo's recommendation'. His acceptance speech, from the chair, promised 'collective leadership' and respect for collegiality and the rights of the Plenum. He then proposed Albrecht and Gierek as new members of the Central Committee Secretariat. Albrecht expressed reluctance and was accused by Khrushchev of shirking responsibility, but did not withdraw. Likewise, Gierek did not decline, though modestly suggested he was not best suited for a secretarial post. However, an alternative candidate, Roman Zambrowski, was proposed against 'the unanimous decision of the Politburo'. His various advocates – all from the 'reformist' tendency in the Party – emphasised his long experience as a Party member they trusted, and his unrivalled expertise in agricultural policy. As they spoke, the Plenum descended into democratic disarray. Members on both sides of the argument were quick to attribute this to the XXth Congress.

Khrushchev was also impatient and could contain himself no longer. Although only listed as an ordinary speaker, and professing himself ignorant of personalities – 'I know Zambrowski a little and don't know the other two at all' – he launched into a rambling oration about Soviet constitutional arrangements: 'Ministers need to take decisions. They send proposals up to the Presidium, which take at least a fortnight to reach a decision. This is damaging.' He expatiated on the need for qualified cadres.[97] At last a break was called, during which Khrushchev, possibly provoked by Staszewski, engaged in extensive indiscretions on Soviet official anti-Semitism. These corridor harangues seemed to satisfy Khrushchev who did not reappear after the interval.

When the Plenum reconvened, Ochab announced that, having taken into account the advice and experience of 'our Russian friends', the Politburo unanimously reaffirmed its two original nominations. It would be inexpedient to enlarge the Secretariat further. After comments from Minc 'with a heavy heart' and prevarications by Putrament, the meeting elected Albrecht and Gierek unopposed. Since there was no further vacancy, Zambrowski's candidacy lapsed.[98] Although the session closed as usual with 'All sang the Internationale', it ended in the balance. Elite politics had not shifted significantly towards a policy of change. The

[96] AAN PZPR, p. 124, t. 80, pp. 1–82. [97] AAN 237/II/13. [98] *Ibid.*

reformist 'young secretaries', Morawski and Matwin, had not been joined by Zambrowski. Ochab and Albrecht can be characterised as 'centrists'.[99] The same could be said for Gierek. They were hence acceptable – at least temporarily – both to 'reformists' and to the 'conservatives' such as Nowak, Zawadzki and Rokossowski.[100]

However, the old guard was now isolated. Bierut had gone, Minc had ceased to play a leading role and the authority of Berman was clearly in question. To maintain the impetus for change in Poland, the 'reformers' decided to approach the Party *aktyw* with a much more candid account of issues raised by Khrushchev's speech.

[99] A. Paczkowski, *Pół wieku dziejów Polski, 1939–1989* (Warsaw, 1995), pp. 298–9.
[100] W. Roszkowski, *Historia Polski, 1914–1991*, enlarged 2nd edn (Warsaw, 1992), pp. 230–1.

4 Flood

> On Stalin's good qualities, an entirely sufficient amount was published in his lifetime
>
> Khrushchev, 1956

Polish archives have three editions of Khrushchev's speech. A red original, numbered '218017', had been given to Bierut at the XXth Congress. Marked 'not for publication', it was intended to enable regional and local CPSU organisations to inform their membership. The copies were to be returned to Moscow within three months.[1] Bierut's copy was made available to selected readers at the top of the Central Committee building. Since many lacked good Russian, the question of translation soon arose. Alone in the bloc, the Polish Party decided to disseminate a text. Hence a blue copy was published under the Party imprint, designated 'exclusively for inner-party use'.[2]

Such documents tend not to remain exclusive for very long. Printers were instructed to exceed the official run (3,000) by a factor of five, and numerous private duplicates were made. The Warsaw Party Secretary Staszewski claims he handed copies 'hot off the press' to correspondents of *Le Monde*, the *Herald Tribune* and the *New York Times*.[3] At home, the text soon found its way onto the black market. Jacek Kuroń recalls it changed hands for 500 złotys.[4] Though a huge sum, this was less than the '$1 million' allegedly paid by the Israeli intelligence service, which passed a copy to the CIA on 17 April.[5]

The latter evidently produced the third edition in archives. Printed on wafer-thin paper, suitable for smuggling or dropping from balloons, this item, 'The Speech of N. S. Khrushchev', appends a litany of further thought-provoking suggestions:

[1] AAN VI, p. 115, t. 38. [2] AAN VI, p. 124, t. 80.
[3] Torańska, *Oni. Stalin's Polish Puppets*, pp. 144–5.
[4] J. Kuroń, *Wiara i Wina. Do i od komunizmu* (Warsaw, 1990), p. 95.
[5] 'Israeli TV Unveils Moscow Spy Coup', *The Times* (London), 20 June 1994.

- Is it just the guilt of Stalin or of the whole Soviet system?
- Can justice be restored without wholesale reorganisation of legislatures, courts and police?
- Does the hierarchical system not throw up such types as Stalin, Dzerzhinsky, Ezhov and Beria?

It rightly adds: 'One can ask thousands more such questions.'[6] Faced with this growing propaganda barrage, the Party sought to regain the initiative. Their educational and *agitprop* apparatuses had been overhauled on 21 March.[7] A mass agitation programme was now launched to 'acquaint the party *aktyw* with comrade Khrushchev's speech'.[8]

The atmosphere was 'heated' amongst party *aktyw* at the Szczecin Technical University (26 March) where 40 comrades asked 110 questions about Khrushchev's speech. The report complained that they were more interested in hurling accusations at the Party than uncovering the historical truth. They demanded:

- What is our guarantee against a reversion to Stalinist methods?
- 'Światło claimed there are Moscow agents working in our Ministries – is this true?'
- Why are 90% of generals in the Polish Army Russians? People heard them talking only Russian at Bierut's funeral.
- Where is the friendship in the Polish-Russian Friendship Society?

The heart of discussion, described by the confidential report as 'an attack on the policy of our party', concerned the status of Poland's own leadership:

- How can we trust Politburo members who have been there for six or seven years to carry out what they now profess?[9]
- Why did Khrushchev stay on in Warsaw after Comrade Bierut's funeral: didn't he select our Central Committee First Secretary?
- In this new situation, don't *we* need to call a Party Congress?

Comrade instructors reported that the final stages of the meeting were 'out of control'[10] well before proceedings closed at 2 a.m.

Secret reports from the provinces show a picture of growing confusion and doubt. Many *aktyw* questioned the Moscow revelations: 'The Khrushchev material might be falsified, just like the materials published

[6] AAN VI, p. 124, t. 80.
[7] See L. W. Głuchowski, 'Poland, 1956: Khrushchev, Gomułka and the "Polish October"', *CWIHP Bulletin*, Spring 1995 (5) (Washington DC), note 49.
[8] R. Werfel, *Trybuna Ludu*, 23 March 1956.
[9] AAN 237/VII/3858, *Meldunki z terenu* 31 March 1956 (24).
[10] AAN 237/VII/3858, *Meldunki z terenu*, 30 March 1956 (23).

in Stalin's lifetime.'[11] Others took the revelations more literally: 'After readings of the speech there was stunned silence. When asked why they were not responding, one comrade stated "What we have just heard is a tragedy for us party members."' Another said: 'Stalin was Poland's executioner.'[12] Zakopane reported that not one Secretary of the Party, satellite parties or youth organisation would contribute, and those from the Kraków apparatus who spoke up did so feebly.[13] *Aktyw* of the Stalinogrod province asked about unreported crimes: 'Was the death of Lenin linked to Stalin in any way?'

Many workers expressed incredulity at the 'Stalin alone' explanation:

- How was he able to decide everything? Where were other members of the Politburo?

Others asked whether Stalin would be deprived of his divinity, posthumously expelled from the CPSU and removed from the Moscow Mausoleum. One disillusioned communist regretted:

- It turns out we were not members of a militant Marxist party but merely mindless marionettes.[14]

Local agitators alleged 'great interest' in the opening of the XXth Congress 'on the part of the working class'. At least initially, such attention was regarded as positive. We learn that 'workers and the technical intelligentsia' in the larger Stalinogrod enterprises referred to Soviet developments as important 'since their economy is parallel to our own'. Many workforces were interested in Congress plans for raising living standards and shortening the working week.[15] Some factories even made production pledges on behalf of the Congress.[16] Daily updates of proceedings were broadcast over loudspeakers. Basic Party Organisation (POP) agitators and leaders of the official union organised collective readings and discussion of the published proceedings. Some expressed surprise at the apparent endorsement of 'Kautsky's theory of a peaceful evolution of capitalism into socialism'. It was noted that Soviet leaders tended to cite Lenin instead of Stalin, especially in Mikoyan's equivocal address.

Mass meetings called to hear and discuss the 'secret speech' concentrated on 'cults' at their own workplace. The Ursus tractor factory

[11] AAN 237/VII/3858, *Meldunki z terenu*, 28 March 1956 (21) (Bydgoszcz, *aktyw*).
[12] AAN 237/VII/3858, *Meldunki z terenu* (21) (Lublin, *aktyw*).
[13] AAN 237/VII/3858, *Meldunki z terenu*, 31 March 1956 (24).
[14] AAN 237/VII/3858, *Meldunki z terenu*, 4 April 1956 (25).
[15] AAN 237/VII/3858, *Meldunki z terenu*, 20 February 1956 (12).
[16] AAN 236/VII/3835, *Informacja*, 24 February 1956 (12).

criticised officialdom at every level. Section chiefs were accused of dictatorial behaviour, and administrative directors of aloofness. Executives and organisers 'in post for years' had become torpid or sunk into routine. Beyond the gates, the Warsaw Party Committee did not concern itself with the factory's problems and simply accepted everything it was told by management. The relevant ministry was failing to supply raw materials.[17] There was much talk of wages and living standards, but the newly announced minimum monthly wage (500 złotys for 200 hours' work) remained pitifully low.[18] It was not mitigated by official talk of decentralising industrial decision-making.

Workers on the coast raised territorial issues:

- Why does Kaliningrad belong to Russia rather than Lithuania or Poland? There is no historical basis for its present attachment to the RSFSR [Russian Soviet Federal Socialist Republic].
- The war with Finland was illegal: the USSR had seized territory from Finland to secure Leningrad.
- Poland is not a sovereign state because the USSR has military air-fields on its territory. The nation does not realise this.

To this the Party Instructor replied cautiously, if not convincingly: 'The Warsaw Pact is a bit different since it facilitates military co-operation.' Another speaker commented:

- At the Potsdam Conference, Stalin guaranteed Polish boundaries, east and west. What will happen now?[19]

Following the lead of the CPSU (3 April), the Party attempted (10 April) to restrict further discussion of the full text to local Party secretaries and their party cells, giving the wider public only a broad general view of 'basic problems arising from comrade Khrushchev's speech'. However, the attempt to rein in the debate had come too late.

The media was inundated with popular responses. An editor of *Nowa Kultura* wrote: 'Like all other newspapers, the radio service and every institution for propaganda on the so-called ideological front – which is becoming simply a tribunal for open discussion between people – we receive hundreds of letters. Letters arrive at present like an avalanche. They testify to the enormous surge of public opinion following the XXth CPSU Congress'.[20]

17 AAN 236/VII/3859, *Meldunki z terenu*, 24 April 1956 (33).
18 Ochab announced an increase of wages for 3.4 million workers, costing the state budget an additional 5 billion złotys over 12 months (*Trybuna Ludu*, 7 April 1956).
19 AAN 237/VII/3858, *Meldunki z terenu*, 29 March 1956 (22).
20 A. Braun (editorial), *Nowa Kultura*, 1956, p. 17.

Discontent soon spread to the countryside. All *powiaty* (districts) in the Łódź voivodship held discussions of the speech (8 April). The Kutno district quoted its local bishop, 'who told us ages ago that Stalin is a murderer', and equated Stalin with Hitler. Most meetings asked whether the Congress would lead to a reconsideration of the (non-communist) Home Army (AK). A number of former AK members spoke up, criticising their present ostracism as 'inappropriate'.[21]

The district of Zielona Góra discussed forced collectivisation. Its district procurator revealed that the local Party and secret police (UB) had put undue pressure on him to conduct 'mass investigation' of the peasantry. When those he had examined withdrew their forcibly extracted depositions in court, leading their cases to be dropped, the Party executive had expelled him for 'an inability to get at the truth'. Białystok voivodship had several embarrassing questions. Was it permissible to use physical means of obtaining evidence for a prosecution? Did socialist construction necessarily entail collectivisation? Was it true that other forms of agricultural organisation, such as cooperative or socialised co-production, 'will not be permitted here'?[22]

Most farmers considered collectivisation to be 'Stalin's invention'. As one explained, 'Lenin gave peasants the land, Stalin took it back.' They increasingly believed the policy would be reversed, typically 'because Gomułka is being released from prison. He is opposed to collectivisation and we peasants will defend him.' On being told that de-collectivisation would not be permitted, a number of peasants in the Bydgoszcz voivodship walked out of a meeting with party activists.[23]

Farmers made numerous protests about compulsory deliveries to the state and low procurement prices. There was a catalogue of complaints, including shortages of building materials, fuel and artificial fertilisers. It was noted that such problems did not beset *kolkhoz* (collective) and state farms, mostly in the Western Territories, which had privileged access to the means of agricultural production.[24] The rumour spread that the policy of collectivisation would be abandoned in Poland and across the bloc.[25]

[21] AAN 237/VII/3869, *Meldunki z terenu*, 14 April 1956 (29) (Krosno). The subject was no longer taboo: J. Ambroziewicz, W. Namiotkiewicz and J. Olszewski, 'Na spotkanie ludziom z AK', *Po prostu*, 11 March 1956; Jerzy Piórkowski, 'My z AK', *Nowa Kultura*, 4 April 1956.

[22] AAN 237/VII/3859, *Meldunki z terenu*, 14 April 1956 (29), and *Meldunki z terenu*, 17 April 1956 (30) (Suwałki powiat).

[23] AAN 237/VII/3859, *Meldunki z terenu*, 26 April 1956 (34).

[24] AAN 237/VII/3859, *Meldunki z terenu*, 34 (26 April 1956). (Lipno, *powiat*).

[25] AAN 237/VII/3859, *Meldunki z terenu*, 34 (26 April 1956). (Poznań voivodship). Collective farms covered less than 10 per cent of arable land. See the policy background in A. Dobieszewski, *Kolektywizacja wsi w Polsce, 1948–1956* (Warsaw, 1993).

Anti-Russian sentiments were widespread. Peasants in Grójec asked: 'When will the Latvian, Lithuanian and Polish nations be freed from oppression?' There were repeated calls for the 'return to Poland' of Lwów, Wilno and other cities.[26] Many asked: 'Is Primate Wyszyński still in detention?',[27] and demanded religious freedoms. By mid-May the central Party apparatus was registering serious disquiet about the 'unhealthy mood' in the countryside. 'Clerical and *kulak* reaction' was strengthening its activity, particularly in malicious propaganda against further collectivisation.[28] Reports noted increasing intimidation of the party *aktyw*, especially of rural teachers. Some peasants openly declared their wish to leave state farms. The homes of those who continued to support collectivisation were being deliberately burned down.[29]

The dismal picture for the Party was completed by the cultural intelligentsia. Long accustomed to regarding themselves as the vanguard of the nation, faced with political and cultural oppression,[30] cultural elites now found themselves simply one part of a much broader protest. The Central Committee's Cultural department noted 'Khrushchev's speech has led to particularly wide discussion in literary circles, with a whole wave of meetings. Writers speak with great vehemence on the problems of freedom of expression.'[31] The report noted a challenge 'to communist writers (Kott, Woroszylski, Braun and others) and their young followers, from liberal critics (Sandauer, to some extent Przyboś, and others) who deny their right to continuing authority in literary affairs and call for "people with clean hands"'.[32]

Several hundred people attended an open meeting of the Writers' Union (ZLP) on 27 April. It was a stormy session with frequent interruptions. An attempt to defend *nomenklatura* privileges, including special shops, came in for ridicule: 'It is not right that ministers and other activists working 14–16 hours a day in offices should have to queue to get a kilo of meat [*Laughter in the hall*].'[33] They condemned special shops 'behind the yellow curtain', multi-roomed villas for families of two or three, holiday homes, and priority access to scarce goods for 'those working in the military, security services, bureaucrats, ministers and Central

26 Krosno, Mielec, Przemyśl and elsewhere.
27 AAN 23/VII/3859, *Meldunki z terenu*, 15 May 1956 (38).
28 AAN 23/VII/3859, *Meldunki z terenu*, 17 April 1956 (30).
29 AAN 23/VII/3859, *Meldunki z terenu*, 15 May 1956 (38).
30 A. Gella, 'The Life and Death of the Old Polish Intelligentsia', *Slavic Review* March 1971 (30).
31 AAN 237/VIII (Central Committee Department of Culture) /150.
32 AAN 237/XVII/I119, 'Sektor Literatury' (First quarter, 1956).
33 AAN 237/V/303, stenographic account, pp. 60–2.

Committee members'. How could one talk of 'justice for all' in such circumstances? There had been much talk about high-ups, but what about all their dependants and hangers-on? Should ministers' children be driven to school or kindergartens in official limousines? Foreign travel paid for by the state was junketing abroad – 'All official go as cultural attaché!' Social inequalities were rife: 'When hospital waiting-lists are long and the sick lie for ages in corridors, is it any wonder that public irritation is aroused by the spectacle of luxuriously equipped and spacious polyclinics reserved for the elect? *(Prolonged applause)*'. Years of negative selection (promotion of those without qualifications or abilities) had resulted in the 'cult' of the incompetent.[34]

Sandauer's speech deplored the triumph of incompetence in culture: careerism, cunning and cynicism, 'teaching us for a decade that the highest virtue is the lack of fixed beliefs'. Culture had been eliminated at record speed: imposing uniformity, gagging publishers, threatening writers with a ban and starvation. But he insisted that anti-Stalinist speeches were not enough. The 'thaw' in culture would remain a façade for as long as it would take to create a new type of institution, and reorganise literary life on the basis of collegiality. Stalinists who had conducted intellectual terror could not be transformed into democrats overnight. 'Our Writers' Union was closed for eight years to those who did not agree with its harmful and mistaken policies.'[35]

After this fiasco, the ZLP Party Committee resolved to meet *in camera*. It took two further sessions[36] to agree a resolution. This declared that the XXth Congress had been 'a decisive turning-point in public life', but inner-Party discussion was being unaccountably held up or blocked: 'The Party leadership is not taking practical account of the *aktyw* critique.' Writers were disturbed by attacks on them in the Party press and speeches, and by the sacking of a censorship official who had passed a protest letter for publication. Materials from the newly radicalised paper *Po prostu* had been confiscated, in contravention of the Constitution. They sought genuine election of Congress delegates and real choice of Party leaders, 'not just a pseudo-democratic fiction'. They also called for calm: 'There is bound to be sharp discussion in a country like Poland where antagonistic classes still exist.' The Party should not tolerate anti-Semitism and racism.[37] Anti-Russian sentiments might spread.[38]

[34] AAN 237/V/303, p. 63. [35] AAN 237/V/303, pp. 128–30.
[36] AAN 237/XVIII/153 (8 June 1956).
[37] K. Kersten, *Polacy, Żydzi, Komunizm: Anatomia półprawd, 1939–1968* (Warsaw, 1992).
[38] AAN 237/XVIII/153.

Po prostu published a signed editorial which rallied the young intelligentsia to social protest. It noted 'students always played a gigantic role in Polish revolutionary movements' and called for such a programme in the present day: 'Put briefly: to struggle together with the whole of our Party, for restoration and development of communist norms of life in building socialism. Over the last decade, our organisation developed many sores and wounds. They will be hard to cure.' The cult of Stalin deformed the system, introducing many elements alien to the ideology of Marxism–Leninism, such as the dictatorship of individuals, in varied spheres and to varying degrees; the paralysis of democracy; contempt for the masses;[39] and jamming of Western broadcasts.[40] A letter to the Central Committee (9 June) stated: 'members of the club are unable to understand why British citizens can listen freely to programmes in English from Warsaw, while Poles may not listen to the Polish Service of the BBC.'

A federation of 'youth discussion clubs' was formed on 15 April. Groups from Kraków, Poznań, Rzeszów and elsewhere empowered the Warsaw Club of Catholic Intelligentsia (KIK) to act as Secretary: to organise and support existing groups and help new ones arise; to represent their interests to the authorities and institutions (particularly where local authorities were being obstructive); to further cooperation between clubs, exchanging experience and information.[41] Discussion clubs mushroomed – for music (including jazz), sculpture and film appreciation. Student theatre and satirical reviews appeared in Gdańsk, Łódź, Kraków and elsewhere. Young people deserted the official ZMP in droves, leading to internal Party investigation of what were now admitted to be 'youth problems'.[42]

With all sections of society now politically engaged, the Party leadership had to act. It announced a widespread amnesty: 35,000 prisoners were released within a month, of whom 4,500 were political, including members of the former anti-communist underground, and socialist and populist politicians. In all some 9,000 politicals were released.[43]

Verdicts in the Stalinist show trials were quashed and their victims rehabilitated. Senior officials from the Stalinist era were dismissed, including the Minister of Culture, Minister of Justice, Prosecutor-General, Military Prosecutor and the last Minister of Public Security before the post's abolition, Stanisław Radkiewicz (demoted to Minister

[39] 'Co robić?' editorial, *Po prostu*, 8 April 1956.

[40] AAN 237/XVIII/161 (Klub Krzywego Koła). [41] AAN 237/XVIII/161, p. 24.

[42] For Party anxieties, see Zofia Zemankowa, AAN 237/V/204, pp. 90–3 (29 March 1956), and special report AAN 237/VII/3859, *Meldunki z terenu*, 28 May 1956 (43).

[43] P. Machcewicz, *Polski Rok 1956* (Warsaw, 1993), p. 53.

of State Farms). Notorious interrogators and torturers, such as Roman Romkowski and Anatol Fejgin,[44] were arrested. It was announced that the number of security personnel (*bezpieka*), would be cut by 22 per cent.[45] Such harsh treatment and public condemnation was bound to demoralise the Party and security apparatus, as their near-paralysis in the face of the 'June events' would soon indicate.

The spring session of parliament (Sejm) was the most vibrant for years. In his opening speech, Prime Minister Cyrankiewicz appeared to welcome the deliberation of its critical committees: 'Without them, decisions of the Sejm become a rubber stamp, going through the motions, without carrying out the proper function of a legislative body.' The XXth Congress had launched a 'democratisation of our political and economic life'. Polish reactions showed the nation had understood it properly: 'The healthy wave of criticism, the increased volume of discussions at Party and non-Party meetings, discussions in the press – the whole great debate in which practically all of us are participating – proves that a never-ending, national conference of political activists on the problems of socialism is taking place.'[46] Every enlightened citizen had become an activist. The political 'thaw' had run ahead of the meteorological one: 'Spring is late this year, there are nightly frosts during April but in no way do they reflect political life in this same month.'[47]

Such optimistic forecasts were echoed by Party leader Ochab in a more conventional idiom. The resolutions of the XXth Congress had a 'tremendous impact on Poland and the rest of the world, whose toiling masses were taking them up in a constructive, Leninist spirit'.[48] A week later, *Trybuna Ludu* announced that the Politburo had 'critically evaluated the activities of Comrade Jakub Berman in the fields over which he exercised control [security, ideology and culture]'. Jakub Berman resigned from his Politburo posts and deputy Premiership.[49] This followed an intensive Politburo investigation (2–5 May) into his past activities.[50] Some of the public welcomed his removal as an anti-Semitic decision: 'Thanks to Berman, a large number of Jews gained positions of power, now that will change.' Another view was that Berman 'had to resign because he was a pupil of Stalin and Bierut and now we are putting things in order'.[51] The routing of the Polish Stalinists was indeed complete.

[44] See H. Piechuch, *Spotkania z Fejginem (zza kulis bezpieki)* (Warsaw, 1990).
[45] W. Roszkowski, *Historia Polski, 1914–1991*, 2nd enlarged edn (Warsaw, 1992), p. 231.
[46] *Trybuna Ludu*, 24 April 1956. [47] *Ibid.*
[48] Ochab, reprinted from *Pravda*, 29 April 1956, by *Trybuna Ludu*, 30 April 1956.
[49] Announced in *Trybuna Ludu*, 6 May 1956.
[50] Z. Rykowski and W. Władyka, *Polska próba. Październik '56* (Kraków, 1989), p. 132.
[51] Reports in AAN 237/VII/3835, *Informacje*, 18 May 1956 (35).

Secret reports on May Day admitted that urban iconography – street and building decorations – was more muted than in previous years, with 'significantly fewer illuminated signs and big banners'. Portraits from the past – Marx, Lenin, Bierut – were more prevalent than those of current Party leaders.[52] Turnout in the countryside was not embarrassingly low: peasants 'often arrived from remote districts on horseback, bicycle or on foot'. But there had been serious shortfalls in the peasants' 'First of May pledges' to speed up sowing, to increase the areas of cultivable land for growing maize, to improve roads, bridges and school buildings, to clear out ditches, plant trees and so on.

By contrast, workers in some cities (Łódź and Stalinogrod) had been more reliable, chanting slogans: 'For Polish–Russian Friendship' and 'Solidarity with the International Workers' Movement'. However, the turn-out of miners had been poor. There was a lack of enthusiasm amongst many marchers. Those parading in Lublin failed to take up official chants and slogans, and in at least one *powiat* the procession went along in complete silence. Even the big parade in central Warsaw was a modest affair which 'lacked militancy'. Overall, the secret report estimated an attendance about 2 million lower than in 1955.[53]

Many young people failed to march or, if they did, 'expressed discontent with the Party and government'. Students of art history at Warsaw University broke into a patriotic song when approaching the review tribunal. Elsewhere in the capital, a banner was unfurled by the Rosa Luxemburg Factory demanding replacement of the Minister for the Motor Industry. There were even counter-demonstrations. One school declared 'Polish Youth struggles with Communism'. RFE and 'anti-government' pamphlets were distributed, while official posters and decorations were defaced or torn down.[54] There had been illegal fliers asking people not to recognise May Day at all: they suggested celebration of 3 May Constitution (of 1793) would be more appropriate.[55]

At a May Day lunch in Moscow, Khrushchev accused the Polish leaders of turning their backs on the Soviet Union. 'We are going to fight against that', Khrushchev shouted, banging his fist on the table. Pointing at the Polish Ambassador, he went on: 'You have your sovereignty, but what you are doing today in Poland is against your sovereignty and against socialism. We deeply regret the death of comrade Bierut who

[52] AAN 237/VII/3859, *Meldunki z terenu*, 4 May 1956 (34).
[53] AAN 237/VII/3859, *Meldunki z terenu*, 4 May 1956 (34).
[54] AAN 237/VII/3859, *Meldunki z terenu*, 4 May 1956 (34).
[55] Jarosz and Pasztor, *W krzywym zwierciadle*.

was a communist internationalist. Ochab has allowed anti-socialist elements to have their own way in Poland. They need to be rapped across the knuckles.'[56]

Poznań

The first workers' revolt against Polish communism did not take place at newly established sites such as Nowa Huta outside Kraków, nor on territories 'recovered' from Germany, but in Wielkopolska, a region long noted for its tradition of efficient work. Perhaps this ethos inspired discontent. As the main historian of 1956 suggests, 'The economic absurdities of Stalinist planning – bureaucratisation, "organised chaos" and massive waste of resources – may have enraged inhabitants to a greater extent than those of less-developed regions.'[57]

The centre of protest was the Stalin Factory (ZiSPO), one of the largest and oldest in Poland, making locomotives and other heavy machinery. Workers sent a delegation to Warsaw with their grievances: recent wage cuts (around 11 million złotys), increased work norms, overlong working-hours (especially for young women), lack of health and safety at work, food price increases and inadequate supplies of domestic coal. The Minister of Machine Industry, Roman Fidelski, made some concessions on the wage issue. He also promised (by some unspecified means) to bring an end to bottle-necks at work caused by shortage of raw materials and semi-finished products. He would refer the other issues, including work norms and prices, to higher officials. Warsaw representatives would visit Poznań in the near future to meet workers at ZiSPO.[58]

Whilst the delegation was away, wage demands escalated. It was now proposed that basic prices be lowered by 50 per cent. Security reports indicated the preparation of banners to be unfurled in the streets, on trams and railways, and at the Meat Production Factory.[59] The visit of Minister Fidelski ended in disarray. He was accused of reneging on promises made earlier in Warsaw. Most sections returned to normal work and others went home. A handful – about twenty workers in one section – felt that the path to negotiation had been blocked and that there was a need for direct action. They prepared to strike.

[56] V. Micunovic, *Moscow Diary* (London, 1980), p. 144. Moscow had been receiving alarmist reports from its Warsaw Ambassador, Ponomarenko. See D. Volkogonov, *Lenin: A New Biography* (New York, 1994), pp. 480–2, 509.

[57] Machcewicz, *Polski Rok 1956*, p. 109.

[58] E. Machowski, *Poznański Czerwiec 1956. Pierwszy bunt społeczeństwa w PRL* (Poznań, 2001), pp. 46–7.

[59] Machcewicz, *Polski Rok 1956*, p. 82.

Their plans were relayed to Warsaw by the security police. The Provincial Party Secretary, Leon Stasiak, rang Ochab late that evening 'having just returned from the Railway Repair Yard where voices made clear that there were now groups organising against People's power'.[60] Thirty-one points were now being addressed to the authorities. There was a sharp critique of 'factory bureaucracy'. The earlier mass meeting had rejected his suggestion of a delegation to discuss issues further, and strike preparations were put in hand. Stasiak realised a crisis was imminent and Ochab agreed. He rang the head of State Security who was just on the point of departure to Moscow 'to discuss the situation in Poznań'. It transpired that the Russians, using radio-telegrams, were better-informed about developments than Polish leaders.

On 28 June, the ZiSPO siren sounded at 6.30 a.m. Hearing this prearranged signal, several thousand workers (at least 80 per cent of the work-force) formed up outside the gates and started marching towards the city centre. They were joined by many other employees, housewives and school-children en route. As the column passed the cathedral, two priests appeared on the steps. Leaders of the demonstration knelt down to receive their blessings.

Banners were unfurled: 'We are Hungry', 'We Want Bread', 'Down with Exploitation of Workers' and 'Down with the Red Bourgeoisie'. A Polish Radio transmission van was commandeered and driven round the city summoning people to the demonstration in the central Stalin (later Adam Mickiewicz) Square. It called out: 'Fewer palaces, more apartments', 'We want fewer Polish children to have tuberculosis and anaemia', 'Food products are being taken out of Poland so our children don't have enough to eat.' Demands soon included 'We want Freedom', 'We want UN-supervised elections', 'Long Live Mikołajczyk'.

Protestors tore down red flags. Patriotic anthems were sung. As Poland's vanished sovereignty was reasserted, it became clear that Polish communists were seen as little more than lackeys of a foreign power: 'Down with the Russians! Down with the Germans! We want a Free Poland.' The atmosphere was cheerful and liberated. When the head of the column approached the Europejskii Café, waiters ran out with trays of drinks and snacks. Militiamen had no inclination to attempt to halt the demonstrators and often offered their support: 'we earn so little too, and we don't like the way things are in Poland these days'. The crowd in front of the Castle, waiting for the authorities to arrive, was put by some observers at 100,000. A delegation entered the local authority building

60 Stasiak interviewed by *Polityka* 13 June 1981, and Ochab by Torańska, *Oni. Stalin's Polish Puppets*, pp. 49–50.

and presented their demands. Top of the list was immediate appearance of a government team to discuss their grievances.

Some demonstrators then moved on to the nearby Provincial Party Committee. Red banners were thrown from the windows, busts of communist leaders (including Bierut's) were smashed and other portraits defenestrated. Only Lenin was spared by being turned to face the wall 'so that he could not observe'. Files were ransacked or incinerated. As crowds entered the building, unofficial tour guides offered the rooms for rent.

Crowd momentum was now unstoppable. It stormed the prison, releasing surprised inmates and procuring rifles and grenades. It attacked the Polish Radio station, destroying equipment used to jam Western broadcasts and surged on to the courts and Procuracy. Only the State Security headquarters did not fall to the demonstrators. However, secret policemen were identified, chased and in one case lynched on the street. Crowds shouted at the Security headquarters 'Fascists' and 'Only the SS, only the Gestapo are defending themselves.'

As Machcewicz shows, the demonstration became an insurrection. The people who had begun the march now began to consider themselves 'The Nation'. As various strands, economic and political, patriotic and religious, converged in a single steam, Poznań crowds came to assume they represented all True Poles from whom a national uprising was anticipated. It was rumoured that similar clashes were taking place in other major cities. Poznań's Security headquarters was held to be the 'last bastion of communism' in Poland. Thus the forces of law and order beginning to be deployed against them were seen as Soviet troops in Polish uniforms. Such sentiments, recurrent in later crises, had some grounds for credence in 1956.

Soviet-trained Minister of Defence, Marshal Rokossovsky,[61] held an emergency meeting with Ochab. Since the local security was incapable of handling such insurgency,[62] he advocated a military response. His demand for a free hand to deal with 'adventurists who attack state institutions'[63] was agreed to by the Politburo. Deployment of 10,000 soldiers and 400 tanks and armoured vehicles left 73 dead and many hundreds seriously wounded. Use of overwhelming force against poorly armed or unarmed civilians led to many tragedies. Even when ordered to

[61] Marshal of the Soviet Union and Poland, Minister of Defence (from November 1949), Vice-Premier (from 1952) and Politburo member (from 1950 to 13 November 1956). On his original appointment, see *Sto sorok besed s Molotovym*, pp. 55–9.

[62] E. Nalepa, *Pacyfikacja zbuntowanego miasta. Wojsko Polskie w czerwcu 1956 r. w Poznaniu* (Warsaw, 1992).

[63] Torańska, *Oni. Stalin's Polish Puppets*, p. 51.

fire into the air, some shots proved fatal. Children who had climbed trees to escape tanks, or for a better view, fell dead like sparrows. Seven soldiers were killed. Future Party leader Gierek and Premier Cyrankiewicz spoke at their funeral.

Since all communications between Poznań and the outside world were blocked, wild rumours abounded. It was said that 30,000 farmers had travelled to Poznań to join the uprising and that Łódź had sent 40,000 workers to assist Poznań. A train bringing Security officials had been blown up. Ochab had died during the disturbances. It was widely stated that, had Poznań held out a few more days, Western military assistance would have been forthcoming and Polish emigrants would have come to the rescue: 'Anders would have brought in an entire armoured corps by air.'[64] Other sources claimed that Polish and Soviet armies had fought pitched battles and that the Soviet consulate in Poznań was demolished. Some said the city had been bombed by Soviet aircraft and that 'all arrested are being taken to Siberia'.[65] One priest maintained that the Poznań incident had been staged by Jakub Berman as a pretext for annexing Poland to the Soviet Union.[66]

Instead of addressing the cause of the protests, Cyrankiewicz made a lurid threat:

> Every provocateur or maniac who dares to raise his hand against People's rule may be sure that, in the interest of the working class, the interest of the working peasantry and intelligentsia, in the interest of the struggle to raise the standard of living of the people, in the interest of the further democratisation of our life and in the interest of our Fatherland, the authorities will chop off his hand.[67]

In the coming weeks, two official alibis were advanced to explain the Poznań revolt. A standard Soviet technique was to categorise all protests as 'mass disorder'.[68] Such vague terminology, enacted as a legal category (Article 79) in the Criminal Code, enabled the authorities to disguise protests. Thus the major strike at Novocherkassk in 1962, the first recorded in the Soviet Union for thirty years, was suppressed and then relegated to 'mass disorder'. Participants were therefore judged under the same heading. This applied equally to hooliganism (gang-warfare

[64] For General Anders' statement on the 'events' in Poznań (29 June 1956), see M. Drozdowski (ed.), *1956. Polska emigracja a Kraj* (Warsaw, 1998), pp. 166–7.

[65] Machcewicz, *Polski Rok 1956*, pp. 128–9. [66] *Ibid.* pp. 130–1.

[67] 'Proclamation to the People of Poznań', 29 June 1956, in Paul E. Zinner (ed.), *National Communism and Popular Revolt in Eastern Europe. A Selection of Documents* (New York, 1956), p. 135.

[68] V. Kozlov, *Massovye besporiadki v SSSR pri Khrushcheve i Brezhneve (1953–nachalo 1980-kh gg.)* (Novosibirsk, 1999).

between bored youths on construction sites), defence of human rights, conscripts protesting against military service, defence of churches against forcible closure and the pro-Stalin marchers in Georgia on the third anniversary of the dictator's death.[69] Likewise, political prisoners were often granted amnesty together with those locked up for violent crimes against other persons. The intention was clearly to smear political protests by criminal association.

Thus the Poznań demonstrators were presented as vandalisers of public property and mindless marauders. The media displayed wrecked premises and sorry photographs of the guilty parties. Cinema newsreel showed four repentant hooligans, now apparently regretting their isolated acts of vandalism against public property, whose looted or incinerated shells were the only evidence offered to the public.[70] Looting does take place under the guise of peaceful demonstrations, and political authorities are capable of fomenting it to discredit protestors (as in 1976). They step forward afterwards as the saviours of public order.

Senior Polish officials, dispatched to Poznań by plane, made no attempt to meet or even understand the demonstrators. Gierek's report to the Politburo placed the blame for disturbances solely on mistakes by local officials. The Poznań events were subversion incited by 'enemies of the people'. Local Party activists had fallen for this provocation. Regional security services and militia had remained passive in the face of agitators in the factories, on the streets, on trains and in repair yards. The central authorities were thus absolved of all responsibility.[71]

Ochab's explanation for the events at Poznań was economic. They were caused by a tightening of shift-working. But when protests were being planned, shortcomings in the security service had prevented ringleaders from being identified and arrested. The militia was disoriented, particularly in the earlier stages: 'It had become demoralised and demobilised by criticisms following the XXth Congress.' Finally, Party organisations, both locally and nationally, had dwindled into passivity and disorientation. A good number had misunderstood democratisation, lawfulness and Leninist norms of party life to mean 'full liberalism, rupturing of Party discipline and tolerating unlimited criticism'.

He added a second dimension. 'Alien elements' had taken advantage of the Twenty-Fifth International Trade Fair in Poznań (17–31 June) to spread the word about their demonstration abroad and to gain publicity for the 'active underground against People's power'. Such

[69] D. Mandel, reviewing Kozlov in *Kritika: Explorations in Russian and Eurasian History* 2003 (4.1), pp. 260–71.

[70] *Polska Kronika Filmowa*, 3 July 1956.

[71] AAN 237/V/237, pp. 5–29.

provocateurs were anti-Russian and envisaged peaceful cooperation with the capitalist world.[72]

Moscow declared that 'imperialist and reactionary Polish underground agents, taking advantage of certain economic difficulties (*sic*), had incited serious disturbances and street disorders' in Poznań. This time, the Polish working class had expressed its 'decisive indignation over the insolent imperialist attack' and rebuffed this action against People's rule. But such foul provocations would continue to be fomented by American monopolists.[73]

Pravda asserted:

> Everyone now knows that this provocation was the work of enemy agents. The American press did not even consider it necessary to conceal the existence of a direct link between the Poznań events and the overseas centres which direct the 'cold war'. The New York *Journal-American* stated on 30 June with cynical frankness 'Senate has decided to allocate within the framework of aid to foreign states the sum of $25 million for financing secret activity behind the iron curtain like that which led to the riots in Poznań'.[74]

Washington seems to have been largely overtaken by the Poznań events. The State Department had concluded earlier in June 1956 that 'Ten years of Sovietisation has eliminated the main obstacles to Soviet domination', such as social movements and local institutional variations. The outcome was a consolidation of Soviet control. The 'New Course' after Stalin's death and denunciation of the late leader were tactical manoeuvres with the same aim as before: the complete Sovietisation of the satellite countries.[75]

Khrushchev denounced 'the subversive activities of the imperialists – in Poznań and Hungary' at the Soviet Presidium (9 and 12 July): 'They want to weaken internationalist ties and in the name of "independent roads" want to foment disunity and destroy [the socialist countries] one by one.'[76] Poznań showed that anti-Stalinism had gone too far and now threatened to undermine the foundations of Soviet socialism. Moscow tried to draw a line between the original anti-Stalin campaign, a necessary stage in which they had taken a bold lead, despite the obvious propaganda weapon this would give to the imperialists, and the new stage in which the time for self-criticism was over.[77] It was not easy to defend the distinction.

[72] AAN 237/V/237, p. 87. [73] *Pravda*, 1 July 1956. [74] *Pravda*, 16 July 1956 (editorial).

[75] P. Machcewicz, 'Stany Zjednoczone wobec Polskiego Października 1956 roku' in *Polska 1956 – próba nowego spojrzenia* (Warsaw, 1997), p. 47.

[76] M. Kramer, 'The "Malin Notes" on the Crises in Hungary and Poland, 1956', *CWIHP Bulletin* Winter 1996–7 (8/9).

[77] *Pravda*, 2 July 1956.

The notion that the Stalin cult, predominant for twenty years, could be eliminated in four months was implausible. The CPSU therefore relied on historicism: 'No malicious or slanderous attacks can halt the irresistible course of the historic development of mankind towards Communism.'[78]

An alternative view was that Poznań sent a signal from which the rulers could learn. Belgrade noted that the Poznań demands were not purely economic: 'It is obvious even to the most superficial observer, that a considerable majority of workers are lending support to tendencies which aim at a democratisation of public life.'[79] It had been a genuine attempt by an authentic working class to make its voice heard. The problem was that the political authorities did not listen.

After Poznań, the mood of the Polish people hardened into resistance.[80] The public realised there might be more bloody defeats or an explosion on a national scale. Once the barrier of fear had lifted, the status quo seemed intolerable. But what forms of change were permissible?

78 *Pravda*, 3 July 1956 (editorial). 79 *Borba*, 1 July 1956.
80 S. Jankowiak and A. Rogulska (eds.), *Poznański Czerwiec 1956* (Warsaw, 2002), pp. 16–17.

5 Polycentrism

> The whole system becomes polycentric, and even in the communist movement itself we cannot speak of a single guide. Togliatti, 1956

In June 1956 a series of nine questions were submitted to the Italian communist leader Palmiro Togliatti concerning communism since the 'secret speech'. He replied that the world communist movement had been changed irrevocably. Even for countries already under communist rule, 'the Soviet model cannot and must not any longer be obligatory'. Progress to socialism would be achieved 'by following paths which are often different'. But one general problem, shared by the whole movement, had arisen from the criticisms of Stalin. Every party must work out its own method of protection 'against the evils of stagnation and bureaucratisation'.[1]

A test case was Yugoslavia. Khrushchev took this as his prime example of Stalin's 'shameful role' in international relations. There had been no substance to the 1948 dispute, which should have been resolved 'through Party discussions among comrades'. Instead, Stalin magnified the issues to a monstrous extent. Showing Khrushchev a letter from Tito, Stalin remarked: 'I will shake my little finger – there will be no more Tito. He will fall.' Yet this did not occur: 'No matter how much or how little Stalin shook, not only his little finger but everything else that he could shake, Tito did not fall.'[2]

Stalin's successors had already tried to mend fences. The Belgrade Declaration (2 June 1955) restored Yugoslavia to the fold. Thereafter Yugoslav communists drew more far-reaching conclusions. Moscow was no longer entitled to a 'monopoly position in the workers' movement, least of all in the sphere of ideology'. It was Stalin's monopolistic claims

[1] '9 Domande sullo Stalinismo' (16 June 1956) in *The Anti-Stalin Campaign and International Communism* (New York, 1956), pp. 138–9.

[2] *The Anti-Stalin Campaign*, pp. 62–3.

that had caused the rift in the first place. They pioneered a new strategy based on self-management, civilian defence and non-alignment.

Poland's Stalinists were nervous of the implications. They nodded towards 'different roads to socialism'. There had been insufficient attention to what was 'innate in our movement, in our historical road, in our methods of construction'. But there should not be over-reliance on notions of national 'specificity'. Indeed there had been 'nihilistic disregard of our achievements' over the past decade. It was important to avoid the 'harmful confusion and ideological chaos' that would come from efforts to 'supplement' Marxism with other sources. Especially dangerous were 'concepts of liberalism, solidarity, relativism, cultural autonomy – autonomy conceived as independent of class struggle, politics and the leading role of the Party'.[3]

On 17 April 1956 Cominform was disbanded and Yugoslav leaders were feted during a long sojourn in Moscow. Towards the end of Tito's visit – his first since the 'split' – a unique Declaration was issued. It marked the first bi-lateral document signed between Moscow and another communist Party. At Yugoslav insistence, it made no mention of 'ideological unity' of the 'socialist camp'. On the contrary, it stated 'the two parties have agreed that their cooperation shall be based on complete voluntariness and equality, friendly criticism, and comradely exchange of opinions on controversial questions'. Socialist development differed according to countries and conditions; there was a 'multipicity of forms'. The two sides agreed that 'any tendency to impose one's opinions on the ways and forms of socialist development was to be avoided'.[4]

The next test-case for polycentrism was Poland. After a brief lull after Poznań (June 1956), popular forces again began to call for political change. Their opening demands were quite modest. After a dormitory power-cut, Wrocław University students held a torch-light procession into town. They stopped official vehicles with the demand 'We want light', and challenged 'those who aren't giving us light'. When they reached the Provincial People's Council (WRN), employees barricaded themselves in and turned out their lights.[5] The militia intervened before protestors could reach the town hall.

Soon afterwards, Warsaw students demanded democratisation in an 'Open Letter to all Students in Poland'. It envisaged a 'new, genuinely revolutionary, political organisation for young people'. It called for

[3] Editorial, *Nowe Drogi*, October 1955.

[4] Moscow Declaration (20 June 1956) in P. E. Zinner (ed.), *National Communism and Popular Revolt in Eastern Europe. A Selection of Documents* (New York, 1956), p. 13.

[5] Machcewicz, *Polski Rok 1956*, p. 150.

'complete openness (*jawność*) in public life', including discussion of the responsibility for Stalinism. Censorship should be limited by statute. There was much attention to the lack of economic democracy. The efforts of workers for self-management should be supported.[6] The idea of 'the revolutionary organisation of students and workers' self-management began to emerge'.[7]

Just before Poznań, Jacek Kuroń and three academic colleagues met Leszek Goździk, the 25-year-old First Secretary of the Factory Committee at the large 'Zeran' factory in suburban Warsaw.[8] Their chosen venue was the staff coffee bar at Warsaw University. Goździk spoke of the ineffectiveness of the workers' council at the factory and the need to introduce elements of democracy.[9] The young lecturers talked rather of Yugoslav self-management. But links between factory workers and intellectuals remained embryonic.

The head of *agitprop* noted that 'the creative intelligentsia, students, etc.' had become politically engaged. By contrast, 'our side' was becoming defensive. While some were speaking candidly, others were glossing over issues, or hiding behind dogma and schematic abstractions. This left the door open to those talking 'obvious nonsense' which had 'nothing in common with the art of Marxism, its science, its method, with our ideology'.[10] The editor of the Party monthly declared: 'The Twentieth Congress stirred up the country, [caused] a healthy storm, a healthy ferment, our ferment', one that could be restorative.[11]

While the Party elite hid its factional struggles behind a façade of unanimity, a stream of resolutions came up from the rank-and-file. The lower echelons now sought a real input into policy-making. Tired of talk about the Stalinist era of 'errors and distortions', they wanted open decisions, more openly arrived at. Many hoped the campaigns leading up to the next Party Congress would provide such a context. Above all, they called for reinstatement of Gomułka. He had been quietly released from detention at the end of 1954 and began to canvass his return to the Party leadership.[12] The Politburo responded to his various missives by dispatching a delegation to see him.[13] On 5 August he was reinstated in the Party.[14]

6 *Po prostu*, 21 October 1956. 7 J. Kuroń, *Wiara i Wina*, p. 102. 8 *Ibid.* pp. 102–3.
9 L. Goździk, 'Byliśmy u siebie w domu' in S. Bratkowski (ed.), *Październik 1956. Pierwszy wyłom w systemie* (Warsaw, 1996), pp. 22–45.
10 AAN 237/V/231 (Stefan Żółkiewski). 11 AAN 237/V/231 (Roman Werfel).
12 Gomułka's letters to the Politburo (9 April) and government (29 April) are published in J. Andrzejewski (A. Paczkowski) (ed.), *Gomułka i inni. Dokumenty z archiwum KC 1948–1982* (Warsaw, 1986, and London, 1987), pp. 76–8.
13 Rykowski and Władyka, *Polska próba*, pp. 132–4.
14 *Trybuna Ludu*, 5 August 1956.

Gomułka

When Gomułka addressed the Politburo (12 October 1956), he claimed not to notice 'groups and fractions' in the Party. The main task was to lead its million and a half members out of a tricky situation. The trust of the working class and the nation had been forfeited. Unless the Party was to rule by bayonets, it must be regained. They must mobilise the factory *aktyw*. Democratisation would prevent a reversion to 'old methods'. Central government should be cut: 'there are too many Vice-Premiers'.[15] The press announced his reinstatement to the Politburo and that the Central Committee was due to meet for its Eighth Plenum on 19 October. Since this had not been cleared with Moscow beforehand, a crisis with the Soviet Union was imminent.

Three armoured columns of Soviet troops, stationed in the north and west of the country, began to advance towards Warsaw.[16] They mostly used side-roads, avoiding major urban centres, notably Łódź. Their tracked vehicles did great damage to roads and bridges: Moscow was later sent a vast bill for compensation. Soviet warships took up positions opposite the Polish fleet in the Bay of Gdańsk and Soviet aircraft patrolled the coast from their Polish bases. Soviet forces in the DDR were put on readiness and similar steps were taken in the Belarussian, Kievian and Carpathian Military Districts. Marshal Rokossovsky put soldiers on alert to seize strategic positions in Warsaw, without informing the Politburo. It seemed that Soviet control of the Polish military would be sufficient to prevent its coming to the defence of a future Gomułka government. However, Soviet influence did not extend to the Polish Internal Security Corps (KBW) and other combat personnel under the Ministry of the Interior.

Some of these, loyal to the Polish Party, were also preparing to secure its leaders and key public buildings in Warsaw, including the radio station. Soviet plans 'to protect the most important state facilities' in Poland, including military installations and lines of communication, had been leaked to Polish officials. The Soviet mobilisation plan was no doubt 'intended as a form of coercive diplomacy rather than to provoke an immediate confrontation'.[17] But brinkmanship brought very present dangers. Potentially the most explosive was conflict within the Polish military and security establishments. KBW troops could be pitted against

[15] Andrzejewski (ed.), *Gomułka i inni*, pp. 96–109.

[16] K. Persak provides a very useful map in K. Kersten (ed.), *Polska 1956 – próba nowego spojrzenia*, Studia i materiały 3 (Warsaw, 1997), vol. III, p. 29.

[17] M. Kramer, 'The Soviet Union and the 1956 Crises in Hungary and Poland: Reassessments and New Findings', *Journal of Contemporary History* April 1998 (33.2).

others under Marshal Rokossovky's command.[18] Ochab did his best to calm the KBW. He told its commanders: 'We will not fight the Red Army. Calm the comrades and keep faith. Do not succumb to panic.'[19]

A Soviet forward unit did reach the suburbs of Warsaw early on 20 October. Met outside a church in Warsaw's Wola suburb, its commander explained he had been ordered to Warsaw where a counter-revolution had broken out and several dozen Soviet soldiers had been killed: 'They were in a hurry to rescue the workers of Warsaw.'[20] When he learned he had been misinformed, he requested petrol for the return journey.

Soviet leaders had already alerted other communist leaders (18 October) about 'sharp differences of opinion' with their Polish counterparts. These involved 'key issues of foreign and internal policy of the [Polish] Party and the state, as well as the composition of the Party leadership. We are seriously concerned about the situation created within the leadership of the [Polish] Party because of the special importance of the Polish position for the camp of socialism, and especially for the Soviet Union.'[21] Though ominous, this telegram did not mention military preparations.

The Soviet Ambassador had told Ochab that Moscow was sending a delegation to Warsaw to discuss the situation in the Party and in the country. Gomułka said later that the Poles replied that 'it would be better if they arrived on the second day of the Plenum, or afterwards, but not before the Plenum. And that must have made them even more nervous, or at least suspicious. They decided to come at once.'[22] Three hours before the Plenum was due to open, two Soviet planes arrived in Polish airspace requesting permission to land. A large 'military–political delegation' disembarked, including Molotov, Mikoyan, Bulganin and Kaganovich. The second plane, with an emotional Khrushchev and security staff, landed fifteen minutes later.

Snubbing the Polish Politburo and state officials, Khrushchev made straight for the Russians assembled on the tarmac. These included Marshal Konev, Commander-in-Chief of the Warsaw Pact, eleven more of the twenty-eight Russian generals currently posted to the

[18] L. Głuchowski and E. Nalepa, *The Soviet–Polish Confrontation of October 1956: The Situation in the Polish Internal Security Corps*, CWIHP Working Paper no. 17 (Washington, 1997), pp. 28–44.
[19] *Ibid.* p. 46.
[20] K. Persak, 'The Polish–Soviet Confrontation in 1956', *Europe–Asia Studies* December 2006, p. 1296 note 25.
[21] *Ibid.* p. 1291.
[22] J. Granville, 'Poland and Hungary in 1956' in K. McDermott and M. Stibbe (eds.), *Revolution and Resistance in Eastern Europe. Challenges to Communist Rule* (Oxford, 2006), p. 65.

Polish army,[23] and Rokossovsky. Turning from 'those on whom I depend', he then bawled at the Poles: 'We know who's the enemy of the Soviet Union here. Ochab's treacherous activity has been detected.'[24] Gomułka was shocked by this loud behaviour: Khrushchev could even be heard by the chauffeurs.

Polish leaders moved to the Belvedere Palace to receive their uninvited guests. The first round of talks was tense. The Russians criticised the imminent personnel changes, including the proposed removal of Marshal Rokossovsky, and told the Poles to strengthen political, economic and military ties with the Soviet Union. Khrushchev announced that the CPSU was ready to 'intervene brutally' in Polish affairs to defend Soviet interests. When Gomułka asked what these were, he received only the vaguest answer, based on West German *revanchisme* and Poland's place in geopolitics. Gomułka stated that the Polish side was willing to listen to 'the complaints of the Soviet comrades', but could not discuss under duress.

Khrushchev recalls him as explaining:

> I ask you to halt Soviet troop movements. You may think it's only you who need friendship with the Russian people. But as a Pole and a Communist, I swear that Poland needs Russian friendship more than Russians need Polish friendship. Don't we understand that without you we won't be able to exist as an independent state? Everything will be in order here, but don't allow Soviet troops into Warsaw, or it will become virtually impossible to control events.[25]

Gomułka also complained about the excessive numbers of 'advisers' within the Polish military and security apparatus[26] – above all, Marshal Rokossovsky. Otherwise, his tone was conciliatory. Poland was committed to the Warsaw Pact and to preserving 'the bloc of socialist states'.

By the next round of talks, Khrushchev was calmer and stated that Soviet troops in Poland were merely 'on manoeuvres'. He would have a word with Marshals Rokossovsky and Konev to bring them to an end. However, external relations were held to be critical. Mikoyan elaborated on the NATO threat, stating that the Americans sought to sunder the Polish–Soviet alliance. Khrushchev accused the Poles of wanting to 'turn your faces to the west and your backs on us'.[27] Both stated that Polish instability would weaken the communications between East Germany, where a huge number of troops were stationed, and their command and

[23] E. Nalepa, *Oficerowie Armii Radzieckiej w Wojsku Polskim 1943–1948* (Warsaw, 1995), p. 86.
[24] AAN, p. 12, t. 46a, pp. 66–8. [25] Taubman, *Khrushchev*, pp. 293–4.
[26] Detailed numbers (for 1944–59) are provided by A. Paczkowski in CWIHP Virtual Archive: 'Document: letter Khrushchev to Gomułka (22 October 1956)', note 1.
[27] L. Głuchowski, 'Poland, 1956: Khrushchev, Gomułka and the "Polish October"', *CWIHP Bulletin* Spring 1995 (5); Volkogonov, *Lenin*, pp. 480–2.

control centres in the Soviet Union. Poland's defection from the bloc would break the link completely. The Russians could never accept such an outcome. Molotov added that, while the Poles merely had to take care of their own affairs, Soviet leaders had 'to take responsibility for the wider issue of the socialist camp'.

The visitors then turned to the question of Polish leadership.[28] They favoured 'old, trustworthy revolutionaries, loyal to the cause of socialism'.[29] There was no meeting of minds. The final communiqué merely noted that the conversation would resume in Moscow at some time in the near future. By the time Soviet leaders had returned to Moscow, the Polish Plenum had reconvened, elected Gomułka First Secretary and removed Rokossovsky from the Polish Politburo.

On his return, Khrushchev told the Soviet Presidium: 'There's only one way out – put an end to what is in Poland.' But he added: 'If Rokossovsky is kept [as Defence Minister], we won't have to press things for a while.' Much of the blame for the Polish situation was placed on Soviet Ambassador Ponomarenko, who was 'grossly mistaken in his assessment of Ochab and Gomułka'. In a somewhat confused discussion, the Soviet Presidium agreed to consider new military exercises and the possible formation of a 'provisional revolutionary committee', consisting of pro-Soviet Polish officials, to displace Gomułka. Meanwhile, a vigorous press campaign would accuse the Polish media of trying to undermine socialism in Poland through 'anti-Soviet slanders'. Khrushchev also advocated summoning leaders of the neighbouring states to a Moscow summit on the Polish crisis. He added, 'Perhaps we should also send Central Committee officials to China for informational purposes.'[30]

The Polish leadership had already taken this precaution. Ochab gives a plausible account of his conversations with Chinese leaders in Beijing at the end of September 1956. It was a mutual effort to break out of isolation. He saw no scope for this with his immediate neighbours: Czechoslovak and East German leaders Novotný and Ulbricht were 'too limited'. Tito was 'too remote' (they did not meet until 1957). This left China as 'something of an independent factor'. Ochab admitted that Beijing perhaps over-estimated Poland's significance within the Soviet bloc. The same was probably true of Warsaw's estimation of China. For Beijing, however, already distanced from Moscow during the anti-Stalin campaign, and perhaps aware that an eventual breach

[28] Paczkowski (ed.), *Tajne dokumenty Biura Politycznego*, pp. 8–12.
[29] M. Kramer, 'Hungary and Poland, 1956', *CWIHP Bulletin*, Spring 1995 (5).
[30] M. Kramer, 'The Soviet Union and the 1956 Crises', *Journal of Contemporary History* (33.2).

was inevitable, any other communist sympathy was welcome. Poland also gave Beijing a good chance to complain to Moscow about 'great-power chauvinism'.[31]

Chou-en-Li told Gomułka later that the Chinese Party had supported the Eighth Plenum and played a 'stabilising role'. He had rung Moscow during the October crisis to suggest that Poland should find its own solutions and urged a peaceful resolution.[32] He emphasised that fraternal parties should base relations upon equality, which had been lacking in the Polish–Soviet case. Fraternity was between brothers: intra-bloc relations should not resemble those of father and sons. Sovereignty should be respected, but so too should the Soviet Union's 'leading role'.[33] Whilst this was a tactful formulation, it may not be fanciful to see here a premonition of the Sino-Soviet split, although this most spectacular piece of polycentrism was not made public until 1961.

When the Russians had left, the Eighth Plenum resumed with an address by Gomułka. After the XXth Congress had sent 'an animating sound current through the Party mass, as silent, enslaved minds began to shake off the poison of mendacity, falsehood and hypocrisy', so working people demanded to know the truth, without omissions or embellishment. They waited patiently for answers. Poznań workers had not taken to the street to protest against People's Poland, but against 'the evil which is widespread in our social system' and distortions of the basic principles of socialism: 'The clumsy attempt to present the painful Poznań tragedy as the work of imperialist agents and provocateurs was very politically naïve.' If the Party lost the confidence of the working class, 'each of us could not in fact represent anything more than ourselves'.[34]

We now know that the most significant workers' self-organisation in October 1956 took place far from the capital. An Australian political scientist found an independent trade union for Seamen and Deep-Sea Fishermen had been formed in October 1956. As the Red Fleet trained its guns on Gdynia, the port of Gdańsk, it was clear that protestors would be shelled if they made trouble. Despite such intimidation, the merchant seamen formed a union with 3,000 members. A wartime *émigré*, recently returned from London, was elected first President. Its initial aim – as in the Gdańsk Shipyard in 1980 – was to defend fellow-workers unjustly dismissed. To some extent this was successful: 'Every seaman who suffered an injustice was rehabilitated and received a verification he could

[31] 'The Emerging Dispute between Beijing and Moscow, 1956–1958' *CWIHP Bulletin* 1995–6 (6/7).
[32] Ochab in Torańska, *Oni. Stalin's Polish Puppets*, pp. 55–60.
[33] AAN PZPR, p. 107. [34] *Trybuna Ludu*, 20 October 1956.

show his wife.' Another grudge was their replacement by raw recruits from the countryside, whose lack of basic training led to many shipping accidents and even wrecks. The fundamental aim was to establish a free trade union. Although this failed for a generation, the interviewee concluded that the initial effort had been an achievement.[35] Whereas the Solidarity movement was born in the glare of world publicity, in 1956 they had been on their own.

Gomułka next told the Plenum that agricultural cooperatives should be voluntary. It was unacceptable to use psychological compulsion to make people join, or economic coercion through taxation and delivery quotas. Cooperatives should be genuinely self-governing and have access to state credits for purchasing the means of production. Collectives could only flourish within a spirit of community. Its broadest expression, which could be termed 'solidarity', was common labour. In an unexpected flourish, he asked: 'Should not the Catholic progressive movement compete with us in the search for forms of collective farms and their realisation? It is a poor idea to maintain that only communists can build socialism, only people holding materialist social views.'

Spontaneous de-collectivisation then took place. Within three weeks, 75 per cent of cooperatives had disbanded. Most others dwindled away. Of almost 10,000 which had existed at the end of 1955, only 1,534 remained by the end of 1957.[36] Land and property was re-privatised. One letter to the Central Committee from Kutno district reports: 'the members are stealing all they can. They are pulling down stone walls, chopping down trees and even pulling up paving-stones on the former collective.' Machinery from co-operatives was driven away to private farms, and state granaries were raided at night. Old scores were settled, often brutally. In Kabulty, Olsztyn province, a gang of fifty congregated at the Red Army monument, knocking down its star, and then headed for the home of the local correspondent of *Chłopska Droga*. They broke his windows but he escaped.[37]

Gomułka's address concluded that the right of 'each nation to a sovereign government in an independent country should be fully and mutually respected'. 'It was unfortunately not always like this in the relations between us and our great and friendly neighbour, the Soviet Union.' Power had been seized there by 'a mediocre man, an obtuse executive

[35] R. Zuzowski, 'An Interview with Włodzimierz Schilling-Siengalewicz' (April 1986), in *The Workers' Defence Committee KOR* (New York, 1992), pp. 265–9.

[36] D. Jarosz, 'Wieś Polska w 1956 roku' in Kersten (ed.), *Polska 1956 – próba nowego spojrzenia*, vol. III, pp. 169–77.

[37] Machcewicz, *Polski Rok 1956*, p. 169.

and a rotten climber'. But the cult did not consist of Stalin alone. There was a 'hierarchic ladder', each country had 'a ladder of cults from top to bottom'.[38] Following publication of his address, huge pro-Gomułka rallies took place on the Baltic Coast, in Poznań, Lublin, Łódź, Kielce, Bydgoszcz and other cities. Such mass mobilisation made alarming reading in Moscow.

The Soviet Presidium on 21 October again considered the options. Although there had been earlier dissent from Molotov and Voroshilov at the 'soft line' towards Poland, there was now unanimous support for Khrushchev's view: 'Taking account of circumstances, we should refrain from military intervention. We need to display patience.'[39] He took the same line at the communist summit on 24 October, also attended by members of a Chinese delegation. According to the Yugoslav Ambassador, Moscow wanted to hear the Chinese viewpoint because 'they were further away from events in Poland and Hungary, and were not directly involved, and could see things better than the Russians who were affected by inertia and the habits of the past'.[40]

Poland's immediate neighbours were the most belligerent. DDR leader Ulbricht and the Czechoslovak Novotný were ready for intervention to 'restore order' in Poland.[41] But Khrushchev wished to avoid 'nervousness and haste'.[42] A political solution looked preferable by far: 'Finding a reason for armed conflict [with Poland] would be very easy now, though finding a way to put an end to such a conflict later would be very hard.'[43] He already knew the intelligence assessment that Polish troops could not all be counted on in such a conflict. Some might fight invaders.

Warsaw Party Secretary Staszewski claimed much later to have issued firearms to defend the capital: 'The KBW distributed 800 rounds of ammunition and a few machine guns and hand grenades to a workers' militia', created in the Żerań Factory outside Warsaw. They were supposed to defend the capital, mainly through political agitation and fraternisation with invading forces.[44] Though unlikely, it seemed a reasonable assumption in Moscow that this could happen.

We also know that a number of Polish officers were considering even more dramatic solutions. General Komar of the Polish Army and General Mus (KBW) began to draft plans for a complete withdrawal of Soviet

[38] *Ibid.* [39] Kramer, 'The Soviet Union and the 1956 Crises'.
[40] Micunovic, *Moscow Diary*, p. 138.
[41] K. Persak, 'Kryzys stosunków Polsko-Radzieckich w 1956 roku' in Kersten (ed.), *Polska 1956 – próba nowego spojrzenia*, vol. III, pp. 37–42.
[42] Kramer, 'Hungary and Poland, 1956'. [43] *Ibid.* p. 54.
[44] Staszewski, *Oni. Stalin's Polish Puppets*, pp. 176–7; Kuroń, *Wiara i Wina*, p. 114.

forces from Poland. As soon as he heard this, Gomułka instructed them to discontinue at once.[45] However, he persisted with the demand for Rokossovsky's recall. By 26 October, the Soviet Presidium regarded this as the 'central question' in Polish–Soviet relations. They considered that 'Gomułka is taking this to extremes.' They noted that even the Chinese, though broadly supportive of Gomułka, were puzzled by his firm stance on this issue.[46]

There was also an economic aspect to the crisis. Warsaw explained to Moscow that:

> Poland is in a catastrophic economic situation. There is a shortfall of 900,000 tons of grain. Coal mining [a major export to the USSR at very low prices] is in a very bad shape too. After the Twentieth Congress, Poland adopted the same social measures as the USSR, but did not have the means to carry them out. That is why Comrade Ochab turned to the CPSU delegation for a loan.

When Khrushchev remarked that perhaps the USA would give them a loan, Ochab said he would ask but expected to be turned down.[47]

The final consideration was a personal one. Gomułka was willing to restore order but on his own terms. The Moscow summit had received favourably two reports on Gomułka. The first was on his published appeal to 'Workers and Youth' which called for 'solidarity, support and trust' in bringing Poland out of its current 'difficulties'. In return, the Party promised 'widening workers' democracy, increased participation of workers in enterprise management, and a greater role for the working masses in running all sectors of national life'.[48] Such platitudes helped to tide Poland over the immediate crisis. The other report concerned his famous oration to 300,000 citizens outside Warsaw's Palace of Culture and Science.

His speech is mainly remembered for its sensational announcement about Soviet troops advancing on Warsaw from bases in the west of the country. Khrushchev had assured him they would return to barracks within forty-eight hours. This statement was edited out of *Pravda*'s text. Russian readers were also unable to learn that the Polish nation 'can completely trust its army and the high command [*ovation*] which in our country, as everywhere in the world, is completely and entirely subordinated to the government'. They could not read that those responsible for past mistakes would be removed from office. However, Moscow

[45] W. Mus, 'Spór generałów o Październik 1956', *Polityka*, 20 October 1990.
[46] Kramer, 'The Soviet Union and the 1956 Crises', p. 389.
[47] M. Kramer, *CWIHP Bulletin* Spring 1995 (5). [48] *Trybuna Ludu*, 25 October 1956.

welcomed Gomułka's statement that Soviet troops were needed in East Germany because of the existence of NATO in West Germany, which was 'rearming the new Wehrmacht and fomenting chauvinism and revisionism aimed at our frontiers'.[49]

There seem to be two main reasons for the Soviet decision to back down. First, they made a shrewd assessment of Gomułka's character and concluded correctly that he remained a loyal communist within the Polish limits of the possible: 'We believed him when he said he realised we faced a common enemy: Western imperialism. We took his word as a promissory note from a man whose good faith we believed in.'[50] Indeed Gomułka's later orthodoxy in domestic politics, and international career as a stalwart of the Soviet bloc, confirmed their judgement. Second, the fear of Polish resistance may have acted as a deterrent. Khrushchev later recalled that, despite Rokossovsky's assurances that the Polish Army would obey his orders, the number of regiments on whom they could rely was unclear: 'Of course, our own armed strength far exceeded that of Poland, but we didn't want to resort to the use of our own troops.'[51] We may assume this calculation was logistical rather than humanitarian: Moscow invaded Hungary two weeks later.

Gomułka's peroration was a disappointment to the highly charged crowd, and to the entire nation listening to the live broadcast. Instead of stirring them to further collective achievements, he declared: 'Enough of meetings and demonstrations. It is time to go back to everyday work – full of faith and confidence that the Party united with the working class will lead Poland on a new road to socialism.' Some 10,000 at the rally refused to disperse. They headed for the Central Committee headquarters shouting pro-Gomułka slogans, 'anti-Soviet epithets' and 'God save Poland.' Protestors demanded the release of Cardinal Wyszyński, the removal of Rokossovsky and closure of Soviet bases in Poland. Some congregated outside the Soviet Embassy before being removed. Others assembled outside the Hungarian Embassy to express solidarity with Budapest. An impromptu gathering outside the Royal Castle site proclaimed 'Warsaw–Budapest–Belgrade'.[52] Gomułka's speech was published in full by *Szabad Nep*, the daily of the Hungarian Workers' Party. There was simultaneously a vast demonstration in Budapest – the onset of the Hungarian Revolution. It supported the changes in Poland, expressed solidarity with the Polish nation and demanded a 'Hungarian road to socialism'.

[49] *Ibid.* [50] *Khrushchev Remembers: The Last Testament* (Boston, 1974), p. 205.
[51] *Ibid.* p. 203. [52] Machcewicz, *Polski Rok 1956*, p. 138.

Hungary

In the last days of October 1956, complexities of managing relations within the communist movement overflowed. A frantic fortnight of shuttle diplomacy took Khrushchev and other Presidium members to Warsaw, Brest, Bucharest, and Tito's private island of Brioni. The pattern of protests was to repeat in 1989. The two years run in parallel. Trouble starts in Poland, finds echoes in Hungary, then spreads to Czechoslovakia[53] and beyond. Eventually, it reaches the USSR itself. In 1989, a peaceful outcome proved possible. Why was one not achieved in 1956?

To understand the Hungarian Revolution of 1956, we need to consider the convoluted trajectory of the country's de-Stalinisation. In response to the XXth Congress, the Hungarian Stalinist Rákosi pronounced himself in 'profound agreement' with the restoration of Leninist norms of Party life, collective leadership and 'elimination of the cult of personality'. The Congress had given impetus to the 'fine policy' laid down by the Hungarians' own previous Congress, which terminated the 1953 'New Course'. Thereby, Imre Nagy's earlier policy was ended, the primacy of heavy over light industry restored and collective agriculture re-imposed. Nagy was removed as Prime Minister and expelled from the Party. The spring and early summer of 1956 saw the paradoxical process of Rákosi presiding over de-Stalinisation and rehabilitating former leaders, above all László Rajk, that he himself had condemned to death on false charges of 'treachery and Titoism'.

From 30 March 1956, some Hungarian writers spoke out openly against Rákosi. They demanded an end to cultural isolation from the West. The Soviet Ambassador to Budapest, Yuri Andropov, reported home (30 April) 'right-wing opportunists and hostile elements have managed to create an impression [amongst the Hungarian public] that the Hungarian Workers' Party leadership, in its current form, is not doing what is needed in Hungary to carry out the decisions of the XXth Congress'.[54] The stability of the Rákosi regime was further challenged by a debating society he himself had promoted for communist youth, the Petöfi Circle.

Its mass meeting of 6,000 members on 27 June, the last before the summer holidays, became a nine-hour debate on the need for a free press. A few speakers widened the scope to the need for political and systemic

[53] J. Matthews, *Majales: The Abortive Student Revolt in Czechoslovakia in 1956*, CWIHP Working Paper no. 24 (Washington, 1998).

[54] Kramer, 'Hungary and Poland, 1956'.

transformation. An ovation greeted the call by veteran writer Tibor Déry: 'Just as people refer to the young people of 1848, so I wish that history will remember the young people of 1956 who will help our nation in creating a better future [*Sustained applause*]'.[55] By midnight, the audience was calling for Imre Nagy to be reinstated to the Party. Three days later, the Petőfi Circle was banned. By then, the Hungarian public had been informed about the Poznań events (28–29 June). When the news broke, a wave of workers' protests and sympathy strikes swept Hungary. Mining communities suggested that 'the communists' game is now up'. The huge Rákosi iron and steel works in Csepel came to a halt. Protest strikes took place at the larger factories in Budapest.[56]

Rákosi himself took the line that Poznań had been an imperialist provocation: 'A few days before the Poznań fair, the Americans had sent many groups of parachuting armed saboteurs.' It was 'the most seriously organised attack against our People's Democracy and against the working class we have seen for some time'. 'The enemy' was trying to 'sow confusion between the Party and the working masses'.[57] A Party Resolution (30 June) declared: 'The Poznań provocation is a warning to every Hungarian worker and honest patriot firmly to oppose attempts at trouble-making.'[58]

Such scapegoating did not impress the Soviet Ambassador. Andropov reported to Moscow (9 July) that in addition to renewed opposition to Rákosi, prominent figures had begun calling for a 'national policy' and a 'national communist movement' which would allow Hungarians independence in which to resolve their own affairs without Soviet interference. He deplored the 'indecision, feeble actions and inadequate vigilance of the Hungarian comrades' and anticipated more trouble.[59] His secret telegram was discussed by the Soviet Presidium on 12 July.

Their analysis was less alarmist. They thought a campaign should be mounted in the communist press, including a contribution from Togliatti, against the 'subversive activities of the imperialists – in Poznań and Hungary': 'They want to weaken internationalist ties; and in the name of independence of paths, they want to foment disunity and destroy [the socialist countries] one by one.'[60] There was concern that 'After the lessons of Poznań we wouldn't want something similar to happen in

[55] Gati, *Failed Illusions*, p. 131. [56] B. Lomax, *Hungary 1956* (London, 1976), p. 39.
[57] J. Granville, 'Hungarian and Polish Reactions to the Events of 1956: New Archival Evidence', *Europe–Asia Studies* November 2001 (53.7), p. 1059.
[58] Zinner, *National Communism and Popular Revolt in Eastern Europe*, p. 331.
[59] Kramer, 'The Soviet Union and the 1956 Crises', *Journal of Contemporary History*, p. 178.
[60] *Ibid.* p. 388.

Hungary.' A Presidium member, Mikoyan, was dispatched to Hungary the next day.

His report from Budapest described the Petöfi Circle as 'an ideological Poznań without gunfire', consisting mainly of students and intellectuals, supporters of Imre Nagy. His primary concern was the Rákosi leadership: 'We should remember that in Poznań there were no direct counter-revolutionary attacks. Thus, the absence of counter-revolutionary slogans in the Petofi Circle should not reassure the Hungarian communists.'[61] Mikoyan bluntly told Rákosi to step down. The change was announced on 18 July. Two days later, visiting Soviet generals signed a top secret plan, code-named 'Volna' (Wave). This provided for the deployment of tens of thousands of Soviet troops, at 3–6 hours' notice if required, 'to uphold and restore public order' in Hungary.[62]

The Hungarian crisis began on 6 October. An estimated 200,000 citizens watched the remains of László Rajk, and other victims of the 1949 show trials, being reinterred in Budapest's Kerepesi Cemetery. The official intention was simply to right a Stalinist wrong, and also to send a conciliatory signal to Yugoslavia that 'Titoism' was a bogey of the past. 'These men', Tito had said of Rákosi and his clique, 'have their hands soaked in blood, have staged trials, given false information, and sentenced innocent men to death. They have Yugoslavia mixed up in all these trials, as in the case of the Rajk trial, and they now find it difficult to admit before their own people their mistakes.'[63] However, the reburials became a political demonstration. Several hundred students marched from the cemetery into the city centre, unfurling flags, singing revolutionary songs and shouting 'We won't stop halfway: Stalinism must be destroyed.' Pausing outside the Yugoslav Embassy, they cheered Tito and the Yugoslav road to socialism.[64] Rákosi's successor Gerő admitted to Andropov that the ceremony had further undermined the Party's standing and emboldened the oppositionists. They were now insolently demanding the return of Nagy to the Politburo. Nagy was reinstated in the Party on 13 October without preconditions.

The storm broke on 23 October. A huge rally in central Budapest expressed approval of events in Poland. Gomułka's speech to the Eighth Plenum had been published in full and Hungarians demanded similar changes. They carried Hungarian and Polish flags, and banners declaring: 'Long live Polish youth.' They demanded 'Full solidarity with

[61] Granville, 'Hungarian and Polish Reactions', *Europe–Asia Studies*, p. 1058.
[62] Kramer, 'The Soviet Union and the 1956 Crises', p. 180.
[63] Gati, *Failed Illusions*, p. 136. [64] Lomax, *Hungary 1956*, p. 45.

Warsaw and with the Polish independence movement', and shouted 'Poland has shown the way; let us follow the Hungarian road.'

Demonstrators marched across the Danube to the statue of General Józef Bem, a hero of the Polish uprising of 1830 and Hungarian rising of 1848. After celebrating Polish–Hungarian solidarity, past and present, and reciting patriotic poetry, columns then dispersed to key points of the city where they demanded 'national independence and democracy'. Sixteen demands were presented for broadcasting at the radio station. The first called for 'the immediate evacuation of all Soviet troops' and the fifth for 'general elections by universal secret ballot ... with all political parties participating'. State security troops, sent to guard the building, opened fire. Stalin's bronze statue was dismembered and pieces dragged through the city. Similar demonstrations took place across the whole country.[65]

Although they had anticipated such an insurrection, Soviet leaders were divided in their response. A majority followed Khrushchev's lead 'in favour of sending troops to Budapest'. Marshal Zhukov stated: 'There is indeed a difference with Poland. Troops must be sent.' He thought martial law should be declared and a curfew imposed. But Mikoyan held out for a political solution. Malin records: 'Expresses doubts about the sending of troops. What are we losing? The Hungarians themselves will restore order on their own. We should try political measures, and only then send troops.'[66] Unable to achieve unanimity, the Soviets sent Mikoyan back to Budapest, accompanied by Suslov, who favoured armed intervention, and the KGB chief Ivan Serov. It was also decided to redeploy Soviet forces in the region. The new directive was to 'establish control over the most important sites in the capital and to restor[e] order', and also to 'seal off Hungary's border with Austria'.

A massive mobilisation of Soviet forces took place overnight. It included 1,130 tanks, 2 fighter divisions (159 aircraft) and 2 bomber divisions (122 planes). This massive show of force strengthened popular resistance. Tanks and armoured personnel carriers, without proper support, were easy targets for grenades and Molotov cocktails. The Hungarian forces had divided loyalties and some sided with the insurgents. By mid-afternoon on 24 October there were at least 25 protestors killed and over 200 wounded.[67]

Reviewing the position on 26 October, the Soviet Presidium criticised the Mikoyan line of non-intervention. Bulganin stated: 'Comrade

[65] Special issue *Europe–Asia Studies* December 2006 (58.8).
[66] Kramer, 'The Soviet Union and the 1956 Crises'.
[67] Kramer, 'The Soviet Union and the 1956 Crises', pp. 184–5.

Mikoyan is maintaining an improper and ill-defined position, and is not helping the Hungarian leaders put an end to their flip-flops. A firm line must be maintained.' Molotov concurred, and stated that Mikoyan should be overruled. Kaganovich stated: 'the real correlation of forces is such that it does not support the conclusions of Comrade Mikoyan. We must adopt a firm position. A Military–Revolutionary Committee must be set up.'[68] He clearly intended such a body to suppress the rising.

When the Presidium next met to discuss Hungary (28 October), Khrushchev admitted that 'the matter is becoming more complicated'. Molotov thought the Mikoyan and Suslov mission was 'gradually moving towards capitulation'. Kaganovich demanded 'decisive action' against the counter-revolution. Voroshilov was most outspoken: 'American secret services are more active there than comrades Suslov and Mikoyan are.' He wanted the troops to stay in Hungary until a new government had been formed. Suslov reported that 'Councils are being formed [spontaneously] at enterprises [around various cities]. There is an anti-Soviet trend in the demonstrations.' Trade unions were now demanding that the events be reclassified as a national-democratic uprising: 'They want to classify it according to the example of the Poznań events.'

Khrushchev was the most constructive. He noted that the uprising had spread to the provinces and that Hungarian troops might go over to the side of the insurgents. The worst alternative would be the formation of 'a Committee which takes power into its hands' (the notes do not elaborate this concept). An appeal to the Hungarian population should be prepared, 'or else we're just shooting'. He also suggested the issue of similar appeals from fraternal parties: Chinese, Bulgarian, Polish, Czechoslovak and Yugoslav.

Polish attitudes were particularly ambiguous. As János Tischler notes, 'When the new Polish leadership, seeking support for systemic change, looked for backing amongst other members of the Warsaw Pact, the orthodox Stalinist line still seemed strong. They thought the one possible ally might be Hungary.'[69] The Hungarian uprising had also taken the pressure off Poland at a time when relations with the Soviet Union were still strained. Given that Hungary was now the prime Soviet concern, Gomułka felt able to press the demand for Rokossovsky's removal.

On 28 October, the Polish Politburo instructed the Foreign Ministry to send a telegram to Beijing thanking it for its support during the Eighth Plenum. It was to confirm to Chinese comrades that 'Poland does not

[68] *Ibid.* pp. 185–6.

[69] J. Tischler, 'Polish Leaders and the Hungarian Revolution' in Kemp-Welch (ed.), *Stalinism in Poland*, p. 126.

intend to demand the removal of the Soviet military.' However, they also decided to issue a press release that Comrade Rokossovsky had 'gone on vacation' and been replaced by a temporary Minister of Defence.[70] Pre-emption worked. Khrushchev told the Soviet Presidium (30 October): 'I said to Gomułka that this is a matter for you [the Poles] to decide.' Finally, they sent a two-man team to Budapest to assess the situation and to urge the Nagy and Kádár leadership to halt further changes.

As Khrushchev had proposed, Warsaw issued an 'Appeal to the Hungarian Nation' signed by Gomułka and Premier Cyrankiewicz:

> Brother Hungarians!
> Stop the shedding of fraternal blood!
> We know the programme of the Hungarian Government of National Unity, the programme of socialist democracy, raising living standards, the creation of workers' councils, full national sovereignty, the withdrawal of Soviet troops from Hungary, basing friendship with the Soviet Union on the Leninist principle of equality.
> We are far from interfering in your internal affairs. We judge, however, that this programme corresponds to the interests of the Hungarian people and the entire camp of peace . . . We are both on the same side: the side of freedom and socialism. We appeal to you: enough of blood, enough of destruction, enough of fratricidal struggle. May peace come to reign in Hungary, peace and unity in the nation, so indispensable for the realisation of the broad programme of democratisation, peace and socialism which has been put forward by your Government of National Unity.

This letter appeared in *Szabad Nep* (Budapest) and all Polish newspapers on 29 October. Given the enormous popular sympathy for Hungarians among ordinary Poles, the Warsaw Appeal was to be read at all Party meetings.

There was an obvious disjunction between calling for withdrawal of Soviet troops from Hungary, and not from Poland. In the tense days that followed, Gomułka began to construct a thesis about the two countries' differing geopolitical positions. Hungary, a small, land-locked state, could afford a form of 'neutrality'; Polish *raison d'état* required a strong Soviet presence to counter-act (West) German *revanchisme*. He also contrived to give the impression that the Hungarian rising would have a favourable end. He told students at Warsaw's Polytechnical University that events there would appear as 'happy and glorious deeds in the annals of history'. Poland would help Hungary 'as far as possible'.[71]

[70] AAN PZPR 1674 k 200.
[71] M. Kula, *Paryż, Londyn i Waszyngton patrzą na Październik 1956 r. w Polsce* (Warsaw, 1992), p. 140.

Indeed, Polish leaders gave what assistance they could. The press and radio covered events objectively, without censorship or destructive editing. An editorial in the Party daily dismissed the notion that 'alien agencies' or counter-revolutionary forces were the main drivers of events in Hungary. Such answers – 'and there was no lack of them after the tragic Poznań events in our country' – could not explain how such isolated agencies could have mobilised vast masses for the struggle. The real source of the 'Hungarian tragedy' lay in the 'errors, distortions and even crimes of the past Stalinist period'. Conservative elements in the Hungarian leadership had caused a conflagration when a 'peaceful manifestation of the Budapest youth had expressed solidarity with the changes in Poland'.[72]

Coded dispatches from his emissaries in Budapest informed Gomułka that none of the Hungarian leaders was able to identify a single 'reactionary centre' in the capital. But they did concede that events were fast slipping out of Party control, which would make military intervention inevitable. That was the line taken at their meetings with Mikoyan and Suslov (29 October), though the Russians did not say that a final decision had been made. All this brought home to Polish leaders how close they had been to that position only a few days earlier.

After a few days' hesitation, Nagy started to grant the demonstrators' demands. On 29 October, his government called for withdrawal of Soviet troops, and the internal security service (AVH) was disbanded. Next day it was declared that a multi-party system would be restored and the holding of free and secret parliamentary elections was announced. Meanwhile, there would be a coalition government based upon democratic collaboration between parties reborn in 1945.

The Soviet Presidium at first responded mildly to these innovations. It appeared to endorse the view of the visiting Chinese delegation that inter-country relations should be based on the five principles of Pancha Shila. These were: respect for territorial integrity; non-interference in domestic affairs; non-aggression; cooperation on the basis of equality and mutual advantage; and peaceful coexistence.[73] These principles had been endorsed by the Chinese and Indian prime ministers two years earlier as a bi-lateral guide, but also to govern 'relations with other countries in Asia and in other parts of the world'. They find their reflection in a 'Declaration by the Government of the USSR' (30 October) on its relations with other socialist states.

[72] *Trybuna Ludu*, 28 October 1956.

[73] T. Robinson and D. Shambaugh (eds.), *Chinese Foreign Policy: Theory and Practice* (Oxford, 1994).

This extraordinary statement appeared to mark a new relationship between Moscow and its allies. After mistakes in the (Stalinist) past, the XXth Congress had restored the 'Leninist principles of the equality of peoples in its [Moscow's] relations with other socialist countries. It proclaimed the need for taking full account of the historical past and peculiarities of each country that has taken the path of building a new life.'[74] There would be a review of deployments in Hungary and Romania, and of 'Soviet military units in the Polish republic on the basis of the Potsdam four-power agreement and the Warsaw Treaty'. It added that 'Soviet military units are not in the other Peoples' Democracies', thus omitting Eastern Germany.

A Chinese statement the next day commented on the previous policy: 'Some of these countries have been unable to build socialism in better accord with their historical circumstances and special features because of these mistakes.' Such misunderstandings and estrangement had led to the Yugoslav situation of 1948–9 and the recent happenings in Poland and Hungary. The demands from these two countries for democracy, independence and equality were 'completely proper'.[75] This appeared to be an explicit endorsement of polycentrism.

However, in conversation afterwards, Mao drew a clear distinction between the Polish and Hungarian uprisings: 'The Party led in Poland. In Hungary, the goal of the Petöfi Club was to break up the Party and government.' It had unleashed an unhealthy campaign, the masses rebelled, and the Party and government ceased to exist. Poland had restoration, but Hungary had counter-revolution and revisionism.[76]

A day after the Soviet statement appeared, the decision was made for re-invasion of Hungary. What caused this overnight *volte-face*?

Khrushchev now advanced a new argument. In earlier Presidium discussions, East–West relations had been a background factor. Thus on 28 October, he simply commented: 'The English and French are in a real mess in Egypt. We shouldn't get caught in the same company. But we must not foster illusions. We are saving face.' Next day, Israel invaded Egypt and the French and British joined their incursions by air and sea on 31 October. Khrushchev gave this operation to regain the Suez Canal, recently nationalised by Nasser, great prominence:

> If we depart from Hungary, it will give a great boost to the Americans, English and French – the imperialists. They will perceive it as weakness on our part and go on

[74] *Pravda*, 31 October 1956.
[75] Zinner, *National Communism and Popular Revolt in Eastern Europe*, pp. 492–5.
[76] 'Conversation between Cyrankiewicz and Mao Zedong', *CWIHP Bulletin* 8 April 1957 (14/15).

to the offensive. We would then be exposing the weakness of our positions. Our party will not accept them if we do. To Egypt they will then add Hungary.[77]

Of course, Soviet leaders did not know that the United States had not been informed of the Anglo-French-Israeli expedition. They assumed its approval.

In fact, the Americans, preoccupied with a presidential re-election, saw the Hungarian rising as a problem, rather than an opportunity. At the National Security Council (26 October), Eisenhower was mostly concerned that a Soviet over-reaction in Hungary might precipitate a more general war. It was decided to send a message to Moscow assuring the Soviets that the USA had no intention of drawing Hungary into NATO. As Dulles put it (27 October): 'We do not look upon these nations [Poland and Hungary] as potential military allies.'

In his important new book, Charles Gati sees this as a moment of truth: after years of rhetoric about 'liberation' and 'rollback', it turned out the cupboard was bare: 'There were no plans whatsoever on the shelves, no diplomatic initiatives had been prepared, and of course no consideration was given to any form of military assistance, let alone direct intervention.' Opinion-making circles canvassed notions of neutrality for Hungary (on Austrian lines), with an equivalent neutralisation of a NATO country, such as Belgium. But Gati concludes that 'in the end, the White House had little to say and nothing to offer. *The excuse of helplessness replaced the myth of liberation and the illusion of omnipotence*.'[78]

Soviet re-intervention in Hungary, on 4 November, was facilitated by the international situation. The Suez venture ruptured the Western alliance and turned world attention away from Hungary. As Khrushchev put in, in talks with Tito, 'They are bogged down there, and we are stuck in Hungary.'[79] Moscow's inaccurate prediction that an 'imperialist victory' in the Near East would be followed by incursions into the heart of Europe made the prospect of a neutral Hungary (mooted in Budapest on 30 October) entirely unacceptable to custodians of the Soviet sphere of influence. Consequently, the Presidium – against the advice of Mikoyan, who favoured negotiations – decided to reverse its policy and re-invade. The intervening days were used to consolidate bloc support for the new line.

There were real fears of 'spill-over' from Hungary into its neighbours. As Shepilov put it (1 November): 'if we don't embark on a decisive path, things in Czechoslovakia will collapse'. There were student demonstrations in

[77] Kramer, 'The Soviet Union and the 1956 Crises', p. 393.
[78] Gati, *Failed Illusions*, pp. 163–5. [79] Micunovic, *Moscow Diary*, p. 134.

Bratislava and other cities (30 October).[80] Czech military officials warned Moscow that 'counter-revolutionary forces' might try to stir up trouble on Slovak territory, especially in areas with many ethnic Hungarians. Likewise, reports from Romania indicated that students in many cities were demonstrating in favour of the Hungarian revolution. As early as 24 October, Romania sealed off its border with Hungary.[81]

Gomułka, Cyrankiewicz and Ochab were summoned to meet Khrushchev, Malenkov and Molotov at Brest (on the Polish–Soviet border) on 1 November. The Russians gave notice of their intention to re-invade Hungary. The Poles took the view that no foreign power had the right to resolve internal crises – whether the current one in Hungary or that in Poland twelve days earlier – by armed force. But they agreed that 'counter-revolution' was at work in Hungary, which needed to be snuffed out. In free elections, the Communist Party would get some 8–10 per cent of the votes. However, they rightly thought that military intervention would lead to a protracted and bloody conflict.

After the meeting had ended without agreement, the Poles reported back to an emergency Politburo in Warsaw. A statement appearing in *Trybuna Ludu* the next day stated that the crisis should be resolved 'by the Hungarian people alone and not by foreign intervention'. Gomułka also offered to convene bi-lateral talks in Warsaw at which the Soviet Union and Hungary could resolve their differences. Nothing came of this initiative.

Khrushchev and Malenkov then travelled to Bucharest, where they met Romanian, Czechoslovak and Bulgarian officials. In contrast to Gomułka, their leaders enthusiastically endorsed armed intervention. The Romanian offer to provide forces for the invasion was declined. Finally, the Russians travelled to Yugoslavia to gain Tito's acquiescence, which they obtained rather easily.[82]

Gomułka accepted the fait accompli. When journalists protested that the Polish public would never forgive such a betrayal of Hungary, he replied calmly:

> You want me to risk Poland's fate? You want me to declare myself for Imre Nagy even though I do not know him or his motives. The only thing I do know is that his government had no communists and that the mob was stringing up communists on lamp posts. And now you, defending such a government, want me to deliver us to the same fate.[83]

[80] Matthews, *Majales: The Abortive Student Revolt.*
[81] Kramer, 'The Soviet Union and the 1956 Crises', pp. 192–4.
[82] Micunovic, *Moscow Diary*, pp. 131–41.
[83] A Werblan, 'Czy los Imre Nagy'a przeraził Gomułkę?', *Prawo i Życie* 1991 (43).

His main fear was that the Hungarian invasion might start a chain reaction in which Poland would be the next victim. Whilst therefore continuing to condemn such military intervention by foreign powers on principle, he accepted it in practice as a lesser evil.

It was not so simple for the Polish public. A wave of rallies and demonstrations swept the country for the rest of the year. They did not simply express support for Gomułka and relief at the peaceful outcome in Poland. Ordinary people felt free to give public expression to their personal beliefs and pent-up emotions. In factories, institutes and universities, and even army barracks, ordinary people openly expressed their views. Many found relief simply in speaking out on issues they had been afraid to raise before. The same spontaneity was later recaptured during the heady sixteen months of Solidarity. For others, it was a settling of accounts, paying-off old scores. Perhaps little was said of lasting value. Some statements were plainly false: 'Rokossovsky is now commanding Soviet troops in Budapest.' But Poles regained freedom of expression, an experience that can be abruptly terminated but cannot be so easily forgotten.

Following the first reports of fatalities amongst Hungarian freedom-fighters, there was a huge wave of public sympathy. To the older generation, their cause recalled the Warsaw Uprising. When Polish Radio called for blood donors to help the 'Hungarian brothers', there was an overwhelming response. The transfusion service had to conscript volunteers and work overnight to cope with the donors: students, workers, soldiers and even pensioners. There were numerous further collections of money, food and medicines.[84] By February 1957, Poles had donated more than eighty wagon-loads of foodstuffs, thread and textiles, shoes and clothing.[85]

There was simultaneous revulsion at renewed Soviet aggression. Security archives used by Paweł Machcewicz are replete with examples. In Bydgoszcz (18 November), a crowd, following heavy-handed treatment by the militia, targeted the local 'Soviet–Polish Friendship Society'. It also attacked and demolished radio-jamming equipment (which had been switched off for some weeks). A week later, Warsaw announced its decision to stop jamming all foreign radio stations. A crowd in Szczecin (10 December) caused late-night uproar outside the Soviet Consulate, which was ransacked and vandalised, with files being destroyed.[86] When asked about the event by foreign correspondents, the Ministry of Interior affected surprise that Szczecin had a Soviet Consulate. Anti-Russian

[84] J. Tischler, *Rewolucja węgierska 1956 w polskich dokumentach* (Warsaw, 1995).
[85] Granville 'Hungarian and Polish Reactions', *Europe–Asia Studies*, p. 1062.
[86] Machcewicz, *Polski rok 1956*, pp. 161–3.

sentiments were rife. There were widespread demands for an end to compulsory Russian language teaching in schools. Pupils would play truant or tear up their text-books. The teaching of Western languages and religious instruction were demanded instead.

Polish–Soviet relations

The peaceful outcome of the Polish October gave pause to the tragic history of Polish–Russian relations. But contended issues remained. The main demands were 'Rokossovsky to Siberia' and the removal of 'Soviet advisers' from the Polish Army (including the twenty-eight generals), the security apparatus, Ministry of Internal Affairs and other ministries. On this issue at least, the public and new leader were at one. In essence, they sought a Warsaw equivalent of the 1955 Belgrade Declaration.

Gomułka had told the Politburo that advisers should have been withdrawn long ago: 'What on earth is happening? These advisers are not needed. Every government must conduct its own affairs. We should go back to those providing the advisers and have them recalled. How can you have respect if you do nothing about this? It is not a matter for discussion – it must be done.'[87] Confronting the Soviet Union on this issue put Polish–Soviet relations on a new footing. Moscow withdrew its 'advisers' from the Ministry of Internal Security and the Polish Army.[88] On 10 November Rokossovsky was removed. A curt resolution offered him thanks and a pension. The withdrawal of other Russian advisers was completed by December.

These were significant gestures to placate the Poles. However, Moscow retained myriad other personnel links within Poland, not least through its swollen Warsaw Embassy. Another channel was secure military communications with its Polish representatives in the Warsaw Pact. Hence the changes were more symbolic than substantive. Even so, Poland moved towards somewhat greater equality in relations with its Eastern neighbour. This did not calm the public. 'Solidarity with the Eighth Plenum' soon turned to indignation, especially in areas where Soviet troops were still stationed. People commonly demanded 'a Polish army for Poland', economic reparations for past Soviet exploitation and the return of eastern territories, including Wilno and Lwów. Some protestors did not want Gomułka to visit Moscow, where previous Polish heroes had perished. But he did head a Polish delegation for talks (15–18 November 1956).

[87] Paczkowski (ed.), *Gomułka i inni*, pp. 94–5 (12 October 1956).
[88] AAN PZPR, p. 112, t. 26, pp. 176–7 (22 October 1956).

The Soviet side agreed that limited Polish sovereignty could be restored. Each country could find its own 'methods, forms and paths for building socialism' in accordance with their 'particular historical conditions and national requirements'. The Soviet model was thus no longer obligatory. This was a major revision of principle. But it did not legitimate all 'methods, forms and paths' in practice. The fate of the Hungarian Revolution was an immediate minatory example. The very controversial matter of repatriations, concerning the millions of citizens deported to the East in the first Soviet occupation (1939–41) or now living in former Polish territories incorporated into the USSR during the period from 1944, was left unresolved.[89]

Poland's meeting in Moscow made clear that many bonds remained. The Warsaw Pact would guarantee Polish territory bordered by the Oder-Neisse line. There would be an agreement governing the stationing of Soviet troops and transit rights through Polish territory.[90] The status under which troops could be stationed on Polish soil was agreed, in a later 'top secret' protocol, which stated they were 'stationed temporarily'.[91] Forces that had marched towards Warsaw one month previously were now 'unable to infringe on the sovereignty of the Polish state in any way'.

Four-fifths of the remaining talks concerned economic relations. It was agreed that debts to the Soviet Union would be cancelled, further credits would be extended. Poland's other needs would be addressed in further discussions. This set the pattern for bi-lateral relations down to 1970. On such issues as the mining and export of coal, and other raw materials, Gomułka looked naturally towards the East for economic cooperation. Unlike his successor, Gierek, he showed no interest in any opening to the West, fearing that socialism's entanglement with capitalism would lead to 'counter-revolution of a new type'. He showed similar disinterest in further political modernisation, seeking solace instead in recognition of geopolitical 'realities'. This was not understood by the public.

Since Gomułka had been a victim of Stalinist repression, his anti-Soviet credentials were taken for granted. The more Soviet leaders piled on the pressure, above all in the third week of October, the more patriotic he appeared to be. Concurrence in the myth suited Soviet leaders quite well. The October compromise which Gomułka made possible was therefore 'extremely illusory'.[92] Democratisation was assumed to be compatible with a communist monopoly of power. However, October 1956 was the

[89] Report by Gomułka in Paczkowski (ed.), *Tajne dokumenty Biura Politycznego*, pp. 19–30 (22 November 1956).
[90] Gomułka's notes in *ibid.* pp. 13–15.
[91] AAN KC PZPR, p. 112, t. 26, pp. 213–20.
[92] K. Kersten, 'Rok 1956 – punkt zwrotny', *Krytyka* 1993 (40).

only time in history that a communist leader was accepted as the tribune of ordinary people, and the spokesman of national independence, without being deposed by outside intervention.

The Church

Faced with the need to curb the population, the Polish leadership took a bold step. It decided to review Church–state relations. Cardinal Wyszyński remained in detention. Half a million believers went on the annual pilgrimage to the Jasna Góra monastery in Częstochowa on 26 August. They saw an empty throne bearing a bouquet of flowers in patriotic colours. His smuggled message was read out to the assembled multitude. But on 26 October, two senior officials (Kliszko and Bieńkowski) visited him at his place of internment. Speaking on behalf of 'comrade Wiesław' (Gomułka's name from the revolutionary underground), they stated that Wyszyński should return to Warsaw forthwith and resume his pastoral duties. This abrupt imperative – ending three years of confinement – was necessary to help pacify the 'the socio-economic and foreign political situations'.

The Primate drove a hard bargain. He was positively disposed towards recent changes in the internal life of Poland, 'designed to calm the situation and break with the errors of the past'. He also accepted that Gomułka's speeches to the Eighth Plenum and at the 24 October mass rally were authoritative 'within the framework of differences which may occur in philosophical outlook'. But he set preconditions for return. First, the 1953 decree governing Church appointments (under which Wyszyński himself had been arrested) must be rescinded. There should be re-instatement of senior clergy removed (by the government) from their posts, and an end to state vetting of appointments below the rank of Bishop. In particular Bishop Kaczmarek of Kielce (victim of the show trial) should be allowed to return. Five new bishops would be appointed in the Western Territories.

To formalise the Church–state dialogue, Gomułka should agree to reinstate a Joint Commission 'as a permanent intermediary body between the Episcopate and the government'. This had been part of the programme of Mutual Understandings with which Wyszyński had become Primate. It duly convened in November 1956. Finally, to enable the Church to function normally, the Catholic press had to be restored 'in the full sense of the word'.[93] Once these conditions were accepted, Wyszyński returned to his palace on Miodowa Street.

[93] *A Freedom Within*, pp. 268–70.

A number of lay Catholic intellectuals were received by Gomułka. The Party leader noted with satisfaction that Soviet intervention had been averted, but added that meant they had responsibility for rebuilding Poland on their own. Echoing his 24 October speech, he declared: 'Socialism should be built by everyone – the whole nation, including Catholics, not just communists.' His visitors would be allowed their weekly newspaper, *Tygodnik Powszechny*. Gomułka was glad they did not wish to set up a Catholic party. Church–state relations would flourish if there was goodwill on both sides.[94]

Lay Catholic intellectuals became a vital channel of communication between the rulers and the ruled. Their 'neo-positivist' approach may be regarded as more dispositional than programmatic. Rejecting Party dogmatism and the romantic nationalism of Polish tradition, its exponents sought to cultivate the political virtues of caution, moderation and toleration. We may take Tadeusz Mazowiecki – in 1989 the world's first post-communist Prime Minister – as an emblematic example.

Even in his student days, Mazowiecki was in trouble for 'clericalism'. He found the confines of the officially recognised Church body PAX unacceptable and resigned in 1955. In place of 'Catholic Stalinism', which subscribed to the Stalinist thesis that 'class struggle intensifies as socialism approaches', Mazowiecki sought conciliation. His group espoused the 'leftist' notions of equality and social justice, against the Party right's fostering of nationalism and anti-Semitism.[95] It pursued the elusive goal of linking their lay Catholicism with the anti-totalitarian ideas of socialism. It founded a Club of the Round Table in 1955 (an idea resurfacing in 1988) and another club named after the French Catholic Emmanuel Mounier, whose outlook may be summarised as 'Catholic Personalism'.

This holds that the individual self, though a biological entity with material needs, can only develop through relating to others. The core value is the inalienable worth of each person. There is thus an obligation to further the dignity of others, to help provide the conditions for their self-development. Personalist humanism is thus also social humanism.[96] The political implications are radical. Liberal capitalism is rejected as unleashing economic anarchy and social injustice, but so too are the communist regimes inspired in reaction to its bankruptcy. Marxism is

[94] J. Zawieyski, diary entry for 29 October 1956, cited by A. Friszke, *Oaza na Kopernika. Klub Inteligencji Katolickiej 1956–1989* (Warsaw, 1997), p. 40.

[95] T. Mazowiecki and J. Mikke, 'List otwarty do Redaktora Naczelnego *Słowa Powszechnego*', *Po prostu*, 29 July 1956.

[96] T. Mazowiecki, *Rozdroża i Wartości* (Warsaw, 1970), pp. 27–8.

the 'rebellious son of capitalism' and the Soviet model of communism is 'totalitarian' by enslaving the Person to the state. In particular, the communist notion of class struggle destroys the cooperation essential between all classes. Communist elites claim to act on behalf of workers, but are in practice not answerable to them. A new order is needed in which people from all classes strive for human rights.[97]

Personalist democracy will come about 'from below'. A populist movement of workers and their sympathisers will press the state for economic and political rights. Such a movement would be peaceful, but Mounier points out that the state, 'itself born of strife but forgetful of its origins', might engender violence. It would treat legitimate protest against injustice as sedition. There are premonitions here of Solidarity and martial law. Politics was the art of the possible. In a one-Party state this meant strict limits indeed. But this should not be made the pretext for passivity or defeatism. It was sometimes possible to redefine the possible. The watchwords were prudence and responsibility; the techniques were compromise and reciprocity.

Mazowiecki helped to construct an informal alliance between the Club of the Crooked Circle and radical Party members working on *Po prostu*. Their common platform was support for Gomułka against any reversion to Stalinism and the rejection of national chauvinism and anti-Semitism in favour of toleration. This informal alliance grew into an All-Poland Club of Catholic Intellectuals which had achieved legal status on 27 October 1956. Some 600 Catholics from four cities attended its inaugural session on 5 November. They supported the Gomułka programme and endorsed the Soviet alliance as the basis for Polish sovereignty. To some, this acceptance of *raison d'état* echoed the views of Roman Dmowski, the pre-war Polish politician who believed that a strong Russia was the best guarantee against German encroachment on Polish sovereignty. At this point, there was no wish to play the role of a political party or to stand in elections: 'Our activity is solely cultural and social.'[98]

Inspired by Mounier's *Esprit*, Mazowiecki sought permission to found a journal. This was eventually granted and the first number of *Więź* (The Link) appeared in summer 1958. Under his editorship, the monthly advocated positive engagement with current Polish society and a willingness to engage in dialogue with Marxism. This put it somewhat to the left of the Kraków monthly *Znak*, though lay Catholics cooperated closely. In 1957, Znak was allowed to present a handful of candidates to the electorate.

[97] J. Maritain, *The Rights of Man and Natural Law* (New York, 1947), pp. 93–4.
[98] A. Friszke, *Opozycja polityczna w PRL, 1945–1980* (London, 1994), p. 188 (Zawieyski).

The Council of State announced there would be fresh elections to the Sejm on 16 December. They were then postponed until 20 January 1957 to enable the Party to regroup and mobilise support from the population.[99] The task was immensely simplified by the placing of all candidates under a single umbrella: the Front of National Unity (FNU). Since no other candidates could appear on the list, the only significant statistics were likely to be the numbers of spoiled ballot papers and abstentions.

The Press and Propaganda Department of the Central Committee addressed the public in posters running to 100,000 copies:

- Workers! The FNU will develop self-management. Take work-place management into your own hands.
- Peasants! Develop and enrich your households with the FNU.
- Scientists and Artists! For full freedom of creative work, support the FNU.
- Young People! For the programme of independence and the Polish road to socialism vote for the FNU.[100]

In the early New Year, Gomułka made a melodramatic radio broadcast to voters: 'Only a socialist Poland can appear on the map of Europe as an independent and sovereign state. The Party is the primary guarantor of this independence, underwritten by the friendship between the Polish and Russian peoples, the guarantor of neighbourly, fraternal Polish–Soviet relations.' His advice to electors was stark: 'To cross out Party (PZPR) candidates is not only to cross out socialism in Poland. It is crossing out our country's sovereignty. It is crossing out Poland from the map of European states.'[101]

Cardinal Wyszyński was asked by Premier Cyrankiewicz to endorse the official list. He agreed. Four days before the poll, the press carried his appeal to 'Catholic-Citizens' concerning the following Sunday. He declared that religious and political responsibilities went hand in hand: 'Catholic citizens are to fulfil their conscience's duty to vote. Catholic priests will conduct their Masses so as to enable the faithful to fulfil their religious duty and their electoral duty without any difficulties.'[102] As Dudek points out, this marked the greatest political concession the Church had made to the powers-that-be. It was tantamount to acceptance of the communist political system.[103] Wyszyński himself came to this opinion. He let it be known well ahead of every subsequent election that he would not be voting.

[99] P. Machcewicz, *Kampania wyborcza i wybory do Sejmu 20 stycznia 1957* (Warsaw, 2000).
[100] *Ibid.* pp. 63–4. [101] W. Gomułka, *Przemówienia* (Warsaw, 1957), pp. 212–13.
[102] P. Raina, *Stefan Kardynał Wyszyński*, vol. II (London, 1986), pp. 150–1.
[103] A. Dudek, *Państwo i Kościół w Polsce, 1945–1970* (Kraków, 1995), p. 50.

The 1957 results showed how effective a Church–state alliance could be. As many as 94.1 per cent of the electorate turned out and 98.4 per cent of these voted for the official (FNU) candidates. Naturally enough, since there were no other candidates. But there has been no suggestion that the result was falsified.

Eight Znak deputies had entered parliament in February 1957. They declared their role to be constructive opposition. High politics could not lead Poland from its post-October crisis. Popular support was needed. To enable this, communism should recognise the rights of all citizens to freedom of expression and of criticism. Social control over those in power, the rule of law and judicial independence were all needed.[104] Since this would transform the system beyond recognition, Znak realised it was not likely to come about. Their stance was criticised from all sides.

Communists proclaimed that Znak proved they had a 'pluralist' political system. Anti-communists accused Znak of 'collaborating' with the authorities. The writer Kiśielewski told the main *émigré* journal that Znak was in parliament but not in government. It was there to represent the non-communist majority of the population and to 'take responsibility for the good of the nation and realism'.[105] A similar defence was offered to Gomułka: 'We don't want to be an opposition in the Sejm but at the same time we have always sought to exercise our right to free criticism, in the spirit of cooperation and moral co-responsibility for the fate of our country.' Gomułka stated 'the Znak deputies are a strange mosaic. But could you tell me: does it represent the Church or not?' Zawieyski replied: 'We don't follow the Church, its hierarchy or the Primate of Poland.'[106]

A reduced group of six entered the next Sejm in 1961. Their 'platform' again emphasised the 'constructive' rather than the oppositional role: 'We do not seek a share in government, but to take part in legislative activity and social control.' They sought the 'creation of conditions and atmosphere for the development of democratic institutions'.[107] It again had an importance out of all proportion to its tiny size.

Mazowiecki's maiden speech caused a sensation. Taking as his text Gomułka's famous remark 'it is foolish to think that socialism can be built only by communists, by those with a materialist world-view', he proposed radical educational reforms. Philosophical debate should be open to all:

[104] Friszke, *Opozycja polityczna*, pp. 195–6.

[105] Interview with *Kultura* (Paris), June 1957. Reprinted in A. Friszke, *Koło Posłów 'Znak' w Sejmie PRL, 1957–1976* (Warsaw, 2002), p. 186.

[106] J. Zawieyski, *Kartki z dziennika, 1955–1969* (Warsaw, 1983) (entry for 22 July 1957).

[107] *Więź* 1961 (6); Friszke, *Koło Posłów 'Znak'*, p. 345.

Catholics and non-Marxists. An integrated socialist society should acknowledge the truth that society is a living organism that draws its vital juices from many sources. A variety of viewpoints should be recognised and respected. There should be no intellectual monopolies, such as Marxism in the social sciences.[108]

[108] Friszke, *Koło Posłów 'Znak'*, pp. 362–3 (14 July 1961).

6 Stagnation

> On receiving Ministerial approval, the Director of our Zoo ordered the construction of a rubber elephant.
>
> S. Mrożek, *Słoń* (Warsaw, 1957)

The year 1956 showed that the Warsaw Pact had a much greater role than NATO in assuring control over its members. But that did not necessarily mean it posed a threat to countries not under its hegemony. This 'dovish' argument was given support by the Soviet XXth Congress at which Lenin's theory of imperialism was formally dropped. The final victory of communism, though still assured, would not now be reached as the successful outcome of a world war, since that would result only in mutual destruction. But where did this leave the 'great contest' between rival systems? Would this doctrinal revision usher in a long duration of peaceful competition, a contest which, assured of the superiority of its own system, each side expected to win? Equally, under the guise of coexistence, the Soviet side might continue to rearm for a final conflict, thus requiring Western vigilance and counter-action.

Super-power competition began to develop a dynamic of its own, driven in part by technological advance. The launch of the earth-orbiting sputnik (4 October 1957) was not simply a scientific achievement, important as a propaganda coup on the eve of the fortieth anniversary of the Russian Revolution. Taken with the previously successful test of a Soviet Intercontinental Ballistic Missile (ICBM), it showed that the Soviet Union had rockets powerful enough to land atomic weapons on any part of the Earth's surface. The American reaction was sharp. To allay American fears that the country was falling behind in the arms race, Eisenhower commissioned the Gaither report to establish the nature of the balance. To his dismay, a 'missile gap' was identified and some of the Commission's more contentious findings were leaked to the press. Although no such shortfall actually existed, the 'missile gap' was used to great effect during the 1960 presidential campaign of John F. Kennedy.

But were such weapons usable? US civilian strategists began to elaborate theories of 'limited' nuclear war. Herman Kahn devised an 'escalation ladder', with forty-four rungs, with nuclear weapons being introduced at rung 15. Hence there were twenty-nine different ways of using nuclear weapons. Kahn replied to critics with *Thinking about the Unthinkable*. Richard Osgood noted that, for deterrence to work, it had to be credible. To be credible, it required that 'the means of deterrence be proportionate to the objectives at stake'.[1] This brought the debate back to policy. Henry Kissinger, echoing Clausewitz, noted that 'The prerequisite for a policy of limited war is to reintroduce the political element into our concept of warfare and to discard the notion that policy ends when war begins.'[2] To Soviet strategists, such talk was fantasy. Once nuclear weapons began to be used against an adversary that possessed them, escalation could no longer be controlled. Indeed, the first outcome of a nuclear exchange would be to destroy the communications channels necessary to call a truce.

There were further objections within Europe itself. Many states would not want to be 'defended' with such weapons, if their territory was to be the battleground. What was the use in inflicting nuclear devastation on a people whose rights to self-determination justified fighting in the first place? One option, pursued by Eisenhower, was nuclear sharing within the NATO Alliance. Faced with the prospect of West Germany joining that club, the Soviet Union and its allies proposed non-proliferation agreements for Europe. Soviet Premier Bulganin unveiled a comprehensive disarmament plan for the abolition of all nuclear forces on 17 November 1956. Following American rejection, this was modified to a prohibition of nuclear testing and a non-aggression pact between the two alliances in Europe.

The Polish Foreign Minister, Adam Rapacki, proposed a nuclear-weapon-free zone for Central Europe (9 October 1957). Following NATO objections, the Rapacki Plan was revised to provide for an initial nuclear freeze, followed by subsequent reductions. The West objected that this did not address the substantive problems: the Warsaw Pact's vast conventional superiority in Europe and lack of progress towards German reunification. Thwarted on disarmament, and alarmed at the prospect of a nuclear West Germany, the Soviet Union precipitated a series of Berlin crises from 1958. They did not subside until the building of the Berlin Wall in 1961.

By then, Khrushchev had boldly declared support for national liberation strategies – previously championed by China in Asia – across the

[1] R. Osgood, *Limited War. The Challenge to American Strategy* (Chicago, 1957).
[2] H. Kissinger, *Nuclear Weapons and Foreign Policy* (New York, 1957).

globe. The success of Castro's revolution in Cuba and subsequent close ties between Moscow and Havana, communist insurgencies in Laos and South Vietnam, and the Katangese secession in the Congo gave credence to Khrushchev's claim that the 'correlation of forces' was shifting in a Soviet direction.[3] But by this point, the Sino-Soviet split was in the public domain. Amazingly, many Western commentators saw it as another trick of the communists. Others saw it posing a new series of challenges as China started to operate as an independent, rogue state, taking bold and aggressive actions, especially in Asia. They failed to realise that the bifurcation of the communist movement was fundamental and far-reaching.

One interpretation of Khrushchev's Cuban gamble was as an attempt to reassert Soviet leadership of international communism at this crucial juncture. The suggestion was that 'acting concretely and decisively to protect the Cuban revolution from "the imperialist aggressor" would eloquently refute Beijing's shrill accusations that the "revisionist" Soviets had shed their revolutionary identity, and were even colluding with Washington to preserve big power prerogatives'.[4] They might recover ground lost to Beijing in Havana itself.

In the aftermath of the Cuban crisis, the two super-powers put in place mechanisms, such as the 'hot line', to prevent a recurrence. There were the first tentative moves towards limiting the testing and spread of nuclear weapons. But massive stock-piling continued, indeed it sped up. In accounting for the accelerating arms race, we can recall President Eisenhower's valedictory address, famously identifying a 'military-industrial complex' driving forward national security policy. A not-too-dissimilar dynamic could be seen in the Soviet Union. Both sides were driven by the fear that the other would find an invulnerable weapon, thus giving it an absolute first-strike advantage. Irrespective of which side 'started' the arms race, it soon developed dynamics of its own. The rule was 'stay ahead', thus providing almost *carte blanche* for weapons procurement.

President Kennedy brought in MacNamara from Ford to the Pentagon, who removed control of policy from the military. New strategic doctrines were devised to overcome reliance on 'massive retaliation'. The main ideas were threefold. First was 'city avoidance', the notion that the military objective in warfare was 'destruction of the enemy's military forces not of his civilian population'. The Pentagon estimated that this

[3] O. A. Westad, *The Global Cold War: Third World Interventions and the Making of our Times* (Cambridge 2005).

[4] J. Hershberg, 'The Cuban Missile Crisis' in *The Cambridge History of the Cold War*, vol. III (forthcoming).

would reduce US casualties from 100 million to a mere 10 million provided the Russians adopted it too. Second was 'assured destruction', 'the ability to inflict an unacceptable degree upon any aggressor, even after absorbing a surprise first strike'. This might require destroying 75 per cent of the Soviet Union's industrial capacity and 33 per cent of its population.

Finally, there was 'flexible response', adopted by NATO in 1967, intended to allow a full range of 'appropriate responses, conventional and nuclear, to all levels of aggression and threats of aggression'. The third idea was predicated on hugely increased defence spending, on the Keynesian principle that such funding would have a multiplier effect throughout the American economy. The Soviet Union responded accordingly and, given the procurement time for major programmes, its global response was ready by the early 1970s. By then, it had a very different style of leadership.

Though Khrushchev's leadership had been secured by 1957, he raised the Stalin question again at the XXIInd Congress (1961). His renewed insistence that Soviet communism tell more of the truth about its own past was impressive testimony to Khrushchev's personal convictions. The 'secret speech' had not been a cynical manoeuvre to oust Stalinists more senior than himself. The Soviet Union now underwent de-Stalinisation more thoroughgoing than before.

Khrushchev himself took the initiative in introducing Solzhenitsyn to other writers and publishing his early stories of GULag life. The camp literature began to include stories of the collectivisation campaign and consequent famine (1932–4), hitherto taboo. Socialist realism went into terminal decline.[5] There was a recovery of intellectual vitality unknown in Soviet life since the twenties. V. P. Danilov began the study of collectivisation[6] and Roy Medvedev pressed forward with his study of Stalinism, a masterpiece, begun in 1956 and intended for publication in the USSR.[7] A new Party Programme (1961) looked forward to full communism. Even completion dates were provided: public transport and education were to be entirely free by 1980.

All this was the unspoken text of Khrushchev's fall. In October 1964, he was accused of adventurism and wild experiments ('hare-brained scheming').[8] After Khrushchev was summoned back from vacation, his chief accuser, Suslov, read out a long catalogue of alleged crimes and

5 M. Hayward, 'The Decline of Socialist Realism', *Survey* Winter 1972.

6 V. P. Danilov, *Rural Russia under the New Regime* (Bloomington, Ind., 1988).

7 It only appeared abroad: *K sudu istorii. Genezis i posledstviya stalinizma* (New York, 1974).

8 R. Medvedev, *Khrushchev*, pp. 237–45.

misdemeanours. Many seemed trivial for such an indictment. But Khrushchev accepted their verdict. Returning home, he threw his briefcase into a corner and announced his retirement: 'They got rid of me just by voting. That is my greatest achievement. Stalin would have had them all shot.' When they were in turn removed, two decades later, his deposers were blamed for 'stagnation'. The charge seems a little unfair. The purpose of replacing the erratic Khrushchev had been to introduce some stagnation. That had already been the policy in Poland for some years.

Throughout the sixties, Poland had a stagnant economy, with growth registering at, at best, 1 per cent or 2 per cent. The state retained the primacy of heavy industry, and consumption was neglected. Politics stagnated too, by the steady elimination from Party ranks of those with reformist aspirations. But the first target was the cultural elites, always seen as the harbingers of trouble. Addressing Czechoslovak reformers much later, Gomułka exclaimed: 'In our country and in Hungary everything began with the writers. It started with the Petöfi Circle in Hungary, and it is the same [in Poland]. The intellectuals have been acting this way since 1956. This time it was again the case with the writers. And in your country it also started with the intellectuals.'[9] Measures to avert this in Poland had been his priority within months of October 1956.

Writers

Deflated expectations of October are perhaps seen in Mrożek's parable, cited above. In his vignette, school-children observe an elephant suddenly take off into the air. After hovering briefly above the monkey house, whose occupants stop chattering, it crash-lands in the Botanical Gardens and bursts on a cactus. It proves to be nothing more than a gas-filled replica. Disillusioned, the pupils play truant and turn to petty crime: 'Above all, they no longer believe in elephants.'[10]

Younger authors, including Mrożek and Hłasko, were elected to the board of the Polish Union of Writers. Its new President Słonimski called for the abolition of censorship and the restoration of the full rights of authors and editors. They demanded a 'return to Europe' of Polish literature. This meant restoring relations with famous writers in emigration, such as Gombrowicz and Miłosz, and establishing normal contacts with the *émigré* community, above all with its Paris-based monthly *Kultura*. They also sent a letter of solidarity to Hungarian writers. Faced with such independence, the Party tried to restore orthodoxy.

[9] J. Navrátil (ed.), *The Prague Spring 1968* (Budapest, 1998), p. 67. [10] Mrożek, *Słoń*.

Polityka was set up as a rival paper to *Po prostu*. Its founder editor demanded cultural leadership based on Marxism–Leninism, since the wish for 'pure liberalism' in cultural policy was utopian.[11] Jan Józef Lipski retorted that the 'bureaucratic model' of cultural policy would destroy initiative which stemmed largely from self-governing social institutions.[12] Since there was no middle ground between these positions, it became clear there would be a conflict over policy. It was also likely that the authorities would win.

Secret censorship reports called *Po prostu* 'oppositional'. Its articles demanded 'permanent revolution' and promoted other negative slogans. It claimed 'Workers' Self-Management is in Danger'[13] and constantly attacked the Party and state authorities as too conservative.

The reports further claimed that *Po prostu* promoted workers' councils as a prototype for 'Councils of other sorts, such as a national union of agricultural circles'. They wished to sunder Poland into self-governing units. It also alleged a deep crisis in intellectual circles, especially 'October left' intellectuals and young activists within the Party. Existing leaders, such as Ochab and Zambrowski, were seen as compromised, demagogic and apologists for the existing system.[14]

When the Politburo reviewed the position, some changes in the stance of *Po prostu* were welcomed. It now gave more space to theorists such as the sociologist Zygmunt Bauman, to discussion between Marxists and Catholics and to regional daily life. But the editorial stance had failed to moderate. It retained the October line of opposition, lacking confidence in the Party to lead a process of renewal, and persisting in its mistaken notion of 'a second stage of revolution'.[15]

All this was illustrated by extracts from 'confiscated, provocative submissions' by the journal. In one, the market-orientated economist Kurowski deplored the bankruptcy of the previous (six-year) plan and decried its five-year successor. Since these plans contained no mobilising ideas comparable to those released in the political sphere – sovereignty, democracy and the rule of law – he thought they would remain dead letters. The consequences were for all to see: 'corruption at every level and nihilism as a social outlook'. In another confiscated item, the editors noted the formation of a privileged class – citing C. W. Mills – using their control over the means of production, and backed by an army of controllers

[11] S. Żółkiewski, *Polityka*, 27 March 1957.
[12] J. J. Lipski, *Po prostu* 28 April 1957 (17).
[13] W. Godek, *Po prostu* 20 January 1957 (3).
[14] AAN 237/XIX/234 (April 1957), pp. 24–5.
[15] AAN 237/XIX/234 (3 May 1957), p. 18.

and enforcers. The political and security elite derived special benefits from running the economy in their own interests, enjoying larger flats and access to shops without the queues and hassle of normal life as lived by millions.[16] The Politburo noted that the journal needed to offer more than mere negations.

Po prostu did indeed draw up a negative balance sheet of achievements since October. An unsigned editorial at the end of May deplored the loss of impetus in the past eight months. Popular enthusiasm and self-sacrifice (*ofiarność*) had subsided into apathy. Workers in particular had become impatient with the growing gulf between expectations and reality. Conferences of Workers' Self-Management were seen as façade institutions, whose members in some cases voted for the tightening of work norms, and hence reduction in real wages. Everyone could observe the spread of 'petty theft, corruption, speculation, disjunction in all branches of the economy and demoralisation of the popular consciousness'.[17]

In early autumn, the head of censorship complained that *Po prostu* contradicted the line of 'the Party and its leadership'. Its editors were hoping to raise social disturbances to a second stage, pushing Poland in the direction of 'bourgeois integral democracy'. He demanded decisive measures.[18] *Po prostu* sent the Party authorities a letter of mild self-criticism and offered a less controversial agenda.[19] The Party Secretariat agreed that *Po prostu* was harmful to the policies of Party and state. The Politburo confirmed 'the decision of the censorship'. Owing to a lack of editorial responsibility, major political blunders and, in a most recent number, adopting anti-socialist positions inimical to the Party, the journal was abolished.[20]

Students tried to hold a protest meeting but were locked out of Warsaw Polytechnical University. The crowd outside were attacked by a massive force – including two battalions of the newly formed force ZOMO – armed with long, heavily weighted truncheons and tear gas.[21] Many peaceful protestors were injured. Noting this was a breach of elementary humanitarian norms, they concluded: 'once again the force of argument has been replaced by the argument of force'.[22]

Over the next few days, young people were confronted by the militia in numerous towns and cities.[23] Arrests ran into hundreds and several

16 AAN 237/XIX/234 (17 February 1957). 17 *Po prostu*, 26 May 1957 (21).
18 AAN 237/XIX/234 (10 September 1957). 19 AAN 237/XIX/234, pp. 50–4.
20 *BIBS* (secret *Information Bulletin*) 10 October 1957 (44), p. 8.
21 A. Dudek and T. Marszałkowski, *Walki uliczne w PRL, 1956–1989* (Kraków, 1999), pp. 69–71.
22 AAN 237/XIX/ 234, pp. 59–60.
23 Dudek and Marszałkowski, *Walki uliczne*, pp. 71–80.

dozen militiamen were seriously injured. Gomułka, brought to power a year earlier on a surge of popular approval, celebrated the anniversary by turning on his former supporters. One Party meeting even heard the view, attributed to 'opinion in the West', that Gomułka had returned to the methods of Stalinism.[24]

A year after October 1956, Gomułka told journalists that the time for dialogue was over. The choice was simple: for socialism or against. Likewise, journalists must choose whether they were with the Party or against it. It was impossible to allow the falsehoods and lies that were being published by *Po prostu*. The paper had been taken over by adventurists: 'These are not students – students are peaceful – but mostly hooligans. Of 28 arrests yesterday: one student, 27 hooligans.' After making polemical remarks directed at Kurowski, Strzelecki, Słonimski and Kołakowski (who was praised for 'special talent'), Gomułka laid down the limits to freedom of expression: 'There cannot be autonomous organisations which usurp for themselves the right of the political centre (*ośrodka*), and represent politics diametrically opposed to the government and Party.' Poland would not return to the pre-October situation, but nor would there be any concessions to capitalism or the bourgeoisie.[25]

The founder editor of *Polityka*, Ziółkowski, fulminated against youthful revisionists.[26] Another official deplored the decline of socialist culture, contaminated in the past two years by contacts with the West, and by a 'reactivisation of clericalism.'[27] The Party announced a membership purge. Expulsions followed. There were many resignations.

A new journal, *Europa*, due to be edited by the Party's foremost writer Jerzy Andrzejewski, and already in proof, was banned. Gomułka announced: 'There will be no *Europa*.'[28] Andrzejewski, Adam Ważyk, Paweł Hertz and several others left the Party. The theatre critic Jan Kott followed soon after. Many more protested to the authorities at this clear attempt to re-isolate Polish culture from the West. Several became significant figures in the subsequent opposition to communist rule.

A political conundrum was the sudden death of a prominent journalist and Party activist, Henryk Holland (21 December 1961). He had been the first Party member to be arrested since 1956 and his funeral became a demonstration by those concerned by the 'retreat from October'. Krysztof Persak's recent reconstruction of Holland's death shows that it was a suicide, forced by intense political pressures. Holland had been accused

[24] AAN 237/XIX/144, p. 191. [25] *BIBS* 10 October 1957 (44), p. 6.
[26] *BIBS* 1957 (44), Appendix 1 (FSO Zeran, 21 September 1957).
[27] *BIBS* 16 November 1957 (46), pp. 22–5 (Kruczkowski).
[28] B. Łopieńska, 'Porwanie *Europy*', *Res Publica* 1987 (2).

of leaking to the Western press remarks by Khrushchev to the XXIInd Congress, concerning the death of Stalin and the ouster of Beria in 1953. He also shows that the tragic episode was engineered and subsequently used by a nationalist faction in the Party around General Moczar, seeking to reverse the more reformist tide within the leadership. Persak concludes that Gomułka too became a victim of this 'nationalist' tendency, with further tragic consequences when Moczar moved again in 1967–8.[29]

The Writers' Union had been further curbed in 1959, when Antoni Słonimski was replaced as President by the politically more pliant Jarosław Iwaszkiewicz. But Słonimski continued to play an important role as the focus of continuity amongst a quite diverse group of writers and intellectuals. A significant protest, the 'Letter of the Thirty-Four' (1964) was drawn up on his initiative, contesting the stringent censorship and repressive cultural policies of the state:

> Limiting the allocation of paper for book production and journals, and sharpening press censorship threatens the development of national culture. The undersigned, recognising the existence of public opinion and the rights to criticism, free discussion, and authentic information as indispensable elements of progress, and guided by their concern as citizens, demand changes in Polish cultural policy in the spirit of rights guaranteed by the constitution of the Polish state and in accordance with the good of the nation.[30]

Signatories included outstanding writers from the older generation, and fourteen full professors.

Furore followed its publication in the West. Ten of the professorial signatories recanted after a severe talking-to by the Prime Minister. Their Letter was now attributed to 'the campaign against our country' by the West. Counter-lists were produced, and counter-counter-lists, perhaps testifying most to the power of the original two sentences drafted in a Warsaw café.[31]

Routine repression followed. Signatories were denied passports, the right to publish (fourteen writers), access to the media, permission to give public recitals and readings and so on. Such sanctions did nothing to diminish the force of their original argument. As Słonimski put it, 'The whole affair of the 34 and the Letter would not have existed had there been no reason to write the Letter. And the reason is the disastrous position of Polish culture. The fruits of October have vanished, censorship has gagged the public, most well-known writers have disappeared from

29 K. Persak, *Sprawa Henryka Hollanda* (Warsaw, 2006).
30 J. Eisler, *List 34* (Warsaw, 1993), and P. Raina, *Political Opposition in Poland, 1954–1977* (London, 1978).
31 Friszke, *Opozycja polityczna*, pp. 177–80.

literary journals, popular books are published in tiny editions.' The Party had done all this, and it was pointless to look for scapegoats.[32]

But scapegoats were sought within the Party. A circular letter reported two currents in the Party: one was healthy and the other wilful. The latter included careerists and persons not immune to agitation from anti-socialist tendencies.[33] After the 1957 election a further circular railed against 'nationalist, chauvinist and racialist opinions' which were inadmissible in an internationalist Party.[34] The corollary was the closure of debate even within the Party, signalled by a new campaign: 'The chief ideological danger in the Party is revisionism.'[35]

Revisionists

Revisionism had a long pedigree in the communist movement. It rent the Second International into a 'revolutionary' and 'evolutionary' wing, whose essential argument was whether communism could be reached by peaceful means, or only (as Marx predicted) by some future, violent, revolution.[36] Given the stabilisation of capitalism in the last quarter of the nineteenth century, tentative introduction of a welfare state and the cautious acceptance of workers' organisations – all predictions that Marx had not made – the case for evolution looked the more promising. This was Bernstein's revisionism. But would it reach communism?

Rosa Luxemburg was convinced otherwise. Considering the stabilisation of capitalism to be temporary, she called trade union activity a 'labour of Sisyphus'. The phrase rankled. Moreover, her rejection of the Leninist Party from its outset caused decades of difficulty for the Polish custodians of her main archives. They wondered how to include her in the pantheon.[37] *Letters from Prison* were published in 1950 with a hostile preface. Preparations for celebrating the eightieth anniversary of her birth (1951) ordered minimal publications, simply a short biographical sketch for the press, and a discussion limited to the Party School and Academy of Sciences. It added that 'the entire campaign must be accompanied by sharply critical exposure of Luxemburgism and all theories derived from it'.[38] A brief selection from her writing on the Russian revolution of 1905 was published, leaving out the critique of Lenin.

32 Cited by Raina, *Political Opposition*, pp. 80–1.
33 AAN 237/V/319 (9 November 1956).
34 AAN 237/V/319 Secretariat PZPR (April 1957).
35 AAN 237/11/19 Resolution of IX Plenum (15–18 May 1957).
36 J. Joll, *The Second International, 1889–1914* (London, 1955).
37 AAN 237/II/18, pp. 135–6.
38 AAN 237/XIX (Press and Publications Department)/55.

Since most Poles knew little about her, it was planned in 1956 to reissue Rosa's brochure *Die russische Revolution* (1922), including her comment that 'degeneration of the socialist revolution becomes inevitable when in the process, law, liberty, and democratic guarantees are eliminated or severely restricted'. But this remained a project. The authorities could not accept her statement that 'It is harmful to propose as a model the experience of the first victorious proletarian revolution which took place under the specific difficulties of a backward and isolated country.'[39]

To the first meaning of revisionism, Stalinism had added a second. Equally pejorative, it arose from Yugoslavia. A number of Polish intellectuals and journalists gave close attention to the 'Yugoslav model'. Eminent economists E. Lipiński, M. Kalecki and O. Lange explored the notion of workers' councils, partly inspired by Yugoslavia.[40] Whilst its federal system seemed inapplicable to Poland, which had attained almost complete ethnic homogeneity from 1945, private agriculture was an attractive option, and the notion of industrial self-management and wider cooperatives also found favour with some revisionists. Attracted to self-management, as a radical alternative to Stalinist central planning, Polish economists organised several study visits to Yugoslavia. Their reports, though not without enthusiasm for some aspects of the 'model', usually expressed practical doubts. How would the system transfer to Polish conditions? What was the applicability of a devolved regional structure with no central banking?[41] Moreover, the political costs were not unknown, particularly with the circulation of Djilas' text on the 'New Class' and its widespread discussion at the KIK and elsewhere. As we shall see, its central thesis was developed by Kuroń and Modzelewski later on.

A third meaning of revisionism followed the denunciation of Stalin: a rethinking of inherited assumptions, and the political structures in which they were incorporated. It was 'a protest, on the part of the intelligentsia, against the mental sterility and mediocrity to which Stalinism had condemned them'. As Isaac Deutscher noted, this went beyond intellectuals' ranks, to a more general search for moral, political and cultural identity. He predicted that 'revision and redefinition of accepted ideas and values [was] a difficult and tragic search that is likely to go on for some years'.[42] In his optimistic view, pressures for democratisation would become irresistible.

39 *Po prostu*, 1957. 40 See *Nowe Drogi*, 1956 (11–12).

41 C. Bobrowski, *Jugosława socjalistyczna* (Warsaw, 1957); W. Brus and S. Jakubowicz, *System jugosłowiański z bliska* (Warsaw, 1957).

42 I. Deutscher, 'Post-Stalin Ferment of Ideas' in *Heretics and Renegades* (London, 1955), p. 211.

During October 1956, new options had indeed opened up. The choices were put with great clarity in Kołakowski's article 'Intellectuals and the Communist Movement', published in the Party monthly. It appeared to herald a new dawn. Communism had a broad vision, requiring the knowledge and imaginative power of intellectuals. Yet communist intellectuals found themselves in an impasse: dialectics was reduced to the incantation of 'four characteristics' and Marxist theory reduced to apologetics for the powers that be. There should be a rebirth of sociology as an independent science, rather than a catalogue of banalities, since 'without it, the Party cannot know or foresee the real consequences of its own decisions'. It was humiliating to have to state that historical documents should not be falsified, that scientific opinions, and the criticism of those opinions, must be substantiated.[43]

Echoing Ossowski, he saw an urgent need for 'construction of Marxism adequate to contemporary needs'. Intellectuals should have no barriers to their search for objective truth. Intellectuals were needed to create 'a socialist culture in its most diverse forms'. Political restrictions on scientific research were inadmissible, above all those stemming from 'untouchable truths'. To predetermine discussion, to announce that conclusions were known beforehand, was to use 'Marxism' as blackmail. Science and scholarship still had social responsibilities. For Kołakowski, at this stage, they were to serve the communist movement. Those interests, however, were not at variance with an objective knowledge of the world. The movement had inherited 'the entire tradition of European rationalism'. Without it would be primitivism, obscurantism and reaction.

This led to questions for Marxism itself. Were all pronouncements by Marx and Engels of permanent validity? Had some of their predictions fared better than others with the passage of time? Kołakowski tries to separate out the two. Marxism was 'not a universal system but a vital philosophical inspiration, a constant stimulus to the social intelligence and memory of mankind'. Its permanent validity stemmed from an ability to allow us to view human affairs through the prism of universal history. Whilst some of the original predictions had not materialised, others, including analytical tools, had been absorbed into mainstream Western thought. Non-Marxists also found illuminating insights for social and economic history, showing how man in society is formed by the struggle against nature and the simultaneous process by which man's work humanises nature. Attention had been drawn to the 'de-masking of

[43] 'Intelektualiści a ruch komunistyczny', *Nowe Drogi* 1956 (9).

myths of consciousness', as the outcome of earlier alienation 'traced back to its real sources'.[44]

Ensuing articles explored the notion of the Left and dwelt at greater length on philosophical aspects of responsibility and history.[45] They tail off into more ironical reflections about inconsistency and a famous piece on the two roles of intellectuals: priest and jester.[46] Kołakowski later repudiated the impulse behind the more political of these articles, especially that in the Party monthly. They had been based on the hope that 'intellectual honesty might be restored within orthodoxy and restore it to health'. Later the author had abandoned such hope and declared: 'I am certain I was mistaken in cherishing it.'[47] Perhaps the paradox is recognised in Kołakowski's 'What is Socialism?' written for *Po prostu* but only published abroad. Seventy-two ironic negations end with 'Now I will tell you: socialism is a good thing.'

The intellectual range of the Polish October is shown by *Po prostu*'s pocket library: from Bertrand Russell's 'Why I am not a Christian', to a critique of Lysenko[48] and essays by Ossowski,[49] reprinting those we have discussed above and others that had had problems with the censor. As Jakub Karpiński points out, his teacher Ossowski's access to print illustrated the cautious and often reversible nature of any 'thaw'.[50] It included the first publication of his 1950 rebuff to Professor Schaff's philippic 'Class Struggle in Philosophy',[51] and a seminal article 'Taktyka i kultura' whose publication had been held up. His Preface attributed the delay not merely to its polemical nature, in raising questions of authority and truth in cultural studies, but also to its addressing more general questions such as the functioning of Marxist doctrine and the role of scientific work in socialist society.[52] He elaborated his conclusion that it was impermissible to 'compromise with truth' in the magisterial *Class Structure in Social Consciousness* (1963).

Contrary to Stalinist simplifications, Ossowski's book shows Marx to use class in at least three senses. First, class is a simple dichotomy: 'The history of all hitherto existing societies is a history of class struggle.' Social

[44] 'Aktualne i nieaktualne pojęcie marksizmu', *Nowa Kultura* 1957 (4).
[45] 'Sens ideowy pojęcia marksizmu', *Po prostu* 1957 (8); 'Odpowiedzialność i historia', *Nowa Kultura* 1957 (35–8).
[46] 'Pochwała niekonsekwencji', *Twórczość* 1958 (9); 'Kapłan i błazen', *Twórczość* 1959 (10).
[47] L. Kołakowski, *Marxism and Beyond. On Historical Understanding and Individual Responsibility* (London, 1971), p. 6.
[48] *Biologia i Polityka. Materiały narad biologów* (Warsaw, 1956).
[49] S. Ossowski, *Marksizm i twórczość naukowa w społeczeństwie socjalistycznym* (Warsaw, 1957).
[50] J. Karpiński, *Nie być w myśleniu posłusznym (Ossowscy, socjologia, filozofia)* (London, 1989).
[51] 'Walka klas i komplikacje dialektyczne' had been submitted to *Kuźnica* in June 1950.
[52] *Przegląd kulturalny* 1956 (13).

structure is divided by a caesura; in crisis it separates into the rulers and the ruled. The *Communist Manifesto* envisages a steady reduction of mankind by capitalism into two antagonistic classes: a small class of immensely wealthy monopolists and a vast and revolutionary proletariat. In modern parlance, it polarises. But in more normal times, outside of crises, Marx admits a second, much more flexible interpretation of class positions, called by Ossowski 'a gradation scheme of intermediate classes'.

Ossowski quotes from volume III of *Capital*: 'in England, modern society is indisputably the most highly developed in economic structures, but even here class stratification does not appear in pure form. Middle and intermediate strata obliterate lines of demarcation.' More complex still, an adequate sociology would have to include those whom Marx omits: not merely 'misfits, Bohemians, drifters', but also the peasantry, whom Marx dismisses for its 'lack of culture', disqualifying it from developing class consciousness.[53] Finally, a third notion of class: the middle classes and professionals in general – 'bourgeois' perhaps, but not caught in the categories of capitalist or proletarian. Ossowski notes they are a third force or potential class, arising from their function in the interdependent division of labour.

The English translation of Ossowski's book contained a curious 'erratum' slip underlining for foreign readers the political significance within the Soviet-type countries of such apparently abstruse debates. It notes that since October 1956 wide possibilities have opened up for deliberate and direct efforts to form a socialist culture:

> The scholar should not overlook, amongst the tasks awaiting work, the duty of watching out for the social consequences of habits of thought left over from the past. I am thinking here not only of the relics of capitalist culture but of thought patterns of more recent origin, dating from the time of grim myth with which those who were reconciled to the existing state of affairs salved their consciences: the myth of historical necessity as revealed to those who wield power.[54]

Similar debates were taking place elsewhere within Marxism. Some economists were still captivated by the 'law of value'.[55] But this stage did not long outlive Stalin. One perceptive visitor noted: 'In Polish economics, the Thaw *means* more rationality and decentralisation: this is almost the whole context. It is universally asserted that there has been

53 D. Mitrany, *Marx Against the Peasant. A Study in Social Dogmatism* (London, 1951), pp. 23–8.
54 S. Ossowski, *Class Structure in the Social Consciousness* (London, 1963).
55 *Ekonomiści dyskutują o prawie wartości* (Warsaw, 1956); *Dyskusja o prawie wartości: ciąg dalszy* (Warsaw, 1957).

far too little of either, due to slavish imitation of the faults of the Soviet Union.'[56] As Oscar Lange twice told his visitors, Poland's switch from Stalinism to Thaw was the move from a war to a peace economy. The appropriate mix between central control and devolution was of course debated between economists, but the need for choice was clear.[57] There was a quite extensive discussion of the socialist idea. But since this trespassed on territory the Party considered its exclusive preserve – to be conducted solely behind the closed doors of the Higher Party School – it was officially discouraged.

Gomułka attacked revisionists as negating the need for centralised democracy as the basis for Party organisation. They had no right to express opinions of their own which had not been agreed by higher Party officials. Kołakowski was taken as an illustration of 'bringing bourgeois ideology into the Party, mixing it up with the ideology of social democracy'. His writings were being reprinted in the bourgeois, and even Trotskyite, press. Gomułka declared that, but for the existence of revisionism, the Party would not have dogmatism. The sociologist Władysław Bieńkowski, a Gomułka ally who lost office in 1959, replied: 'without dogmatism there would be no revisionism'.

The Warsaw Club of the Crooked Circle had been meeting since 1956. It included academics and artists, publicists and other opinion-formers, who met on an informal basis, originally in private apartments. It grew to around 300 members, even admitting Bieńkowski. Whilst differing strands could be distinguished, both radical and conservative, their most significant attribute was mutual tolerance. It was a forum in which like-minded intellectuals could meet to exchange and modify their ideas. In addition to the undoubted pleasure of belonging to the 'chattering classes', membership helped to integrate a common milieu. As Jan Józef Lipski puts it, 'every participant in the discussion widened the circle of people with whom it was easy to find a common language'.[58] The club was closed down in 1962.

A Discussion Club for members of the Warsaw University Party and the Communist Youth Organisation (ZMS) was then founded by Karol Modzelewski.[59] Revisionist-inclined professors addressed their meetings. Its other animating spirit was Kuroń – like Modzelewski, an assistant lecturer at Warsaw University. He recalls Marx's early *Economic and*

[56] P. Wiles, 'Changing Economic Thought in Poland', *Oxford Economic Papers* 1957 (2).
[57] E. Lipiński, 'Model i reformy', *Przegląd kulturalny* 1957 (42); Lipiński, *Rewizje* (Warsaw, 1958).
[58] J. J. Lipski, *KOR. A History of the Workers' Defense Committee in Poland, 1976–1981* (Berkeley, 1985), p. 13.
[59] Kuroń, *Wiara i Wina*, pp. 169–70.

Philosophical Manuscripts, with its analysis of alienation, and Trotsky's *Revolution Betrayed*, published in the face of Stalin's terror, as particularly influential for his thinking.

A police raid confiscated a text on which the group had been working for six months. According to the secret police they were 'an illegal, anti-state group' preparing to disseminate 'a so-called programme, bordering in character on demagogic revisionism and anarchism, based on a total negation of the achievements of People's Poland'. On 27 November 1964, a special session of the Party's Teaching Committee at Warsaw University, attended by Andrzej Werblan (head of the Central Committee's Department of Science and Education) and Józef Kępa (Party Secretary in Warsaw), expelled Modzelewski and Kuroń from the Party. Also excluded were the sociologist Bernard Tejkowski, author of a master's thesis on 'The Social Function of Bureaucracy'; a second sociologist, Andrzej Mazur (University of Łódź); and an economist, Stanisław Gomułka, who lived in the flat which was raided.[60]

Kuroń and Modzelewski responded with an 'Open Letter' the following spring. It explained that they had revised the text confiscated by the secret police. Not knowing whether the new text – a densely packed fifty pages – would lead to further administrative measures or the decision for a trial, they asserted 'the *full right* to address an open letter to the political organisation which had removed them from its ranks, in order to explain to the wider membership of such bodies our point of view and the motives for our action'. They were indeed re-arrested and – despite a major rumpus at home and abroad – sent to prison for advocating the overthrow of the political and social system by force. They sat in prison until May 1967.

Their extraordinary manifesto argued that no alternative ideology had been generated since the shattering of Stalinism. Poland's rulers had resumed their 'class goal', defined as continuous expansion of production – 'production for production'. They here echoed Marx's central critique of capitalist production: 'Accumulate, accumulate! That is Moses and all the prophets!' This was an end in itself, the *raison d'être* of a 'socialist state' which paid no heed to consumers. During the 'anti-bureaucratic revolution' of 1956–7, Polish and Hungarian societies had mounted their first challenge to the central bureaucracy. The Hungarian dictatorship had been restored by Russian tanks and by the Revolution's international isolation: 'How could Poland's bureaucracy retain power by peaceful means?' Largely, it seemed, by default. The

60 AAN 237/XVI/404.

'October Left' had been divided and unable to act decisively. Failing to produce a programme, it was soon sidelined or co-opted as 'a leftist appendage to the ruling liberal bureaucracy'. But the latter, being barren, and bereft of ideas beyond its own self-preservation, could only insist upon its own ideological monopoly and devote the resources of Party and state to snuffing out any signs of intellectual independence.

The remedy was revolution by the working class. Compelled by their hopeless situation, Polish workers would overthrow the bureaucracy. To this end they must organise Workers' Councils to run the factories. Federated through a nationwide system of Workers' Delegates, headed by a Central Council, these would both formulate and supervise the enactment of economic policy. Such huge powers would be mitigated by the abolition of preventive censorship and all other impediments to the working class organising itself along diverse political lines. Once formed, membership of such parties would no longer be limited to workers. Moreover, alongside their Councils and Delegates, workers would have 'trade unions completely independent of the state and with the right to organise economic and political strikes'. A literary peroration envisaged the liberation of the working class. It must be emancipated from political police and from the regular army: 'both by their very nature, tools of anti-democratic dictatorship. As long as it is maintained, a clique of generals may always prove stronger than all Parties and Councils.' To ensure democratic control, 'It must introduce a multi-party system, providing political freedom to the whole of society.'[61]

Whilst the language was to be modified in the years that followed, this analysis was retained in one key sense. Functionaries and their dependants are set apart from the great majority of the population, which therefore feels excluded and at intervals rebels. In the seventies, this developed into a new opposition. For the moment, though, oppositional thinking was in an impasse. It had also lost touch with Polish society. Kuroń wryły remarks that Polish workers started behaving in 1970 as Marx had predicted, just when he himself was abandoning Marxism.[62]

It is easier to compile a list of revisionists and of their views than to identify their programme. In retrospect, the revisionist project seemed self-defeating. Revisionists sought to keep their disputes within the Party.[63] They felt that debate should be freely conducted, but not in front of outsiders, particularly not students. Socialism must not be undermined by 'non-Marxist criticism'. Critique would help 'alien forces', who would take comfort from every crumb of self-criticism that fell from the

61 J. Kuroń and K. Modzelewski, *List otwarty do partii* (Paris, 1966).
62 Kuroń, *Wiara i Wina*, p. 310. 63 J. Gross, 'O rewizjonizmie', *Kultura* (Paris) 1969 (1).

communists' table. Revisionists still thought – or pretended to think – that Party membership made sense.

Like the Old Bolsheviks' 'last opposition' to the Stalinist ascendancy, the only chance of success for the Polish revisionists would have been to take the debate to the public at large. An open debate could have harnessed the popular momentum of the October tendency. Behind closed doors, revisionists could only be isolated and condemned as 'splitters' in breach of basic Party discipline. By agreeing to confine debate to the inner sanctums of the Party, and increasingly to its upper echelons, they sealed their fate.

Was there a more pragmatic strand to Polish revisionism? In addition to reviving socialist thought, did they seek an institutional reform to achieve socialist aims in practice? They thought it meant 'changing the apparatus', but could this be done? Do institutions not determine behaviour? Pomian thought revisionism required a wider transformation of the ways in which politics, economics, culture and even ethics were conducted.[64]

The revisionists sought to limit the powers of the Party apparatus, and favoured elections to democratise its structure. This required the licensing of differing points of view – thus reversing Lenin's temporary 'ban on factions' (in force since 1921) – and securing the rights of minorities (as well as majorities) to their particular views. As Friszke remarks, this would have transformed the Communist Party into a social-democratic organisation. He draws attention to other social democratic experiences, such as, for instance, that of Julian Hochfeld, a former member of the PPS.[65] But the practical record in this regard was one of defeat. Those leaders thought most reliable by the 'revisionist tendency' were removed without much delay: Morawski in 1960, Albrecht in 1961, Zambrowski and Matwin in 1963. Their replacements conformed more closely to the 'conservatism' of the Party leader.[66]

On the tenth anniversary of the Eighth Plenum (21 October 1966), Kołakowski addressed an extraordinary gathering at Warsaw University. He noted that this date had been ignored by the Party. They were right 'since there is nothing to celebrate'. The talk caused a sensation amongst some 250–300 staff and students crowded into a hall built for 100.[67] According to the transcript, recorded for Party leaders by the secret police, there were two main themes. First was lack of lawfulness (*praworządność*). In large part, law was used as an instrument of repression. The Small Penal

[64] Interview with K. Pomian, *Mówią wieki* 1991 (10).
[65] Friszke, *Opozycja polityczna*, pp. 133–65. [66] Paczkowski, *Pół wieku*, p. 330.
[67] On the fortieth anniversary, Kołakowski was again the main speaker (Warsaw University, 21 October 2006).

Code of 1945 was so constituted that anyone could be arrested simply following a denunciation. Constitutional rights were empty phrases, as in the 1952 Stalin Constitution. Despite the hopes of October 1956, 'We are still a country without genuine elections, without freedom of assembly, without freedom to criticise or freedom of information.' Those in top posts had become isolated and over-confident. There was no contact between those in power and the powerless. The second theme was social. Like the state, society had succumbed to stagnation. It was ground down by material impoverishment, notably in housing. There was a 'pauperisation of the spirit, lack of air in which to breathe, lack of hope, a feeling of stagnation'.[68]

The other invited speaker, Krzysztof Pomian, talked about the demoralisation of young people, and the obstacles placed in the way of any free spirits within student organisations. The historians Jerzy Holzer and Andrzej Garlicki – later chroniclers of the Solidarity movement and the fall of communism – then made what the secret police called 'demagogic interventions'. Seweryn Blumstayn spoke on the failure of the October 'Left' to press ahead with its programme in the face of the authorities' argument of '*raison d'état*'. A motion calling for the immediate release of Kuroń and Modzelewski was put to the meeting, and endorsed by Adam Michnik. The Dean of History – interestingly in attendance – advised against the motion.

Kołakowski was expelled from the Party immediately afterwards. Politburo member Zenon Kliszko explained that his dissent had deep roots. He produced a letter Kołakowski had sent to the executive of the Philosophy Faculty at Warsaw University (2 January 1958) declaring the key post-October question to be whether 'Stalinism, broadly understood as a system of governing, of economic management, of Party life, and as a style in culture, will be effectively overcome by the progress of reform'. In Klizko's view he had succumbed to 'bourgeois-liberal views', including the sentiment that 'mono-Party authority leads to degeneration'.[69] Michnik and other student participants received disciplinary warnings. A petition to the Rector, defending their right to speak and the general principle of freedom of expression, carried 1,036 signatures from students and 150 from senior researchers.[70] Collecting them was a formative moment in a growing movement for student self-defence.

Despite stagnation, disagreements in high politics still continued. Given the public façade of unanimity, and the doctrinal claim to infallibility, this caused a difficult 'double-think' for Polish leaders. Policies could be jettisoned and replaced by their opposite, but they could not so

[68] AAN 237/XVI/408. [69] AAN 237/XVI/408, pp. 201–2.
[70] Friszke, *Opozycja polityczna*, pp. 233–4.

easily be modified without admitting culpability. It was politically easier to abandon a policy altogether than to modify it. Such politics favoured passivity and conformity – waiting to see if the line would change and then, when it had, boldly asserting the opposite of yesterday. Those who thought differently were forced into silence, or obliged to continue their cogitation from outside. Policy-makers abroad pondered an apparent impasse.

Bridge-building

Shortly before the ouster of Khrushchev, US Secretary of State Dean Rusk instructed all US diplomatic missions to revise their terminology for East European countries. The old terms 'Soviet satellites' and 'satellites', long used to characterise subservience to Moscow and conformity to the Soviet model, were no longer an adequate description of the relations of these countries to the Soviet Union. Staff should substitute the longer, but more accurate, designation 'East European communist countries' or 'East European countries'. Likewise, the phrase 'Soviet bloc' was outmoded. A more accurate description might be 'Soviet-oriented countries', while the term 'Sino-oriented countries' could be used to refer to North Korea, North Vietnam and Albania.[71] Such semantic revisions were shortly followed by a new policy initiative, 'Bridge to Eastern Europe'.

The aim was to give substance to John F. Kennedy's notion of 'peaceful engagement'. This expressed the hope that 'constructive change within the Communist bloc might bring within reach solutions which now seem beyond us'.[72] Policy planners were now invited to grapple with a series of issues which one defined as 'Why do we wish to build what kind of bridges to where?' One answer was:

> the most effective and dramatic move to 'build a bridge' to Poland would be an informal, personal statement by the President, similar to that of President de Gaulle, affirming the permanency of Poland's Oder–Neisse frontier. This would complicate Khrushchev's problems by implicitly raising the question of Poland's eastern frontier. It would also, however, complicate US relations with the Federal Republic of Germany.[73]

Nonetheless, it was beginning to be seen that improved relations between the USA and Eastern Europe could not be separated from a framework for European reconciliation as a whole.

71 LBJ Presidential Library, NS File, Country File Europe, Box 162 (4 March 1964).
72 American University, Washington DC (10 June 1963).
73 NS Security File, Box 163 (June–July 1964).

An 'Action Program for US Relations with Eastern Europe' (June 1965) noted promising trends in the region, which were expected to accelerate in the years to come. This 'quiet revolution' was held to comprise: internal liberalisation, a measure of national independence from Soviet control, pragmatism in facing economic problems and 'progress in re-association with the West'. The Program's eventual goal was the dismantling of the Iron Curtain and the free association of Eastern Europe with the West. However, there were road-blocks to increased traffic on the Soviet side of the bridge. Such impediments included 'the dead weight of Soviet bureaucracy', pervasive ideological and cultural controls and dollar penury.[74] It looked like a policy to make haste slowly.

Impatient with this, Marshall Shulman noted that 'frenetic and simplistic preoccupation with the Cold War' tended to distort the generous impulse of US aid programmes. Soviet policy had evolved in response to changes in the world environment. The globe had moved from bi-polarity to a triangular competition between the Soviet Union, China and the West. The United States and its Western allies 'are becoming aware that anti-Communism is not an adequate response to the total situation in which we live'.[75] But even in this optimistic assessment, which noted the 'trends towards greater autonomy in Eastern Europe', it was expected that Soviet domination of the region would continue for 'many years, probably many decades'.[76]

Reviewing the domestic impasse, political sociologists asked 'How non-monopolistic can a monopolistic Party be?'[77] Raymond Aron replied that communist regimes had not produced any justification for single-Party rule, still less for their retention of power for all time. They simply asserted that utopia would be achieved one day, rendering all forms of rule unnecessary. But would utopia come? Had Soviet communism become fossilised in transition? Western democratic theory saw political debate as a permanent, necessary and desirable process whereby 'different interests are conciliated within a given system of rule'. By contrast, communist politics was teleological. It held that one day all conflicts – 'contradictions' – would be resolved, and the necessity for political rule in any form would cease. According to Engels, the state would lose its political – class – character. Politics would be reduced to impersonal administration 'of things'. The extensive interim was bound to be conflictual. During the transition, the authorities would respond negatively

[74] National Security Action Memorandum (NSAM) no. 304.
[75] M. Shulman, *Beyond the Cold War* (New Haven, 1966), pp. 84–5. [76] *Ibid.* pp. 101–2.
[77] 'Can the Party Alone Run a One-Party State?' *Government and Opposition* January–April 1967 (2.2) (discussion of 20 May 1966).

to those who wanted to interfere with the historical process, normally with police and judicial repression.

The classic sociologist Pareto had taught that governing elites can retain power only for as long as they do not lose confidence in themselves. Commenting on the sudden re-emergence of political pluralism during the heady days of the Hungarian Revolution a decade earlier, Aron remarked: 'Having won with tanks, the victorious oppressors denounced pluralism as "counter-revolution".'[78] But if monolithic politics could only be sustained by force, and the costs of the use of force were high, the question arose of how far communist parties could relinquish some of their power in order to retain the rest of it. Could political opposition have any place? If so, where was such opposition to come from? The answer was counter-culture.

[78] T. Aczel (ed.), *Ten Years After. A Commemoration of the Tenth Anniversary of the Hungarian Revolution* (London, 1966), pp. 19–31.

7 Counter-culture

Be Realistic: Demand the Impossible! Parisian graffiti, 1968

During the late sixties, informal groups began to challenge Cold War certainties. Not simply in universities – 'Down with the Pedagogic Gerontocracy' – but also in the wider society, a post-war generation began to articulate a new critique. The moral authority of political systems and war machines, as well as academic institutions run by middle-aged, middle-class white males, came under serious scrutiny. Not only was the ability of political leaders to deliver on promises questioned, but also the values which they maintained were contested. The interaction between social movements and diplomacy brought new patterns of relations between peoples, cultures and governments.[1]

In order to contain dissent at home, governments frequently resorted to force against their own populations. The result was to radicalise the people rather than to legitimise government rule. Thus 'Rudi' Dutschke, who escaped from East Germany to study at the Free University in West Berlin, called for a 'third front' to challenge both capitalist and communist hegemonies. He invoked a new gallery of inspirational figures – such as Che Guevara – to symbolise the revolution against existing institutions.[2] Paradoxically, as super-power relations began to stabilise in the aftermath of Cuba, the societies they sought to govern became more disruptive. In the United States, the main driver was Vietnam.

Herbert Marcuse was an emblematic figure for these young radicals. Abandoning the analytic rigour of the Frankfurt School of critical theorists, he addressed a manifesto to the forces of liberation. He claimed a linkage between revolutionaries in Vietnam, Cuba and China, guerrilla movements in Latin America, ghetto populations in the United States

[1] J. Suri, *Power and Protest: Global Revolution and the Rise of Détente* (Cambridge, Mass., 2003).

[2] J. Suri, 'The Cultural Contradictions of Cold War Education: The Case of West Berlin', *Cold War History* April 2004 (4).

and student opposition 'spreading in the old socialist as well as capitalist countries'. Their commonality was a Great Refusal to be contained by 'the massive exploitative power of corporate capitalism even in its most comfortable and liberal realisations'.[3] Answering questions at West Berlin's Free University (July 1967), Marcuse explained that the Refusal was not to participate in the blessings of the 'affluent society' on the part of both those for whom it was a given and those in the Third World for whom it was not. But he saw a major discontinuity – perhaps a historical turning-point – in Vietnam where 'the human will and the human body with the poorest weapons can keep in check the most efficient system of destruction of all times'.[4]

According to the press, a 'world-wide student conspiracy' had emerged. Student leaders such as Mark Rudd at Columbia University (New York) and Daniel Cohn-Bendit at Nanterre (Paris) were 'acting in harness with unnamed students to overturn civil authority at such diverse schools as the Universities of Belgrade, Cracow, Warsaw and Prague'.[5] But were these 'agents of liberation' too diverse to mount a coherent threat to the status quo? Asked to comment, the CIA made the pragmatic reply that 'there is no evidence of collusion between student activists in the West and in the Soviet bloc'. It also noted a difference of target: 'Dissidents enrolled in Belgrade, Moscow etc., seek to operate within the state-sanctioned system and hope to enlist the sympathy of regime leaders, as those at Belgrade have done in the case of Tito. Students in the West are after far more sweeping changes in university administration, with or without official support.' In a covering note to the White House, the CIA Director added: 'Contagion not necessarily collusion would appear to be the order of the day.'[6]

Adam Michnik later reflected to fellow-radical Cohn-Bendit, on the period 1965–8: 'Those years were interesting because a few friends and I managed to function as a legal opposition group within a system that didn't admit the existence of a legal opposition. It's thanks to the University [of Warsaw] that we were able to exist.' He noted various attitudes amongst the academics: 'Many professors had liberal opinions, and some were Party members ... But their honour and dignity incited them to defend us. We, the protestors, were nonetheless their students, the legitimation of their conformity. We represented their entrance into history. We justified their existence. That's why many of them protected

[3] H. Marcuse, *An Essay on Liberation* (Boston, 1969), pp. vii–viii.
[4] H. Marcuse, *Five Lectures* (London, 1970), pp. 75–87.
[5] Drew Pearson, *Washington Post*, 14 June 1968.
[6] National Security Agency File, CIA – W. Rostow (14 June 1968).

us, albeit reluctantly.'[7] The students' shared background is characterised by Jan Lityński as that of being children from families of a pre-war communist tradition who did not believe parental assurances that they now lived in the best of all possible worlds.[8]

They debated and argued at the 'Club of Seekers after Contradictions' and sang songs of the Russian 'dissidents' Galich and Okudzhava. Sometimes they sallied forth to ask difficult and embarrassing questions at meetings of their elders: about the Ribbentrop–Molotov Pact or the fate of Polish soldiers at Katyń. Following such paratroop-like raids on discussion meetings they were nicknamed the 'commandos'. Kuroń and Modzelewski were role models for these youthful rebels and many actions were attempted in their defence.

Michnik sent copies of their 'Open Letter' to Paris. It was published in Polish by the émigré monthly *Kultura* and in French by the Trotskyite *Ligue communiste révolutionnaire*. The text was widely circulated by students occupying Paris universities in May 1968.[9] Soon after the authors' release from prison, in autumn 1967, a new issue presented itself. The twin themes of national independence and cultural freedom were neatly entwined.

March 1968

Mickiewicz's classical drama *Dziady* (Forefathers) was put on at Warsaw's National Theatre to mark the fiftieth anniversary of the Russian Revolution. Although the play had been required reading in Polish schools at least since independence was regained in 1918 and had been performed regularly during the communist period, it is not clear why its subject, Poland's struggle for freedom under the Russian partition, was thought suitable by the theatrical censorship. However, performances began on 25 November 1967 and high dignitaries of Party and state attended.

Audience reactions to the anti-Russian passages steadily grew. This alarmed the authorities, who banned the play from 30 January 1968, which happened to coincide with a favourable notice in *Pravda*. The last performance was packed out. Public interjections increased. As the curtain fell, Modzelewski called from the gallery 'Independence without Censorship'. Afterwards, about 300 members of the audience marched

[7] Interview with Daniel Cohn-Bendit (May 1987) in A. Michnik, *Letters from Freedom. Post-Cold War Realities and Perspectives* (Berkeley, Calif., 1998), p. 36.

[8] J. Lityński, 'My z Marca', in *Krajobraz po szoku* (Warsaw, 1989).

[9] A. Paczkowski, 'Marzec kontra Maj?' *Krytyka* (28/29).

out to the Mickiewicz statue nearby, festooning it with flowers and banners. This first street manifestation by students for more than a decade shocked the Party leadership.

In the next few days, Warsaw University students collected signatures for a two-sentence petition to the Sejm: 'We, Warsaw youth, protest against the decision to ban performances of Adam Mickiewicz's *Dziady* at the National Theatre in Warsaw. We protest against a policy cutting us off from the progressive traditions of the Polish nation.' There was strong support, particularly in the departments of Philosophy, History and Political Economy and in halls of residence. By 5 February, there were 400 signatures.[10] When brought before parliament (16 February) it had 3,000 signatures.[11] Despite secret-police harassment and intimidation, some 75 protest letters reached the Sejm. Students stated this proved they were not 'a small isolated group'. They were defending national culture and elementary principles of democracy. These included 'the right of society to control moves by the authorities'.[12]

The issue became international when two of the 'commandos', Michnik and Henryk Szlajfer, were interviewed for *Le Monde* by Bernard Margueritte. Their account of current events was widely reported abroad and was broadcast back to Poland on RFE. In reponse, the authorities expelled them from Warsaw University. Protests began in literary circles, with letters and petitions to the state-run ZLP. Another was drafted to President Ochab about the decision to close *Dziady*. Słonimski and Jasienica tried to mobilise the PEN Club, including its Information Centre in London. At a PEN Club meeting in Warsaw they attacked censorship and other aspects of cultural policy.[13] They also referred to the trial and imprisonment of the Russian writers Sinyavsky and Daniel.[14]

Polish writers called for an emergency Plenum of their Union, which met in closed session on 29 February. The 400 writers present heard a defence of the ban from the Minister of Culture, who claimed the theatre audience had exploited a tendentious production. In response, writers made the sharpest attacks on the Party's cultural policy for a decade. Kołakowski called the state's arrogation to itself of the right to determine theatrical interpretations a return to 'Zhdanovism', the policy of Stalin's cultural commissar: 'We have reached the shameful situation in which the

[10] AAN 237/XVI/586 'Wydarzenia marcowe' (6 February 1968).
[11] J. Eisler, *Marzec 1968* (Warsaw, 1991), pp. 158–9.
[12] AAN 237/XVI/586 'Wydarzenia marcowe' (21 February 1968).
[13] AAN 237/XVI/586 'Wydarzenia marcowe' (7 February 1968).
[14] L. Łabędz and M. Hayward (eds.), *On Trial. The Case of Sinyavsky (Tertz) and Daniel (Arzhak)* (London, 1967).

world drama from Aeschylus through Shakespeare to Ionesco, has become a catalogue of allusions to current Poland.' Any critical voice was deemed 'anti-socialist, an enemy of the system, and dedicated to restoring capitalism. But this is blackmail.'[15] Kisielewski, a writer of *feuilletons*, attacked the scandal of censorship. Instead of serving the public on a legal basis, it had become a state within a state: white gaps indicated where the censor's pencil had carried out acts of 'spiritual vandalism', often giving the opposite of the sense intended.[16] A few days later he was attacked and beaten up by 'persons unknown'.

Słonimski declared that little was left of the achievements of October 1956. Writers censored themselves before submitting their work to editors and publishers. Censorship was not merely an Office, it was ubiquitous. Current Party leaders had carried out the first stages of de-Stalinisation, restoring the rule of law, but these were now distant memories. He welcomed very recent changes in Czechoslovakia, where the Stalinist dictator Novotný had just been removed. He hoped that country would not suffer the same disappointment as Poland had since 1956.

In autumn 1967, a humane and enlightened form of socialism had begun to emerge in Prague. As in Warsaw, the first rumblings came from students, but the response was very different. Pawel Machonin, head of the Institute of Marxism–Leninism, regarded the student body as 'a real social group, with its own specific position, its own interests, its social psyche and even a developing ideology'.[17] Their ideological target was Novotný. The Slovak Party leader Dubcek echoed their complaints and called for a 'long-term Party programme' to channel discontents. Seriously alarmed by these divisions, Brezhnev paid a two-day visit to Prague (8–9 December). Crisis discussions convinced him that Novotný was entirely out of touch with the popular mood. He was replaced by Dubček on 5 January 1968. Speaking on 22 February, the twentieth anniversary of the 'Prague coup', Dubček called for 'a true invigoration and unification of all constructive and progressive forces in our Republic'. This was a necessary precondition for 'a new start to socialism'. All problems should be looked 'boldly in the face'.[18]

Criticism had focussed on the economy at least since 1963, when Czechoslovakia recorded the first negative growth rate in the history of communist Eastern Europe. Professor of Economics Ota Šik severely

[15] G. Sołtysiak and J. Stępiań (eds.), *Marzec '68. Między tragedią a podłością* (Warsaw, 1998), pp. 111–14.
[16] *Ibid.* pp. 122–4.
[17] H. Gordon Skilling, *Czechoslovakia's Interrupted Revolution* (Princeton, N. J.,1976), p. 76.
[18] Navrátil (ed.), *The Prague Spring, 1968*, pp. 53–4.

criticised central planning and advocated 'profit' and other new indicators of enterprise performance. The move from a command economy would be a 'long, slow process', but it was essential to end 'subjectively determined material proportions' set by the centre. His institutional alternatives were radical. The Planning Commission should become just one ministry amongst many, with an Economic Council established to co-ordinate the economy. Above all, individual enterprises, the real entrepreneurs, should have genuine initiative. Workers should have the power to elect factory directors and to dismiss them. There should be consumers' rights and 'the right and real possibility of various groups of the working people and different social groups to formulate and defend their economic interests in shaping economic policy'.[19]

The most far-reaching discussions concerned political institutions. This took place in a research team under Z. Mlynář, who had studied at Moscow University in the early 1950s with Gorbachev. They called the inherited system dictatorial and monopolistic. It was based on the 'false thesis that the Party is the instrument of the dictatorship of the proletariat'. There should be genuine discussion at the top. The Central Committee should no longer merely ratify decisions taken in advance, nor should it decide everything: 'The Party does not want to, and will not, take the place of social organisations.'[20] It should not act by *fiat*. On the contrary, a democratic system should allow 'different social interests and needs to play a real part in the creation and execution of policy'. How such a transformation would come about was not entirely clear. It was a social and political experiment under difficult conditions. As Mlynář later noted: 'This was a development towards political pluralism under conditions in which the economic, social, political and institutional supports of classic bourgeois political pluralism had been destroyed and society gradually had to build up new supports.'[21]

When the Soviet Politburo had discussed events in Czechoslovakia (18 January), the Ambassador to Prague reported that Dubček was 'unquestionably an honourable and faithful man and a staunch friend of the Soviet Union'. But the leadership was weak and divided, and Dubček 'vacillating'.[22] They resolved to keep a close watch on developments. Fears of 'democratic infection' were also expressed in neighbouring states.

[19] Skilling, *Czechoslovakia's Interrupted Revolution*, p. 114. [20] *Ibid.* Ch. 12.

[21] Z. Mlynář, *Notions of Political Pluralism in the Policy of the Communist Party of Czechoslovakia in 1968*, Working Paper no. 3 (Vienna, 1979), pp. 3–4.

[22] M. Kramer, 'The Czechoslovak Crisis and the Brezhnev Doctrine' in C. Fink, P. Gassert and D. Junker (eds.), *1968: The World Transformed* (Cambridge, 1998), pp. 122–3.

East German and Polish leaders were the first to raise concerns about 'contagion'. Gomułka gave Dubček a long lecture on this subject (7 February). He stated: 'We want your Party to be stronger. Your being in a good situation helps us. If your situation gets worse, our hostile elements will rear their head again. We have trouble right now with writers and students about the Mickiewicz *Dziady* in the theatre.'[23] Gomułka was correct. Czechoslovak changes were a catalyst for further protests in Poland. There was a new popular slogan: 'Poland awaits her own Dubček.'[24]

The 'commandos' met at Kuroń's flat in early March 1968 to plan a new protest. Fliers called students to a mass meeting 'in defence of democratic freedoms' and university autonomy. The mass meeting at Warsaw University (8 March) declared 'We will not permit anyone to trample on the Constitution', and pointed out that Article 71 guaranteed freedom of speech, press and assembly. The 'shameful' banning of *Dziady* was an open violation of this provision. After expressing solidarity with the expelled colleagues Michnik and Szlajfer and a number of others subject to disciplinary proceedings, the meeting affirmed: 'We will not permit our rights to defend the democratic and independent traditions of the Polish nation to be removed from us.' Students shouted 'No Bread without Freedom' and 'No Science without Freedom'. Pro-Rector Rybicki appeared on the balcony, hatless despite the snow.[25] He gave the crowd fifteen minutes to disperse.

With Gomułka and other top leaders absent at a summit in Sofia, the major figures in the capital were Warsaw Party Secretary Jōzef Kępa, and a political general, Mieczysław Moczar. They had sent several bus-loads of plain-clothed police to the University two hours before the students' peaceful protest was to begin. The coaches were marked 'excursion'. Their occupants, according to the internal Party bulletin, were 'workers' *aktyw*' who had become impatient with students living 'at our expense, and acting against us'. They had therefore to secure the socialist order against 'hooligans'. Students started to leave. As they reached the main gates, heavily armed police charged them, chasing many across the campus, some down to the river, beating and clubbing indiscriminately all they could reach. There were at least seventy arrests.

Secret-police reports all stressed the students' aggressiveness. They had loudly shouted 'Freedom and Democracy' and 'Down with the

23 A. Garlicki and A. Paczkowski (eds.), *Zaciskanie pętli. Tajne dokumenty dotyczące Czechosłowacji 1968r.* (Warsaw, 1995), p. 46.

24 Eisler, *Marzec 1968*, p. 346.

25 Photo: *Biuletyn Instytutu Pamięci Narodowej* 2003 (3/4), p. 7.

Gestapo' and passed a provocative resolution on 'guaranteeing the freedom of citizens, etc.'. They had been unreasonable, greeting the Pro-Rector with cries of 'Where's the Rector?' and insulting decanal mediators Stanisław Herbst (History) and Czesław Bobrowski (Economics) with cries of 'Provocation, Lies, Hypocrisy!' Likewise, the 'workers' *aktyw*' had been denigrated as 'bandits, fascists, Gestapo, mercenaries, black crosses and so on'.[26] Snowballs had been thrown at their buses. Such 'excesses' had made police intervention – including deployment of a 300-strong group of ORMO (the Voluntary Reserve of the Civic Militia) – inevitable.

In response, there was an unprecedented intervention. The Znak group of Sejm deputies addressed two questions to the Prime Minister:

(i) What measures will the government take to halt the brutal action of the militia and ORMO against young academics and to establish responsibility for their brutal treatment of youth?
(ii) How will the government set about answering the highly relevant and burning questions posed by young people concerning the democratic freedom of citizens and the cultural policy of the government?[27]

Their letter also called for steps to calm the situation, and expressed alarm that the press was inflaming it even more. It was wrong to see students as hostile to socialism. The irresponsible shouts to which some had given vent were often caused by police brutality. The communist authorities had no experience of being addressed in such a direct manner, and took a while to decide what line to take. Eventually, the Party Secretariat decided that the Prime Minister would respond at the next Sejm.

The Znak group elected to the Sejm of 1965 normally maintained a stance of critical, but not disloyal, opposition. It debated legislation, putting forward amendments, sometimes casting negative votes, sometimes abstaining.[28] For the communist authorities, this was a fairly harmless distraction. The 'interpolation' of March 1968 was a different matter. Znak was the first public body to speak against the brutal attacks at Warsaw University. Whilst such protests became commonplace a decade later, this pioneering example gave the authorities pause. However, the letter was never answered, nor its receipt acknowledged.

Instead, student mail was intercepted and phone lines monitored. But news spread fast. The 'Warsaw events' became widely known, not least through RFE. Some students managed to travel, despite a banning edict

[26] M. Zaremba (ed.), *Marzec 1968. Trzydzieści lat później*, vol. II: *Aneks źródłowy* (Warsaw, 1998), pp. 17–25.
[27] Friszke, *Koło Posłów 'Znak'*, pp. 488–9. [28] Summarised in *ibid.* pp. 513–20.

at train and bus stations and even road blocks. Warsaw University student Jan Gross reached Kraków on 10 March, where his meetings were monitored by the secret police.[29]

The authorities decided on smear tactics. Student leaders were portrayed by the Party daily as the 'golden youth', living at home, feeding on bananas (an unobtainable luxury) and smoking American cigarettes. In addition to abusing free higher education, they were sponging off their parents, many of whom had retired from or still occupied high positions. How could they have brought up such 'parasites'? And now there was a more insidious charge. Building on the thesis that the 'commandos' were mainly Jewish, the article stated they were using Mickiewicz to disguise their real interests.[30] This ferocious attack on students evoked an immediate response.

The first posters went up at the Jagiellonian University (Kraków) early on the morning the article appeared: 'Help Warsaw' and 'Down with Censorship'.[31] 500 Kraków students were demonstrating at the Mickiewicz statue by mid-day. 1,000 attended a mass meeting and passed a resolution in support of Warsaw students.[32] The Rector's appeal for calm discussion of the matter in hand was initially well received. He withdrew, however, when a much more extended agenda emerged. The students put forward five demands: observance of the Constitution; release of the students and researchers arrested; full information to be made public about the course of events; a special commission to establish the facts, which would proceed in public; autonomy for higher education in Poland. They called for publication of the programme within forty-eight hours.[33]

The initially mild reaction by the Kraków authorities was later accounted for by the comparative liberalism of the local leaders, who did not wish to inflame tensions.[34] But it is also attributable to the sheer speed of events, which took the secret police and militia by surprise. They had had no experience of such protests since 1956. This did not deter them from considerable brutality thereafter. A 'pacification' operation, which included raids with gas and water on the University campus, took four days and resulted in the arrest of 128 students.[35]

[29] Sołtysiak and Stępiań (eds.), *Marzec '68*, pp. 225–6.
[30] *Trybuna Ludu*, 11 March 1968.
[31] Sołtysiak and Stępiań (eds.), *Marzec '68*, pp. 194–5 (11 March 1968).
[32] AAN 237/XVI/587 'Wydarzenia marcowe na wyższych uczelniach' (11 March 1968).
[33] Sołtysiak and Stępiań (eds.), *Marzec '68*, p. 196.
[34] J. Kwiek (ed.), *Marzec 1968 w Krakowie w dokumentach* (Kraków, 2005), pp. 11–12.
[35] Dudek and Marszałkowski, *Walki uliczne*, pp. 234–6; Kwiek (ed.), *Marzec 1968*, pp. 13–14.

The next revolt was in Lublin, home both to the Catholic University (KUL) and the state university named after Maria Skłodowska-Curie. Having heard the RFE broadcast, students circulated fliers 'in solidarity with the young students of Warsaw'. According to official estimates, about 1,000 assembled (including school-children) on 11 March. Their 'aggressive' behaviour was countered by 'a 300-strong group of workers', supported by militia with batons. A total of 43 demonstrators were arrested, including 20 students from KUL. Amongst student demands set out the next day, were:

– The press slanders us. We cannot allow this. We demand an apology.
– They accuse us of supporting Warsaw students when we know nothing about them and have not been there. We just want to show our solidarity. How many of us have been to Vietnam?
– We are struggling to make Poland free.[36]

Thereafter, student protests spread nationwide.

Some 800 students took part in a silent protest at the Fedro monument to the victims of Hitler in Wrocław. Another 200 students met in the Łódź University Library to choose a delegation to the Rector. His only response was to shut the building. In Gliwice, some 200 students from the Silesian Polytechnical University sang patriotic anthems, the 'Internationale', and laid flowers at the Mickiewicz statue. In Gdańsk, Foreign Minister Rapacki delivered a lecture to Party faithful on the 'German Problem', while 500 students mounted a demonstration outside and shouted that the press was slandering them.[37] In Poznań, 400 students from Adam Mickiewicz University demonstrated peacefully at the poet's statue. It was rumoured in Łódź that Warsaw University's Department of Philosophy would be closed. Students declared 'Solidarity with Kołakowski' and 'We Demand *Dziady*.'[38]

Some 4,500 students from all higher-education institutions in Wrocław declared a 48-hour sit-in.[39] They drew up an eleven-point resolution, issued a call for the establishment of a Sejm Commission to review their demands, and appealed for solidarity from the working class. Their slogans stated: 'Workers we are with you', 'Workers, support our interests', 'Workers – we're your children', 'Workers and peasants!!! We are waiting for Your support!'[40] A further syllogism explained: 'Workers plus Students equals Socialism.'[41] Official placards stated 'Students Back to

36 Dudek and Marszałkowski, *Walki uliczne*, pp. 234–6.
37 AAN 237/XVI/587 (12 March 1968). 38 AAN 237/XVI/587 (14 March 1968).
39 W. Suleja, *Dolnośląski Marzec '68. Anatomia protestu* (Warsaw, 2006), Ch. 3.
40 *Ibid.* p. 92. 41 AAN 237/XVI/587 (14 March 1968).

their Studies', a sentiment widely echoed in Western Europe during student protests later in the year.

Massive counter-rallies were held by the authorities.[42] Their size and organisation far outnumbered anything the students could muster. One in Kraków passed eighty resolutions, all unanimous in their support of the Party and its leadership.[43] Of course, those shouting support for the authorities at rallies might harbour private doubts. The response from factory workers remains unclear. We know that strikes and occupations did not take place in support of students, though they did on other issues. But some evidence supports the claim by students that 'there does not exist a divergence between the wishes of the working class and of students. We protest against the attempts to drive a wedge between these two circles.'[44]

A student delegation from the Technical University was admitted to the Gdańsk Shipyard and permitted to explain their aims: freedom of expression and the fight against censorship. Their words did not make much impression. The dilemma was later portrayed in the famous confrontation between the father and student son in Wajda's *Man of Iron*.[45] After coffee with the Director, they received a more hostile welcome at the Shipyard gates, where ORMO members engaged in a well-paid exercise of student-bashing. Such brutality aroused sympathy and led to a counter-demonstration later in the day.

Figures for the arrested in Gdańsk included only 21 students, alongside 83 young workers (58 from shipyards), 26 young clerks, and the rest schoolchildren.[46] Similar proportions apply to Poland as a whole. Of 2,725 arrested (in the month from 7 March), 937 were young workers. There were instances of workers' protests outside the workplace, as individuals or in small groups within larger street demonstrations.[47] It is also possible that worker involvement was greater than official statistics showed, since it was common to classify those detained as 'hooligans', allegedly engaged in non-political activities. Given that the vast majority of those arrested (and more not included in official statistics) were under thirty, one might expect them to become part of a new protest generation. Some do not reappear. Their youthful detention, followed by police surveillance and lack of promotion in their later careers, were likely

42 L. Kamiński, 'Jesteśmy z wami, towarzyszu Wiesławie', *Biuletyn IPN* 2003 (3/4).
43 Cited by Zaremba (ed.), *Marzec 1968*, vol. XI, p. 163.
44 Sołtysiak and Stępiań (eds.), *Marzec '68*, p. 229.
45 L. Wałęsa, *A Path of Hope* (London, 1987), pp. 52–4.
46 *Informacja*, 16 March 1968 (37), cited by Zaremba (ed.), *Marzec 1968*, vol. XI, p. 156.
47 A. Friszke, 'Ruch protestu w marcu 1968 (w świetle raportów MSW)', *Więź* 1994 (3).

deterrents. But others, who joined the seventies opposition, had little left to lose.

The mixed response to student protests may have other explanations. Students are an easy target in any country where higher education is open only to a tiny minority. In 1968, the percentage in Poland with higher education was less than 3 per cent of the total population. As we have seen, they were immediately presented as ungrateful beneficiaries of special privileges. One private farmer (from the Kraków region) commented thus: 'What is going on? Young people today have good [living] conditions, halls of residence, stipends and all they need for studying. Why are they making so much trouble?'[48]

The public had yet to hear from Gomułka whose eleven-day silence was broken on 19 March. Addressing 3,000 Party activists in the Congress Hall of the Palace of Culture, broadcast on live radio and television, he stated that, far from being spontaneous, student protests had been incited by the writers' Plenum and, in particular, by Kisielewski and Jasienica. Their second source of 'inspiration' had been academics in the humanistic faculties of Warsaw University, such as Professors Brus, Baczko, Morawski and Bauman, long known in the Party for their revisionist views. Third came a more sinister charge: 'An active part in the events was played by young academics of Jewish origin.' In a novelty for political sociology, he divided Jews into three categories: Zionist, cosmopolitan and those loyalists 'who regard Poland as their only fatherland'.[49] At the mention of a Jewish question, parts of his audience erupted, some shouting aggressive epithets, others chanting the name of Silesian Party Leader Edward Gierek. It seems the intensity of this reaction took Gomułka by surprise. Someone else had planned the demonstration.

Poland had broken off relations with the state of Israel, following its victory in the June 1967 war. Now it was claimed that these students were its agents, and had supporters (and fathers) in high places. The parallel with Israeli 'commandos', victors in the recent war, was perhaps more redolent than the authorities intended.

Anti-Zionism

In numerical terms, Polish Jewry hardly still existed. Around 10 per cent of the Polish population before the Second World War, they were now 0.1 per cent. In addition to the Holocaust, there had been two waves of

[48] M. Zaremba, 'Biedni Polacy '68' in M. Kula, P. Osęka and M. Zaremba (eds.), *Marzec 1968. Trzydzieści lat później*, vol. I (Warsaw, 1998), p. 150.

[49] D. Stoła, *Kampania antysyjonistyczna w Polsce 1967–1968* (Warsaw, 2000).

legal emigration, in the later 1940s and from 1956 to 1958. By 1967, no more than 30,000 remained amongst a population of 32 million. The majority were ageing, whilst their offspring, brought up in communist Poland, tended to be secular and assimilated. The Jewish community did not have a single qualified rabbi.[50]

In summer 1967, Poland followed the Soviet line of support for the Arab cause in the Near East. Gomułka publicly accused Polish Jews of supporting Israeli aggression and American imperialism. They were a subversive 'fifth column'. His comment that 'one should have only one fatherland' led the writer Słonimski to observe 'Yes, but why should it be Egypt?' Indeed, it would have been curious if ordinary opinion in Poland had not favoured Israel, in the sense that it had just inflicted on the Soviet ally such a crushing defeat. The Ministry of the Interior started to screen prominent people in search of 'Zionists'. As Dariusz Stoła points out, this term was doubly misleading. It was firstly code for 'Jewish' and secondly signified 'Jew' even if the person called 'Zionist' was not Jewish.[51]

A witch-hunt began within the military, which started to dismiss Jewish officers. A plot was hatched to remove Defence Minister Spychalski (in post since 1956). Supporters of General Moczar spread the rumour that he was an inefficient commander whose (Jewish) wife had sinister ties with Israel: 'A full report on how the Jews have stolen military secrets should be given to the Polish people.' It was alleged that Jews had been to the Israeli Embassy in Warsaw to enlist in the Israeli army. Moczar's men also declared that 'the Party Central Committee should be dissolved and replaced by a purely Polish body'.[52] They meant that Jewish communists should be removed. This hate campaign was by no means the first in Poland's troubled history. There is a growing literature on anti-Semitism in early post-war Poland.[53] But it *was* distinctive for the communist period in that the communists themselves now adopted a legacy and terminology with which they had themselves been attacked.

The second wave resumed in spring 1968. Three days after the start of the 'March events', the state media attributed disturbances to Zionists and bankrupt politicians. Thus in addition to 'Zionists in Poland [who] took orders from the Federal German Republic', there were Jewish

[50] D. Stoła, 'Fighting against the Shadows. The "Anti-Zionist" Campaign of 1968' in R. Blobaum (ed.), *Anti-Semitism and its Opponents in Modern Poland* (Ithaca, 2005), p. 285.
[51] Stoła, *Kampania antysyjonistyczna*, p. 7.
[52] LBJ Presidential Library, NS File Country File Poland vol. 11, CIA Special Report (28 September 1967).
[53] See B. Szaynok, 'The Role of Anti-semitism in Postwar Polish–Jewish Relations' in Blobaum (ed.), *Antisemitism and its Opponents*, pp. 265–83.

ex-Stalinists in Party positions who were responsible for the mistakes and terror of the Stalin period. In a remarkable study of this campaign, which swept the country for several months, Stoła shows how extraordinary accusations were summoned up. Thus, Jews were:

> Marxist revisionists, that is carriers of a dangerous ideological disease; they have an inclination to oppose the Party line in general and Comrade Gomułka in particular. Another crime is the Jew's disrespect for the Cold War division of the world, since they have families and friends in the west; they are open (or hidden and thus even more dangerous) sympathizers with Israel and, therefore, with Israel's imperialist backers.[54]

Gomułka told the Politburo (8 April) that it was 'an unhealthy tendency to attack every Jew just for being Jewish': 'Revisionism not Zionism is the main danger.' Of course, they might overlap. Subsequently, he extended the list of enemies to socialism to 'forces of reaction, revisionism and clericalism.'[55] All were more dangerous than Zionism.

During the 'March events', the Episcopal Conference issued a clear endorsement of the students' aims. It accepted that 'the latest student demonstrations have a social and cultural, not a political, character'. Rather than being in revolt against the system or state authorities, they were appealing for the Constitution to be observed. It would therefore be wrong either to see these demonstrations as politically motivated, or to dismiss them as anonymous acts of hooliganism. The Church deeply regretted that the students had not been addressed by the University authorities, but rather intervened against by violent police measures 'especially in the streets of Warsaw, Poznań, Katowice, Gliwice, Kraków, Gdańsk etc.'. Such methods had discredited the state: 'A truncheon is never an argument in a free society: it arouses the worst memories and mobilises public opinion against the existing order. The state cannot replace commonsense and righteousness by the police baton.' Disinformation by the press with regard to students' demands and intentions was well understood by the Episcopate 'since they have themselves experienced the bitter fruits of an unscrupulous press'. The state should free all those arrested, make the real demands of students publicly known, and cease the 'anachronistic repressive measures which awaken in our Nation disgraceful memories of the past'.[56]

Instead of heeding this calming missive, the Party Secretariat planned severe measures to handle 'the strike of students and disorganisation of

54 Stoła, 'Fighting against the Shadows', in Blobaum (ed.), *Anti-semitism and its Opponents*, p. 292.

55 P. Machcewicz, *Władysław Gomułka* (Warsaw, 1995), pp. 65–7.

56 Raina, *Political Opposition*, pp. 144–5 (21 March 1968).

science at Warsaw schools and other academic centres'. Warsaw University would dismiss the academics who had supported student trouble-makers. This began with the sacking of Professors Brus, Baczko, Morawski, Kołakowski and Bauman.[57] Even so, in the light of 'excesses' at Warsaw University, sixty-three students and ten junior staff were arrested. The range of Faculties purged was quite extensive – Mathematics and Physics, Geology, Chemistry and Biology, as well as the more usual suspects: Social Science, History and Law.[58] Thirty-four students were expelled from the University, and many more were suspended. Some managed to finish their studies externally or in other universities such as Michnik in Poznań and Lityński in Wrocław. Instead of isolating such individuals, this had the opposite effect of spreading and consolidating ideas of an incipient opposition.

A protest meeting at Warsaw University (28 March) declared the sackings of professors was 'a new and threatening stage of intervention' by the authorities in scientific and cultural life: 'There can be no Polish school of sociology without Bauman and Hirszowicz, no Polish school of philosophy without Baczko, Kołakowski and Stefan Morawski nor Marxist political economy without Brus.' This was a state intervention without precedent.[59] The meeting passed a 'Declaration of the Student Movement', mainly drawn up by three assistant lecturers at the University, Jakub Karpiński and Jadwiga Staniszkis (Sociology) and Andrzej Mencwel (Political Economy). Bringing together the earlier strands of thought, it was the most significant document of social protest since 1956.[60]

The starting point was radical criticism of official youth organisations. However, the creation of alternative structures was blocked. Representatives from nine cities with higher education institutions managed to meet in Wrocław on 25 March. According to police reports, they discussed the need to coordinate activities and discussed the future of the 'students' movement'. Sporadic boycotts followed. But by the end of April most of those involved were under lock and key. Counter-demonstrations on May Day did not take place, though some student marchers produced protest banners as they passed the reviewing stands.[61]

The second theme was political economy. Official discussions about differing 'models' within the scope of socialism had not gone very far. Yet there was a range on offer, including workers' and territorial

[57] Stoła, *Kampania antysyjonistyczna*, pp. 319–20.
[58] Zaremba (ed.), *Marzec 1968*, vol. XI, pp. 198–201.
[59] *Ibid.* p. 249. [60] Friszke, *Opozycja Polityczna*, p. 245.
[61] Friszke, 'Marzec 1968', *Więź*, March 1994.

self-management, which should be considered in order to determine the most suitable for Polish conditions. The existing centralised model was dysfunctional. Rather than pre-empting discussion, the declaration called for open debate. This required giving the public accurate information about the current state of the economy, respecting rational accounting, keeping 'strict and effective social control' over the planning mechanism, and appointing competent people to run the economy.[62] The implication that the *nomenklatura* system promoted the incompetent was not concealed.

A third theme concerned 'administrative monopoly over information', especially in conflict situations. The public needed freedom of discussion: 'We demand the abolition of censorship.' This clearly echoed developments in Czechoslovakia, where censorship had been lifted from February. Students also sought secrecy of correspondence and telephone conversations as guaranteed by law (Article 73 of the Constitution), and changes to the criminal code to set out rules under which officials could refuse a passport for travelling abroad or issue a call-up for military service. As it was, 600 students were called-up as a punishment for the 'March events'.[63]

Finally, the students demanded legality. There should be a greater role for the Sejm in debating legislation. It was intolerable that the judiciary could be used as an instrument of political repression. It concluded: 'We seek a socialist and democratic Poland, freed from chaos and lawlessness.'[64] That same day, the sociologist Jerzy Jedlicki wrote to the Academy of Sciences claiming that both Party and public life were being conducted through 'terror, slander and reaction'. He returned his Party card.[65]

The Rector of Warsaw University announced the abolition of the Faculties of Economics, Philosophy, Sociology and Psychology; the third year of Mathematics and Physics was also disbanded. Some 1,616 students were dismissed from their studies in Warsaw alone, and the purge was extended to other university cities. The most extensive was at Wrocław Technical University, where 1,553 students were expelled from three departments. An even more dramatic purge took place in the high offices of state. Between March and May, 483 senior officials were summarily sacked, including 4 ministers, 14 vice-ministers, 7 directors-general and 51 departmental heads. These measures were replicated with greater severity outside the capital. The reasons for their dismissal were alleged 'pro-Zionist' views, Jewish origin, or both. As a result of the

[62] Zaremba (ed.), *Marzec 1968*, vol. XI, p. 252. [63] Friszke, *Opozycja polityczna*, p. 248.
[64] *Ibid.* pp. 252–3. [65] *Ibid.* p. 250.

campaign, which continued until 1971, Poland lost about 15,000 citizens through emigration.[66]

Absurd arguments were advanced to explain this exodus. In early April, for instance, a PAX leader called 'the political line of Znak an amalgam of Zionism and political clericalism'. It allegedly wished to replace the Soviet Union by West Germany as Poland's foreign orientation and (simultaneously) to bring 'Jewish-liberals' to power. In conversations with Catholics abroad, the group did not hide their solidarity with Israel. Their 'Interpolation' of 11 March was one strand in this strategy[67]. Such abuse could not go unanswered. For Znak, one cardinal principle could not be broken: complete religious toleration. Strident nationalism, particularly in its anti-Semitic form, was an absolute anathema. The group was divided on the best approach to take at the forthcoming session of the Sejm.[68]

Psychological tension was heightened by the politicised ferment within that normally staid Chamber. Its first full day heard an opening harangue from the Prime Minister, vociferously applauded from a normally empty public gallery, now packed with security policemen.[69] There followed a 'witches' Sabbath' – two days of attacks on the Znak intervention.[70] In response, the senior Znak deputy, Zawieyski, read the Sejm a lecture on toleration. He called the beating-up of his fellow deputy Kisielewski (on 11 March) an attack on Polish culture without precedent in the communist period. Instead of demagogy and brutality, debate required dialogue.

He defined this term. Widely used 'in political, ideological, philosophical and even papal circles', dialogue assumes a plane of possible agreement between opposed positions. In order to take place at all, certain preconditions had to be observed: 'goodwill on both sides, based on respect for someone else's point of view'. There had to be a recognition of each other's rationality before dialogue could occur. This did not mean that all issues could be resolved by consensus. But it did mean that parties to discussion required the same starting-point: 'solidarity – the spirit of fraternity'.[71] The only response of the authorities was to sack Zawieyski from the Council of State.

Shortly afterwards, Znak deputy Stomma spoke in defence of students. His point was simple: in contrast to the national uprising in 1956, when

[66] Dudek and Marszałkowski, *Walki uliczne*, p. 166.

[67] A Friszke, 'Trudny egzamin. Koło posłów "Znak" w okresie Marca 68' in Kula *et al.* (eds.), *Marzec 1968*, pp. 189–90.

[68] *Ibid.* pp. 190–2. [69] Mazowiecki, interviewed by Eisler, *Marzec 1968*, p. 329.

[70] A. Micewski, *Współrządzić czy nie kłamać? Pax i Znak w Polsce 1945–1976* (Paris, 1978), p. 210.

[71] Friszke, *Koło Posłów 'Znak'*, p. 499 (10 April 1968).

'anti-Russian sentiments were very strong', the recent demonstration had contained no such tendencies, or even slogans. Yet they had been brutally attacked. Znak's original point to the Premier, the need to halt the violence and take students' democratic demands into account, had yet to be addressed.[72] Students had simply been suppressed.

Kliszko, regarded as second only to Gomułka in the Party hierarchy, repeated the Premier's taunt that the Znak letter had been addressed 'to the streets and to abroad' (RFE) not to the government. It was rabble-rousing for reactionary purposes. Not patriotism at all, it supported Zionist and revisionist elements working to undermine the Polish state. Its machinations would not succeed: the populist rhetoric of Znak could not disguise its political isolation.[73]

In a speech at the end of the year, Mazowiecki looked back on the 'sharp criticism we received in this Chamber last April'. Znak had not sought to challenge the Party's leading role, nor – as many had alleged – to foster an 'erosion' of socialism. But socialism could only develop when criticism was listened to, rather than dismissed as a political challenge to those in power. He noted that Polish society remained as reluctant to take control over its own affairs as was the Party to relinquish it. The stalemate of March had been confirmed by the year's other 'grievous event': the Warsaw Pact invasion of Czechoslovakia.[74]

Prague Spring

Polish protestors were keenly aware of events across the border. One of their key chants was 'Long Live Czechoslovakia'. Solidarity developed between academics. The Czech philosopher Karel Kosík defended the 'Marxist humanists of Poland' such as Baczko and Kołakowski, after their dismissal: 'It would be in keeping with the principles of human solidarity if these persecuted Polish thinkers could come to Prague, permitting them freely to continue their work and to propagate progressive socialist opinions.'[75] As in Poland in the mid-fifties, there was a dramatic thaw. Sociology no longer had to masquerade as 'applied Marxism', following its famous denunciation by Stalin in 1931 as a 'bourgeois pseudo-science'. Pawel Machonin's team investigated the paradoxes of power and inequality.[76] Literary critics reviewed Kafka. No longer dismissed as

72 *Ibid.* pp. 500–4. 73 Eisler, *Marzec 1968*, pp. 331–2.
74 Friszke, *Koło Posłów 'Znak'*, pp. 508–10.
75 *Literární listy* (4 April 1968), cited by Raina, *Political Opposition*, p. 146.
76 E. Gellner, 'The Pluralist Anti-Levellers of Prague', *Government and Opposition* Winter 1972 (7).

bourgeois or decadent, he was recognised as the chronicler of alienation in an absurd, bureaucratic environment.

Soviet leaders were increasingly concerned by swift changes, pushed through on the wave of public opinion, which removed key figures in the Party, Ministry of the Interior and armed forces. The channels of Soviet influence were rapidly eroding. Andropov, who had served in Budapest in 1956, informed the Politburo (15 March) that the events in Czechoslovakia 'are very reminiscent of what happened in Hungary'. Brezhnev added: 'our earlier hopes for Dubček have not been borne out'.[77] Events in Czechoslovakia were making the traditional methods of subordination to Moscow less operable.

At an emergency summit in Dresden (23 March), Warsaw Pact leaders spoke frankly, unaware that their talks were being recorded by the East German Security Service (the Stasi). Ulbricht was concerned both about the 'contamination effect' and by possible geo-strategic consequences. A reformed Czechoslovakia might seek rapprochement with West Germany. There was indeed a precedent since Romania had unilaterally established diplomatic relations with Bonn in early 1967.[78] Even more alarming, from Ulbricht's point of view, was that Moscow – driven by both economic and strategic needs – might seek an opening to West Germany. The timing seemed promising. Even a staunch anti-communist such as Adenauer accepted the need for improved East–West relations in Europe.[79]

After Ulbricht, the most vehement opponent of the Prague Spring was Gomułka. Dismissing Dubček as naive, he developed the comparison with Poland:

> I don't want to remind you comrades of the student events in our country because I have already talked about this subject very fully before the Warsaw Party *aktyw*, gave an extensive evaluation of the situation. I have the impression that this evaluation fits your situation 90%, Czechoslovak comrades. The more you look at it and exchange some facts, the more it looks the same.

He explained that trouble always starts with the arts: 'Under the flag of the defence of culture and the defence of freedom, under this mask, the enemy, the counter-revolution works, foreign intelligence services work. They want to stir people up and achieve their goals this way.'[80] The hero

77 Kramer, 'The Czechoslovak Crisis and the Brezhnev Doctrine' in Fink *et al.* (eds.), *1968*, pp. 123–4.

78 *Ibid.* pp. 128–9.

79 J. Suri, 'Developed Socialism: The Soviet "Thaw" and the Crucible of the Prague Spring, 1964–1972', *Contemporary European History* (15.2), 2006.

80 Navrátil (ed.), *The Prague Spring, 1968*, p. 67.

of the Polish October had no time for the Prague experiment: 'Counter-revolution has reared its head and the process is growing.'[81]

Brezhnev reported that the Soviet Politburo had spent 'dozens of hours' analysing the Czechoslovak events: 'We have put all our other work aside, have looked at documents, have evaluated everything from the political point of view, and have perceived the very dangerous trend of events.' He then addressed the Czechoslovaks directly: 'We would like to tell you as friends: we are still convinced that the situation can be changed, that the counter-revolution can still be dealt a blow. But one needs the desire, the will-power and also the courage in order to implement the necessary actions.'[82] Czechoslovak leaders did not heed these warnings, nor fully brief their comrades on the strength of allied feeling at the Dresden summit.

Gomułka told the Soviet Ambassador (16 April) that 'the process whereby socialist Czechoslovakia will be transformed into a bourgeois republic has already begun'. He deplored statements about 'the liquidation of democratic centralism, leeway for bourgeois expression, trade unions without communists, national committees without communists'. Since many Poles wished to emulate what was happening in Czechoslovakia, 'events developing there have an increasingly negative effect on Poland'.[83] It was impossible to remain an indifferent observer whilst counter-revolutionary plans were being implemented.

A major landmark in the blossoming Prague Spring was the Party's Action Programme (10 April). Rejecting the Stalinist thesis of antagonistic classes – which 'no longer existed' – it advocated a 'frank exchange of views and democratisation of the whole social and economic system'.[84] The CIA regarded this as 'a bloodless but nevertheless very real revolution in Czechoslovakia'. They assessed that Soviet leaders had conceded, albeit grudgingly, that the Czech Party was right to try to reform itself and attempt a communist 'democratisation'. Brezhnev and Kosygin, however, were bound to fear the spread of such concepts to their own countries. Even so, the report cited *Rudé Právo* (19 April) which defended the Czechoslovak 'socialist model' while stating clearly that 'no-one can prescribe for any Party what is and what is not its international duty'.[85]

The implications were considered by the NSC (24 April). Significant differences were noted between the various countries of Eastern Europe,

[81] Garlicki and Paczkowski (eds.), *Zaciskanie pętli*, p. 52. [82] *Ibid.* p. 66.

[83] Navrátil (ed.), *The Prague Spring 1968*, p. 103.

[84] R. Remington (ed.), *Winter in Prague. Documents on Czechoslovak Communism in Crisis* (Cambridge, Mass., 1969), pp. 88–137.

[85] LBJ Presidential Library, CIA Intelligence Memo 'Czechoslovakia in Transition' (23 April 1968).

held to be a positive result of 'bridge-building'. But experience showed that 'further progress is likely to be subject to interruptions and even, as in the case of Poland, substantial retrogression'. While the State Department 'declined to discuss recent Polish events', it did note 'the tragic consequences that have resulted from the encouragement of anti-Semitism'. By contrast, the Czechoslovak Action Programme emphasised national reconciliation, with some compromises based on recognition of individual and group rights. It should be the US position 'to make clear informally and discreetly to the Czechs, on appropriate occasions, that we welcome the steps they are taking towards liberalisation'. But care should be taken not to embarrass Czech leaders – presumably by sounding too fulsome – nor to complicate their delicate relations with the Soviet Union and Eastern European neighbours.[86]

US Ambassador Bohlen expressed concern that the Czechoslovak developments would go too far and provoke a Soviet reaction. He too advocated quiet diplomacy. There was a further danger, if tensions grew within Eastern Europe, that East Germany might try to create tension with the West. That too meant 'Play in very low key. Avoid shouting. No interference. Difference between rape and seduction in diplomatic terms.'[87]

Soviet, East German, Polish, Hungarian and Bulgarian leaders next met (8 May) without their Czechoslovak counterparts. The Hungarian leader Kádár was most conciliatory. He dismissed the Action Programme as mere words; he had told Dubček: 'They can write 8,000 pages for you, and argue about words and specific formulations, but it won't mean a thing.' It was 'a big zero – a nothing'. Gomułka retorted: 'Comrade Kádár, this is not a zero; it is the main document against which we will have to fight not only in Czechoslovakia but in other countries as well.' Of course, there was not counter-revolution in the sense of weapons on the streets, 'But we are not children. As politicians, we know that imperialist circles do not act like that in socialist countries.' Imperialism subverted socialism under the guise of its improvement or democratisation. Fortunately, the working class would not tolerate such impudent approaches.[88]

The Czech novelist Vaculík's famous 'Two Thousand Words that Belong to Workers, Farmers, Officials, Scientists, Artists, and Everybody' (27 June) stated bluntly that, after twenty years of unchallenged rule, Party leaders were weakened and debilitated. Truth was not prevailing: 'Truth is merely what remains when everything else has been

[86] LBJ Presidential Library, NSC (585) (24 April 1968).
[87] *FRUS*, vol. XIII, p. 70. [88] Navrátil (ed.), *The Prague Spring, 1968*, p. 104.

frittered away. So there is no reason for national jubilation, simply for fresh hope.' The Action Programme, though drawn up by communists, should be elaborated 'in public in every district and community'. Citizens should demand removal of those officials who embezzled, acted brutally or were simply incompetent. Peaceful means of pressure were proposed: 'public criticism, resolutions, demonstrations, demonstrative work brigades, collections to buy leaving gifts for bosses "on their retirement"'. There could be strikes and picketing of front doors, but no rude letters.[89]

Moscow saw the 'Two Thousand Words' as subversion. It was a political platform 'to denigrate the position of the entire communist party in the eyes of the Czechoslovak people and in front of world opinion'. Civic committees would undermine the legal authority of government. They were a call to arms, to destabilise all the socialist states. The Warsaw Pact was under threat from a revanchist and militarist West Germany – 'the true political heir to Hitlerite Germany'.[90]

Gomułka opened a Warsaw Pact summit in the Polish capital (14–15 July) by regretting that Czech colleagues had declined to attend another multilateral meeting. They refused to recognise that the process taking place in their country was a 'peaceful transformation of a socialist state into a republic of a bourgeois type'. Such a 'peaceful counter-revolution' was unprecedented in the history of communist states. It was not an armed counter-revolution of the type seen in Hungary in 1956, nor was it simply the restoration of capitalism of the classical type, since the class basis for restoring the old order had been destroyed. However, neo-capitalism had reared its head, particularly amongst intellectuals, who were using the slogan 'freedom of expression' to create a climate of 'moral and political terror'. The Party had been captured by revisionism. Re-privatisation of the socialised economy would inevitably follow.[91]

There was now unanimity of view. Even Kádár saw the situation as dangerous and deteriorating. Though still reluctant to call it counter-revolutionary, he thought the situation was beginning to resemble that of Yugoslavia. He also thought the next stage would be restoration of the bourgeois order.[92] The five leaders' 'Warsaw Letter' addressed Prague bluntly: 'We are not appearing before you as representatives of an old order trying to prevent you from correcting errors and shortcomings, such as violations of socialist legality that took place in the past.' They had no objection to a more rational economy or to improved relations between Czechs and Slovaks. However, 'we cannot agree to hostile forces pushing

[89] *Literarni listy*, 27 June 1968.
[90] Navrátil (ed.), *The Prague Spring 1968*, pp. 194–8 (4 July 1968).
[91] Garlicki and Paczkowski (eds.), *Zaciskanie pętli*, pp. 120–7. [92] *Ibid.* pp. 132–7.

your country from the socialist path and threatening to tear Czechoslovakia from the socialist commonwealth'. It was necessary to block the path of reaction through the 'solidarity and comprehensive assistance of fraternal socialist parties'; 'This matter is no longer yours alone.'[93]

Twenty Warsaw Pact divisions assembled on Czechoslovakia's borders by the end of July. The Czechoslovak Ambassador to Warsaw reported that 'in the event of disturbance in Warsaw, Soviet units deployed in the vicinity of Warsaw were to intervene'.[94]

During last-ditch negotiations, in a railway carriage on the Slovakian–Ukrainian border, Brezhnev delivered a new doctrine: 'The fate of the socialist gains of the Czechoslovak people and of Czechoslovakia as a socialist state, bound by allied obligations with our country and the other fraternal countries, is not purely an internal affair of the Czechoslovak Communist Party. This is the common affair of the whole commonwealth of socialist countries and of the entire communist movement.'

The Soviet Central Committee believed it had an international duty to see that all measures led to the strengthening of the Czechoslovak Communist Party, to the protection and strengthening of socialism in Czechoslovakia and to the defence of Czechoslovakia from imperialist conspiracies: 'This, I repeat, is our international duty, it is the international duty of all fraternal parties, and we would cease to be communists if we refused to discharge it.'[95]

The five-power invasion of Czechoslovakia, on the night of 21 August 1968, did not cause a major international crisis. At no point was there a likelihood that war would result. On the contrary, American forces in Europe were pulled back some 200 kilometres. When the US Cabinet met (22 August), President Johnson stated, somewhat defensively, 'we did not assume there would be no military intervention'. They had noted the massing of troops on the borders, though the balance of advice had been that they would not go in.

The CIA Director Helms had previously told him (10 August) that the Czechoslovak crisis 'is eased, not over. The Czechs want to reduce commitments to the Warsaw Pact. They made certain assurances. Prague meetings will take place in September. Soviets seek to bring about reforms.'[96] A carefully crafted statement tried to cover the

[93] *Pravda*, 18 July 1968.
[94] Navrátil (ed.), *The Prague Spring, 1968*, p. 298. [95] *Ibid.* p. 286.
[96] LBJ Presidential Library, 'Tom Johnson's Notes of Meetings', Box 3, LBJ Ranch Meeting (10 August 1968), p. 1.

American position. The USA had no commitment to intervene militarily and it would not be in Czech interests for them to do so. Dean Rusk added: 'if there were military intervention [by the US] there would be a world war'. However, 'the "Cold War" was not over' and US relations with the Soviet Union were 'in transition'. The President would go anywhere at any time to further the interests of peace.[97]

This evidently referred to two communications delivered to the President immediately before the invasion. Ambassador Dobrynin gave Secretary Rusk a hand-written note inviting President Johnson to the Soviet Union. It suggested that early October would be convenient.[98] Premier Kosygin wrote to the President agreeing to hold general negotiations on SALT (strategic arms limitations) and ABM (defence systems against ballistic missiles). He suggested the talks convene on 30 September.[99]

NATO had accepted Soviet reassurances that the invasion posed no threat to them. There was not even a general alert. Yet for home consumption, the Soviet Union had argued the opposite: that the invasion was to forestall Western *revanchisme*, even informing incredulous Czechs that West German divisions were massing on their borders. The lessons of US passivity were not lost on Johnson's successors. As we shall see, National Security Adviser Brzeziński was determined that White House inactivity should not be repeated in the crisis over Solidarity. Washington later praised Dubček's calmness in face of the invasion. They told him that any other response would have 'posed a danger, and a danger not only for you, but one that could have meant a catastrophe for all of Europe and ultimately, perhaps for the whole world'.[100]

Popular feeling in Poland continued to support the ideas of the Prague Spring. Flyers appeared in Wrocław: 'Down with the aggression against Czechoslovakia' and 'Crimes against Czechoslovakia'. One anonymous pamphlet drew a parallel with March 1968. Just as Polish society had been silenced by truncheons, tear gas and imprisonment, now the Polish army 'is taking part in the murder of the freedom of our Czechoslovak brothers'. It ended with a call on factory workers to strike: 'Long Live free Czechoslovakia. Long live Polish workers and students. Down with the executioners of freedom'.[101]

97 LBJ Presidential Library, Cabinet (22 August 1968).
98 LBJ Presidential Library, NSF Files of Walt W. Rostow, Box 11 (19 August 1968).
99 LBJ Presidential Library, NSF Files of Walt W. Rostow, Box 15 (20 August 1968).
100 Interview with Dubček of 1990, quoted in LBJ Presidential Library, NSF Files of Walt W. Rostow, Box 15 (20 August 1968), p. 307.
101 Suleja, *Dolnośląski Marzec '68*, pp. 338–9.

In Warsaw, intellectuals' responses were muted. Andrzejewski protested by open letter.[102] Mrożek, now abroad, protested from Paris. But when the Warsaw KIK held a meeting to hear representations from the Kraków KIK on the need for a protest resolution, the proposal was rejected.[103] Jerzy Zawieyski – one of the only two Znak deputies who survived to stand in the elections of 1969 – confided to his diary that it was 'the beginning of the end, which may take a very long time. Communism lies in the mud of Czechoslovak streets. Disgorged and abominated. Nothing can rescue it.'[104]

Czechoslovaks themselves offered a sustained display of passive resistance to an invasion which they had stated in advance would not be met by force. A range of tactics, from fraternisation with invading troops to non-violent civilian resistance, made the post-military part of the invasion most difficult to perform. The American Secretary of State noted that: 'Although the military operation went smoothly, the Russians badly miscalculated the political reactions of the Czechs. All Czechs opposed the movement of Soviet troops into their country. Their performance and discipline were superb. The Russians were unable to organise a puppet government to take over and legitimise their invasion.'[105]

Under a tacit deal, during Husák's extended 'normalisation', economic benefits were promised in exchange for political conformity, passivity and acquiescence. Some 450,000 ex-communists were excluded from this deal, and lost both their Party cards and employment, or took work far below their qualifications. The result was an impasse. On the tenth anniversary, Adam Michnik noted: 'A long wave of neo-Stalinism engulfed Czechoslovakia. One would like to believe that Polish forces will never again be used to offer this kind of "fraternal assistance".'[106]

A CIA round-up report 'Restless Youth' noted a generation gap in Poland. Half the population was under twenty-five but these younger Poles did not favour a return to private ownership or the pre-war social system. They appeared most 'to oppose the stagnation and lack of movement, the exclusiveness and corruption of the establishment'. Communist ideology was seen as irrelevant: 'a dead letter with only its institutional forms still prevailing'. Like most ruling communist parties, the Polish Party was seen as a 'core of a stagnant society rather than a dynamic stimulant to change'. In attitudes, 'students favoured a form of West-European social democracy', a non-sectarian approach to religion

[102] *Le Monde*, 27 September 1968. [103] Friszke, *Oaza na Kopernika*, p. 101.
[104] *Ibid.* p. 104. [105] LBJ Presidential Library, NSC (590), 4 September 1968.
[106] A. Michnik, *Letters from Prison and Other Essays* (Berkeley, 1985), pp. 155–9; *Gazeta Wyborcza*, 4 July 1989.

and experimental freedom in the arts.[107] Their nationalism was tempered by 'vague feelings of supra-nationalism and a strong allegiance to Europe as an entity'.[108] It was this last concern that East European leaders, including Gomułka, began to address.

[107] See Z. Ośinski, *Grotowski and His Laboratory* (New York, 1986); Klara Kemp-Welch, 'Excursions in Communist reality: Tadeusz Kantor's Impossible Happenings', *Object* (UCL) 2005/6 (8).

[108] LBJ Presidential Library, NSF, CIA Report 'Restless Youth' (September 1968).

8 *Détente*

The crushing of the Prague Spring was a turning-point in the conduct of the Cold War. For the first time, the Soviet Union, 'in collusion with other powers, acted as a deliberate aggressor without even the pretence of legality behind it'.[1] Unlike the Hungarians in 1956, the Czechs and Slovaks had remained loyal to the Warsaw Pact. A joint document, signed in Bratislava on 4 August, affirmed the sovereignty of Czechoslovakia and the inviolability of its borders. Since this had been torn up less than three weeks later, the question arose whether the Soviet government could be trusted in international relations again.

The invasion had two further consequences. Whilst spillover in Moscow was short-lived – a small demonstration in Red Square and student murmurings – citizens in other Union Republics became more engaged. The Politburo complained (11 September) that 'events in Czechoslovakia are still giving rise to illegal nationalist activities' in Ukraine. Nationalists were 'disseminating vile sentiments and malicious fabrications' intended to stir up bourgeois notions of an 'independent Ukraine'.[2] Secondly, the impact on Sino-Soviet relations was severe. The 1968 invasion, and the border clashes which began on the Ussuri River in March 1969, were reasons given by the Chinese Premier for naming the Soviet Union as China's 'main enemy'. Faced with Soviet expansionism, China would seek a common front with the USA.[3]

NATO was initially alarmed that Moscow might move elsewhere in Europe. The most likely target was thought to be Romania. Rusk told the NSC of the possibility of the movement of nineteen Soviet divisions into Romania within two or three days. There was also potentially an attack on Yugoslavia and Albania or even neutral Austria or Finland.

1 P. Windsor and A. Roberts, *Czechoslovakia 1968. Reform, Repression and Resistance* (London, 1969), p. 3.
2 Kramer, 'The Czechoslovak Crisis and the Brezhnev Doctrine' in Fink *et al.* (eds.), *1968*, p. 163.
3 *Ibid.* p. 165.

Did this mean an end to the *détente* which had become an important Western objective? The NSC was inclined to see August 1968 as 'a cold *douche* for the future of *détente* or the progressive rapprochement of East and West'. Though progress had been undermined by the invasion, the West's 'relatively limited actions' did not preclude 'the possibility of return in due course to the pursuit of *détente*'.[4]

Soviet diplomats continued to reassure the White House. Ambassador Dobrynin told President Johnson (4 September) that US state interests were not affected by the Soviet action. The President replied that 'US interests are involved in Berlin where we are committed to prevent the city being overrun by the Russians.' He told the NSC that for the past five years the greatest problem had been how to improve relations between the two powers: 'Many Pen Pal letters have been sent in an effort to establish greater confidence.'[5] The strong indication is that both super-powers wished *détente* to develop. However, there were grounds for thinking that the relationship could not continue as before.

Vojtech Mastny argues that 1968 was a 'strategic watershed' of the Cold War. It helped to highlight the unreality of the super-powers' nuclear rivalry. In additional to massive stock-piling beyond any possible use, both sides had an incoherent strategic doctrine. They were preparing for a military conflict in Central Europe which would not involve nuclear weapons. Yet neither side was able to show its alliance partners, particularly those living in the potential battlefield of Central Europe, how such an escalation could be avoided. The Czech General Staff concluded that, because of their country's geographical location, 'annihilation in a nuclear war was all but certain'.[6] Similar conclusions had already been reached in Western Europe.

The French right had questioned the NATO alliance at least since Suez. It appeared that Soviet–American collusion had created a new condominium after Cuba, which suited the super-powers much more than its client states, especially in Europe. De Gaulle therefore sought *détente* in Europe as an alternative to the continent being permanently divided by the super-powers.[7] The replacement of the 'adventurist' Khrushchev seemed a good moment to seek a more stable relationship with the East. While being careful not to alarm Moscow, where he made a spectacular visit in June 1966, De Gaulle also sought to woo the East

[4] LBJ Presidential Library, NSC (590), 'The US, Europe and the Czechoslovak Crisis', 4 September 1968.
[5] LBJ Presidential Library, NSC (590), 4 September 1968.
[6] V. Mastny, 'Was 1968 a Strategic Watershed of the Cold War?' *Diplomatic History* January 2005 (29.1).
[7] F. Bozo, *La Politique étrangère de la France depuis 1945* (Paris, 1997).

European states, particularly Poland and Romania with which France had pre-war ties.

His visit to Warsaw (September 1967), however, met with a stinging public rebuff from Gomułka: 'Between the two world wars, Poland and France were linked in a political and military alliance. For many reasons which I shall not mention today, the alliance functioned badly, and it did not save either Poland or France from the catastrophe of defeat. Reborn Poland has drawn all the conclusions from this historic experience.' Poland's overwhelming need was an alliance with its great Eastern neighbour as 'the basic guarantee of its security'. The Soviet alliance had enabled Poland to return to 'a permanent and important place in Europe, a place which our Fatherland has been unsuccessfully seeking since the eighteenth century'.[8]

Gaullists questioned the division of Europe into 'blocs'. They sought to foster a process whereby the Soviet Union became more cooperative towards the West and less restrictive of its alliance partners, while simultaneously allowing Western Europe to become more autonomous of its transatlantic super-power. But the debate within NATO had reached a quite different conclusion. The Harmel report (December 1967) called for *détente* to become a NATO policy.[9] It was to be a *détente* between the blocs whose functioning Gaullism had sought to diminish.

A second opening to the East, Brandt's *Ostpolitik*, may be traced back to 1961. It was a response to the building of the Wall when he was Mayor of West Berlin. Division of the city had joined division of the country as a permanent part of *Realpolitik*. The principal ideas of the new policy have been excellently summarised by Gottfried Neidhart: (1) while post-war realities should be accepted, increased East–West communication could lead to gradual change; (2) just as the West had legitimate strategic interests, so too did the other side. Recognition of the status quo was a precondition for overcoming it; (3) this applied particularly to Soviet predominance in Eastern Europe, which should be acknowledged as a prelude to change; (4) the division of Germany would last for as long as the division of Europe itself, and could only be overcome through cooperation with the Soviet Union; (5) as part of the process, West Germany 'should look after its interests with respect to the East in a more vigorous way'.[10] As Foreign Minister in the 'Grand Coalition' from November

[8] W. Gomułka, *Trybuna Ludu* 12 September 1967.

[9] J. Stromseth, *The Origins of Flexible Response. NATO's Debate over Strategy in the 1960s* (New York, 1988).

[10] G. Neidhart, 'Ostpolitik. The Role of the Federal Republic of Germany in the Process of Détente' in Fink *et al.* (eds.), *1968*, pp. 175–6.

1966, Brandt accepted that *détente* in Europe was a precondition for resolving the German–German question. He argued that the policy must continue despite the invasion of August 1968. The Soviet intervention in Czechoslovakia merely confirmed what had already been acknowledged in principle (3) above.

Brandt's *Ostpolitik* did not sit easily with the ideas of the incoming Nixon administration. Nixon and Kissinger were intent on bi-lateral *détente* with the Soviet Union and were reluctant to have this overshadowed by initiatives from West Germany.[11] The solution was to coordinate both policies closely. As Kissinger put it: 'If *Ostpolitik* were to succeed, it had to be related to other issues involving the (Atlantic) Alliance as a whole: only in this manner would the Soviet Union have incentives for compromise.'[12] This was a form of linkage that Brandt both understood and was willing to accept.

Hanhimaki sees Kissinger as a 'Flawed Architect' who was unable to break out of the more persistent paradigms of the Cold War. Making the containment of Soviet power the central goal of American foreign policy, he pursued bi-lateral – and later, with China, tri-lateral – diplomacy. His designs failed to take into account the complexities of ongoing regional conflicts. Soviet–American *détente* was undermined particularly by the 1973 Middle East War and the conflicts in Southern Africa. His *Realpolitik* 'proved a poor match with the realities of the third world'.[13]

A more radical notion sees *détente* as having a social origin that scholars have neglected: 'It was a convergent response to disorder among the great powers.'[14] Faced with turbulent populations, political leaders drew back from their ideological differences. Both East and West colluded to stabilise their domestic societies and stay in power: 'The promise of *détente* became a stick with which to beat domestic critics.'[15]

Perhaps the most lasting legacy of *détente* was one least expected: the Conference on Security and Cooperation in Europe. First mooted by Molotov back in 1954, the proposal made clear that the United States and Canada were not invited. The initiative was revisited by the Polish Foreign Minister Adam Rapacki, at the United Nations General Assembly in December 1964. It was reaffirmed by the Warsaw Pact a month later. Soviet leaders envisaged a pan-European gathering at the 'highest political level', preferably crowned by a banquet in the Kremlin,

[11] J. Hanhimaki, *The Flawed Architect. Henry Kissinger and American Foreign Policy* (Oxford, 2004).
[12] H. Kissinger, *White House Years* (Boston, 1979), p. 410.
[13] Hanhimaki, *The Flawed Architect*, Preface.
[14] Suri, *Power and Protest*, p. 2. [15] *Ibid.* p. 261.

to put the post-war European settlement on a more formal footing. Following this grand initiative, junior officials could sort out technical details behind the scenes. But the West, thinking the devil is in the detail, thought talks should come first. An open invitation 'to discuss measures ensuring collective security in Europe' was not easy to refuse. But in what sense was it compatible with Brezhnev's Doctrine?

Brezhnev explained the invasion of Czechoslovakia, at the Fifth Polish Party Congress in November 1968, as 'an extraordinary step, dictated by necessity'. He offered no justification for the use of military power and no basis in international law. Instead, he clothed the unprovoked attack within the broadest ideological framework. The inevitable struggle between socialism and imperialism had reached a new stage. Having been held at bay by the threat of nuclear retaliation, imperialism was still playing its old game. Using 'anti-socialist' elements in senior positions, it hoped to subvert the Communist Party. Czechoslovakia's gradual conversion to a Western orientation, through economic ties, would lead to eventual secession from the Warsaw Pact.[16] Once this had happened, Brezhnev continued – this time to a gathering of 'Polish workers' – there would be a change of regime in Poland and the DDR, the assimilation of East into West Germany and denunciation of the Warsaw Pact. Faced with these audacious aspirations, the socialist commonwealth had acted in self-defence. Czechoslovakian state sovereignty, whilst still intact, had to take second place to the 'sacred duty' of acting on behalf of 'the socialist solidarity of the socialist commonwealth'.

This argument was circular. The Warsaw Pact would invade (itself) wherever socialism was in danger: but the defining of danger, and of socialism, was done in Moscow. In 1956, the Hungarians had abandoned the monopoly of their Communist Party and left the Warsaw Pact. The Czechs and Slovaks had done neither, yet the outcome was just the same. Brezhnev's Doctrine seemed a *carte blanche* for interventionism.

One Western option was to offset the Brezhnev Doctrine by addressing the Soviet Union's wider aim: recognition as a global super-power. Moscow's chosen instrument was *détente* and the main means was arms control with the United States. It hoped for rapid expansion of East–West trade to remedy the growing lag of Soviet technology in many spheres. Military competition, with the huge increases in expenditure under Kennedy–McNamara, and the corresponding rises that ushered in the Brezhnev period, encouraged a mutual recognition that the costs of the arms race were becoming prohibitive. There might be the makings of a

[16] Navrátil, *The Prague Spring 1968*, pp. 502–3.

package here. But could Moscow be trusted as a partner in any deal following her so recent military intervention? And if the Soviet Union did settle down as a global super-power, with the United States' active assistance, would this leave Europe a permanent victim of bi-polarity?

British diplomats interpreted the Soviet move as calculated to prove 'usefully divisive' of the Western Alliance. It did indeed put the West at a disadvantage, however it responded. Acceptance could set the Yalta division of Europe in stone, thus freezing the status quo on the continent indefinitely. Rejection would give 'the Russians and their allies a propaganda line which they would be able to put to good effect'.[17] Western governments therefore advanced a cunning addendum. This supplemented the Soviet strategic (military) and economic agenda, with a 'third basket' to enshrine human rights, proposed by NATO in May 1970. Western policy-makers were confident that this would discourage the Soviet Union from pressing ahead with its project. If, however, Moscow did persist, it would eventually have to sign up to a newly formulated set of common principles for the future of Europe. These might include an explicit statement of humanitarian objectives which could have beneficial consequences, though no one at this stage envisaged quite how influential they would be. The prevalent assumption was that, even if formally accepted, they would be acknowledged mainly by non-observance.

Super-power *détente* was a combination of talks and competition.[18] Talks sprang from the need for strategic understandings to rebuild confidence following the near *débâcle* over Cuba. Competition continued almost to the end of communist rule. For the super-powers, the Cold War in Europe required a permanent division of the continent. But Europeans themselves canvassed alternatives almost from the outset. The Polish historian Oscar Halecki elegantly suggested that the balance-of-power system, to which Europe had been reduced for centuries, remained incomplete when the third, and possibly fourth, 'basic region' of Europe was ignored.[19] He meant 'West-Central' and 'East-Central' Europe, existing or seeking to exist between East and West.

Ostpolitik

All her neighbours shared fears of German reunification, but West Germany insisted that this was its objective. In this sense, the Germans

[17] G. Bennett and K. Hamilton (eds.), *Documents on British Policy Overseas*, series III, vol. II (London, 1997) (20 March 1972).

[18] A. de Tinguy, *US–Soviet Relations During the Détente* (New York, 1999), pp. 147–8.

[19] O. Halecki, *The Limits and Divisions of European History* (London, 1950), pp. 125–41.

were the only people who did not accept the post-war settlement on the continent. Europe's post-war generation, while pleased to see an end to Franco-German confrontation, was uncomfortable with the call for eternal loyalty to one or other of the over-arching blocs that had sprung up so recently. Though the Warsaw Pact (formed in 1955) was periodically overt in assuring domestic control, it did not necessarily pose a military threat to non-member countries. Despite the XXth Congress's abandonment of Lenin's theory of imperialism, Moscow still held the final victory of communism to be assured, but not as the outcome of a third World War since that would only result in mutual annihilation.

Younger Europeans were prone to question, if not to reject outright, the need for large standing armies in peacetime. History had no precedent for sovereign nations pledging to defend each other and all members in a permanent alliance. The stationing of new and ever more lethal weapons in Western Europe, to compensate for the Red Army's conventional superiority, invariably provoked political questions. Many citizens found Europe's division into two military blocs unacceptable, and, when ascribed solely to the machinations of Soviet imperialism, simplistic. Of course, one problem for such youthful critics was the Soviet Union's periodic confirmation of the thesis. But its Eastern European military incursions could also be seen as the rearguard of a status-quo power, struggling to hold on to reluctant allies. That suggested scope for a change of relations.

The view emerged fitfully in Europe, though more consistently in Germany, that the two power-blocs were not immutable. A stalemate might suit the big two, but was mightily uncomfortable for those who lived under it, not least because NATO strategy was based on first use of nuclear weapons to offset conventional inferiority. Even if explained as a relic of history, perhaps entered into by muddle or mistake, the status quo seemed dangerous. But could it be unfrozen without upsetting the delicate 'balance of terror'? Where would that leave the 'great contest' between rival systems?

European *détente* was given impetus by *Ostpolitik*: openings to the East within Europe itself. Whilst following the general oscillations of superpower relations, the German approach had aspects of its own. Under the Hallstein Doctrine (1955), Bonn alone could represent the German state: thus the DDR was denied any recognition, as were states that conferred recognition on it, apart from the USSR. But, from the end of 1966, the newly installed West German Foreign Minister, and later German Chancellor, Willy Brandt pursued a diplomatic path towards his Eastern neighbours. *Ostpolitik* confronted the Germans with 'the reality of their military defeat in 1945, which had created boundaries and new realities which needed to be respected'.[20] Originally, he had intended to take the route to Berlin via Warsaw, with which talks began in February 1970. On Russian insistence, the diplomacy started further east.

To Brandt, openings to the East were necessary steps on the road to German reunification. To the East German leaders, they were an opportunity for greater legitimacy and 'statehood'. Moscow concurred, insisting that full legal recognition of East Germany was a precondition for Bonn–Moscow negotiations. In the event, the Moscow Treaty (12 August 1970) did not include such recognition, though this was the first official document in which the Federal Republic acknowledged that the DDR existed. A separate note to the Soviet Foreign Ministry stated the West German goal of eventual German unity.[21]

The Treaty undertook 'unconditional respect for the territorial integrity in their present borders of all the countries of Europe'. Only one was in serious dispute, as recognised in Article 3: 'All European borders are inviolable both now and in the future, including the Oder-Neisse line, which constitutes the western border of the Polish People's Republic and the border between the Federal German Republic and the German Democratic Republic.' Whilst critics of *détente* claimed that this was a 'brilliant diplomatic success' for the Soviet Union, gaining recognition for an East European regime based principally on brute force,[22] there were wider implications for Europe. Poland in particular was the beneficiary. As a German author memorably noted: 'A nation that has for two hundred years been partitioned, conquered, suppressed, treated as inferior and regarded as incapable of forming a state, and finally threatened with permanent slavery and extermination needs certainties upon which to support itself internally and externally.'[23] The key was boundaries. For Poles, 'the frontier question is the national question for the whole country'.[24] It was now to be sanctified on home soil.

Kneeling before the monument to fighters who fell in the Warsaw Ghetto,[25] marking its rising against German occupation in 1943, Willy Brandt

> expressed what words could not say adequately, the acceptance of guilt, the sorrow for unspeakable crimes committed by Germans against millions of innocent people. This gesture captured the imagination of the world and did a great

[20] B. Marshall, *Willy Brandt: A Political Biography* (London, 1997), p. 3.
[21] M. Sarotte, *Dealing with the Devil. East Germany, Détente, and Ostpolitik 1969–1973* (Chapel Hill, 2001), pp. 68–9.
[22] A. Ulam, *Dangerous Relations. The Soviet Union in World Politics, 1970–1982* (Oxford, 1983), p. 64.
[23] P. Bender, *East Europe in Search of Security* (London, 1972), p. 52. [24] *Ibid.* p. 53.
[25] W. Brandt, *People and Politics. The Years 1960–1975* (London, 1978), p. 399.

deal to restore respect for Germany. It singled out Brandt as a politician with a moral dimension which had been lacking in his predecessors.[26]

Another Treaty was concluded which recognised the Oder-Neisse line as Poland's western frontier and declared existing borders inviolable. West Germany and Poland had 'no territorial claims on each other and will not raise such claims in the future'. They would settle all future disagreements by political means, and refrain from 'the threat or use of force in all issues concerning European or international security as well as in their mutual relations'. They established diplomatic relations, and set in motion the transfer of population which eventually resettled 125,000 Polish citizens of German origin.

The Treaty was significant for two further reasons. Firstly, by putting to rest the spectre of 'West German *revanchisme*', Poland's communists abandoned a long-standing propaganda weapon for domestic consumption. It undermined the *raison d'état* argument they had long relied on. Prior to the Treaty it could be asserted that Russia acted as Poland's protector, and was therefore at worst a necessary ally in the struggle against West German *revanchisme*. Once West Germany had ratified the Treaty, that argument became void. Secondly, Poland was granted access to the largest and most dynamic economy in Europe. In return, West Germany agreed to promote and co-finance Poland's economic growth through Western borrowings. It was an opening both sides exploited fully in the coming decade.

Signing the Polish–German Treaty (7 December 1970) was the apex of Gomułka's international career. Brezhnev had acclaimed him at the recent Polish Party Congress as 'a true son of his nation, immutable Leninist, distinguished activist of the international workers' movement and great friend of the Soviet Union'. Yet the immutable Leninist fell, as a result of workers' protests, within a fortnight.

Polish workers

By November 1970, many Polish families spent half their budget on food. A decade's stagnation of real wages left them in no position to pay more. But the Politburo resolved on increases of 40 per cent on basic foodstuffs. They were to be accompanied by reductions on expensive durables (television sets, kitchen appliances). Since these were way beyond the reach of ordinary households, this clumsy attempt at camouflage would cause additional resentment. Some Party leaders wanted to 'start the New

[26] Marshall, *Willy Brandt*, p. 72.

Year with new prices' and others to begin at once. A compromise date was agreed: ten days before Christmas. This proved to be Gomułka's last Politburo.

In retirement, he pointed out that his successor – despite subsequently claiming to have been absent – had confirmed the price rises.[27] When asked to predict reactions 'from the working class and society' in his region of responsibility, Gierek had replied: 'It will be tough, but we can handle it.'[28] Silesia did indeed remain quiescent. Beyond such routine consultation, Gomułka refused all debate. When one member, an academic, challenged the policy, he replied, 'Don't lecture me on Marxist economics.'[29] This was possibly the last mention of Marxism in the Politburo.

Protests were expected. Riot brigades and 'special operational groups' were placed on full alert, to protect 'public order' during the misleadingly entitled 'Plan for Securing Enactment of National Economic Reform'. Secret-police informants were to report on the oppositional groups they had infiltrated and recommend preventive arrests where necessary. 'Price changes' were nodded through the Politburo (11 December) which then moved on to appoint a new Ambassador to Lebanon.[30] An explanatory letter was to be read to the Party faithful.

Readings led to indignation amongst the *aktyw*, not least because their own obedient support was taken for granted. Party audiences greeted the announced rises with shock and dismay, some tearfully, and a few with bitter laughter. There were numerous 'breaches of Party discipline' – some members tore up their Party cards on the spot and many meetings dissolved in chaos. Such nationwide responses were immediately conveyed to Warsaw. Hence the authorities' later claim that public protest could not have been anticipated was invalid.

The increases were announced on TV and radio on Saturday evening. Shops opened specially on Sunday with the new prices. To most citizens, the timing was provocative. They needed to make provision for Christmas Eve. Why had the authorities not delayed the increases until January? The 'spectre of hunger' arose. Older citizens recalled the 'change of money' in 1950 which had rendered their savings worthless and talked of withdrawing their current savings from the National Bank. During the day, secret policemen collected numerous flyers and

27 Andrzejewski (Paczkowski) (ed.), *Gomułka i inni*, pp. 194–6.

28 J. Eisler, *Grudzień 1970. Geneza, przebieg, konsekwencje* (Warsaw, 2000), p. 79.

29 J. Eisler and S. Trepczyński (eds.), *Grudzień 70 wewnątrz 'Białego Domu'* (Warsaw, 1991), p. 93.

30 P. Domański (ed.), *Tajne dokumenty Biura Politycznego. Grudzień 1970* (London, 1991), p. 9.

pamphlets calling for strike action. Monitoring sermons, they found just a handful commenting on the increases, then mostly in passing. But one Bishop, Kominek of Wrocław, had preached that they would ruin low-income families.[31]

The Gdańsk region became the centre of worker protests. Social anthropologists explain that the former Danzig had been re-populated, following the enormous civilian war casualties, flight of refugees, imprisonment and expulsion of remaining Germans, and resettlement of persons displaced from the East.[32] Sociologists note the high concentration in this region of young workers, most of whom had joined the labour force after 1956, thus escaping both wartime tribulations and Stalinism.[33] Housing shortages were the major problem of daily life, with hundreds put up in shipyard dormitories. The waiting-time for a tiny apartment was ten years.

On Monday 12 December, Party officials at the Gdańsk Shipyard met at 5 a.m. to discuss tactics. They settled on a simple argument. Since the increases could not be changed, protest was pointless. As the day shift came on, supervisors urged them straight to work. Ignoring their instructions, workers loitered in the locker-rooms, talking together in small groups. They were not yet on strike, simply failing to start up machinery. The atmosphere became tenser. Workers formulated their first demand: that the price increase be rescinded. Foremen and Party officials began to melt away. This removed a critical buffer between the authorities and the workforce. Some 3,000 employees gathered outside the Director's office.

The Director pointed out he did not formulate macro-economic policy of the state. Nor was he in any position to explain. Protestors replied he could use the hotline to Warsaw. Workers sat on their safety helmets, ignoring calls for a return to work and the promise of cash bonuses. While they waited, about 1,000 workers formed up at Gate Two and marched into town, joined by passers-by en route. The crowd sang patriotic anthems and the 'Internationale'. The mood was calm, though determined. A number of unflattering epithets were aimed at the authorities: 'Thieves from the Polish Working-Class' and 'Down with the Red Bourgeoisie'. The procession halted outside the provincial Party building, whose windows and blinds had been closed. Officials peered out occasionally. A delegation was admitted but did not reappear. Rumours spread that they had been arrested.

[31] J. Eisler (ed.), *Grudzień 1970 w dokumentach MSW* (Warsaw, 2000), p. 54.

[32] C. Tighe, *Gdańsk. National Identity in the Polish–German Borderlands* (London, 1990), pp. 210–12.

[33] R. Laba, *The Roots of Solidarity. A Political Sociology of Poland's Working-Class Democratization* (Princeton, 1991), pp. 118–19.

At noon, a delegation of top officials arrived from Warsaw, including the Gdańsk Party Secretary Kociołek. As in Poznań in 1956, they drove straight to Party headquarters and remained behind closed doors. No-one came out to address the crowd. Faced with an ominous silence, they rigged up a loudspeaker system and speeches began. They all made clear that responsibility for the price increases lay with the political authorities. Such instant escalation of claims can only be explained by the structure of the one-Party state. There were soon calls for the resignation of Gomułka and members of his team.

Workers broke through the locked gates of Gdańsk Technical University and confronted the Rector. They attempted to enlist support. But most students, threatened with expulsion, stayed within their dormitories and were soon sent home early for Christmas. Some did join the protest, and students were amongst the categories of citizens arrested by the militia. In the late afternoon, riot police were brought up, with their long, heavily weighted batons and tear gas, to disperse the demonstrators. They tried to clear a path through crowds, now swollen by schoolchildren.

An initial show of force failed to silence the protests. The crowds continued chanting 'We want bread! We want truth!' In the early evening, the Party building came under attack from two groups of arsonists from the increasingly frustrated crowds. Another flash-point was the main railway station. About 10,000 people went on the rampage. Looting took place, particularly of luxury items such as furs. Symbols of privilege and status, such as cars parked in front of the Hotel Monopol, were set on fire. Twenty militiamen were hospitalised, five with serious injuries. No figures for civilian casualties were recorded. The militia announced 16 arrests 'for vandalism and petty theft'. This figure was rightly disbelieved. Secret reports to Warsaw reported 330 arrests.[34] Release of all those detained became a new demand.

Telegraphic communications were severed between Gdańsk and the outside world. Intended to isolate and demoralise the strikers, this had the opposite effect. Gdańsk protestors assumed, wrongly, that the rest of the country was also on strike. Secret-police reports show a patchy response elsewhere, mostly confined to flyers bearing legends such as 'Shipyard workers – we are with you.'[35] Only in the port of Szczecin were there any serious stirrings.

Next day, the strike spread across the Gdańsk region. Workers marched to the militia headquarters, which they attempted to storm

[34] Eisler (ed.), *Grudzień 1970 w dokumentach MSW*, pp. 56–7. [35] *Ibid.* pp. 62–4.

with stones and improvised weapons, leaving many injured on both sides. The first fatality occurred. A militiaman pulled out a pistol and shot dead a demonstrator: 'He had no chance to fire again. The crowd was on him. Everyone wanted a souvenir. He was pulled to pieces.' Shooting began from the roof of the police building. When the first tanks appeared, two demonstrators were squashed to death.

Beaten back, the insurgents returned to the Party headquarters, which had been garrisoned by 160 Internal Security troops overnight. It was soon surrounded by at least 10,000 demonstrators, with new arrivals all the time from the electric railway linking the three cities of Gdańsk, Gdynia and Sopot. Wine bottles filled with petrol were lobbed through the first floor windows. The building was soon on fire. Soldiers were allowed out. The militia were asked to surrender, but had no order to do so. It was pointed out to them that little help would come from the helicopter with ropes hovering overhead. Many took off their insignia and protective clothing. They were carried to safety on trucks and their uniforms were raised up on flag poles.

Gomułka convened an emergency cabinet to consider the news from Gdańsk. Emphasis was put on the wounded militiamen, the burning of public buildings, and general disorder. A local state of emergency was declared, with a curfew from 6 p.m. to 6 a.m. Gomułka gave the order that firearms were to be used by army and police to defend lives (including their own) and public buildings. Following warnings, including shots in the air, approaching crowds could be halted by rounds of live ammunition: 'salvos to the legs'.[36] This decision was immediately communicated to General Korczyński, commanding a five-man 'task force' on the coast. Some 27,000 troops were dispatched to Gdańsk and Szczecin, with 550 tanks and hundreds of armoured vehicles.[37] They were under the direct command of the Minister of Defence, General Jaruzelski, who would be responsible for issuing any orders to fire. Other large-scale forces were deployed in twelve industrial centres, including Kraków, Łódź and Wrocław. They had standing orders to break any supporting strikes that might occur.[38]

Finding tanks and armoured vehicles stationed outside the Gdańsk Shipyard was a novel experience for workers. Occupiers of the yard wondered how things had come to such a pass. A young electrician, Lech Wałęsa, recalls a complex of emotions: 'despair, desire for revenge and a confused sense of immunity. Most people didn't believe that the

[36] Eisler, *Grudzień 1970 w dokumentach MSW*, p. 136.
[37] Domański (ed.), *Tajne dokumenty BP*, p. 85.
[38] A. Michta, *Red Eagle. The Army in Polish Politics, 1944–1988* (Stanford, 1990), pp. 68–9.

army or security forces were really getting ready to attack our workers, or that the decision to fire would be made.'[39]

Soldiers were told that 'hooligans' had taken over the Shipyard. As they drew up in front of the Gates, their orders were ambiguous: 'Shoot in the air at first; then, depending on the situation . . .'. They had received a packet of cigarettes a day, and hot meals, but 'no pills'.[40] The public was reluctant to believe they had anything other than blanks, but soldiers fraternised and showed their live ammunition. A number of conscripts surrendered to the crowd when they realised that it consisted of Poles such as themselves, not the invading 'Germans' of their official briefing. But no wider communication with the soldiers was effected. Since Shipyard management was not willing to get involved, continuing to treat the protested issues as beyond their competence, and the higher authorities offered nothing, tragedy was now obviously imminent.

On the Tuesday, a group of young workers sallying forth from Gate Two were met with a salvo of bullets, killing two outright and fatally wounding a third.[41] The corpses were taken inside. As Roman Laba puts it: 'In this desperate situation, the workers called on ritual and symbol. Like an antique chorus in a Greek tragedy, they turned the massacre into a kind of national rite in which the dead workers were the human sacrifices.'[42] The making of their martyrdom was begun. With a police helicopter circling overhead, and armoured vehicles impeding ambulances coming to the many wounded on the ground, the workers' slogan became 'Murderers'. The national flag was flown at half-mast. A new stage of the strike had begun. Polish radio and television news made their first reference to disturbances in Gdańsk, attributing them to hooligans and criminals. There was no mention of strikes.

Next day in Szczecin, shipyard workers at the vast Warski yard sought talks with the Director. But his only response was 'Don't march on the city or we'll have another Czechoslovakia, another Hungary.' Ignoring his advice, they marched into town. The notion was to present demands to the Party Secretary, but he refused to address 'the mob'. No senior official was found inside the Party building, which was set on fire. The enraged crowd then moved on to the prison to release those arrested earlier in the day. Other official buildings were incinerated, including the procuracy and headquarters of the trade unions. As the police and army opened fire, the crowd scattered, leaving bodies on the ground.

39 Wałęsa, *A Path of Hope*, pp. 69–70.
40 Finnish TV film *Monument*. Shown in the UK on 12 February 1985.
41 Eisler, *Grudzień 1970 w dokumentach MSW*, pp. 175–80.
42 Laba, *Roots of Solidarity*, p. 44.

Confrontation in Gdynia was even grimmer.[43] Early-morning trains brought in thousands of commuters, answering a televised appeal for a 'return to normal work'. As they pushed towards the Shipyard gates, to make way for hundreds more arriving on the next trains, loudspeakers gave the impossible command to halt and disperse. It declared that the Shipyard was closed. If anyone should attack the Shipyard, it would be defended.[44] It was a trap, with no way out. Automatic rifles firing warning shots at the pavements were sufficient to cause havoc as they ricocheted from cobblestones. At least 1,164 were wounded. Then the order was given to fire machine guns directly into the crowds. The dead from Gdynia's 'Black Thursday' were carried through the streets on make-shift biers. The armed forces fired on intermittently, causing further casualties. The official death toll (forty-four) was an underestimate.[45]

The Soviet Politburo sent its Polish counterpart a 'top secret' letter expressing 'active disquiet' about the 'complicated situation' in Poland. Pleading lack of full information, it hoped there would soon be the restoration of order. It saw an 'unstable political situation' in which 'the crucial connection between the Party and the working class is currently weakened in several cities'.[46] This had allowed 'the activisation of anti-socialist elements'. The conflict should be resolved as soon as possible 'by political means, by persuasion'. But Moscow did not show how this could be achieved. Gierek commented afterwards that the Russians could support 'only political [means], only economic and so on'.[47]

Szczecin workers declared occupations.[48] A city-wide committee was formed from their delegates. This was a vital precursor to the Interfactory Strike Committee in the Gdańsk region a decade later. Minister of Defence Jaruzelski told the Politburo: 'The situation in Szczecin is critical, in effect a general strike.' Openly anti-Party and anti-Russian statements had not been manifest. Rather, it was 'characteristic of the events in Szczecin' that demands did not go beyond the economic sphere. The human costs of 'pacification on the coast' numbered thirty-five deaths so far, including one militiaman. He had received disquieting signals from other regions. There were strikes in seven voivodships. Soldiers were

[43] W. Kwaśniewska, *Grudzień '70 w Gdyni* (Warsaw, 1986), pp. 40–80.
[44] H. Kula, *Dwa Oblicza Grudnia '70. Oficjalne-Rzeczywiste* (Gdańsk, 2000), pp. 217–37.
[45] P. Jeglinski (ed.), *Grudzień 1970* (Paris, 1986), p. 73 note 1.
[46] Paczkowski (ed.), *Tajne dokumenty Biura Politycznego*, pp. 661–2.
[47] E. Wacowska, *Rewolta Szczecińska i jej znaczenie* (Paris, 1971), p. 37.
[48] M. Szejnert and T. Zalewski, *Szczecin: Grudzień-Sierpień-Grudzień* (Warsaw, 1984), pp. 27–49.

being addressed as 'Gestapo' or 'Murderers' and the families of officers had been threatened.[49]

A few voices of moderation were heard. Mieczysław Jagielski, the Politburo member vital to the peaceful settlement of August 1980, saw a double conflict: between the working class and the Party, and between the rank-and-file Party organisation and the leadership. Military means could not resolve the situation, which required a political solution without delay.[50] Jędrychowski – the only Politburo member to have opposed the price increase – saw economic decisions as vital. The working class should be given 'something specific' as soon as possible. Further delay could only inflame the situation. He supported the view that Gierek should become acting First Secretary since Gomułka was now in hospital.[51]

Gomułka received scant support from Moscow. After haranguing Soviet Ambassador Aristov to no avail,[52] he had a telephone conversation with Brezhnev. The Russians were unresponsive to his explanation that 'counter-revolutionary elements, diversionaries inspired by imperialist circles' had caused the events in Poland. Nor were they convinced by Gomułka's explanation that a portion of the working class had mutinied – like the sailors at Kronstadt in 1921 – and needed to be pacified, as Lenin had done, by military means. The Kremlin would not support military repression on the coast. However, it would provide 'political support and credits, including hard currency, to rescue the parlous material position of the Polish economy'.[53]

Leadership change had already seemed implicit in the Moscow letter. Its silences were eloquent. The use of force was not endorsed. Gomułka, in power since 1956 and elder statesman of the bloc, was not even mentioned. The snub suggested that Soviet confidence in him, and his handling of the December crisis, had been exhausted.

Gomułka and four close associates, including the Prime Minister, Cyrankiewicz, were removed from the Politburo. New First Secretary Gierek declared modest ambitions. At fifty-eight, he was nearing the end of his career. Top offices might in future be filled by rotation. He did not rule out proposing another candidate for First Secretary to the next Party Congress.[54] But Gierek did not reiterate these innovative proposals to an emergency Plenum.[55] He ruled for a decade.

[49] Domański (ed.), *Tajne dokumenty BP*, pp. 87–8. [50] *Ibid.* p. 91. [51] *Ibid.* p. 94.
[52] Eisler, *Grudzień 1970*, p. 202. [53] *Ibid.* pp. 238–41.
[54] A. Dudek, A. Kochański and K. Persak (eds.), *Centrum Władzy. Protokoły posiedzeń kierownictwa PZPR. Wybór z lat 1949–1970* (Warsaw, 2000).
[55] Domański (ed.), *Tajne dokumenty BP*, pp. 121–5.

After announcing the leadership changes on television, Gierek reconvened the Politburo. There would be a revision to the coming five-year plan (1971–5). It would include financial compensation for price increases. But they still stood. There would be talks with the Episcopate on normalising state–Church relations. The leaders of fraternal communist parties would be informed of recent 'problems arising'.[56] Whilst this suggested attempts to conciliate, there was no analysis of society's demands.

Analysis of demands

Disregarding the fine tradition of Ossowski, Polish sociology in the 1960s assumed an apologetic character. The abstractions of loyal functionaries concerning 'developed socialism' contributed little to knowledge or understanding.[57] It was left to independent scholars to investigate the views of the Polish population during the December crisis. Most importantly, these unofficial researchers recovered and analysed thousands of strikers' 'demands'. The word itself merits attention.

In Polish, *postulaty* mean proposals put forward for negotiation. They can thus be understood as more than individual expressions of opinion. Whilst the workers' *cahiers de doléances* were deliberately not political manifestos, nor can they be described as a-political. As in eighteenth-century England, the protestors subscribed to 'definite, and passionately held, notions of the common weal'. They acted in the belief that they were upholding a general good and hence had the backing of consensus in the wider community. This enabled them to overcome the barriers of fear and deference in favour of 'a form of direct popular action, disciplined and with clear objectives'.[58]

Polish protestors not only sought to be heard, they also wanted to be answered. This helps explain the language in which their demands are often expressed. In contrast to the direct and earthy language that workers used towards each other, their demands were formed 'more under the impact of political jargon and a *sui generis* verbal convention of the communist state, as the result of an insufficient model in the strikers' own political vocabulary'.[59] By 1980, strikers had got rid of 'illusions and

[56] Dudek *et al.* (eds.), *Centrum Władzy*, p. 412.

[57] J. Kurczewski, *The Resurrection of Rights in Poland* (Oxford, 1993), names Professors Wiatr, Wesołowski, Widerszpil and Sufin as official social scientists (p. 145).

[58] E. P. Thompson, 'The Moral Economy of the English Crowd in the Eighteenth Century', *Past and Present* 1971 (5).

[59] B. Chmiel and E. Kaczyńska, *Postulaty. Materiały do dziejów wystąpień pracowniczych w latach 1970–71 i 1980 (Gdańsk i Szczecin)* (Warsaw, 1988), pp. 15–48.

linguistic habits from the previous period, when they had often served to placate the authorities'.[60]

But in 1970, such self-confidence was minimal. In any case, it was not clear that interlocutors could be found. Management at the Gdańsk Shipyard only agreed to open talks 'as a last resort'. Even this concession infuriated emissaries from the Politburo. Fulminating against 'counter-revolution', they asked how local officials could arrogate to themselves 'the right to carry on some kind of discussion'.[61] That was made impossible in Gdynia by the arrest of entire strike committees.

Independent analysis indicates a prevalence of political or ideological postulates. Typically, the workers demand justice and equality, particularly in public institutions. This call becomes even more prevalent after repressive action against strikes. There was nothing new in this. As Kaczyńska shows, workers' demands stretched back to the 1890s, in that they sought not only material improvements but also the right to use the Polish language and form their own organisations. In 1905, the demands for national culture and freedom of speech and civil rights became universal, even though some of those on strike were illiterate.[62]

Equally, analytical distinctions between categories have little practical meaning in a monopolistic state. Should the demand to end special privileges for the secret police, militia and military be treated as political or social?[63] An economic demand – for lower prices or higher wages – had to be sent to the political authorities who set them. Was 'changing the composition of workers' councils; replacing Party with non-Party members'[64] purely political? Enterprise managers could honestly reply that they had no jurisdiction over such matters; they could only make representations, like the protestors. But that raised a further set of questions about their functions. If they had no real responsibility, why did they enjoy special benefits and privileges? If they were not accountable for their frequent waste of public funding, who was responsible?

Of particular interest are organisational demands. Turning their back on state-sponsored unions, workforces sought to establish bodies distinctively their own. A new stage in self-organisation had begun. The fruits would be seen a decade later.

After the December massacre, workers frequently questioned the role of official trade unions, in particular their failure to articulate and channel the grievances that led to so tragic an outcome. Their impotence was indeed apparent. In Szczecin, the same persons were 'elected' to the same

[60] *Ibid.* [61] Laba, *Roots of Solidarity*, p. 42.
[62] Chmiel and Kaczyńska, *Postulaty 1970–71 i 1980*, pp. 5–14. [63] *Ibid.* p. 13.
[64] Eisler (ed.), *Grudzień 1970 w dokumentach MSW*, pp. 61–2.

union posts for decades. Rotation of offices was demanded at all levels. Free elections should replace time-servers with those who had gained public confidence during the recent protests. New *aktyw* 'from production' should be brought in to replace those whose entire career had been in administration.

Further criticisms were directed at the state-run Central Council of Trade Unions. Union members wished to know how their dues were being spent. It was politely suggested that gentlemen in high posts might have forgotten 'whose money they live on'. It would be appropriate to repay their debt by genuine effort to improve workers' welfare. It was also indicated that union officials should become better-versed in labour law in order to be able to defend the interests of those they represented. Above all, speakers sought to wrest more jurisdiction and independence for trade unions from Party and state control.[65]

It was sometimes suggested that unions could be turned into a form of 'institutional opposition'. Unions had become side-tracked into bureaucracy, implementing production norms, paper-work and organising recreational activities. They had lost their original purpose of defending workers against 'both big and little bosses who disregard our vital interests'. Genuine and independent unions would act as a fire alarm 'signaling any deviation from the law in political and economic matters'. Workers' self-government had been reduced to an empty shell. It should be restored to its authentic functions. At micro-level, it would oversee industrial disputes and decision-making, and an open division of the wage-fund. At national level, one article suggested unions be given a veto over decisions of the Price Commission to avoid a repeat of the *débâcle* of December.[66]

Within twenty-four hours, the Gdańsk Shipyard workers had disbanded their 'official' strike committee, from which Party members were not automatically disbarred, and elected one of their own. It only became clear much later to 'intellectual independent opinion-creating circles', that this was an innovation of a constitutional character.[67] Far from being incidental, it is the key to workers' protests of the period. The strike committees had a second and decisively important feature: they reached out to other workplaces. In addition to providing strength in numbers and mutual support, the formation of joint strike committees meant that the authorities could not crush sites of protest piece-meal, picking them off one by one, as they were able to do under martial law (December 1981).

[65] Radio Gdańsk, 13 January 1971. [66] *Głos Szczeciński*, 27 January 1971.
[67] Kurczewski, *Resurrection of Rights*, pp. 143–4.

The Gdańsk workers also found a popular tribune. In additional to astonishing oratorical talents, entirely untutored, Wałęsa brought into Polish politics a set of attitudes that had not been articulated before. His generation, reaching adulthood in the sixties, was 'ready for dialogue and compromise [but] not very receptive to officially-launched doctrines, and mistrustful of empty declarations and senseless slogans, quite knowledgeable on general subjects, but lacking a full knowledge of the system under which they live'.[68] Wałęsa became the emblematic figure of working-class discontent.

Development of strike techniques was greatest in Szczecin, where the first slogan was 'Solidarity with Gdańsk'. After days of violence, workers occupied the giant Warski Shipyard and considered how to enter into peaceful negotiations. As one put it:

> When we gathered, we were doing something that had never been done or discussed in our public or social lives. It was a conflict of the people with the state. We had to open negotiations with them. Who they represented and who we represented was not in doubt. But how were we to do it, how to organize all this? We had to improvise, with no previous models, patterns or instructions.[69]

They chose a committee to run every aspect of the strike, and sent emissaries to other yards. A common front was formulated for negotiations with the communist state. The workers in Szczecin were joined by a total of ninety-four striking workplaces in the region. Cognisant of the fundamental threat this posed to its own *raison d'être*, the Party fought back with every means at its disposal. The purpose was to re-erect the barrier of fear which coastal workers had managed to overcome. In a sustained and brutal process of recriminations, strike leaders from 1970–1 were weeded out, demoted, sacked or attacked. In several cases, they were murdered by 'persons unknown'. Others, such as Bałuka, the leader in the Szczecin Shipyard, were forced into emigration.

The demands have additional importance for comparative purposes. Many concerns of 1956, such as more secure borders and more equal relations with the Soviet Union, had disappeared. This was the permanent legacy of the Gomułka era. On the other hand, they did contain requests for freedom of speech, truth in public life and education, and – above all – independent self-governing trade unions. Analysis shows how little these changed between 1970 and 1980. Their reappearance indicates the ineffectiveness of changes Poland underwent during the 'new deal' of the 1970s. The events of 1980 had a precedent. August 1980

[68] A. Drzycimski, 'Growing' in *The Book of Lech Wałęsa* (London, 1982), p. 69.
[69] Laba, *Roots of Solidarity*, p. 66.

became exceptional simply because an agreement was reached, with all the consequences that followed, rather than by the demands being articulated. Most had been heard before, though clothed in a language thought more suitable for addressing those in power, thus – perhaps unconsciously – absorbing some of the limitations of official thinking.

Such popular resistance is seen by Kurczewski as a 'resurrection of rights', whereby society moved its repressed normative structure to the publicly communicated surface of its collective life.[70] Thus a contested notion throughout the communist period is law itself: whether law can be used for purely political purposes, as an allegedly impartial instrument, in practice subordinated to class rule. Political protests expressing well-justified grievances and a sense of solidarity amongst protestors were commonly dismissed as 'rioting' by the political authorities. This was also used as an underlying justification for the entire system. As the unofficial discussion group 'Experience and the Future' observed later:

> It is hard to avoid the impression that law, in a great many cases, performs a quasi-class role. It serves to defend privilege and inequality, it is an instrument for the dictatorship of groups and individuals whose aim is unrestricted legal authority, for the sake of egotistical self-advantage, even though the essence of a legal order is to limit arbitrariness.[71]

The new team

Gierek and his new team were greeted with enthusiasm by social scientists in the West. Canadian Professor Adam Bromke noted that they were the first generation to come to power whose entire career had been made in 'People's Poland'. Not only did they displace former Stalinists, or members of the communist underground, it was also the case that 'for the first time since the eighteenth century the country became ruled by people who had made their entire political career in the Polish state'. Unlike their ideological predecessors, the new elite was both relatively educated and experienced in pragmatic administration. Of course, this was tempered by the communist loyalties instilled during the 'intense political indoctrination' of the Stalinist period, and they owed their careers entirely to the Party, but Gierek enjoyed both unquestioned authority within the Party and 'popularity in the country'. Bromke foresaw Gierek's voluntary resignation before the end of the decade to make way, via a

[70] Kurczewski, *Resurrection of Rights*, Ch. 10.

[71] *Poland: The State of the Republic. Reports by the Experience and the Future Discussion Group (DiP) Warsaw* (London, 1981).

smooth transition, for younger people who might undertake 'some new political changes'.[72]

The 'man for all seasons' of Polish politics, Party politician M. F. Rakowski,[73] provides an unfailing barometer of prevailing orthodoxy. His *volte-face* after the crisis of 1970–1 is characteristic. Gomułka, his previous hero and first patron, is abruptly rejected. He had become oblivious to the 'socio-economic forces of discontent' which had flared on the Coast. The new Party leaders were no longer wedded to the puritanical concept of socialism. They recognised that the demands of the demonstrating workers were 'exclusively socialist' in character. Rakowski did not mention the massacre on the Coast. Instead, he criticised the 'routine bureaucratic approach to both people and problems' still visible in the Party's daily work (for which no remedies were suggested). Progressive elements in the Party had started to put forward a long-term programme. This planning exercise had brought great satisfaction to the toiling masses: 'Polish society today possesses a perspective; this, in itself, has brought about extremely positive effects.'[74] But the content of key words such as 'socialism' and 'society' is not defined.

As the result of such propaganda, Poland's image abroad, and the results of policy at home, began to diverge very radically. Perhaps because fashioning the Western image lay mainly in the hands of publicists – the purveyors of short-term perspectives, eager for good copy – elements of change were greatly exaggerated. Such enthusiasm was not in itself problematical. It was an external counterpart to the domestic 'propaganda of success' masking the proliferation of waste, chaos and lack of planning that came to characterise economic management. However, so much was written about 'Gierek's Poland' that ordinary Poland was overlooked. When political protest resumed, there was surprise.

Within Poland, Gierek's accession was received with acquiescence that many came to regret later on. But its opening phase was not unpromising. The new team did appear willing to address public concerns, even the most critical ones.

The Szczecin strike committee was reconstituted in January 1971[75] to take up unresolved issues. It called for immediate and legally binding elections to trade union posts, and to the workers' councils. 'Following the wish of a majority of Party members', there should be democratic

[72] A. Bromke, 'La nouvelle élite politique en Pologne', *Revue de l'Est* 1974 (3).
[73] L. Tyrmand, 'The Hair-Styles of Mieczysław Rakowski', *Survey* Summer 1982.
[74] M. F. Rakowski, 'December 1970: The Turning Point' in A. Bromke and J. W. Strong (eds.), *Gierek's Poland* (New York, 1973), pp. 24–35.
[75] Szejnert and Zalewski, *Szczecin*, pp. 50–9.

elections to basic Party cells and to youth organisations. The security services should cease harassing, intimidating and arresting those on strike. The right to protest was defended: 'To go on strike is not an offence: nothing in the law forbids it.' Finally, they demanded that the new Party Secretary and Prime Minister come in person to the Warski Shipyard 'to enter into immediate and permanent dialogue with workers' representatives on the Strike Committee.'[76] To the amazement of everyone, apart perhaps from the workers themselves, they came.

There followed a tumultuous exchange lasting eight hours. Strike delegates used this unprecedented opportunity to pour out their hearts to the newly appointed First Secretary. For their part, the authorities tried to lend a sympathetic ear while simultaneously winning the support and trust of the delegates for an improvised and somewhat nebulous reform programme.

Gierek's opening address mentioned objective problems, such as failures in agriculture and financial exploitation by the West. But more important were 'subjective conditions', the faults of individuals, above all Comrade Gomułka, 'in whom we had unlimited confidence for so long'. He would brush all criticism aside: 'You know nothing. I know best.' Opposition to his leadership did exist, but little could be changed and even that was immediately sabotaged by 'the bureaucracy'. A front of 'unanimity' was always presented to the general public. Colleagues had warned Gomułka against the price increases, which were sure to result in strikes. Too arrogant to listen, high-handed and 'exceptionally autocratic', he denied even senior colleagues any real voice in decision-making.[77] They often learned about important decrees from newspapers.

Gierek's self-defence became rhetorical. What were Gomułka's critics, Gierek included, supposed to do? Resign? Desert the country in its hour of need? He was a simple worker, just like the audience. He had no relatives in high places. He lacked personal ambition and would retire in two or three years' time. He was looking forward to his pensions, including one from working in the mines in France and Belgium. He had taken the post of First Secretary for patriotic reasons. Without him, there would have been a bloodbath. The appeal came down to: 'I am only a worker like you: Help me!'[78]

Delegates had never had the opportunity to address such dignitaries in person, let alone in public, on vital and contended issues of the day. The need for permanent dialogue with the Party was a recurrent theme. Many emphasised that, for dialogue to be possible, workers had to be treated

[76] Chmiel and Kaczyńska, *Postulaty 1970–71 i 1980*, pp. 110–12 (24 January 1971).
[77] Wacowska, *Rewolta Szczecińska*, pp. 29–39. [78] *Ibid*. p. 32.

with dignity, as equal and respected partners in discussion. This would require the evolution of a common language. It was also connected to sharing a common world.

The delegate from Shipyard Section K-1 called those in charge 'an aristocracy that is going to steal everything', prompting an ovation. It was workers who paid their salaries through taxation, which funded many parasites at the workplace, who were paid large sums without lifting a finger. Some Poles lived in splendour, while many others had not enough to feed their families.[79] Another delegate, a Communist Party member from its inception in 1944, put this plainly: 'Comrades, our society is divided into classes. Some people no longer know what to do with their socialism and are looking for something better [*indistinct*]. Their socialism is like that because they have too much money and too many ways of making it.' Class divisions were imposed from the top. Poles had been talking about abolition of inequalities between peasants and workers since the thirties: 'Money should be taken back and given to those who need it for their basic bread.'[80]

Their ambiguity towards the new leader was captured by the delegate from Section K-3: 'Comrade Gierek has promised us nothing. He blames the economic situation.' Poles needed guarantees. Yet Comrade Gierek should be given a chance: 'We should trust him. Of course, we also trusted Gomułka in his time, and were let down. But in my view, he is the right kind of man [*applause*]. Let's give him a year or two and then see the results. If they are good – all will be well. Then the working class will give Comrade Edward Gierek 100% support.'[81]

Political responsibility preoccupied many delegates. It was considered to operate at all levels. The delegate from K-1 thought changes should begin at the base: 'A fish rots from the head. But, as every house-wife knows, it must be de-scaled from the tail.'[82] Responsibility for the shooting of workers was placed directly on the Minister of Defence: Wojciech Jaruzelski.

Jaruzelski, also present as a local Sejm deputy, replied that the decision to use armed force was taken at the highest political level: 'Would the military dispute decisions of a legally constituted government? No! We are at your service and always will be. Our soldier will always defend the people's government; with you he will defend the Party.'[83] In his professional opinion, soldiers had behaved with dignity during the troubles, well beyond what could have been expected of young boys. What were professional soldiers to think when they saw their precious equipment – which had raised Poland's army to the status of the second

[79] *Ibid.* pp. 93–4. [80] *Ibid.* pp. 102–5. [81] *Ibid.* pp. 71–2.
[82] *Ibid.* p. 65. [83] *Ibid.* p. 135.

largest in the Warsaw Pact – going up in flames? No soldier had the right to surrender his precious, hard-earned weapons. Junior officers had conducted themselves with 'such tact and moderation' that a catastrophe had been averted.

Jaruzelski offered two further alibis. The army was in place locally to protect Poland's western frontiers. Despite the recent Treaty, not yet ratified, West German patrol vessels were just over the horizon, whilst aerial surveillance by the Bundeswehr took place day and night. The Baltic was an open frontier. There were also enemies within: 'Aliens, who want to destroy our unity. They want to separate the Polish People's Army from the working class, from the masses. Together we will thwart them. You will not allow it, nor will we. We are at your service and always will be.'[84] His final question was prophetic: 'Comrades, workers, friends, do you want an army that carries out regime change, as in South America and Africa? Do you want a government of colonels and generals?'[85]

Jaruzelski's recent biographer explores at length the role of the military in the 1970 crisis.[86] The top priority, once the violence of 'Black December' (1970) had ceased, was damage limitation, above all to the army's public standing and its own morale. The two were intimately connected. In cases revealed much later, soldiers had refused orders to mobilise against or fire on civilians.[87] Others had deserted on discovering they were being deployed against fellow-citizens. There was general dismay that they had been tricked into a battle against 'hostile forces' allegedly attacking the Polish coastal cities. The collapse of morale was critical for military planning. As Michta puts it, 'For the Russians, the continuing use of Polish soldiers against civilians was fraught with the imminent danger that another key Northern Tier, non-Soviet Warsaw Pact army would thereby be rendered operationally useless, only two years after the disintegration of the Czechoslovak army in the aftermath of the 1968 invasion.'[88] Lessons were not lost on the Polish high command. Over the next decade, attempts were made to reconnect the country's armed forces with ordinary civilian life. Jaruzelski himself wrote in 1975, 'The Polish army is deeply enmeshed in the life of society, takes an active part in the development of the country, stands first in the front line of education and scholarship, economy and science, technology and culture.'[89]

[84] *Ibid.* pp. 138–9. [85] *Ibid.* p. 135.

[86] L. Kowalski, *Generał ze skazą. Biografia wojskowa gen. armii Wojciecha Jaruzelskiego* (Warsaw, 2001), pp. 329–58.

[87] *Tygodnik Solidarność* 1981. [88] Michta, *Red Eagle*, p. 70.

[89] T. Rosenberg, *The Haunted Land. Facing Europe's Ghosts After Communism* (London, 1995), pp. 157–8.

The Church was slow to react during the December crisis, but Mazowiecki and another Znak deputy travelled to Gdańsk to try to determine what had taken place. Avoiding contact with the local authorities, they met several dozen members of the public under church auspices.[90] On returning to Warsaw, they lobbied a Politburo member, Józef Tejchma, who agreed to pass to Gierek their 'categorical demand' for a special parliamentary commission to investigate the 'events on the coast'.[91] But the only response was the removal of Mazowiecki's name from the list of candidates for the next parliament. He remained excluded until the elections of 1989.

Gierek still stood by the price increases. He told strike delegates in Szczecin: 'There can be no return, no return whatsoever', to the prices of 12 December 1970.[92] It took the textile workers of Łódź to succeed where coastal protesters had failed.

Faced with a strike 12,000 strong, mostly women, the Politburo decided to dispatch the Prime Minister to tell them that compensatory wage increases were out of the question.[93] But this time, the charm offensive – which had also worked in Gdańsk – was to no avail. When Jaroszewicz and his official party arrived to address them, in the Grand Theatre, Łódź, the audience made obscene gestures. He scuttled back to Warsaw convinced that 'a change in economic strategy' was unavoidable.[94] The Politburo accepted his advice. An announcement that price increases would be rescinded from 1 March was agreed the next day. The Polish Prime Minister was to call Kosygin to ask the Soviet government for emergency hard currency credit ($100 million) to import deficit items.[95]

A number of sops were given to the workforce on the Coast. As they put it: 'First they kill our people, then they build us a playground.' Wałęsa was caustic about cosmetic changes offered to Gdańsk workers under the new slogan 'Better and Better'. Cheerful music now blared out in the locker rooms, as did the local radio station with cultural and sporting news items.[96] But nothing of substance changed. Workers' organisations for self-defence were rapidly emasculated. Once and future workers' leaders such as Wałęsa continued to ponder their predicament.

90 'Relacja Tadeusza Mazowieckiego [October 1981]' in Jegliński (ed.), *Grudzień 1970*, pp. 205–6.
91 Domański (ed.), *Tajne dokumenty BP*, p. 203 (13 February 1971).
92 Wacowska, *Rewolta Szczecińska*, p. 40.
93 Domański (ed.), *Tajne dokumenty BP*, pp. 202–3 (13 February 1971).
94 Eisler, *Grudzień 1970*, p. 360.
95 Domański (ed.), *Tajne dokumenty BP*, pp. 204–5 (15 February 1971).
96 Wałęsa, *A Path of Hope*, p. 79.

External forces did not seem to offer a complete explanation. The protests of 1970–1 had not been a re-run of 1956. Then, national sovereignty had been at the top of the agenda. This was not so now because of the very success of October 1956 in restoring Polish sovereignty within the limits prescribed by the Cold War. But was the Cold War mutable, perhaps by the Europeans themselves?

Helsinki

Proponents of European *détente*, to whom the Cold War was a mistake born of misperceptions, now saw an opportunity to mitigate one of its most unacceptable consequences: permanent division of the continent. Their hopes included an eventual reunification of Germany and a gradual re-orientation of Poland away from the Soviet sphere. Of course, Poland could not (as wits suggested) change places with Spain or Portugal. Long-standing boundaries between the blocs were not going to dissolve overnight, nor were more recent walls going to tumble down. However, there could be a policy shift from the strident rhetoric of anti-Sovietism to a subtler approach, drawing the Soviet Union into more constructive international relations, above all to maintain the peace in Europe's volatile and highly militarised arena.

Hawks replied that this ignored the Soviet Union's continuing military build-up. For the first time in Russian history, its navy had a global reach. The use of Cubans for proxy wars in southern Africa was a disturbing sign of expansionist ambitions. Many American politicians and military experts saw SALT 1 (1971) as a one-sided Soviet victory, for the first time enshrining the essential strategic equivalence of the two superpowers.[97] Given the large conventional advantage the Soviet Union had long enjoyed in Europe, this seemed a significant shift in what Moscow called 'the correlation of forces'. The response to any Soviet attack on Western Europe now lay not in American superiority but in the less tangible area of deterrence, whereby Washington kept open the option of using nuclear weapons first, whilst knowing that the Soviet Union had the capacity to retaliate against its own cities. The visit of Nixon to Beijing (February 1972) was insufficient to restore a balance. Even so, there was a sense in which its newfound global status, and its own conflict with China, might lead Moscow to welcome an *aggiornamento* on its European flank.

[97] Ulam, *Dangerous Relations*, pp. 65–9.

When the Warsaw Pact returned to the idea of a Conference on Security and Cooperation in Europe (CSCE), in its Budapest Appeal (17 March 1969), there were no limits to participation. The Soviet Union had dropped its objection to the USA and Canada attending. Hence its implicit agenda of excluding and eventually dissolving NATO disappeared. Two months later, the Finnish President offered his capital as a suitable site for such a conference. Talks started in Helsinki in November 1972. It soon proved to be a protracted forum as many of the smallest states represented sought to have their say in full. This led to a certain impatience from the super-powers, particularly in Washington, where National Security Adviser (and from 1973 Secretary of State) Kissinger was alternately disinterested or sceptical.[98]

Moscow showed a new openness in economic relations with the capitalist world. Brezhnev told business leaders in Washington (June 1973) that 'we have been a prisoner of old trends and to this day have not been able fully to break those fetters'. Now, he assured them, the Soviet Union sought a new era based on stability and permanence. This was marked by the signing of a mutually advantageous grain deal, to compensate for fluctuating Soviet harvests. The super-powers declared that international relations were to move from 'from confrontation to negotiation'.

Moscow's charm offensive offered rich pickings to the West and helped convince many of the sceptics. Even if this were a temporary manoeuvre by the Soviets, a cunning ruse to be reversed later, it was worth a try. As Brezhnev put it: 'To live in peace, we must trust each other, we must know each other better.'[99] It was quite widely believed that mutual self-interest through bi-lateral trade, credits and even shared technology would eventually lead to a convergence of the two systems.

Foreign Ministers engaged in extensive final discussions from mid-1973, leading up to a signing ceremony in July 1975. At Helsinki, the High Representatives of participating States adopted a new set of principles on security in Europe, starting with sovereignty. The thirty-five signatory states would 'respect each other's right freely to choose and develop its political, social, economic and cultural systems, as well as its right to determine its laws and regulations'. This contradiction of the Brezhnev Doctrine was underpinned by clauses on 'Non-intervention in internal affairs'.

Echoing the UN Charter, the Helsinki preamble declared that states would not intervene in 'the internal or external affairs which fall within the domestic jurisdiction' of another signatory. They would therefore

[98] J. Maresca, *To Helsinki: The Conference on Security and Cooperation in Europe, 1973–1975* (Durham, N. C., 1985).

[99] Cited by W. Laqueur, *A Continent Astray. Europe, 1970–1978* (Oxford, 1979), pp. 180–4.

'refrain from any form of armed intervention or threat of such intervention against another participating State'. Likewise, there would be 'no other act of military, or of political, economic or other coercion designed to subordinate to their own interest the exercise by another participating State of the rights inherent in its sovereignty and thus to secure advantages of any kind'.

This was given a positive aspect under 'Respect for human rights and fundamental freedoms'. There would be promotion and encouragement of 'the effective exercise of civil, political, economic, social, cultural and other rights and freedoms all of which derive from the inherent dignity of the human person and are essential for his free and full development'.[100] Citizens in a number of the signatory states took this latter clause literally.

The document then proceeded to delineate three areas in which the signatories would strive 'to make *détente* both a continuing and an increasingly viable and comprehensive process, universal in scope'. Firstly, the signatories would refrain from the threat or use of force, except where allowed under the Charter of the United Nations. They would respect each other's 'sovereign equality' – leaving this tautology unexplained – and territorial integrity. There would be confidence-building measures, such as prior notification of military manoeuvres 'exceeding a total of 25,000 troops'. Efforts would be made 'to complement political *détente* in Europe' with disarmament. Signatories would also allow free scope for others to choose their own 'political, social, economic and cultural systems'. Secondly, there should be cooperation in the fields of economics, science and technology and of the environment (oceanography and glaciology were mentioned). Tourism should be promoted in a positive spirit, including provision of 'the formalities required for such travel' (i.e. the issuance of passports and exit visas). Finally, in Basket Three, there was to be cooperation in 'Humanitarian and Other Fields'.

Basket Three provided an unexpected argument for human rights.[101] It enabled Eastern European dissenters to address their governments in terminology and on principles to which they had voluntarily adhered: 'We are merely asking you to keep your international agreements.' Helsinki monitoring groups were founded by independently minded citizens in Moscow, Kiev, Tbilisi, Erevan and Wilno. All were much persecuted by the authorities. They found counterparts in Bucharest and Berlin, and most notably in Prague.[102]

[100] *Conference on Security and Cooperation in Europe. Final Act* (London, 1975), pp. 1–5.

[101] D. Thomas, *The Helsinki Effect: International Norms, Human Rights, and the Demise of Communism* (Princeton, N.J. 2001).

[102] H. Gordon Skilling, *Charter 77 and Human Rights in Czechoslovakia* (London, 1981).

Polish human rights groups used the Helsinki Agreement and its bi-annual monitoring, starting in Belgrade in October 1977, to gain Western support.[103] They found their government had become more sensitive to its international image, though its growing economic dependency on the West was more decisive.

Gierek's drive to revive the Polish economy was based on Western credits.[104] The growth strategy envisaged large-scale borrowing from Western countries – in order to modernise the industrial structure through technology transfer – rather than restricting domestic consumption, as Gomułka had done. The debts would be repaid by boosting exports to the West. 'Building a Second Poland' – to emulate the golden-age Poland of Kazimierz the Great – was a not-ignoble goal. From the early seventies, prestige projects, such as building Fiat cars under licence, appeared to put Poland 'on wheels' and gave the country a more modern look. But millions of dollars pumped into coal and steel failed to improve the profitability of these industries and made Poland one of the most polluted countries in Europe. Lack of management reform left Polish enterprises unable to innovate and absorb technology at a rate sufficient to compete in the West. Imported machinery remained uninstalled or was not properly integrated into the production process, whilst unsold output lay rusting outside factory gates. Bottle-necks and waste also demoralised the workforce. Moreover, the investment strategy was itself questionable. As Portes comments: 'To expand heavily into steel, motor vehicles, ship-building and petro-chemicals in the mid-1970s was clearly unwise.'[105] A particularly startling instance of mis-investment was the Katowice Steelworks, begun in 1974, with imported Soviet ores. But even with better investment management, the timing would have sent it hopelessly awry.

The oil crisis of 1973 sent the West into immediate recession, and its monetary policies tripled interest rates. Recycled petro-dollars enabled Poland to borrow readily without taking the harsh choices at home needed to restore internal balances. While the Western market for its manufactures shrank, domestic consumer expectations outran export capabilities. Though it was not immediately apparent, by mid-decade the hard-currency debt had reached a serviceable maximum. It was rapidly coming to absorb the total of Western earnings.

[103] Raina, *Political Opposition*, pp. 423–33.

[104] W. Brus in A. Nove (ed.), *The East European Economies in the 1970s* (London, 1982), p. 123.

[105] R. Portes, *The Polish Crisis: Western Economic Policy Options* (London, 1981), pp. 7–8.

The only available domestic remedy was the one that had removed Gomułka: sharp price increases to reduce state subsidies on basic goods in order to release funds for the servicing of overseas borrowings. Political prudence suggested this should be averted if possible. But the time-horizons shrank rapidly from 1975. The government could no longer afford the staggering 12 per cent of GDP being spent on food subsidies, a legacy of previous political crises. As one commentator observed, Gierek had been pursuing 'simultaneous and increasingly hectic love-affairs with Polish housewives, and Western bankers'.[106] He would have to drop one partner and it was unlikely to be the bankers.

[106] P. Green, 'Third Round in Poland', *New Left Review* February–April 1977.

9 Opposition

> The future of Poland will depend upon how many people are mature enough to be non-conformists.
>
> Pope John Paul II, during his Polish pilgrimage (June 1979)

If 'opposition' meant simply rejection of state authority, then most Poles have been in opposition since the Partitions. A narrower definition, however – the organised attempt to change political leadership and its policies – discloses three major forms of opposition during the communist period. First is the struggle for power, competition for office and influence at the top, which performed the task of opposition in a liberal democracy in replacing one ruling team by another. However undemocratic in actual conduct, this was the usual means by which political succession took place in communist countries.[1] A second form was revisionism, the effort, after Stalin died, to revive the Party, economy and Marxism from within. Its supposition was that no irreconcilable division existed between society and the Party apparatus, which would respond to pressures from 'in-system reformers' and make concessions of substance from above.[2] As we have seen, the events of 1968 – the Polish pogrom and the fate of the Prague Spring – put paid to this expectation.

This seemed to leave only one further source of political pressure: non-Party opposition from below. Yet student protests of March 1968 had achieved minimal resonance within the wider society. Moreover, the next round of worker demonstrations in winter 1970–1 received scant support from other classes. From exile, Kołakowski attributed this to a loss of hope: 'The fact that a large part of the Polish intelligentsia has been persuaded to believe in the complete inflexibility of the shameful system under which they live is almost certainly responsible for the regrettable passivity they displayed during the dramatic action of the Polish workers in 1970.'[3]

[1] L. Schapiro (ed.), *Political Opposition in One-Party States* (London, 1972), p. 5.
[2] M. Rakovski, *Towards an East European Marxism* (London, 1978), pp. 130–4.
[3] L. Kołakowski, 'Theses on Hope and Hopelessness', *Survey* June 1971.

Expanding the thesis of hopelessness, he draws attention to the monopolistic aspirations of the Party apparatus, underpinned by the final sanction of Soviet power, and the pattern of servility and subordination to which these reduce legitimate public activity. No monopoly can be partial. However, there were grounds for thinking that the Party-state could show flexibility when this was perceived to be necessary for the maintenance of its rule. The necessity for technological progress, for instance, required a relaxation of information policy to permit the flow of innovative ideas essential to both international competitiveness and the satisfaction of domestic consumerism. Whilst passivity increases the inflexibility of the system and repression, every instance of resistance, however tiny, serves to revive civil society.

Jacek Kuroń added the idea of 'self-organisation' by society.[4] The idea was not yet that a more independent culture and society could one day develop into an effective political opposition. Rather, the development of autonomous groups, unofficial initiatives and eventually social movements can *in themselves* constitute an opposition. Participants would actively enjoy the benefits of self-organisation and freedom of expression, across an increasing range of social activities. A non-coercive sphere for engaged citizens with a sense of common purpose could reclaim the public space monopolised by the Party and promote democratic values. Social activity could take place outside the officially sanctioned realm, by-passing the 'leading role' of the Party and state-controlled instruments, such as elections and the parliament.

Kuroń's 'Notes on Self-Government' stressed that this prospect was not utopian, but rooted in the politics of Poland over the post-Stalin period. Thus private farmers had reasserted their independence during the spontaneous de-collectivisation of autumn 1956. This had become a permanent achievement. Though workers' protests had been at a heavy cost, some demands had been met. Writers and scholars had made efforts to restrict censorship and keep alive ideas of intellectual independence, dignity and truth. Finally, the Polish Catholic Church was a mass social movement which remained uncompromised, unlike a number of its counterparts in the Soviet bloc. Since 1956, the interdependence of all four social groups had constituted 'an essential feature of our social reality'. None would have been successful on their own.[5]

According to Michnik's 'New Evolutionism', the opposition should address its programme to the public at large – above all, the working class. Workers had managed to force the authorities to make spectacular

[4] J. Kuroń, 'Polityka i opozycja w Polsce' (1974) in J. Kuroń, *Polityka i odpowiedzialność* (London, 1984).

[5] J. Kuroń, 'Notatki o samorządzie' in *Polityka i odpowiedzialność*.

concessions on several occasions: 'Without doubt, the power elite fear this social group most.' Strikers in the Szczecin and Gdańsk Shipyards in 1970–1 achieved a new form of independent self-defence. It was not possible to predict how and when more permanent workers' representation might be formed, but it was already clear that working-class consciousness had grown. The future would depend upon a convergence of independent groups with the interests of the working class.[6]

The Church presented a model of opposition to the communist authorities which even those on the secular Left eventually came to admire and seek to emulate. From the mid-seventies, the possibility of compromise began to be discussed. Political activists previously far removed from the Church began to discover in it a source of democratic and humane values. Young Marxists, reared on the dialectic of class struggle and alienation, now embraced the Christian categories of love and sacrifice. Religion was no longer merely 'opium of the people' or the product of 'false consciousness' but contained sacred mysteries of its own. By encountering and attempting to grasp these teachings, the nascent democratic opposition could further ground itself in popular culture.

Adam Michnik noted two tendencies in Polish Catholicism: the European and the ethnocentric. Wyszyński was in the latter category: 'Like General De Gaulle, he was a great anachronism. His greatness lay in his flawless decoding of the nature of communism and his brilliant strategy of resistance. In this the Cardinal was remarkably modern.'[7] And there was a wider Church with a diversity of approaches to the democratic opposition. Whilst Bishop Ignacy Tokarczuk (Przemyśl) helped parishioners construct a church that had been forbidden by the authorities, another bishop was seen publicly voting for the Sejm. Cardinal Wojtyła (Kraków) defended students from repression and allowed church premises to be used for this purpose, whilst another bishop accused hunger strikers of 'cynically trespassing' on church grounds.[8]

Michnik saw an evolution in the Church's own teachings. From the anti-communist jeremiads against communist 'godlessness', the constant refrain since communist rule began in 1945, its pastoral letters had begun to emphasise the right to truth and defence of human freedom and dignity. The Church had come out in defence of workers' rights, including the right to strike and to form independent trade unions. Consequently, it

[6] A. Michnik, 'The New Evolutionism' (October 1976) in Michnik, *Letters from Prison.*

[7] A. Michnik, 'Preface' to Michnik, *The Church and the Left*, tr. Ost (Chicago, 1993), pp. xii–xiv (trans. of Michnik, *Kościoł, Lewica, Dialog*).

[8] 'A Response to Critics' (July 1981) in Michnik, *The Church and the Left*, p. 236.

had become the forum for all those seeking to defend the International Convention on Human Rights and to extend civil liberties.

He also examined geopolitics: 'The Soviet military and political presence in Poland is the factor that determines the limits of possible evolution, and this is unlikely to change for some time.' Polish resistance had long been constrained by the spectre of Soviet tanks, and memories of Budapest and Prague led many Poles to believe that change was impossible. But on closer inspection, the prospects seemed more complicated. Given the propensity of Poles to fight, a war would ensue: 'Poland would lose on the battlefield but the Soviet Union would lose politically.' Thus Poland should seek to evolve within the parameters of the 'Brezhnev Doctrine'.[9]

June 1976

The most sensitive topic in Polish politics in 1976 was still the price of meat. An index of society's well-being, and intrinsic to family hospitality, it was a cost the state put up at its peril. Such decisions went to the Politburo and had lost the previous Party Secretary his job. Gierek eventually rescinded Gomułka's increases and renewed the undertaking for four more years. In the mid-seventies, the population was still paying sixties' prices for many basic goods.

Party leaders therefore decided to put up basic meat prices by 50 per cent, with better cuts and quality sausages up by as much as 90 per cent. Many other staples would increase by 30 per cent and the price of sugar would double. Party economists calculated that much of the population could afford to pay. The 1970 increases followed a decade of stagnation in real wages, but since then average earnings had risen by up to 10 per cent per annum, and strategically placed groups – miners and shipbuilders, functionaries, the police and military – had done better still. For the first time in communist Poland, many citizens had begun to believe in the possibility of profiting from the existing system. Those who had missed out during the 'dash for growth' quinquennium were to receive compensation in the forms of cash supplements to wages and pensions, increased family and child allowances and student grants. Giving these concessions, the government felt bold enough to act. But extensive covert measures were taken to preempt any social veto.

At the start of June 1976, known 'troublemakers' were called up for military service. They included student leaders from 1968, members of

[9] 'The New Evolutionism' in Michnik, *Letters from Prison*, pp. 143–5.

strike committees during the protests of 1970–1 and many others who had come into conflict with industrial management or Party organisations. Some 7,000 people were thereby removed from the scene of potential disturbances.[10] Next, the 'pricing operation' (*operacja cenowa*) was carefully prepared.

Provincial Party Secretaries were summoned to Warsaw to discuss its enactment. They reported an improved public attitude towards 'problems of prices', tactfully attributed to recent Congress speeches by Gierek and Premier Jaroszewicz. Although still the subject of intense popular debate and speculation, it 'had ceased being a taboo'. 'Working-people in general, and the Party *aktyw* in particular', had come to understand the necessity for changes. There was a 'good atmosphere' in large industrial enterprises, though railway workers were a particular problem: awash with gossip and rumours. Teachers were dissatisfied with low pay, as were health sector workers. Several Secretaries spoke of the need to prepare the Church for the price increases.[11]

The gist of two days' discussion (8–9 June) was that sporadic protests might be anticipated but they were, with proper handling, containable. Provincial Secretaries asked to be excused from attending the Sejm session at which increases would be announced, which implied they wished to be on the spot if trouble occurred. But one would not have expected any to single out their own fiefdoms as ungovernable.

The Ministry of Internal Affairs dispatched numerous circulars to local police headquarters on the policy; the operation was now named 'Summer '76'. On 10 June they called for 'vigilance' in view of possible threats to public order. 'Prophylactic-operational' measures should isolate 'destructive elements', who should be kept away from capitalist diplomats and visitors. Efforts should be made to cultivate prominent journalists and figures in culture and the arts as speakers against those enemies threatening the social, political and economic well-being of the country. There should be efforts to influence opinion-formers, such as the Polish Economists' Association. A special watch was to be kept on students and even school-children.[12]

The 'price changes' were ratified by a full Politburo on 15 June. The word 'increase' was evidently taboo. No word of dissent is recorded in the protocol,[13] simply matters of implementation. State propaganda was to be mobilised for this purpose. Senior officials boasted about the expected smoothness of the operation. For the first time in People's Poland, they told each other, the element of shock had been removed.

[10] J. Eisler (ed.), *Czerwiec 1976 w materiałach archiwalnych* (Warsaw, 2001), p. 34.
[11] *Ibid.* pp. 86–92. [12] *Ibid.* pp. 93–6. [13] *Ibid.* p. 31.

The changes they had resolved on would be decided through democratic, parliamentary mechanisms. 'Public consultation' was ensured, though the timetable was very tight.

The Premier would make the 'changes' public in the Sejm on Thursday 24 June. On Friday, consultation groups, including Party workers, would meet in major enterprises to discuss the measures. The Sejm would re-convene to approve the measures on Saturday night. They would come into force on Monday.

On the eve of the announcement, Party Secretary Kania held a meeting with the Episcopal Secretary, Archbishop Dąbrowski. Reminding his interlocutor that the authorities had recently given permission for the construction of thirty new churches, he remained evasive on prices. Admitting it was 'the major question of the moment', he stated that various options were under discussion. The Bishop retorted that popular opinion had been considering the question for some time and the level of anxiety was high, given the threat of real poverty.[14] This was well founded. The government had rejected rationing scarce goods as an alternative to inflation. Yet independent estimates showed almost one third of the population living below the officially defined 'social minimum'.[15] Moreover, the system of compensation for new prices was strongly regressive, leaving millions of Poles unable to pay.

Parliament duly approved the Premier's proposal 'for certain changes in the structure of prices and social recompensation for the effects of these changes'. They would reconvene to consider a report on 'consultations' with representatives of enterprises and workplaces. Officials and activists of the state-run Central Council of Trade Unions (CRSS) were taken to be 'representatives of working people'. All these subterfuges were to no avail. Public rejection of the new prices was instantaneous and nationwide.

According to inner-Party information, almost half the forty-nine voivodships reported protests. Major enterprises in Warsaw stopped work; those at Ursus Tractor Factory blocked the international railway line, imprisoning the express to Paris for several hours. Sixteen enterprises in Łódź came to a halt. Protests took place along the entire Baltic coast. There were stoppages in Silesia. There were day-long disturbances in Płock.[16] The most dramatic events were in Radom.

[14] P. Raina, *Rozmowy z władzami PRL*, vol. I: *1970–1981* (Warsaw, 1995), pp. 252–5.

[15] A. Tymowski, *Próba określenia minimum spożycia* (Warsaw, 1971). Also *Polityka*, 4 October 1980, and *Więź* 1980 (11/12).

[16] K. Dubiński, *Rewolta radomska. Czerwiec 76* (Warsaw, 1991), includes Ministry of Internal Affairs (MSW) reports; A. Friszke, *Opozycja polityczna*, p. 338.

The trouble started at the 'General Walter' armaments factory, the city's largest enterprise, at 7.10 a.m. A group of fifty or sixty workers held an 'advisory meeting' during a 'break in work' around 9 a.m. Not yet declaring a strike, they articulated their practical concerns and demands:

1 Changes in the scale of compensation [to make it less regressive]
2 Higher allowances for children and non-working mothers
3 No increase in the price of sugar and butter
4 How will piece-rates be worked out?
5 How will we pay for pre-schools, holidays and summer camps if food costs more?
. . .
10 Why do shops lack sugar, flour, *kasza* [groats], etc.?
11 Will there be enough supplies in shops after the increases?
12 Cancel the export of goods
13 Will the increases be calculated in alimony payments?
14 Everything should cost less, not more, because we have productive agriculture
15 Will apartment rents go up?[17]

The Director made no attempt to defend the increases, which he said were inevitable. A working mother explained to him that they would reduce her family to penury. The Director, a life-long 'Party-bureaucrat', explained that everyone would be adequately compensated and said they should now get back to work.[18] The manner of the increase was criticised as much as its substance. Its abrupt announcement exposed the fictitious nature of public 'consultation'. To the population, it underlined once again that trade union and other 'workers' organs' were 'for them and not for us'. A new slogan emerged: 'Let's go to the Party headquarters'.[19]

They sallied forth onto the streets and, joined by workers from adjoining enterprises – the shoe and leather factory, a cigarette factory, and the railway repair shop – they marched into town. The procession was joined by school-children and housewives en route. A crowd of 6,000 reached the Party building on 1 May Street.[20] The Party Secretary would not come out to the crowd, but offered to meet a delegation. This was rejected as a trap, for fear their delegates would be arrested. His deputy was sent out to calm the crowd, but had nothing specific to say, and was chased away in disgrace.

Realising that disaster could soon ensue, the Party Secretary spoke from the window, promising to ring Warsaw with their demands. He

[17] Eisler (ed.), *Czerwiec 1976*, pp. 100–1.
[18] W. Mizerski (ed.), *Radomski Czerwiec 1976*, vol. I, 2nd edn (Lublin, 1991), pp. 34–7.
[19] 'Radom 1976', *Karta* 1998 (25), p. 28.
[20] Dudek and Marszałkowski, *Walki uliczne*, pp. 228–34.

rang the Politburo, as promised, demanding a decision within two hours, 'because it was the only chance to save the situation'. The crowd agreed to wait. When no answer came, they entered the premises, and protestors ran down the red flag.

As the Polish flag was unfurled in its place, the crowd responded with the national anthem. Another group raided the Party functionaries' buffet, finding luxury items – including best-quality ham – not seen for years in ordinary shops. Protestors showed the strong public disdain for the inequality in resource allocation. Members of the *nomenklatura* enjoyed special-access shops. These not only sold scarce goods, but did so at below the normal price. Enraged, the crowd broke into filing cabinets, demolished furniture and equipment, and threw sofas and televisions from the windows. The Party headquarters was set on fire.

Around 40,000 demonstrators marched to other official buildings, heavily guarded by the militia, who attacked with gas and long, heavily weighted truncheons. The insurgents responded with improvised barricades (on which two of them were killed). Molotov cocktails were thrown. Militia vehicles were set alight, and other buildings, including the Passport Office, incinerated.[21] The whole city turned to revolt. Brutal treatment was dealt out on the streets and at police headquarters. Estimates of the number of protestors injured are put at 2,000.[22]

An emergency Politburo met in the late afternoon and decided to withdraw the 'price reform'. That evening, Premier Jaroszewicz stated on prime-time television that the 'government project, presently before the Sejm and the whole of society as a proposal' had not been finally decided upon. That would come later after the government had addressed 'problems which this project had given rise to amongst working people'. There would be further consultation at major enterprises across the country. Strikes were not mentioned.

The Party moved quickly to cover up this astonishing *débâcle*. Everyone could now clearly see the powerlessness of the monopolistic state. At mass rallies arranged in selected cities, carefully chosen audiences proclaimed their allegiance to the Gierek leadership. The Party declared it would 'solemnly and tenaciously' consult the working population on matters of socio-economic policy. The mass media attributed the 'recent disturbances' to agitators, parasites, criminals and anti-socialist elements: 'Drunken hooligans and hysterical women led the crowds.' The full force of the mono-Party judiciary was mobilised for summary trials, *in camera*, of those deemed responsible for the protests.

21 Photos in *Karta* 1998 (25), pp. 26–52.
22 Mizerski (ed.), *Radomski Czerwiec 1976*, pp. 139–40.

The Church raised its voice in their defence. Preaching to the annual pilgrimage to the country's most holy icon, the 'Black Madonna' of Częstochowa, on 26 August, Cardinal Wyszyński called for clemency for arrested workers and condemned the state's 'system of torture'. Its heavy-handed methods could do nothing to restore social peace. State violence could only undermine its own authority. In a carefully worded communiqué on 10 September, the Conference of Bishops considered that 'the state authorities should respect citizens' rights, conduct a genuine dialogue with society and take its voice into account when making decisions concerning society as a whole'. The state should end its repression of workers. Those already sentenced should be amnestied.[23]

A second protest came from fourteen Warsaw intellectuals who declared their solidarity with Polish workers. Price increases had been fixed behind the closed doors of the Council of Ministers. Dialogue could not take place under conditions of repression. Authentic nationwide debate required democratic freedoms, including a free press. Workers needed genuine representation: 'Recent events have shown yet again that the official trade unions are completely fictitious.'[24] Referring back to the tragic events of Poznań in 1956 and the Baltic coast in 1970, they asked if Poland could break the vicious circle and introduce a more democratic form of politics based upon force of argument rather than the argument of force.

One signatory, Kuroń, added that, as in 1956 in Poznań and 1970 on the Baltic coast, Polish workers had paid in blood for the mistakes of those in power. The root cause of the most recent repression was denial of workers' rights. The 'consultation' on price increases had been a 48-hour fiction. Workers had reacted spontaneously against it. Yet they had no legal means by which to make their views known, or to defend their interests. Despite ruling for thirty years, those in power had learned nothing and understood nothing. Kuroń foretold a further tragedy with international implications. His prediction took the form of an 'Open Letter' to the foremost Eurocommunist Enrico Berlinguer who published and responded positively to the letter.[25] His reply took the form of a letter from the Italian Communist Party to its Polish counterpart. It has not been published. But shortly afterwards, Gierek instructed the courts to lighten their sentencing of the accused workers. They were eventually amnestied. As Kuroń comments, 'It is the one occasion I know for certain that I managed to release people from prison.'[26]

[23] Z. Hemmerling and M. Nadolski (eds.), *Opozycja demokratyczna w Polsce 1976–1980. Wybór dokumentów* (Warsaw, 1994), pp. 97–8.
[24] *Aneks* 1976 (12). [25] *L'Unita*, 20 July 1976; *Kultura* (Paris) 1976 (9).
[26] J. Kuroń, *Gwiezdny czas* (London, 1991), p. 9.

A further appeal was addressed to Western intellectuals, through *Le Nouvel Observateur*. It followed the Warsaw trials of Ursus workers for 'active participation in outbreaks of hooliganism'. It pointed out that elementary norms of jurisprudence were absent: the defending counsels were all state appointees. Only immediate family were admitted to the courtroom, leaving many foreign journalists, and a large group of students and intellectuals, locked outside. Three- to five-year sentences were handed down. Closed trials had also been held in Radom, with sentences of up to ten years' imprisonment. The letter stated that responsibility for the June disorders lay solely with the authorities. Their behaviour had led to the emasculation of Workers' Councils established in 1956, and transformed trade unions into 'an inert, fictitious organism, subject and obedient to the apparatus of power'. The way to avert disorder in future was not repression but restoration of workers' rights: 'Demand the release of those who participated in the workers' protests in Poland.' The thirteen signatories appealed to all those who had defended the persecuted in Chile, Spain, Czechoslovakia and the USSR. Eight French writers were addressed by name, as were Günter Grass and Heinrich Boll, Arthur Miller and Saul Bellow, Stephen Spender and Robert Conquest.[27]

KOR

On 23 September, a Committee for the Defence of Workers (KOR) was formed, to offer medical, financial and legal help to those being persecuted for their part in the June protests and to their families. The initial inspiration came in the courtrooms themselves, when independent intellectuals attempted to witness the trials of those being punished or made scapegoats for their protests. Its foundation was announced in the form of an open letter by the writer Jerzy Andrzejewski to the Speaker of the Sejm and in an 'Appeal to Society and to the Authorities of the Polish People's Republic'.

After noting that acting illegally was nothing new for the Polish government, the Appeal stated: 'It has been a long while since the repressions have been as massive and as brutal as in recent times. For the first time in many years, arrests and interrogations are now accompanied by physical terror.' Tortured victims had no redress from those institutions supposed to help them: 'Trade unions are pathetic. Social welfare agencies also refuse to help.' Consequently, society must organise its own means for self-defence. It had 'no other means of defence against lawlessness other than solidarity and mutual aid'.[28]

[27] *Libération* (Paris), 28 July 1976. [28] Lipski, *KOR*, pp. 467–9.

Two elements in KOR's outlook are worthy of special comment. First, uniquely amongst Polish oppositionists, they acted openly. Public statements attached the names of signatories and their professions; addresses and home telephone numbers were given. That naturally made the authors prey to police repression, but it also gave credibility to their statements. In calling for civic courage from others, they showed the way themselves. Partly through KOR, it became apparent to the wider public that communist claims to subservience and obedience could be resisted. It became possible to say 'no' to demands by the state. Workers in June 1976 had shown the way – forcing the government to abandon its price increase overnight. There was a negative veto.

Second, KOR insisted that its activity – whatever the state might say to the contrary – was legal. In seeking legal ground for such activity, reliance was placed on the Helsinki Final Act, the Polish Constitution and various other laws and conventions. Attempts by the state to argue for its illegality were countered by the comment that the group had never applied for official 'registration'. A body became illegal only if it continued to act after being denied registration. Those which did not apply could exist in a form of legal limbo.[29] In KOR's case, even the notion of 'group' was understood informally. There was a membership, but no other trappings of an organisation: no membership fees, officials, rules or regulations. There were no elected posts, no minutes of meetings or any bureaucracy beyond the need for someone to man the telephone to summon the committee to meet, as occasion demanded, in private flats. Almost all members lived in Warsaw, reducing travel costs to a minimum and the need for funding to the costs of printing and paper.

As Joseph Kay commented: 'Despite the efforts of official detractors to present KOR as an isolated band of renegades and traitors, this tiny group of intellectuals began to exert an influence out of all proportion to their size. They set new standards of social behaviour. Consistently they have tried to break down the barriers between social classes.'[30] Public opinion, often considered impossible within a communist state, now became a political factor working on behalf of the opposition both at home and abroad.

Against all expectations, the initiative was rather effective. Reviewing its position one year later, KOR noted that all those sentenced for their part in the June protests were now free. Most had been re-employed, though in some cases at lower positions. However, the demand for identification and punishment of those responsible for torture and other violations of the rule of law had not been met. Nor had the call for

[29] *Ibid.* pp. 44–5. [30] Joseph Kay, 'The Polish Opposition', *Survey* Autumn 1979.

impartial investigation of the June events by a Special Commission of the Sejm been answered. In the course of its first year, moreover, the Committee had been approached by numerous other persons unjustly persecuted for political reasons not connected with the June events. KOR had learned of many other illegal actions by the police, secret police, judiciary and prison system. Rather than falling redundant, therefore, as the authorities no doubt hoped, the Committee broadened its scope to the protection of the whole society, establishing the 'Social Self-Defence Committee' (KSS), retaining the label 'KOR' for nostalgic reasons. They explained: 'We will continue our activity because we are convinced that the most effective weapon against the use of coercion by those in power is the active solidarity of the citizens.'[31]

Despite their rhetoric of diminishing class struggle, and their distant ideological goal of introducing classless societies, communist governments devoted immense resources to keeping social classes apart. In the Soviet Union, this had the effect of leaving the intelligentsia atomised. Though steadily enlarged to consist, by the Brezhnev period, of all those with higher education, its relations with other classes were virtually non-existent. The practice of intellectual 'dissent' and the periodic instances of workers' uprisings had no impact on each other: there was no perception of a communality of interest in respect of the monopolistic state. This now began to alter in Poland. Three areas of activity promoted by KOR have longer-term significance: contacts with students, with private (independent) farmers and with workers themselves. We will take each in turn.

Students

On 7 May 1977, a student at the Jagellonian University in Kraków was found dead in suspicious circumstance. Stanisław Pyjas, a KOR supporter, had last been seen alive collecting signatures for an appeal for a Sejm commission to investigate abuses by the security services following the June 1976 events. Pyjas had recently received death threats. Fellow-students had received anonymous letters denouncing him as a police informer. It urged them to 'settle the matter once and for all using every possible means at your disposal'. In a dignified reply, the students reminded the State Prosecutor that the right to petition was guaranteed by law.[32]

His requiem mass was held in the Dominican church in Kraków on 15 May. Many seeking to attend from other cities were arrested (including members of KOR) or detained en route. Nonetheless, the substantial

[31] Lipski, *KOR*, pp. 469–71. [32] Raina, *Political Opposition*, pp. 274–5.

congregation included around 2,000 students. That evening some 5,000 students held a candle-lit procession through the streets. Gathering beneath the Royal Castle (Wawel), they heard speakers calling the death of Pyjas political murder, and a declaration was passed forming a Students' Solidarity Committee (SKS) as 'authentic and independent student representation'. The Speaker of the Sejm was informed of this initiative the next day. The students' new body would be 'completely open and transparent'. The names and addresses of its founders were given.

Programmatic statements soon followed. These criticised the state's Socialist Students' Union, formed in place of four disparate unions in 1973, and thereafter treated as the independent representative of Polish students. The objections were that 'it does not represent the real interests of students', and that it was centralised in structure and the exclusive province of privileged elites. The 'Socialist' title was an affront to Catholic students. An early action of the Kraków SKS was to challenge the requirement that passport applicants receive from the state's union a statement of their 'proper moral and political position'.

By contrast, the SKS was 'to operate outside the officially sanctioned forms of socio-political activity, which are dependent on the Communist Party'.[33] It would be open to all students, irrespective of their worldview. It would organise itself in self-defence against further reprisals, and to this end would 'give strong moral support' to the work of KOR. In future, it would press for a more democratic structure for universities, curriculum reform to enable higher education to perform its functions of full development of the personality and enhancement of human rights and fundamental liberties: 'Higher education cannot function properly without autonomy.'[34]

It sought further to encourage 'independent self-organisation of Polish students outside officially recognised institutions'. The pattern was repeated in many university cities. Kuroń summed up this activity as 'the struggle for pluralism in every area of social life, in schools, scientific institutes, in film and in literature, in the Church, and in peasant households'.[35]

Independent farmers

Polish farmers have their own political traditions. A smallholder, Witos, was Prime Minister in the 1920s. Peasant political parties were federated in 1931 and a surge of political involvement culminated in a peasants'

[33] Hemmerling and Nadolski (eds.), *Opozycja demokratyczna*, pp. 176–8.

[34] *Bratniak* (Gdańsk) 1 October 1977 (1) (statement of 25 May 1977).

[35] J. Kuroń, 'List otwarty do zespołu *Bratniaka*', *Bratniak* March/April 1979 (16).

strike of 1937. During the Second World War, peasants had their own battalions. Peasant cultural activities also included a youth organisation (*Wici*), publishing enterprises, a press and a People's University. All this occurred in opposition to the state. Indeed, the latter was regarded – long before the post-war authorities closed all independent peasant organs down – as a repressive and alien institution.

Contacts with the state swung from the pole of bitter hostility during the period of partial collectivisation (1948–55),[36] towards regulated, if unfavourable, market relations. In Soviet terms, the shift was from Stalinist to Bukharinite approaches.[37] There were mutual misgivings. To the state, the Polish peasantry were the most backward element in their ideological and industrial programmes. To private farmers, the state was a perpetual source of intervention which led to resistance, sometimes expressed through civil disobedience.

In summer 1978, a new pension scheme was introduced for peasants, which required premiums to be paid at once for benefits to be received in 1980. Some 400,000 peasants withheld contributions. They organised token strikes against the policy, withholding milk deliveries to the state, and promised further protests if the authorities persisted in forcible attempts to collect the premiums.[38] Soon broader issues began to be raised. Inadequacies of infrastructure were criticised, especially of roads, schools and public transport. Peasants criticised the wastage of fallow land, nominally taken over by the state. They reported chronic shortages of supply. At the heart of these grievances lay an awareness of inequalities between town and countryside. Peasants noted that, unlike urban dwellers, they had to build their own communal facilities, at their own expense. This did not remind them of 'social action', as the communists called it, but of *szarwarki* - unpaid service to the landlord in the olden days.

Private farmers started to form Self-Defence Committees on KOR lines. Begun in the poorer, central and eastern voivodships, Lublin and Rzeszów, these spread to the semi-urban, Grójec region.[39] Resolutions were passed at open meetings, and published unofficially (without state censorship), with peasants' names and districts appended to them. A number of sharp statements were issued against harassment of their

[36] D. Jarosz, *Polityka władz komunistycznych w Polsce w latach 1948–1956 a chłopi* (Warsaw, 1998).
[37] V. P. Danilov, 'Bukharin and the Countryside' in A. Kemp-Welch (ed.), *The Ideas of Nikolai Bukharin* (Oxford, 1991), pp. 69–81.
[38] *Głos* 1978 (8) (30 July 1978, Lublin region).
[39] *Robotnik*, 25 September 1978 (21/22); Hemmerling and Nadolski (eds.), *Opozycja demokratyczna*, pp. 288–90 (9 September 1978, Zbrosza Duża).

most articulate members, who were commonly held in preventive detention for the duration of meetings.

Peasant protests gave the authorities an awkward choice. Outright repression, which would only cause counter-violence, was excluded: there was no return to Stalinist methods. However, the use of the market mechanism always operated in peasants' disfavour. Thus compulsory quotas for the delivery of slaughtered animals, cereals and potatoes had been lifted in 1972. But they were not replaced by cash incentives sufficient for the peasantry to increase production. The political opposition did not have an easy answer to this problem. But they pointed out that the peasantry needed confidence-building measures, to reassure them of the good intentions of their major buyer, the state. This meant restoring some of the previously abolished independent peasant institutions.

Yet any efforts at organising the peasants, whether from outside or amongst peasants themselves, had to confront traditional antagonisms towards the state. Here education was essential, as peasants themselves recognised when they reopened the Peasant Universities in February 1979. The first lectures considered peasant culture and national culture; peasant history, including the activities of the Polish Peasants' Party; human rights and the experience of KOR. Further lectures were planned on the wartime peasant battalions, on administrative law, economics and ethnography. In June 1979, a peasants' Centre for Knowledge was established to work for peasant self-government which, it noted, could not be organised from outside: 'All organisations must grow organically in particular villages.'[40] An amalgamation of Peasant Self-Defence Committees, a Provisional Committee of a Peasants' Independent Trade Union[41] and an association of religious believers contributed to this revival. Such strivings were the genesis of Rural Solidarity.

The Party's response was sharp indeed. Localities were regularly patrolled. Private cars were stopped and searched. People on the way to visit families were turned back. The authorities tried to prevent intellectuals from attending meetings of the Peasant University. Authors, experts, oppositionists and members of the Academy of Sciences were all prevented from delivering lectures. Peasants drew their own conclusions:

> The example of this small and embryonic social institution discloses the real intentions of the authorities. For them, the peasant should be ignorant, for only then will he be a willing slave. He must not think about democracy,

[40] *Robotnik*, 25 November 1978 (25), 15 December 1978 (26).

[41] Hemmerling and Nadolski (eds.), *Opozycja demokratyczna*, pp. 291–2 (10 September 1978, Lisów).

self-management or social history. He must labour, plough and raise pigs, but cannot even listen to an expert lecture on pig rearing.

Despite their own ignorance, peasants would not abandon the search for free thought: 'Only he who wants to be a slave will become one.'[42]

Workers

Determined to break through the division between workers and intellectuals, the latter initiated a bi-monthly *Biuletyn Informacyjny*. Modelled on the Russian uncensored *Chronicle of Current Events*, it was assembled by four Warsaw intellectuals, whose names and addresses appeared. The basic idea was to break the state's information monopoly and collate basic materials for social self-defence. Thus the first issues published details of police searches, confiscations, charges, sentences and brutalities from all over the country following the June events. It gave detailed coverage of trials of workers from Ursus, Płock, Poznań, Łódź and Radom; the harsh sentences handed down; the flimsy evidence; judicial irregularities; and harassment of correspondents.[43] Following this initiative, members of KOR sought more permanent means of cooperation for self-defence.

At first, the signs were not good. Workers looked askance at the project of 'free trade unions', pointing out that they had unions already, and that there seemed little purpose in supplementing one set of dummy institutions with another.[44] Social links between workers themselves outside the factory proved tenuous, making solidarity with the repressed difficult and external organisation almost impossible. It looked as though the existing pattern, workers' acquiescence punctuated by sudden outbursts of suppressed fury, would inevitably recur. But one channel of continuing communication with workers and between them was established. A news-sheet, *Robotnik* (Worker), was compiled and edited by KOR members and supporters. Its modest, semi-legible first issue explained the paper was one in which 'workers may publish their independent opinions, exchange experiences and build contacts with workers in other enterprises'. It could also help in practical ways: 'defending workers' interests through solidarity; increasing the part employees could play in setting wages, conditions and hours of work, social conditions and housing; supporting the independent representation of workers, which should replace the moribund Trade Unions'.[45]

42 Peasants' University, *Communiqué*, in Kay, 'The Polish Opposition', *Survey*, p. 13.
43 *Robotnik* November 1977 (5).
44 J. Lityński, *Labour Focus on Eastern Europe*, January 1980.
45 *Robotnik*, September 1977 (1).

Within eighteen months, the print-run rose – in offset – to 40,000. It reached workers in all major industries: Silesian miners, Kraków steel-makers, shipbuilders on the Baltic coast, textile workers and light-industrial employees in Central Poland. At one stage, distribution was done openly at the gates of factories and shipyards – this action was one of Wałęsa's first contacts with the political opposition. More usually, news-sheets were carried into work places for covert distribution. The existence of such a publication, which reached 100,000–200,000 workers, had no precedent in communist Eastern Europe.

The first articles dealt with basic issues: the lack of meat, high prices and inflation, and infringements of the labour code. These were followed by broader topics: 'Socialist Equality in Practice' (issue 12); 'Falsification of History', concerning Polish boundary changes in Soviet atlases (13); and a series of anniversaries – Poznań '56 (17), June '76 (18) – culminating in a special number, 'Czechoslovakia, 1968–78' (20). Polish workers' struggles were reported alongside those of miners in Romania and the unemployed in the Soviet Union.

A diversity of politics appeared, as *Robotnik* correspondents in Gdańsk, Silesia and Grudziądz (near Toruń) emerged as spokesmen for local issues. Thus, *Robotnik* printed a protest from citizens of Grudziądz, who listed the consumer shortages in their town. They catalogued the absence of children's clothing and domestic utensils, and asked why so many goods were available only in foreign-currency shops. Pointing out that 'we receive our wages and pensions in *złotys*', they demanded 'all goods be available in our currency'. Turning to social policies, they noted that the promised school and sports stadium for the town (which had 50,000 inhabitants) lay abandoned. Transport and housing were inadequate.[46] The petition, with almost 1,000 signatures, collected by Edmund Zadrożyński, was presented to the Sejm. Its only response was to send him to Toruń gaol.

While persecution of *Robotnik*'s correspondents was considerable, there was also a process of learning how to avoid repression. Strikes gained mass support only when they showed signs of being successful. The word 'strike' was often avoided: workers prefered to call their actions *awarie* (breakdowns), *przestoje* (bottle-necks), *przerwy w pracy* (breaks in work) or simply *zebrania* (meetings). Employees were aware that strike action would bring down on them the full force of factory managers, state administrators, Party and trade union officials, and possibly judges and militiamen.[47] Yet it regularly occurred.

[46] *Ibid.* 30 April 1979 (32). [47] J. Sreniowski, *Robotnik*, 17 June 1978 (17).

A common pattern was the occupation of a plant or factory until specific requirements – supply of meat to the town, restoration of old work-norms – were met. These actions were often successful. Such protests were almost invariably defensive responses to measures that the authorities had already taken. Much less frequent was the canvassing of new demands. Joseph Kay noted: 'Workers are not necessarily less interested in political freedoms than, say, scientific researchers, but are simply more pragmatic than intellectuals in assessing present possibilities. Such freedoms do not head a manual workers' agenda, but, once the authorities are on the run, "economic" demands from workers quickly escalate into the political domain.'[48]

To this end *Robotnik* published a Charter of Workers' Rights. The editors did not imagine that printing the Charter would at once improve the situation. Rather they hoped that formulating a more general programme would lead to gradual betterment of conditions, focus latent working-class discontent and so help ward off the next explosion: 'The sense of impotence should be shaken off'; 'If we do not begin to defend our interests today, the situation will only worsen.' The signatures came from twenty-six towns and cities. They included founders of the Free Trade Union on the Coast, Andrzej and Joanna Duda-Gwiazda, Anna Walentynowicz and Lech Wałęsa in Gdańsk, and all the editors of *Robotnik*.

A Preamble catalogued the present position:

- Citizens are deprived of the right to participate in decisions that concern them
- Basic rights of working people are restricted, such as the rights to safe and sensible work, to proper wages, and to rest
- A sense of inequality and social injustice is deepening
- A lack of institutions to defend working people – official trade unions are certainly not doing so
- Workers are deprived of a basic right to self-defence, that is the right to strike
- Society is bearing the cost of all mistakes by the authorities, and the costs of the present crisis. Our long-term aim is the setting-up of a self-defence system for working people, above all to create independent trade unions

The Charter then proceeded to immediate problems. First, wages should be inflation-linked and all workers guaranteed an independently assessed social minimum. 'Blatant and unjustified wage differentials' should be eliminated. Second, the country should move from the present 46-hour working week to one of 40 hours, without a reduction of wages. There should be no more (compulsory) week-end shift working for miners, and free Saturdays should be guaranteed across-the-board. Finally, safety at

[48] J. Kay, 'The Polish Opposition', *Survey*.

work should be observed in all cases, giving inspectors real powers, including those to shut down the enterprise when necessary. Factory medical facilities must be independent of management; 'Night work for women must be eliminated; women must not be forced to perform hard physical labour.' There was, however, no economic analysis to show that such measures were affordable.

The remaining clauses moved to wider issues.

1. *Evaluation of work done and promotion* 'cannot be based on Party membership, political opinions or worldviews'. Privileges such as bonuses, apartments and free holidays should be distributed publicly, with a list of the beneficiaries. It is necessary to eliminate the privileges of groups connected with the authorities (militia, Party *apparatchiks*) and to end special allocations of scarce goods 'housing, land, building materials, cars, special Medicare, luxury holiday villas, special pension rights etc.'
2. *Pressure to act against one's conscience.* No-one should be forced into immoral acts, to inform on others to superiors in the Party or secret police, or to take part in witch-hunts. No-one should be forced to produce shoddy goods, work in dangerous conditions, cover-up accidents at work or falsify reports.
3. *The 1975 Labour Code should be radically amended.* Article 52, used as an anti-strike law after the events of June 1976, must be changed. The right to strike must be guaranteed by law. Grounds for dismissal must be given in writing and be contestable in court, where the dismissed should have the right to be represented. Union activists, chosen by employees, should be immune from dismissal until their term of office had ended.[49]

The Charter tried to convince workers that it was possible to influence decision-making by the authorities. Strikes were effective, but only in the short run. Openness of information could achieve effective results. It was worth speaking up at meetings, and pressure should be put on officials of the state-run trade unions to speak up for their members. Yet such means of constant pressure remained embryonic: 'Only independent trade unions, supported by the workers they represent, have any chance of resisting the authorities; only they can constitute a force with which the authorities will have to reckon and with which they will negotiate on the basis of equality.'[50] Even the Chartists thought this was a distant goal.

Members of KOR had outstanding records of resistance to one form of authoritarian repression or another. It included thirteen members who took part in the underground resistance to Nazi occupation. A number of others were victims of show trials in the Stalinist and post-Stalin era. In political orientation it contained several former Party members, most

[49] *Robotnik* 18 July 1979, Special Issue (35). [50] *Ibid.*

notably the eminent economist Edward Lipiński who styled himself 'a socialist since 1906'. He was expelled from the Party in April 1977.

The relationship between KOR and Polish workers is complex and has often been debated.[51] Roman Laba, who spent some months at Solidarity's Gdańsk headquarters while it was an underground organisation and later wrote a very valuable account of earlier protests and worker organisations on the Coast, identifies an 'elite thesis' in Western literature. Expounding it, Laba cites a comment by Tim Garton Ash that 'KOR worked very much as Lenin recommended [in 'What is to be Done?'] that the conspiratorial communist party should work, raising the political consciousness of the proletariat in key industrial centres.'[52] Laba thinks Western writers were overly influenced by their intelligentsia contacts: 'Especially in repressive situations, intellectuals act as gatekeepers who interpret their own societies for foreigners.'[53] He criticises the claim that Polish intellectuals brought revolution to Polish workers *from outside*. He does not think they were attempting to circumvent the Marxian fix that 'false consciousness' – put simply, mental retardation – prevented all but the most 'advanced' workers from finding revolution for themselves.[54]

Joseph Kay, in 1979, was less theoretical:

> Perhaps surprisingly to Western critics who dub the Polish opposition 'Marxist', KOR subscribes to no all-embracing ideology. On the one hand, this means rejection of Marxism as propounded by the political authorities as an ineffectual catechism unrelated to socialist reality. On the other, it involves rejection of Western theories as having little relevance to the new societies of Eastern Europe.[55]

Kay saw KOR using 'social pressure, not socio-philosophical cogitation' as the more likely means to influence the authorities. The Leninist idea of bringing leadership to the working class from outside would have been anathema. But making no contact would have served only to perpetuate mono-Party rule.

It is not clear that the 'Workers or Intellectuals?' dichotomy captures the sociology or politics of Poland in this period. Neither label fits the categories – still less the activists – concerned: 'The new social entity that opposed the party-State can be conceptualised as *workers* only at the cost of serious distortion.'[56] Jan Kubik proposes 'a class of wage employees

51 M. Bernhard, 'Nowe spojrzenie na Solidarnośé', *Krytyka* 1992 (38). pp. 231–45.
52 T. Garton Ash, *The Polish Revolution* (London, 1983), pp. 24–5, 43.
53 Laba, *Roots of Solidarity*, p. 7. 54 *Ibid.*
55 J. Kay, 'The Polish Opposition', *Survey*.
56 J. Kubik, *The Power of Symbols against the Symbols of Power* (University Park, Pa., 1994), pp. 230–35.

and groups professionally active in the state sector, not occupying higher managerial positions'.[57] He concludes that, through evolving a common cultural framework, they came to be a new cultural-political class, in the Weberian sense, which heralded the demise of state socialism in Eastern Europe.

Pluralism

As the barrier of fear lifted, a growing number of activists engaged in politics beyond the boundaries of Party-imposed legality. Uncensored publications poured forth;[58] independent education initiatives flourished. A further source of counter-culture was academic. Sixteen staff dismissed from Warsaw University, including Andrzej Celiński, took the initiative to revive an older institution, the 'Flying University.'[59] The idea was to offer an alternative source of higher education, to raise subjects which state education held taboo (such as the history and culture of neighbouring national minorities) and to keep contacts alive between students and dismissed lecturers. Seven courses were offered in the first session: on post-war politics, economic thought, sociology, contemporary political ideologies, social psychology, literature and culture. After serious physical assaults, open lectures were abandoned. They were replaced by smaller seminars with invited speakers. The first lecture to be published was 'The Language of Propaganda'.[60]

As society spawned an astonishing array of institutions for self-government and self-defence, the familiar tendency in Polish history for citizens to carry on regardless of the state was accompanied by weakness at the top. Having had its key policy vetoed by workers' power, the Party was in no hurry for further humiliation. They preferred paralysis.

A 'Letter of the Fourteen', who included former leaders headed by Ochab, criticised Gierek's passivity in forthright terms. They called on the Party *aktyw* to formulate a 'daring yet realistic' programme of economic and social reform. 'Healthy forces' within the Party needed to assert themselves against the 'Party bureaucratic machine' which fostered only insincerity and torpor, depriving the mass membership of any scope for initiative or action.

57 *Ibid.* pp. 237–8.
58 As many as 6,506 are catalogued in *Bibliografia podziemnych druków zwartych z lat 1976–1989* (Warsaw, 1995).
59 Founding Declaration (Warsaw) in Hemmerling and Nadolski (eds.), *Opozycja demokratyczna*, pp. 231–4.
60 *Język Propagandy* (Warsaw, 1979).

The signatories, including three 'revisionist' CC Secretaries removed by Gomułka,[61] defined inner Party democracy as 'free discussion of an open character and an end to presenting opinions anonymously'. Lower echelons should have the right to criticise those above. There should be statutory rotation of high offices, and a struggle against privilege and flattery. Trade unions should become 'equal partners with the state administration and economic managers on all questions of pay and social policy'. Workers' Councils, co-opted after October 1956, and workers on the shop-floor should have a larger say in management.[62] The Gierek team ignored the letter, privately dismissed as a pathetic whinge from pensioners.

Even so the economic crisis of the late seventies seems to have obliged the authorities once more to broaden the range of opinions it considered, even to the extent of allowing rather critical documents to circulate as uncensored self-publications (*samwydaw*). Outstanding amongst these was the extensive survey 'Experience and the Future', whose preface explains how it was written. The group's inaugural seminar had been held in November 1978, with 100 public figures attending, but 'unfortunately the group was prevented by the authorities from performing its intended activities'. The first meeting was thus the last. Instead, a questionnaire was sent to some fifty figures in public and academic life, 'Party and non-party, atheists and believers', and a small editorial board collated their responses. These were collated in a 'Report on the State of the Republic and Ways to Rectify it', which was made public in May 1979.

It reflected a wide variety of viewpoints. However, all characterised the communist ('post-war') period as one of *fiat*, in which public consent was withheld from policies in whose formulation they had no involvement. It was difficult to discern any area of social life in which 'the rules of the game were recognised by all parties concerned'. Compromise, accommodating the interests of different social groups and reconciling the interests of individuals in society, had been entirely lacking. As a result, ordinary citizens had become steadily more distanced from the authorities and had come to look upon 'all public institutions – whether state, trade union or local – as "for them and not for us"'.

Earlier crises had provided the preconditions for reaching understandings, agreements and compromises with the widest sections of society. But these had been squandered. Such changes as did occur were simply handed down from above, and not subjected to any subsequent process of public scrutiny to ensure they were carried through. The inevitable

[61] Albrecht, Matwin and Morawski. [62] Raina, *Political Opposition*, Annex 1, pp. 444–51.

outcome was 'to increase the polarisation of politics and society'. The report discloses a general view that radical changes in the Polish socio-political 'model' are absolutely inevitable, yet simultaneously impossible, and tries to show that this need not be so.

Post-war history is analysed as a 'vicious circle': popular uprisings, followed by reform, withdrawal of reform and further popular explosions. It adds that the effect of every crisis was 'to limit and withdraw self-regulation, to blot out spontaneous initiative and hence to imprint ever more firmly the division between rulers and the ruled'. On law, for instance, one respondent commented: 'It is hard to avoid the impression that law, in a great many cases, performs a quasi-class role.'

The editors found that the basic problem was that post-war institutions lacked legitimacy: 'Over this whole period the regulations and norms of social life were not accepted.' Like KOR, they saw the basic need to build institutions that would genuinely mediate between the citizens and the state authorities. One reply stated Poland suffers from: 'pseudo-planning, pseudo-science, culture and, education; pseudo-legislation and consultation; elections that are not elections; the pompous opening of half-completed factories; a pseudo-struggle with apparent difficulties; pseudo-legality – so that no one believes what actually is the case, of which empirical investigation is anyway disallowed'.[63] The criticism continues through agriculture, wages and investments, local government and many other areas of public life.

The diagnosis is institutional: that nothing mediates between the closest circle of family and friends and the state, with disastrous social consequences – 'People drink and steal. They take and offer bribes. They make deals. They sneer at everything. Everything is "terrible" and "depressing".' But the remedy proposed is weaker. A minimum programme is put forward: to separate the Party from the legal and economic apparatuses and from the state; to extend powers of representative organs such as the Control Commission (NIK) and the Sejm; to restrict censorship and to build up legal guarantees against abuses, by legislative and administrative reform. But this first draft did not show what social or other pressures would lead to reform being achieved.

In March 1977, a new group was founded in defence of human rights (ROPCiO).[64] Its 'Appeal to Polish Society' outlined four basic foundations for protection of human rights in the country. The first was history: 'Respect, and demand for respect of human rights is one of the most

[63] 'Raport konwersatorium "Doświadczenie i Przyszłość"', in Hemmerling and Nadolski (eds.), *Opozycja demokratyczna*, p. 37.

[64] G. Waligóra, *Ruch Obrony Praw Człowieka i Obywatela, 1977–1981* (Warsaw, 2006).

valuable traditions and achievement of Polish culture.' A quintessential part of national consciousness, the rights of man, and of citizens, dignity of the individual, freedom and mutual tolerance had been venerated and celebrated down the ages: 'They are generally accepted as indispensable to our life as a society.' A second guarantee was the UN Universal Declaration of Human Rights (1948) and the UN International Convention on Human Rights (1966), which became part of international law following sufficient ratifications in early 1976 and was now binding on Poland following its signature on 7 March 1977. Thirdly, the Helsinki Final Act was held to raise respect for the rights and liberties of the individual as there defined 'to the level of a norm governing inter-state relations on our continent'. Finally, the Polish Constitution affirmed civil liberties that were essential not only for the spiritual well-being of the country, but also for the development of its economy and national culture. The founders were 'not forming any organisation or association'. They would simply keep watch over the observance of civil liberties, make known any infringements to both public opinion and the appropriate authorities, assist and protect victims, and cooperate in defence of human rights with external bodies 'so that the principle of freedom may triumph all over the world'.[65]

Introducing a symposium on political opposition in one-Party states,[66] Leonard Schapiro analysed the preconditions for interest-group activity. In the late seventies they started to appear in Poland. Polish public opinion certainly did exist. Part of the domestic opposition was attempting to reach and mould it. The tightening of censorship and other controls in the mid-1970s pushed many cultural figures out of public life, confronting them with the choice of silence or of opposition.

The outcome was a plethora of self-publications. Originally belletristic, it disseminated through independent publishing. An uncensored literature sprang up through independent publishing-houses, such as NOWA. Some of it came from banned authors (Tyrmand or Konwicki), some was in translation (Orwell and Günter Grass). The poetry of Mandelstam and Brodsky appeared, with that of Barańczak and (under the imprint of the Dzerzhinsky Institute of Satire) Szpotański. *Feuilletons*, literary criticism and reviews came out in the journal *Zapis*, edited in Poland and re-published in London. Soon the subject-matter broadened to major issues of public concern.

65 Hemmerling and Nadolski (eds.), *Opozycja demokratyczna*, pp. 165–7.

66 L. B. Schapiro, "Introduction", *Political Opposition in One-Party States* (Basingstoke: Macmillan, 1972)

At first, this simply gave the public information that had been withheld by state-censored publications. All governments use their executive powers to conceal information, and this was very much the case under communism. A key aim of opposition was to eat into this monopoly by independent research into problems of society and the economy. Leakage from official bodies was utilised, as welfare statistics filtered out of the Central Statistical Office and economic prognoses from the Planning Commission. The insistence on truth and accuracy opened up a gulf between unofficial and state publications. This was highlighted by the dramatic defection of a young censorship official to Sweden, where he revealed both the censors' rulebook and documentation of their interventions.[67]

Widely circulated in the country, and published in full abroad, these documents provide depressing testimony to the readiness of the authorities to censor vital information (such as the discharge of poisonous effluent into the Vistula) rather than acknowledge errors and inform the public.

There was now an international dimension to this activity. The United States' election of 1976 brought to the White House a President who sought a moral dimension to foreign policy. Republicans distanced themselves from what they saw as Carter's over-zealous and counter-productive espousal of human rights. Their criticism has been reiterated in subsequent historiography. Yet normative foreign policy had much resonance at the time. Within the USSR, dissidents such as Sakharov insisted that resolute and sustained pressure from the West was necessary. It was indeed the only way to make communist governments respect their Helsinki undertakings on human rights. A considerable number of Poles agreed.

Brzeziński took the view that the USA should encourage 'polycentrism' and pluralism in Eastern Europe. Presidential Directive 21 (13 September 1977) set out a policy giving preference to countries which were relatively more liberal internally and/or more independent of the Soviet Union. Carter's first major world trip included Poland. Brzeziński thought it would 'encourage the process of liberalization that was gathering momentum there'.[68]

Carter used his Polish visit (29 December 1977) to praise Poland's respect for human rights and religious freedom. ROPCiO engaged in various public activities at the time of Carter's visit but was denied access to his press conference. Instead, they supplied written questions, to which

67 *Czarna księga cenzury PRL*, 2 vols. (London, 1977–8).

68 Z. Brzeziński, *Power and Principle. Memoirs of the National Security Adviser 1977–1981* (London, 1983), pp. 296–300.

the President replied before leaving Warsaw. The key question concerned Poland:

Opinia [Opinion]: If movements and parties independent of the Government of Poland begin to engage in activity in Poland, would that, in the President's opinion, have influence on the policy of *détente* in Europe – and if so, what sort?
Carter: I think it inappropriate for me to comment on the internal politics of another country. I do, however, also feel that *détente* must involve not only governments but must also be supported and encouraged by non-official individuals and groups.[69]

The Party now made a serious attempt to improve relations with the Church. The change in policy was signalled in autumn 1977 by a meeting of the Party leader with Cardinal Wyszyński – the first with a Party leader since 1963. Gierek paid a visit to the Vatican at the end of the year. Then relations were transformed by the election of October 1978 which brought a Pole to the Papacy.

John Paul II was quickly recognised abroad for his acute political mind. Meeting him in June 1980, Brzeziński found 'a man of extraordinary vision and political intelligence. In a sense, I think it is fair to say that today he is *the* outstanding Western leader.'[70] At home, the Party put on a brave face, claiming the election to be a victory for all Poles (and indeed that it took place under their stewardship). There were, however, strong misgivings behind the scenes.

Arranging the Pope's visit was difficult.[71] The initial Episcopal proposal that this should coincide with the feast of St Stanisław (a bishop martyred by the king) was vetoed. The suggested itinerary was restricted to exclude the mining regions of Silesia. There were to be no days off for workers to see the pontiff; a special tax of $350 was to be imposed on foreign correspondents. Despite these obstacles, the papal visit (2–10 June 1979) became a massive festival in which the nation experienced itself as a community. As many as 12 million Poles saw the Pope in person and heard his cycle of thirty-two sermons. They called for an authentic dialogue between Church and state, while recognising their 'diametrically opposed concept of the world'.

An essential message was the dignity of labour. This could not be reduced to technology or even economics, but concerned fundamental principles and human rights. It became clear later in John Paul II's Papacy that making necessary statements against communism did not mean uncritical acceptance of the 'Western model' of economic competition and social

[69] Raina, *Political Opposition*, pp. 542–4. [70] Brzeziński, *Power and Principle*, p. 463.
[71] A. Friszke and M. Zaremba, *Wizyta Jana Pawła II w Polsce 1979. Dokumenty KC PZPR i MSW* (Warsaw, 2005).

pluralism.[72] Another theme was geopolitics. Though tactful towards the Soviet Union, the papal message was clear: 'It is necessary to work for peace and understanding amongst peoples and nations of the whole world. It is necessary to seek reconciliation. It is necessary to open the borders' (Kraków, Błonie Meadow). He mentioned forgotten and neglected nations. Recalling the tragedy of the Warsaw Uprising, he declared: 'There can be no just Europe without the independence of Poland marked on its map' (Warsaw mass). Thus the crippled and divided Europe, sanctioned at Yalta, required redress. There should be a change of the 'balance of forces' without using force itself.

At Auschwitz he commented on totalitarian coercion which deprives a person of his most fundamental rights. He condemned 'an ideology in which human rights are arbitrarily subordinated to the requirements of the system': 'No nation may develop at the expense of another, at the cost of another's enslavement, exploitation or death.' He recalled both those gassed at Auschwitz-Birkenau (Oświęcim-Brzezinka) and those frozen in the Siberian camps. The death camps were a contemporary Golgotha. He paused and pondered plaques in Hebrew and Russian, as well as Polish ones. The place was a symptom of war, a disproportionate growth of hatred, destruction and cruelty. War gave opportunities for positive values – courage, heroism and patriotism – but the losses were greater.

On arrival, he had stated 'Peace and understanding amongst nations can only be built on principles of respect for the objective rights of every nation, such as the right to exist, to be free, to respect social and political subjectivity, to create its own culture and civilisation' (Belweder – the Presidential Palace). His departure from the Kraków meadows was watched by 2 million people. The authorities left stewarding of these vast gatherings to the Church itself. There had been a temporary displacement of the communist state.

On the eve

Warnings of impending catastrophe abounded but the Gierek leadership was in no mood to listen. Even Brezhnev complained of his complacency: 'All we ever heard was: "Nothing is going on, no opposition exists, the Polish government and Party are in control of the situation."' He blamed this on 'stupidity, over-confidence or excessive ambition'.[73]

Gierek's New Year message for 1980 described Poland's economic 'difficulties' as temporary, the product of 'a dry summer and a harsh

[72] J. Lityński, *Robotnik* 20 June 1979 (34). [73] Kramer, *Special Working Paper*, pp. 41–2.

winter'. The Prime Minister was sacked but his replacement Babiuch, a Gierek ally, had no economic experience. Parliamentary elections were held, at which 99 per cent of voters were said to have supported the official list. The Episcopate stated that the 'dangerous economic situation' required the opening of an immediate dialogue. But their offer to mediate between the authorities and society was declined. There was immobility in policy and decision-making. There were two major problems.

Firstly, Poland's external debt had risen from $1.2 billion (1971) to $20.5 billion (1979).[74] Debt servicing as a share of export earnings grew in the same years from 12.4 per cent (1971) to 81.8 per cent (1979). By 1980 this had reached unity, taking up all total export earnings, despite the IMF practice of treating a 40 per cent debt service ratio as the manageable limit.[75] Since the country was unable to pay, rescheduling of interest and principal repayments was negotiated with Western governments (the so-called 'Paris Club') and commercial banks. Despite loans and aid from Comecon partners, Western imports had to be drastically cut back.

These included cement, metallurgical products and plastics, as well as pharmaceuticals, fertilisers and foodstuffs. Shortage of inputs reduced production. Bottle-necks occurred, sending the economy into a downward spiral of late completion dates, impossibility of completion and wasted investment. That in turn led to underused capacity, imported technology and equipment lying idle in yards and fields, and extensive employment imbalances. A labour surplus developed in some areas – mitigated by early retirement and guest-working abroad (principally in West Germany) – while other sectors lacked labour.

Secondly, prices did not reflect production costs and possibilities of supply. Rather than expressing an economic rationale, Polish prices were a good index of political instability. They fell by 1.2 per cent (1971) after Gierek's eventual reversal of the December 1970 increases. There was officially no inflation in 1972 and then modest increases until mid-decade. Further increases were held back by the 1976 protests. Then they rose steadily: 4.9 per cent (1977) 8.7 per cent (1978), 6.7 per cent (1979). To keep food prices relatively stable within this inflationary context absorbed increasing quantities of the state budget.[76] They were unsustainable. A further 'economic manoeuvre' was announced, but no reform.

Instead, the authorities again embarked on price increases. In theory, the population in 1980 was still paying 1960s prices for basic goods,

[74] *Rządowy raport o stanie gospodarki* (Warsaw, 1981), p. 124.
[75] D. Nuti, *The Socialist Register 1981*, p. 107. [76] *Ibid.* pp. 107–9.

although wages had more than doubled during the interim. Government food subsidies, especially for meat, had risen steeply. Overall, food subsidies rose from 19 billion złotys (1971) to 166 billion złotys (1979). In an effort to curb them, the government had introduced a two- (and later three-) tier system of pricing through the institution of 'commercial' (and later 'super-commercial') shops, selling superior cuts of meat at much higher prices.

Unlike in 1970 and 1976, the new round was unannounced. Better cuts of meat and meat products simply began to appear at higher prices, which had sometimes doubled. The public thus encountered them by chance. Driving from Łódź to Warsaw, one could find state shops selling the same cuts of meat at four different prices – a novelty for the planned economy. At Huta Warszawa, the works canteen alternated the new and old prices, sometimes several times a day.

But the public reaction was again negative for three main reasons. First, despite the irritating claim of 'consultation', increases were introduced without prior warning. Second, they were introduced through 'commercial shops', selling scarce goods at much higher prices, with a further innovation being the PEWEX shops (at which Polish goods were sold exclusively for hard currency), whose very existence offended a population which surveys found to be strongly egalitarian.[77] Finally, price rises were often accompanied by the announcement of stiffer work norms in many enterprises. It proved a fatal combination.

At first, the authorities did not respond to disturbances. The Politburo hoped that protests would soon die down. Secret-police reports avoided the word 'strike'. At the Ursus tractor plant near Warsaw they noted: 'The interruption of work had a spontaneous character at first. Participants did not put forward specific demands. The predominant theme of discussion was linked with higher wages.' They added: 'it took place peaceably, with no damage to equipment or office furniture.'[78] On 3 July, a few dozen employees stopped work at the Gdańsk Shipyard, but a wider strike did not develop. Short strikes also occurred at the Cegielski Works (formerly ZiSPO) in Poznań and numerous smaller enterprises. Until 10 July the secret police reported them as 'Interruptions in Work and Expressions of Disquiet'. Then they were promoted to 'Social Unrest and Conflicts in the Workplaces'.

Wherever protests occurred, enterprise managers were under instructions to pay compensating wage increases, usually between 10 per cent and 15 per cent, and, above all, to settle protests quickly. However, the

[77] S. Nowak, 'Values and Attitudes of the Polish People', *Scientific American* (1981).

[78] K. Dubiński, *Zeszyty Historyczne* (Paris) 2000 (133). (Hereafter *Meldunki MSW*.)

case-by-case series of settlements served to escalate rather than diminish demands. Those who had earlier settled returned with fresh claims on hearing of more favourable awards elsewhere. Such leap-frogging was inevitable and vitiated the purpose of putting up prices in the first place. This was not solely to restore domestic equilibrium, but also to offer evidence of prudent management and greater economic rationality to external creditors. The shift of food exports and consumer goods to the internal market would make Polish borrowing in hard-currency money markets more difficult and increase the need for further Western credits.

KOR announced it would keep the public informed about the strike actions. Its supporters Andrzej Gwiazda and Joanna Duda-Gwiazda were detained on 4 July for hawking leaflets with 'inflammatory contents'.[79] But the authorities did not arrest KOR's leading activists for another six weeks. Kuroń joked that bugging his telephone perhaps helped the authorities to keep abreast of developments and anticipate planned protests. His Warsaw apartment was also a vital source of information for the Western press.

KOR issued an appeal to 'the workforce all over Poland'. It urged them to avoid all forms of protest which the authorities might use to provoke violent disturbances. The most effective form of action would be self-organisation at the workplace, electing workers' representatives to put demands in the name of workers and conduct negotiations with the management. The most essential requirement was solidarity. This was the only way to protect those on strike, and to prevent the powers-that-be from taking punitive action against their representatives.[80]

The strike agenda widened. Aircraft workers in Świdnik refused to listen to the Minister for Machine Industries and demanded that Gierek come in person to address the workforce.[81] Instead he appeared on television during a conference of Party *aktyw* which confirmed the commercial prices, though they were to be limited to two categories of meat, to lard, certain poultry and a number of tinned meats. He described the situation as 'complex'. He did not add that in some workplaces price increases were seen as the outcome of an arbitrary politics which needed regulation through workers' control.[82]

The July strikes, though sporadic and uncoordinated, formed a new pattern. Street protests, which had ended tragically in December 1970, were avoided. Protestors stayed within the workplace. Rather than issuing a straight ultimatum – withdrawal of the price increase, as in

79 *Robotnik* 12 July 1980, Special Issue (57). 80 Lipski, *KOR*, p. 365.
81 J.-Y. Potel, *The Summer before the Frost. Solidarity in Poland* (London, 1982), p. 35.
82 *Ibid.*

June 1976 – demands were now more nuanced. Strikers sought compensation for price increases and then shifted the discussion towards economic management in general. This led on to questions of representation and independent unions that would ultimately require reconstruction of the political system. Politicisation was reflected in the secret-police *Bulletins*. By mid-July, they recorded fourteen stoppages.[83] By far the most significant was in Lublin.

A 'stoppage committee' had been formed at Lublin's 10,000-strong lorry factory (FSC). Enraged by simultaneous prices increases and higher work norms, they called for negotiations with management. When the Director deplored the cost of lost work and appealed to patriotism, this grew to a strike committee of eighty members. Demands included abolition of hard-currency shops and special outlets 'for privileged social groups'. The same prices should be paid by all social groups 'including the state apparatus'. Everyone's family allowances and other benefits should be raised to levels received by the army and militia (a 1,000 per cent increase). Faced with such escalation, the Director declared that someone from the central authorities would come to meet them.[84]

Whilst the FSC soon settled for much less than demanded, urban transport came to a halt and railway workers threatened to strike. The railway station was blocked by seventy locomotives.[85] Since Lublin lay on the strategic line between the Soviet Union and East Germany, where many Red Army divisions were stationed, this was escalation indeed. Blackleg workers from Siedlce, sent in to break the strike, went home after hearing an appeal from the strike committee. Rumours spread that Polish shops were empty because goods had been carried off to Moscow, where the Olympics were due to open on 19 July. Strikers stayed strictly within their gates, remembering clearly the violence in neighbouring Radom four years earlier. This was in effect a general strike, but without the negotiating powers of an inter-enterprise strike committee.[86]

The Politburo met in emergency session (11 July). Gierek reiterated the remarks he had made on television: that the purpose of government was to improve the living conditions of working people through restoring the economy, but higher prices were needed in the interests of good economic management and effectiveness. It was the business of workplace directors to make this understood.[87] A group of managers was

[83] *Meldunki MSW* (12 July 1980), pp. 87–9. [84] *Ibid.*
[85] *Meldunki MSW* (18 July 1980), pp. 100–1.
[86] M. Dąbrowski, 'Lubelski lipiec 1980', *Miesiące. Przegląd Zwiazkowy* (NSZZ Solidarność Lublin) 1981 (1); D. Singer, *The Road to Gdańsk* (London, 1981), pp. 214–17.
[87] Z. Włodek (ed.), *Tajne dokumenty Biura Politycznego. PZPR a 'Solidarność' 1980–1981*, (London, 1992), pp. 19–20.

flown to Warsaw that day and told to buy 'social peace' through material concessions. Other Politburo members demanded more significant initiatives. Babiuch thought the strike wave, already almost a fortnight old, had no end in sight. He thought the Party *aktyw* should be mobilised to defend the increases. Kania also expressed urgency: 'Time plays a great role. We are faced with great insecurity.'[88] But even he had no specific measures to propose.

KOR issued a statement the same day: 'The authorities should realise that they cannot avoid negotiations with society and that it principally depends on them whether these will take place peacefully or in an atmosphere of sharpening conflict.'[89] Reprisals against 'independent social and political activists' should cease. The powers of the militia and secret police should be restricted. An independent judiciary should be restored and all political prisoners released immediately.[90]

Lublin was still the centre of attention. Following the sharp downturn in wages and supplies in the preceding months, announcement of higher work norms had led to a four-hour stoppage on the railways.[91] Links developed between protestors and the intellectual opposition, both within the local Catholic University and through Father Jan Zieja, a member of KOR. As the strike spread, news was transmitted to Kuroń in Warsaw, thence abroad, and broadcast back to Poland through RFE. Lublin began a new manner of protest: peaceful stoppage in support of workers' rights.

On 18 July, the Politburo learned that Lublin had come to a complete standstill: 80,000 were on strike from 177 workplaces. Party *aktyw* in striking enterprises had melted away. Negotiations to reopen the railways had come to nothing and occupation of the State Railways Board was being planned. There were rumours of a rally next day, to coincide with the opening ceremony of the Moscow Olympics. Faced with this new crisis, Gierek reiterated old themes: 'We need a campaign to strengthen the effectiveness of economic management (*gospodarowania*).' 'Exorbitant demands' were unacceptable. It was a 'positive sign' that unrest was restricted to Lublin and Stalowa Wola. However, he conceded that the rail strike was a 'strategic blow' at supply-lines for the Russian armies in the DDR: 'If it drags on, we can expect questions from the Russian comrades.' General Jaruzelski was more explicit: continued stoppages would pose a 'threat to the [Polish] nation'.[92] The idea of a

88 *Ibid.* pp. 20–1.
89 *Robotnik*, 12 July 1980 (57), and Lipski, *KOR*, pp. 365–6. 90 *Ibid.*
91 M. Choma, 'Strajk Lubelskich kolejarzy', *Biuletyn IPN* 2002 (12), (15 May 1980).
92 AAN 235/V/1816, pp. 2–3.

televised appeal 'To the People of Lublin' was mooted and kept in reserve. A Politburo letter was thought too difficult to distribute, given reluctance to publish it in the press. Gierek thought militarisation of the railways would be difficult to enforce, but that things would calm down if people acted 'honestly'.

Instead, Lublin was sent a Government Commission, headed by Mieczysław Jagielski, a senior government official with broad economic experience. A former Minister of Agriculture, he had been promoted to Gierek's first Politburo, in which he became a key member of the new economic team as Chairman of the Planning Commission and Poland's permanent representative to the Moscow-based COMECON. His mission to Lublin, for which he was also a Sejm deputy, became a dress rehearsal for the Gdańsk talks in August.

An agreement to end the strike was signed the following evening, in a ceremony attended by 'guarantors' from both the strike committees and city and provincial officials. The points agreed included fresh elections to the official trade unions, in which members of the former strike committees could stand as candidates. There were wage compensations, increased supplies and withdrawal of 'commercial prices'. The financial costs of this settlement were prodigious. The state simply issued more currency. One observer remarked: 'the rulers could still use the printing presses to save their necks'.[93] Such apparent generosity led Kuroń to predict that the authorities would renege on their promises, thus precipitating fresh protests in the autumn.

On 20 July, the CIA sent the first of several 'Alert Memos' on Poland to the President. It considered that the Soviets 'would be extremely reluctant to take military action under any conditions', especially during the Olympics. Satellite surveillance and other sources had noted no special activity on the part of the two Soviet divisions stationed in Poland, or of Soviet forces on the Western border with Poland. But there were other possible scenarios. Moscow would be hopeful that Gierek could bring the situation under control, as he had in 1970 and 1976, and would offer him full support for the third time. However, there were circumstances in which this wager on Gierek might break down. The Polish leadership was relying on patriotism – by implicitly raising fears of Soviet intervention – and on the Church to help calm the situation behind the scenes. The strategy might not work: 'Festering labour unrest could degenerate rapidly into violence, however, and the regime could be obliged to introduce force. If the Polish leadership proved incapable of restoring order in a

[93] Singer, *The Road to Gdańsk*, p. 216.

situation that had deteriorated into violent confrontation, we believe the Soviets would, as a last resort, intervene.'[94]

For the moment, though, the Polish authorities relaxed. Assured by Kania that there was no need to delay or cancel his holiday and that all would remain under control in his absence, Gierek left for three weeks in the Crimea. This compulsorily included an annual interview with Brezhnev, also vacationing on the coast. Their first encounter (31 July) was somewhat difficult. In contrast to the usual 'complete identity of views on all issues', there was a more cautious communiqué on 'complete mutual understanding'. That suggested considerable divergences.

Instead of passivity, Brezhnev urged Gierek to take the initiative on two fronts. Given the peculiar idiom of Soviet Leninism, they needed some translation into the language of Polish daily practice: 'Foster socialist internationalism, while decisively rebuffing all attempts to use nationalism to stir up anti-socialist and anti-Soviet sentiments, distorting the history of Soviet–Polish relations and the nature of relations between the USSR and People's Poland.' We are not told what illustrations Brezhnev gave of these tendencies: 'Undertake vigorous propaganda against efforts to slide over the class content of socialist patriotism under the slogan "All Poles in the world are brothers" and to idealise Poland's pre-Revolutionary past'.[95] The reference here was doubtless the surge of national pride following the election of the first Polish Pope, and the inclusive nature of his pilgrimage in early summer 1979. To the long-standing Soviet phobia of 'clericalism' was now added the potential links (especially at local level) between the Church and the sporadic, but swelling, strike movement.[96]

Strikes continued. There were protests in ten regions on 5 August alone.[97] Even so, the Party Propaganda Secretary (Jerzy Łukaszewicz) told foreign journalists on 12 August that the 'strike' wave was over. This was the first time the word had been used officially. Commenting mildly that 'they are not a good way of making progress', he added that they must be settled exclusively by negotiations, through which the position of trade unions could be reviewed and their role modified.[98] Two days later, the most momentous of all Polish strikes began: the birth of Solidarity.

[94] *National Intelligence Daily* (hereafter *NID*), 21 July 1980 (NSA).

[95] M. Kramer, *Soviet Deliberations during the Polish Crisis, 1980–1981*, Cold War International History Project Special Working Paper no. 1 (Washington, April 1999) (hereafter Kramer, Special Working Paper), pp. 42–3.

[96] M. Choma, 'Strajk Lubelskich kolejarzy', *Biuletyn IPN* 2002 (12), (15 May 1980).

[97] *Meldunki MSW* (6 August 1980), pp. 136–9.

[98] K. Ruane, *The Polish Challenge* (London, 1981), p. 10.

10 Gdańsk

> We understood a simple truth: people can organise themselves! This is a revolution – the most peaceful one you can imagine
>
> Kuroń, *Samorządność* (Gdańsk) 1981 (3)

Western historians have interpreted Solidarity in two main ways. Minimalists view Solidarity simply as the culmination of workers' protests, begun in 1970, against the Party's repressive and incompetent management of the economy. As Tony Judt puts it: 'They were not in themselves a harbinger of the downfall of communist power.'[1] Maximalists see Solidarity as the start of the Soviet Union's collapse. Martin Malia dedicates his study 'To Solidarity which began the task of dismantling communism in 1980, eventually completed by Democratic Russia in 1991'.[2]

Animated discussion of the Lublin events had taken place amongst the Free Trade Unionists on the Coast. But Anna Walentynowicz notes that 'even we thought there was little prospect of doing the same. Shipyard workers were still too frightened. We anticipated at least two more years of misery before society at large would be ready to act.'[3] Wałęsa agreed: 'I was haunted by the idea that August [1980] had come too soon, that we needed a year or two more of hard work to prepare.'[4] Despite their hesitations, an opportunity for immediate action was now presented.

Walentynowicz was summarily dismissed from the Gdańsk Shipyard on 9 August, just five months before she was due for retirement. This vindictive form of dismissal, which meant automatic loss of pension rights, led to protests from the Free Trade Unions, and from the editors of *Robotnik Wybrzeża*, Bogdan Borusewicz and the Gwiazdas. Their

[1] T. Judt, *Postwar: A History of Europe since 1945* (London, 2005), p. 589.

[2] M. Malia, *The Soviet Tragedy: A History of Socialism in Russia, 1917–1991* (New York, 1994), p. iii.

[3] 'Opowiada Anna Walentynowicz' in M. Chojecki (ed.), *Gdańsk-Sierpień 1980* (Warsaw, 1981), p. 5.

[4] Wałęsa, *A Path of Hope*, p. 118.

statement 'To the Workers of the Gdańsk Shipyard' related that Walentynowicz had worked there since 1950, first as a welder, latterly as a crane driver, as an exemplary employee, with medals to prove it. But management had changed their attitude as soon as she involved herself in unofficial union activity. By defending colleagues who had been unjustly persecuted, she brought sanctions upon herself. The appeal stated that this had implications for everyone: 'The best way of defending our own interests is to defend one another. That's why we are calling on you to defend Anna Walentynowicz.'[5]

On 14 August, three workers arrived early for the first shift. They put up seven posters: 'We demand a wage increase of 1,000 złotys and reinstatement of Anna Walentynowicz.' As other workers came in, they handed out 500 copies of the appeal and *Robotnik*. Borowczak told them: 'Lublin rose up, now it's our turn to fight.'[6] Groups gathered round the posters and discussion began. The temperature rose when an official attempted to pull the posters down. Then Borowczak led a small group to the larger ships' hull department.

Somewhat later, the Party Secretary drew up at the gates in his Fiat 1300. He explained that Walentynowicz had been sacked for 'disciplinary reasons'. Reminding him that she had worked there for thirty years and gained three service medals, the crowd, now swollen to 1,000, moved on. The workers observed a minute's silence for the victims of December 1970 beneath Gate Two and sang the national anthem. Borowczak declared 'We must defend Walentynowicz. If they can sack people like her, what will they do to us? We have nothing to lose.' The Director's car was sent to fetch her.

A Strike Committee was created at the Gdańsk Shipyard, with a special appeal to older and trusted workers to come forward. Borowczak explained: 'I wanted no repeat of 1970 and 1976, when two department heads were on the Strike Committee and simply sold us out.' The twenty chosen included Walentynowicz and Wałęsa. A list of demands was formulated, including the reinstatement and the wage increase, but also social and political issues. These included dissolving the discredited factory and section council and creating free trade unions, a monument to the victims of the December 1970 massacre on the Coast, and release of political prisoners.[7] The Director climbed up on a bulldozer and appealed for a return to work. Nobody listened. Wałęsa, forewarned of the protest by siren and hoisted into the Yard over the steel fence,

[5] *Ibid.* pp. 116–17.
[6] Account related to K. Wyszkowski in *Tygodnik Solidarność* 1981 (20).
[7] *Meldunki MSW* (15 August 1980), pp. 156–7.

scrambled up alongside him and took charge of the strike. Broadcast of negotiations within the Shipyard and reinstatement of Walentynowicz were set as preconditions for holding talks.

Technicians rigged up loudspeakers in the health and safety building and two delegates from each department assembled there for talks with management. On one side of the table sat Wałęsa, Borowczak and Felski, on the other the Director, his assistant and the Party Secretary (Wójcik). The latter made a tortuous speech to which the strikers responded: 'Why don't you use our language? Whom are you addressing? Speak simply and clearly.'[8] Management rejected the proposed memorial, citing planning restrictions and loss of parking facilities. Wójcik mentioned the Shipyard already had a tablet commemorating victims of Nazism. The strikers replied: 'We want a monument, not a plaque.'[9]

They called for discussion of their demands and suggested that the new Prime Minister Babiuch come to hold talks 'because he has the authority to do so'. The Director announced that he would receive authorization 'on the hot line' at any moment. But it was nearing 4 p.m. (the end of office hours) and nobody believed him. Wałęsa announced: 'We stay the night.' By early evening, the strike included the whole Gdańsk Shipyard, the Repair Yard (2,000 workers) and many smaller enterprises.[10]

Kania told the Politburo that a 'meeting' of workers in the Gdańsk Shipyard had formed a committee for talks with the Director. But they had not listened to him and he had no impact. The position was therefore insecure, with demands escalating. Anti-socialist elements were operating, in particular the 'recently sacked Wałęsa, who has links to the Kuroń group'. Counter-measures had been taken to protect the yard from sabotage and to regain the political offensive. Militia reinforcements were being sent to Gdańsk and three army regiments put on alert.[11]

The Politburo thought the public should be addressed on television, but was not clear what line to take. Should they admit to 'work stoppages'? They deplored the role of *Robotnik* in fomenting protests, particularly its recent article 'How to organise strikes'. They sent a plane to the Crimea, to bring Gierek back to Poland forthwith. Gierek returned to face the music, which he began to suspect was being orchestrated by political opponents. In retirement he cites the security apparatus, and Kania in particular, as perceiving advantages in his removal.[12]

8 *Tygodnik Solidarność* 1981 (20).
9 A. Drzycimski and T. Skutnik, *Zapis Rokowań Gdańskich. Sierpień 1980* (Paris, n.d.). Reissued as *Gdańsk Sierpień '80. Rozmowy* (Gdańsk, 1990), pp. 13–55.
10 *Meldunki MSW* (15 August 1980), p. 158.
11 Włodek (ed.), *Tajne dokumenty*, pp. 24–5.
12 J. Rolicki (ed.), *Edward Gierek: Przerwana dekada* (Warsaw, 1990), pp. 155–60.

Kania reported to the Politburo that, whilst Szczecin remained calm despite an attempted strike, the Gdańsk region was virtually paralysed. Demands had escalated beyond the 'social', which he defined in economic terms. They now included 'other postulates', such as raising family allowances to the levels received by the military and militia, and the reinstatement of Walentynowicz and Wałęsa.[13] This could get out of control, either through adventurism, or (more likely) because of a level of public support for strikers which meant that a policy of rejecting their demands was bound to fail.

Propaganda chief Łukaszewicz called the demands 'political', citing the call for 'new trade unions, monuments commemorating victims of December 1970, and release of political prisoners'. KOR activists were now appearing openly and publicly as leaders. By contrast, the (official) trade unions were inactive and the Party rank-and-file passive.[14] Gierek conceded that a dangerous situation had arisen, in which 'use of force' might become necessary. A state of 'serious threat to domestic security' was declared within the Ministry of the Interior. It drew up contingency plans (known by the code-name 'Lato-80'), headed by a deputy minister of defence, General Bogusław Stachura.[15]

Under these secret orders, commandos dropped by military helicopters would storm the Gdańsk Shipyard. Gdańsk would be cut off from the outside world until pacification was complete. It was assumed this would involve mass arrests. The allies were kept fully informed and ready to provide whatever 'assistance' became necessary. The Soviet News Agency (TASS) announced 'routine manoeuvres' of the Warsaw Pact in East Germany and the Baltic Sea. However 'Lato-80' was never put into effect. Whilst General Stachura contended that military action would quickly 'exterminate the counter-revolutionary nest in Gdańsk', most Politburo members were less sanguine. Kania's view that no large-scale crackdown could be enacted so soon eventually prevailed. Negotiations were now the best option.

Political risk assessment in Washington reported that 'the regime apparently is getting ready to use force if necessary. We have sighted police disembarking from aircraft, and party security boss Stanisław Kania has been in Gdańsk at least since Monday.'[16] But they also noted the apparent endorsement by Moscow of Gierek's handling of the crisis. In public, at least, the Soviet Party was expressing confidence that their Polish counterpart could restore order, and that economic assistance would be forthcoming for this purpose. However, mindful of the impact

[13] Włodek (ed.), *Tajne dokumenty*, p. 28. [14] *Ibid.* pp. 29–31.
[15] K. Dubiński, *Zeszyty Historyczne* 133. [16] *NID* (20 August 1980), p. 2.

of Polish events on its own population, Moscow had resumed the jamming of Western broadcasts for the first time since signing the Helsinki Agreement.

The Gdańsk region now had 50,000 people on strike, and the ripple was still spreading. At the Shipyard, negotiations with management dragged on. It was clear the Director intended to restrict the agenda to the wage demand, and, further, to split the strikers by insisting on differential increases, rather than accepting the strikers' demand for 2,000 złotys across the board. Stalemate ensued. But one significant new proposal was read out. Strikers at the Northern Shipyard proposed free trade unions and factory councils, 'independent of the administration and political apparatus'. They would be created through immediate free elections in which Strike Committee members could be candidates.[17]

The evening's television address by Premier Babiuch was not well received. According to first reactions, picked up by informers, it contained nothing specific, had no time-table for action, and showed scant responsibility for the future of the country. Commentary in Kraków likewise noted it offered nothing in response to society's needs. After the speech had been relayed to strikers in the Gdańsk Shipyard, one remarked, 'We want to talk to the Prime Minister, not listen to him.' Consensus in the Szczecin Shipyards was that the vacuous speech demonstrated the government had no programme and had no-one capable of restoring the economy.[18]

A 'coordinating team for central authority activity until the strikes are ended' was established under Kania, who now essentially took charge of the crisis. A very political general, Baryła, head of the Main Political Administration of the Polish Army, was added to the team. He became one of the most vigorous opponents of Solidarity. A report from Gdańsk noted that a new issue had emerged: 'creating "free trade unions"'. This was 'a success for KOR'.[19]

The Gdańsk authorities had managed to narrow negotiations down to the wage question. The Director repeated his earlier offer of 1,200 złotys, while mandated departmental delegates all insisted on 1,500. When the Director withdrew to consult with higher authorities, the free trade union issue re-emerged and a list of 'founder members' was circulated. But what they were founding was extremely unclear as no free trade union statute yet existed, nor any programme other than its name. Then the Director returned to announce acceptance of the 1,500 złotys. It was, however,

[17] Drzycimski and Skutnik, *Zapis Rokowań*, p. 83.
[18] *Meldunki MSW* (16 August 1980), pp. 163–4.
[19] Włodek (ed.), *Tajne dokumenty*, pp. 34–5.

conditional on an immediate evacuation of the Shipyard 'for security reasons' and a return to normal work on Monday. Debate amongst strike delegates ensued.

Wałęsa tried to close discussion: 'Let's not be provocative. This is enough.' Others reminded him this was a matter for collective decision. A remaining issue concerned guarantees for what had been agreed. Strike delegates were adamant that oral promises would not do: 'Kociołek appealed to us to return to work next day [15 December 1970] and machine guns were waiting for us.' When the Director offered his word of honour and asked 'Why are you afraid?' the answer came 'December: So many corpses'.[20] It was agreed that guarantees would be signed by Gdańsk Party Secretary Fiszbach.

In the early afternoon, when guarantees were given, Wałęsa asked the Shipyard workers over the loudspeaker whether they confirmed the delegates' decision to end the strike.[21] They did so and he asked – in accordance with the agreement – that the Shipyard be evacuated within the next three hours. As delegates filed out of the hall, they encountered members of the strike committees at other enterprises – the Repair and Northern Shipyards, Urban Transport (WPK) and various factories – who accused them of accepting worthless guarantees and abandoning the smaller workplaces which would now be 'crushed like flies'.[22] Pandemonium ensued.

Wałęsa changed his mind on the spot and tried to countermand the evacuation order, but the loudspeaker system was already disconnected. Walentynowicz rushed to Gate 3 in order to explain the need for a strike in solidarity with smaller enterprises. No-one listened. As she recalls: 'Someone shouted' "You want to strike? Go ahead." I burst into tears, but Alinka [Alina Pieńkowska] jumped onto a barrel and began to speak about the need to show solidarity with those who supported us. Someone in the crowd called out "She's right. They're not going to forgive us these three days either." The Gate was closed.'[23] The scene was repeated at Gates 1 and 2.[24] When the last Gate was shut, about 2,000 employees remained in the Shipyard. An Interfactory Strike Committee (MKS) was elected and a fresh list of demands drawn up. The Solidarity strike had begun.

[20] *Ibid.* p. 147.

[21] W. Giełżyński and L. Stefański, *Gdańsk-Sierpień 1980* (Warsaw, 1981), p. 44.

[22] S. Cenckiewicz, 'Kalendarium Sierpnia '80. Wypisy źródłowe z dokumentów MO i SB', *Biuletyn Instytutu Pamięci Narodowej* 2005 (7–8).

[23] 'Opowiada Anna Walentynowicz' in *Gdańsk-Sierpień 1980*, p. 8.

[24] A useful plan appears in S. Persky, *At the Lenin Shipyard. Poland and the Rise of the Solidarity Trade Union* (Vancouver, 1981), p. 15.

The Shipyard strike

Bishop Kaczmarek of Gdańsk, a septuagenarian, was an indefatigable mediator. He persuaded the city authorities that open-air mass should be celebrated at the Gdańsk Shipyard. A 6,000-strong congregation heard Father Jankowski's sermon which sought a 'path of dialogue' and 'above all peace on the *terrain* of Gdańsk.'[25] After mass, he blessed a makeshift cross in honour of the dead of December 1970. Bishop Kaczmarek also acted as the main conduit between the strikers and the Vatican. The assurance that the Pope was following events on the Coast encouraged the workforce.

Premier Babiuch, Łukaszewicz and Barcikowski went to Szczecin, where 25,000 people had stopped work and formed an Interfactory Strike Committee at the Warski Shipyard. A second team went to Gdańsk, where Kania, Jabłoński (the Head of State) and various chiefs of staff attended a 'widened session' of the local Party Committee. It heard a first-hand account of the strike from local Secretary Fiszbach, who emphasised its 'genuinely working-class character' and stressed the need to find a 'political solution'. Kania said the strike proved the necessity for 'agreement between the authorities and the nation, the Party and its class'. We are told that this conciliatory line was echoed by Admiral Janczyszyn, who stated that the armed forces could not do anything 'to loosen their connections with society'. We have no record of which way President Jabłoński spoke. The meeting concluded that 'political methods' were the 'only possible means'.[26]

Gierek spoke on national television that evening – his first public comments on the crisis. His tone was conciliatory. There would be a revision of both annual and quinquennial economic plans. He promised food imports and a reform of wage and pricing policies, including progressive increases for all groups of workers. Trade unions were cumbersome and should be streamlined, perhaps at their November Congress. The speech was relayed into the Gdańsk Shipyard while evening mass was being celebrated. Workers talked it over. One commented: 'In 1970, I was optimistic about Gierek's nomination, now I only trust ourselves.' Another said: 'Let him talk to Party members. Let *them* help him.' Wałęsa, as usual, caught the mood: 'Nothing to do with us. We have our demands. We'll talk to a government team. We stay on strike until they turn up.'[27]

[25] Drzycimski and Skutnik, *Zapis Rokowań*, pp. 107–13.
[26] Giełżyński and Stefański, *Gdańsk-Sierpień 80*, pp. 66–7.
[27] 'Opowiada Anna Walentynowicz' in *Gdańsk-Sierpień 1980*, p. 10.

Trade Union Chairman Jan Szydlak complained to the Politburo that, instead of becoming exhausted, the strikers were maintaining good order and providing for welfare needs.[28] Anna Walentynowicz recalls: 'We issued permits for food shops to reopen. Delivery lorries still operated, so too did the bakeries. The canning factory stayed at work so that the fish would not be wasted. The factory making tins had to work as well, as did the transport. Drivers wore red and white arm-bands and flags were flown outside the shops.' As Joanna Duda-Gwiazda put it:

> We have taken power in this town, we had better get things organised. We had a wealth of experience from 1970 and knew that success would depend on our calmness and prudence. We used our influence to stop the sale of alcohol, in order to prevent disturbances. Even the sale of beer was prohibited. All this was directed by the eighteen-member Strike Committee, mainly workers. Only one of us, Andrzej Gwiazda, was an engineer and Gruszecki had a doctorate in chemistry.[29]

The MKS now represented 200 enterprises. It alone was authorised to conduct negotiations with the central authorities (not the local ones). The decision to end the strike rested with the MKS. Afterwards, it would not dissolve, but would 'oversee implementation of the demands and organise free trade unions'.[30] Such solidarity was timely. A Deputy-Premier, Tadeusz Pyka, had been appointed Chairman of a Commission 'to investigate grievances of workers on the coast'. His real orders were to divide the strikers. Pyka ignored the MKS and instead sought separate settlements with individual workplaces, letting it be known that he had the 'personal authorisation' of Gierek to sign agreements.[31]

Pyka was approached by small groups which somewhat diffidently presented the Twenty-one Demands (discussed in detail below). To their astonishment, he led them to believe that all were acceptable. His assurances were repeated to representatives of seventeen enterprises that evening[32] and a formal ending of the strike was agreed. Pyka made further magical promises on meat imports, free Saturdays and censorship. A small team stayed behind to edit the final agreement. This done, Pyka abruptly declared the document would have to be submitted to the Council of Ministers for approval. An answer soon came: of the twelve-point agreement, they accepted only three, minor ones at that. The MKS, which now represented 304 strike committees, drew its own conclusion: 'Individual Strike Committees should not negotiate any of our common

[28] AAN 237/V/1816 Politburo (20 August 1980), p. 6.
[29] AAN 237/V/1816, pp. 11–12. [30] Communiqué no. 1 MKS.
[31] Gielżyński and Stefański, *Gdańsk-Sierpień 80*, pp. 74–8.
[32] Listed in Drzycimski and Skutnik, *Zapis Rokowań*, p. 132.

demands with the state authorities.'[33] This became a condition of membership in the MKS.

KOR expressed its solidarity with striking workers. In a joint statement with *Robotnik*, it reported the formation of the MKS. It would have the sole right to represent strikers and end the strike, after which it would take a 'permanent legal form as a Provincial Council of Free Trade Unions'. Since the old trade union (CRZZ) was discredited and works' councils were hopelessly compromised, the only way out was the formation of independent trade unions. Strikes had so far been peaceful and prudent, despite the authorities' pressure on strike committee members, threatening their families, searching their apartments, putting them under surveillance and attempting all sorts of threats and provocations. Once again, police methods had been used against citizens who took genuine and independent initiatives: 'Negotiations should be suspended whenever the political police intervene, whether overtly or in a covert manner.'[34]

Jan Lityński, already under house arrest, was detained and beaten up on 19 August. Jacek Kuroń's home was raided, and a dozen more KOR members were arrested the next day. The Gdańsk MKS noted: 'Workers are not surprised by the vile methods of psychological warfare conducted by the authorities. Everybody knows that they are deliberately deferring negotiations.'[35] Copies of a leaflet signed by Director Gniech promised them a 1,500 złotys rise for everyone and called for a return to work.[36] It was ignored.

A confidential circular to all Party members stated that national survival was endangered by a group of 'political enemies', terrorising and intimidating anyone who was not with them. Poland's independence could not be taken for granted: 'Our security and independence have not been given to us once and for all time.' Disturbances in Gdańsk and on the coast 'have already emboldened West German *revanchistes*, who openly admit that recent events are very welcome to their revisionist plans'.[37]

Senior officials began to adopt a menacing tone, exemplified by that of Jan Szydlak. Addressing carefully selected *aktyw* in Gdańsk, he attributed the strike to 'hostile forces and terror' and issued the memorable *dictum*:

[33] Statement no. 1 (20 August 1980); a report from the somewhat chaotic meeting with Pyka is in Drzycimski and Skutnik, *Zapis Rokowań*, pp. 114–23 (19 August 1980).

[34] Hemmerling and Nadolski (eds.), *Opozycja demokratyczna*, pp. 710–13; Lipski, *KOR*, pp. 367–8.

[35] Statement no. 2 (21 August 1980).

[36] Gielżyński and Stefański, *Gdańsk-Sierpień 80*, p. 87.

[37] Obtained and reprinted in *Solidarność* 24 August 1980 (2).

'We will not give up power, nor will we share it with anyone.'[38] The Strike Bulletin declared: 'Although he considers himself to be representing workers, he in fact represents the institution which is responsible for the current situation in the country.'[39] The MKS decided on an immediate withdrawal from the state-run unions.

Gierek told the Politburo that the 'crisis of confidence' in the authorities was widespread, but did not accept the claim that government was 'passive and doing nothing'. A new generation had grown up, making new demands. The previous Premier Jaroszewicz was not a scapegoat. They all needed to rebuild confidence in the Party.[40]

The Politburo was dissatisfied with Pyka's progress. Babiuch called his monetary concessions 'a time-bomb under the entire economy'. He suggested Gierek hold talks with each member individually to ascertain their views, implying that the Politburo was split. Kania suggested that the Vatican should be asked to make a 'calming statement'. Jaruzelski reported that Polish events were disquieting 'our Russian friends'. The longer the crisis went on, the more 'dissident elements' gained experience and grew in confidence. Whilst use of military force, 'both ours and allied', was ruled out, they must ensure free and unimpeded transit for Warsaw Pact forces through Poland.[41] Pyka was removed as head of the Government Commission.[42]

His replacement, Jagielski, was not yet authorised to recognise the MKS, which now included 350 enterprises on strike.[43] Even so, they welcomed the change: 'Bravo! So we are waiting for Jagielski, waiting for Jagielski in this hall. At the Gdańsk Shipyard! We are waiting here for him. Please bring news that he is coming to us as soon as possible!'[44] But no date was set for talks, though they had begun in Szczecin.

The economy worsened daily. The USSR and DDR were asked for emergency supplies.[45] Premier Babiuch had already offered his resignation. He wished to go at once so that a new team could be formed: 'We must save the Party and the country. We must change policy and re-group cadres, because this situation really might end tragically. The economic team must begin to speak a language other than the one used up to now.'[46]

[38] Drzycimski and Skutnik, *Zapis Rokowań*, p. 142; Gielżyński and Stefański, *Gdańsk-Sierpień 80*, p. 87.
[39] Statement no. 1 (20 August 1980). [40] AAN 237/V/1816 (20 August 1980), p. 10.
[41] AAN 237/V/1816 Politburo (20 August 1980), pp. 1–8.
[42] AAN 237/V/1816 (21 August 1980), p. 1 (Kania).
[43] Listed in Drzycimski and Skutnik, *Zapis Rokowań*, pp. 164–74.
[44] *Ibid.* pp. 161–2 (Wiśniewski). [45] AAN 237/V/1816 (21 August 1980), p. 5.
[46] AAN 237/V/1816, pp. 47–8.

Gierek saw no point in a reshuffle for its own sake: Babiuch had only been in office six months. This would be better discussed when the situation had calmed down. He mentioned a letter from Brezhnev. This seems to have expressed qualified support for Gierek, though its contents were not minuted.[47] But Moscow's patience was fast dissolving. Kruczek was candid: 'Comrade Brezhnev's letter, like those that Husak and Honecker could send, shows disquiet.' Instead of communist government, they saw 'dual power on the Coast, counter-revolutionary rule, to which Western trade unions might give support'.[48]

Church leaders declared that tensions, the consequence of 'accumulated errors' over many years, could only be corrected 'in an atmosphere of calm and internal peace'. An honest dialogue should now take place between the strike committees and government representatives: 'Poles must know how to talk to each other, resolve their problems themselves and put their own house in order.' The statement appended a comprehensive catalogue of human rights including 'the right to assemble, to elect independent representatives and autonomous committees'. On the key issue, they were adamant: 'Amongst elementary human rights is the right of workers to free association in unions which genuinely represent them.'[49]

Practically the whole Baltic region from Szczecin to Elbląg was now on strike. The MKS had been joined by over 400 workplaces. Wałęsa tried to defuse tensions: 'From the start, I made clear that we are purely a trade union. We are not getting mixed up in politics, or any state entanglements. And we are going to keep to this. There are provocations, insinuations ... So we can't go that way. We must put an end to them. Only and exclusively trade union matters. Is that clear? [*Applause*].'[50]

He referred to KOR, the Young Poland Movement and the political opposition as the 'hook' with which the authorities were trying to catch the strikers. Yet everything those people had done 'was for us'. Wałęsa was categorical in their defence: 'I state officially that unless the authorities stop arresting activists of KOR and other social-political organisations, there will be no negotiations WHATEVER [*Prolonged applause. Shouts of 'Bravo'*].'[51]

Kania accepted the advice of local Party officials that the strikers were 'tired but determined'.[52] He authorised Jagielski to receive their delegation, which tried to reassure him that those on strike were not inspired by

47 Rolicki (ed.), *Edward Gierek*, p. 177. 48 AAN 237/V/1816 p. 8.
49 *Solidarność* 24 August 1980 (2).
50 Drzycimski and Skutnik, *Zapis Rokowań*, p. 160. 51 *Ibid.* p. 219.
52 Włodek (ed.), *Tajne dokumenty*, p. 51.

any 'political' or 'anti-socialist' aims. Jagielski proposed the expulsion of three 'militants' – Gwiazda, Wałęsa and Walentynowicz – from the Presidium, as a precondition for talks. It was agreed that there would be a preparatory meeting with the Prefect of the Gdańsk Region.[53]

The Prefect came to the Shipyard to meet four representatives of those on strike. Wałęsa explained to anxious delegates: 'Some people have doubts about this four-man commission. It's only preparatory. It has to sort out when, where and what we talk about. Someone has to talk to them. If we all talk at once, we'll get nowhere.'[54] This paved the way for negotiations.

Twenty-One Demands

Negotiations were based upon demands which the Strike Presidium selected from hundreds put forward by its constituent committees. Some had been formulated at the 'Elmor' enterprise, where a distinction had been made between 'political' demands addressed to the central authorities and others directed towards the local management. During editorial work at the Gdańsk Shipyard, a member of KOR, Borusewicz, argued for exclusion of demands for the abolition of censorship and free elections, citing the fate of the Prague Spring. They were duly omitted. The main points were:

Free trade unions

Before the 1980 strike, Polish trade unions were organised in twenty-three branches, according to particular industries. They were federated in a Central Council, to which 95 per cent of the labour force compulsorily belonged. The apparent right to form other unions granted by the Labour Code was qualified, if not removed, by the 1949 Trade Union statute which laid down that 'every new trade union must join the Federation'. Failure to do so would result in dissolution.

In arguing their right to form unions of their own, the strikers relied on Conventions of the International Labour Organisation. In particular, Gwiazda quoted no. 87, 'The Freedom of Association and Protection of the Right to Organize Convention, 1948': 'Workers and employers, without distinction whatsoever, shall have the right to establish and,

53 L. Bądkowski, 'Przepisy dnia (z dzienników Gdańskich 14 VIII – 1 IX 1980)', *Zapis* (Warsaw and London) January 1981 (17).

54 A. Kemp-Welch, *The Birth of Solidarity*, St Antony's College / Macmillan Series, 2nd edn (London, 1991), p. 36.

subject only to the rules of the organisation concerned, to join organisations of their own choosing without previous authorisation.' Poland had signed this Convention in 1956. Gwiazda thus remarked that this demand had been accepted twenty-four years ago.[55]

Further paragraphs of the Convention elaborated:

- Workers' and employers' organisations shall have the right: to draw up their constitutions and rules, to elect their own representatives in full freedom, to organise their administration and activities and to formulate their programmes.
- The public authorities shall refrain from any interference which would restrict this right or impede the lawful exercise thereof.
- Workers' and employers' organisations shall not be liable to be dissolved or suspended by administrative authority.

The strikers also referred to ILO no. 98, 'The Right to Organise and Collective Bargaining Convention, 1949' (also ratified by Poland) which provides, *inter alia*, that: 'Workers shall enjoy adequate protection against acts of anti-union discrimination in respect of their employment, in particular to acts calculated to cause dismissal of, or otherwise prejudice a worker by reason of union membership or because of participation in union activities'. They adduced further arguments from natural justice, of which the international conventions were held to be an expression.

Free unions in communist Poland had a short and unpromising history. Their founding father, Kazimierz Świtoń, had been arrested on numerous occasions.[56] His colleague in Silesia, Władysław Sulecki, had been demoted, persecuted and driven into exile.[57] Activists in the Gdańsk region were treated almost as harshly.

The authorities were willing to allow reform of the old unions. They even welcomed the candidature of Strike Committee members. This promise had helped to end the strike in Lublin a month earlier, but was not now acceptable. Workers on the Coast insisted that new unions, independent of the Party and state, should be created. As Kurczewski points out, the primacy given to this demand transformed the strike from 'a diffuse, spontaneously arising and withering away activity, into an organised social movement'.[58]

The right to strike

Soviet theory treated strikes as a weapon for securing the liberation of the working class from capitalist exploitation. The abolition of capitalism thus

[55] Drzycimski and Skutnik, *Zapis Rokowań*, p. 228. [56] *Robotnik* 24 January 1979 (28).
[57] *Ibid.* 25 September 1978 (21/22). [58] Kurczewski, *Resurrection of Rights*, pp. 191–4.

removed the need to strike. Admittedly, some passages in Lenin do seem to recognise the need for a workers' organisation to protect them from 'bureaucratic' features of the communist state. These were extensively quoted in Yugoslavia, the one communist country where strikes were legalised. In the USSR itself they were ignored.[59] All the Soviet officials met by an ILO delegation in 1960 declared that remaining differences could be resolved through the various organisations in which workers were represented – unions, production conferences and so on – by 'social pressures' on management: 'It was therefore felt that the need for strike action was nonexistent.'[60]

The Polish Constitution made no provision for a right to strike but did not preclude it. However, Article 52 of the Labour Code, introduced in 1975, entitled management to dissolve a work contract 'without notice' – a so-called 'disciplinary dismissal' – where an employee was found guilty of a 'serious breach of basic duties of an employee, in particular by causing a serious breach of the peace or good order at the workplace; or of unjustified absence from work'. This clause was widely used to dismiss workers after the strikes of June 1976. Its repeal was regularly canvassed in *Robotnik*, whose 'Charter of Workers' Rights' called it an 'anti-strike statute' and urged that the right to strike be legally guaranteed.[61]

At issue here are two separate notions of strikes, stemming from radically different views of society. The 'Soviet' view saw society as a unity with common interests and values in which strikes are 'dysfunctional, destructive of the social fabric, non-rational responses to the work situation, indicative of ignorance, prejudice and the presence of alien influences and values'.[62] The second view, a pluralist one, regards strikes as a rational and legitimate means of putting pressures upon an employer to put right a grievance or to meet a demand when all other remedies have failed. The difficulty arises, of course, when the employer is also the state. The distinction between an 'economic' grievance against an employer and a 'political' demand of the state is thus narrowed, if not obliterated. The Government Commission therefore sought to circumscribe its 'political' implications, while the strikers sought de jure status for an activity that did de facto exist.

Freedom of expression

Free unions, if permitted, could not function without freedom of expression. At the least, they would need their own newspapers and the right to

59 B. Ruble, *Soviet Trade Unions* (Cambridge, 1981), pp. 100–3.
60 *The Trade Union Situation in the USSR* (Geneva, 1960), p. 66.
61 *Robotnik* 18 July 1979 (35).
62 See L. MacFarlane, *The Right to Strike* (Harmondsworth, 1981), p. 62.

print what they wished in them 'whether or not this suits the authorities'. Thus censorship, sometimes thought to be simply an 'intellectual' concern, became a major issue for the striking workers. As one striker put it, during the negotiations, 'It is enough to call something "political" and then it won't be published. But these are not political matters. They really aren't. That's simply what this apparatus of ours got used to calling them. They take the easy way out. They say it's "political" and the matter is closed.'[63]

Impetus for this demand came from Gdańsk writers whose letter was read to the MKS on 22 August. Declaring their 'moral responsibility as writers', they supported a 'profound reform of the state' through peaceful and controlled evolution. Integral to this process, and its guarantor, would be the formation of 'new trade unions possessing an independent position in relation to Party–state institutions'. They sought representation at all levels, up to the Sejm. A new statute on censorship should limit its interventions to clearly defined interests of state. Enacting such proposals would help heal the 'political culture of society as a whole'.[64] Following their enthusiastic reception,[65] the leader of the delegation was co-opted, at Wałęsa's suggestion, onto the Strike Presidium.[66] His name was added simply as 'Lech Bądkowski – writer'. A novelist, previously banned from journalism 'for life' for political reasons, he became Solidarity's first Press Secretary.

Gdańsk writers sought to replace the official censorship body with a parliamentary statute restricting censorship to 'the most essential elements of state security and its international alignment'.[67] The intention was not to abolish censorship but to bring it within legal jurisdiction and to institute a right of appeal.

The need for an alternative channel to the state's monopoly of information was amply demonstrated during the strike itself. Whilst the world's press was in the Shipyard and relayed events fully, the Polish media remained silent. However, the strikers were assisted by Konrad Bieliński and Mariusz Wilk who produced the bulletin *Solidarność*. Dissemination of strike news was undertaken by KOR. Another channel was the Church. As Anna Walentynowicz put it: 'To protect ourselves from lies and slander, such as that spread during the occupation strike of 1970 – "the Germans have attacked Gdańsk again" – we decided to let the

[63] Kemp-Welch, *The Birth of Solidarity*, p. 51 (Wiśniewski).
[64] Drzycimski and Skutnik, *Zapis Rokowań*, pp. 206–7.
[65] L. Bądkowski, 'The Man of What?' in *The Book of Lech Wałęsa* (London, 1982), pp. 110–11.
[66] *Zapis* January 1981 (17). [67] Drzycimski and Skutnik, *Zapis Rokowań*, pp. 206–7.

truth about the situation within the Shipyard be known through the Bishop's Curia in Gdańsk. The news reached the Polish Episcopate and the Pope, which gave us added confidence.'[68] Interestingly, for an overwhelmingly Catholic country, the demand also added that officially published works and broadcasts should present 'a variety of ideas, opinions and evaluations'. There should be access to the media for 'all denominations'.

Release of political prisoners

The official attitude, repeated by Jagielski in the talks, was that Poland had no political prisoners. The strikers, however, gave specific examples of 'social activists' who had been sentenced on trumped-up criminal charges. Their release was requested. They also repeated the demand from the first stage of the strike for reinstatement of those dismissed from the Shipyard for participation in the 1970 and 1976 demonstrations, together with students expelled in 1968. Finally, there were the numerous strike supporters detained on the coast and inland. A list of those arrested in Warsaw was brought to the Shipyard with a request that the Strike Presidium press for their release, which became a major issue in the last hours of the strike.[69] Quite apart from solidarity with the repressed, there was the very justifiable fear that the strikers themselves, and especially their leaders, might become the next victims. Gwiazda was not just being rhetorical when he asked the Deputy-Premier: 'What guarantee is there that false witnesses will not be found to prove that the entire Interfactory Strike Committee is a gang of criminals?'[70] There *was* no guarantee.

Economic reform

Since the Party claimed a monopoly on economic decision-making, this demand was also political. To contest a price rise was also to challenge the Party's central planning. To condemn an economic privilege was also to question the legitimacy of its beneficiaries. Government negotiators made a lame attempt to defend such privileges as special meat deliveries to private homes of high officials. Delegates greeted with derision their claim that 'it is not right that officials working long and selfless hours for the good of the state should also have to spend additional hours in meat queues'.

68 'Opowiada Anna Walentynowicz', in *Gdańsk-Sierpień 1980*, p. 6.
69 E. Milewicz, 'Ja, happening, Stocznia', *Biuletyn Informacyjny* Aug.–Sept. 1980 (40.6).
70 Kemp-Welch, *The Birth of Solidarity*, p. 99.

The strikers were far from presenting a fully fledged economic programme, but they did demand that 'definite steps be taken to lead the country out of its present crisis'. They wanted a more democratic means of decision-taking based upon 'giving the public full information about the social and economic situation and enabling all social groups to participate in discussion of a reform programme'. Yet workers had no wish simply to ratify decisions already taken by management, still less to share the stigma of support for unpopular measures. It was eventually agreed that the trade unions should 'have a real chance to express their opinion in public on the major decisions which determine the living standards of working people'.

As Martin Myant argues, economic policies were the arena in which the authorities' failings were most plain. All employees and consumers could see the consequences of their secretiveness, corruption, incompetence and sheer contempt for ordinary people.[71] The contrast between unfulfilled promises – the propaganda of success – and the high living of some political elites – was exacerbated by the hardships of everyday life. The public was unused to external alibis, such as the 'crisis of capitalism'. They had been taught that superiority of the socialist system lay in its ability to overcome the anarchy of capitalism and bring 'impersonal market forces' under human control.

The strikers wanted politicians to address problems of the real world – as Gwiazda put it in the negotiations, 'real life as experienced by working people'. Poland's problems were systemic. Could the leadership come up with and implement solutions despite decades of 'negative selection' and the *nomenklatura*? Point 12 proposed that 'people in leading positions should be chosen on the basis of qualifications rather than Party membership'. The Government Commission replied that it had been Party policy for years that those appointed to responsible positions should possess the appropriate qualifications. The strikers then formulated the point more sharply. They demanded abolition of the *nomenklatura*. Jagielski told them this was non-negotiable.

Negotiations

The Gdańsk negotiations were unique in history. Never before had workers been accepted as partners in discussion by a communist state As strikes spread from the seaboard to the whole country, Polish society started to speak a language distinctively its own. Liberated from

[71] M. Myant, *Poland: A Crisis for Socialism* (London, 1982), p. 99.

double-speak (*nowa mowa*), freely elected spokesmen began to address the authorities in terminology not used before. A plainer vocabulary evolved, shorn of the abstractions enshrouding 'real socialism'. In place of a linguistic molasses in which no movement was possible, the language of 'real life' began to enter public discourse. This often clashed with the discourse of those in power.

Government negotiators arrived by bus. Running the gauntlet of striking workers was a novel experience for such dignitaries. A number of unflattering epithets were aimed at the authorities. Jagielski complained afterwards that their reception had been 'humiliating, disgraceful'.[72] Wałęsa escorted them across the yard, then through the hall of delegates from 370 enterprises on strike, and finally into a small room suitable for negotiations. He then welcomed the visitors:

Wałęsa: The fact that we represent hundreds of thousands of people makes us feel sure that the cause we are fighting for is just. Coming here may bring home to you what a shipyard is like when workers are governing themselves. You can see for yourselves how orderly it all is. The serious matters we must settle require us to act prudently and without haste. We have been waiting patiently for nine days and we have plenty of patience left. We hope that today's meeting will be the first step towards a speedy ending of the strike.[73]

Every word was being relayed to thousands of strikers assembled outside. In this intimidating context, Deputy-Premier Jagielski began quite well: 'It is my intention, as well as my duty and responsibility, to conduct these talks in a straight-forward and constructive manner.' He would start with Point One. He understood the wish of strikers to make trade unions the 'real, authentic and effective representatives of the interests of all employees'. This matter was not within the competence of the government: it was up to trade unions themselves to determine their statutes and functions. Even so, he could express an opinion.

Polish trade unions had 1.5 million officials: 'If the public feels that the unions do not fulfil their functions satisfactorily, and that its overgrown structure has become outmoded, then it must be changed.' He noticed that on the strike committee with which he was negotiating there were people with 'genuine authority and real talent: natural activists'. Why should they not join factory councils or unions at some level?

He thought trade unions should have a greater role in shaping 'social policy as a whole'. New draft laws on trade unions and on workers' self-management would be presented to parliament soon. But this could not

[72] AAN 237/V/1816 Politburo (24 August 1980).
[73] Kemp-Welch, *The Birth of Solidarity*, p. 39.

be rushed into without proper consideration. Similarly, the right to strike could not be debated in such an emotional atmosphere. 'Often-justified resentment and grievances are being expressed', but this would not lead to a good law. The existence of a problem was undeniable, but its resolution required a calm and widespread public debate.[74] Concluding this point, he stated that those engaged in the present strike, apart from anyone engaged in theft or destruction of property, would not suffer any consequences.

At this, the Strike Committee erupted:

Wałęsa: We don't see it like this. Plenty of people are sitting in prison, and plenty more are beaten up. These are the facts. Since we were to speak frankly, I think this matter should be made known.[75]

Wiśniewski: Prime Minister, the problem is not so simple. It looks different from your position. We work on the shop floor. I have worked in trade unions for many years and know that the problem is really serious. At the moment, it looks difficult from the legal angle because the Labour Code is presently formulated so that anyone who goes on strike can get the sack.[76]

Within minutes, the strike issue was being widened to the whole conduct of government. The authorities began to be addressed with frankness previously unknown to ruling circles.

Gwiazda: Prime Minister, until recently the press said all was well with our industry and our economy. The obligatory official line was that, despite some minor difficulties, everything was running smoothly. Now it transpires that great deficiencies were being deliberately concealed or glossed over. Don't you think, Prime Minister, that something similar may be happening with the administration of justice? Why should it be any different?[77]

A further concern of the strikers was to get their truth out. Relations between the two sides were not improved by Party Secretary Zieliński who offered a novel explanation of the communications blockade:

A hurricane passed through Warsaw last night, destroying buildings in large areas of the city. I was in Warsaw at the time, to be exact just after the hurricane. You can see whole streets – such as the avenue to the airport – where huge trees, beautiful limes, are completely demolished along half the route. The central telephone exchange was completely demolished.[78]

As one of the strikers commented, when telephones had been cut off a week ago, there was no mention of any hurricane.

The session ended with a long résumé by Jagielski, which the strike *Bulletin* considered 'vague, platitudinous, inept in places and devoid of definite proposals'.[79] Wałęsa's riposte was colourful and apposite:

[74] *Ibid.* pp. 39–42. [75] *Ibid.* p. 43. [76] *Ibid.* pp. 50–1. [77] *Ibid.* p. 53.
[78] *Ibid.* p. 53. [79] *Solidarność*, 25 August 1980 (4).

Wałęsa: Thank you, Mr Premier, we have listened to you very carefully. It seems, though, you didn't explain why we keep coming back to the same place. This time it took ten years. I expect that in another ten we will be back where we are now. We must prevent this. But in order to prevent it and draw conclusions, we must know the causes. We have not found out from what you say why we keep going round in circles and ending up at the same spot.[80]

The joint communiqué was anodyne. It noted that the two sides had met, that the Government Commission had presented its position on the Twenty-One Demands, and the Strike Committee had put further arguments forward. Talks would continue when Jagielski returned from Warsaw.[81]

Jagielski told the next Politburo that talks were 'dominated by political issues'. The 'strike staff' aimed to prolong the dispute and to win at all costs. Wałęsa had also been joined by a team of special advisers. Jagielski had crossed paths with them at Warsaw Airport. Kania foresaw a nationwide stoppage within ten days. In a swipe at Gierek, he stated that the Politburo had been treated with 'total contempt'. Jaruzelski agreed: 'Pressure and criticism grow, deep changes in the Politburo are expected.'[82] Gierek was obliged to drop six of his closest allies. These sweeping changes were confirmed by the Central Committee at a special Plenum next day. In the sixties, such an 'avalanche' would have been sensational. But workers now on strike seemed unmoved. They expected little from a reshuffle. The events of 1970 had shown that new faces were not enough. The stuff of Polish politics was shifting from 'personalities' to institutions.

When Mazowiecki and Bronisław Geremek arrived in the Shipyard the next day, Wałęsa again seized the opportunity to have specialists at his side. He explained to delegates: 'Our Presidium decided we must appoint a team of experts to help us do well. You all know we have to act wisely. This will be a good start. Did we do the right thing? [*Applause*]' Mazowiecki added a characteristic note of caution: 'Since our arrival we have been impressed by your great prudence (*rozwaga*). We hope you will manage to maintain it and preserve your greatest strength: your Solidarity [*applause*].'[83] He added that the experts would be purely advisory. All decisions would remain in the hands of the Strike Presidium.

The new arrivals were signatories of the 'Appeal of the Sixty-Four [Warsaw intellectuals]' read out to strikers the day before.[84] This blamed

80 Kemp-Welch, *The Birth of Solidarity*, p. 66.
81 *Ibid.* 82 AAN 237/V/1816 Politburo (24 August 1980).
83 Kemp-Welch, *The Birth of Solidarity*, p. 35.
84 Drzycimski and Skutnik, *Zapis Rokowań*, pp. 213–14.

the Polish crisis on 'ill-conceived economic policies over many years; the authorities' blind confidence in their own infallibility; broken promises and suppression of criticism and trampling on citizens' rights. Once again it has been shown that the nation cannot be governed without listening to its voice.' Talks should start immediately: 'The tragedy of ten years ago must not be repeated: there must be no more bloodshed.' Even an hour's delay was inadmissible since 'it can create irreversible or dangerous facts'.[85]

Kania called this a 'new element' in the situation. Propaganda chief Łukaszewicz advised a calm response. They should 'interview' some of the signatories. The original authors – including historians and philosophers, economists and sociologists and well-known writers – were joined within three days by 170 further names, including 51 full professors. Werblan observed that no KOR members were amongst the original 64.[86]

Mazowiecki and Geremek invited a small team of experts to the Shipyard.[87] None of them envisaged a radical break with the status quo. As one puts it: 'we almost all arrived with grave doubts about the feasibility of this First Point' (free trade unions). Geremek had advised the newcomers to reserve judgement on key issues until after talking to the workers on strike. The opinion of the strikers was unanimous: 'During the course of a whole week's negotiations, I did not meet a single striker or delegate who was willing to compromise on this issue.'[88] Asked by Wałęsa how long the experts could stay, Mazowiecki replied that they would remain to the end, whatever the outcome. This helped cement the solidarity between strikers and their intellectual advisers.

The experts' role in drawing up the final text, preliminary drafting of which took place in a joint 'working group' between the plenary sessions, together with many details about the intense discussions amongst the Strike Presidium behind the scenes, have been described by the political economist, Dr Tadeusz Kowalik. He reveals that it was Mazowiecki who contributed the important notion of reciprocity on which the entire Gdańsk Agreement was based.

Mazowiecki insisted that the role of experts was mediatory: to help secure an Agreement, by influencing both sides where necessary. Their status did not extend to changing the substance of any demands. Their

85 Hemmerling and Nadolski (eds.), *Opozyjca demokratyczna*, pp. 714–16; Friszke, *Oaza na Kopernika*, pp. 205–6.

86 Włodek (ed.), *Tajne dokumenty*, pp. 44–6.

87 Dubbed 'self-appointed' by J. Kurczewski, in I. Maclean, A. Montefiore and P. Winch (eds.), *The Political Responsibility of Intellectuals* (Cambridge, 1990).

88 T. Kowalik, 'Experts and the Working Group' in Kemp-Welch, *The Birth of Solidarity*, p. 151.

function was to help 'express the demands in the language of negotiations' without altering their content in any way.[89] Andrews summarises it well. They were 'put to work drafting and marshalling arguments for the negotiations, analyzing Party proposals, and preparing counter-proposals'.[90]

Point one was crucial and would be decisive for relations between the strikers and their advisers. Geremek recalls:

> It was vital to find wording that would fully retain the basic aspirations, expressed in the Twenty-One Demands, and at the same time avoid both subservience and hostility with regard to the language of the ruling political ideology. The problem of verbalisation turned out to be a fundamental one. We spent days and nights pondering not how to devise new ideas and programmes, but how to express in words those incessant altercations between the authorities and the Strike Committee, how to mark out the terrain of negotiation.[91]

The experts' role became even more complicated when the government side introduced their own team, summoned onto the platform at the second meeting by Jagielski: 'I see there are experts present. So, let ours be called. Please tell Professors Pajestka and Rajkiewicz, I have sent for them.' They appeared a few minutes later, accompanied by a Professor of Labour Law from Gdańsk University. Experts on both sides had much in common. Most of them were brought up in the same Warsaw intellectual and political milieu. They had attended the Party's Higher School of Social Sciences or trained in the Lange-Lipiński school of reformist economic thought. Geremek had been a Party member until 1968. Jagielski had known his opposite number Kowalik for twenty-five years but did not show any sign of recognition. He was a gentleman.

The Strike Presidium contained both young activists and more experienced members, some veterans of the 1970 strike. Strikers themselves had acute political minds. They were unencumbered by Cold War 'realism'. It was rather the experts who had to liberate themselves from 'the ingrained realism of Warsaw political and intellectual circles, a realism that was too tame'.[92] Workers' realism was expressed simply: 'either we get what we want or there is no point in talking because it means we have lost'.[93]

The Strike Committee wanted 'experts' to supply the skills, above all verbal ones, which they felt sure they would lack in negotiations. Strikers

[89] *Tygodnik Powszechny*, 12 October 1980.
[90] N. Andrews, *Poland 1980–81. Solidarity versus the Party* (Washington, 1985), p. 33.
[91] B. Geremek, 'Eksperci w Gdańsku. Wspomnienie', *Widnokrąg* 1986 (3/4).
[92] T. Kowalik in Kemp-Welch, *The Birth of Solidarity*, p. 152.
[93] *Widnokrąg* 1996 (3/4).

also realised that once talks got driven into semantic *cul-de-sacs*, or elevated to elegant abstractions such as the meaning of the Party's 'leading role', they would lose. Many felt the experts intended to quieten protestors down. Mutual trust only came about when the experts abandoned any attempt to be 'objective' and declared their allegiances, thereby showing whose side 'they were really on'.[94] The experts found no support whatever for the 'so-called Variant B'. Instead of Point One this was simply a radical reconstruction of the old unions. But before the Variants were put to a vote – which took place in deep secrecy in a disused canteen – workers insisted the experts themselves declare which proposal they backed. It was a defining moment. Thereafter, those experts had to act solely on behalf of the Strike Presidium, rather than as third-party mediators.

The lawyer Lech Kubicki had already withdrawn, stating he had expected to be an adviser to both sides. The sociologist Jadwiga Staniszkis – who had gone there independently of Mazowiecki's team – left later, stating that the experts had sold the strikers down the river.[95] Her stormy departure gave rise to much debate.[96]

The local Party Secretary complained that the strikers had experts in the hall, who were KOR sympathisers: 'They should not be there. The Government Commission was conducting talks with goodwill. It could not act under *dyktat*.' Strikers replied: 'We have lived under a *dyktat* for years. This is not a *dyktat*. We will not give up our advisers.'[97]

Soviet concerns grew. When Warsaw welcomed proposals to improve existing trade unions, which should be 'modernised', made more democratic and opened to electing some of those presently leading the strike, this was too much for Moscow. *Pravda* censored Gierek's promise of 'elections for new governing trade union organs at enterprises whose collectives consider them necessary. These elections must be completely democratic, secret and with an unlimited number of candidates.'[98]

The Polish Party hoped to 'isolate the extremists' in the MKZ, by separating 'anti-socialists' from those willing to support a Party–government line.[99] A new Secretariat was appointed to enact the policy. Premier Pińkowski was joined by a batch of new Vice-Premiers. They included Jagielski and Barcikowski, joint heads of a new 'Commission for Realising Demands made on the Coast'. There were

94 *Ibid.*
95 J. Staniszkis, *Soviet Studies* April 1981, and in *Labour Focus on Eastern Europe* (4.46) 1981, p. 13.
96 Summarised by Kowalik in Kemp-Welch, *The Birth of Solidarity*, pp. 184–7.
97 *Ibid.* 98 *Pravda*, 26 August 1980.
99 AAN 237/V/2254 (Secretariat, 25 August 1980).

now stoppages in Wrocław, Krosno, Łódź and at Nowa Huta, and the halting of public transport in many towns. Kania told the Politburo that attempts should be made to isolate Gdańsk and Szczecin by blocking off the coast, and also closing borders with the West. He thought the Party should use exclusively political means. Yet demands advanced in Gdańsk were unacceptable: 'The Strike Committee is being steered by Mazowiecki and Bądkowski.'[100] In the confused discussion which followed, Jagielski reported that Wałęsa was willing to settle on all issues except trade unions. But Wałęsa had actually said: 'If we get agreement on all points except Point One, then there will be no Agreement.'

Point One was the core issue at the Second Meeting (26 August). Jagielski now proposed a 'renewal of trade union activity'. Fresh elections were to be held without delay. They would be democratic, by secret ballot, to show whether 'the authority of representatives who emerged so recently in certain factories proves lasting'. If it did, they would find themselves in the new union leadership. It was the Party's view – 'in this sphere I speak for the Party, since trade unions are not subordinate to the government' – that the primary function of trade unions was to defend the interests of employees.

On Point Two (the right to strike) he thought it would be sensible to 'include regulations within the law, which, so to speak, lay down conditions and procedures for work stoppages as a form of pressing workers' claims when all other remedies, more expedient and appropriate from the social point of view, have been exhausted'.[101]

At this, a metal-worker lost patience:

Sobieszek: I would not like to ridicule anyone, but I think there is simply a misunderstanding here. Our demand for free trade unions is clear but the Prime Minister just sticks to his conditions about modernising the old ones. That's not what we're after. That's not it at all. It's just fudging the issue. [*Noise in the Hall*][102]

Jagielski then agreed that discussion should be transferred to a working group, with experts from both sides. Their findings would not be binding: 'They are only to define positions more precisely on the basis of the International (ILO) Convention.' The strikers accepted this procedure.

Jagielski told the Politburo that the entire Coastal population was behind the strike. Their determination was total, they were very well organised and had rejected all his arguments. He thus disabused his

[100] Włodek (ed.), *Tajne dokumenty*, pp. 60–5 (Politburo, 26 August 1980).
[101] Kemp-Welch, *The Birth of Solidarity*, pp. 76–7. [102] *Ibid.* p. 86.

colleagues of any hope that strike leaders could be somehow separated from 'honest workers'. He saw little scope for further prevarication on the key issue. They wanted a clear answer 'to whether we agree to the formation of free trade unions, in accordance with the Geneva Convention': 'Today the workers are still asking our permission. Tomorrow they may not bother to ask us.'[103]

Kania pointed out that Agreement on the Coast would not be the end of the matter. It would create a working-class organisation of considerable power. Gierek commented: 'Today they are demanding unions, tomorrow they will be storming the Party, government and Sejm.' It was 'a political act with incalculable consequences for the whole socialist bloc'.[104]

The next Politburo saw a 'decomposition of the state, which is rapidly spreading and deepening'. They needed to act quickly: every day passing was a day lost. It now accepted that 'Problem number one is [determining] our attitude to the main political question: to the political organisation of separate trade unions.' They should have no illusions: workers thought that new unions would guarantee them strength against the authorities and enable them to press demands through strike action. Gierek now admitted that it was not simply political 'adversaries' who were pushing this demand. It had mass support, as shown by wide-scale enrolments. Collection of funds had already begun. Donations from two Western unions had also been reported.

Since a crisis-point had now arrived, extreme measures were discussed. In addition to the arrest of oppositionists, these included schemes 'to capture the ports of Gdańsk and Świnoujście'. This could not be entrusted to the army. Seizure by the militia was being considered. But it was not an easy matter. Even if the ports were captured, 'What then? Who will run them? Skilled personnel will be needed.'[105]

The hawkish Olszowski offered to appear on television with a good speech 'spelling out what the new union business is about, unmasking it. Tell workers that we want union renewal, and elections where needed. That we don't fear criticism. But that unions are their affair and not for helpers from outside.' He would also point out that 'the Party was responsible for the country and could not agree to setting-up anti-socialist structures at will. Mention the dangers involved (Czechoslovakia, Hungary).'[106]

[103] Włodek (ed.), *Tajne dokumenty*, pp. 70–2 (Politburo, 26 August 1980).
[104] *Ibid.* pp. 75–7. [105] AAN 237/V/1817 (Politburo, 27 August 1980).
[106] AAN 237/V/1817 (Politburo, 27 August 1980).

Instead, the more conciliatory Jagielski appeared on Gdańsk Television that evening. He still argued that the strike was economic. The government was rectifying the situation, for example by improving the supply of meat through imports (30,000 tons). The introduction of rationing to guarantee supplies was not ruled out. He acknowledged a 'crisis of confidence' in the existing unions but maintained their 'shortcomings' could be rectified within the existing framework: 'The sick body can and must be cured, however painful the cure may be.'[107] Independent unions were not mentioned. His speech was repeated by the national media the next day.

Jaruzelski advised Politburo colleagues 'to demonstrate our goodwill'. But they should take a much tougher line with Wałęsa, warning him that they had 'entered a phase in which he has undertaken responsibility for public order'. The use of force could simply result in a spontaneous solidarity movement under the slogan 'Hands off Gdańsk'. And sending in the army would mean the use of fire-arms. However, ZOMO was trained for such operations, with long, heavy truncheons and tear-gas, rather than live ammunition: 'Society should be prepared for such an eventuality.'[108]

Kania thought the priority was 'to get the workforce back to work'. The demand for free trade unions did not come from workers, but from 'anti-socialist gamblers, grouped around Kuroń', who had no interest in defending workers but wished to attack the system and interrupt the normal functioning of the state: 'We must defend the unity of our union movement' against those who raised the slogan of 'free trade unions' in order to undermine the socialist state.[109]

A top secret 'Party–state Crisis Staff' (*Partyjno-rządowy Sztab Kryzysowy*) had been set up under the new Premier Pińkowski, including the head of National Defence Jaruzelski and Party Secretaries Barcikowski and Olszowski. One of its functionaries was Colonel Ryszard Kukliński, a top aide to General Jaruzelski. Kukliński, a close confidant of, and speech-writer for, Jaruzelski, was Chief of Strategic Planning and Deputy Chief of Operations for the Polish army until a month before martial law was imposed in December 1981. He was also a foreign agent. Following the shootings of December 1970, he had decided to keep the CIA informed.

Over the next decade he provided the Kremlin's 'crown jewels' to the West: Soviet war plans for Europe, weapons systems, Warsaw Pact

[107] P. Raina, *Independent Social Movements in Poland* (London, 1981), pp. 545–50.
[108] AAN 237/V/1817 (27 August 1980), pp. 9–10.
[109] AAN 237/V/1817 (27 August 1980), pp. 1–5.

targeting, the location of tactical nuclear weapons. He now reported that the 'Crisis Staff' intended to keep any Gdańsk Agreement as vague as possible. Once the mutinous population had returned to work, concessions made 'under the strike pistol' would be clawed back. Should such administrative measures prove insufficient, a second stage would be the imposition of martial law.[110]

Premier Pińkowski considered the options. 'Administrative measures' would remain problematical 'until we can make our decisions stick'. This was a coded reference to martial law. The military option was discussed by the Polish Politburo the next day.[111] Though feasible, members thought force was a last resort. This left a third option: 'political struggle' to win the propaganda war. Three further actors pointed towards this peaceful outcome.

The Church

Cardinal Wyszyński's homily at the shrine of Jasna Góra (26 August) spelled out three areas of responsibility in national life: religious–moral, family and socio-professional. Only the third touched on current troubles. He noted that workers were striving for 'social, moral, economic and cultural rights': political ones were not mentioned. Such values were necessary for the normal development of the nation, but the country's primary need was calm. Consequently, 'We must work honestly, with a sense of responsibility and conscientiousness. We should not squander, we should not waste, but should economise, because we should remember that we are a nation still on the path to prosperity.'[112] This failure to endorse strike action was welcomed as responsible by Kania in the Politburo.

The Cardinal emphasised the responsibility of Poles to work for the good of Poland. The authorities showed some of the sermon on prime-time television. The first broadcast of a Catholic leader for decades could have been a national sensation. But the reception amongst strikers was lukewarm. They thought the Cardinal was overcautious and growing old. The Party's rank-and-file also wondered what on earth was going on.

An Episcopal communiqué was issued under Wyszyński's chairmanship, later the same day. The bishops declared the source of present tensions was mistaken government policies for many years. The only

[110] 'Wojna z narodem widziana od środka', interview with Kukliński, *Kultura* (Paris) 1987 (4).
[111] Kramer, Special Working Paper (29 August 1980).
[112] Hemmerling and Nadolski (eds.), *Opozycja demokratyczna*, pp. 724–34.

hope for restoring social peace was effective dialogue between the Strike Committee and the political authorities, to resolve disputed issues peaceably in the interests of the nation. The watchwords were dialogue and a willingness to make concessions on both sides. Both sides should reach an agreement and respect it: *Pacta sunt servanda*. However, social peace was unobtainable without the respect for civil and human rights, 'to be upheld in reality, not simply as declarations'.

There followed a full catalogue of these rights: freedom of religion, a decent existence for every family, the rights to truth, to freedom of opinion, to bread, to private property in agriculture, to the dignity of labour, to a fair day's wage for a fair day's work, and to autonomous representation. On the last point, the Second Vatican Council had stated: 'The right to set up free trade unions is a fundamental human right.' Unions should genuinely represent their members, all of whom should be guaranteed the right to participate in their activities without fear of reprisal.[113] There was a splendid lack of ambiguity about this pronouncement.

The Episcopate also publicised a papal message, formally addressed to Cardinal Wyszyński, in which the Pope assured compatriots that he was with them 'with all my heart and in all my prayers'. During the 'present difficult days' when Poland occupied the centre of international attention, he hoped the Episcopate 'will be able to help the nation in its struggle for daily bread, for social justice and a natural right to its own way of life'.

Moscow

The Soviet Politburo set up a Commission under Suslov to monitor developments (25 August). It was to pay 'close attention to the situation unfolding in Poland and to keep the Politburo systematically informed about the state of affairs and about possible measures on our part'. It contained Foreign Minister Gromyko, Defence Minister Ustinov and Andropov, head of the KGB.

Also included were Chernenko (a Brezhnev successor), Rusakov, Arkhipov and Leonid Zamyatin who was to play a prominent role during the Solidarity sixteen months. According to its Secretary, Georgii Shakhnazarov, the body met at least fortnightly throughout the Polish crisis, and more frequently when needed, until its eventual discontinuation in the early Gorbachev period. It is described by Mark Kramer as 'a

[113] *Ibid.* pp. 734–6.

core decision-making group'. On several occasions, the four key members drafted documents on Poland, published afterwards as 'Central Committee Resolutions'. The Central Committee itself was convened infrequently to express its 'ardent and unanimous approval' of Politburo decisions.[114]

The first product of the 'Suslov Commission' was a top-secret 'special dossier' on 28 August, planning how 'to form a group of forces in case military assistance is provided to Poland'. The political analysis was curt: 'The situation in Poland remains tense. The strike movement is operating on a country-wide scale.' But the military option was spelled out in detail:

> Taking account of the emerging situation, the Ministry of Defence requests permission, in the first instance, to bring three tank divisions (1 in the Baltic Military District and 2 in the Belorussian Military District) and one mechanised rifle division (Transcarpathian Military District) up to full combat readiness by 6 p.m. on 29 August.

Mobilisation would also require up to 25,000 reservists and 6,000 vehicles, half of them to replace vehicles redeployed to help the harvest. Full mobilisation would require up to 100,000 reservists and 15,000 vehicles. Such deployment would become necessary 'if the situation in Poland deteriorates further' and 'if the main forces of the Polish army go over to the side of the counter-revolutionary forces'.[115] The reliability or otherwise of the Polish armed forces was a growing preoccupation for both Polish and Soviet leaders, as the Solidarity period developed.

Deployment of Soviet forces could prove decisive. By the same token, the military option looked unpalatable to Moscow. The Soviet Union had recently moved beyond its normal sphere of operations to shore up an ailing communist regime. The misguided invasion of Afghanistan in December 1979, massively condemned by the international community, had important implications for Poland. The Soviet Union could not afford another Afghanistan – least of all in the middle of Europe.

East German communists privately considered Gierek weak and out of touch.[116] At talks between East German Security (represented by Marcus Wolf) and the Polish generals Stachura and Milewski, the Stasi gained the impression that the Polish leadership was prepared to meet all Twenty-One Demands except the first – free trade unions – which had been imported into the strike by (unnamed) agents. The Polish Party intended 'to isolate the centre of counter-revolution in the Lenin Shipyard' and reach a political solution without the use of force. But there was the

[114] Kramer, Special Working Paper, pp. 11–12. [115] Kramer, *CWIHP Bulletin* (II), p. 108.
[116] *PRL w oczach STASI*, vol. I (Warsaw, 1996), pp. 38–41.

danger that the MKS would escalate the situation into a general strike. Thus chances of a peaceful outcome were only put at 50:50.[117]

Washington

In its first public statement on the Gdańsk events (18 August), the US State Department emphasised that current difficulties were for 'the Polish people and the Polish authorities' to work out by themselves. It was privately considered that US statements on behalf of 'rebel workers' in the past had been counter-productive. Nothing should be done now to show a 'red flag – or a trigger – to the Soviets'.[118] These cautious utterances were accompanied by strong protests against the resumption of Soviet jamming of Western broadcasts as a breach of the Helsinki Agreement.

On 25 August, National Security Adviser Brzeziński 'urged the President to underline American interests in these [Polish] developments through Presidential Letters' to Western European leaders. The purpose was to initiate an exchange of views 'so that a common Western policy would emerge'. It would also express American concern about possible Soviet intervention without saying so to Moscow directly.[119] Brzeziński included the Pope in this purview.

Carter wrote to French, German and British leaders that 'events in Poland are of such importance that I should very much like to have your personal assessment of them, and also to share mine with you'. The outcome 'could precipitate far-reaching consequences for East–West relations and even for the future of the Soviet bloc itself'. He was sympathetic towards Polish efforts to reform the system, while urging restraint on all parties. Above all, the West should avoid any interference which 'could be seized upon by the Soviets as a pretext for intervention'.[120] Carter expected a peaceful outcome. He thought Gierek had Soviet support and the majority of Poles also favoured evolutionary changes without recourse to violence. He was also heartened by the conciliatory approach adopted publicly by the Pope and by Cardinal Wyszyński.

Giscard d'Estaing wrote to Gierek in the same spirit, though more mutedly. He saw the optimal outcome as a non-violent accord between the Polish authorities and the people: 'Such an accommodation could

117 *Ibid.*
118 T. Cynkin, *Soviet and American Signalling in the Polish Crisis* (Basingstoke, 1988), p. 42.
119 Brzeziński, *Power and Principle*, p. 464.
120 State Department telegram 'Presidential Letter (27 August 1980)' (1 September 1980).

well transform the character of the Polish system, leading possibly to a more liberal and democratic model.'[121]

Washington's 'Special Analysis on Poland' thought that 'At the very least, the Church's actions and statements will raise serious questions of conscience for the striking workers.' The Church would become even more directly involved if the situation seemed to worsen: 'Through sermons and the activity of local priests, the Church could try to prevent the spread of strikes. Cardinal Wyszyński could lay his prestige even more directly on the line by going to Gdańsk. Finally, the Pope could make a more direct appeal.'

In this analysis, the key variable remained the willingness of the strikers to compromise. The CIA account saw 'militant workers' as the problem. The identity of non-militant workers was not clarified. Tough talk would be needed 'to bring the militant strike leaders round to the view that the dangers inherent in the situation have come to outweigh the gains they seek'; 'The most effective means of pressure would almost certainly be sabre-rattling from Moscow.'[122]

The next 'Special Analysis' saw the Soviet Union willing to go along with some political concessions, short of independent trade unions and the abolition of censorship (not a strike demand), in the hope of clawing them back once the immediate crisis was past. If the crisis dragged on for some weeks, Moscow would be likely to give an open warning of political intervention, including military manoeuvres, 'to impress the strikers and the Church with the gravity of the crisis. If these measures failed, Moscow might urge that Gierek be replaced.' A final option would be to advise the Polish Party to use force, and then join in if this did not solve the problem. The costs, though enormous, would be acceptable if this prevented the Polish regime from collapsing.[123]

MacEachin indicates that the possibility of an eventual Soviet military intervention had preoccupied US officials virtually from the start of the stoppages in early July. There was little confidence that Polish forces would be successful in carrying out an internal crackdown, 'even if it was willing to try, which most analysts doubted'. Forces moved to Gdańsk in the first week of the Shipyard strike carried with them the risk that they might refuse to perform. The 'rising civil opposition had substantially eroded the reliability of militia and other forces, and the attempt to use them could result in violence spreading beyond the regime's control'.[124]

[121] Włodek (ed.), *Tajne dokumenty*, vol. II, p. 83.
[122] *NIB Special Analysis*.
[123] *NIB Special Analysis* (28 August 1980).
[124] D. MacEachin, *US Intelligence and the Confrontation in Poland, 1980–1981* (University Park, Pa., 2002), pp. 2–28.

Gdańsk negotiations did not resume on 29 August. The strike *Bulletin* commented:

It is high time the Government Commission showed greater understanding of the strikers' demands at a moment when the country stands on the brink of a general strike. The avalanche set in motion by the workers on the coast can only be contained by a radical change in the attitude of the authorities towards working people. The time has come when the government can no longer remain deaf to what society is saying and demanding. We hope they have realised this by now.[125]

Jagielski flew back to Gdańsk the next day. A Fourth Meeting came back to Point One. Gwiazda read out the draft protocol relating to trade unions. Immediately afterwards, Jagielski signed the draft. It became the centrepiece of the Gdańsk Agreement. Under this historic document, the government accepted the formation of free trade unions, to be self-governing and independent of the state. They would have the right to strike and access to the mass media. Political prisoners would be released and the public would have the opportunity to influence economic policy.[126]

The signing of the Gdańsk Agreement was greeted by general euphoria. As Anna Walentynowicz put it: 'I thought this was a real breakthrough, that a new life would begin. I had no idea what difficulties were to follow, how much bitterness and disappointment.' Yet she ends her memoir, a year later, on a prophetic note: 'If we had to start again from the beginning, I would do the same without a moment's hesitation, perhaps with more experience'; 'Where did the name Solidarity come from? Since Deputy Premier Jagielski could not let the phrase "Free Trade Unions" pass his lips, we consulted the experts. This was a "solidarity" strike and our *Bulletin* was called *Solidarity*. So the name chose itself.'[127]

Wałęsa pondered the future. Solidarity the pauper, relegated to a back room, suddenly finds himself co-owner of Poland. The other tenant, the Party, reviews his position. He would certainly draw up a glowing report on his earlier stewardship.[128] He might also wish to regain ownership.

125 *Solidarność*, 29 August 1980 (9).
126 For full analysis, and comparison with the Szczecin Agreement, see T. Kowalik in Kemp-Welch, *The Birth of Solidarity*, pp. 180–7.
127 'Opowiada Anna Walentynowicz' in *Gdańsk-Sierpień 1980*, p. 14.
128 Wałęsa, *A Path of Hope*, pp. 139–40.

11 Non-invasion

Poland's present situation recalls the year 1921 in the Soviet Union: the struggle of the Bolsheviks with anarcho-syndicalists.

Ambassador Aristov, August 1980

Moscow understood the historic nature of the Gdańsk negotiations. Prior to the August Agreement, Soviet Ambassador Aristov told Gierek that Poland in 1980 confronted anarcho-syndicalism: one of the most dreaded heresies in the communist lexicon.[1] He was referring to the 'Workers' Opposition' which had presented 'Theses on the Trade Union Question' to the Xth Party Congress (1921). This trenchant document explained their origin 'from the depths of the industrial proletariat in Soviet Russia' as an outgrowth not only of the unbearable conditions of life and labour in which 7 million industrial workers found themselves. They were also 'a product of vacillation, inconsistencies and outright deviation of our Soviet policy from the previously expressed class-consistent principles of our communist programme'.[2] Working-class creativity was being replaced by communists inside the unions. But what communists were they? In this process, they saw great degeneration, the direct negation of the self-activity of the masses: 'Some third person decides your fate: this is the whole essence of bureaucracy'.[3]

Their remedies were elimination of non-working-class elements from administrative positions within the Party and freedom of discussion and publication within the Party. But decisions of the Xth Congress terminated both freedom of expression and political opposition inside the CPSU. During the proceedings, sailors on Kronstadt (a fortress in the Gulf of Finland) came out in revolt against Soviet power.[4] Congress adjourned while the mutineers were stormed across the ice. Afterwards, Lenin pushed through a Congress resolution that banned 'factions' in the

[1] Włodek (ed.), *Tajne dokumenty* (28 August 1980), p. 78.
[2] A. Kollontai, *The Workers' Opposition*, Solidarity Pamphlet 7 (London, 1968), p. 1.
[3] *Ibid.* pp. 24–43. [4] Ida Mett, *La Commune de Cronstadt* (Paris, 1938).

Party.[5] Introduced as a temporary measure, it remained in force for seventy years.

Still mindful of this debate in 1980, Soviet leaders sent their Polish counterparts rambling dissertations on the 'Leninist theory' of trade unions. Lenin had taught that trade union 'neutrality' was a hypocritical delusion. It existed nowhere in the world. Thus the concept of 'free' trade unions was a false notion. As Lenin had asked: 'Free from what or whom?' It was a subversive slogan espoused by counter-revolutionaries. 'So-called free unions' would inevitably be drawn into political struggle against the Party. Bourgeois circles in the West were already treating the 'Gdańsk Interfactory Committee of Lech Wałęsa' as 'the first stage of Poland's transformation into a pluralist system'.[6] Lenin had warned repeatedly against this 'extremely dangerous trend'. He had argued both against 'splitting-off' trade unions from the state, and the opposite notion of the incorporation into the state (*ogosudarstvleniya*) of trade unions.[7]

To permit 'self-governing' unions in Poland would sunder the working class, on whose unity Party rule was based, and undermine the Party's 'leading role' in both society and the state. The 'leading role' was defined as setting priorities for social development, forming the governing bodies of state and social organisations at all levels, and realising the policy of socialist economy. The purpose of trade unionism was to assist this by working together (*sotrudnichestvo*) with government and ministries.[8] In the Soviet view, such cooperation was working satisfactorily in some of Poland's socialist neighbours. In Hungary, for instance, government and trade unions held discussions at six-monthly intervals. This was the regular operation of responsible trade unionism. But the proposed 'self-governing' trade unions in Poland contained many worrying tendencies. The recent slogan 'Let's form trade unions without communists' was blatant counter-revolution.[9]

Political risk assessment carried out under Andropov in Moscow resolved that all means short of military ones were to be used to stop the rot. KGB weekly briefings were held without stenographers – partly to promote blue-skies thinking – and the position papers on which analysts presented their conclusions remain deeply buried in security archives. However, one 'top-secret' instruction to Warsaw, encrypted by the KGB, has been uncovered. Confirmed by the Politburo on 3 September, it took

[5] L. B. Schapiro, *The Origin of the Communist Autocracy* (London, 1955), Ch. 17.
[6] AAN 237/V/2255 (Kania's Secretariat).
[7] V. I. Lenin, *Polnoe sobranie sochinenii*, 5th edn (Moscow, 1958–65), vol. XVI, pp. 427–37; vol. XLII, p. 268.
[8] I. Deutscher, *Soviet Trade Unions* (London, 1951), pp. 42–59.
[9] AAN 237/V/2255 (Kania's Secretariat).

the form of 'theses for discussion with representatives of the Polish leadership'.[10] The main recommendations were:

(i) **Restore Leninism**. The Gdańsk Agreement was held to breach a cardinal principle of the Leninist state by legalising an 'anti-socialist opposition'. 'So-called united strike committees' contained non-worker oppositionists, mendaciously disguised as defenders of the working class. Though not named, KOR is clearly meant. They harboured political aspirations on a national and even international scale and were counting on assistance from abroad. Such hostile forces would be encouraged, rather than restrained by the Agreement. Consequently, 'the compromise that has been achieved will be only temporary in nature'. Concessions made under duress would be clawed back.

(ii) **Regain the initiative**. The Polish Party was under pressure from 'anti-socialist forces', which had briefly gained the ascendancy. The need was now to counter-attack and regain territory lost 'amongst the working class and the people'. This should be spear-headed by the ruling Party, around its 'strong, healthy core', and by the state apparatus. The ranks should be purged and a dynamic programme for economic and social recovery promulgated by a special Congress. No elaboration was offered, nor any explanation of how a crippled economy could rapidly revive. As a last resort, the 'contemplated administrative measures' should be employed. This no doubt referred to the top-secret 'Party–state leadership staff' whose first meeting convened on 24 August.

(iii) **Revive trade unions**. Every effort should be made to prevent the existing trade unions from disintegration. The date of their next Congress should be brought forward. They should hold new elections to secure their own nominees *before* the new union had time to organise. Then, reliable Party *aktyw* should be infiltrated into the 'so-called self-managing trade unions'. The old unions should come forward with bold initiatives to bolster their authority and restore the severed link with the toiling masses. The Gdańsk and other Agreements should be watered down: 'Abide by certain provisions and at the same time adopt all measures to limit and neutralise the effect of the most dangerous articles.' This evidently meant Points One (the right to independent unions) and Two (the right to strike).

(iv) **Develop a new role for the military**. The Soviet system had always kept the military at arm's length from political rule. But now it was stated that the army's Political Directorate should provide new cadres for

[10] Kramer, Special Working Paper, pp. 35–43.

Party leadership. Admission that the Party alone might be inadequate for the tasks ahead was implied by the suggestion that 'army command personnel perform Party-economic work as well'. But anxiety about their political reliability was implied by the injunction to 'devote special attention to the military-political preparation of soldiers'.

As an additional measure, Party supervision of the media must be stepped up. Any new press law should explicitly forbid any statements against socialism. Censorship should put an end to 'the wide circulation of anti-communist publications, films, and television productions in Poland' and maintain strict control over sources of information from Poland, including the activity of bourgeois journalists. Programmes should be put out to 'show that events in Poland have not been caused by any shortcomings of the socialist system *per se*, but by mistakes and oversights, and also by some objective factors (natural calamities, etc.)'. In a parting shot, Soviet leaders reminded the Poles of the advice from Brezhnev to Gierek, given in the Crimea a year earlier. The implication was clear: had it been followed, August 1980 would not have happened.

As principal architect of this débâcle, Gierek was disposable. He was admitted to Warsaw's Institute of Cardiology on 5 September. His removal from power went smoothly. Stanisław Kania, who had been in effective charge for the past fortnight, was installed as First Secretary. Kania reported to colleagues a congratulatory call from Brezhnev promising him moral, political and economic support. The Soviet leader had expressed his good-will towards Poland's other leaders and to the country as a whole.[11]

US policy

As Solidarity started to change the face of communism in Europe, the Soviet Union and its allies met to plan military intervention, and that in turn precipitated the last Cold War crisis on the continent. But the Warsaw Pact did not invade Warsaw. The non-invasion of Poland surprised the West. Policy-makers and most observers assumed that Poland's experiment would go the way of other reform movements in Eastern Europe, thus confirming the rigidity and immobility of Soviet rule. Some, however, saw that Solidarity was raising issues that Soviet communism had not faced before. To crush working people in Poland, who had so recently and solemnly been promised civil liberties, would put paid to European *détente*. It would also expose as fraudulent the claim that workers ruled in the workers' state.

[11] Włodek (ed.), *Tajne dokumenty*, p. 95.

US policy towards Poland was evolving rapidly. A primary aim was prudential: to 'calm the Poles down' and stabilise the domestic situation. Washington wished to deter any hopes in Poland that an armed uprising would receive military assistance from the West, such as that being provided to insurgents in Afghanistan. The fact that such an uprising was not being contemplated by Poles did not necessarily change the argument.

The second and opposite aim of Washington was to stiffen Polish resistance. Poland should be freed from 'Marxist–Leninist totalitarianism', thus advancing the day which would finally emancipate the entire region from Soviet hegemony. Advocates of this second policy objective saw the Polish crisis in retrospect as the 'last major, protracted cold war battle in Europe, involving competition by the two super-powers over the international orientation and domestic system of one of the major nations of Europe'.[12] However, many Western European states, 'perceiving Polish events as destabilizing and hopeless', were inclined to distance themselves from attempts to moderate Soviet policy. This attitude 'left the US alone vis-à-vis Moscow and significantly reduced Washington's ability to influence the outcome of the power struggle in Poland'.[13]

An uneasy compromise between these strategic goals was the 'Sonnenfelt Doctrine' that Eastern European governments should be differentiated, and rewarded according to the degree they were distanced from Soviet orthodoxy. President Carter thus welcomed the Gdańsk Accords in his Labor Day address (1 September): 'Americans look with pleasure and admiration on the workers of Poland. We have been inspired and gratified by the peaceful determination with which they acted under the most difficult of circumstances, by their discipline, their tenacity and their courage. The working men and women of Poland have set an example for all those who cherish freedom and human dignity.'

These fine words were followed by an aid package for Poland, twelve days later. This advanced $670 million for an emergency food programme, new credits for grain purchases and a rescheduling of hard currency debt. So large was the debt, however, that 85 per cent of the new credits went to service the old. Moreover, the US Administration attempted to dissuade Lane Kirkland of the American Federation of Labor Congress of Industrial Organisations (AFL/CIO) from sending a modest donation of $25,000 to Solidarity on the ground that Moscow

[12] A. Rachwald, *In Search of Poland. The Superpowers' Response to Solidarity, 1980–1989* (Hoover, Calif., 1990), p. xii.

[13] Rachwald, *In Search of Poland*, p. 56. Mrs Thatcher is not mentioned.

would 'misinterpret the move'. When Kirkland demurred, Secretary of State Muskie informed the Soviet Embassy in Washington of the imminent donation and declared that it did not have official backing.

The predominant view behind closed doors in Washington was 'the likelihood, as most people saw it, of Soviet military intervention, sooner or later, to crush the Polish reform movement'. East European and Soviet specialists were mindful of 1956 and 1968. Though Poland (which had not been invaded since the Second World War) was regarded as a more complex military target, from which resistance could be anticipated, so too was its strategic position more vital for the Soviet Union. It was generally believed the USSR would not hesitate for long before 'stamping out a threat to Polish Communist rule and its own hegemonic position'.[14]

The US National Security Adviser, Zbigniew Brzeziński, expected Moscow to give Polish leaders some time to attempt an internal resolution of their political crisis. But he had already called for a CIA report on signs of preparation for an invasion. President Carter had been widely criticised for not making public the accumulating evidence of the Soviet military action in Afghanistan. This was not a critique his administration would wish to face again. He also recalls that:

> Throughout this period, I was guided by the thought that the United States must avoid the mistake it had made in 1968, when it failed to communicate to the Soviets prior to their intervention in Czechoslovakia the costs of such an aggression to East–West relations and to the Soviet Union specifically.
>
> Accordingly, my strategy was to generate advance understanding of the various sanctions that would be adopted, and to make as much of that publicly known as possible, so that the Soviets would know what would follow and that we were politically bound to react. I realised this would not be a decisive factor in Soviet calculations, but I felt that under certain circumstances it could make more than a marginal difference in the event of any internal Kremlin disagreement.

This seemed pertinent as the Warsaw Pact was stepping up pressures. Eight days of Soviet and East German military manoeuvres took place on Poland's borders.

According to diplomatic reports sent back to Washington, Warsaw officialdom was increasingly concerned about possible Soviet military intervention. While not 'in a panic' as yet, continued verbal attacks by the Soviet press on 'anti-socialist elements' in Poland could be seen as laying the groundwork for a future military attack. There were regular philippics in *Pravda*.[15] Kania was seen to have very little latitude domestically. Stronger action against sporadic strikes might consolidate them

14 F. J. Meehan, 'Reflections on the Polish Crisis', *CWIHP Bulletin* Winter 1998 (11).
15 By 'Petrov' in *Pravda*, 1, 6, 20 and 27 September 1980.

into a mass protest. But inaction could reinforce a view in Moscow that Kania was weakening, might make further and far-reaching concessions, or lose control altogether. That would necessitate a Soviet intervention 'to restore order'.[16]

The NSC's 'Special Coordination Committee on Poland' met in the White House on 23 September. In the CIA's view, 'Kania had not yet turned the corner on controlling events. Industrial unrest was spreading.' They reported that 'the Soviet military were taking some steps similar to those they took in the Czech crisis of 1968'. But they had not yet made up their minds to invade Poland. Such an invasion would require thirty divisions and their mobilisation would give the USA two to three weeks' warning time.[17] According to subsequent calculations, a further fifteen divisions might be needed if there was a reaction from Polish military forces; but fifteen in all might suffice if Soviet divisions were to enter Poland 'by invitation'.[18]

Brzeziński tried to use diplomacy to deter a Soviet invasion. One potential pressure was from Western Europe, where the French President and German Chancellor were seen as the most significant figures. In reality, however, reliance on Chancellor Schmidt proved worthless. He told a meeting of the four-power (QUAD) conference (with Britain, France and the United States) that *détente* should not become the victim of any Soviet intervention. Should it take place, German relations with the Soviet Union and its allies would be unimpaired. It would be business as usual. A dismayed Brzeziński remarked: 'This is the best proof yet of the increasing Finlandisation of the Germans.'[19]

A second deterrent was 'strong Polish resistance to any invasion'. There was a CIA consensus that Poles would fight, though it was not clear how organised such resistance would be.[20] Tacit encouragement of Polish resistance might seem a risky strategy, which might even lead to a war in Central Europe, but the dangers of passivity were greater. The example of 1968 was considered minatory. President Johnson's Administration had treated the potential Soviet invasion of Czechoslovakia as more or less a domestic affair. Brzeziński ordered a review of the effectiveness or otherwise of American policy at that time 'to see if it had any applicability to the current crisis'.

The third deterrent sought to play on Soviet fears of China. In none-too-subtle a threat, the US government signalled to Moscow that intervention

[16] US Ambassador to Moscow (T. Watson) to the Department of State (19 September 1980).
[17] 'Summary of Conclusions', NSA (23 September 1980).
[18] NSA (4 November 1980).
[19] Z. Brzeziński, 'White House Diary, 1980', *Orbis* Winter 1988. [20] *Ibid.* pp. 32–3.

in Poland would lead to increased American–Chinese military collaboration. In particular, advanced weaponry could be sold to China in the event of Soviet invasion of Poland. Brzeziński thought this would enhance Moscow's phobia of 'encirclement'. As Kissinger quipped, the Soviet Union was the only country surrounded by hostile communist states.

Kania's policy

Kania's new team wondered how to get Poland back to work. Gomułka had achieved this by a single speech in 1956. Gierek had regained worker support by personal appeals in 1971. The public would not respond again to such performances.

The Polish Sejm held its most lively session for years.[21] Deputies made trenchant criticism of Party and government, and the practice of cloaking social and economic problems in censorship was roundly denounced. The session confirmed Pińkowski as Prime Minister. His acceptance speech gave orthodox pledges to further enhance and strengthen the fraternal alliance with the Soviet Union and to rebuff all anti-socialist forces. He also promised a radical programme to reform the economy. However, no such programme existed nor would circumstances have favoured introducing one. Public expectations were far in excess of anything the economy could conceivably deliver. Debts to the West exceeded $20 billion. Warsaw's allies rallied round with emergency aid, including Soviet hard-currency credits amounting to $550 million.[22] They were palliatives.

Kania foresaw a 'breathing space'. Solidarity had only just begun to organise internally and had yet to develop wider momentum. However, new unions were springing up like mushrooms, as the rest of the country wanted what coastal workers had already achieved. Their action typically took the form of a sit-down strike until the Twenty-One Demands were agreed at their own workplace. They sometimes went further than those on the Coast. Thus the Jastrzębie Agreement in Silesia accepted the ending of the four-brigade system for miners and an end to compulsory Saturday working. This later became a national issue. Strikers often included sharp criticism of the local administration at factory and provincial level. There were many calls for the resignation of local Party Secretaries.

The Party was being deserted in droves. As the younger *aktyw* turned towards new unions, it was being steadily reduced to a central apparatus

[21] N. Ascherson, *The Polish August* (London, 1981) covered it (pp. 181–3).
[22] Włodek (ed.), *Tajne dokumenty*, p. 614.

of older functionaries. Jaruzelski admitted later: 'a drastic breach had opened up between the doctrine of real socialism and the expectations of ordinary people'.[23] Dummy institutions of real socialism were exposed as fraudulent. Thus, the public ignored the efforts of the state-run Trade Union Council to achieve some credibility through asserting workers' rights, while denigrating its rival, Solidarity. The industrial branches on which it was based started to disaffiliate.[24] As Moscow feared, the old unions disintegrated.

Putting on a brave face, leaders expressed satisfaction that recent events, the 'largest social conflict in Party history and in the socialist camp' had ended without bloodshed. This allegedly showed 'public confidence in our activity'. A rallying call was issued by Andrzej Żabiński: clearly one of Moscow's 'healthy forces'. He had been promoted to Party Secretary in charge of a new department for 'trade unions, worker self-government, social policy and working conditions' to supervise and implement the recently signed Agreements. Żabiński's line was to retain the old unions, whilst recognising the nationwide demand for new ones. This had to be accommodated, but 'without capitulating or making any compromises'. Rather than blame the 'healthy' working masses, political deviation was attributed to outside influences. He singled out the Confederation of Independent Poland (KPN), whose leader Moczulski was re-arrested, and KOR. Kuroń was treated to special criticism.[25]

A KOR statement declared 'full solidarity with the strikers and admiration for the courage and wisdom of the striking workers on the Coast'. It thanked workers for their solidarity in setting the release of members of the democratic opposition as a precondition for ending the strike. The authorities had 'abandoned the methods of terror which they always used to quash workers' demands' but there must be no reversion to old ways. KOR insisted that 'only a dialogue between the authorities and democratically elected representatives of the work force can lead to effective political solutions'.[26]

KOR members gravitated naturally into the Solidarity structure at various levels. Lityński built on the links with *Robotnik* contributors, particularly in Lower Silesia. Many others were turned to, as trusted and experienced oppositionists, to head the Solidarity groups at their local workplaces. They continued to offer advice and provided technical help for the burgeoning Solidarity press, set up to spread information within the organisation and to overcome the official blackout of news on

[23] W. Jaruzelski, *Stan wojenny ... dlaczego* (Warsaw, 1992), p. 14.
[24] Włodek (ed.), *Tajne dokumenty*, p. 101.
[25] AAN 237/V/2254, pp. 4–25. [26] Lipski, *KOR*, pp. 503–5.

its development. But this was in no sense a leading role. Its Intervention Bureau, run by Zbigniew and Zofia Romaszewski, remained active, in order to protect activists in the newly formed movement from repression, and drew on KOR's Social Self-Defence Fund for this purpose.[27]

Although formally existing for another year, KOR met very infrequently and its statements were rarities. Seeing the mass union as an incomparably more effective vehicle for the realisation of its goals, KOR took the view that its main task was done. Henceforth, Polish society would organise itself.

On 1 September, the MKS in Gdańsk re-formed. It became the Interfactory Founding Committee (MKZ) of the NSZZ 'Solidarity'. Its temporary premises, the Hotel Morski, rapidly filled up with eager helpers. Wałęsa was again elected its head and chaired its first plenary session on 3 September. This was also attended by expert advisers: Kuroń and the veteran economist Edward Lipiński (both founders of KOR) and the local lawyer and KOR activist Lech Kaczyński. The tasks to be undertaken were practical: to ensure fulfilment of the Agreement, starting with compensation for the price increases and ensuring basic living standards ('the social minimum'). A more democratic system for elections to factory councils was proposed, and health and safety issues were identified. They would also strive for legal registration in order to be able to act alongside other (state-run) unions.[28] Similar meetings took place nationwide. On 4 September, the Warsaw region 'Mazowsze' elected Zbigniew Bujak as its Chairman and the Łódź region convened under Andrzej Słowik.

There was movement in academic circles to revive the Society of Scientific Courses (TKN) which had previously operated outside the law, as the 'Flying University'. It endorsed the call by students in several cities for the foundation of self-governing and apolitical students' organisations, to run alongside those controlled by the state. Professional associations of artists, writers, film-makers, architects, teachers and many others sought to form autonomous organisations of their own. The mass media maintained their silence towards these social initiatives.

On 10 September, the Gdańsk MKZ issued its own statement: 'We are struggling for Independent Self-Governing Trade Unions, not only for ourselves, but for society as a whole.'[29] A week later, the first national meeting of MKZ delegates, representing more than 3 million workers in

27 *Ibid.* pp. 432–3.
28 K. Kosiński, *Ku rejestracji NSZZ 'Solidarność'. Kalendarium wydarzeń 1980 r.* (Warsaw, 1998), pp. 15–16.
29 *Ibid.* pp. 19–20.

3,500 enterprises, convened in Gdańsk. On the same day, students formed a free union, also based there.

As Solidarity set out on the road to registration, the state moved promptly to preserve its monopoly on power. The Council of State decreed on 14 September that the registration of new unions would be through the District Court in Warsaw, which would consider whether the statute proposed by the founding committees of a new union was compatible with the Polish Constitution and other laws. In the event of a rejection, an appeal could be made to the Supreme Court. On 22 September, the District Court rejected the first application for the founding of a new union, from Huta Katowice. Its reasons included an objection to the intention that the union operate nationwide. The union for the national airline (LOT) was the first to be registered, and by early October twenty-seven unions had done so. But there were strong hints that Solidarity's draft would not pass key tests: particularly its failure to endorse the Party's 'leading role'.

Crisis-management within the Polish leadership now took a more serious turn. Hopes that signing the Agreements of August and September would pacify the population had proved unfounded. Delaying tactics by the authorities had stiffened popular resolve and Solidarity had not collapsed into disarray. On the contrary, its application for legal registration was about to be adjudicated by the Warsaw District Court. Two days before the hearing, the Polish military began top-secret preparations for the imposition of martial law. Thus, moves to suppress Solidarity were afoot even before it had been granted legal personality.

Kukliński reported that by 22 October 1980 further plans were enacted to enable the removal of Solidarity under a 'state of war'. Jaruzelski, as Minister of National Defence, instructed the General Staff of the Polish Army under General Siwicki to draft the plan as a matter of great urgency. A feasibility study, including draft decrees and designations of what should be suspended, de-legalised and militarised, was to be ready by early November.[30]

These were then reviewed by the Committee for National Defence (KOK). The main elements of the plan were to:

1. precede a martial law declaration by calling up 250,000 reservists
2. introduce legislation allowing the conscription of students and recent graduates
3. militarise all factories and enterprises
4. call up a million other people into Civil Defence units.[31]

[30] R. Kukliński, 'Wojna z narodem widziana od środka', *Kultura* (Paris) April 1987.
[31] *Ibid.*

It was agreed that the Polish army was to be restricted to policing roles within cities and the countryside. Strike-breaking and the storming of occupied factories was to be carried out by mobile units of ZOMO (Motorised Units of Civil Militia, or riot police), supplied with additional ammunition and weaponry from the military. Jaruzelski told the Politburo such plans should be used only in political extremities. He noted that no such provision had existed even in the 1940s, and there were many practical problems. He asked prophetically: 'Could a state of war be carried out effectively against millions of strikers?'[32] The plan was approved but kept on hold.

On 24 October, the District Court told an open hearing that it accepted Solidarity's application for registration. But once the cheers of supporters died down, the judge announced changes to the statute. Exceeding his mandate, simply to accept or reject the application, he unilaterally inserted statements about the Party's leading role in the state (incorporating Point One of the Gdańsk Agreement). The Court also weakened paragraphs referring to the right to strike: 'If the union, in defending the basic interests of workers exhausts all other possible methods, it may decide to call a strike.' It added, however, that 'a strike must not run counter to the laws in force'. Since the law did not provide for strike action, this was curtailment indeed.

As Solidarity pointed out, the District Court's judgement contravened both the international conventions and the Polish legislation on which the Gdańsk Agreement had been based. It also abrogated the joint commitment to social agreement and dialogue between the authorities and society. Finally, since the 'corrections' (*poprawki*) were clearly inspired by the Party, the verdict marked a sad decline in the standing and independence of the Court, and of Polish jurisprudence more generally.[33] Nonetheless, Solidarity would exercise its right of appeal to the Supreme Court.

The 'Registration Crisis' began. For most in Solidarity, it seemed that the authorities were already reneging on the Gdańsk Agreement. At the National Committee in Gdańsk only two delegates out of forty-two thought the 'corrected' statute acceptable. A national strike was set for 12 November. In a moment of hubris, the Prime Minister was summoned to the Shipyard within twenty-four hours.

The Politburo considered its response (28 October). It rejected the registration of Solidarity's statute within three days, and the ultimatum

32 Włodek (ed.), *Tajne dokumenty*, p. 169 (Politburo, 8 November 1980).

33 Krajowa Komisja Porozumiewawcza (National Coordinating Commission (of Solidarity)) Statement, 24 October 1980.

that Pińkowski should attend the Shipyard. Jagielski was sent instead.[34] Minister of Interior Milewski reported that grass-roots pressure for Solidarity's statute was enormous and growing. Catholic intellectuals had been shocked by the Court's ruling. Mazowiecki and the veteran lawyer Siła-Nowicki led the protests. 'Enemy activists' were regrouping in various directions: 'extremists' determined on confrontation; 'moderates'; and those who concentrated on social-welfare issues. There was one consolation: the Church was behaving 'loyally and peacefully'.[35]

Olszowski attacked 'the adversary' for seeking to create a two-party system, either de facto or formally. Solidarity sought to become a political force equal to the Party. The situation was worst in Gdańsk. It was imperative to separate Solidarity's leaders from its intellectual advisers, particularly Kuroń. The Party should not retreat into 'bunker psychology'; it should conduct robust conversations with the working class.[36] Another 'hard-head', Grabski, saw Solidarity as 'pushing the government onto its knees, pulling it by a lead', through constant pressure.

Rumblings abroad grew louder as the 'allies' looked askance at Poland's handling of its crisis. Frontiers with East Germany and Czechoslovakia had already been closed to most Polish travellers, in breach of the Helsinki Agreement on free movement. In Bulgaria, Party leader Zhivkov circulated a Letter to the Politburo, contrasting the position of Poland unfavourably with that of his country and of 'world socialism'. His main thesis was that, while Bulgaria had developed successfully, the same could not be said of Poland. On the contrary:

> The underestimation of the class approach on the part of the Polish comrades, the distortions in the management of the economy connected with the over-centralisation and bureaucratisation of public life, the incorrect notions of democracy and the mistaken liberalism brought to a crisis the trust in the party and led to the disintegration of the political system of the socialist order in some spheres.

The Polish Party was now paralysed and demoralised. Its leadership was divided and disunity was being compounded from abroad.

The United States alone had 'some twelve million Poles', some of them, such as Brzeziński and Muskie, in high places. A new and very dangerous form of counter-revolution was being prepared by international reactionary forces, designed to shift the balance of power in Europe and worldwide 'in favour of the new military strategy of American imperialism'.[37] According to Zhivkov, the next target was Bulgaria.

[34] AAN 237/V/2254 Politburo (28 October 1980), pp. 10–11.
[35] AAN 237/V/2254 (25 October 1980), pp. 3–4. [36] AAN 237/V/2254, pp. 5–6.
[37] AAN 237/V/2254 Politburo (21 October 1980), pp. 1–5.

Resuming a few days later, Zhivkov's eventual successor Mladenov took up the comparison with Czechoslovakia in 1968. While their aims were similar, the scale was quite different. In 1968, the Pelikans and Dubceks had emerged as individual heroes; the Polish masses had come out in their millions. There was talk of 8 million in the Solidarity trade union. Yet, the Polish leadership was supporting 'renewal'. De-coded, this word meant a new model of socialism, differing from what the Bulgarians understood by 'socialism', perhaps on the Yugoslav model. Alternatively, the Polish leadership may be seeking a model closer to that of Sweden and Austria under Kreisky, 'which would have pluralism in the sphere of politics, of ideology'. He suggested that Zhivkov write to Brezhnev proposing a bi-lateral or multi-lateral meeting of the socialist countries with Polish leaders. The latter would be advised 'to control and gain command of the situation'.[38] A bi-lateral meeting of Polish and Soviet leaders was set for 30 October.

Brezhnev considered the cardinal point to be Poland's failure to eliminate, or even identify, the 'enemies of the nation (*vragi naroda*)' who were fomenting counter-revolution. He noted that even Yugoslavia had taken opposition more seriously, recently putting 300 people into prison. Andropov declared that 'anti-socialist' elements, such as Wałęsa and Kuroń, wanted to seize power from the workers, but there was nothing about this in the Polish media. The purpose of the meeting was to impress on Polish comrades the gravity of the situation and to spur them into action, while at the same time reassuring them that the Soviet leadership had confidence in their abilities to overcome the crisis they faced.

In fact, this confidence was not shared by the Soviet leadership. Minister of Defence Ustinov noted that the position of the Polish army was becoming less certain, that there was wavering in the ranks: 'But the Northern Group [of Soviet forces] is ready and in full military preparedness.' Foreign Minister Gromyko was categorical: 'We absolutely cannot lose Poland.'[39] There followed a discussion about the current Polish leadership, in which Moczar was mentioned. This indicated that Moscow was pondering some alternative combination, though one had not yet been found.

Unlike their Soviet counterparts, Polish leaders did not dwell on political struggle with counter-revolution. Their policy was to build a 'broad front of common sense and realism', inclusive of non-Party people and members of allied parties. As Kania pointed out, no other line was compatible with the decisions of the recent Party plenum. His colleagues

[38] AAN 237/V/2254 Politburo meeting (25 October 1980), pp. 1–3.
[39] Kramer, Special Working Paper, pp. 44–54, CPSU Politburo (29 October 1980).

suggested some further items for the Moscow conversations. Jaruzelski saw scope for bi-lateral economic cooperation in boosting exports and further integration with the Russian economy, and Olszowski stated that Poland could learn from the experiences of fraternal states about the importance of the primacy of central planning.[40]

In the Moscow talks, both sides agreed that the activities of anti-socialist forces in Poland had been stepped up, though the Polish comrades were reluctant to call them counter-revolutionary. It was also understood that, at some point in the future, the country and its Eastern ally 'will abruptly be faced with a critical situation, which will require extraordinary and, one might even say painful decisions'. But when asked directly what emergency measures the Poles would take, Kania prevaricated.

He confirmed that there existed a plan for making arrests and using the army. But this was not seen as an easy option. The Russians concluded: 'All things considered, they are not yet prepared to take such a step and have put it off to the indefinite future.' One reason was the West, which held a potential veto by refusing to extend the already crippling hard currency debt: 'The Polish economy is directly dependent on the West.' The Soviet side offered to extend short-term relief as a matter of urgency, for which Kania paid public tribute on his return to Warsaw. However, he had told Moscow that he was reluctant to reveal the full extent of their conversations, even to some of his Politburo colleagues, who might leak them to the West. Brezhnev noted: 'it is essential for the Polish leaders to forestall any hints that they are acting at the behest of Moscow.'[41]

Shortly afterwards, Brezhnev wrote to Honecker to solicit hard-currency contributions for Poland, which could be used to service its external debt and for additional imports of food and other products. The proposed means of doing this was to cut supplies of Soviet oil to its Eastern European allies and sell the surplus for convertible currency to the West. Brezhnev asked Eric (Honecker) to treat this 'suggestion' with sympathy, since he was convinced that 'such a manifestation of fraternal solidarity will allow our Polish comrades to weather this difficult hour'.[42]

Not dissimilar arguments were heard in Washington. Muskie chaired a Policy Review Committee (5 November), to discuss economic assistance to Poland. He argued that the US government could make a gesture to help give the Polish government more time to stabilise the situation. Brzeziński concurred. Short-term economic aid which eased the situation, thus averting the worker unrest which might precipitate a Soviet

[40] Włodek (ed.), *Tajne dokumenty*, pp. 149–50.
[41] Kramer, Special Working Paper, pp. 55–9, CPSU Politburo (31 October 1980).
[42] NSA Brezhnev–Honecker (4 November 1980).

invasion, would cost considerably less than 'spending billions of dollars later in terms of sanctions and other measures'.[43] He felt this was a major strategic decision that should be referred to the President.

On 31 October, a large Solidarity delegation headed by Wałęsa was received by Premier Pińkowski on behalf of the Council of Ministers. A somewhat chaotic session followed, indicating the need, already discussed with Jagielski in Gdańsk, for some permanent means of contact between the government and Solidarity. The talks focussed initially on the 'unconditional' registration of Solidarity, and a date was set for a Supreme Court appeal (10 November) whose verdict would be considered final. But there was no agreement on any other matters.

The Party rejected the demand for the registration of an independent farmers' union, 'Rural Solidarity', as beyond the scope of the Gdańsk and other Agreements. Its draft statute had already been rejected by the Warsaw District Court. There was no progress on the remaining political demand: for reinstatement of those dismissed from work as a result of the protests in 1970, 1976 and 1980. The meeting even failed to issue a joint communiqué when Prime Minister Pińkowski withdrew his signature at the last moment, apparently on direct instructions from Kania. As a minor consolation for Gdańsk Solidarity, the weekly *Polityka* carried an interview with Wałęsa, Gwiazda, Pieńkowska, Borusewicz and Bogdan Lis, with their group photograph on its front page.[44]

A constantly contested issue was access to the mass media. The broadcast of Sunday mass on Polish Radio, agreed at Gdańsk, was quickly enacted.[45] During Warsaw talks, the new union was promised its own weekly newspaper, once technical matters had been resolved. These included access to printing presses (among them those donated from abroad), to paper (Solidarity suggested reallocation from the official union's paper, *Głos Pracy*) and some financial security. It proved to be a long discussion: the first issue of *Tygodnik Solidarność* appeared on 2 April 1981. Access to television, even a ten-minute bulletin for union members, or a possible announcement by Wałęsa withdrawing the threatened strike, was persistently denied. Continued censorship was heavily criticised at a special Congress of the Union of Polish Journalists in late October, which elected Bratkowski to head a new leadership.

The Party Secretariat ordered members at factory level to be mobilised in opposition to the threatened strike. Given the mass defection of the rank-and-file to the new union, and the fact that many more were opting for dual membership (as already held by Bodgan Lis), it seemed very

[43] NSA, 5 November 1980. [44] *Polityka*, 1 November 1980.
[45] *Tajne dokumenty Państwo-Kościół 1980–1989* (London, 1993), pp. 5–11.

unlikely that this traditional lever would still operate as normal. Propaganda was to be stepped up to spell out the catastrophic political and economic consequences of strikes. Strikes were to be described as social unrest stoked up by anti-socialist elements.[46] Olszowski anticipated a confrontation, which he perhaps relished, by mid-November.[47] Party leader Kania also foresaw the danger that mass strikes would turn into a trial of strength, with demands escalating beyond registration to the question of 'who rules?'[48] This he preempted categorically: 'We will not tolerate dual power, although some think we might.' Despite the strike threat, they should stand firm. But strikes hit the economy, ruptured renewal (*odnowa*) and normalisation, and heightened social tensions.[49] By implication, a peaceful resolution of the Registration Crisis should be found.

The government negotiated through Mazowiecki behind the scenes. In his view, the opening seven clauses of the Gdańsk Agreement, the political ones, could be attached as an appendix to the Solidarity statute. Mazowiecki did not think the whole National Commission would support this idea, but thought it could nonetheless go forward.[50] The veteran lawyer Siła-Nowicki put the suggestion of an appendix to a member of the Supreme Court. The Politburo discussed the matter on 8 November. One observer rightly remarked: 'so much for the independence of the courts!'[51]

Kania phoned Brezhnev the next day to brief him on developments. He drew attention to 'new elements in the situation', among which the threatened strike was undoubtedly paramount.[52] Around this time, Moscow reminded Warsaw of its economic dependence on the USSR for fuels and raw materials. Specifically, the Soviet Union threatened to reduce supplies of natural gas, phosphorus, iron ore and cotton by 50 per cent and petrol exports by even more.[53] Thus, while urging Poland to put its house in order, the Soviet Union was also threatening to bring about economic and social dislocation on a massive scale.

The Registration Crisis subsided on 10 November when the Solidarity statute was approved by the Supreme Court. An appendix included the ILO Conventions on Freedom of Association (87) and on the Right to Organise and to Collective Bargaining (98), both ratified by Poland. It

46 AAN 237/V/2255 (4 November 1980), p. 4.
47 AAN 237/V/2255 (2 November 1980), pp. 5–6.
48 Włodek (ed.), *Tajne dokumenty*, (4 November 1980), p. 159. 49 *Ibid.* pp. 160–1.
50 *Ibid.* (7 November 1980), p. 163 (Grabski).
51 Garton Ash, *The Polish Revolution*, p. 85. 52 *Ibid.* (8 November 1980), p. 164.
53 Jaruzelski, cited by M. Dobbs, *Down with Big Brother: The Fall of the Soviet Empire* (New York, 1997), p. 73.

also appended seven Points of the Gdańsk Agreement, including the First Point delimiting the union's political role. The structure of the union thus formally emerged.

Membership was open to all those who did not belong to any other union. Its overall purposes were defined in paragraphs 6 and 7 as 'to protect the jobs, dignity and interests of workers' in a variety of ways including strikes 'in especially justified cases'. Once all other remedies had been exhausted, a strike ballot could be held amongst union members. Whenever possible, a real strike would be preceded by a warning strike of not longer than half a working day. There were several safeguards against preemptive action against union activity. Repression for strike action or of its leaders empowered the employees to strike immediately. If strike action in one factory was ineffective, union officials could call on other enterprises to start a strike in solidarity. All members could become union officials, unless they held executive posts at the workplace, such as enterprise directors and their deputies. Also disbarred from office were those who 'fulfilled managerial functions in political organisations'.

A relieved Politburo met the next day. Kania considered registration was 'our success, though not a turning-point'.[54] Olszowski declared it to have been a positive step that should lead to further constructive dialogue with Solidarity. But he was quick to identify divergent tendencies within the new union. He saw it more as a coalition of various forces than as an organisational monolith. There were both the 'social-democratic, under the influence of KOR, unwilling to compromise' and the better-disposed 'Christian-democratic, linked to the Church, very realistic, understanding that socialism is irreversible'. Finally, there were fringe elements and hangers-on. Elections to factory councils should be used to eliminate such 'adventurists and extremists'.[55]

No-one present realised the cost of this quarrel. But it was soon apparent that this first trial of strength with Solidarity, one in which the Politburo had given way, led to over-estimation of the potency of the strike threat by Solidarity's rank-and-file which came to see it as a universal remedy for points of contention with the authorities. The Party's rank-and-file, watching the initial firmness and subsequent retreat of its own leaders, became ever more demoralised. They started to desert in droves. Those who remained became infected with democracy. Barcikowski reported that ordinary members were bombarding Warsaw with decisions, resolutions and written statements demanding a IXth Party Congress be held urgently and under a new voting system.[56]

[54] Włodek (ed.), *Tajne dokumenty* (11 November 1980), pp. 173–5. [55] *Ibid.* p. 172.
[56] *Ibid.* (18 November 1980), p. 618.

Kania had a good Registration Crisis. He emerged from the shadows of his long career in security as a reasonable, amiable figure. His first official meeting with Wałęsa took place at the Party headquarters on 14 November. Kania's principal concern was to find some way to institutionalise Solidarity within the existing system, making it co-responsible for resolving the country's problems. But Wałęsa refused to be pinned down and instead raised numerous practical questions of interest to his membership. Wałęsa recalls this as the start of a series of unsatisfactory encounters. The problem was not one of personalities, but of circumstance: 'Kania seemed to have his back up against the wall; he was tense and the talks plodded on.' In their talks, the scenario was always the same. The Party would begin with a general *tour d'horizon*, stressing the lack of resources and the complexity of the issues before them. But there was no movement on any of the issues discussed, and no positive impetus towards a solution on the Party's side. They prevaricated and stalled, frequently leading Wałęsa to lose his temper about the lack of progress. He always came away frustrated, feeling that nothing had been achieved.[57]

The Gdańsk Agreement had guaranteed the new trade union a real voice in the management of the country. Its agreed purpose was 'to provide working people with appropriate means for exercising control, expressing their opinions and defending their own interests'. But how was this to be implemented? Clearly the new union could not take responsibility for the management of the economic system, but equally it could not remain indifferent to the economic situation or to necessary reforms. One answer being canvassed was the revival of workers' self-management in a radically reformed manner that gave workers effective control at the point of production. But that would undercut a basic function of the communist *nomenklatura*.

A further problem was the development of negotiating strategies. As Mazowiecki told KIK (7 October), normal union activities needed to replace the instant recourse to strike action. But in order for negotiations with management at every level to retain the support of union members, it would have to bring results. Otherwise the workforce would conclude the powers-that-be were just going through the motions and playing games with workers' representatives: 'One of the greatest concerns among new union leaders is the fear of losing contact with the workers.'[58] Hence any attempt to co-opt them onto government committees was instinctively rejected.

57 Wałęsa, *A Path of Hope*, pp. 179–80.
58 Speech to the Warsaw KIK (7 October 1980), *Głos* October 1980 (9).

To Michnik, speaking at Warsaw University (14 November), the crisis stemmed from the authorities' lack of credibility. A crucial moment had come in 1976 when Polish workers exercised their veto over government policy. By forcing it to back down, in a manner that recalled the *liberum veto* of the *szlachta* (squirearchy/gentry) in the seventeenth century, they precipitated a disintegration of state power. The state continued to exist, but could no longer sustain its task of 'creating and modelling social situations'. Solidarity was the supreme achievement of a process through which society learned to organise itself independently of the state. For the process to continue, there needed to be 'a democratic equilibrium resulting from the constantly renegotiated compromise between different social forces'. Society would need to master the virtues of patience and moderation, in addition to the sheer courage to resist the pressures of a state which 'remains in place and will no doubt endure'. Political compromise, enshrined in the Gdańsk Agreement, must be sustained at all costs. It had 'institutionalised the dialogue between the rulers and the ruled'.[59]

Michnik's words were turned on their head at the next Politburo meeting. Kruczek called them 'an aggressive political attack'. None of those present made any mention of compromise. Their talk was entirely adversarial. Milewski observed a change of tactic by the 'adversary': 'While officially demonstrating the wish to be a constructive influence in calming tensions, in fact he launches attacks on the system and the authorities.' Kania thought the 'aggressiveness of Solidarity is growing unmistakably'. It was seeking new ways to extort concessions from those in power. There was talk of creating a political party on the basis of Solidarity, and putting up their own candidates for the Sejm. A big show was being prepared for the tenth anniversary of December 1970. But the Party's rank-and-file remained oblivious to the dangers of the situation. Instead of warding off the threat to socialism, they were calling for a Congress, with delegates selected on the basis of 'an anarchical voting method', and the rotation of Party officials.[60]

Premier Pińkowski wanted Kania's report to the Seventh Plenum to enshrine basic principles of Leninism: democratic centralism, reassertion of the Party's leading role 'in the new conditions' and consolidation around the Party of all healthy forces. The alternative was anarchy. Żabiński declared: 'we must not hesitate to use the law against those who break it. Anarchy – No!' Jaruzelski agreed. Despite its declared realism and loyalty, Solidarity was under the control of evil influences,

[59] Lecture, Warsaw University (14 November 1980) in *L'Alternative* (Paris) Jan.–Feb. 1981 (8), pp. 9–12.

[60] AAN 237/V/2255 Politburo (18 November 1980), pp. 1–6.

using 'terror, discrimination, rumours and pamphlets' to upset law and order. The anti-socialist forces lurking behind Solidarity and adopting pseudo-democratic slogans confirmed that 'anarchy is the enemy of democracy'. Olszowski elaborated a definition of democracy: 'not deliberative, *szlachta*-like, and a universal panacea, but as the democracy of the new socialist society – integrated and disciplined'.[61]

Ceauşescu considered the Polish problem to be an internal issue for the Poles to resolve themselves. Although he did not and would not support any Warsaw Pact intervention, there seemed to be a significant caveat: 'The independent labor movement in Poland could embolden dissatisfied elements in Romania.' He also indicated that intervention might be necessary 'if the Polish party could not maintain control'.[62] A clear call for intervention was indeed imminent.

Honecker considered the Gdańsk Agreement was unacceptable[63] since 'no-one other than the Party itself, with the aid of scientific socialism, can express and realise the class interests of the Party'. By the end of September, the SED concluded an analysis of the current Polish situation which compared events to Czechoslovakia in 1968 and found 'in both their essence and their goals, and also partly in their methods, there is a striking continuity'. Registration of Solidarity was a 'capitulation' by the Polish Party leadership to counter-revolution. Honecker told Olszowski that 'this compromise was an immense shock to everyone who was still hoping you could resolve your problems on your own'. Although armed force was a last resort, it had become necessary in Berlin in 1953, and again in 1956 and 1968. Honecker added: 'We cannot be indifferent to the fate of the Polish People's Republic. We will act accordingly. You can count on us, on our aid, on every form of assistance.'[64]

On 26 November, Honecker wrote to Brezhnev clearly canvassing such a step: 'Counter-revolutionary forces are on the constant offensive, and any delay in acting against them would mean death – the death of socialist Poland. Yesterday our collective efforts may perhaps have been premature; today they are essential; and tomorrow they would already be too late.'[65] It was unfortunate that the timely advice Kania had been given on his day trip to Moscow (30 October) failed to have the 'decisive influence on the situation in Poland which we had all been hoping for'. Honecker therefore suggested that offering Kania 'collective advice and possible assistance from fraternal countries' could only be to his benefit. He cited

61 AAN 237/V/2255, pp. 6–12.
62 NSA, US Ambassador to Belgrade (21 November 1980).
63 *PRL w oczach STASI*, vol. II: *Dokumenty z lat 1980–1983* (Warsaw, 1996), pp. 6–41.
64 Honecker–Olszowski, NSA. 65 *CWIHP Project Bulletin* 5, p. 124.

Husak and Zhivkov as also in favour of an urgent meeting of Warsaw Pact members, to take place immediately after the next Polish Party Plenum (scheduled for 1–3 December).

Poland had now plunged into its next internal crisis. A secret-police search of Solidarity's Warsaw headquarters – Mazowsze – on 20 November recovered a classified document from the General Prosecutor's office, dated 30 September. Entitled 'Notes on Hitherto-Employed Methods of Prosecuting Participants in Illegal, Anti-Socialist Activities', it mainly rehearsed the history of political opposition in Poland from Kuroń and Modzelewski's 'Open Letter' (1965) up to the birth of Solidarity. But in the latter part, the General Procuracy outlined a series of counter-measures to be taken in a future prosecution of Solidarity. These are best described as 'categorical breaches of lawfulness'.[66]

A day later the police arrested Jan Narożniak, a doctor in mathematics who was also a print worker for NOWA and Mazowsze, and Piotr Sapiełło, the Procuracy clerk who had leaked the document to him. This first arrest of a Solidarity activist, on a ninety-day detention order, inflamed the population. The Ursus tractor plant and several other Warsaw enterprises came out on strike, calling for their release, demanding the authorities repudiate the anti-Solidarity sentiments expressed in the leaked memo. Mazowsze's measured statement noted that, though the document was marked 'secret', some facts should not be concealed in this way.[67] Tension increased sharply when the Mazowsze leader, Zbigniew Bujak, himself an Ursus worker, added a raft of fresh demands.

He called for a parliamentary commission, including Solidarity members, to investigate the lawfulness of actions by the Procuracy, secret police and militia, and for control of expenditure by the Ministry of the Interior. It should identify and punish those responsible for the repression of workers in 1970 and 1976 (Ursus and Radom). Political prisoners should be released, including leaders of KPN. The underlying concern was expressed in a warning poster: 'Narożniak today – Wałęsa tomorrow – the Day afterwards: You!'

Solidarity's National Commission endorsed the strike call. It accepted its view that Procurator Czubiński's document posed a threat to all union members, who could in the new circumstances be labeled 'anti-socialist'. It also deplored the evident fact that the Prosecutor-General was encouraging the secret police to break the law in search of evidence that would later be used to charge the opposition with preparing to overthrow the government by force.

[66] Kuroń, *Gwiezdny czas*, p. 153. [67] Cited by Lipski, *KOR*, p. 440.

As strikes spread, the Solidarity leadership became aware that its decentralised structure, deliberately chosen from the outset, would lay itself open to the charge from the authorities of an inability to control its own organisation. After a two-hour stoppage on the railways, the Soviet Union began to express strategic concerns, emphasising its vital interest in keeping open communications and logistical links between the group of Soviet forces in East Germany and the USSR.[68]

The CIA issued an 'alert', stating that the Polish leadership now faced its 'gravest challenge' since the August settlement, and predicted a yet more dangerous stage. Events were heading towards either 'coercive measures' within the country or 'possibly a Soviet military invasion'.[69] President Carter authorised Brzeziński to canvass government reactions in Washington to possible consequences for the Soviet Union that might follow a military intervention. At the top of his list was the notion that it would rupture the political *détente* in Europe. Brzeziński did not speculate whether *détente* was viable given the recent election victory of Ronald Reagan, but simply noted the need to get the incoming American administration 'more on record'.[70]

Kania reported a wide range of strikes to the next Politburo on 26 November. The Ursus call for a general strike had support from Solidarity in other cities. The steel mill Huta Warszawa, a former bastion of the Party in Warsaw, whose main activists had all gone over to Solidarity, was also adamantly in favour of the Bujak demands. Opinions differed on the appropriate response. Jaruzelski stated that, since the dispute had 'unfortunately an overall-political character', they should set up a Special Political Staff to plan for the future.[71] Its membership should include the chief of the General Staff.

Kania thought preparations for a confrontation with Solidarity should begin at once, revoking its special status with regard to strike action. A state-of-war decree should be prepared to 'ban strikes and assemblies, and stiffen censorship and propaganda'. But the confrontation, which even Jagielski now thought 'inevitable, sooner or later', should not have the same 'political-repressive character' as that of 1970, 'whose effects dog us to this day'. Instead, there should be an honourable compromise.[72]

Through the good offices of the journalists' leader Stefan Bratkowski, a mediator acceptable to both sides, it was agreed that the two arrested would be released in exchange for Solidarity calling off the general strike. Huta Warszawa balked at so small an outcome, achieved at so much cost.

[68] *Izvestiya*, 24 November 1980. [69] Gates, *From the Shadows*, p. 165.
[70] 'White House Diary', *Orbis*.
[71] Włodek (ed.), *Tajne dokumenty*, pp. 183–4 (26 November 1980). [72] *Ibid.* pp. 184–8.

A whole package of attendant measures, concerning the militia, had yet to be addressed. Following Bujak's failed attempt to calm the workforce, Wałęsa and Kuroń were brought into action. Their insistence on the need to keep to, rather than go beyond, the Gdańsk Agreement eventually prevailed.[73]

KOR noted that the birth of Solidarity through the August accords 'constitutes the most important achievement of Polish society, a model of self-organisation for everyone and a radical breakthrough in relations between the authorities and society. Centralised dictatorship over the whole of social life is no longer possible.' But there were lines that could not be crossed: 'Independent social organisations cannot and should not undertake actions leading to changes in the system or to the overthrow of the government.' It added: 'The external threat defines the boundaries of possible change.'[74]

In late November, the Soviet Ambassador Aristov and Marshal Kulikov, Supreme Commander of the Warsaw Pact, now a regular visitor to the Polish capital, began to assemble an alternative to the Kania leadership. The new team, referred to by Kukliński as the 'Targowica' (the Pro-Russian Confederation, opposed to the free Polish Constitution of 1791), was to consist of Polish politicians willing to suppress Solidarity by armed force in accordance with instructions from Moscow. The move would be preceded by a large-scale invasion of Poland by Soviet and other Warsaw Pact forces. The Russians envisaged neutralisation of the Polish army which they regarded as unreliable.[75] Although dismayed by this latter prospect, Jaruzelski agreed to send two high-ranking officers to Moscow to finalise the invasion plans. They travelled by special aircraft on 1 December.

Under the plan, Poland would be entered, on the pretext of 'Soyuz '81' joint manoeuvres, by fifteen Soviet divisions, two from Czechoslovakia and one from the DDR. They were to be ready to move at midnight on 8 December. The Baltic would be blockaded by the Soviet Baltic Fleet and the East German Navy. All major Polish cities, particularly industrial ones, were to be sealed off. Polish forces were to remain in their bases while their 'allies' regrouped on Polish territory. At Jaruzelski's request, this was modified by the planned attachment of a few Polish units to the invading Czechoslovak and East German armies, but his attempt to exclude East German forces altogether was rejected. He found the entire scenario deeply dispiriting, and remained inaccessible, even to his closest associates, for some time. Paralysis set in. Kukliński reported that 'no-one

[73] Kuroń, *Gwiezdny czas*, pp. 154–5. [74] Lipski, *KOR*, pp. 505–8.
[75] Kukliński, 'Wojna z narodem'.

is contemplating putting up active resistance against the Warsaw Pact action'. There were one or two who thought that the presence of such vast forces on Polish territory 'may calm the nation'.[76]

The Polish General Staff concluded that the Russians had totally misjudged the situation: 'They were unaware of the popular mood and were underestimating the strength of Solidarity.' Instead of having a calming effect, the invasion 'might result in still greater social unrest and even in a nationwide uprising'. There were further efforts to stir Jaruzelski into action. General Siwicki proposed he canvass alternative scenarios with the Russians, such as imposing martial law immediately, without waiting until conditions became more favourable. Another general, Molczyk, suggested Jaruzelski present Moscow with a plan for the immediate crushing of Solidarity and the opposition, by Polish forces alone. He apparently added 'History will never forgive us if they do the job for us.'

Satellite and intelligence sources convinced decision-makers in Washington that a Soviet invasion of Poland was imminent.[77] Brzeziński urged a joint *démarche* from the President and President-elect, expressing concern and stating that a Soviet or Soviet-led invasion would have adverse consequences for US–Soviet relations. Such superpower deterrence was to be fortified by positive action from the Poles themselves. Warsaw should make every effort 'to consolidate the gains and not produce a showdown'. They should reassure Moscow that key pillars of orthodoxy would not be shaken, including membership of the Warsaw Pact and the political monopoly of the Communist Party. But they should also indicate that a Soviet invasion would be met by resistance from both people and government. This would prevent the Soviet Union from expecting a 'walkover as in Czechoslovakia in 1968'.[78]

But he was not unaware that raising an unnecessary war-scare too publicly with the Washington press corps could be counter-productive. It would create the impression that a Soviet invasion was inevitable, and 'in a curious psychological way' almost legitimate it. Endorsing the external threat to Solidarity's survival did the Soviet Union's work for it. Both sides in the Polish conflict made this point to American Ambassador Meehan. For the Party, Rakowski claimed the exaggeration of a Soviet threat had the positive consequence of slowing Solidarity down and making it act more responsibly. The Solidarity leader Bogdan Lis thought it helped the government by making the reform movement more cautious when it should have been exerting maximum pressure for change.[79]

[76] NSA, telegram from Kukliński (early December 1980).
[77] NSA, telegram from Kukliński (early December 1980). [78] 'White House diary', *Orbis*.
[79] *CWIHP Project Bulletin*, 'F. Meehan Reflections'.

Ambassador Meehan was also somewhat sceptical of the value of President Carter's letter to Brezhnev, sent on 3 December. This brief message affirmed the intention of the United States 'neither to exploit the events in Poland nor to threaten legitimate Soviet security interests in the region. I want you to know that our only interest is the preservation of peace in Central Europe, in the context of which the Polish government and Polish people can resolve their internal differences.'[80] At the same time, it made clear that the imposition of a solution by force would most adversely affect US–Soviet relations. The President-elect was not a party to the letter, which was signed 'Best Wishes, Jimmy Carter'.

In Meehan's view, this message, while no doubt taken seriously in Moscow, as was any other statement from Washington, was a largely *pro forma* exercise. To the Russians, the imponderability of taking military action in Poland was a far more crucial consideration.[81] A further concern in Moscow was the willingness of the Polish leadership to take policy in the desired direction, by crushing Solidarity, or indeed its ability to continue to rule at all. These were the subjects on which Kania was to give account when summoned to address a Warsaw Pact meeting scheduled for Moscow immediately after the Polish Plenum.

The Party's rank-and-file became steadily more frustrated by their leaders' inability to take the country out of crisis. The problem was compounded by the Party's vertical structure. Under democratic centralism, local bodies existed solely to enact decisions taken from above. Unlike local Solidarity committees, which were springing up like mushrooms in most workplaces, they had no scope for initiating action. Where Party committees did act, they were held to be in breach of Party discipline. Zbigniew Iwanow, local Party Secretary at the Towimor factory in Toruń, developed horizontal links with Party members in other enterprises. This became a *cause célèbre* for which he was shortly afterwards expelled. The 'horizontal movement' struck at the Party apparatus by demanding contested elections for leadership posts, to be held by secret ballot. Inspired by Solidarity, they too sought to restore the sovereignty of popular assemblies. In one effort to channel these frustrations through normal channels, the Kraków Party set up a Resolutions Committee headed by Hieronim Kubiak. A huge range of Congress resolutions was generated, including numerous proposals for reforming the Party.[82]

In October and November alone, 500 Party functionaries were dismissed. Reporting this to the Seventh Plenum (1–2 December 1980), Kania took a tone of reasonableness: 'Since the July–August crisis the

[80] *Ibid.* [81] *Ibid.* [82] *Trybuna Ludu*, 22 December 1980.

majority of the rank-and-file has chosen the path of accommodation and renewal.' No-one could accuse the Party of lacking patience and readiness to reach a compromise or even make concessions. But nothing could be done which threatened to undermine the socialist order: 'The defence of socialism is the highest national value, the defence of Poland's *raison d'être.*'[83]

Gierek was held responsible for 'voluntarist economic and social policies, ignoring the laws of economics and disregarding critical opinions'. He was also culpable for a mistaken cadres' policy, particularly at the highest levels. Accordingly, other pillars of the *ancien régime* were disgraced and even removed from parliament: the longest-serving being Premier Jaroszewicz, Babiuch, Szydlak, Wraszczyk, Żandarowski and Pyka.

A new note was entered by General Baryła, head of the Main Political Administration of the Polish armed forces. A virulent critic of Solidarity since its inception, he now turned his fire on the Party:

> Opportunities presented by the Sixth Plenum have been wasted. The Party has not taken the offensive in the realm of propaganda and direct Party action. The present Plenum can fulfil the hopes of the Party's rank-and-file and of the entire society only on the condition that the Party will manage to lead, and that its decisions and resolutions will immediately become a weapon of direct, consistent and active struggle.

He reported anxiety from the military that 'many people and many units within our Party have acted as if they had lost the sense of their historical and political rationale, as if they were shy or even ashamed and helpless. This situation cannot be tolerated much longer.'[84]

As Michta points out: 'The army's propaganda campaign, ostensibly aimed at building up support for the party, in fact underscored the *apparatchiks*' inability to govern.'[85] Such attacks on the Party for a failure to confront and defeat Solidarity also served as a private warning to civilian leaders that military patience was running out.

At the Warsaw Pact summit on 4–5 December, Brezhnev remarked: 'the crisis in Poland of course concerns us all. Various forces are mobilising against socialism in Poland, from the so-called liberals to the fascists. They are dealing blows against socialist Poland. The objective, however, is the whole socialist community.' Kania would speak first, reporting on the Seventh Plenum. Following this would be a discussion 'here in the circle of friends' of measures to be taken to overcome the crisis.[86]

[83] Włodek (ed.), *Tajne dokumenty*, p. 620.
[84] Cited by Michta, *Red Eagle*, p. 90. [85] *Ibid.* p. 89.
[86] *CWIHP Bulletin* II, p. 110.

Kania's speech, his first in such a forum, gave a frank account of the difficulties. The Polish crisis was 'burdensome for socialism. Anarchy and counter-revolution have appeared' but arose from the justified dissatisfaction of the working class. It was one of a series stretching back to the bloody events in Poznań in 1956, student street demonstrations in 1968, the 'very dramatic events' on the Coast in 1970, and 1976 when there was a sharp reaction in Radom and at Ursus to projected price increases. It was right to have resolved the conflicts of 1980 by political means: 'Any other mode of resolution could have led to bloodshed, with incalculable consequences for the world of real socialism. We had no way out other than to agree to new trade unions.' While the recent strike phase was now over, its after-effects were still felt daily: 'Recent protests had a mass character, extending beyond the working class to other parts of the population, notably to young activists.' It produced new structures, in particular new trade unions, which had been penetrated by enemies of socialism. The position of the Church had been strengthened, as the defender of the social rights of workers, particularly in Silesia and on the Coast.

It was neither the Party itself nor socialism that had led the country into crisis, but mistakes of policy and the violation of Leninist norms of inner-Party life. That was why the Party had adopted the notion of 'renewal'. There were many calls for those who committed mistakes to be brought to account. The premature proclamation that a 'developed socialist society' had been reached overlooked the fact that much of agriculture remained in private hands, and the same was true of private trade.'

Measures were in hand to restore rank-and-file confidence in Party leaders, which had led to many voivodship First Secretaries being changed. But unity was required, not factionalism. The Congress should be postponed because circumstances were not right for the election of Marxist delegates. While the state's sectoral unions had only 5 million members, Solidarity had 6 million, and its leader Wałęsa, a figurehead steered by others, was exploiting his personal popularity. A further problem was the 'young, radical, kamikaze' leaders of Solidarity, for example in Gdynia, aged twenty-two, and Mazowsze, aged twenty-six.

Kania stated that opposition activities had necessitated the setting up of a Committee for Administrative Measures: 'There is an operative body working alongside the Prime Minister which is prepared for the introduction of a state of emergency. Combat-ready units are being set up by members of the Party and they will be armed. Today these number 19,000, by the end of December they will reach 30,000.' In an emergency, these units would launch surprise arrests of the main opposition elements, and would take control of the mass media, railways and principal strategic points.[87] It is highly unlikely any such distribution of weapons had taken place. The passage was omitted from the Polish text.

Honecker expressed dismay at the Supreme Court's decision. It was inconceivable to him that the Party's 'leading role' could be a mere appendix to the statute. Polish leaders had again retreated in the face of counter-revolutionary forces: 'There is obviously no disagreement amongst us that already the capitulation towards the strike committees in Gdańsk, Szczecin and Jastrzębie was a mistake.' This first error was followed by strikes and riots, spreading throughout the country, whose original social demands had increasingly given way to political slogans. Forces behind Solidarity had taken advantage of the situation and 'in the shape of a union they today already have a legal political *party*'. They must now destroy the counter-revolutionary conspiracy and stabilise the government:

> If the workers' and peasants' government is at risk, if it has to be protected from counter-revolutionary forces determined to go all the way, then there remains no other choice than deploying the security organs of the workers' and peasants' state. This was our experience in 1953. This became evident in the 1956 events in Hungary, about which comrade Kádár spoke.

He recalled a conversation with Dubček during the Dresden meeting (March 1968): 'For an hour, Dubček tried to convince me that what was happening in Czechoslovakia was not a counter-revolution but a "process of democratic revival of socialism". Everybody knows what happened later. The Czechoslovak comrades under Comrade Husak have composed a document about this that taught us a lot.' Husak himself endorsed the parallel with 1968, but thought the present Polish leadership to be 'better than the one we had then'. The lesson to be learned from spring and early summer 1968 was the need for a 'consistent and united leadership'. The Czechoslovak Party had been slow to act, had no clear-cut programme and lost the initiative, which had to be regained through outside intervention. His advice to Poland was: 'You need a Marxist–Leninist party to defend socialism adequately and to defeat the opportunist, counter-revolutionary and revanchist forces.'

Zhivkov also canvassed an internal solution to the Polish crisis. Healthy forces – the army, security forces, and the larger part of the Party and population – should be mobilised to defend the socialist system. Western strategists were planning to put a different system in place in Poland, which 'diverges from real socialism and heads towards liberal socialism, a model which could pose an example and provoke changes in the social

[87] Hungarian Socialist Workers' Party 'Report to the Politburo', 8 December 1980, p. 3.

order in the other countries of the socialist commonwealth'. Brezhnev concluded that the Polish leadership must 'turn the course of events around, and not wait until the enemy has the Party with its back to the wall'. The Party had retreated again and again, emboldening hostile forces. Practically speaking, there was dual power in Poland today: 'The counter-revolutionary centre accelerates processes: it seeks to form a party on the basis of the Solidarity organisation.' Wałęsa was already boasting that he had deposed one leader and could, if he wished, depose his successor. On top of that, a Christian Democratic party was about to be formed.

The 'counter-revolutionary centre' was working towards a bourgeois electoral system. It was gradually taking over the mass media and 'becoming active even within the army, where it exerts its influence with the help of the Church'. Death threats had been made against communists and their families. In the name of 'legitimate protest', there were occupations of factories, universities, government buildings and 'the nerve centres of transport and media, which affect the vital interests of the Warsaw Pact Organisation'. The Party's leading role must be restored and an offensive launched to normalise the situation: 'A precise plan has to be developed as to how army and security forces can secure control over the transport and the main communication lines, and this plan has to be effectively implemented. Without declaring martial law, it is useful to establish military command posts and introduce patrolling services along the railways.'[88]

The failure to implement plans for the use of armed force on 8 December 1980 was partly the outcome of coolness under potential fire by the Polish leader. In a dramatic tête-à-tête with Brezhnev after the summit, Kania took the line that military intervention in Poland would be greeted by a national uprising: 'Even if angels entered Poland, they would be treated as bloodthirsty vampires and the socialist ideals would be swimming in blood.'[89] Brezhnev evidently took the point, but ended their meeting on an ambiguous note. To Kania's assurance that Poland's 'constitutional order' would not be ruptured, Brezhnev reportedly replied 'okay, we will not go in'. According to Kania, he added, 'But if there are complications, we will go in. We will go in. But without you, we won't go in.'[90] Kania pondered this parting shot on his return flight. It could have been an expression of confidence or a warning of his personal dispensability. He was indeed removed the following autumn.

[88] *CWIHP Bulletin* II, pp. 110–12. [89] *Wejdą nie wejdą* (Warsaw, 1993).
[90] S. Kania, *Zatrzymać konfrontację* (Warsaw, 1991), p. 91.

The position was equally unclear in Washington. Diplomatic reports from Europe inclined to the view that the Moscow meeting had given Poland a last chance to solve its problems on its own. The short-notice summit had given the Poles a final warning that they had better master the situation quickly. There were limits to Soviet tolerance and the Brezhnev Doctrine still applied. Likewise, the observed military build-up could be intended to intimidate Poland, as well as to intervene.

The CIA had expected an attack on the morning of 8 December. It described the mode of intervention as 'peaceful': 'the Soviets will enter Poland in conjunction with security there'. Bloodshed would ensue. Brzeziński thought that if the CIA analysis was correct, Soviet intervention would be preceded by a Polish security operation 'to seize Solidarity leadership and other key centers and then to break the psychological back of any disorganized resistance the Soviets will encounter'. Should this scenario be confirmed, there was a moral obligation to warn Polish dissidents and the free trade union movement, giving them time to hide and make contingency plans. But there was also a doubt that all Polish leaders would collude with such extreme measures, in which case some signs of protest could be expected from them.

President Carter took the view that intervention was inevitable. The Polish economic crisis would drive the Soviets in. He felt that Soviet Ambassador Dobrynin was preparing the diplomatic groundwork. Nonetheless, some moves could still be made. In order to remove the element of surprise, to encourage Polish resistance while simultaneously calming the Poles down, and to deter the Soviet Union, Carter's hotline warnings to Russia were made public. There followed a flurry of unprecedented diplomacy. In an apparent breach of protocol, Brzeziński called the Vatican switchboard and had a ten-minute conversation with the Pope. Carter's message on the prospective invasion to European leaders was forwarded to India, which Brezhnev was due to visit the next day.[91]

Kania's brief report to the Politburo on the Moscow talks stressed their positive aspects. The allies' anxieties were legitimately expressed since Polish events had an impact on their own countries. It was not always possible to agree with their assessments. Even so, allied confidence in the Polish leadership's ability to calm the situation was reassuring and helpful.[92] He did not mention any differences of emphasis between the allies nor the threat of force expressed by two of them.

Suslov noted that Kania was more robust in Moscow than at home: 'If you compare the [Moscow] speech by comrade Kania with the statement

[91] *Ibid.* pp. 82–97.
[92] *Tajne dokumenty*, p. 189 (6 December 1980).

he made to his Politburo and at the Plenum back in Poland, he was more self-critical, more vibrant and more incisive.' In Moscow, he had been much more explicit about 'the ability of the Party, the Polish people and the nation's healthy forces, armed forces, state security and police, who support the Party, to use their own forces to rectify the situation and normalise it.' Gromyko considered that both the Polish and other leaders had left the meeting satisfied with the outcome: 'They received a necessary infusion of energy and instructions on all matters concerning the Polish situation.'[93]

Poland itself was calmer. Solidarity's press spokesman, Karol Modzelewski, noted on the day of the Moscow summit that no strikes were taking place in Poland, nor were any planned. A closed session of the Solidarity leadership called for a 'social alliance representing wisdom, common sense and responsibility'. On the tenth anniversary of the massacre on the coast, a vast martyrs' memorial was dedicated in front of the Gdańsk Shipyard. The spectacle, stage-managed by Andrzej Wajda, brought together heads of the great players in the new Poland: Solidarity, Church and state.

The Politburo relaxed. Despite some adventurist elements, it noted greater signs of moderation in Solidarity.[94] Kania spoke of the need for contacts between government representatives and Solidarity but 'on the basis of their being one single authority in Poland'. Dual power was impossible. Solidarity was a trade union being invited into co-government (*współrządzenia*).[95]

In this conciliatory spirit, the Politburo also agreed to rebut a recent TASS communiqué from Moscow accusing 'counter-revolutionary groups' in Poland of 'switching over to open confrontation'. The agency alleged a *putsch* at a factory in Kielce where insurgents had disarmed the guards and dismissed the managers. Kania told Rusakov that it was a 'provocation' (deliberate falsification) and Polish Foreign Minister Czyrek said the same to the Soviet Ambassador Aristov.[96] The communiqué was withdrawn as an 'editorial error'.

Tensions arose from a new quarter. Whilst the Episcopate called for domestic peace to stabilise social life, its Secretary Orszulik broke with convention to make a sharp attack on KOR. He told foreign journalists that Kuroń in particular harboured political ambitions and was damaging the state and the Polish nation.

Kuroń himself saw no possibility of reining in a 'tremendous social democratisation movement in all spheres', with Solidarity part of it and

[93] CPSU Politburo (11 December 1980). [94] AAN 237/V/2255 (9 December 1980), p. 5.
[95] AAN 237/V/2255, p. 11. [96] AAN 237/V/2255, p. 9.

emblematic of the rest: 'This movement can no longer be stopped.' The Narożniak affair had shown that any conflict between Solidarity and the government, however small, would release the pent-up frustrations and antipathies experienced by the population for thirty-five years. Popular support for Solidarity was overwhelming, whereas any agreement with the government aroused disfavour or even disappointment. Should cooperation with the government begin to achieve more results, then the radical and more conciliatory wings within Solidarity would start to diverge. Inner tensions, pushed into the background by conflict with the government, would re-emerge. Solidarity had tremendous power but no experience or tested organisational forms.

The Party's monopoly of power was broken, but the democratic reforms sought by society had not been introduced. Solidarity should therefore press forward, not just on the union front, but with the creation of a democratic, pluralist society: 'corporations, cooperatives, consumer associations, economic self-management', together with rural self-management and nationwide discussion clubs and other citizens' initiatives. The heart of the new order should be self-management,[97] to coexist with the communist monopoly of the police, military and foreign affairs. If not established quickly, the worst scenario could come about. Given a failure to establish pluralist institutions to absorb conflict and reach peaceful solutions, the danger zone (of intervention) would be reached: 'the fall of the communist government which is in charge of maintaining Soviet influence in Poland'.[98]

[97] J. Zielonka, *Political Ideas in Contemporary Poland* (Aldershot, 1989), Ch. 3.
[98] Interview with Kuroń, *Der Spiegel* (15 December 1980).

12 Martial law

> There would be nothing more fatal for Poland than to have a traitor at the head of the Government. Jean-Jacques Rousseau, 1772[1]

Poland continued to be central to super-power relations throughout 1981. Recalling the first year of Reagan's Presidency, his CIA chief notes: 'Nothing in foreign affairs took as much time and energy as the Polish crisis, which dominated the foreign policy agenda from Inauguration Day [20 January 1981] nearly until Christmas. And none would have as important consequences for the future as did Poland.'[2]

President Carter's valedictory message to Congress highlighted the unfinished problem:

> Now, as was the case a year ago, the prospect of Soviet use of force threatens the international order. The Soviet Union has completed preparations for a possible military intervention against Poland. Although the situation in Poland has shown signs of stabilising recently, Soviet forces remain in a high state of readiness and they could move into Poland on a short notice.

He re-asserted the basic American position that 'the Polish people should be allowed to work out their internal problems themselves, without outside interference' and added the admonition: 'we have made clear to the Soviet leadership that any intervention in Poland would have severe and prolonged consequences for East–West *détente*, and US–Soviet relations in particular'.[3]

The Reagan line was continuity. The USA would seek to discourage Polish insurrection by making clear that Western military assistance would not be forthcoming: 'We should avoid any statement or action that might encourage a hopeless armed resistance on the part of the Polish people.' But the new administration would also tell the Soviets, 'in plain

[1] C. Kelly (ed.), *The Collected Writings of Rousseau*, vol. XI (Dartmouth, 2005), p. 239.
[2] Gates, *From the Shadows*, pp. 227–39.
[3] T. Cynkin, *Soviet and American Signalling in the Polish Crisis* (Basingstoke, 1988), p. 83 (16 January 1981).

words, and on every possible occasion, that intervention in Poland would severely damage Soviet–American relations and imperil the prospects of agreements on questions vital to Moscow.'[4] In such an event, sanctions would be aimed at the USSR and 'those in Poland responsible for the outrage'. To help stabilise the current situation, Washington discussed short-term aid, financial and material, to alleviate Poland's 'desperate economic situation'.

Secretary of State Haig sent a blunt warning letter to Gromyko on 24 January. It stated that any Soviet intervention in Poland would have long-term consequences for *détente*.[5] The threat was made public at a press conference (28 January) which drew attention to Soviet military activity in relation to Poland and warned of the 'gravest consequences' of armed intervention.[6] On 1 February, he made explicit a linkage between Soviet non-intervention in Poland and Soviet–American arms control negotiations.[7] This caused a diplomatic flurry. Ambassador Dobrynin personally delivered a retort to Haig: the outgoing Carter Administration had made much of human rights, and not much had come of it. He thought the new Administration sounded very like the old pre-Carter policy which 'will cause great puzzlement in Moscow'.

Haig replied that US policy was new in the sense that it was now backed by a popular consensus. Recent statements from the Polish government sounded heavy-handed, whereas the Polish people should be allowed to work through the situation themselves. Dobrynin replied: 'Nothing happened in Poland today. We have put off consideration of the Polish problem until tomorrow.'[8] Moscow would prefer dialogue to megaphone diplomacy. He then produced Gromyko's unequivocal reply on Poland (some of which Moscow made public a few days later). This declared that the 'internal affairs of a sovereign socialist state' could not be made a subject of discussion between other countries, such as the USSR or the USA. However, if the question of outside interference were to be raised, he might mention 'the provocative and instigatory broadcasts of the "Voice of America"', aimed at stirring up unfriendly sentiments towards the Soviet Union. He further asked what purpose was being served by the attempts of the American side to introduce the 'Polish topic' into Soviet–American dialogue.[9]

Despite this bluster, it was clear that dialogue could not be resumed, at least in public, until the Polish crisis had been resolved. Dobrynin's

[4] A. Haig, *Caveat. Realism, Reagan and Foreign Policy* (London, 1984), p. 240.
[5] *Ibid.* p. 90. [6] *Ibid.* Cynkin, *Soviet and American Signalling*, pp. 84–5.
[7] Cynkin, *Soviet and American Signalling*, p. 90. [8] Haig, *Caveat*, p. 103.
[9] Cynkin, *Soviet and American Signalling*, p. 86.

comments implied that resolution would take place within a few months, and not in favour of Solidarity. This was presented as 'sphere of interest' politics: Soviet hegemony over Eastern Europe had been sanctified at Yalta. But was the wartime settlement unchangeable? Was the Brezhnev Doctrine permanent? Alternatively, was Moscow inviting the incoming Administration to enter a new form of super-power condominium?[10] Answers would clearly depend on Soviet conduct in Poland.

The US State Department moved quickly to endorse the NATO statement of December 1980 that any Soviet intervention in Poland would have lasting consequences for East–West relations. On 12 December, NATO had noted that '*Détente* has brought appreciable benefits in the field of East–West cooperation and exchange. But it has been seriously damaged by Soviet actions. It could not survive if the Soviet Union were again to violate the basic rights of any state to territorial integrity and independence. Poland should be free to decide its own future.'[11] The incoming President received information on Poland through a redesigned Daily Brief, with a regular country report and periodic updates of American intelligence assessments. Two merit particular attention. A Special Analysis considered the prospects for political reform within the Polish Party. Internal pressures for reform came from the younger rank-and-file, who argued for a clean sweep of office-holders and the restriction of future officials, to be elected by secret ballot, to fixed terms. However, the Analysis noted that permanent officialdom, at both middle and lower rank, opposed such changes, which would in many cases remove them from post. Kania had therefore opted for a middle course, under the somewhat elastic notion of 'renewal'. A called-for Party Congress to enact structural changes was likely to be deferred, not least because the imminence of such a reforming Congress in Czechoslovakia, due in early September 1968, was thought to have precipitated the Soviet-led invasion.[12]

A second saw 'communist rule in the Warsaw Pact' as facing its most broadly based challenge since 1968. A conjunction of political, economic and 'emotional' factors created 'an increasingly anarchic situation which no single authority seems capable of controlling'. The Soviet Union would not allow this deterioration to continue indefinitely and had undoubtedly established a timetable within which Kania was to reverse the slide. Developments which could lead to military intervention included: breakdown of internal order, frontal assault on regime authority (such as a general strike), withdrawal from the Warsaw Pact. Short of

[10] Haig, *Caveat*, p. 106. [11] Cynkin, *Soviet and American Signalling*, p. 75.
[12] NSA, 'NID Special Analysis: Poland: Pressures for Party Reform' (19 January 1981).

these challenges to its vital interests, and mindful of the huge costs such an armed operation would involve, the Soviet Union was likely to grant Kania more time to restore the *status quo ante*. They would not, however, countenance any further concessions. On the contrary, they wished to reverse the existing trend, already 'decidedly negative'.[13]

The report raised two further points: mobilisation time and the likelihood of Polish armed resistance. It considered that 'if the Soviets foresaw the possibility of significant, organised resistance from the Polish armed forces, they would intervene with a force of at least 30 divisions'. That would take up to a fortnight to set in motion. A concealed incursion, under the guise of joint manoeuvres, would need perhaps twenty divisions and could be ready within a week. Though a smaller force could be assembled in two or three days, 'we think it unlikely, given the possibility of resistance, that the Soviets would actually intervene with such a small force'.[14]

Soviet concerns

Two Soviet teams were sent to Poland in early 1981. A military delegation was led by the Commander-in-Chief of the Warsaw Pact, Kulikov, and included all his deputies. Ostensibly visiting to verify the readiness of Polish forces for the Soyuz-81 exercises by touring all military districts, they paid no attention to the combat readiness of troops but focussed exclusively on their attitudes towards Poland's 'counter-revolution'. They wished to know the morale and discipline of Polish officers. In one case, a group of Polish officers was asked directly how they would respond to orders to break a strike and to remove occupiers forcibly from factories.[15]

Under cover of the exercise, the visitors also gave close scrutiny to strategic locations: Warsaw Airport, the Radio and Television Centre, Huta Warszawa, the Żerań motor works, the Gdańsk Shipyard and many other enterprises in key cities. Marshal Kulikov insisted that Soviet army groups scheduled to take part in manoeuvres should be located in forests near large industrial and urban centres. Reporting on this reconnaissance to the Soviet Politburo, Defence Minister Ustinov gave Kulikov's opinion that no serious 'turnaround' (*perelom*) had yet taken place: 'We need to keep constant pressure on the Polish leadership, to chase them the whole time.' Military manoeuvres would be held there in March: 'It seems to me

13 NSA, 'National Intelligence Assessment: Poland's Prospects over the Next Six Months' (listed 27 January 1981), pp. 1–3.
14 NSA, 'National Intelligence Assessment', p. 3.
15 Kukliński, 'Wojna z narodem', pp. 31–2.

we should boost these manoeuvres somewhat, that is, to make clear we have the forces ready to act.'[16]

The second team was a civilian group led by Leonid Zamyatin, head of the CPSU International Information department. During the visit, he repeatedly mentioned his 'special mission on behalf of Secretary-General Brezhnev and the Russian government' to determine the means and methods of overcoming Poland's crisis. At every meeting, they recited 'in a highly emotional manner' a lengthy catalogue of concerns: the role of the Church and oppositional political groupings and the scale of strikes, particularly in the defence and military-related industries. Solidarity was 'not a movement for union rights and social conditions for working people but a political force [aiming at] becoming a political party, inimical to socialism, closely linked with foreign subversive circles'.[17] The genesis of Solidarity was ascribed to an intelligentsia group in the late 1970s, seeking to turn the economic crisis to its own ends, by de-stabilising the situation in Poland. The union had fomented the crisis by organising strikes ('warning, hunger, solidarity or general'), destabilising the market, and preventing the government from governing. Imperialists, knowing that military means could not prevail, had turned to ideological diversion. President Carter was cited as stating that radio stations were more effective than rockets in psychological warfare.[18]

Zamyatin reported back to the Soviet Politburo that the Polish Party was regrouping, but its most serious test had yet to come. It was a victim of past mistakes: 'The working class has many reasons for dissatisfaction. This is especially true of young workers, who have not yet suffered hardships. They are being exploited by Solidarity.' However, Solidarity itself was heterogeneous. Zamyatin defined it as 'a fundamental movement with which the Polish Party must come to terms';[19] 'Solidarity is now essentially a political party, which is openly hostile to the PZPR and the state.' But, in further differentiation of Solidarity's ranks, Zamyatin noted that 'the group around Wałęsa, backed by the Church, wields great strength'. He thus seemed to advocate a dual policy. One was to isolate the 'extremists', by 'reducing the role of the militant wing of Solidarity to a minimum'. This would be achieved by severing Solidarity from KOR. At the same time, strengthening the Communist Party and (official) trade unions would restore trust amongst the masses and make clear to them that oppositional plans had no prospect of succeeding. This meant, in

16 Kramer, Special Working Paper, pp. 79–85, CPSU Politburo (22 January 1981).
17 AAN 237/V/4762 (Kania's Secretariat), p. 4.
18 AAN 237/V/3982 (Kania's Secretariat), pp. 1–4 (meeting in Katowice).
19 Kramer, Special Working Paper, pp. 79–85, CPSU Politburo (22 January 1981).

practice, striking at 'enemies of socialism without implying that Solidarity as a whole is identical to the hostile forces that exist within the organisation'.[20] Chattering was rife in the mass media, 'where one often finds debates about the Polish model of a socialist society, about liberalisation, about the need to revise Marxism–Leninism, about pluralism in public life, and so on'.

The Soviet Politburo was not reassured. Gromyko thought it 'impossible to overstate the danger posed by Solidarity. Solidarity is a political party with an anti-socialist bent. We must constantly remind the Polish leadership of this point.' He deplored the porousness of public life in Poland: top-secret Politburo proceedings were known by the entire population the very next day. Gromyko did not believe that Polish leaders would adopt emergency measures, 'despite our recommendations'. In fact, he thought they had abandoned the idea altogether.

By contrast, Rusakov, CPSU Secretary for intra-bloc relations, thought Soviet influence was being effective. He noted that Brezhnev telephoned Kania on an almost weekly basis and could continue to use these calls to 'tactfully raise all the issues and seriously indicate to comrade Kania what he should do'. But the policy needed greater coordination. He therefore mooted a 'Working Group' – from the CPSU apparatus, KGB, military and Foreign Ministry – to 'monitor and decide questions about Poland'. This was soon appointed and presented the Politburo a programme in February 1981. This called for a sharp increase in Soviet and neighbourly pressures on the Polish leadership, through a mixture of political and military means.[21] Suslov summed up the outcome as supporting the (current) Polish leadership where it was taking the required steps but also applying necessary pressure where it was not.[22] It went without saying that this meant elimination of the main problem: Solidarity.

Jaruzelski

On 7 February 1981, General Jaruzelski became Prime Minister, whilst remaining Minister of Defence. In all previous communist history, the military had been kept in check. On the rare occasions it acted openly – such as Marshal Zhukov's intervention to save Khrushchev in 1957 – the incursion was short-lived. Civil–military relations had never been an

[20] Politburo, *Special Dossier* (16 April 1981), cited by Kramer, Special Working Paper, note p. 91.
[21] Kramer, Special Working Paper, note p. 85. [22] *Ibid.*

issue. Despite the lack of precedent, Jaruzelski's further promotion did not ring alarm bells in Poland.

First of all, the Polish armed services enjoyed a public respect not given to any other communist-dominated institution. Second, there were pragmatic concerns. Someone was needed to restore the ruined economy and rebuild trust in state institutions, imperatives which seemed to many to transcend the more mundane issue of the Party's 'leading role'. Though little was known about Jaruzelski's policy orientation, he was quite widely thought to be the man for the moment. No-one realised yet that this was the beginning of the decomposition of the Party and its replacement – by the end of the decade – by the Presidency of General Jaruzelski.

Finally, there was the personal factor. As a career officer who lived modestly, Jaruzelski was not regarded as politically corrupt. Careful camouflage had prevented his being held personally responsible – as Minister of Defence – for the massacre of 1970. Though common sense suggested that the order to shoot could not have been issued without his approval, popular myth gave currency to the contrary. It was even considered that he had opposed the decision and had his resignation rejected. The Politburo was told that Jaruzelski had accepted the post reluctantly and for a trial period. Such reluctance had been a permanent feature of his advancement. Jaruzelski's first steps looked positive. He appointed the chief government official at the 1980 Gdańsk negotiations, Jagielski, as Vice-Premier and head of a new Committee for Economic Affairs.[23] Its programme, outlined to parliament (11 February), sounded conciliatory. Government and trade unions were both learning the difficult art of compromise, which meant 'negotiation and understanding their partner's point of view'. Economic problems were attributed principally to work stoppages.

Premier Jaruzelski then called for a moratorium on strikes for 'three hard-working months, ninety peaceful days', during which the new government would formulate a strategy to stabilise the economy. A ten-point plan would address such key issues as rationing, prices and incomes, investment and exports. Legislation would be brought forward on workers' self-management and rural self-government, enterprise autonomy, reform of state administration and the banking system.[24] In a positive response, Solidarity's spokesman endorsed the desire for negotiation and compromise. He stated that Solidarity also sought strong government because it would be able to honour accords reached, including the Gdańsk Agreement. Poland's crisis could not be overcome

[23] Włodek (ed.), *Tajne dokumenty*, p. 267 (Politburo, 7 February 1981).
[24] *Trybuna Ludu* 13 February 1981.

without respect for Solidarity as a partner.[25] Mazowiecki considered the Jaruzelski government to be 'the last chance of a peaceful solution in Poland'.[26]

Top officials from the Ministries of Defence and the Interior played a war game at the Internal Defence Forces headquarters in Warsaw (16–20 February). Under the supervision of Soviet military and KGB delegations, they simulated martial law. All participants agreed that such a plan, if realised, could lead to the greatest drama in Polish history. They were sworn to secrecy. Their report to Jaruzelski made four main recommendations:

- in order to eliminate the multi-million-strong Solidarity, it was essential to achieve surprise;
- resistance would be least if the action were launched at a weekend, preferably midnight on Saturday or the early hours of Sunday, or between Friday night and a work-free Saturday;
- some 6,000 Solidarity activists should be interned, along with others from independent union and social bodies. This should take place at least six and preferably twelve hours prior to the formal declaration of a state of war to minimise resistance;
- in case of 'confrontations with the population', ZOMO and the secret police would storm workplaces. By contrast, the role of the military would be restricted to patrolling, policing and enforcing a communications blockade.[27]

Jaruzelski approved this policy, code-named 'Operation Springtime', with minor alterations, and took it to Moscow for the XXVIth Party Congress on 22 February.

His memoirs comment on the age of its Presidium. On the platform sat Suslov (81), Brezhnev (76) and Gromyko (72). But in the corridors he met numerous fellow officers. He felt familiar both with them and with Russian culture: 'Above all, I understood the so-called Russian soul, the Russian mentality, customs and literature.'[28] At the end of the Congress, the Polish delegation was called back to the Kremlin for a grilling.

The Brezhnev Doctrine was re-invoked to remind the Poles that developments in their country were of concern to 'the whole socialist coalition'. Although Jaruzelski presented the plan for eventual martial law, his seven interlocutors were deeply sceptical: 'Our explanations [for postponement] were received with great reservations. This could be seen in

[25] K. Modzelewski, *Życie Warszawy* 16 February 1981.
[26] *NSZZ Solidarność agencja prasowa* (hereafter *AS*), no. 8, p. 005.
[27] Kukliński, 'Wojna z narodem'. [28] Jaruzelski, *Stan wojenny*, pp. 47–9.

their facial expressions, gestures and the cold good-byes.' It was clear that continued Soviet support would depend on a tougher stand against Solidarity. There was also a wider agenda. The final communiqué stated:

> Participants in the talks noted that imperialism and internal reaction were counting on the economic and political crisis bringing a change in the balance of forces in the world and the weakening of the socialist community, the international Communist movement and the whole liberation movement. This makes it especially pressing to give a firm and resolute rebuff to such dangerous attempts.[29]

Brezhnev had one-to-one discussions with every East European leader attending the Congress. All expressed concerns about Poland. Most vociferous was the East German leader. As Brezhnev put it, 'Comrade Honecker's alarm at the situation in Poland was very much in evidence.'[30] Brezhnev summarised the position: 'All of us are clearly united in believing that the Polish comrades must start taking more forceful measures to restore order in the country and to provide stability.' The government was now headed by Comrade Jaruzelski, 'a good, intelligent comrade, who exercises great authority'.[31]

The Soviet Union announced joint military manoeuvres to keep up the pressure. When Soyuz-81 started (16 March), Soviet fighters flew over Polish airspace, and troops in Czechoslovakia and East Germany massed on Poland's borders. The twelve Soviet divisions stationed in and around Poland were moved to high alert, support facilities were brought up and moves taken to guard Soviet installations in Poland. On the face of it, this was an abrogation of sovereignty, even amongst allies. But the manoeuvres were accepted by Jaruzelski's team with apparent equanimity. One explanation for their cooperation – which had been absent during the previous December – could be the integral part played by the manoeuvres in Jaruzelski's domestic martial law plan. Soviet forces in particular would act as re-insurance if his resources failed. Some 30,000 Soviet troops in Poland and 120,000 poised on the borders could be deployed rapidly. This could become necessary if Solidarity managed to start a general strike, potentially assisted by desertions from the Polish armed forces.

Bydgoszcz

After being evicted from a provincial council meeting in Bydgoszcz (19 March 1981), two prominent Solidarity leaders and one member of

29 Ruane, *The Polish Challenge*, p. 127.

30 Honecker in Kramer, 'Beyond the Brezhnev Doctrine', *International Security* Winter 1989/90 (14.3).

31 Kramer, Special Working Paper, pp. 86–8, CPSU Politburo (12 March 1981).

Rural Solidarity were badly beaten up. Though 200 uniformed militia were at the scene, eye-witnesses reported that plain-clothed secret police (SB) were responsible. This was the first use of force against Solidarity. An outraged National Coordinating Commission demanded an independent inquiry, punishment of those responsible and a commitment from the authorities to renounce coercive measures in future. Further demands were added: registration of Rural Solidarity and release of all detained for political activities since 1976. The incident was described as 'an obvious provocation aimed at the government of General Jaruzelski'.

Although Jaruzelski quickly sent a legal official (Procurator) to investigate, and appointed a commission of inquiry under the Ministry of Justice, some Politburo colleagues were determined to prejudge its findings. Olszowski saw the incident as political, a deliberately destructive event caused by Solidarity activists who had occupied a public building.[32] Milewski reported verbal abuse aimed at the secret police, militia and his Interior Ministry, though he thought 'the Bydgoszcz action is not yet a global confrontation'. When that came, it would be 'a trial of strength to see whether Solidarity is able to decide the situation in the country'.[33] He added, the next day, that the whole country was tense, with numerous rumours and pamphlets falsely accusing the secret police and militia of further beatings and arrests.[34] Subsequent investigation by Andrzej Paczkowski provides strong indications that the incident took place with the fore-knowledge of some elements in the Warsaw Ministry of Interior, though the extent they were acting under authorisation or on their own initiative is still unclear.[35]

Wałęsa realised that Bydgoszcz was more than a routine incident. Events there 'reflected the divisions, political confusion and internal contradictions that marked the whole period. If real problems are neglected they reappear in unexpectedly dramatic form.'[36] But within Solidarity's leadership he was the moderate: he felt that a general strike should only be called when all other remedies had been exhausted. Bujak (the young leader of the Warsaw region) noted Solidarity was being accused of sowing anarchy, trying to destabilise the country and fanning the flames of tension. In his view, Solidarity, a social movement of 10 million members, was remarkably well disciplined.[37]

[32] Włodek (ed.), *Tajne dokumenty*, p. 286 (Politburo, 21 March 1981).
[33] *Ibid.* pp. 288–9. [34] *Ibid.* p. 296 (Politburo, 22 March 1981).
[35] *O stanie wojennym. W sejmowej komisji odpowiedzialności konstytucyjnej* (Warsaw, 1997), pp. 143–4.
[36] Wałęsa, *A Path of Hope*, pp. 185–6.
[37] *AS*, no. 8, *Wydanie specjalne Bydgoszcz*, p. 002.

The experts counselled caution. Geremek called the decision before them 'the most dramatic choice since August [1980]'.[38] This was not an overstatement. To Kuroń, the March events were a moment of truth. In his view, the new union must show its strength: now or never. This did not in itself guarantee a victory, but anything less than a general strike would be a defeat. The time had come to confront the government openly. The opportunity for changing the communist system would not recur.

Wałęsa understood how crucial the crisis had become, and was willing to face it, though in his own time and in his own way. As his chief of staff put it: 'Wałęsa was convinced of one thing: that Poland is not really a sovereign country and that it is just a pipe dream to think that we could, by our own efforts, effect the slightest change in her status.'[39] Though he never articulated this view, and would in any case not have used such language, Wałęsa was led to be cautious by geopolitics. This always made him attentive to the voices, including those of experts, who advocated moderation. In the end, their view prevailed. The National Coordinating Commission decided that only if talks with the government on trade unions proved fruitless would there be a 'warning strike'. As a last resort, and only if this did not bear fruit, a general strike was set for 31 March.

Rakowski used the talks to make a frontal assault on Solidarity. He read out a polemical text (later repeated on television) which stated Solidarity's campaign of threatened strikes abrogated the Prime Minister's call for a three-month strike moratorium. From being a trade union, it was well on the way to becoming an anti-communist political party. He added at the meeting the unsubtle threat that the Soyuz-81 manoeuvres had been extended 'not just for fun'. The threat was palpable: 'All this has gone on long enough.' The government side did not address any of Solidarity's demands, nor offer any positive proposals. It simply called for support for Jaruzelski's government. After an hour's harangue, Wałęsa had had enough: 'We must get some sleep gentlemen, and prepare ourselves for tomorrow.'[40]

The next day was unique in the history of communism. From 8 a.m. till noon, a four-hour 'warning strike' took place all across Poland. Whilst essential services were maintained, such as hospitals, and certain types of enterprises (such as steel mills) kept running for safety reasons, the rest of the country came to a halt. In addition to complete solidarity amongst members of Solidarity (around 9.5 million of a 12.5 million labour force), there was also widespread further support. Not merely students, but even

[38] *Ibid.* p. 005. [39] A. Celiński in Wałęsa, *A Path of Hope*, pp. 189–90.
[40] *AS*, no. 9, pp. 103–4.

school-children absented themselves from lessons in droves.[41] Most worryingly for the Party, the strike was joined by many of its 3 million members even though they had been explicitly instructed to stay at work. Strike participation of up to 50 per cent was recorded in some voivodships, and up to 80 per cent in large enterprises.[42] The carnival atmosphere of flags and posters – many of them humorous – is well captured by a careful observer.[43] The amusement was not shared in Moscow.

Two Soviet delegations – a military team led by Marshal Kulikov and General Gribkov, and a KGB team led by its deputy chairman Kryuchkov – were in Warsaw on the same day to finalise the plans for martial law. They pored over the war-game documents, and modified and endorsed them. Kania and Jaruzelski then signed them. Together with a 'Framework for Economic Measures', drawn up with a further Soviet delegation, led by the Chairman of the State Planning Commission (Gosplan), they formed the conceptual basis for martial law. Implementation directives were also provided, for which Kania and Jaruzelski simply needed to insert the date on which martial law would begin and sign the orders. Soviet leaders were insistent that they should do so promptly since the political situation in Poland could only deteriorate. Brezhnev told Kania during telephone calls on 27 March: 'There is an upsurge of aggressiveness and anti-Russianness' in Poland;[44] 'A deadly threat to socialism has been created. Soon the proclamation of martial law will no longer be avoidable.'[45]

Washington's intelligence and policy communities believed martial law could be invoked within days – possibly involving Soviet military intervention – and drew up sanctions accordingly. These included giving high priority to improvements in NATO, and deployment of more advanced weapons systems in Europe. Another scheme was for the President to proclaim a 'Polish Patriots' Day' in the event of a Soviet intervention.[46] US intelligence considered a Polish compromise could still be reached if the authorities managed to rein in Solidarity through appeals to the Church, hints of martial law or threats of military force. But Polish workers had lost some of their fear and were determined to resist the use of force by the police. The chances of martial law had therefore

41 Włodek (ed.), *Tajne dokumenty*, p. 318 (Politburo, 27 March 1981).

42 *Informacja*, iii/125/81 'Przebieg strajku ostrzegawczego 27 BM'; Włodek (ed.), *Tajne dokumenty*, pp. 231–6.

43 Garton Ash, *The Polish Revolution*, pp. 155–7.

44 Włodek (ed.), *Tajne dokumenty*, p. 320 (Politburo, 27 March 1981).

45 Jaruzelski, *Stan wojenny*, p. 95. 46 Gates, *From the Shadows*, pp. 230–1.

increased 'even though it risked provoking widespread disorder and a military intervention by the Soviets'.[47]

As usual in a crisis, the Church came forward as mediator. On 26 March, Jaruzelski held a private conversation with Cardinal Wyszyński (the only time they met). Jaruzelski took the view that the Bydgoszcz incident had blown out of all proportion. An avalanche had been set in motion: 'The situation is threatening. We have received signals that if certain limits are crossed, it will cease to be an internal matter.' The fate of Poland was at stake.[48] Wyszyński spoke in favour of legalising a farmers' trade union. The same day, a papal message to Wyszyński urged agreement between 'the state authorities and representatives of the world of work'. This would strengthen 'domestic peace in the spirit of the renewal (*odnowa*)' that had begun the previous autumn.[49]

The Pope met the Soviet Ambassador to Italy in private for two hours (28 March). The pontiff told his staff afterwards that he reached an agreement with the envoy. A senior official from Poland would travel to the Vatican in April to discuss implementation. Meantime, Moscow offered an assurance that it would not intervene in Poland for six months.[50]

A US Alert Memorandum concluded: 'the Soviets are now capable of intervention with a force of 12 to 20 divisions with little further warning. Whether the Soviets believe such a force is adequate is known only to them.'[51] President Reagan sent a strongly worded message to Brezhnev warning against extension of the Soyuz-81 manoeuvres into an invasion of Poland.[52] But there were also carrots. Should force be eschewed, the White House offered Poland an attractive package: (i) $200 million in addition to the $670 million loan guarantees already offered for the fiscal year; (ii) sale of dairy products at concessionary prices, plus $70 million in surplus butter and dried milk; (iii) an emergency donation of wheat, under 'food for peace' legislation; (iv) rescheduling some $80 million in debt repayment due by 30 June.[53] This stabilisation package was offered to Jagielski at a meeting with Vice-President George Bush.

Bydgoszcz also increased tensions within the Polish Party. Some 350 resolutions and letters had reached the Central Committee in the previous few days, mostly from Party members in large enterprises. They

47 CIACO, 'NID Special Analysis. Poland: Possible Turning Point' (25 March 1981).
48 Jaruzelski, *Stan wojenny*, p. 88.
49 Włodek (ed.), *Tajne dokumenty*, Kalendarium, p. 629.
50 Gates, *From the Shadows*, pp. 240–1.
51 CIACO NID Alert Memorandum (3 April 1981).
52 Cynkin, *Soviet and American Signalling*, p. 111.
53 *Ibid.* pp. 106–7; Rachwald, *In Search of Poland*, p. 53.

demanded positive action to bring the country out of its political crisis and called for an understanding with Solidarity.[54] There were also signs of state censorship breaking down. The official news agency published an 'Open Letter' from Stefan Bratkowski which made a frontal attack on hardliners in the Party: 'those who would like to drive our Party away from the path of social agreement'. They did not even want agreement with the Party's grass roots and sought to present themselves as the protectors of the apparatus against the rank-and-file: 'These are the men who try to set the forces of public order against their own community.' But 'In reality they constitute no force.'[55] All this was reflected in the tenor of the Plenum. Speakers roundly condemned hardliners and several resignations were tendered from the leadership. None was accepted, but the policy of a compromise agreement with Solidarity was strongly endorsed.[56]

Accordingly, Rakowski's Committee for Trade Union Affairs reached a settlement with Solidarity representatives on 30 March. Under the 'Warsaw Agreement', it admitted mishandling the Bydgoszcz incident and accepted demands that security forces should not be used to resolve social conflicts by political means. It agreed to withdraw militia units from the Bydgoszcz region. Legal recognition for Rural Solidarity would be facilitated by a change in the law on trade unions or a new draft law on rural self-management. Moreover, the issue of freedom of expression (Point Four of the Gdańsk Agreement) would be the subject of further negotiations.[57] In return, Wałęsa unilaterally rescinded the next day's general strike.

This led to a major storm within Solidarity. Wałęsa was accused of dictatorial behaviour. He later called it a 'breaking point' for the organisation. Splinter groups appeared opposed to his leadership, his chief-of-staff Andrzej Celiński was voted out, and Press Secretary Karol Modzelewski resigned over the 'monarchical' functioning of a union in which one man was king.[58] Mazowiecki, ever the moderator, called for the restoration of trust within the union since 'Solidarity is the one guarantee of democracy in Poland'. It was essential that local conflicts should not again cause a national conflagration. Members should take a realistic approach towards negotiations. Demands could not be achieved 100 per cent.[59]

Soviet leaders were appalled by the turn of events. When Kania complained that he had been criticised at the Plenum, Brezhnev retorted

[54] Włodek (ed.), *Tajne dokumenty*, Kalendarium. p. 630.
[55] Ruane, *The Polish Challenge*, p. 143.
[56] Włodek (ed.), *Tajne dokumenty*, p. 327 (Politburo, 31 March 1981).
[57] The weekly *Tygodnik Solidarność* eventually appeared on 3 April 1981.
[58] His resignation speech is in *AS*, no. 10 (31 March 1981), p. 8 (007).
[59] *AS*, no. 10, p. 9 (008).

'They were right. They shouldn't have just criticised you; they should have raised a truncheon against you. Then, perhaps, you would understand.' Kania acknowledged that he had been too lenient and needed to be more forceful. Brezhnev exclaimed: 'A general strike has been averted, but at what price? At the price of a subsequent capitulation to the opposition.' He added, 'You can't keep making endless concessions to "Solidarity". You always speak about a peaceful path, but you don't understand (or at least don't wish to understand) that a "peaceful path" of the sort you're after is likely to cost you blood.'[60]

Moscow saw the Polish leadership as 'moving steadily backwards'. Minister of Defence Ustinov commented: 'With regard to Polish leaders, I think it difficult to say who is best. Earlier we regarded Comrade Jaruzelski as a stalwart figure, but now he has proven to be weak.'[61] There was a perceived shift in the potential reliability of Polish armed forces. The earlier evaluation had been upbeat, a view shared by General Gribkov, in Poland under the prolonged Soyuz-80 exercises.[62] Post-Bydgoszcz, Kania 'insisted that they could not rely on the [Polish] army and security organs and could not be certain that they would support the Party and state leadership if the situation reached a critical point'. Jaruzelski endorsed this view.

Spelling this out, Ustinov stated: 'If we are candid about the matter, we have to recognise that Kania and Jaruzelski are scarcely inclined to pursue a confrontation, bearing in mind the Bydgoszcz conflict'; 'The results of this conflict showed that even if just two people from Solidarity are somehow injured, the whole country will literally be up in arms, and that Solidarity was able to mobilise its forces quickly.' He thought that Polish leaders would retreat still further, with all the gains of socialism being lost: 'Bloodshed can't be avoided: it will occur.'[63]

Marshal Kulikov, reporting on Soyuz-81, considered that comrades Kania and Jaruzelski lacked depth in their analysis of the Polish crisis: 'A realistic evaluation of the counter-revolution in Poland from a class standpoint is unfortunately not to be found with either.' They had not understood that 'Solidarity is increasingly gaining power and has the goal of ending the Party's leading role.' The Polish counter-revolution was being aided and abetted by West Germany and the USA and was aiming

60 Kramer, Special Working Paper, pp. 92–102, CPSU Politburo (2 April 1981).
61 *Ibid.* p. 99.
62 A. I. Gribkov, '"Doktrina Brezhneva" i pol'skii krizis nachala 80-kh godov', *Voyenno-istoricheskii zhurnal* 1992 (9).
63 Kramer, Special Working Paper, pp. 92–102, CPSU Politburo (2 April 1981).

further to bring difficulties to East Germany, Czechoslovakia and the Soviet Union, 'so as to shake violently the whole Soviet bloc'.[64]

The two Polish leaders were summoned to an overnight harangue in a railway carriage near Brest (4–5 April). Soviet leaders Andropov and Ustinov were struck by the 'dejected (*podavlennoye*) condition' of their interlocutors. But they advised the Soviet Politburo that 'we still need this pair to stick together and strengthen their relations'.[65] Soviet leaders had not established an alternative leadership of 'healthy forces' in Poland and still expected that Jaruzelski would do their bidding. Even so, there started to emerge informal pressure groups within Polish communism, evidently with Soviet backing. The Grunwald Patriotic Union and the Katowice Party Forum were outspoken critics of Solidarity and the Kania–Jaruzelski 'soft line'.

The Suslov Commission presented its most gloomy report so far. Solidarity was able 'to paralyse the activity of Party and state organs and take de facto power into its own hands'. They had only been restrained from such action by the fear of Soviet troops. It hoped it could 'achieve its aims without bloodshed and by means of a creeping counter-revolution'. A new tactic had emerged. Realising that geopolitics deprived them of the chance to obstruct the Warsaw Pact or undermine the Party's leading role, the opposition 'have clearly decided to undermine the Party from within, to bring about the Party's "rebirth" and thus to seize power "on a legal basis"'.[66]

Between July 1980 and mid-June 1981, over 300,000 members resigned from the Party. This still left a mass organisation 2.8 million strong, but many Party members also joined Solidarity, which was by now 9.5–10 million strong. A Plenum (29–30 April) decided to hold an Extraordinary Party Congress in July at which the issue of Party 'renewal' would be debated and decided. Attention thus turned to the election of delegates to the Congress. During this campaign, proponents of the 'horizontal' structures, who favoured a radical reconstruction of the Party, bringing it much closer to the social democratic parties of Western Europe, were defeated. They held a major conference in Toruń on 15 April. But hardly any of its supporters reached the Congress. But nor did the increasingly strident ideologues.

Elimination of both Party radicals and the most orthodox elements meant that the Congress could rally around what Party 'centre' there was – variously referred to as moderates, pragmatists or realists. Duraczyński

64 DDR Ministry of Defence (7 April 1981).
65 Kramer, Special Working Paper, pp. 103–11, CPSU Politburo (9 April 1981).
66 M. Kramer, *CWIHP Bulletin* Spring 1995 (5), pp. 130–2.

summarises their priorities as: preserving unity within the Party, resolving Polish matters without the assistance of foreign intervention and leading the country out of its economic recession. Any accommodation with Solidarity was abandoned as incompatible with 'the systemic reality of the eastern bloc' and functioning without Soviet acceptance was 'unthinkable in the long-run and even unimaginable at the time'. But the Congress did not bring forward any remedies for the economy through structural reforms because it was incapable of doing so.[67]

There were three strands of Party thinking in relation to Solidarity. The first (represented by Kania) was a genuine effort to incorporate the social movement within the existing system. It was clearly collapsing by this point. A second strand (handed to Rakowski) was to treat Solidarity as a political player, and win. Subsequently, the defeated Solidarity could be castigated as confrontational, and later out of control. The third course (Jaruzelski) was a more cynical time-play by those who remained loyal to Moscow. They presented a façade of compromise and reasonableness, while in fact giving nothing away. Lack of results was bound to inflame Solidarity's mass membership, who would become simultaneously enraged and worn down, thus helping to prepare the ground for the 'lesser evil' of martial law.

Moscow was delighted by the disintegration of the Party's 'horizontal movement'. Following a flying visit to Warsaw, Suslov declared they had been 'creating total disorder in the organisational structure of the Party and are completely at odds with Leninist organisational principles for the structure of a Marxist–Leninist party'. But the rest of his report was negative. Brezhnev commented, on Polish leaders, 'even though they listen to us, they don't do what we recommend'.[68]

A Moscow letter, handed to Kania by Ambassador Aristov (5 June), did not mince words: 'Mortal danger now looms over the Polish people's revolutionary achievements.' During talks at the highest level, Polish leaders had been given friendly warnings which 'were not taken into account and even ignored'. There was now a critical situation in which the enemies of socialist Poland had declared their intentions: 'They are waging a struggle for power and are already in the process of achieving it.' Counter-revolution 'has been using Solidarity's extremist faction as a strike force'. One position after another was being surrendered. This was being assisted by imperialist reaction 'hoping to change the European and world balance of forces in its favour'.[69]

[67] E. Duraczyński, 'The Polish United Workers' Party in Crisis', *Jachranka* November 1997.
[68] Kramer, Special Working Paper, pp. 115–18, CPSU Politburo (30 April 1981).
[69] The letter appeared in *Le Monde* 10 June 1981.

The Party Congress (14–19 July) was the first attended by 90 per cent of delegates. At their insistence, the new Central Committee and First Secretary were elected by secret ballot. Kania was re-elected First Secretary by 1,311 votes to Barcikowski's 568. Only 4 of the original 11 Politburo members were reappointed: Kania, Jaruzelski, Barcikowski and Olszowski. The Party Secretariat was similarly decimated. Of the 49 provincial Party Secretaries from the Congress of February 1980, only 2 survived.[70] Even though 40 Solidarity members had joined the 200-strong Central Committee, and one was even elevated to the Politburo, the composition of Party bodies did not augur well for policy renewal. While increased democracy could strengthen cohesion between central leadership and regional roots, it did not provide any solution to national problems.

Working-groups of the Congress considered current issues, but did little to suggest ways out of the country's economic crisis. As Kania put it to Brezhnev (21 July): 'Economic circumstances in Poland are terrible. Due to the shortage of market supplies, the possibility of rioting is most likely.'[71] Shortly afterwards, the government announced increases in the prices of food and other consumer goods and a 20 per cent cut in meat rations for the coming two months. Protests erupted across Poland. Hunger marches took place in towns and cities. Bread rationing was introduced in a province north of Warsaw. Solidarity leaders held a special meeting in Gdańsk (24–26 July) to discuss reactions.

Discussion was introduced by Wałęsa's close adviser Andrzej Celiński. He saw Solidarity as autonomous but lacking independence. Some elements of the authorities had taken initiatives, as in stirring up the Bydgoszcz provocation, but Solidarity emerged from each crisis weaker than before. Kuroń then took the floor. He saw a revolution in progress 'in which the existing order has been overthrown and no attempt has been made to construct a new one'. Solidarity could not create one. This must be done by the whole of society. Yet such a revolution must be self-limiting or 'the USSR will definitely march in'. Modzelewski argued that the union should overcome the crisis through self-management.[72]

August was a fraught month for Polish society. A protest parade of lorries and other vehicles blocked the traffic roundabout (Rondo) in central Warsaw. The failure of food supplies continued to dominate the Solidarity agenda. Their suggestion of taking part in food rationing and allocation was rejected by the authorities. In tense meetings between

[70] NSA, CIACO NID 81 (6 July 1981).
[71] Hungarian National Archives, *Jachranka* Document 41 (22 July 1981).
[72] *AS*, no. 26 (21–27 July 1981) pp. 105–11.

Wałęsa and Rakowski (3–6 August), their first since 25 June, the government called this proposal 'a programme for the takeover of power'.[73] In an ominous retort, which lingered long in the popular memory, Rakowski declared 'who has food has power'. Wałęsa responded with an 'Appeal to Union Members and the Whole Society' (12 August). This called for a moratorium on street protests and a return to voluntary work on 'free Saturday'. But it also demanded the rebuilding of local administration through democratic elections.[74]

On 14 August, Kania was received by Brezhnev in the Crimea. It was his last such visit as Party Secretary. The Soviet leader came straight to the point: 'You hoped that events would begin to turn around in some definite way after the [Party] Congress. But in actuality, the situation has continued to deteriorate and the counter-revolution is stepping up its onslaught.' Kania countered that the Polish Party now had a programme and was seizing the initiative. But a new obstacle was mentioned: 'Poland's foreign debt has grown astronomically ... They don't give us loans as a gift. Credits are extended to us at very high rates of interest of up to 20 per cent.'[75] In fact, both the USSR and the USA delayed Polish repayments by rescheduling agreements reached later that month.

Solidarity's First National Congress opened in Gdańsk (5 September) with 896 delegates representing some 9.5 million members. In an atmosphere which resembled the founding Congress of the Second International (Paris, 1879), there was the same excitement, confusion over credentials, medley of flags and internationalism. When Wałęsa began with 'Otwieram Nasz Zjazd' (I open Our Congress), there was a five-minute standing ovation. International speakers included the Secretaries of some twenty Western trade unions, though Lane Kirkland, Chairman of the AFL/CIO, had been denied a visa. Likewise, all East European guests of the Congress had been barred from Poland. To remind delegates about geopolitics, Soviet warships began a week of manoeuvres in the Bay of Gdańsk.

The Catholic Church made every effort to preserve an atmosphere of calm. At mass before the second day, the Congress' chaplain, Father Józef Tischner, described the meeting as 'an event in the history of the culture of Polish work'. Their shared concern was the 'independence of Polish work', which did not mean divisiveness, but rather reciprocity, agreement, multi-faceted dependence and communion. The country converged as a great river grows by collecting its tributaries. Thus the Vistula, near whose estuary they were meeting, collects the waters from

[73] Andrews, *Poland 1980–81*, pp. 189–92. [74] *AS*, no. 29 (10–12 August 1981), p. 301.
[75] Kramer, Special Working Paper, pp. 125–36.

most of the rivers of Poland and from the Tatra Mountains where 'as we know, we are close to the heavens'. Polish independence would depend upon the independence of work. His homily ended with a reference to Polish history. After the uprising of 1830, its defeated soldiery were exiled in Paris: 'All the powers of Europe were against them. Nonetheless, it was they who were right.'[76]

Tischner taught Solidarity that the precondition for any dialogue is for people to come out of their sanctuaries, to approach each other and exchange opinions. Dialogue cannot be on the basis of 'I am entirely right.' There has to be a reciprocal acceptance that the other partner is also right, to some extent. Another person's notion of truth has to be acknowledged as a starting-point for discussion.[77] Secondly, the interlocutors have to find a language which allows for concept formation outside the official sphere of communication. For any interchange of views to become possible, words such as 'strike', 'election' or 'party' have to have a meaning beyond those imposed by those in power. This collision of discourse had been seen most clearly in the Gdańsk negotiations of August 1980.

A third precondition is that dialogue is entered into without the result being known beforehand. It requires recognition that political debate or demands cannot be won '100 per cent'. To compromise on some issues is not a moral disgrace or defeat, but a way to progress. For many Poles, this challenged the romantic tradition under which a heroic defeat becomes a spiritual victory, since struggling for a just cause kept the national idea alive. Equally, political realism was distrusted as the rationalisation of moral surrender. This left the field of politics open to others and also enabled communists to claim a monopoly of political realism in post-war Poland.[78]

Before lunch on the fourth day, a bearded figure from the Gdańsk negotiations, Andrzej Gwiazda, made his way slowly to the microphone, looking like a monk at prayer. He read out a brief 'Message to Working-people in Eastern Europe' who had been excluded from visiting Poland. It conveyed greetings and support to the workers of Albania, Bulgaria, Czechoslovakia, the DDR, Romania and Hungary, and to all the nations of the USSR: 'As the first independent trade union in post-war history, we are profoundly aware that we share the same destiny.' 'Contrary to the lies spread about us in your countries', Solidarity was an 'authentic,

[76] J. Tischner, *The Spirit of Solidarity* (New York, 1984), pp. 96–100.

[77] J. Tischner, *Etyka Solidarności* (Kraków, 1981; Paris, 1982), pp. 15–17.

[78] A. Walicki, 'Three Traditions in Polish Patriotism' in S. Gomułka and A. Polonsky (eds.), *Polish Paradoxes* (London, 1990), pp. 28–39.

10-million strong representative of working people, created as the result of workers' strikes'. Solidarity supported all those who had decided to embark upon the difficult road of struggle for a free and independent labour movement: 'We believe that it will not be long before your representatives and ours are able to meet to exchange experience as trade unionists.'[79] To the consternation of the platform, and contrary to the wishes and advice of the experts and advisers, the message was passed by acclamation after a standing ovation.[80]

The Soviet Press Agency immediately denounced this 'villainous appeal' as the product of counter-revolutionaries and imperialist agents seeking to restore the bourgeois order in Poland.[81] In fact the message had been written by Congress delegate Jan Lityński and given to Gwiazda.[82] TASS insisted that the Gdańsk Congress had become an 'anti-socialist and anti-Soviet orgy'.[83] Brezhnev denounced the message at the next Politburo (10 September) as a 'dangerous and provocative document'.[84] The Central Committee's Propaganda Department would draft outraged replies from major Soviet enterprises (none of whose workers had read the message). Gorbachev, a comparative newcomer to the Politburo, commented: 'I consider that Leonid Il'ich [Brezhnev] was completely right to propose that workers' collectives in large enterprises speak out, and that the activities of "Solidarity" should be unmasked in our press.'[85] Soviet patience with Kania had reached its end. Brezhnev told leaders of the neighbouring states that 'Comrade Kania is displaying unacceptable liberalism and we must apply strong pressure on him'.[86]

We have only Brezhnev's side of his next telephone conversation with Kania (11 September): "I'll speak frankly: you should wake up again and think about who is controlling the situation in Poland. Has the fulcrum of power already changed there? The leaders of Solidarity are acting so brazenly (*vol'no*) that one cannot avoid this question.' He considered the Gdańsk Congress (by then in recess) as 'in no way a congress of workers'. He stated that a quarter of delegates were from KOR or KPN (Confederation of Independent Poland) and were bent on humiliating the Party government and forcing it to its knees. Even Poland had become too small for Solidarity. The message to the East was an attempt to

79 *Tygodnik Solidarność* 18 September 1981 (25).
80 Those of us observing from the gallery also leaped to our feet.
81 Ruane, *The Polish Challenge*, p. 233.
82 J. Holzer, *Solidarność 1980–1981. Geneza i Historia* (Warsaw, 1983), p. 180.
83 B. Kaliski, *'Antysocjalistyczne zbiorowisko?' I Krajowy Zjazd Delegatów NSZZ Solidarność* (Warsaw, 2003).
84 Kramer, Special Working Paper, pp. 137–40, CPSU Politburo (10 September 1981).
85 *Ibid.* p. 146. 86 *Ibid.* CPSU Politburo (17 September 1981), p. 146.

'impose its subversive ideas on neighbouring countries and interfere in their internal affairs'. Solidarity was creating combat groups to terrorise communists and patriots. Within economic management, one position after another was being transferred to Solidarity's control. There was the demand for fresh elections.

Above all, Poland was forcing 'the socialist commonwealth to confront the even thornier question of how to maintain security in the centre of Europe'. What would happen to 'strategic lines of communication' if Solidarity ruled Poland? How could the Warsaw Pact 'ensure the preservation of the results of World War Two, which were codified in well-known political and international legal documents'?[87]

The Pope issued his delayed encyclical *Laborem Exercens* (On Human Work) the next day.[88] Two sections seemed to address Poland most directly. One noted that 'Worker Solidarity' was, in the nineteenth century, 'sometimes described as the proletariat question' and had evolved later under various forms of neo-capitalism and collectivism. But it was much broader than that. To achieve social justice in various parts of the world, and between them, 'there is the need for ever new movements of solidarity of the workers and with the workers'.[89] A second stated that unions were not mere reflections of 'class struggle' – they act for social justice. Working people had the right to strike without being penalised. But the strike weapon should not be used to paralyse the whole of socio-economic life.[90]

According to Kukliński, Kania attended his first session of the National Defence Committee (KOK) on 15 September. He seemed shocked to discover that almost all members supported the introduction of martial law. It was unanimously endorsed at Jaruzelski's behest. General Kiszczak gave details of how the operation would be conducted, noting that Solidarity had obtained them through an unknown source. The Ministry of Interior would seal off major areas of Warsaw and other cities six hours before the announcement was broadcast and make mass arrests.[91] All that remained was to choose the most favourable moment.

Solidarity went to some lengths to deny a pretext. Its absolute commitment to non-violence meant the authorities were unable to provide any evidence of military preparations against martial law. The claim that 'extremist elements' were preparing Molotov cocktails with which to

[87] *Ibid.* pp. 141–5.
[88] Publication had been delayed by the Pope's recuperation from the attempted assassination in May, two days before it was to be issued.
[89] *Laborem Exercens* (London, 1981), pp. 26–30. [90] *Ibid.* pp. 72–6.
[91] Kramer, *CWIHP Bulletin* II, p. 55 'Telegram from R. Kukliński ("Jack Strong")' 15 September 1981.

assault government buildings turned out to be Ministry of Interior fabrications.[92]

During the Solidarity Congress' second round (28 September), Wałęsa was re-elected leader with 55 per cent of the vote. There were three other candidates. It was not a rousing endorsement. One major criticism was his undemocratic conduct in recent negotiations with the government on a parliamentary bill on Workers' Self-Management.[93] Even so, the new legislation was far closer to Solidarity's preferred draft than to the Party's. Parliament had not acted as independently since 1947.

Wałęsa restated to delegates his determination since summer 1980 that no-one with designs upon Solidarity, 'whether the Party-administration, Church or KOR', would take it under their control. For its part, KOR now disbanded, saying that Solidarity could better discharge its tasks. Wałęsa paid a generous tribute: 'As you know I grew up close to the KOR movement.'[94] After announcing the end of KOR, the veteran economist Professor Edward Lipiński received a standing ovation. But the session ended early when another founder and historian of the group, J. J. Lipski, collapsed at the microphone.[95]

The concluding session of the Congress (7 October) empowered the newly elected National Commission to initiate talks with the government. These began on 15 October when a Solidarity delegation presented a set of proposals for both economic policy and management of the economy. The latter was to be transferred to a Social Council of National Economy, entirely independent of Party and government. It would act through parliament, where it could initiate legislation. After some thirty-six hours of inconsequential discussion, the government side declared this proposal non-negotiable.[96]

The Party's Fourth Plenum (16–18 October) strongly criticised Kania's leadership. He resigned and Jaruzelski replaced him, by a vote of 180 to 4, while still remaining Prime Minister and Minister of Defence. He took a fourth post, head of the Military Council for National Salvation, in December. The Plenum called for an end to strikes and a firm rebuff to 'anti-Soviet propaganda'. A nationwide one-hour strike took place on 28 October to protest at the government's lack of progress in forming the Social Council. In response, Jaruzelski asked parliament to ban strikes altogether and to grant 'extraordinary powers' to defend

92 Gates, *From the Shadows*, p. 232.
93 S. Jakubowicz, *Bitwa o samorząd 1980–1981* (London, 1988).
94 *AS*, no. 42 (29 September – October 1981), pp. 101–9.
95 *AS*, no. 40 (26–28 September 1981), p. 301.
96 *Rozmowy z rządem PRL. Negocjacje pomiędzy NSZZ 'Solidarność' a rządem w dniach 15–18 października 1981* (Warsaw, 1998).

the state. Neither request was granted. Jaruzelski decided to proceed without them.

'State of war'

Jaruzelski indignantly rejected the claim at Jachranka (oral history conference, 1997) that he asked for Soviet military intervention should the domestic forces be unequal to the pacification of the nation. Such remonstrance was essential to sustaining his claim that his 'state of war' had saved the nation from a 'greater evil'. Yet evidence shows that Jaruzelski did call on Soviet forces to provide an ultimate back-up for martial law, as a last resort to save Polish communism and his own place in power.

Yet it seems unlikely that incoming forces would have wished to retain the *ancien régime*. The post-invasion treatment of Imre Nagy (executed in 1958) and Alexander Dubček (abducted to Moscow and removed after a few months) were not encouraging precedents. In his memoirs, Jaruzelski suggests that he realised this and told Rakowski that the honourable course in such an eventuality was suicide. On the other hand, Jaruzelski seems to continue the Targowica line of Polish collaboration with Russian imperial power. The US Defense Secretary Weinberger called him a 'Russian general in Polish uniform'.

When Poland disappeared from the map of Europe in 1795, the disloyal Count Potocki declared: 'I no longer speak of Polishness and the Poles. This state, this name, has vanished as have many others in the history of the world. The Poles should abandon all memories of their Fatherland. I am now a Russian forever.'[97] But his Confederates of Targowica were rarities compared to the ensuing choruses of romantic patriotism. Andrzej Walicki suggests that, by espousing political idealism, Poles salvaged their moral reputation but simultaneously allowed the cause of realism to be monopolised by people with dirty hands. Is the imposition of martial law a modern example?

Doubts about Jaruzelski's behaviour and intentions surfaced in Moscow during 1992. A retired army general, Anatolii Gribkov, long-standing Chief of Staff and First Deputy Commander-in-Chief of the Warsaw Pact, denied that martial law in Poland was imposed to forestall a Soviet invasion. He argued, on the contrary, that Jaruzelski explicitly demanded guarantees of military assistance from Moscow if the Polish situation should become 'critical'. When this was turned down, at the highest political level, Jaruzelski apparently retorted that 'if military

[97] Cited by A. Blejwas, *Realism in Polish Politics: Warsaw Positivism and National Survival in Nineteenth-Century Poland* (New Haven, Conn., 1984), p. 5.

assistance is not offered, Poland will be lost to the Warsaw Pact'.[98] Gribkov attributed this last-minute request to 'the nervousness and diffidence that the top Polish leaders were feeling about their ability to carry out the plans for martial law'.[99]

A further Soviet source revealed at Jachranka was the notebook kept by Viktor Anoshkin, *aide-de-camp* of Marshal Kulikov, in Poland from 7 to 17 December 1981. This shows that Jaruzelski called Brezhnev early on 10 December to inform him that the Polish Military High Command (not the ruling Party) had agreed overnight on the final decision to implement martial law. He then asked whether Poland could count on military assistance if the situation in the country became 'critical'. Brezhnev's noncommittal reply was clarified shortly afterwards. Kulikov was instructed to tell Jaruzelski that 'the Poles themselves must resolve the Polish question. We are not preparing to send troops onto Polish territory.'

Next day, Jaruzelski sent an urgent cable to Moscow (through the Soviet Embassy in Warsaw) asking 'Can we count on military assistance from the USSR and the sending of troops?', to which Moscow replied: 'No troops will be sent.' A dismayed Jaruzelski exclaimed: 'This is terrible news for us. A year and a half of chattering about sending troops and now everything has disappeared.' He made the same request to Andropov, warning that military assistance was needed urgently, but received the curt rebuff: 'There is no question whatever of sending [Soviet] troops.'[100] It seems likely that Jaruzelski's nerve was failing by this point.

The Soviet Politburo (10 December) heard that Jaruzelski was reverting to indecision and was 'extremely neurotic and diffident about his capacity to do anything'.[101] Rusakov reported Jaruzelski envisaging a form of military dictatorship of the Piłsudski type: 'He indicated that Poles will accept this more readily than something else.' But Jaruzelski was also saying that 'if Polish forces are unable to cope with the resistance put up by Solidarity, the Polish comrades hope to receive assistance from other countries, up to and including the introduction of armed forces on the territory of Poland'. In expressing this hope, he cited earlier remarks by Marshal Kulikov.[102] Whilst Kulikov may or may not have given some

98 P. Machcewicz, 'The Assistance of Warsaw Pact Forces Is Not Ruled Out', *CWIHP Bulletin*.
99 A. Gribkov, 'Doktrina Brezhneva', p. 52.
100 M. Kramer, 'Jaruzelski, the Soviet Union and the Imposition of Martial Law in Poland'.
101 Kramer, *CWIHP Bulletin* II, pp. 5–39, Special Working Paper, pp. 157–70, CPSU Politburo (10 December 1981).
102 *Ibid.* pp. 162–3.

such reassurances to Jaruzelski, the Soviet Politburo was resolved not to honour them.

The transcript of this Politburo shows unanimity. But like many a formal protocol, it may well have been preceded by a franker debate off-the-record. Gromyko indeed mentions 'very intense discussions of Poland' earlier in the day. Later he states: 'There cannot be any introduction of troops into Poland.' Defence Minister Ustinov agrees, but seems dubious about Jaruzelski's ability to do the job. Suslov sums up the debate: 'If troops are introduced, that will be a catastrophe. I think we have reached a unanimous view here on this matter.'[103]

Jaruzelski requested that a high-level Soviet delegation fly to Warsaw for urgent consultations. Kiszczak confirms that Jaruzelski called Brezhnev (12 December) and that Suslov took the receiver instead.[104] The Soviet refusal of military assistance rendered any flying visit unnecessary. More details about the request came later from Gorbachev, always well-disposed towards Jaruzelski personally. While denying any Soviet invasion threat in December 1981, he also reports the call from Jaruzelski. In reply, Suslov had stated that the Soviet Union would continue to guarantee Poland against 'external threats' but declined to counter 'internal dangers'.[105]

On 13 December, Poles woke up to the national anthem. Television viewers then saw General Jaruzelski in full uniform, sitting next to a huge Polish flag and not wearing dark glasses. He informed them: 'Our country finds itself on the brink of an abyss. The achievements of many generations, the house erected from Polish ashes, are being destroyed.' After patriotism, he turned to law and order: 'Strikes, warning strikes, protest actions have become the norm. Even school-children are dragged in ... Acts of terrorism, threats and mob justice, together with direct coercion abound.' The country had descended into criminality and chaos. This was the doing of Solidarity.

Whereas millions of Poles had welcomed the great national accord (summer 1980) as a chance to deepen democracy and broaden the range of reform, 'the Solidarity leaders were absent from the common table'. They had announced a policy of confrontation at their most recent meetings (Radom and Gdańsk) which could only lead to a national catastrophe. A Military Council for National Salvation had therefore been formed ('today') and had introduced a 'state of war' throughout

[103] *Ibid.* p. 168.

[104] W. Bereś and J. Skoczylas, *Generał Kiszczak mówi ... prawie wszystko* (Warsaw, 1991), pp. 129–30.

[105] Interview with *Trybuna*, 9 November 1992.

the country from midnight. He announced the internment of 'extremist Solidarity activists and activists of illegal anti-State organisations'. Those responsible for past mistakes, including former Party leader Gierek and long-serving Premier Jaroszewicz, had also been detained.

In the next few days, ZOMO troops systematically broke strikes across the whole country. The pattern of 'pacification' was the same everywhere. Tanks broke down factory gates or walls, and ZOMO charged in, using flares at night to light up the enterprises. They broke down doors with axes and crowbars and herded occupiers out to open spaces. Those on the list for detention were taken away. Factory equipment was spared in these raids, but Solidarity offices were smashed to smithereens. All printing equipment, typewriters and office furniture were demolished.

The greatest single loss of life was at the Wujek Colliery in Silesia, where nine miners were killed. Jaruzelski's followers – including Rakowski – later boasted that the loss of life was minimal by Latin American standards. Indeed, Jaruzelski's address had stated: 'We are not striving for a military coup, for a military dictatorship.' Did he recall his questions to the strikers of Szczecin in 1971: 'Do you want a government of colonels and generals?'[106]

In later evidence to the Sejm Commission on Constitutional Responsibility for Martial Law, which sat from September 1992, Andrzej Paczkowski characterised the whole operation as 'a legal coup d'état'. This stemmed from the absence of any executive orders based on the Polish Constitution's Article 33, which authorises the Council of State to declare martial law. Instead, emergency measures were prepared in secret, by the military, in response to the creation of Solidarity as an independent social movement. The Council of State, Party and government institutions were excluded from this planning, even though Soviet officers and KGB functionaries received and amended them on at least two occasions. Paczkowski also notes that directives were usually hurried through at times of crisis, notably August 1980 and late March 1981. Despite their entrustment to the military, the measures were aimed against internal democratic forces, rather than defending the country against foreign threat. He concluded that the process involved extensive violations of individual freedom, natural law and national sovereignty.[107]

The Pope's response to martial law was unequivocal. He wrote to Jaruzelski (18 December):

> During the past two centuries, the Polish nation has endured great wrongs, and much blood has been spilled in the struggle for power over our Fatherland. Our history cries out against more bloodshed, and we must not allow this tragedy to

[106] See p. 196. [107] *O stanie wojennym*, pp. 134–52.

continue to weigh so heavily on the conscience of the nation. I therefore appeal to you, General, to return to the method of peaceful dialogue that has characterized efforts at social renewal since August 1980. Even though this may be a difficult step, it is not an impossible one. It is demanded by the good of the whole nation.[108]

Jaruzelski's reply (6 January 1982) recognised the state's need for social support. In return, the Pope questioned whether this required 'the "shock" of the state of war, interning thousands of leading "Solidarity" activists and imposition of a whole array of harmful sanctions on the world of work and culture'. His conclusion was forthright: the state needs to discover 'another model of exercising power than that conducted by the state of war'.[109]

There was fury in Washington. Richard Pipes recalls: 'the six or seven weeks following the crackdown were extremely tense and busy in the White House. In my two years in Washington they were the most intense and harrowing, because not only was the [incoming] administration confronted with its first major crisis, but the National Security Council was without a Director.' President Reagan 'did not conceal his outrage at what was happening in Poland'. Convinced that appeasement in the 1930s had led to the Second World War, he was determined to respond to Soviet aggression before it was too late.[110] But formulating an effective response, and coordinating it with allies, proved highly problematical.

The German Foreign Minister took the view that Poland's crisis was an internal matter. No West German sanctions or conditions on aid were being considered. He suggested that Reagan write to Brezhnev in mollifying terms to help diffuse a tense situation. Instead, Reagan wrote a personal letter to Jaruzelski in protest at recent events. The first American sanctions were announced on 23 December.

The initial package was aimed at Poland. It ended credits for food and other consumer purchases, cancelled export credit insurance through the Export–Import Bank, and terminated civil aviation landing rights in the USA and fishing permissions in US waters. But humanitarian aid would continue. On 29 December, a raft of measures was aimed at the Soviet Union, seen as the principal author of martial law. These included cancelling export licences for gas pipeline equipment, other technological embargoes and postponing a new long-term grain agreement.[111] Such sanctions were mainly symbolic since the Soviet Union had no difficulty

[108] Wałęsa, *A Path of Hope*, pp. 224–5. [109] AAN 237/V/ (6 January 1981).

[110] R. Pipes, 'American–Soviet Relations and the Polish Question' in J. Black and J. Strong (eds.), *Sisyphus and Poland. Reflections on Martial Law* (Winnipeg, 1986), p. 127.

[111] P. Marantz, 'Economic Sanctions in the Polish Crisis' in Black and Strong (eds.), *Sisyphus and Poland*, pp. 114–15.

in finding other sources of supply. As often, sanctions did not 'fail' so much as fail to be applied. Marantz notes: ' "Non-sanctions" were bound to produce a resounding "non-effect".'[112]

A NATO communiqué (12 January 1982) indicated three steps that would improve the Polish situation: lifting martial law, freeing political detainees and renewed dialogue between the government, Church and Solidarity. But there was little unity in the Western Alliance. The German Chancellor, Helmut Schmidt, expressed sympathy for Polish workers (2 January). But his main point was not to endorse US sanctions against Poland and the Soviet Union. Explaining this decision, Schmidt stated that any attempt to disrupt the 'spheres of influence' established at Yalta could precipitate a new European war. The implication was that Solidarity and US sanctions were doing the disrupting. Indeed the line was being developed that 'Solidarity went too far: it provoked the government.'

Anticipating that argument, Kołakowski wrote: 'In the same sense, blacks who want equal rights in South Africa go too far; the government cannot accept that. People in Argentina who ask about the fate of the "disappeared" go too far; the rulers cannot tolerate that. Whoever in whatever despotic country is not satisfied with the despotism goes too far. Serves him right.'[113] Later, Rakowski added the thought that Jaruzelski would have closed Solidarity down even if the Soviet Union had not insisted. The greater threat for Polish communists was Solidarity, not the Soviet Union.[114]

Solidarity's reliance on non-violent resistance had prevented a much greater national tragedy, but it had also failed. The notion of non-violent action continued to be adhered to and there was interest in Western theoreticians of the technique.[115] Gene Sharp was translated into Polish.[116] But it was impossible to avoid the conclusion that Solidarity had been woefully unprepared for a State of War which so many had predicted. As the fragmented underground re-established its contacts, two difficult questions had to be confronted.

First, what was the possibility of resistance? Kuroń's contribution, smuggled out of an internment camp, 'Theses on a Solution to a Situation Without Solution' (February 1982), proposed that 'Polish society prepare to liquidate the occupation through collective action'. This strategy was regarded in the underground as short-term and too

[112] *Ibid.* p. 118. [113] *Wall Street Journal* 31 December 1981.
[114] Rosenberg, *The Haunted Land*, p. 217.
[115] A. Roberts (ed.), *Civilian Resistance as a National Defence. Non-violent Action Against Aggression* (London, 1969).
[116] G. Sharp, *Walka bez stosowania przemocy* (Gdańsk, 1984); 'Non violence active [*sic*] – wybór materiałów', *Spotkania* 1984 (19/20).

dangerous. In its place, Bujak proposed factory-based struggle for the right to trade union activities and construction of an independent and decentralised opposition movement dedicated to society's autonomy from the state. This was the strategy of the 'long march'. By contrast, Frasyniuk sought a 'short leap'. Rather than fostering intellectual and cultural circles, he advocated formation of factory organisations to prepare a general strike.[117] It was, however, recognised that one single region could not succeed on its own.

Borusewicz, a veteran of free trade unions on the Coast, considered both assessments erroneous. The public put up massive shows of resistance. ZOMO did not intervene against the counter-marchers on May Day 1982. But when the public turned out again on 3 May (anniversary of the 1791 Constitution), ZOMO took its revenge. There were pitched battles in sixteen cities, with unprecedented police brutality.[118] Borusewicz noted: 'We called on people to stay at home. But they took to the streets. They were more radical than we were. It is certain that, had we called for demonstrations, they would have been larger than they were. But they were already large enough to shake the authorities and demonstrate the degree of social solidarity.'[119]

The second difficult question concerned the continuing relevance of the Solidarity programme. Documents passed by the First Congress, reflecting the spirit of the 1980 Agreements, assumed that cooperation with the authorities was possible. This had proved not to be the case. It was therefore insufficient to continue to demand 'independent and self-governing trade unions'. There needed to be a transformation of the system. But how? One answer seemed to lie with the 'underground society' itself. Bujak calculated that some 300,000 activists were still involved in union work, and some 1,200,000 paid their union dues and read the underground press.[120] In the circumstances, this was an impressive number, yet the authorities of the day still seemed to have the whip-hand, even though their vaunted programme to lift Poland from the abyss had proved vacuous.

On 11 November 1982, Wałęsa was released from detention. Throughout, he had maintained his independence and rejected all blandishments from the authorities.[121] He was now a 'private citizen'. He soon made contact with the Solidarity underground. On the last day of 1982, the authorities 'suspended' martial law. It was officially 'terminated' the following July.

[117] M. Łopiński, M. Moskit and M. Wilk, *Konspira. Solidarity Underground* (Berkeley, 1990), pp. 78–83.
[118] Dudek and Marszałkowski, *Walki uliczne*, pp. 284–95.
[119] Łopiński *et al.*, *Konspira*, p. 89. [120] *Ibid.* p. 184.
[121] Wałęsa, *A Path of Hope*, pp. 220–43.

13 Amnesty

> Some say '*perestroika* is better than anything'. But it would have been much better had we not needed *perestroika*. A. Yakovlev, 1987

Gorbachev became Soviet leader in March 1985 with little prior experience of international affairs. Conscious of this shortcoming, he turned to Alexander Yakovlev for an analysis of US policy under Reagan. Yakovlev's account started from the assumption that the USA would continue to be the world's strongest power for another quarter of a century. However, it would move from a position of dominance within the capitalist world towards one of dominant partnership and eventually relative equality. This transition gave the Soviet Union an opportunity to reorient its foreign policy 'in terms of gradually and consistently developing relations with Western Europe, Japan, and China'. A potent factor in possible political pressure on the USA 'is the interest of Europeans in a relaxation of tensions'. The tenth anniversary of the Helsinki Agreement (August 1985) would be a good opportunity to 'revive the process of *détente* in the political as well as in the military sphere'.[1]

The Kremlin was wary of trouble from Eastern Europe. Disturbances there would threaten Soviet domestic reform, since those opposed to change at home would point to them as the inevitable consequences. Mindful of the post-Stalin succession, they knew it could also destabilise their own positions. So the new leader stressed continuity of policy towards Eastern Europe and sought to strengthen intra-bloc institutions. In April 1985, the Soviet Union and its allies renewed the thirty-year-old Warsaw Pact for a further thirty years. This may have run counter to the wishes of East European officials, some of whom would have preferred a five- or ten-year extension. The move indicated a priority for integration, which included closer ties within the Council for Mutual Economic Assistance (COMECON) and calls for greater cohesion across the Soviet bloc.[2]

[1] NSA, 'About Reagan' (12 March 1985). [2] Kramer, 'Beyond the Brezhnev Doctrine'.

In June 1985, an authoritative statement in *Pravda* set out an orthodox agenda for Eastern Europe:

1. The East Europeans must defend the 'fundamental principles of socialist economic management'. These included: socialist ownership rather than revisionist attempts to extend the private sector, which were dangerous and could raise social tensions; and central planning, to be defended against bourgeois apologists who allege that the socialist system is unable to develop in a dynamic way. 'Despite problems', the socialist economy had demonstrated its superiority over capitalism and was 'the more dynamic of the two'.
2. The East European Parties must strengthen Marxist–Leninist theory. The class enemy was trying to disturb the general laws which govern socialist construction. Such laws have permanent validity and cannot be regarded either as an abstract concept or as a historical legacy 'correct only for some period in the past'.
3. National models of socialism were championed in the West in an attempt to gain leverage upon 'one or another socialist state, from without or from within'. Nationalism continued to be the chief hope of the class enemy. Western propaganda tried to cultivate the worship of Western civilisation and to exaggerate 'injustices' or 'black spots' in the history of Soviet relations with a number of fraternal countries.
4. 'Small Countries' had no special role in international relations. Efforts by others to mediate between the super-powers were meaningless because the foreign policies of the USSR and the 'Marxist–Leninist nucleus of world socialism' were identical.[3]

The full text was republished in East Germany, Czechoslovakia and Bulgaria, but not in Poland, Hungary and Romania.

The US commentator Seweryn Bialer, who left Poland in 1956, argued that this article 'clearly embodied Gorbachev's own views'. Gorbachev had not revised the policy of his predecessors, but, if anything, strengthened its key dogmas. His approach to Eastern Europe constituted an all-out hard-line policy: 'It includes much stronger insistence on political orthodoxy, particularly in Poland and Hungary; crackdowns on dissent; encouragement of a siege mentality and crude anti-Western propaganda; greater pressure against economic egalitarianism; and rapid reaction to social and political unrest or to signs of greater independence of satellite leadership.'[4] However, this judgement proved premature for several reasons.

[3] 'O Vladimirov', *Pravda* 21 June 1985.

[4] S. Bialer, *The Soviet Paradox: External Expansion, Internal Decline* (London, 1986), pp. 205–6.

Firstly, the *Pravda* statement had no sequel of similar severity. Secondly, personnel changes took place at the probable place of authorship. In March 1986, Vadim Medvedev was appointed Secretary responsible for the Central Committee department that oversaw Eastern Europe (officially entitled the CC Department for Liaison with Communist and Workers' Parties in Socialist Countries). He replaced Oleg Rakhmanin ('O Vladimirov') with the reform-minded Georgii Shakhnazarov,[5] who in time became the closest of Gorbachev's advisers on Eastern Europe. Later, the department itself was merged into an expanded International department placed then under a new Commission on International Policy, headed by Aleksandr Yakovlev. Kramer considers that this reorganisation of the central apparatus 'contributed directly to the looser Soviet policy in Eastern Europe'.[6]

A third sign of change was that alternative views of Eastern European futures began to appear in the Soviet media. The Party's theoretical monthly devoted a section to 'Coordination of Economic Interests and Policy under Socialism'. One contributor was Oleg Bogomolov, a member of the 'Inter-departmental Council' set up by Andropov (in 1983) to advise the Politburo on the relevance to the Soviet Union of economic reform experience in Eastern Europe. He began with a favourite quotation from Engels: 'the economic relations of a given society present themselves in the first place as interests'. His conclusion was that interests could not be identical for all socialist states since each country has 'individual interests, its own overriding preoccupations'. East European states were at 'different stages of economic development; have differing economic and political structures and traditions'.[7] This was the ground-work for a major reappraisal. But when did the essential rethinking first appear?

One landmark statement may be Gorbachev's address to a meeting of COMECON in November 1986. He proclaimed that relations between socialist states were based on 'the independence of each Party, its right to make sovereign decisions about problems of development in its country, its responsibility to its own people'. Hertle considers that Gorbachev's intention was to stabilise the socialist community on new principles of independence and autonomy. He did not intend to dissolve the alliance.[8] The point seems well made. Yet as the East European empire starts to unravel, Moscow makes little effort to stem the tide. The most prominent feature of Gorbachev's relations with most East European allies, up to and including 1989, is non-intervention.

[5] See R. Hill, *Soviet Politics, Political Science and Reform* (Oxford, 1980).
[6] Kramer, 'Beyond the Brezhnev Doctrine', *International Security*, p. 37.
[7] *Kommunist*, July 1985. [8] H.-H. Hertle, 'The Fall of the Wall', *CWIHP Bulletin* (12/13).

US responses

Gorbachev's initiatives engendered a more active US policy towards Eastern Europe. Kennan's essentially negative policy of containment and the passivity reinforced after the Hungarian uprising of 1956 had reached an impasse.[9] As we have seen, *détente* had positive aspects but did not change fundamentally the geo-strategic division of the continent. Were opportunities to do so now opening up?

A hawkish view in Washington saw Gorbachev's 'new thinking' as more window-dressing. The Soviet Union, on this analysis, remained what it had always been. In response, Charles Gati argued that, rather than trying to 'test' Gorbachev's intentions in Eastern Europe, the United States and its allies should leave well alone. Soviet – East European relations were difficult enough, and the processes of change so fraught – with much of Eastern Europe lagging behind Moscow's reform programme – without the other super-power raising awkward questions. The term 'Eastern bloc' had become a misnomer. The West should do nothing to increase the region's instability. On the contrary, it should 'withdraw' from the area except in so far as it could promote positive developments.[10] A compromise between these views began to emerge: conditionality.

American sanctions on Poland imposed in immediate response to martial law remained harsh until mid-1986. They included a block on further IMF credits – 'we kept our thumb firmly on that' – leading Jaruzelski to complain that 'the air was cut off'. But Washington began to stress to Warsaw officials that sanctions would be lifted in direct proportion to the liberalisation of Polish domestic politics. The main demands were

(1) ending martial law, extended later to respecting human rights;
(2) release of political prisoners;
(3) resumption of a dialogue with Solidarity.[11]

Asked what positive assistance they would provide, following political progress in Poland, American diplomats replied: 'the US government would respond to a genuine amnesty [for political prisoners] by signing an agreement on scientific and technological co-operation. If the amnesty was a full one, and went so far as including Bujak for example, the US would lift its embargo on credit for Poland. In the final phase, Poland could regain the most-favoured-nation trading status.'[12]

[9] Ambassador John R. Davis Jr, Międzeszyn, 21 October 1999.
[10] C. Gati, 'Gorbachev and Eastern Europe', *Foreign Affairs* 1987 (5).
[11] John R. Davis Jr in A. Paczkowski (ed.), *Polska 1986–1989*, pp. 43–5.
[12] AAN 237/XIA/1422: reports of 10 and 29 July 1986 (L. Pastusiak and B. Sujka).

Jaruzelski commissioned a series of memos for his eyes only, on options for change. They were to re-examine relations between the authorities and society and suggest ways the Party could devise a political strategy to eliminate the roots of conflict.[13] But the changing international context was also noted. One top-secret memo blamed Washington for coordinating Western policy against Poland. America was 'disciplining its allies and deliberately hampering the tendency to speed up the process of normalising relations with Poland'. It noted that this new approach was not achieving much resonance in Germany. But other Western European states were 'linking their readiness for normal political relations with Poland to the development of the internal situation in our country in the direction expected by the West'. Even the latest Italian coalition under Craxi was setting preconditions for Jaruzelski's visit to Italy: the release of Michnik and his two fellow political prisoners.

'Emigré circles of the former "Solidarity"' were making play with 'Basket Three' of the Helsinki Agreement, and demanding human rights from its decennial review in Vienna. As a further irritant, Western ambassadors in Warsaw were taking advantage of national holidays to invite 'alongside official representatives, "prominent" members of opposition circles', particularly through increased contacts with Wałęsa. The report proposed to exert influence through 'members of the administrative authorities, members of the State–church commission, members of the Episcopate and even the moderate circles of "legal opposition" in the name of higher interests of state, to restrict Wałęsa's active contacts with the West'.[14]

Solidarity

The ending of the 'state of war' (July 1983) had been accompanied by a partial amnesty for political prisoners. However, the threat of a show trial of major leaders of 'former Solidarity' was maintained and its activists continued to be put on trial.[15] A major underground leader Lis was eventually captured (June 1984) and charged with treason, which carried a possible death sentence. Wider repression culminated in the murder of the 'Solidarity priest' from a north Warsaw diocese, Father Jerzy Popiełuszko (October 1984). Finally, on 13 February 1985, Frasyniuk, Lis and Michnik were rearrested while meeting Wałęsa, and faced serious new charges. These were eventually dropped at the end of the year.

[13] Stanisław Ciosek, Międzeszyn, 21 October 1999.
[14] AAN 237/V/314, unsigned memo (6 August 1986).
[15] A. Swidlicki, *Political Trials in Poland, 1981–1986* (London, 1988).

The uneasy stalemate continued until 11 September 1986, when the authorities announced a general amnesty. Some 225 political prisoners were released, including major Solidarity leaders and advisers: Bujak, Michnik, Frasyniuk and Bogdan Lis. One observer regards the decision as removing 'the first obstacle on the way to the eventual compromise' between the opposition and those in power.[16] It showed that the authorities had decided to abandon political repression as their sole instrument of policy.

In the main underground newspaper, Lityński wrote: 'The authorities have taken their most significant decision since the declaration of martial law.' Although Solidarity still had no legal basis, it had re-emerged as a political fact. A 'post-December [1981] period' had begun which, he predicted, would be an era of gradual and limited compromise.[17] Indeed, senior officials, such as Rakowski, now recognised that repression was ineffective and old methods of handling the situation were outmoded. They even admitted, behind closed doors and partly for tactical reasons, that the 'previous model of socialism is out of date'.[18]

Whilst welcoming the amnesty, Solidarity noted that it alone did not resolve anything: 'To carry out the tasks that stand before society, there must be reinstatement of trade union pluralism, a rebuilding of the economic system and creation of a situation in which independent social activity is possible.'[19] The release of prisoners was only one precondition for dialogue. In a clear and conciliatory hint to the authorities that the reinstated union would work within the law, Wałęsa called for trade union pluralism 'in the framework of the Constitution'.[20] A quid pro quo was beginning to emerge. If reinstated, Solidarity would cooperate in rescuing the economy. A newly formed Provisional Council of Solidarity (TRS) put itself forward as a suitable body for negotiating with those in power.

Wałęsa and his most senior advisers (including Geremek and Mazowiecki) publicly appealed to the American government to lift economic sanctions. The American *chargé d'affaires* told Party Secretary Czyrek that Washington had responded positively to the changes in Polish affairs. There was scope for improving Polish–American relations if there was a 'sustaining of the present situation in Poland since the amnesty'. Czyrek welcomed the improved atmosphere but replied that the normalisation of Polish–American relations could not be made

[16] J. Skórzyński, *Ugoda i Rewolucja. Władza i Opozycja 1985–1989* (Warsaw, 1995), p. 19.
[17] J. Lityński, 'W nowym układzie politycznym', *Tygodnik Mazowsze* 22 September 1986.
[18] M. Rakowski, *Jak to się stało* (Warsaw, 1991), p. 101.
[19] *Tygodnik Mazowsze* 1 October 1986.
[20] Letter of L. Wałęsa to the Council of State (2 October 1986) in P. Machcewicz, 'Poland 1986–1989: From "Cooptation" to "Negotiated Revolution"', *CWIHP Bulletin* Fall/Winter 2002 (12/13).

contingent on 'a group of oppositional extremists in Poland, who might attempt to sabotage the process'. The American left this jibe unanswered.[21]

When talks about power-sharing eventually began, in 1988–9, Poland seemed a more promising candidate than most of its neighbours. In Solidarity, there was someone with whom the Party could share. However, it was Solidarity's experience that formal agreements reached with the authorities, notably that in Gdańsk of summer 1980, were brutally ruptured. Many members of Solidarity, extensively persecuted under martial law, had lost confidence in any pact with the authorities. None looked viable without genuine guarantees.

Solidarity was much diminished from its heyday of 1980–1. In place of the legal union's 10 million members, there were perhaps 4,000 in an underground movement. Their principal means of expression were clandestine journals and bulletins published outside state censorship.[22] Moreover, its identity semed uncertain. The programme of the 'self-governing republic' adopted at its 1981 Congress, designed to take economic management out of the hands of the Communist Party, now looked anachronistic. How much else of the original Solidarity project had retained its relevance? One view saw Solidarity as still a potential instrument of enormous power, which should be retained at least as a symbol, particularly to sustain Wałęsa's public profile. This project was advocated from the time of the amnesty by the key adviser Geremek. Several Western governments concurred.

Given that some eventual *entente* between the authorities and society was probably inevitable, Jaruzelski realised that Solidarity might be a potential partner for negotiations. But this was a very long way off, and, he hoped, would not be needed at all. Instead, his next tactic was to offer wider access to a 'consultative' process in government. Invitations were sent out to join a Social Consultative Council to advise him as Head of State. It was addressed to 'individuals representing opinion-making circles who do not have contacts with the highest state authorities'.

In its cautious reply, the Episcopate noted that the amnesty had created possibilities for 'a broader social dialogue'. This was much needed, given the rapidly deteriorating social and economic situation. There was a lack of perspective for the future, particularly amongst young people and 'a lack of trust of the authorities, frequently connected with deep aversion to them'. But any such dialogue required 'the truly independent character of

[21] AAN 237/V/320, 'Notatka' (30 October 1986).

[22] K. Łabędź, *Spory wokół zagadnień programowych w publikacjach opozycji politycznej w Polsce 1981–89* (Kraków, 1997).

invited participants' and a return to trade union pluralism. They appended nine further questions including: 'Is there a possibility of holding proper consultations with Lech Wałęsa on the participation of people from the "Solidarity" circles?'[23]

The authorities replied robustly. They denied the claim that trade union pluralism was indispensable in the long run: 'Consultations with Wałęsa are not envisaged without [his] fulfilling the condition about which the government spokesman [Jerzy Urban] had explained on television, that is cutting himself off from other "Solidarity" leaders.' They accused the Episcopate of a lack of response to the authorities' 'new and startling' initiative.

A number of prominent Catholic intellectuals were also invited to join the Consultative Council. After a lively internal debate,[24] most of those approached declined to advise Jaruzelski. They emphasised that 'the majority of society is passive, has no confidence and is sceptical towards the authorities'. Jerzy Turowicz (editor of *Tygodnik Powszechny*) stated that 'normalisation' was perceived negatively by society 'and seen as a means to reinforce the totalitarian system'. Yet the need for systemic reform was palpable. He did not agree that the 'Solidarity' advisers Mazowiecki and Geremek could be excluded as 'extremists'. On the contrary, they were reasonable and moderate people.[25]

Solidarity responded with a set of conditions to elevate the Council from a decorative to an efficient institution. They called for 'undistorted social and economic data' and access to mass media. The new body must have the power to initiate legislation.[26] The authorities retorted that recognition of Solidarity would be a 'return to chaos', that it was too divided to provide positive programmatic alternatives and, anyway, irrelevant since it had lost public support. The Consultative Council held bi-monthly meetings on general issues (from 6 December 1986). It was described by one participant as 'a kind of debating club'.[27]

Beyond this, the authorities made no further move towards dialogue. The momentum and hopes generated by the amnesty were thus dissipated. There was a return to routine repression, confiscation (even of motor cars), arrests and fines. As Jan Skórzyński puts it, this restricted the public appearances of the political opposition 'to court houses, church premises and the drawing-rooms of Western ambassadors'.[28] In previous

[23] *CWIHP Bulletin* (12/13). [24] Friszke, *Oaza na Kopernika*, pp. 245–52.
[25] *CWIHP Bulletin* (12/13) (18 October 1986).
[26] *Tygodnik Mazowsze* 12 November 1986.
[27] A. Tymowski, 'Widziana z wewnątrz', *Polityka* 20 June 1987.
[28] Skórzyński, *Ugoda*, p. 27.

impasses, the Party had turned to the Church. Once again, communist leaders tried to play this card.

In a private audience in the Vatican on 13 January 1987, Jaruzelski assured the Pope that since their last conversation (on his 1983 pilgrimage) Poland had become 'more stable, the authorities stronger, taking bolder and further steps on the road to reform and to a developed form of socialist democracy. Many of these steps have an original, even pioneering character.' Overcoming the economic crisis inherited from the 1970s would require a 'great national effort, a feeling of citizens' responsibility' during the inevitable rigours of the second stage of economic reform. Good relations with Gorbachev gave Poland an exceptionally favourable position. Poland's 'new and unprecedented solutions in domestic politics' received a degree of prominence in the Soviet press.

He told the Pope that both the Polish Church and state faced inner oppositions. The Episcopate had difficulty in restraining some of its more 'provocative' priests, such as Wałęsa's confessor, Father Jankowski. Likewise, the state apparatus was sharpening its distrust and unwillingness for dialogue. Yet 'dialogue is inevitable and we on our side will promote it in all spheres'.[29]

In his laconic reply, the Pope noted that the historical experience of the Polish nation, its lack of statehood for 123 years, had made Poles particularly sensitive to questions of national independence and self-determination. Though sometimes assuming an exaggerated form, this was an objective fact, which one should take into account. It was worth recalling the long Polish tradition of tolerance: Zygmunt August had accepted the crown (in 1548) on condition that 'I will not be king of your consciences.' He also cited Wyspiański's *dictum* that a nation can only develop within its own state. This might be an exaggeration, since a national culture can develop without a state, but in the last analysis the state has a 'huge and indispensable role in securing in a full sense the subjectivity of its citizens'.[30]

The Catholic publicist Peter Raina tells us that 'the Pope considered the first step in this direction to be the legal activity of Solidarity. Only the process of democratisation could guarantee domestic peace.' He advised Jaruzelski 'to instruct the responsible state officials to invite Wałęsa and other representatives of society for talks at one table, so a social agreement could be reached by direct contact'. Raina concludes that it was 'in the Vatican that the phrase "Round Table" was first heard'.[31] Not much

[29] AAN 237/V/336 (20 January 1987), pp. 2–8. [30] AAN 237/V/336, p. 8.

[31] P. Raina (ed.), *Droga do 'Okrągłego Stołu'. Zakulisowe rozmowy przygotowawcze* (Warsaw, 1999), pp. 157–8.

evidence for this version appears in Raina's three 'follow-up' documents. General Kiszczak commented afterwards that he would not put much reliance on Wałęsa in helping to keep social calm during the Pope's projected visit to Gdańsk: 'He thinks one thing in the morning and does something else in the afternoon.'[32]

Prior to the Pope's next pilgrimage to his native land, anxiety arose that the authorities might use the visit to legitimise their 'state of war' and the consequent 'normalisation' of Poland without Solidarity. To allay public concern, and to express Poland's right to sovereignty and national independence, Wałęsa convened a meeting of political activists and Solidarity sympathisers in a Warsaw church. Amongst the sixty-two participants were other Solidarity leaders (Bujak, Jedynak and Onyszkiewicz) and advisers, as well as many prominent figures in intellectual and cultural life.

Their statement affirmed the right of all Poles to live in democracy, freedom and under the rule of law. This required that all citizens be guaranteed equality before the law, 'elimination of privileged social classes' and the realisation of 'the basic social ideals handed down by the Polish historical tradition and the social teachings of the Church'. Democracy entailed both free elections and freedom of association for trade unions and other bodies, and freedom of expression and belief.[33] As yet, Wałęsa's advisers issued no overt political challenge to the authorities. But the group evolved over the coming months into a Citizens' Committee dedicated to the rebuilding of the economy and state.

The Pope's third and longest pilgrimage (8–14 June 1987) confounded the sceptics. The itinerary, reluctantly agreed by the authorities, now took in the Baltic coast, including Szczecin and Gdańsk, and also the major industrial centre of Łódź. He was expected to attract congregations of many millions, with many more lining the route. His progress was to be followed by 574 accredited foreign journalists from press, radio and television. Fearing the consequences, Jaruzelski had dispatched Barcikowski and Ciosek to see Vatican advisers in an attempt to steer the Pope away from the contemporary political situation onto neutral and uncontested territory. They expressed the hope that the Pope would focus on such themes as: peace at home and abroad, Poland's 'Recovered Territories' in the west, the importance of citizens' rights broadly conceived and the need for hard work on behalf of the Fatherland. Papal advisers calmly replied that His Holiness had not the slightest wish to destabilise the existing system.[34]

[32] *Ibid.* p. 160 (Kiszczak and Dąbrowski, 16 January 1987).
[33] *Tygodnik Mazowsze*, 3 June 1987.
[34] AAN 237/XIA/1464, 'Notatka dot. rozmowy z prof. G. Barberinim' (10 June 1987).

The Church was offered the services of the Polish secret police and militia 'to neutralise oppositional attempts' to upset the visit. It refused. Likewise, the Episcopate was furnished with daily reports 'on the plans of post-Solidarity extremists' and were warned that any 'anti-state slogans and banners must be eliminated'.[35] But the whole occasion passed off peacefully.

During his sermons, homilies and beatifications, the Pope avoided contemporary reference. But his language – which the authorities called 'clerical double-talk' – was unambiguous. Constant emphasis was given to the necessity for protecting human rights, including the freedom of association. In Gdańsk, he spoke of the need for independent, self-governing trade unions 'as was emphasised in this very place', and stated that the Gdańsk Agreement of August 1980 remained to be fulfilled. It was plainly the place of the Church to carry on the struggle for the dignity of labour which Solidarity then began and the political authorities had discontinued.

The Vatican Press Bureau tactfully described his unofficial encounter with Wałęsa, after the formal end of his visit, as a meeting 'with the Nobel Prize winner'. The Italian press endorsed the notion of Józef Tischner, a close papal associate, that the Church supported conciliation rather than contestation, endorsing those circles in Polish society which sought dialogue and compromise. Jaruzelski's advisers somewhat over-optimistically treated this approach as an end to the 'Wałęsa myth' and the 'extremist wing of Solidarity'.

The Church was willing to act as a moderator in times of crisis, and arbiter (and later guarantor) when state and society sought to reach agreement. But it rejected the role of co-partner with the atheist state. It was a witness and observer, not taking sides. As Bishop Dąbrowski put it later:

> This is because it does not want to be a political force; it must not replace society in deciding the fate and future of the nation. At a time when society was deprived of its identity and even voice, it [the Church] had to take its place out of necessity. When the dialogue finally came about, the Church's role as a substitute was over.[36]

A sense was growing in the Jaruzelski team that more decisive action must soon be taken. Jaruzelski reminded the Secretariat (on 4 April 1987) that, of all the crises faced by the Party over the decades, the most severe had been those of 1980 and 1981, 'when there was the departure of a very large part of the working class from the Party, when there was and remains an almost total rupture between young people and the Party,

[35] AAN 237/V/355, 'Wizyta papieża w Polsce', p. 10. [36] Statement of 5 April 1989.

and the Polish Church is at its strongest since 1939, particularly amongst the intelligentsia'. Jaruzelski began to express his impatience with the Party itself. Instead of being 'an intellectually innovative *avant-garde*', its prevalent mentality was 'technocratic–bureaucratic managerialism'. There were fundamental questions about its *raison d'être*: was the Party supposed to be 'a government or super-government', or simply an institute or discussion club?[37] This identity crisis was clearly perturbing to a professional soldier. New partners were now sought.

The KIK was attended by Czyrek as head of a 'Party-state delegation' on 11 July. This encounter was not the outcome of a formal Party decision: 'The Politburo was shocked to learn there had been contacts between Czyrek and Andrzej Święcicki [former President of KIK] and then with Professor Stelmachowski [his successor].'[38] There were also strong reservations on the other side. Some members of KIK held the meeting, vaguely attributed to 'various contacts with the authorities over recent months', to be unwise. They feared legitimising the authorities in return for empty rhetoric.[39] To avert this danger, it was decided to introduce a substantive agenda.

Stelmachowski opened the meeting by defining democratisation. Although Polish society was at present pluralistic, state institutions remained monolithic. Under the doctrine of the 'leading role of the Party', all initiatives had to emanate 'from above'. There was no space in which to realise citizenship or exercise the constitutional right to self-organisation, hence no freedom of association for workers, nor pluralism of trade unions. By contrast, the Poland of 1980–1 had evolved 'something new, not merely imitating Western-type parliamentary democracy', to which the Pope had drawn attention on his recent pilgrimage. This stemmed from social agreement. Yet the return to dialogue had certain preconditions, including respect for the identity of the negotiating partner and a presumption of goodwill on both sides.[40]

Czyrek replied that the political authorities were 'ready for dialogue'. It had given him satisfaction to hear the professor endorse the existing state structure, and accept its *raison d'état*. It was necessary 'to search for a new role for the Party, as a political force in coalition with other forces'. This would require working out a programme that could command support in

37 AAN 237/V/83, Secretariat (4 April 1987), pp. 48–54.

38 Marian Orzechowski, Międzeszyn, 21 October 1999.

39 Friszke, *Oaza na Kopernika*, p. 256 (prior discussion in KiK, 30 June 1987).

40 Archiwum Kazimierza Czaplińskiego (zbiór Andrzeja Friszke), 'Zebranie Zarządu KIK Wrocław (lipiec 1987)', pp. 1–3 (report on Warsaw meeting, 11 June 1987). Also present were representatives of many KIKs from other cities, and editors of the Catholic periodicals *Tygodnik Powszechny*, *Znak* and *Więź*.

wide circles: 'It is possible to reshape social relations on the basis of the internal dialogue of a great national coalition, including all those who do not seek to overthrow the existing system.'[41] But members of the audience were dubious. Unlike Czyrek, they spoke of the need for dialogue with Solidarity and criticised the restriction of free debate through the tightening of state censorship.[42] The consensus was that Czyrek's visit confirmed official goodwill but that the Party line remained implacably opposed to any contact with the political opposition. Stelmachowski commented: 'The five-hour discussion did not lead to any specific results, but at least it was open and sincere.'[43]

An internal Party report considered that recent liberalisation measures, such as allowing the independent monthly *Res Publica* to publish legally, 'have little resonance with society and give little help in improving the standing of the government. One can advance the thesis that their reception is greater in narrow circles of the so-called moderate opposition and in some circles in the West, than amongst broader public opinion at home.' It noted that discontent was rising steadily in all sections of society. The 'adversary' knew this and was biding his time. As government becomes weaker and ever more discredited, 'It is sufficient to sustain a [public] mood of justified anger, wait and then join – at the right moment – the eruption of dissatisfaction, as in 1980.'[44]

By September 1987, Jaruzelski's advisers were presenting him with a stark picture: 'We face the most threatening and challenging situation of the last five years.' The present social peace was illusory. It was necessary to seize the initiative through 'revolutionary economic reform'. The second stage of economic reform, announced in April, remained on paper. The prevalent public view was that 'The second stage of reform is only a second stage of hot air.' While there was always the danger that radical change would be destabilising and cause an 'eruption of discontent', a decision not to reform would carry even greater risks. There followed somewhat anodyne suggestions of 'intensified dialogue' with the Church, a rebuilding of confidence in the Party amongst scientific and artistic circles (such as the PEN Club) and a public discussion on electoral reform. The most dramatic proposal came at the end: to recognise Wałęsa officially by offering him a seat on the Consultative Council of the Council of State.

[41] Archiwum Kazimierza Czaplińskiego, 'Zebranie', pp. 3–4.
[42] Friszke, *Oaza na Kopernika*, p. 257.
[43] A. Stelmachowski, *Kształtowanie się ustroju III Rzeczypospolitej* (Warsaw, Jaktorów, 1998), p. 40.
[44] A. Paczkowski papers (28 August 1987).

The advisers explained that this would overcome the problem that Wałęsa already enjoyed a 'semi-official status' through meetings with Vice-President Bush 'and a host of other foreign visitors'. Wałęsa would soon travel abroad – much better if he did so as an officially sanctioned and institutionalised 'leader of constructive opposition'. He would no doubt set preconditions: that a group of his colleagues should also join the Consultative Council and that the authorities should allow 'trade union pluralism'. But even if he declined, the offer would show the authorities in a positive and constructive light. Negotiations with him could be conducted through Catholic intermediaries who would obviate the need for direct contact.[45] There would not have to be a Polish equivalent of Gorbachev's telephone call to the exiled Russian dissident Andrei Sakharov (December 1986), followed by his triumphal return to Moscow.

Further advice was offered by Rakowski. His widely circulated document, aimed at promoting discussion in the Party, also suggested that Wałęsa could be offered a seat on the Council of State's Consultative Council, though he might refuse. Rakowski suggested the Consultative Council be broadened to include non-Party intellectuals and the editors of *Res Publica*. He suggested policies to isolate a 'core opposition' from more reasonable elements. The former should be 'rapped over the knuckles'.[46] Since he advocated police measures, as part of a more aggressive strategy against the opposition, there was little in Rakowski's tract to encourage genuine dialogue.

Kuroń wrote that martial law had achieved its objective in the atomisation of society, which was unable to exert effective pressure upon the privileged *nomenklatura*, the only effective social base of power. It used this base 'to pacify society of which it is afraid' and to block reform. It was time for Solidarity to lay aside the 'martial law' structures and mentality of 'war' and 'conspiracy' and learn a new language with which to engage reform-minded Party members in discussion about agreements. This was a risky strategy, fraught with difficulties, but the alternative was endless reiteration of the desire for an agreement with the authorities, while simultaneously acting as though no-one believed agreement to be possible.[47] Lityński declared that 'The time for negation is over.' The authorities now sought social support. Their change in tactics necessitated a new

[45] A. Paczkowski, 'Nastroje przed bitwą', *Zeszyty Historyczne* (Paris) 1992 (100).
[46] Published unofficially as: *Tajny referat Rakowskiego. Uwagi dotyczące niektórych aspektów politycznej i gospodarczej sytuacji PRL w drugiej połowie lat osiemdziesiątych* (Warsaw, 1988), p. 28.
[47] J. Kuroń, 'Krajobraz po bitwie', *Tygodnik Mazowsze* 2 September 1987.

modus operandi for the opposition. Solidarity should cooperate with all those – irrespective of political colour – who wished to carry out reforms.[48]

Solidarity dissolved its underground structures. In their place it created a single leadership body, a National Executive Committee (KKW), to function in public. The next move was to invite 'representatives of independent circles' to discuss 'problems of political reform'. They met in the crypt of a Warsaw church on 7 November.

Wałęsa's welcoming address stressed their legality: 'We are not here to plot against the authorities.' He had called on 'knowledgeable and able people, with moral authority and with the confidence of their social circles, to debate what can be done to turn our aspirations into reality'.[49] The authorities had recently announced that they would ask the public in a referendum whether they supported the Sejm programme for overcoming the economic crisis and whether they wished a democratisation of political life. But Wałęsa retorted that Poles did not have to be asked whether they wanted a reform of the state and the economy. That had been quite evident since August 1980.[50] The more important questions were, given the existing system in Poland and the present situation in Poland and the Eastern bloc, can a democratic model of power holding be formed? Is the 1980 programme of social agreements still valid following the experience of the 'state of war'? What chances exist for mobilisation and self-organisation of society – including social, professional and neighbourhood groups – as well as groups of individuals?[51]

Stelmachowski saw the Polish crisis as symptomatic of a more general crisis of 'real socialism'. Those in power increasingly replaced Marxist ideology with a peculiar 'quasi-ideology' of their own, largely emptied of content. Idealistic communists were being phased out. But the democratic opposition also faced a crisis of confidence and growing sense of hopelessness, as Kuroń's 'Landscape after Battle' had described. One could venture the suggestion that neither the Party nor the opposition had won the social struggles of the 1980s. The real victor had been the Church, but this did not solve the systemic crisis because the Church was unwilling to associate with any form of political system. Nonetheless, the system was reformable. An option for the central authorities was to restrict their sphere of influence to 'key issues', delegating the rest to

[48] 'Skończył się czas negacji', *Tygodnik Mazowsze* 21 October 1987.
[49] Archiwum Senatu, 'Komitet Obywatelski: Spotkanie 2' (AS KO:2) (7 November 1987), pp. 5–6.
[50] 'Wobec referendum. Oświadczenie', *Tygodnik Mazowsze* 21 October 1987.
[51] AS KO:2, p. 2.

lower echelons of self-government. To begin with, this would enhance the power of lower-Party bureaucrats – 'admittedly the most conservative and corrupt' – but in due course Solidarity and the democratic opposition could begin to operate within the public spaces newly opened up.[52]

Solidarity regarded 'consultation' as cosmetic. Institutions such as the Consultative Council were little more than talking-shops, whose more pliable non-Party members could be paraded before Western visitors as evidence of Poland's 'socialist democracy'. But belated publication of an interview with Geremek was an 'important psychological moment'.[53] For the first time since martial law, the official press gave space to the views of Solidarity. Hitherto Geremek could only be mentioned in a negative context, even, according to the government press spokesman, that of espionage. Now, despite the belittling by-line introducing him as 'adviser to the former Solidarity', he was associated with a significant initiative, designed to channel public frustrations in a positive direction.

Geremek's interview suggested that both sides had learned from the early eighties. Society now realised that its aspirations and demands must be confined within strict limits; the authorities understood that without authentic social forces there could not be the turning-point (*przełom*) which so many wanted. Geremek noted that society must respect the rule of law 'based on the leading role of the Party'.[54] In recognising this, Geremek hoped to induce more reasonable Party leaders to consider that Solidarity could work within the confines of political realism. A positive response came from the higher Party echelons. Ciosek mentioned to the Episcopate that 'Geremek is a highly intelligent man, and it is a pity he doesn't stand on the Party's side.'[55]

Geremek proposed an 'anti-crisis pact'. In return for helping the authorities to rebuild the economy, thereby extracting the Party from its political impasse, Solidarity sought freedom of association and 'trade union pluralism', including its own legal reinstatement.[56] Public life would be divided into two spheres: state and society. In the former, the Party would continue to exercise its monopoly of power; in the latter, there would be institutional pluralism, guaranteed by law. As part of the bargain, Solidarity would withdraw its macro-political objectives, such as the installation of a multi-party system that had sometimes

[52] AS KO:2, pp. 2–3.
[53] Geremek in *Rok 1989. Geremek opowiada. Jacek Żakowski pyta* (Warsaw, 1990), pp. 9–10.
[54] *Konfrontacje* February 1988 (1).
[55] P. Raina (ed.), *Rozmowy z władzami PRL. Arcybiskup Dąbrowski w służbie Kościoła i narodu*, vol. II: *1982–1989* (Warsaw, 1995), 3 June 1988, p. 242.
[56] *Tygodnik Mazowsze* 9 December 1987.

figured in its pronouncements.[57] As a result, power would be delimited and divided, rather than shared. But the authorities ignored even this limited formulation. It took no further initiatives for some months. Instead, the crisis came.

Student protests

The Secretariat considered public order on 11 January 1988. Their primary concern was that the independent student movement (NZS), banned since martial law, planned celebrations of its seventh anniversary (17 February). Further demonstrations were to commemorate the twentieth anniversary of the 'March events' of 1968, a turning-point in the political experience of many Poles.

For Geremek, 'March' had been an anti-intellectual and anti-zionist campaign arising from within the Party leadership. He had resigned from the Party at this point. For the younger generation, expulsion from Warsaw University was a further landmark. It turned them to permanent political activity, which others (such as Blumsztajn and the Smolar brothers) continued from abroad. In a move towards greater *glasnost'* (openness) about its own history, and to cast light on the internal crisis which had remained the most resistant to historical explanation, the Polish Party received in December 1987 a proposal to reconsider the March events. The question was how far to go in opening up this most murky episode in the Party's post-war past?

The Secretariat recognised that the 'anti-socialist' opposition were going to use the anniversary to organise 'anti-state political demonstrations'. They were sure to 'hold us responsible for the events of spring 1968 and impute to us anti-semitic tendencies and anti-intelligentsia policies'. Setting the record straight, in a spirit of opennness, would give the lie to hostile domestic propaganda and also lead to a positive reaction from abroad.[58] However, as Dariusz Stoła notes, an investigation might also expose the conduct of the only Party leader still in office from those times: Jaruzelski.[59] Indeed, he had been promoted to the post of Minister of Defence in April, just in time to prepare for the invasion of Czechoslovakia.

The Secretariat decided to review the 'causes, chronology and consequences' of the 'March events'. The Academy of Social Sciences

[57] 'Z Bronisławem Geremkiem doradcą b. KKP NSZZ "Solidarności" rozmawia Jerzy Szczęsny', *Konfrontacje* February 1988 (1) (interview held the previous December).
[58] AAN 237/VII/88, Secretariat, December 1987.
[59] Stoła, *Kampania antysyjonistyczna*, p. 263.

(founded 1984) and relevant Central Committee Departments (Ideology, Socio-Legal, Propaganda) were to speed up and deepen their research on this part of the 'complex history of People's Poland and the PZPR' and make public some of the 'causes, course of events and consquences'.[60] No such general history ever materialised, but the weekly *Polityka* published a calendar of the 'March events', the first ever to appear in a Party newspaper, and a 3½-page article came out in the Party daily.[61] Asked about its provenance by Italian journalists, the Polish press spokesman Urban replied that the paper had expressed 'the authoritative account of the Party, identical to the views of the Polish authorities'.[62] While it was bound to fall short of oppositional notions of objectivity, the public admission by the Party that its former policy had been mistaken was a politically small but psychologically significant step towards agreement with the opposition.[63]

Student protests gathered momentum slowly. On 17 February 1988, pamphletting by the NZS passed off peacefully in Gdańsk, Olsztyn, Warsaw and Wrocław. An evening march by a large crowd of some 1,500–2,000 students at the Jagiellonian University in Kraków apparently took the militia by surprise and they did not intervene.[64] The reaction to the next commemoration was very different. After a meeting at Warsaw University on 8 March, students spilled out into the streets where various columns of protesters, some throwing coins and stones at the militia, were broken up by police batons. Some broke through the police cordon and made their way to the Old Town for an anniversary mass, after which police batons were again used. In Kraków, some 2,000 students sallied forth from the university towards the Market Square. Just as in 1968, the protesters were met by a police blockade and threw up impromptu barricades against advancing militiamen, who made forty-seven arrests. Subsequently, smaller demonstrations in Kraków passed off without police intervention. Student protests also took place in Wrocław, Lublin and Gliwice.[65]

The Church tried to protect students from state violence during their peaceful protests in Warsaw and Kraków. The Episcopate asked General Kiszczak afterwards whether the attacks on them had been ordered 'from

60 AAN 237/VII/88, Secretariat, 25 January 1988.
61 Z. Rykowski and W. Władyka, 'Marzec '68', *Polityka* 20 February 1988; J. Janicki and M. Jaworski, 'Marzec 1968', *Trybuna Ludu* 2 March 1988.
62 *Życie Warszawy* 9 March 1988. Also Z. Kozik, 'O wydarzeniach marcowych 1968 r.' *Nowe Drogi* 1988 (2), and B. Łopieńska, 'Komu to służy?' *Res Publica* 1988 (3).
63 Skórzyński, *Ugoda*, p. 58.
64 A. Anusz, *Niezależne Zrzeszenie Studentów w latach 1980–1989* (Warsaw, 1991).
65 Dudek and Marszałkowski, *Walki uliczne*, pp. 372–3.

above'. He replied that there had been no such order, on the contrary his instruction had been to preserve the peace. He had looked into the matter personally and his research had revealed that not a single person had been admitted to hospital as a result of the protest. In future, street protests would be recorded on film so that it could be established 'who had used force and if it was within their instructions'.[66]

Church representatives also took the opportunity to quiz Kiszczak on high politics. They asked what credence should be given to recently circulating rumours about a weakening of General Jaruzelski's position? Kiszczak replied no-one advocated a more liberal policy than Jaruzelski. The former architect of martial law now explained that there was no solution to political problems through 'weapons, force and police batons'. The way forward required talks with students and with the opposition, 'to meet and to enter into dialogue'. Kiszczak saw no potential successor to Jaruzelski. Amongst the names the Church had put to him, he stated that Kociołek was tainted by a sexual scandal from 1985 when he was Ambassador to Moscow, and his role as Gdańsk Party Secretary in December 1970 – ordering strikers to return to work and firing on them when they did – had never been fully clarified.

The Church had mentioned that Rakowski was much disliked in Solidarity circles for his arrogant behaviour towards them.They noted that Rakowski had attracted much international attention through his journalistic contacts with the West. RFE had commented on his report which had been highly critical of the Party leadership. Why had he since been promoted to the Politburo? Kiszczak simply replied that on many points Rakowski was right and, on many others, including relations with the Church, he was quite wrong.[67]

For the first time since 1968, students were again in the vanguard of social protest. The authorities took the potential threat with utmost seriousness. A secret-police report told of preparations at the Mickiewicz University, Poznań, where meetings took place under the auspices of the local KIK. As part of the campaign for re-legalisation of the NZS, they had approached intermediaries: the lawyer Władysław Siła-Nowicki with a request that he raise the issue at the Consultative Council, and also planned to approach Professor Ewa Letowska, the newly appointed Ombudsman. The secret-police report also noted that they planned to invite 'well-known anti-socialists such as Kropiwnicki, Kuroń and Michnik' to the March meeting, which might be held in the Dominican church.[68] In the meantime, they had

[66] Raina (ed.), *Rozmowy* (13 April 1988), p. 218. [67] *Ibid.* p. 218. [68] AAN 237/VII/88.

collected some 2,000 signatures to an appeal for a more liberal statute on higher education.

The Party Secretariat was alarmed by such initiatives. Woźniak sought to direct them into harmless channels: 'creation of clubs, leagues, circles and associations to promote computing, ecology, improved trams or solar energy'. Kiszczak complained that clubs would register under an innocuous name – 'The Association of the Lovers of Temperance and Work' – and then act quite politically. Baryła saw motives for forming new organisations to lie in the 'fossilised and bureacratised nature of most existing mass organisations'. These could only be counteracted by mobilising those organsiation that did have a chance to lead the country out of crisis and respond to new needs.[69]

Jaruzelski thought that the Party 'should not block, but rather promote social initiative and activity'. But he expressed concern on behalf of the coalition partners (ZSL and SD) at talk of forming fourth and fifth political parties. He thought the partners would be particularly worried since 'they are more threatened by competition than we are'. There had been discussion amongst the Party's political scientists (led by Jerzy Wiatr) on clarifying 'the concept of the model of functioning of the socialist state at the present historical stage'. One suggestion was the setting-up of a second Marxist party. Jaruzelski did not think that wider dissemination of such ideas would be opportune: 'Publication now, when the Party is weak, could be destabilising.'[70]

Wider evidence of weakness came in an internal Party report, predicting the most likely social and political reactions to the average 40 per cent price rises on basic foods and services due to take place on 1 February. The prognosis was gloomy. Public optimism was at its lowest level since surveys began in the late 1950s. Earlier experience had shown that outbursts could take place, as in 1976 and 1980, when the index of 'social optimism' dipped below 20 per cent. Now only 13 per cent thought things would get better. The older generation of Party *aktyw* (now a majority) responded with 'great scepticism and distrust of policies towards: the Church, methods of achieving social justice, cadres policy and the process of democratisation', and felt excluded from political decision-making. All research showed that the attitudes prevailing amongst members of allied parties were 'even worse'.

More positive for the Party core was a report that the 'political adversary' was undergoing a process of 'decomposition and disintegration'. It was questioning Wałęsa's ruling group and contesting the purpose of

[69] AAN 237/VII/88, pp. 4–6. [70] AAN 237/VII/88, pp. 7–10.

continuing opposition under the rubric of Solidarity. But, even in disarray, it was able to mount a political challenge and could exploit the potential social conflict to give 'reminders of their existence'. The most dramatic of three scenarios outlined saw price rises leading to a 'sharp explosion' from society, perhaps some weeks after the increases came into effect. The report noted that (despite martial law) memories of 1980–1 were still very much alive, and gave the public grounds for both fear and hope.[71]

The Secretariat soon returned to the question of a new law on associations (8 March). Cypryniak asked: 'Are we supposed to tolerate an organisation that will attack us?' Rakowski noted that legalising the 'adversary' would please the West, but that *perestroika* (restructuring) was engendering all sorts of anti-socialist organisations. Poland should 'risk a democratic statute' but build in restrictions to safeguard the interests of the state.[72] Jaruzelski referred back to the 1970s when there was 'one, small, illegal organisation' (clearly KOR): 'We thought we were strong and then everything suddenly collapsed.' He now sought safeguards.

Faced with compaints in letters to Party organisations about bureaucracy, confusion, corruption and bribery, the Party needed to take 'some decisive, even spectacular action'.[73] But freedom of association should come as a package including various social organisations, such as an officially mooted Social Committee on Human Rights. There would inevitably be competition between new organisations for youth, culture and the Church and existing ones. Collisions and confrontations should be avoided in the name of national agreement.

A number of new associations applied for registration in early 1988. Those rejected included a Gdańsk Political Club named after Lech Bądkowski (the writer who had joined the Shipyard strike committee in August 1980) and student organisations in several cities. The authorities likewise rejected the Warsaw Economic Association and Social Educational Association, the organisation of those opposed to capital punishment and even the association for Polish–American Friendship.[74] The non-communist Left attempted to recombine. Jan Józef Lipski told a meeting on 4 January 1988 that a revived Polish Socialist Party (PPS) should help the public to distinguish genuine socialism from its distortions by the Party. He thought it should focus on correcting the mistakes of the ruling Party rather than competing for office,[75] but was challenged in mid-summer by the appearance of a 'left PPS-Rewolucja

[71] AAN 237/VII/88, Politburo, 26 January 1988.
[72] AAN 237/VII/88, Secretariat, 8 March 1988, pp. 6–7.
[73] A 63-page summary in AAN 237/VII/88 (Secretariat, 11 January 1988).
[74] Skórzyński, *Ugoda*, p. 57. [75] AAN 237/VII/88, 11 January 1988.

Demokratyczna'. The Confederation of Independent Poland (KPN) was joined by various other 'Independence' movements characterised by the authorities as containing 'right-wing anti-communists' and linked to the 'London camp'.[76]

A peace movement appeared and held an 'international peace seminar' in Warsaw (5–7 May 1987). There appeared an alternative Ecological Social Movement (RSA). Happenings were staged by the Orange Alternative in Wrocław (1 June 1987). Janusz Korwin-Mikke led a 'Movement of Real Politics' committed to a legal path to bourgeois democracy and private property. There were local 'independent youth movements' in many cities.[77] Increased fringe activity even extended to one of the ruling 'coalition' partners, the ZSL (United Peasants' Party), which began agitating for a monument to their former leader Witos.

Perennial inefficiencies in the Polish economy had reached yet another crisis point. External debt had doubled to $48 billion and annual inflation reached 80 per cent by 1988. It was obvious that the economy could not be rescued without drastic reforms and that these could not be enacted without much greater social support. Party leaders learned from the surveys of 'social opinion' conducted solely for them, and sometimes cited during meetings of the Politburo,[78] that public attitudes towards state intervention in the economy had shifted significantly.

The proportion of Poles who thought large wage differentials acceptable – if not based on undeserved (i.e. *nomenklatura*) privileges – had risen from 54 per cent (1980) to 83 per cent (1988). Those who thought full employment essential had dropped from 78 per cent to 60 per cent in the same period (and to 53 per cent in 1984). While these anti-egalitarian shifts were to facilitate the Balcerowicz reforms in the post-communist period, they made sorry reading for the captains of a command economy. Rather than responding to the clear desire of society that the Party withdraw from much of its economic activity in favour of a restored market system,[79] the government resorted to an age-old expedient. Instead of making structural reforms, it increased the price of basic foods and services by an average of 40 per cent (from 1 February 1988). Social

[76] AAN 237/V/402, 2 March 1988.

[77] K. Łabędź, *Spory wokół zagadnień programowych w publikacjach opozycji politycznej w Polsce, 1981–89* (Kraków, 1997); P. Kenney, *A Carnival of Revolution: Central Europe 1989* (Oxford, 2002).

[78] AAN 237/V/402. Many were later published in *Społeczeństwo i władza lat osiemdziesiątych w badaniach CBOS* (Warsaw, 1994).

[79] See J. Eysymontt, 'Reform in the Polish Economy' in R. A. Clarke (ed.), *Poland: The Economy in the 1980s* (London, 1989), pp. 29–44.

pressures on the authorities, in abeyance for several years, resumed shortly afterwards.

Workers' protests

A key player in the Polish drama, silenced by years of martial law and economic deprivation, now re-entered the political stage. Its re-emergence, as usual, took other actors by surprise.

Transport workers halted all bus and tram services in Bydgoszcz on 25 April. Party officials told them that their 'work stoppage' was improperly constituted and therefore illegal. They replied: 'This is a spontaneous reaction by employees. The [official] trade unions did not organise it. But they support the employees' demands.' One demand was for 'a different attitude from the Director towards employees'.[80] Though the other nine demands were financial, their political implications were clear. In his telex to the Politburo asking for instructions, the local First Secretary blamed 'lack of vigilance by the Party factory committee, enterprise managers and security service' as sources of this 'surprising form of conflict'.[81]

The Lenin Steelworks in Kraków began a ten-day strike the next day. Some 4,500 workers demanded wage increases to compensate for higher prices, reinstatement of four colleagues who had been sacked, and immunity for members of the strike committee.[82] A sympathy strike at Huta Stalowa Wola (29 April), supporting the demands from the Lenin Steelworks, called for the release of Solidarity activists and supporters, supplying a list of names, and demanded trade union pluralism.[83] They meant re-legalisation of Solidarity, as well as the re-employment of those sacked for Solidarity activities.

The strike at Stalowa Wola was top of the agenda at a meeting of Party leaders later in the day. Kiszczak reported that the 'illegal committee' organising the strike had stiffened its position. Solidarity *aktyw* had held a meeting overnight in the apartment of 'a priest known for his hostile attitudes'. They called a strike which swelled to 4,000 participants and elected a strike committee headed by Wiesław Wojtas, a 'former' Solidarity activist dismissed on 25 April for organising an illegal demonstration at the steel mill four days earlier. The demand that the Director re-instate all dismissed Solidarity activists would be supported by an

[80] AAN 237/VII/88, 'Chronologia strajków i nielegalnych wieców w okresie od 25 kwietnia do 10 maja1988 r.'
[81] AAN 237/VII/88. [82] P. Smoleński, *A na hucie strajk*... (Warsaw, 1988), pp. 20–1.
[83] AAN 237/VII/88, 'Chronologia strajków', pp. 2–3.

occupation if not acceded to by midday. There followed ten demands on trade unions. In answer to Jaruzelski's question, 'Political demands or economic?', Kiszczak said 'Political pluralism as well'.[84] A strike at the Steel processing mill in Bochnia added fresh demands for reinstatement of those 'dismissed groundlessly in 1981'; for the removal of 'alien services' from the workplace, including the secret police (SB) and ORMO; and guaranteed security for all those at mass meetings and negotiations.

Kiszczak also reported on Warsaw University where 'former activists' of the NZS had put up posters in support of the Kraków steelworkers. A banner stating 'Students Support the Workers' Strike' had been draped across the main gates. Gathering round, about 100 'very aggressive students' shouted hostile political slogans. The Rector was nowhere to be seen (Jaruzelski ordered a search for him). Kiszczak also reported signs of workers' solidarity with those on strike from many other regions. There were 'pre-conflict situations' in Sanok, Elbląg and Szczecin.[85]

Difficulties were compounded by the imminence of the May Day parades. Jaruzelski envisaged an 'event of colossal significance', during which 'millions of people [were] to turn out, all of them in an orderly fashion, to show their confidence and support for the government'.[86] But the balance of forces was shifting, as the public was losing the sense of fear instilled by martial law. The re-emergence of Solidarity's National Executive posed a challenge the authorities could not publicly ignore much longer. Yet the opening of negotiations came at a difficult time. As Jaruzelski put it, 'They are speaking to us from a position of strength, while we speak from a position of weakness.'

The next approach from Solidarity was a letter to the Party's most high-ranking economists, Vice-Premier Zdzisław Sadowski and Władysław Baka, President of the National Bank. Wałęsa's carefully worded epistle cordially invited them to discuss the economy with representatives of 'various tendencies in Polish social opinion'. It added that 'by taking part, you gentlemen will contribute to a fruitful debate, based on a citizen's sense of responsibility'. Attached were preparatory materials drawn up by two independent experts, Wielowieyski and Bugaj, which took for granted that economic reform was not possible without political change.

While accepting much of their draft programme, Jaruzelski noted that 'the main point dividing us is the question of pluralism'. There was also a protocol problem. The document called for cooperation between government forces and 'independent social circles' to form a social

[84] AAN 237/VII/88, Secretariat, 29 April 1988, p. 6.
[85] AAN 237/VII/88, pp. 243–5. [86] AAN 237/VII/88, p. 332.

consensus for a programme to take the country out of the current crisis. Geremek's 'anti-crisis' pact in all but name, this would increase confidence in financial circles abroad. But could the Party negotiate with 'independent forces'?

According to Jaruzelski, the official trade unions (OPZZ) were independent ('Just ask the government'). He claimed that accepting Wałęsa's offer would be seen as a snub by the Consultative Council, which, 'despite the clumsiness and idiocy of Siła-Nowicki and others', was starting to feel and behave like part of the establishment. He would prefer to develop the Council and 'other institutions of the KIK type with which we are achieving partnerly contacts'.[87] The normally conciliatory Ciosek also favoured spurning Wałęsa's letter and concentrating instead on finding 'other forms of union, various alliances, pacts and forms of understanding'.[88] Summing up his negative response, Jaruzelski suggested that Vice-Premier Sadowski himself should host a meeting on the economy and invite Wałęsa, although he might not come. Such an offer was conveyed by Czyrek and Ciosek to Wielowieyski on 3 May.

Jaruzelski's May Day address was broadcast live to the nation. Simultaneously, Wałęsa addressed a crowd outside St Brygyda's Church in Gdańsk. Resuming after mass, Wałęsa responded to calls for Gdańsk to join the strike action. One feature of these demonstrations was generational. New militants pitted themselves against the veterans of 1980.[89] Unlike their elders, they saw little room for compromise, which was indeed regarded as moral disgrace. A primary demand was the reinstatement of Solidarity as a legal body, at least at factory level.

Following a Gdańsk Shipyard strike (2 May), the authorities returned to the use of force. ZOMO carried out simulated attacks and intimidating shows of strength outside for several nights.[90] In Szczecin, students held thirty-two illegal meetings. Further protests took place in Gdańsk, Warsaw, Wrocław, and Kraków where a student solidarity meeting at the Jagiellonian University was followed by scuffles with the militia.[91]

The Episcopal Conference stated (3 May) that 'no government, nor any political camp will succeed in solving the urgent problems of our country without extensive participation by society'. This was spelled out further by the statement of the Social Council of the Episcopate 'on the necessity of dialogue between the authorities and society'. It declared

87 AAN 237/VII/88, Secretariat, 29 April 1988, pp. 261–71.
88 AAN 237/VII/88, pp. 327–8.
89 B. Szczepula, 'Pragmatycy i fundamentaliści' in L. Mazewski and W. Turek (eds.), *'Solidarność' i opozycja antykomunistyczna w Gdańsku 1980–1989* (Gdańsk, 1995).
90 Dudek and Marszałkowski, *Walki uliczne*, pp. 378–89. 91 *Ibid.* p. 374.

bluntly that it was difficult to 'sustain a position in which the majority of working people are deprived of their own voice and are represented by an organisation [OPZZ] which they do not support'.[92] The Warsaw Episcopate dispatched mediating missions to the main places of protest. On written authority from the Church, Stelmachowski, Olszewski and Halina Bortnowska went to Nowa Huta.[93] Mazowiecki and Wielowieyski went to the Gdańsk Shipyard.[94]

During crisis talks with Wielowieyski, the Party Secretaries Czyrek and Ciosek told him that Jaruzelski had agreed to talks with Wałęsa. But this information proved wildly premature. No official recognition was given to the striking workforces. After an eight-day stoppage, Wałęsa and Alojzy Szablewski led a march out of the Gdańsk Shipyard to end the strike.[95] Despite its apparent success in coping with these protests, the Party's inner advisers saw a serious confrontation ahead.

A 'team of experts' reported to Jaruzelski during the protests: 'We are to an increasing degree dealing with a real political crisis.' They thought everything possible had to be done to calm social tensions and bring the present unrest under control. In their view, the ZOMO option – widespread use of force – could only inflame the situation and possibly lead to bloodshed. Society's patience was running out. The threshold of fear had risen considerably and the public was no longer afraid of the authorities: 'Memories of martial law no longer have a restraining impact.'

They saw only one way to pacify the situation – 'political means', code language for rejection of violence and an opening towards society. However, they warned that rhetoric from the government about 'socialist renewal' would not suffice.[96] A new government should be formed on the basis of 'wide social agreement between all constructive forces'. But this analysis was weak on remedies. The OPZZ should open their ranks to some activists from Solidarity, and their leader Miodowicz might initiate some meeting with Wałęsa or other representatives of Solidarity. However, the rebirth of Solidarity or formation of new political parties should be rejected.[97]

To Jaruzelski, the spring events had shown the Party's weakness, 'which is no surprise'. Local officials had failed to take the initiative during workers' protests on the Coast. Instead of relying on political

[92] P. Raina (ed.), *Kościół w PRL. Kościół katolicki a państwo w świetle dokumentów. 1945–1989*, vol. III, *1975–1989* (Poznań, 1996), pp. 584–5.

[93] W. Giełżyński, *Gdańsk, maj 88* (Warsaw, 1988); A. Stelmachowski, *Kształtowanie się*, pp. 40–1.

[94] Giełżyński, *Gdańsk, maj 88*, p. 131. [95] *Ibid.* pp. 183–95.

[96] W. Baka, *U źródeł wielkiej transformacji* (Warsaw, 1999), pp. 62–6.

[97] AAN 237/V/409, 5 May 1988.

argument, they had simply waited for police batons. This produced the paradoxical effect that the socialist authorities were seen as dictatorial and anti-democratic whilst in reality they were sluggish and incapable: 'We have spent the last seven years blocking the organised activity of the adversary. What has the Party done in this period? It has aged, young people have left. This is a catastrophe.'[98] Exhorting his colleagues, he relied increasingly on slogans such as 'strengthen socialist pluralism'.

One close observer, Dubiński (later Secretary to the Round Table), suggests:

> the authorities were unable to decide what they actually wanted: whether to press ahead with dialogue, or to make limited changes in the method of exercising power while not changing its principles, or to leave everything be, use force and wait until things sorted themselves out. In fact, the principle emerged that all solutions could be attempted simultaneously, the best example being the handling of the strike at Nowa Huta.

His several attempts to investigate this schizophrenic approach had failed: 'I do not think they knew themselves. Their awareness of the need to change wrestled with the retention of old habits.'[99]

Instead, the Party made overtures to more trusted partners. Ciosek told the Episcopate that Poland could never become a democracy unless there were stable relations between Church and state.[100] The already-favourable attitude of the Party to church-building, and other concessions to the Church agenda, could be enhanced. But such bribes did not achieve the desired results. Another approach was to non-Party intellectuals, whom the authorities hoped to charm or cajole into cooperation. New bodies were conjured up for this purpose, such as a Polish Club of International Relations.

Czyrek told its founding meeting on 11 May that Poland was in need of a broad 'pro-reform coalition or anti-crisis pact'. The Party would like to achieve this through 'wide social dialogue' in which the Club members could play a part. Their 'prominent representatives of various circles and orientations' could help put the country on the road to 'pluralism and agreement (*porozumienie*).[101] While still ignoring Solidarity, the Party came forward with dramatic proposals of its own. On 16 May, Czyrek publicly floated the notion of replacing the existing government, 'which had shown its incapability of leading the country out of crisis', with a 'pro-reform coalition' including members of the opposition.[102]

98 AAN 237/V/409, Secretariat, 16 May 1988.
99 Bereś and J. Skoczylas, *Generał Kiszczak mówi*, p. 260.
100 Raina (ed.), *Rozmowy*, p. 232 (25 April 1988).
101 Archiwum Andrzeja Stelmachowskiego.
102 *Trybuna Ludu* 16 May 1988.

The Dutch scholar André Gerrits sees these initiatives as offering 'consultative democracy' which led to a 'failure of authoritarian change'. He draws attention to a pattern of policies to cope with a 'crisis of political participation'.[103] By reluctantly admitting the existence of independent public opinion, and admitting its inability to silence it, the Jaruzelski team attempted to direct political opposition into its desired channels. Dummy institutions of participation under martial law having been ineffective, the Party attempted 'to consult and integrate the people it had chosen and the organisations it had established itself', in order to carry out authoritarian change. Characteristic of its consultative bodies were a lack of formal competence (or legal standing), a self-evident absence of representativeness (the Party hand-picked politically reliable members and sought to veto others) and its subordination to those above.[104] Despite these limits, Jaruzelski's team took a more startling initiative.

Ciosek amazed the Episcopal Secretary, Orszulik, by proposing (3 June) that parliament should be more freely elected from a wider list of candidates, thereby ending single-Party rule. Under new constitutional procedures, the 'ruling coalition' (the Party) would have 60–65 per cent of seats in the lower chamber, but only a minority – say 35–40 per cent – in the Senate. He suggested that the Church should play a substantial role in setting up this new political order.[105] Rejecting Ciosek's proposal of a pact between the Church and the government, Orszulik suggested the authorities seek 'agreement with independent opinion'. The first step towards social agreement would be trade union pluralism and re-legalisation of Solidarity. He proposed some interlocutors. Suitable people, '"anointed" by the Church from afar', would be Stelmachowski and Geremek, Wałęsa himself, the Gdańsk political theorist Aleksander Hall and 'young people from Jastrzębie [in Silesia] who are not on strike'.[106]

Jaruzelski told a Party Plenum (13 June) of plans to change the system governing Poland. Its core would remain the PZPR and 'coalition' partners. A second circle would include Catholic and lay Catholic organisations and the Patriotic Movement for National Rebirth (PRON). A third, outer circle would include those 'ready to participate in reform and building an understanding'. Much of his speech was devoted to differentiating the opposition into patriots and the others (apparently a sizeable proportion) who gave their allegiance to foreign courts.[107] The new

[103] A. Gerrits, *The Failure of Authoritarian Change. Reform, Opposition and Geo-Politics in Poland in the 1980s* (Dartmouth, 1990), p. 95.
[104] *Ibid.* p. 37. [105] Raina (ed.), *Rozmowy*, p. 256.
[106] *Ibid.* p. 257. [107] *Trybuna Ludu* 14 June 1988.

system would come into being through a 'Round Table'. This would be a discussion forum between various social groups on such issues as re-drafting the law on freedom of association. An offer couched in these somewhat nebulous terms was unattractive to the opposition and received little comment in Solidarity circles. The system, albeit modified, would remain monocentric.

Whilst geopolitics still seemed to prescribe some limits to political concessions by the ruling team, it looked as though the external landscape was shifting rapidly. Jaruzelski's *troika* of advisers noted that 'Profound changes taking place in the Soviet Union, and the withdrawal of Russian forces from Afghanistan [agreed in Geneva on 14 April], are interpreted by the opposition and its external inspirers as limiting the danger of outside intervention in Poland or even "pressures from outside".' At the same time, *perestroika* weakened the Polish authorities vis-à-vis their own society.

Genuine reform within the Soviet Union would make its absence in Poland all the more glaring, a contrast the opposition would not fail to make.[108] Equally, removal of the Soviet 'bogey' might make domestic pressure in Poland harder to contain, as Jaruzelski's closest advisers now began to point out. His *troika* feared the loss thereby of an important 'safety valve'.[109] A further memo, from Rakowski, asked Jaruzelski, not perhaps rhetorically, what would happen if there was another explosion in Poland which the authorities declared might lead to 'someone's intervention', but that 'someone', considering their own interests, refused to interfere.[110] There was growing evidence from Moscow that this was likely.

[108] J. Kuroń, 'Krajobraz po bitwie', *Tygodnik Mazowsze* 2 September 1987.
[109] A. Paczkowski, 'Nastroje przed bitwą', *Zeszyty Historyczne* (Paris) 1992 (100).
[110] Rakowski, *Jak to się stało*, p. 101.

14 Consultation

> The most dangerous moment for a bad government usually comes when it begins to reform itself.
> De Tocqueville, 1860

Soviet leaders were rethinking their relationship with Central and Eastern Europe. Obtained under Stalin for security, the region had proved chronically unstable. This necessitated the constant threat, and periodic practice, of Soviet military intervention. But signals given to the 'allied' communists to reach what accommodation they could with their own societies had been widely ignored. Most Central and East European leaders thought either that Gorbachev did not mean his rhetoric encouraging them towards independence, or that, if he did, he would soon be replaced by a new Soviet leader restoring orthodoxy. In either case, a policy of wait-and-see seemed prudent.

Gorbachev lacked political allies in Eastern Europe. To begin with, he saw some positive prospects for Hungary, which he had visited several times in his previous post as CC Secretary for Agriculture (1978–85). However, as *perestroika* accelerated, the long-serving János Kádár (now seventy-six) seemed left behind. As a Hungarian oppositionist remarked, it was 'an irony of fate that Kadarist politics entered the depths of stagnation and decay when Soviet politics was in the process of leaving them'.[1] After three decades of skilfully defending Hungary from cold winds blowing from Moscow, and introducing the most open economy in the region, Kádár and his entourage no longer had the energy or skill to navigate through the more favourable climate. On the contrary, together with many other regional leaders, he thought Gorbachev's reign would be short-lived. The prudent policy was thus to hold fast until Gorbachev was removed by less reform-minded successors.[2] But the reverse occurred.

Kádár's successor recalled that it had been extremely difficult to persuade him to retire. Prior to Gorbachev, the prospect had been possible,

[1] J. Kis, *Politics in Hungary: For a Democratic Alternative* (New Jersey, 1989), p. 22.

[2] B. Lomax, 'Hungary: From Kadarism to Democracy' in D. Spring (ed.), *The Impact of Gorbachev. The First Phase, 1985–90* (London, 1991), p. 160.

but in 1988 Kádár 'saw himself as the captain of a ship in peril and refused to leave the helm, believing that he alone had the experience to steer it clear of the worst'. By then he had decided that Gorbachev's policies would bring catastrophe to the USSR and he had expressed this view to other members of the communist movement, including Soviet visitors. Even so, Gorbachev took no direct step to remove Kádár. After his ouster (18 May 1988), he commented to Kádár: 'I would not have expected you to take any other decision. I was convinced you would take it when it became necessary.'[3]

The prospects for change in Poland looked more promising. Gorbachev believed he had one genuine ally amongst the East European leaders: General Jaruzelski.[4] During bi-lateral talks in Warsaw (11 July), Jaruzelski told his Soviet counterpart that the Polish 'process of democratisation' was essential and would be taken further. But there were two boundaries his country would never cross. He assured Gorbachev that 'we will not permit trade union pluralism [and] we will not permit the formation of opposition parties'. His reassertion of Leninism did not preclude 'participation in representative and social organisations of persons presenting various political or even oppositional points of view and opinions'. Summing up, Gorbachev stated that both countries were 'seeking new mechanisms' and that these had 'colossal historical significance'.[5] He asked Jaruzelski to send a report on the possible legalisation of Solidarity. Comments started to emanate from other Soviet officials that 'trade union pluralism is not a heresy'.[6] However, it took the return of industrial unrest to put the issue back on top of the Polish agenda.

August 1988

Poland's summer truce ended with a strike at the Manifest Lipcowy coalmine in Jastrzębie, on 15 August 1988. Legalisation of Solidarity was the main demand. Strikes spread to other mines in Silesia and the Baltic within days. Jaruzelski admitted to a meeting of the Committee for National Defence (KOK) on 20 August that 'the opponent is strong – and senses our weakness and our mistakes'. Strikes were not simply inspired from abroad, but were spontaneous demonstrations 'dominated by young people filled with emotion'.[7]

[3] J. Levesque, *The Enigma of 1989: The USSR and the Liberation of Eastern Europe* (Berkeley, 1997), p. 66.
[4] *Ibid.* p. 67.
[5] Perzkowski (ed.), *Tajne dokumenty Biura Politycznego i Sekretariatu KC*, pp. 8–9.
[6] Levesque, *The Enigma of 1989*, p. 112.
[7] L. Kowalski, 'Stan wyjątkowy – okrągły stół', *Arka* 1993 (2/3).

The Ministry of the Interior was told to plan for a state of emergency. This would include widespread use of the Security Service for a major assault on oppositionists.[8] But this was not being considered as an immediate contingency. Indeed, the option of the use of force was hardly mentioned at the Politburo meeting the next day. Instead, space for a bold political initiative was being created.

The Politburo heard of two contacts with opposition. Stelmachowski's initiative stemmed from a meeting in the Warsaw KIK (19 August) which had considered ways to help the striking workers. It decided to approach Czyrek.[9] Stelmachowski signalled the readiness of the former Solidarity for talks, though only with the participation of the 'Electrician' (Wałęsa). He reassured Czyrek that Wałęsa had grown more realistic. Solidarity had learned that its political ambitions were realisable in a less confrontational way. Wałęsa would agree to talks in return for extinguishing the new wave of strikes, but only if re-legalisation of Solidarity was on the agenda. Czyrek thought that dialogue should be pursued with the specific condition that the 'strike pistol' was removed first. General Kiszczak could then conduct talks for the government side. He noted, as if in passing, that dialogue with Wałęsa would mean re-legalising Solidarity.

The second channel consisted of Kiszczak's own talks with the lawyer and veteran human rights activist Siła-Nowicki, who had recently acted as an independent mediator during the strikes in Silesia. Siła-Nowicki had warned of potential uncontrolled outbursts from workers in both mines and factories. He had rung Kiszczak from Katowice to warn that the occupation by thousands of coal-miners could end in tragedy. Jaruzelski reported great anger amongst local Party *aktyw* that the centre (Warsaw) was doing nothing to end the strikes. They awaited decisive action, but the provincial Party Secretary Gorywoda saw no way to end the strike by force. Strikes were also threatened in Warsaw factories where Party cadres 'do not feel strong enough and fear that we will not be consistent in the tasks that face us. Memories of 1980–81 [the Solidarity era] are returning.' Apart from one brief question on whether to deploy warships in the ports of Szczecin and Gdańsk, force was not considered. A consensus for talks was emerging.[10]

On 24 August, Ciosek met Orszulik and proposed a new political structure. His conception was tri-partite: a Presidency on top; a Senate (apportioned equally between the 'ruling coalition', the Church and independents); and a lower house (60 per cent 'ruling coalition' and

[8] L. Kowalski, 'KOK wobec opozycji politycznej i Kościoła w latach 80-tych', *Zeszyty Historyczne* (Paris) 1995 (113), pp. 125–47.

[9] Stelmachowski, *Kształtowanie się*, p. 42.

[10] AAN 237/V/421.

40 per cent 'opposition and our non-Party friends'). To this unexpected offer of a coalition, Orszulik replied that organisations were better built from 'timber' rather than from the roof down. The long-standing demand to reconstruct trade unions was a case in point. Ciosek replied that trade union pluralism was unacceptable from the economic point of view and also from the political angle, given what a force they had become in 1981. To Orszulik's riposte that the new era was quite different, Ciosek replied: 'You think the Brezhnev Doctrine is no longer operative? Gorbachev is making *perestroika* but against him is a whole army!'[11]

On the same day, Czyrek told Stelmachowski that he wanted written confirmation that Wałęsa sought dialogue. He travelled to the Gdańsk Shipyard, where Wałęsa signed a letter, drafted and edited by Mazowiecki and Michnik, which set out three initial proposals for discussion at a future Round Table. These were: restoration of the workers' and citizens' rights set out in the Agreement of August 1980, in particular trade union pluralism; social and political pluralism, including freedom of political clubs and association; and bringing the country from crisis by economic reform. The latter could be done through cooperation and strengthening the Sejm. The Episcopal Conference appealed for social peace and conflict resolution through mutual agreement. It declared the need to 'find ways leading to union pluralism and the creation of associations'.[12]

Kiszczak's appearance on television later that day was a revelation. Three days earlier, he had been threatening to introduce a curfew and other extraordinary measures. He was now a model of calm. The extinguishing of illegal strikes had created a new situation. 'As Chairman of the Council of Ministers Committee on the Enforcement of Law, Public Order and Social Discipline', he would hold an urgent meeting with 'representatives of various social and occupational circles'. This could take the form of a 'Round Table'. He set no preconditions or agenda for the talks, and no participants were excluded except those who 'reject the legal and constitutional order of the Polish People's Republic'.[13]

Czyrek's report to a special Party Plenum (27–28 August) offered the opposition a place in parliament, as the expression of a 'wide coalition of reform and renewal (*odnowa*)'. A Round Table could work out a joint election programme. It could consider electoral reform, creation of a second chamber and the (enhancing of) the office of the President. However, the return to trade union pluralism was decisively rejected.[14]

[11] Raina (ed.), *Rozmowy*, p. 256. [12] Dudek, *Kościół w PRL*, p. 586 (26 August 1988).
[13] K. Dubiński (ed.), *Okrągły Stół* (Warsaw, 1999), p. 35.
[14] *Trybuna Ludu* 29 August 1988.

Skórzyński sees this manoeuvre as an 'escape forwards',[15] in which the Party offered to make more political concessions than the opposition had expected, in return for abandonment of Solidarity.

The meeting between Kiszczak and Wałęsa took place on the eighth anniversary of the Gdańsk Agreement. Wałęsa was accompanied, at his own insistence, by a senior churchman, Bishop Jerzy Dąbrowski, as a witness. Ciosek was present for the other side. Kiszczak set the ending of strikes as a precondition for the Round Table. His agenda for the talks centred on the planned electoral reform, opening places in the Senate and other parts of public life to 'constructive opposition'. Pluralism was accepted in general terms, but there could be no departure from the principle of 'one trade union in one workplace'. Those invited to the Round Table would be 'people of "Solidarity" but without "Solidarity"', and only those who did not reject the 'existing legal order'. Wałęsa replied that 'matters of the Round Table are important, but the matter of Solidarity is more important, followed by pluralism'.[16] A cryptic announcement from the official press agency (PAP) noted that they had met to discuss a Round Table meeting, but the bulletin gave equal weight to a meeting of Kiszczak with the leader of PRON and most space to his meeting members of the Consultative Council, editors of *Res Publica*, coalition partners and academic administrators.[17]

Wałęsa kept his side of the bargain,[18] extinguishing strikes on his own authority as Solidarity leader, elected at the 1981 Congress. But there were ructions behind the scenes. Resistance to any arrangement with the Party was strongly felt amongst union fundamentalists, who regarded any deal with 'the reds' as tantamount to a betrayal. Wałęsa had acted wisely in taking a Church 'witness' to the talks. Jaruzelski regarded the accusations against Wałęsa as a positive sign of dividing 'realist and constructive currents from the extremist and destructive'.[19]

Party activists also started bombarding their Warsaw headquarters with questions, anxieties and doubts about the volte-face towards Wałęsa. Most voivodship committees signed a memorandum to the Central Committee opposing official talks with Wałęsa. One lapidary passage stated: 'We were told for seven years that Wałęsa is an idiot; we now ask: has the idiot become wise and the government idiotic?'[20] However, 'hysteria and shock' within the Party *apparat* was also combined with a

[15] Skórzyński, *Ugoda*, p. 90. [16] Dubiński (ed.), *Okrągły Stół*, p. 15. [17] *Ibid.* p. 52.
[18] Stelmachowski, *Kształtowanie się*, p. 45.
[19] AAN 237/V/427, Secretariat, 1 September 1988.
[20] Stelmachowski, *Kształtowanie się*, p. 46.

sense of relief that the summer strikes had been ended without force, and awareness that some price had to be paid for the peaceful outcome.[21]

To placate the voivodship Party committees, Warsaw sent out a teleprinter message, 'The Question of Talks with the Opposition'. Its (italicised) key point was that '*We stress that in conversations with L. Wałęsa no guarantee has been given about the registration of Solidarity*'; 'People's power must not misuse the argument of force as a legitimation of government'. Partners to dialogue must be found. This meant sounding out all 'realistically thinking partners' with whom to reach lasting solutions to social unrest.

By advocating a Round Table, the Party had regained the initiative and undercut the argument of enemies at home and abroad that 'we don't want to talk, that dialogue is fictitious and agreements a façade'. It also stole a march on the opposition which – aside from slogans about political pluralism – had little to say about actual policies: on the economy, on securing social peace and 'averting anarchy'. Wałęsa was taking part in talks 'as a citizen, not as the leader of the former Solidarity'. Unlike August 1980, he was just one participant amongst many; the talks were taking place with the Minister of the Interior in Warsaw rather than a government commission in Gdańsk. Wałęsa himself was taking risks, and being criticised for making concessions to the authorities, by a new, very radical, generation of opposition *aktyw*. Finally, Wałęsa was 'being used in the West's political game towards Poland (the Nobel Prize, honorary doctorates, talks with politicians visiting Poland). Talking to him deprives the West of a basic argument in their propaganda war with us.'[22]

Party propaganda moved into top gear. Its daily started a regular column: 'Leading Up to the Round Table'. Television showed carpenters and joiners busily assembling an appropriate piece of furniture. Proceedings were expected to begin within two or three weeks.

Wałęsa's preparatory note to Kiszczak (4 September) proposed two steps towards the Round Table: fulfilment by the authorities of their undertaking that those who took part in the recent strikes would not suffer any penalties, and that there should be 'trade union pluralism and under it the legalisation of Solidarity'. A tripartite discussion should then resume, resulting in a 'sincere debate on economic and political reform in our country'.[23] Wałęsa envisaged a process of negotiation with full Church participation. Talks about talks resumed through the Stelmachowski–Czyrek channel the next day.[24]

21 AAN 237/V/427 (Głowczyk).

22 Perzkowski (ed.), *Tajne dokumenty Biura Politycznego i Sekretariatu KC*, pp. 44–8.

23 T. Tabako, *Strajk '88* (Warsaw, 1992), pp. 331–2.

24 They held a total of eighteen meetings: Stelmachowski, *Kształtowaniesię*, p. 47.

Stelmachowski presented the Wałęsa letter and a memorandum of his own which defined pluralism in a very broad sense, as covering political organisations and including other trade unions, such as Rural Solidarity (for private farmers). Czyrek suggested a second working meeting of Kiszczak and Wałęsa to be followed by a Round Table whose agenda consisted of:

(1) the socio-political system and the economic system. He stated this would include work on democratisation (joint election programmes) and agreement to reshape the most important state structures (parliament, government, head of state (meaning a 'presidential system'));
(2) pluralism of types of association (to be carried out by the end of the year);
(3) the model of trade unions ('we will agree a statute on this'). This, of course, reversed Wałęsa's agenda, postponing Solidarity's revival to some unstated future date.

'Putting his cards on the table', Czyrek declared that 'in reaching a decision over Solidarity's re-legalisation, the authorities would like to know how Solidarity sees its place within the political system. They would like to see Solidarity as a constructive factor, not one undermining the system'. They were not demanding Solidarity's incorporation into the system as it presently existed, but that it would cooperate and take co-responsibility within a reformed system.[25]

Co-responsibility for a reformed system without legal restoration was not an attractive proposition for Solidarity. As Mazowiecki pointed out, to ignore the issue of re-legalisation, or to postpone it indefinitely, was to omit the most crucial question. Only after progress on this issue could attention turn to other things.[26] Others saw Czyrek's vision of the Round Table as yet another attempt by government to drum up support, and as a new name for bodies discredited earlier – PRON, the Social-Economic Council of the Sejm, the Consultative Council and the Council of National Agreement (first mooted by Jaruzelski at the end of 1981) – and revived in the recent Czyrek conversation.[27]

A fourth meeting of the 'group of sixty' Solidarity advisers and independent intellectuals was summoned by Wałęsa to St Brygyda's Church in Gdańsk on Saturday 11 September. Working groups had prepared materials on three subjects: trade unions (Kuroń, Wujec and others); the economy (Wielowieyski, Bugaj and G. Janowski); and pluralism of association (Geremek, Szaniawski, Paszyński, Bratkowski and M. Król).

[25] Tabako, *Strajk '88*, pp. 333–6 (report to Wałęsa, 6 September).
[26] *Tygodnik Mazowsze* 7 September 1988.
[27] Skórzyński, *Ugoda*, pp. 99–100.

While the need for talks with the authorities was not questioned, their necessary outcome – trade union pluralism – was also uncontested. Bugaj added that the need was not to recreate 1980, a 'duopoly of the authorities and Solidarity' but to establish plural institutions, trade union and social, through which public opinion could influence central decision-making.[28] A resolution reiterated the need for Solidarity's re-legalisation if it was to play an effective part in reforming the country.[29]

The following Monday morning (13 September), Ciosek protested to Orszulik (but 'in a cheerful voice') that Saturday's meeting in Gdańsk had 'wrecked the prospects' of a Round Table. More seriously, he told Orszulik that the meeting of Kiszczak with Wałęsa had unleashed a 'storm' in the Party apparatus. There had been very heated discussion and a large number of activists had resigned from the Party. Others had poured out hatred against Wałęsa and accused the Party leadership and government of vacillation and weakness.

Ciosek suggested that the Church should use its influence on Wałęsa and Solidarity activists to moderate their demands, and in particular to remove their *iunctim* (linkage) between reform of political structures and the registration of Solidarity. In their proposed changes, the authorities wished 'to go as far as giving the opposition real participation in power'. Some factories could have Solidarity and others OPZZ (the official unions). An increase in central unions would not be a problem, though he feared the proliferation of different unions in single workplaces. He also remarked that the Brezhnev Doctrine was 'still valid'.[30]

In autumn 1988, the OPZZ attempted to emerge as an independent political actor. On 6 September, its Council passed a vote of no confidence in the government. Miodowicz began to bombard the Politburo (of which he was a member), and Jaruzelski in particular, with letters fulminating against price rises and other measures detrimental to its 'own' constituency, the working class. When the Politburo discussed 'The Model of Trade Unions and National Agreement' (8 September) much time was given to the prospects for the OPZZ, but its contribution to solving the country's problems was entirely negative. It opposed both trade union pluralism and any move towards liberal economic reform. But nor was Solidarity seen as a solution. The Politburo rejected its call for registration as 'institutionalising anti-communist opposition' and expressed concern that its 'rotten history' might recur. This included a whole catalogue of its alleged crimes and misdemeanours: 'the evolution of Solidarity as a political movement, a species of political counter-system,

[28] Cited in *ibid.* pp. 100–1. [29] *Tygodnik Mazowsze* 14 September 1988.
[30] Raina (ed.), *Rozmowy*, pp. 258–63.

anarchistic strikes, empty shelves, rejected offers of agreement, escalation of divisions, threat of civil war, weakening of Poland's international position, loss of confidence amongst trading partners'.[31]

This tactic was repeated by Kiszczak at his next meeting with Wałęsa (15 September). He read out an accusatory list: strikes had cost 54 billion złotys, $20 million and 9 million roubles; 'To this negative balance must also be added irretrievable moral, social and political losses.' The authorities had to consider their own base: 7 million trade unionists; 2.2 million Party members and their families; the officer corps; members of 'our great coalition' (ZSL and SD); Catholic and Christian associations and many non-Party people 'who do not want anarchy, do not always cry "Hosanna" for strikes, for Solidarity or for union pluralism'. Despite Wałęsa's good offices in extinguishing recent protests, Solidarity was presenting itself as the 'party of strikes, as it was in 1981'.[32]

Wałęsa restated the position: 'there is no freedom without Solidarity'. The 1980s had so far been a negative decade. But after a seven-year break, in which positive proposals had not come from either side, there was now a chance of development. The way forward was 'pluralism, with a place for Solidarity in it, not that from 1981 but renewed, coming to a Round Table with specific proposals'. While rejecting this, Kiszczak made certain gestures of goodwill: ceasing prosecutions for recent strike activity and cancelling the practice of calling-up Solidarity activists for military service exercises.[33]

A preparatory meeting of the Round Table took place at Magdalenka (outside Warsaw) the next day. Of twenty-five participants, ten represented the 'Solidarity-opposition', thirteen the 'ruling coalition', and two were Church observers. Kiszczak welcomed them to the start of a 'great debate for the good of the Republic'. No topics were taboo but they should concentrate on the most important: economic reform – a new economic model based on developing all forms of property-ownership – and political reform – a new model of the state, empowering the Sejm to carry out projects for political reform. The latter could include a new model of union movements and proposals defining their place in the political system.

Wałęsa explained that Solidarity did not seek to displace the official trade unions: 'We don't want a monopoly, we want an equal chance', which re-legalisation would provide. His advisers concurred. For Mazowiecki, re-legalisation was not 'a preliminary condition but the key point'. Until

[31] Perzkowski (ed.), *Tajne dokumenty Biura Politycznego i Sekretariatu KC*, pp. 49–51.

[32] Dubiński (ed.), *Okrągły Stół*, pp. 65–7. For Orszulik's account, see Raina (ed.), *Droga do 'Okrągłego Stołu'*, p. 219.

[33] Stelmachowski, *Kształtowanie się*, pp. 49–50.

there was a clear declaration regularising Solidarity's place in the political life of the country, it would not be possible to make progress on other issues, such as economic reform. Stelmachowski, despite his role as intermediary, was equally categorical: 'The essential problem is the legalisation of Solidarity as a fully legal partner in the life of the country and Round Table talks'.[34] Stalemate ensued. The authorities refused to move and the future Round Table seemed in jeopardy. Eventually, the Solidarity side conceded to a final communiqué, which noted only that 'the shape of the Polish trade union movement' would be discussed at the forthcoming Round Table.

Although Solidarity did not achieve its goal, its advisers came away with the sense that the meeting did amount to de facto recognition. The authorities were talking to Solidarity again in all but name. A key actor in the restoration of relations was the Catholic Church. The Primate had delegated Bishop Bronisław Dembowski to the meeting, with the single instruction 'make sure the first round of talks is not the last'. The Bishop later recalled that the Church was a witness for both sides. This protected Wałęsa, in meeting Kiszczak, from being disqualified in the eyes of society, and Kiszczak, in meeting Wałęsa, from being disqualified in Party circles. Moreover, once agreement had been reached, 'Our role was to act as guarantor for both sides.'[35]

During an interval in the talks, Kiszczak had suggested to Wałęsa and Mazowiecki that outstanding problems could be resolved after the next meeting of the Sejm which was set to dismiss the government. The demise of the government duly took place on 27 September by 359 votes to 1 (with 17 abstentions). The first communist government to leave office by 'parliamentary arithmetic' marked an end to seven decades of Leninism. In the current climate, it passed almost unnoticed.

Solidarity moved ahead with preparations for negotiations. It sought answers to procedural questions, such as the size of working groups and the deadline for completion of various stages. It set up seven interim teams to advise Wałęsa on key issues. The most important were: trade union pluralism (under Mazowiecki), economic matters (Wielowieyski), social pluralism (Szaniawski) and political reforms (Geremek).[36] These sub-tables were accepted in talks on 28 September.[37] Czyrek also stated that

[34] Accounts in Dubiński (ed.), *Okręgły Stół*, pp. 68–82; Raina (ed.), *Droga do 'Okrągłego stołu'*, pp. 224–35 and Stelmachowski, *Kształtowanie się*, pp. 50–6.

[35] B. Dembowski, 'Od Białołęki do Magdalenki i dalej. Wspomnienia świadka' in *Książka dla Jacka. W sześćdziesiątą rocznicę urodzin Jacka Kuronia* (Warsaw, 1975), pp. 47–8.

[36] Stelmachowski, *Kształtowanie się*, p. 56.

[37] Czyrek rejected two further groups, saying that law and the legal system (Olszewski) could come under the political heading, and that the issue of mining (Pietrzyk) was

the Round Table would consist of some fifty to seventy people drawn from three main categories: representatives of 'Solidarity'; 'Party–government' with 'allies'; and a third category of 'others', to include well-known persons without immediate affiliation to either side. The Round Table would also include Church representatives. Even a timetable was proposed (17 October – 11 November) so that the outcome could be celebrated on the seventieth anniversary of Poland's regaining independence.[38]

The Party leadership now realised the urgency of handling an unprecedented and rapidly developing situation. Czyrek told the Secretariat (4 October) that public opinion, initially sceptical, now welcomed the Round Table and expected it to reach a national understanding: 'This proves that our initiative has fallen on fertile social ground!'[39] Kiszczak was much more fearful. Emboldened by three meetings with him, Solidarity was reactivated. Under the guise of dialogue and the need for an understanding, they were feverishly preparing to seize the initiative and impose their own concept of talks, 'above all eliminating the Party's dominant influence over economic and socio-political life'. It was driven on by a younger generation, which had been particularly militant in the recent strikes: 'We should be fully aware that the legalisation of Solidarity is the first, mild stage in the opposition's struggle for power. Later stages will be much harder for us.'[40] A further worrying phenomenon stemmed from the 16 September meeting: 'While representatives of the Church and Solidarity were speaking *en bloc* from a unified proposition, our negotiators often used different languages and voices. We must not let that recur at the Round Table.'[41]

Yet another anxiety was the conduct of the 'coalition partners' (United Peasants' and Democratic parties). Kiszczak stated bluntly, 'we don't have any allies amongst the allies'. They now adopted the same position as Solidarity and claimed always to have opposed its dissolution. This enabled Wałęsa to argue: 'You see, General, it's only you, the PZPR, who are against reactivating Solidarity.'[42] Cypryniak noted that 'coalition partners', Catholic groupings and all shades of opinion wanted political reform to bring the rapid results expected by society. They openly expressed the view, a predominant one in the country, that 'the obstacle

already being discussed outside the Round Table: Perzkowski (ed.), *Tajne dokumenty Biura Politycznego i Sekretariatu KC*, p. 58 (Secretariat, 4 October 1988). Stelmachowski was for some time unwilling to give up his own group on agriculture.

38 Archiwum Andrzeja Stelmachowskiego, letter to Wałęsa (1 October 1988).

39 Perzkowski (ed.), *Tajne dokumenty Biura Politycznego i Sekretariatu KC*, p. 55.

40 *Ibid.* pp. 62–3. 41 *Ibid.* p. 65.

42 *Ibid.* p. 84. But a conciliatory interview with Wałęsa was published: 'Inaczej, mądrzej, lepiej', *Tygodnik Powszechny* 2 October 1988.

is the PZPR'. This raised the question: 'What is our Party, will it recover its strength?'[43]

Poland's internal debate was taking place during dramatic changes in Moscow. On 30 September, Gorbachev ousted much of the 'old guard', including Gromyko. The Polish Church paid great attention to these manoeuvres: as Orszulik put it to Ciosek, 'We will see which way it flows there.'[44] It was also mooted that a political uprising in Poland, perhaps following a failed Round Table, would seriously damage *perestroika*. Gorbachev's own advisers considered this possibility.

Shakhnazarov's position paper for the Soviet Politburo of 6 October stated that the possibility of any 'extinguishing' of crisis in socialist countries by military means must now be completely excluded: 'Even the old [Brezhnev] leadership seems to have realised this, at least with regard to Poland.' Yet there were real dangers: several countries, including Poland, were on the verge of bankruptcy; there could be another round of trouble-making in Poland. He advocated a high-level body to 'ask the sharpest questions' and share the results at a meeting of East European leaders the following February.[45]

An unusually outspoken communiqué from the Polish Episcopal Conference (5–6 October) noted that the August strike wave had given rise to hopes of 'building the initiative of a wide political opening' through the idea of a Round Table. Bishops believed that the rights of employees, in particular workers and farmers, included trade unions chosen by free elections. They also thought that agreement on fundamental values was the basis for 'reform of the state, its structure and the national economy'.[46]

Opposition leaders discussed prospects for a national accord. Lityński thought the lull in strikes might be interpreted by the authorities as a sign of weakness. This raised the 'eternal dilemma: whether the best way of achieving reforms is social peace, or rather social pressure and a policy of faits accomplis'. There were many concerns about the future: 'Would the Party be ready to relax its monopolistic grip on the economy? What about the *nomenklatura*? Will talks end with the establishment of just another bogus conciliatory body, like the Consultative Council?' Lityński added that both sides were now weak and this could be a positive sign. In 1981 both were sure of their strength and had the temptation to destroy each

[43] Perzkowski (ed.), *Tajne dokumenty Biura Politycznego i Sekretariatu KC*, p. 95.
[44] *Ibid.* pp. 66–7. Orszulik's account is in Raina (ed.), *Rozmowy*, pp. 281–3 (30 September 1988).
[45] G. Shakhnazarov, *Tsena svobody: Reformatsiya Gorbacheva glazami ego pomoshchnika* (Moscow, 1993), pp. 367–9.
[46] Raina (ed.), *Kościół w PRL*, pp. 592–3 (12 November 1988).

other – 'Now, their respective weakeness will induce them to seek a compromise.'[47]

The Party tried to contain the Round Table by eliminating the most outspoken of Wałęsa's proposed delegation. Ciosek told Orszulik that Jaruzelski personally had been 'shocked' to find such names as Kuroń and Michnik, Onyszkiewicz and Romaszewski, Jan Józef Lipski and Jan Józef Szczepański.[48] A polite note from Wałęsa to Kiszczak proposed that neither side should interfere in the composition of each other's delegation.[49] But Kiszczak's Interior Ministry drew up a black-list of those disbarred from the Round Table under any circumstances: (1) the 'KOR' group (Kuroń, Michnik, Onyszkiewicz); (2) 'so-called political parties' (PPS, KPN, PPN and others); (3) 'extremists active in illegal structures' (forty members of Solidarity in major cities).[50]

Jaruzelski elaborated his anxieties to the next session of the Secretariat. Wałęsa could say that he would make concessions but for his radicals, so 'Why can't we say we have radicals gripping us by the throat, massing and protesting and so on. It would be good to have a burst of resolutions on this.'[51] He was also concerned by an inopportune, though unavoidable, US visitor. Deputy-Secretary of State John Whitehead was due in Poland (12–14 October) as part of an American policy to differentiate between the socialist countries, rewarding those that distanced themselves from orthodoxy. Jaruzelski had little faith in the altruism of this approach:

> Frankly speaking, we are going to lose on this. He will boost Wałęsa; he will boost all of them. Because the key point of the Round Table is, as we said earlier, Solidarity. They don't give a damn about other things. They know that all the democracy we are promising, second chambers and all that will just drop down from the tree once Solidarity is there. Because Solidarity will sort out everything, commune [*sic*] and socialism included.[52]

There was no point in deluding oneself that acceding to American demands would lead to an easing of their financial pressures on Poland. Irrespective of what the Party did or said, Whitehead would go home and tell the Americans to back Solidarity to the hilt and 'we won't get a penny'.

Papers, prepared by an interdepartmental team of the Central Committee, proposed a new political structure. There should be a

47 *Tygodnik Mazowsze* 5 October 1988.
48 Raina (ed.), *Rozmowy*, pp. 286–7 (meeting of 7 October 1988).
49 Dubiński (ed.), *Okrągły Stół*, p. 92. 50 *Ibid.* pp. 111–13.
51 Perzkowski (ed.), *Tajne dokumenty Biura Politycznego i Sekretariatu KC*, pp. 134–5 (10 October 1988).
52 *Ibid.* pp. 154–5.

Council of National Agreement (based on the Consultative Council model) with a tri-partite membership: one third each for the ruling coalition, social organisations of the political centre, and people from the opposition. A supporting press article declared that the existence of an opposition did not contradict the classics of Marxism–Leninism.[53] However, the Council would not be open to members of extremist organisations such as 'Fighting Solidarity' and KPN, or 'so-called political parties acting against the constitution (PPS)'. Thus, the proposed 'socialist reform' would not depart from 'the basis of the leading role of the Marxist–Leninist party in society'.

The old 'transmission model' would be transformed into a 'multi-directional model of persuasion and negotiation', conducted through social dialogue, compromise and agreement. Half of the second chamber (to be called the Senate) would be occupied by members of the 'centre and opposition'. Above both would stand a President, who would be a member of the Party, on a seven-year term of office (renewable).[54] The Party would fulfil two other major functions: taking programmatic initiatives after 'dialogue with other political forces', and playing 'an active role as mediator and arbiter in social life'. This would be achieved through 'inspiration, consultation, negotiation, working-out compromises, seeking social consensus or majority approval'.[55]

A 'top-secret' document candidly admitted that public pessimism had increased greatly since August, and there had been 'a major fall of confidence in the socialist institutions of public life'.[56] Indeed, most authors of letters to the Central Committee, while welcoming the Round Table, looked to it for real results. They told the Party centre that they would support a real discussion 'for the good of the fatherland', but not an 'auction' between narrow circles of political representatives.[57] The document also considered various outcomes of the Round Table. A successful Round Table required reaching a consensus on union pluralism, but the Wałęsa plan for a reactivation of Solidarity was a limit beyond which the Party could not cross. So there would have to be agreement on some 'intermediate' way to allow 'pluralism without Solidarity'. Alternatively, there could be an impasse during which the opposition returned to strikes as a means of putting pressure on the authorities, or the talks might break down completely. If so, they might be retrieved by

[53] K. Janowski, 'Opozycja polityczna w Polsce', *Trybuna Ludu* 20 October 1988.
[54] Perzkowski (ed.), *Tajne dokumenty Biura Politycznego i Sekretariatu KC*, pp. 169–75.
[55] AAN 237/V/433.
[56] Dubiński (ed.), *Okrągły Stół*, pp. 114–22 (15 October 1988). See also *Społeczeństwo i władza. Wokół problemów okrągłego stołu* (reports 387, 400).
[57] AAN 237/V/435 (18 October 1988).

some spectacular piece of crisis management by the Church hierarchy, on the lines of 'State–Church and Poland–Vatican' talks.[58]

The possibility of agreement with Solidarity receded further with Jaruzelski's address to worker-activists at the Ursus tractor factory in Warsaw. While noting that trade union pluralism existed *de jure* (in 1982 legislation), he stated it could not be realised in practice until many preconditions – economic, political, legal and international – had been fulfilled.[59] These postponed actual pluralism to an indefinite future. As Stelmachowski complained to Cardinal Glemp, the economic precondition (restoring an equilibrium that workers' demands could not upset) implied that economic reform could be carried out without widespread social support, while trade union pluralism was 'a sort of luxury that could be added later'.[60]

The Round Table was in effect suspended. The opening slipped from 17 to 28 October and finally – like the piece of furniture itself, dismantled and put in storage – disappeared from view. Disruption of opposition newspapers resumed: *Tygodnik Mazowsze* was raided on 10 October. Student activists were harassed, particularly those emboldened towards radical actions after speeches by university authorities at the start of the new academic year. A brief statement by Wałęsa was, as ever, conciliatory. He reaffirmed a willingness to talk. But, 'without the restoration of Solidarity', he saw no chance of Poland overcoming its problems.[61]

The new Premier, Rakowski, co-architect of martial law, had long shown impatience at the ineffectiveness of previous premierships. Apart from self-advancement, his aims may be characterised as 'enlightened absolutism'. He accepted the need for critical discussion, from which ideas for change may emerge, but then insisted that the monopolistic Party, rather than independent social forces, should enact them. He thought his government could regain the political initiative through a few bold and cleverly constructed steps. Abroad, both west and east, he had retained the reputation of a reformer, but this opinion was not shared at home. Solidarity remembered Rakowski as a major obstacle to reaching an agreement with the government from spring 1981, and they were still rankled by his intemperate attacks upon them – including Wałęsa personally – during a confrontation at the Gdańsk Shipyard in 1983. All the independent intellectuals approached declined to join his government.[62] One commented

[58] Dubiński (ed.), *Okrągły Stół*, p. 118. [59] *Życie Warszawy* 24 October 1988.
[60] Stelmachowski, *Kształtowanie się*, p. 58.
[61] Dubiński (ed.), *Okrągły Stół*, p. 136 (statement of 27 October 1988).
[62] W. Trzeciakowski and A. Paszyński (economists) and J. Auleytner and A. Micewski (advisers to the Episcopate).

that positions proposed to them amounted to taking responsibility for foreign debt and housing shortages.[63] Suspicion of Rakowski was even found at the heart of the government. Kiszczak described him to Orszulik as 'intelligent and able' but could not support his tactics and politics, 'in which he is too megalomanic, big-headed and bumptious'.[64]

Rakowski's approach to Solidarity was confrontational. He told the Secretariat: 'We need to put on a show of strength towards them – even if we don't have it to a sufficient degree.' The refusal to re-legalise Solidarity would lead to a confrontation on a large scale: 'We must prepare ourselves, of course in strict secrecy, for such a confrontation.' Agreeing to a Round Table was right, but 'possessing such a plan for confrontation is also essential'.[65] His team followed a familiar pattern: twenty members of the 'ruling coalition' and two independents. He told the world's press (14 October) that Poles were more interested in having their own tables well-stocked than in a Round Table.[66]

Rakowski offered economic decentralisation instead of political reform. Market elements were to be reintroduced. A self-made millionaire, M. Wilczek, became Minister for Industry. On 31 October, the new government announced that the Gdańsk Shipyard, birthplace of Solidarity, was to be closed 'on economic grounds'. Solidarity replied that the decision was 'a sinister and dangerous political act, which shows that the Rakowski government is taking advantage of its special powers to preserve and consolidate the Stalinist model of managing the economy'. Such decisions should be decided 'by the laws of the market and not by arbitrary political decisions'.[67]

The decision came on the eve of a visit by Margaret Thatcher. Her original letter, stressing her intimate relationship with Gorbachev, had stated that a short trip to Gdańsk would be well received by millions of people.[68] Jaruzelski replied that he much appreciated her wish to visit the monument to the heroes of Westerplatte, where the Second World War had begun almost fifty years before. Her honouring the dead would be appreciated 'by the millions of Europeans in our long-ago alliance'.[69] In private, he noted that they could not prevent her going to the monument to Gdańsk Shipyard workers shot dead in 1970 (when Jaruzelski was Minister of Defence) or to the tomb of the murdered Warsaw priest Father Jerzy Popiełuszko. This private part of her visit was most

[63] See A. Paszyński, 'Dlaczego nie wchodzę do rządu Rakowskiego', *Tygodnik Mazowsze* 5 October 1988.
[64] Kiszczak to Archbishop Dąbrowski (27 July 1988) in Raina (ed.), *Rozmowy*, p. 252.
[65] Perzkowski (ed.), *Tajne dokumenty Biura Politycznego i Sekretariatu KC*, pp. 90–2.
[66] *Trybuna Ludu* 15–16 October 1988. [67] National Executive (5 November 1988).
[68] AAN 237/V/418 (letter of 15 July 1988). [69] AAN 237/V/418.

unwelcome: 'Horrid woman. Those Anglicans don't tolerate the Papists at all and yet she starts everything from Popiełuszko.' He regarded it as 'an incomprehensible demonstration, particularly from a country where they are murdering one another in Ireland and she starved some to death in prison'.[70]

In the event, the Polish Foreign Ministry adjudged the visit of the 'well-known anti-communist' a success. Prime Minister Rakowski read her a lecture on economic reform: 'We should not forget that the present form of socialism in Poland grew under the influence of Stalinist concepts. Its cardinal sin was the dominant role of the state'. He attempted to portray decisions of his government, such as the announced closure of the Gdańsk Shipyard, in the spirit of British 'privatisation'. It was necessary to break the state monopoly of industry.[71] The British Prime Minister did not endorse this 'Thatcherite' approach. She stated the transition from a centralised economy to private enterprise and competition was difficult. It was not just a matter of changing economic policy – there had to be 'personal, political and spiritual change'. Unlike Rakowski, she had a mandate for change, given in 1979 and renewed in two subsequent elections.[72]

In his meetings, Jaruzelski praised Mrs Thatcher's curbs on Brtitish trade unions. She retorted that 'people in Britain do not have to rely on trade unions as a means of expressing their political views because we have free elections'.[73] Jaruzelski insisted that the Gdańsk Shipyard closure was on economic grounds and expressed the hope that it would not be used as a pretext (by the opposition, evidently) to break off talks about a Round Table. The authorities had not proposed the Round Table as a tactical gambit but in good faith. Unfortunately, a similar initiative to create a Council of National Agreement in late 1981 had come to nothing since Wałęsa, who had originally accepted it, returned to Gdańsk and changed his mind: 'Solidarity, despite bandying around the slogans of democracy and pluralism, was not a partner to talks.'[74]

Wałęsa stated, in a letter to Kiszczak, that the decision to shut the Gdańsk Shipyard could not be understood as anything other than blocking the way to the Round Table. Delays in reaching the Round Table stemmed from fundamental issues. Above all, there needed to be a declaration by both sides that the Table would deal with the most

70 Perzkowski (ed.), *Tajne dokumenty Biura Politycznego i Sekretariatu KC*, p. 156 (ten IRA prisoners had died on hunger strike).
71 AAN 237/V/418, pp. 25–6.
72 M. Thatcher, *The Downing Street Years* (London, 1993), p. 779.
73 *Ibid.* p. 780.
74 AAN 237/V/418, pp. 11–12, 23.

important matters facing the country, with the 'Solidarity' question as one of them.[75] Kiszczak managed to reply at length without referring to the Gdańsk Shipyard or the Solidarity issue.[76] The same day, unofficial celebrations of Independence Day (11 November) passed off peacefully in many cities. Those in Gdańsk, Poznań and Katowice, however, were attacked by the militia.[77] An uneasy stalemate prevailed. The Church made further efforts to mediate.

Taking up the issue of the Gdańsk Shipyard with Ciosek, Episcopal Secretary Orszulik commented bluntly:

> no-one at home or abroad believed or believes that the decision was purely economic. Not only Solidarity, but the foreign press, including the communist one, considers the decision to be political. The decision came as a shock not only to public opinion, but to all those working at the Shipyard, including management and the party organisation. This is a typically dictatorial approach to economic reform, in which the workers' opinions count for nothing.[78]

Ciosek replied lamely that the new Premier, dissatisfied with the lack of progress towards the Round Table, had to press ahead himself with decisions on economic reform in order to release foreign credits. Orszulik retorted that 'the whole society must take part in political and economic reform, not simply the Party elite, since the effect of reform falls, above all, on society'.[79] An Episcopal statement the next day made one of its strongest condemnations of government policies for many years. Closure of the Gdańsk Shipyard was 'a political act which does not favour reconciliation'. The government should conduct talks with society and 'avoid actions which make dialogue with society difficult'.[80]

The Church convened a further meeting between Kiszczak and Wałęsa on 18–19 November, at Wilanów. But prospects for agreement were damaged beforehand by Jaruzelski's instructions to Kiszczak that the official communiqué could not mention the word 'Solidarity'.[81] Kiszczak's opening address ignored Solidarity entirely. He did, however, mention trade unions, by which he meant the 7-million-strong OPZZ, 'with an identity and opinions of its own on matters of national importance'. This Union, he said, should have the same size of delegation to the Round Table as that of 'persons finding themselves on Mr Wałęsa's list'.[82] Wałęsa reiterated the demands for union pluralism and a re-legalised

[75] Dubiński (ed.), *Okrągły Stół*, p. 139 (5 November 1988).
[76] *Ibid.* pp. 140–1 (11 November 1988).
[77] Dudek and Marszałkowski, *Walki uliczne*, pp. 382–5.
[78] Raina (ed.), *Droga do 'Okrągłego stołu'*, p. 243 (9 November 1988). [79] *Ibid.* p. 244.
[80] Signed by Archbishop Dąbrowski, 12 November 1988.
[81] Dubiński (ed.), *Okrągły Stół*, p. 19. [82] *Ibid.* pp. 144–7.

Solidarity. Accused of 'repeating the old mistake: playing for all or nothing', Wałęsa replied calmly: 'I'm in no hurry. We have time. We will wait.'[83]

The deadlock was broken in an unexpected way. The OPZZ Chairman proposed a television debate with Wałęsa. Miodowicz's challenge was evidently issued on his own initiative: he was eager for the contest and expected to win. His political masters expressed strong reservations behind the scenes. Jaruzelski referred to him as 'rushing like a moth to the flames'.[84] Consulted by Solidarity, the US Ambassador advised that simply appearing on television after being an 'unperson' for seven years would guarantee Wałęsa victory.[85] Solidarity also considered it essential that editorial intervention would not be able to distort Wałęsa's words. Thus a clock would be shown throughout the broadcast, so that any cuts could be easily identified, and an independent camera would film the debate, as evidence in any subsequent dispute. This was manned by Andrzej Wajda and his production team from his film *Man of Iron*.

A day before the broadcast, the Party stated that 'in the television discussion with L. Wałęsa, comrade A. Miodowicz will be speaking in his own name, not in the name of the Politburo of the Central Committee'.[86] It was a timely disclaimer. In what the underground press called 'forty minutes of freedom', Wałęsa dispelled seven years of state propaganda.

'Yesterday's opponent', 'the political adventurer', 'the post-Solidarity extremist', 'the Electrician, Mr Wałęsa' turned out to be a moderate and reasonable politician with constructive ideas for the future of Poland. He skilfully referred to Soviet developments: 'In 1980, in 1981, external conditions did not exist for the reforms Solidarity proposed: first and foremost – as I once said, perhaps not too seriously – because Brezhnev lived two years too long.' Now there was a good climate in almost all the countries of the system, above all the Soviet Union: 'Over there they are going further in their reforms. After all, over there they are truly doing what Solidarity has been fighting for then and right up to the present day. That is why we shouldn't hamper *perestroikas*, but in our country we should – after all the experience we have had, on both sides – we should move further.'

However, the Stalinist experience had yet to be overcome: 'The Stalinist era isn't over yet ... And where did Stalin come from? He came because there was no political pluralism. We were the ones who

83 *Ibid.* pp. 148–9 (notes by Dubiński).
84 Perzkowski (ed.), *Tajne dokumenty Biura Politycznego i Sekretariatu KC*, p. 200.
85 J. Davis, Międzeszyn, 21 October 1999.
86 Perzkowski (ed.), *Tajne dokumenty Biura Politycznego i Sekretariatu KC*, p. 191.

built Stalin up, all of us, at that time. There were no controlling organisations, no pluralism, and he runs all this right up to this day.'[87]

By contrast, Miodowicz came across poorly to most viewers. A poll of 250 Warsaw residents the next day found that 1 per cent thought Miodowicz the victor, while 64 per cent gave the advantage to Wałęsa. The programme increased support for Solidarity from young people (under thirty), the intelligentsia, skilled workers and those who had been members of Solidarity prior to 13 December 1981. Miodowicz followers were typically members of OPZZ and of the Party and were much older (over-forties). A supplementary question found that 3 per cent of respondents were opposed to the re-legalisation of Solidarity, while 73 per cent were in favour.[88]

Kiszczak admitted to the Politburo, the day after the broadcast, that it had 'completely ruined the previous stereotype of Wałęsa's personality put out by Party propaganda'. Party members were accusing the Party leadership and its propaganda apparatus of deceiving them. In putting forward an attractive alternative to official politics, Wałęsa had skilfully played the 'Russian card'. Pointing out the progress of *perestroika*, and to reforms in Hungary, had enabled him to present the idea of Solidarity in the wider context of the development of real socialism. Wałęsa's thesis that remnants of the Stalinist model still needed to be eliminated had been particularly effective, though Kiszczak noted he had borrowed the idea from an OPZZ adviser at a previous meeting. The television debate had definitively closed the present phase of preparations for the Round Table, and Wałęsa had done so to the advantage of Solidarity.[89]

Jaruzelski immediately authorised a more active phase of preparations for the Round Table. As a goodwill gesture, Wałęsa was given a passport to visit France. Ciosek told Archbishop Dąbrowski on 2 December that this permission, which had already been communicated to President Mitterand, created 'a new political fact'. He pressed the Church for another 'working meeting' between Kiszczak and Wałęsa before he left for Paris. Dąbrowski replied that the real point was to decide on holding negotiations with Solidarity. Ciosek was somewhat more specific the next day: 'We want to create conditions for the political formation of Solidarity. You want to anchor Solidarity in the workplace, while we evacuate the Party. We are giving you [a new law on] associations. We are restricting the *nomenklatura*. We don't want to destroy the formation of Solidarity. The presence of the Party in the workplace is an

[87] Polish TV, 7 p.m. GMT, 30 November 1988.
[88] *Społeczeństwo i władza*, pp. 383–6. [89] Dubiński (ed.), *Okrągły Stół*, p. 151.

anachronism.'[90] But there was still no agreement on the legalisation of Solidarity. The 'problem of Solidarity', as the authorities put it, could be discussed at the Round Table.

Jaruzelski realised the 'unfortunate broadcast' had changed the public perception of Wałęsa and of Solidarity. But his own colleagues were bereft of ideas. The Party was dividing between those who 'fear its disintegration, weakening its identity, its distinctive doctrinal base' and others who saw the opportunity for the Party to retain its role, albeit exercised in a different way. He favoured an escape forwards (*ucieczka do przodu*[91]) and refloated his old notion of the 'Big Three' meeting from 1981, to include himself, Wałęsa and Cardinal Glemp.[92] Nothing came of this suggestion. Nor did a further 'working meeting' materialise. Instead, the Politburo set up a 'Coordination Staff for activities in the political struggle with the opposition and political opponents'.[93] Its composition was quite conciliatory. It was headed by Czyrek, and included Ciosek, Press Secretary Urban (who was now converted to the idea of a dialogue) and Aleksander Kwaśniewski, a rising star.

Ciosek informed Church mediators that the Politburo had considered 'various options for solving the problem of Solidarity', but a decision would have to wait until the political analysis of the next Party Plenum, in a week's or a month's time.[94] Barcikowski told Dąbrowski and Orszulik (9 December) that 'the Politburo has no mandate to allow the legalisation of Solidarity'. Its mandate could only be renewed by a Party Plenum.[95]

Just before Wałęsa's visit to France, his first foreign trip since martial law, the Soviet Union made a major policy announcement on Central Europe. In a dramatic statement to the General Assembly of the United Nations, Gorbachev formally revoked the 'Brezhnev Doctrine'. Declaring that force would no longer be a factor in relations between socialist states, he also announced unilateral withdrawal of 50,000 Soviet troops from Czechoslovakia, Hungary and the DDR.

A 'prognosis' from the Polish Foreign Ministry saw an acceleration of change in the socialist countries. The neo-Stalinist model, based on centralised direction of the economy and heavy industry through command-administrative methods, had led to a systemic crisis. It could only be overcome through essential reforms and profound democratisation, particularly in the Soviet Union, Poland and Hungary.[96]

90 Raina (ed.), *Rozmowy*, p. 313.
91 Perzkowski (ed.), *Tajne dokumenty Biura Politycznego i Sekretariatu KC*, p. 197.
92 Dubiński (ed.), *Okrągły Stół*, p. 19.
93 *Ibid.* pp. 154–5 (facsimile of Politburo decision).
94 Raina (ed.), *Rozmowy*, pp. 315–17. 95 *Ibid.* p. 320.
96 Perzkowski (ed.), *Tajne dokumenty Biura Politycznego i Sekretariatu KC*, p. 206.

Their report predicted that relations with the in-coming US Administration would not be easy, at least initially. President-elect Bush had made clear that he would continue a policy of 'rewarding' internal liberalisation and independence in foreign policy. The USA had made a clear linkage (*iunctim*) between the development of relations with Poland and political concessions to the opposition. Without such concessions, improved dialogue with America would not be possible. A new agreement on restructuring Polish debt needed to be reached with the International Monetary Fund by 1 January 1989. Otherwise, Poland would find itself 'in the position of a debtor unable to meet its obligations'.[97]

A domestic 'prognosis' for the Politburo found problems no less pressing, above all the resolution of 'the central matter, the question of Solidarity'. Several options were considered. Rejection of Solidarity was deemed disastrous, leading to an inevitable further social confrontation which the authorities might well lose. A further casualty would be any prospect of economic reform. But if the Party was to accept the inevitable, should it do so actively or passively? To await events would subject both the Party and the law to further attacks, as Solidarity came into de facto, yet illegal, existence. Acceptance of reality, however unpalatable that might be to 'certain of our allies abroad', was the recommended course. It could be agreed as part of a package at the Round Table setting out 'a new model of union movement in our country'; 'Legalising Solidarity is a risk for us. But if we don't re-legalise, who can guarantee its disappearance?'[98] No one could guarantee it.

On return from his triumphant visit to France, in which he was accorded treatment worthy of a visiting head of state, Wałęsa summoned a fifth meeting of 'advisers'. Some 128 assembled in the crypt of a Warsaw church on 18 December. They included 48 Solidarity activists and advisers, 28 representatives of Catholic groups, 16 presidents of creative unions and associations, 6 rectors or former rectors of higher schools, and other intellectuals, experts and distinguished guests.[99] After a résumé by Mazowiecki of the past three months of negotiations with the authorities, the gathering discussed the prospects for and purposes of a Round Table. Adam Michnik, developing a position he had first outlined in prison during 1986, argued the need to compromise with a 'pro-reformist core' inside the Party.[100] This pre-supposed such a 'core' existed, but, even if it only consisted of 5 per cent of the total Party membership, it was

[97] Perzkowski (ed.), *Tajne dokumenty Biura Politycznego i Sekretariatu KC*, p. 210.
[98] *Ibid.* pp. 213–23 (21 December 1988). [99] Skórzyński, *Ugoda*, p. 165 note 27.
[100] A. Michnik, *Takie czasy . . . Rzecz o kompromisie* (Warsaw, 1986).

still worth investing in, because failure to reach a compromise would mean return to confrontation and the road to civil war.[101]

Jacek Kuroń foresaw an 'explosion of social anger' and open conflict breaking out within the next few months, providing an urgent deadline which should drive participants towards the Round Table.[102] Testimony to the growing radicalisation of young factory workers and miners was confirmed by first-hand reports from Jerzy Puciata and Mieczysław Gil.[103] A visitor, Kołakowski, reminded them that the contemporary Polish communists had no leader with the public support of a Dubček or Gomułka (as in 1956). They had no-one who could address the public (or even the Party), with the admission that 'although we have made great mistakes, we are correcting them and will build real – not false – socialism'. The lesson of the past thirty years was that communism was unreformable, in the sense that its ideology and politics could not be made to operate in accordance with the aspirations of society.[104]

The constitutional business of the meeting was introduced by Wielowieyski. It passed a motion to transform Wałęsa's informal consultants into regular teams of experts to prepare for the Round Table. The most important of the fifteen portfolios were trade union pluralism (Mazowiecki); political reform (Geremek); law and administration of justice (Stelmachowski); and economic policy and reform (Trzeciakowski). There was to be no permanent Chairman, but Henryk Wujec became Secretary, with two assistants. Marcin Król described the team, prophetically, as a 'shadow cabinet', though it is unlikely that anyone took this literally at the time. This was reflected by a change of title, at Osmanczyk's suggestion, to a 'Citizens' Committee attached to the Chairman of NSZZ "Solidarność"'.[105]

The Party's preparations for the Round Table included a 'long and lively discussion' by the Secretariat on 20 December.[106] At issue was whether the Party was willing to countenance a dialogue with the opposition. Since a precondition for successful negotiations was unity in Party ranks, it seems safe to assume that those who lost this argument also lost their positions in the Party leadership. The depth of the division 'above' accounts for the sweeping personnel changes made on the opening day of

[101] Archiwum Senatu (AS), Komitet Obywatelski: Spotkanie 5 (18 December 1988), pp. 87–9.
[102] AS, Komitet Obywatelski: Spotkanie 5, pp. 108–10.
[103] AS, Komitet Obywatelski: Spotkanie 5, pp. 98–9 (Puciata); pp. 95–6 (Gil).
[104] AS, Komitet Obywatelski: Spotkanie 5, pp. 93–4.
[105] AS, Komitet Obywatelski: Spotkanie 5, pp. 113–34.
[106] Perzkowski (ed.), *Tajne dokumenty Biura Politycznego i Sekretariatu KC* (Politburo, 21 December 1988), p. 212.

the Party's Tenth Plenum (20 December). Eight out of fifteen Politburo members were removed, as were four of the eleven Central Committee Secretaries. Those promoted to full membership of the Politburo included Stanisław Ciosek, a key negotiator with Solidarity, and Janusz Reykowski, a university professor of psychology.

On the second day of the Plenum, Rakowski declared the need for a dialogue with Wałęsa and Solidarity.[107] Jaruzelski stated that the dilemma of December 1988 was no less dramatic than that of December 1981 and concerned the same issue: whether to recognise Solidarity, accept it as a party to negotiation and share power in a new political formation, or to stubbornly defend the status quo. This time, he opted for the former.[108] But so far-reaching a decision could not be confined to the Party's upper reaches. The Plenum would have to approve legislation to re-legalise the opposition. It therefore adjourned while preparations were made for a second round.

Czyrek told the Secretariat (23 December) that the issue of pluralism could split the Party. Delegates to the Plenum should be carefully groomed by an Ideological Conference and special meetings of the Party School, as well as 'individual consultations' with *aktyw*.[109] The opposition was playing for time and the Party could adopt a similar tactic. The line should be: 'we are in favour of pluralism, but we need to introduce it by creating appropriate conditions and constructive activity'. This would include the careful drafting of a resolution: 'The Position of the Central Committee with Respect to Political and Union Pluralism'. It was important that the leadership did not prejudge the question of legalising Solidarity before the Plenum.[110]

Jaruzelski agreed that the Plenum would have to take a stance on the question of the Round Table. He set out 'elementary preconditions' for pluralism. These included 'social peace' and 'not disturbing the stability of the state, not paralysing economic reform and not agitating (*skłócenie*) the working class'. The idea of power-sharing was not extremist, since the Party was amenable to all constructive forces. Orzechowski, Ciosek and others should disseminate this message to 'opinion-forming circles'.[111] Ciosek himself had wondered: 'What are the state of consciousness, role and wishes of the Party on this issue? What will be the reaction of the Party base? Will two weeks be enough to find out?'[112]

107 Rakowski, *Jak to się stało*, pp. 170–2.
108 Baka, *U zródeł wielkiej transformacji*, pp. 67–8. 109 AAN 237/V/93.
110 AAN 237/V/93, Secretariat (23 December 1988), pp. 3–5.
111 AAN 237/V/93, pp. 6–7. 112 AAN 237/V/93, p. 3.

A fortnight later, Czyrek admitted that the Party still harboured many 'doubts, reservations and disorientations'.[113] The economist Baka, promoted to the Secretariat the previous June, saw the basic problem as 'adapting the work of the Party *apparat* to new socio-economic and political demands and overcoming the party bureaucracy'.[114] While this was no doubt true, much the same could have been said for the past thirty-five years. As politics within the Party had reached an impasse, social tensions were rising, fuelled by the inflammatory demands from the official trade unions. Party leaders turned again to the Church, adding Rakowski to the negotiating team.

In talks with the Church hierarchy, held at Gierek's former villa (4 January 1989), Rakowski presented a grim picture. The national economy was in a bad state: there had been 80 per cent inflation in 1988, falling hardest on fixed-income groups such as pensioners. The position would deteriorate still further. But the government was 'not so stupid as to believe that economic reform can be carried out without political and social reform'. Despite 'attacks from left and right, including some from Solidarity', he wished to clear the ground for economic reform within the next three months. The prospects for political change were much better than seven years earlier and incomparably better than those thought possible by (his newspaper) *Polityka* in the 1970s. Elections to the Sejm in April would stabilise the political situation. They would be preceded by a 'genuine national agreement' on a common programme and shared seats. It would be a non-confrontational election.[115]

There was nothing here about re-legalising Solidarity. Rakowski relegated the issue to a post-election period, when a formula would be negotiated. Even then there were numerous preconditions. Solidarity would have to give no-strike guarantees and undertake not to force through wage demands. It must sever its links with the nationalist KPN and base itself on the Polish Constitution. It would have to give up being financed from abroad. Wałęsa should stop shifting his opinions, saying one thing in Paris and another when he got back. He should acknowledge that 'Solidarity today is not what it was in 1981.' There had to be guarantees against anarchy. The accession of Gorbachev had created a unique situation for the socialist countries, which were 'for the first time entirely independent in furnishing our own house'. But this did not mean that all the neighbours accepted *perestroika*: 'The DDR says we have gone mad. Only Hungary understands us.' Even within Poland, the reactions of the military, secret police and Party *apparat* were unpredictable.[116]

113 AAN 237/V/93, p. 3. 114 AAN 237/V/93, p. 8.
115 Raina (ed.), *Rozmowy*, pp. 329–30. 116 *Ibid.*

Mazowiecki pressed Solidarity's case in two further meetings with Ciosek (6 and 11 January). Agreement to elections was dependent on the Party's prior acceptance of a process for re-legalising Solidarity. Ciosek was equivocal and reluctant to agree a timetable on various pretexts, such as: 'We are frightened of an eruption of [Solidarity's] demands.' After a long discussion, Orszulik proposed a document presenting the views of each side. This began by stating that the Party Plenum (set to resume on 16 January) would pass a resolution on union pluralism, opening the way for Solidarity to act legally as a trade union. It would be enacted no later than March and followed by elections in May. Mazowiecki stated that the division of seats in the next parliament needed to be made public: 'This is not only a political problem, but also a moral one. We must make progress honestly before society.' The tri-partite division of seats that Ciosek proposed might possibly cover the first election but could not be binding for the next.[117]

In the meantime, Wałęsa was allowed to form an Organisational Committee, which could convene at once, on condition it abandoned strikes and other means of pressing economic demands. The historic significance of the moment was not lost on the participants. Czyrek referred to their agreement as 'a political conclusion to the state of war'.[118] Ciosek saw the Round Table as sketching out 'a new social agreement'. It could resume negotiations begun in Gdańsk (in 1980).[119] Ciosek himself 'crossed the Rubicon' on 15 January by including the word 'Solidarity' in the draft to be put before the next day's Party Plenum.[120]

The Plenum was tempestuous, as Politburo members complained on the evening of 17 January (their third Politburo meeting within twenty-four hours). Jaruzelski stated plainly that the Central Committee discussion was an attack on the leadership, 'sharp and undiluted, hardly sparing anybody'. Speeches made clear that the *aktyw* had lost confidence in the leadership[121] and 'that we were creating a very dangerous crisis situation'. There were only two ways out: either the Central Committee should pass a vote of confidence in the present leadership, resulting in the implementation of accepted resolutions, or they should resign. He was authorised by comrades Rakowski, Siwicki (Minister of Defence) and Kiszczak to state that if they did not receive a vote of confidence they would resign: 'This is not blackmail. If anyone else feels strong enough to proceed, please go ahead, the road is clear.'[122]

[117] *Ibid.* pp. 339–44. [118] *Ibid.* p. 337. [119] *Ibid.* p. 341. [120] *Ibid.* p. 349.
[121] See Skórzyński, *Ugoda*, pp. 171–3.
[122] Perzkowski (ed.), *Tajne dokumenty Biura Politycznego i Sekretariatu KC*, p. 229.

In discussion that followed, Professor Reykowski took the view that the crisis of confidence in the leadership should be brought to a head: 'Of course this move is dangerous, but what is the alternative?' The alternative was conservative, but acting boldly had a chance of victory over the voices that had dominated in the discussion.[123] Kiszczak thought the Central Committee should be made to see the gravity of the situation: 'It cannot go on like this. Either things are so bad that we should leave, or they are not so bad, there is confidence, and we can stay.'[124] A closed session of the Politburo decided that the entire leadership would submit itself to a vote of confidence. The ballot, chaired by a senior Central Committee member, Henryk Jabłoński, was decisive. All voted to support the leadership, with 4 abstentions. The resolution on union pluralism and agreement with Solidarity went through by 143 votes in favour, with 32 against and 14 abstentions. For the first time since the 'Partisan' movement of the 1960s, the Party had a significant minority, consisting of perhaps one quarter of the Central Committee.[125]

In accounting for Jaruzelski's victory, Paczkowski notices the comparative weakness of the inner-Party opposition. It lacked leadership of stature or charisma: the most prominent of the 'concrete' (*beton*) were demoted in 1985 – Kociołek, Milewski, and Olszowski who had even emigrated.[126] In defeating what Ciosek called a 'putsch', planned by the Warsaw and Katowice Party organisations, Jaruzelski was assisted by the loyalty of the police and military. The plotters also knew that – unlike the position in the early 1980s – they had no support in the Soviet leadership.[127] It was also known that the easing of Western credit restrictions was still dependent upon accommodation with the opposition. Finally, we should note Jaruzelski's own skill in crisis management. When it came to the vote, Party discipline largely prevailed, no doubt assisted by awareness that an open split would greatly strengthen Solidarity.

Solidarity's leadership gave the Union resolution a cautious welcome (20–21 January). It 'opened the possibility of negotiations' on Solidarity and national issues. The re-legalised union would 'cooperate in the struggle with the crisis' according to an agreed reform programme subject to social control. To do so, the normal preconditions of political pluralism would have to be restored: freedom of association, judicial independence, freedom of speech and access to the media, including state television. For

[123] *Ibid.* pp. 229–30. [124] *Ibid.* p. 230.
[125] Paczkowski (ed.), *Polska 1986–1989*, pp. 29–30.
[126] A. Paczkowski, 'The "Great Historical Experiment" or the Demise of Real Socialism in Poland', *Intermarium* (1.1).
[127] Raina (ed.), *Rozmowy*, p. 351 (20 January 1989).

the first time, a statement by the KKW was published in the Party press.[128] However, concern was also expressed about the authorities' real intentions towards the revived Solidarity. Geremek warned that they would insist it give up its regional structure, and function only at local level. Kuroń rejected the call to give up the right to strike.[129] Participation in elections on a common programme, which the Party had set as a precondition for re-legalisation, was not mentioned at all.

Opinion polls showed that the Solidarity issue divided the Party rank-and-file. Ciosek told the Episcopate (23 January) that their views were split 50–50. As Barcikowski added, 'Enough for two parties'.[130] The Central Committee Secretaries added that the Party rank-and-file ('the Bottom') consisted largely of 'primitive populists'. The official unions were disoriented – some members pleased that progress had been made, others calling it a betrayal.[131]

The scope of change was discussed by the Secretariat the same day. Jaruzelski insisted that the absolute priority be given to preparing the Round Table, 'which is our initiative, consistently presented from the beginning and not a tactic'. The Plenum had endorsed 'not only pluralism, but an opening to economic and political reform, creating a new model of political forces'. Yet Jaruzelski clearly felt the initiative was slipping away. A week had passed since the Plenum, yet little had been done: 'Further delay is disastrous.'[132] A very specific set of tasks was allocated, to be completed by the next meeting in four days' time.[133]

One reason for his urgency was the behaviour of other political parties. A Labour Party (*Stronnictwo Pracy*) had re-appeared. Under the leadership of Siła-Nowicki, it was clamouring for recognition.[134] More ominous for the Party was the behaviour of its 'coalition' partners. Dormant for decades, they had suddenly shown signs of independence. Their insubordination had even extended to demands for the rehabilitation of Mikołajczyk, the United Peasants' Party (PSL) leader, driven out of government and into exile by the rigged elections of 1948.[135] Czyrek complained that the 'allied parties', hiding behind the slogan 'the right

[128] 'Oświadczenie KKW NSZZ "Solidarność"', *Trybuna Ludu* 23 January 1989. This was done on Ciosek's initiative: Raina (ed.), *Rozmowy*, p. 354.

[129] Skorzyński, *Ugoda*, pp. 177.

[130] *Tajne dokumenty Państwo-Kościół 1980–1989* (London, 1993), p. 558.

[131] *Ibid.* pp. 559–63.

[132] Perzkowski (ed.), *Tajne dokumenty Biura Politycznego i Sekretariatu KC*, pp. 235–9.

[133] *Ibid.* pp. 241–3.

[134] It was officially registered on 12 February 1989.

[135] A. Paczkowski, *Stanisław Mikołajczyk czyli klęska realisty (zarys biografii politycznej)* (Warsaw, 1991); S. Mikołajczyk, *The Pattern of Soviet Domination* (London, 1948).

to opposition within the coalition' were acting by fait accompli.[136] Kiszczak noted that coalition leaders were passive in the face of 'autonomous tendencies and critique of their leadership for collaboration with the Party' from their rank-and-file. In consequence, he predicted ominously, 'the constellation in the Sejm may become unfavourable to us'.[137]

Secretary Cypryniak thought that the new Sejm should form a government of national unity in which the opposition would 'share responsibility for extricating [the country] from crisis'. A Party government could 'extend the comfort of exercising power, but only for a short time'.[138] Solidarity was also the key point for Secretary Czarzasty, but he sought a fresh start – a 'zero option' – under which all trade unions began anew, with fresh elections and statutes. Thus, 'new Solidarity' would not be able to rely on resolutions passed before 13 December 1981, and could not set up vertical or horizontal structures prior to registration. In the interim, it could take part in the President's Consultative Council.[139]

Jaruzelski agreed that Solidarity was the major problem. They could try to argue that the Pope, on his Gdańsk visit in 1987, had referred to 'solidarity' (in the lower case) 'in the sense of a spiritual legacy, not an organisation'. Divisions within Solidarity should be exploited, and, while keeping to the spirit of the Plenum resolution, it should not be assumed that re-legalisation was a foregone conclusion. 'Facts against the law' which might block the talks should be collected and used in Party propaganda. At the same time, the Party should strongly emphasise its own goodwill.[140]

When both sides met at Magdalenka on 27 January, Wałęsa immediately sought to take the debate forward. The issue was no longer whether to legalise Solidarity, since the Plenum had agreed to that, but only 'how to do it and who wants to reform our country'. The open discussion he proposed lasted for eleven hours, with a number of tense interludes, calmed down by Bishop Tadeusz Gocłowski. The most controversial debate surrounded Solidarity's insistence that the sine qua non for its participation in a non-confrontational election was an agremeent between the authorities and society which included its own legalisation. The would-be non-contestants made their differing intentions rather plain:

GEREMEK: We cannot accept a situation in which we are plunged into a *nomenklatura* electoral system. We want to find an electoral system that people accept as democratic. We must find a method that gains social acceptance.

CC SECRETARY GDULA: Like every government, we want to organise elections in order to win them.

[136] Perzkowski (ed.), *Tajne dokumenty Biura Politycznego i Sekretariatu KC*, p. 238.
[137] *Ibid*. p. 234. [138] *Ibid*. p. 245 (Secretariat, 27 January 1989).
[139] *Ibid*. p. 246. [140] *Ibid*. p. 247.

STELMACHOWSKI: I understand that the agreement is for one election only. We need to give society a glimpse of democratic elections for the future.

KACZYŃSKI: You gentlemen are proposing us a coalition.

INTERIOR MINISTER KISZCZAK: We want your representatives to join the government after the elections. Poland must extract itself from crisis with united forces.

MAZOWIECKI: In reaching agreement we will take responsibility for the state, but not for governing . . .

GEREMEK: We understand that the government wants to win, but we want much greater freedom and these two concepts need to be brought together.

KISZCZAK: We say that we want to win the elections, but we also want to go two steps forward and we do not want confrontation.

WAŁĘSA: We don't want to win the elections. We are not barging into government.[141]

Sympathy for the dilemmas of Polish communism was expressed in Hungary, where events in Poland were being closely watched.

On 11 January, Budapest drafted legislation allowing for the formation of independent political groupings. There was no longer any mention of the Party's 'leading role'. On the other hand, the revised Constitution was to define Hungary as a 'socialist state'.[142] Reports in the Polish media were construed as telling of permission for the formation of new political groupings. To scotch such rumours, Andrzej Gdula demanded a Polish statement that 'there will be no new political parties in the near future'. He wanted this to be announced by the President of the Supreme Court.[143] No such statement materialised and events in Hungary continued to occupy Polish attention. Though almost simultaneous with those in Poland, they took a somewhat different trajectory.

Jaruzelski tried to explain the 'origins, necessity and prospects of the Round Table' during a visit to Prague on 1 February. His sceptical hosts were themselves the butt of growing domestic protests. Jaruzelski argued that it would be better to neutralise Solidarity now by making it take co-responsibility for reform than to wait another year or two, by when problems could be considerably more severe: 'The game is about swallowing up the opposition by our system, and their participation in (re)shaping it. This is a great historical experiment, which – if it works – can have an importance extending beyond Poland's borders.'[144]

141 Raina (ed.), *Rozmowy*, pp. 360–79 (transcribed by Episcopal Secretary Jacek Ambroziak, 1 February 1989).

142 See A. Bozóki, 'The Hungarian Road to Systemic Change: The Opposition Round Table', *East European Politics and Society* 1993 (7.2).

143 Perzkowski (ed.), *Tajne dokumenty Biura Politycznego i Sekretariatu KC*, p. 236.

144 *Ibid.* pp. 260–2.

15 Abdication

> We don't want to win the elections.
> We're not barging into government.
>
> Wałęsa, February 1989, cited in Raina (ed.), *Rozmowy*, p. 374

In early 1989, Alexander Yakovlev commissioned four reports on Eastern Europe.[1] Their purpose was to review for the Soviet Party leadership the implications of changes so far. They were also asked to predict the directions of future change. We do not know what direct influence they had on Gorbachev himself. But the documents do show that he had a very perceptive range of analyses before him which anticipate some – though by no means all – of the drama of 1989.

The International Department of the Central Committee noted that the 'transition to the principle of equality and mutual responsibility, launched in April 1985' had reached a crucial stage. Former types of relations had been terminated, but new ones had yet to be established. Ruling parties could not continue to rule in the old ways but 'new "rules of the game" – of managing the group interests that are pouring out, of finding a social consensus' – had yet to be worked out. They recommended a differentiated response according to the countries concerned.

Poland and Hungary were moving towards pluralism. The ruling parties could only preserve their positions within a framework of political alliances. That required involving the opposition in constructive cooperation. In these two countries, 'The chances of preserving internal stability and obligations to allies are very high' if the initiative for democratic changes, towards a parliamentary or presidential system, originates from within their ruling parties. Thus the Polish Party could 'realistically become just one, and maybe not even the main [part] of the power structures. However, Polish geopolitics is such that even the opposition understands the need to preserve some form of alliance with the USSR.'

[1] Three of the reports were obtained by J. Levesque, *The Enigma of 1989*, Ch. 5, and placed in the National Security Archive. The fourth remains buried in the former KGB archive.

The position was less favourable elsewhere. Tensions were rising considerably in Czechoslovakia: 'The 1968 syndrome is still present, which interferes with the Party's ability to define its position towards *perestroika*.' It tinkered with the economy, believing that genuine democratisation and *glasnost'* could be postponed to some later stage. Likewise, the conservative East German leadership, 'to a large extent under the influnce of personal ambitions', was striving to avoid the problems of renewal. In Bulgaria, Zhivkov was engaging in a pseudo-*perestroika*, making loud declarations about a 'comprehensive reconsideration of Marxist–Leninist theory', accompanied by endless reshuffles and manipulation. This gulf between theory and practice 'discredits the Party, and socialism and casts a shadow on *perestroika*'. Finally, Romania lay under 'the oppressive personality cult of Ceauseşcu's authoritarian rule'. Overall, they concluded, 'it is very unlikely we would be able to re-use the methods of 1956 and 1968 both as a matter of principle and because of unacceptable consequences'. But 'we should leave a certain vagueness as far as our concrete actions are concerned'.[2]

Bogomolov's Institute of the Economy of the World Socialist System, reporting somewhat earlier, noted that the rapid acceleration of developments across the region over the past twelve to eighteen months had left Stalinist, neo-Stalinist and Soviet-inspired methods behind. Most countries were seeking a new model of socialism. But the outcome of transition was unpredictable. One possibility was a collapse of the socialist idea. Common across the region was a crisis of confidence in the ability of communist parties to govern: 'Dogmatic social sciences are incapable of working out a convincing ideological rationale for long-needed reform.' Public opinion, particularly amongst the young, 'spreads apathy, a sense of doom, nostalgia for pre-Revolutionary times (pre-war or even earlier), a lack of faith in the potential of socialism'. Bi-lateral trade with the USSR was falling and interest had faded in greater socialist integration through direct ties and cooperation in technology.

The chances of a social explosion were highest in Poland, Hungary and Yugoslavia, where adverse social response to policies of 'socialist Thatcherism' brought increasing protests. Their reform projects faced a formidable ideological obstacle. Marxist–Leninist parties saw themselves as the workers' vanguard, yet economic modernisation would impact hardest in core working-class constituencies: mining, metallurgy, shipbuilding and other traditional industries. In the case of Yugoslavia, the geopolitical and geo-strategic impact of protests on the Soviet Union

[2] NSA, 'Towards a Strategy of Relations with European Socialist Countries' (February 1989).

would be marginal: 'But the course of events in Hungary and especially Poland will affect us very directly and very painfully by buttressing the position of [our] conservative forces and breeding doubts about the survival of *perestroika*.' Here the analysis became sombre.

Pressures for change in Eastern Europe were irresistible. To attempt to thwart them 'would be tantamount to fighting time itself, the objective course of history'. The use of force by Moscow would be disastrous in the countries concerned, strengthening the conservative wing 'in the upper echelons of power' and halting the process of reform, thus making the domestic crisis worse: 'The direct use of force by the USSR, its intervention in the course of events on behalf of the conservative forces that are alienated from the people, will most evidently signal the end of *perestroika*, the crumbling of the trust of the world community in [our reforms].' A further casualty would be the improved super-power relations.

Soivet new thinking was changing the priorities of the 'architects' of American foreign policy. They now preferred to support *perestroika* in the USSR and the creation of an external environment favourable to its success: 'Serious Western politicians warn against playing on the problems of the socialist community.' Positive cooperation with reformists would achieve more than 'attempting to pull socialist countries from the sphere of influence of the USSR one by one'. This provided an opportunity for Moscow: 'Renunciation of the *diktat* with regard to the socialist countries of Eastern Europe will nurture a more benevolent image of the USSR in the public opinion of these countries and around the world, and it will make the USA seriously correct its foreign policy towards Eastern Europe.'

The emergence of a 'mid-way position on the continent' would have many advantages for Soviet foreign relations. Western Europe would become more interested in the economic and political stability of Eastern Europe. That would stimulate disarmament and *détente* on the continent and worldwide. The emergence of a 'European factor', and a 'common European house', would help to contain 'an anti-Soviet consolidation of the Western world'. That in turn would 'alleviate the economic burden of the USSR'. Finally, Moscow would gain in prestige if the process took place as the result of a conscious 'revolution from above' rather than being forced by 'revolution from below'. Self-limitation favourable to the progress of reforms in socialist Eastern Europe would also have 'a powerful side-effect on the processes of internal *perestroika* in the USSR'. Modernised economies with market relations in Eastern Europe would 'help to overcome a beggar-thy-neighbour (*izhdivenchestvo*) philosophy in their economic relations with the USSR'.

Bogomolov's report envisaged three possible scenarios for Poland. An optimum outcome of the Round Table would be an unstable compromise between the Party (and allies) and Solidarity (and 'the forces of the opposition intelligentsia'). At its best, this could co-opt representatives of the present opposition into the government and facilitate a process of gradual reform during which social tensions were reduced, though mini-crises would periodically recur. The second possible outcome, failure to reach an 'anti-crisis pact', would produce an extended deadlock, with growing anarchy transforming Poland into the chronically 'sick man of Europe'. Worst of all, the collapse of talks would lead to a further explosion (most probably in spring 1989) followed by renewed martial law or an approximation of civil war – 'Afghanistan in the middle of Europe'. Success of the first scenario would depend on Party traditionalists keeping to the recent Plenum resolution and on Solidarity managing to contain mass protests and maintain a two-year moratorium on strikes. Even the most favourable prediction did not augur well for socialism in Poland. The country was much more likely to evolve into a 'classic bourgeois society of the Italian or Greek type'.[3]

Round Table

The inaugural session of the Polish Round Table took place on 6 February 1989. There were twenty-nine delegates from the 'Party–government' team, twenty-six from the Solidarity-led opposition, and three Catholic observers. They sat under a magnifient chandelier in the Hall of Columns in a Warsaw palace.[4] The opening speeches were shown on television, but not live.

Having welcomed all delegates personally, shaking hands with those he had until recently held prisoner, General Kiszczak stated he sought an end to confrontation. He presented four basic propositions for agreement:

1. The authorities wished to govern according to socialism 'with a democratic and humanist face'. Politics should recognise a diversity of views and interests.
2. Both conservative obstructiveness and [radically] unreal proposals and pressures should be avoided. Renewal (*odnowa*) required social peace, respect for partners and the path of dialogue between state and society.
3. Everyone should accept the need for gradual change, and recognise that stirring up conflict could only hamper this complex process.

3 NSA, M. Sil'vanskaya, 'Changes in Eastern Europe and their Influence on the USSR' (February 1989).

4 Photos appear in Dubiński (ed.), *Okrągły Stół*, pp. 305, 481.

4. There was no place for a negative assessment of the historical achievements of socialism in Poland, which could only dissipate social energies and lead to moral disintegration.[5]

Wałęsa accepted these propositions for negotiation, but his starting-point was quite different. Whilst the General sought a 'top-down' renewal, keeping exisiting authority, his analysis was 'bottom-up'.

Forty years of political monopoly had brought Poland to ruin. This had not been caused by gremlins, but by the mode of governing. It was 'the result of a bad system, the result of the lack of freedom. We still feel the spirit of Stalin on our shoulders.' But faced with national catastrophe, Poles had retained their instinct for self-defence. This had led to trade union pluralism, to Solidarity: 'We want Solidarity and we have the right to it.' Likewise, private farmers and students needed their legal associations. Trade union and social pluralism would create 'the space for freedom which Poles need like air'. There should be a re-building (*przebudowa*) so that the state reconnected with nation and society, and families could have confidence in their fatherland. Poland needed to be a new country, based on co-responsibility for governing.[6]

It was already clear that two versions of the Round Table were on offer. Amazingly, Miodowicz, on behalf of the official trade unions, offered a third. In an address not cleared with Politburo colleagues, he rounded on Solidarity as traitors to the workers' cause. They had gone underground in 1982, leaving other trade unions to defend workers' interests. Though a self-appointed spokesman for 'true people of labour', he noted the Round Table was composed largely of elites. He made radical new proposals of his own: free elections to the Sejm, formation of a second chamber from organs of self-government and the abolition of censorship.[7]

This intervention caused general consternation. It challenged the Round Table on key assumptions. First, Miodowicz detached himself from the 'Party–government' team, thus starting a tendency that was increasingly to worry the ruling elite, as its 'coalition partners' began, for the first time, to show signs of independence. Second, his agenda went far beyond the Magdalenka Agreement. At the next Party Secretariat, Jaruzelski noted curtly that even Kuroń was not now calling for free elections. It was a 'counter-revolutionary slogan of 1981'.[8] Finally, the charge of 'elitism' was not easy to refute. The two sides had come to the Round Table with a shared interest. The Party's top leaders, faced with renewed industrial unrest, realised they could no longer govern without recognising an opposition. Jaruzelski explained thus: 'We have

[5] *Ibid.* p. 215. [6] *Ibid.* pp. 221–4. [7] *Ibid.* pp. 225–7.
[8] Perzkowski (ed.), *Tajne dokumenty Biura Politycznego i Sekretariatu KC*, p. 276.

undertaken a pioneering political experiment. The Party wants to share power, but wisely.'[9]

The Solidarity leadership was aware of being regarded as the 'old guard' by younger and bolder workers. Its own ability to deliver acquiescence, whether to end a strike or to reach a compromise with government, was under strain. The challenge to its mandate was made explicit a few days later when a group within Solidarity, also elected by the 1981 Congress, charged Wałęsa with ignoring intra-union democracy in favour of reaching an agreement with the authorities. Noting that the announcement of a Round Table (the previous summer) had been met with social support, they stated that its numerous delays had lowered public expectations. It was no longer seen as sufficient cause to stem spontaneous strikes. Further, the undemocratic composition of the Solidarity delegation – excluding their working group – could mean that other groups might not feel bound by any understanding reached. Above all, there was fear of a secret deal to accept terms far below society's aspirations and even, they added, of agreement to some future repression against its opponents.[10]

During the negotiations, a curious osmosis took place. Having entered the talks with a strong hand, expecting to co-opt the opposition, the 'Party–government' team became ever more adept at compromise. This ability was most noteworthy in Aleksander Kwaśniewski, a future President. As an astute observer commented, 'the communists have at last produced a politician. But I think it is too late.'[11]

Negotiations were overseen by the Church observers. In one sense they were present as passive witnesses. But they also served as a channel to keep the Vatican abreast of proceedings. Orszulik told Ciosek and Mazowiecki that the Pope was very positively disposed to the Round Table.[12] And they had a further function in verifying the content of proceedings that had no printed record. As the Solidarity leader Bujak explained to the press: 'Nothing is written down. Everything is oral. When one side claims the other does not keep to an agreed condition, they ask church observers to recall who was right. They have already given a number of verdicts, some favouring one side, some the other.'[13]

The format of privacy helped 'Party–government' officials to foster unorthodox solutions. Hence its representatives were able to move even

[9] *Ibid.* p. 277.

[10] Letter from Andrzej Słowik (Łódź) to the Chairman of the Round Table, *CWIHP Bulletin* (12/13) (12 February 1989).

[11] Jan Lityński, to the present author (Warsaw, January 1989).

[12] AAN KC PZPR X1A/1427 (14 February 1989).

[13] K. Gebert, *Mebel* (London, 1990), p. 58.

further from the Party apparatus which had opposed talks in the first place. As Wiktor Osiatyński observes, 'the leadership left the *nomenklatura* behind'.[14] The gap grew so wide by the end of the process that top Party negotiators came to perceive the Party apparatus as 'them' and their ertswhile adversaries across the table as 'us'. In the very difficult months afterwards, this helped the Party leadership to keep its side of the agreement. But there was also a concern that the public should not expect too much from the Round Table. An inner Party instruction to the mass media stated it should be presented as 'one element of a national agreement, not a panacea for eveything'.[15] Given that Solidarity spokesmen, including sub-table chairmen, were now given television time, the Politburo expressed concern that 'the explosion of open indoctrination by the opposition' could disorient the public.[16]

The Round Table had three major panels and a plethora of sub-tables and working groups, involving a total of 452 persons, of whom 230 were from Solidarity.[17] The main coordinators of the two sides were Ciosek for the 'Party–government' and Geremek for Solidarity. General Kiszczak and Lech Wałęsa took part in key sessions in the Council of Ministers and at the extended Magdalenka, as well as the signing ceremony on 5 April. General Jaruzelski was kept, formally speaking, above the fray. But as we shall see, his potential role as President-in-waiting was to prove a decisive and contested issue.

At the panel on trade union pluralism, which convened on 9 February, Mazowiecki called for the re-legalisation of Solidarity by a single legislative act, enabling the union to resume as a national and regional body. Responding, Kwaśniewski demanded guarantees that it would not seek to function as a political movement. Mazowiecki replied that this would not depend on Solidarity but on the political situation: 'If there will be political pluralism, the union will limit itself to trade union activities. If there is not pluralism, objective reality will politicise the union.'[18] To this, the Solidarity leader Frasyniuk added enigmatically: 'the one guarantee will be free citizenship'.

The first session on political reforms (10 February) developed issues outlined by Kiszczak and Wałęsa at the opening session. For the 'Party–government' side, Professor Reykowski admitted that the monocentric

14 W. Osiatyński, 'The Roundtable Talks in Poland' in J. Elster (ed.), *The Roundtable Talks and the Breakdown of Communism* (Chicago, 1996), p. 59.
15 AAN KC PZPR V/476 (5 March 1989).
16 AAN KC PZPR V/476 (Position paper for the Politburo) (7 March 1989).
17 A. Friszke, 'Okrągły Stół. Geneza i Przebieg' in Paczkowski (ed.), *Polska 1986–1989*, vol. I, p. 107.
18 Dubiński (ed.), *Okrągły Stół*, pp. 258–9.

system was outmoded and should be opened up by 'free elections'. The Party was the main stabiliser of the political order and principal safeguard of systemic identity. But it did not follow that it should be 'the only sovereign or the only subject of political life'. He envisaged a new form of parliament. When elections were held, 'very important social groups' would not have to enter a contested ballot. While they would be guaranteed seats in the chamber, a 'significant number' of opposition delegates would have the chance to stand. Their election would enable them to promote the issues of their greatest concern, local self-government, access to the mass media and various reforms. Legalisation of Solidarity was not mentioned. In the bargaining that followed, this initial position was mitigated in crucial respects.

Geremek saw the legalisation of Solidarity as the essential starting-point. The state needed to adjust to the new situation. There was a crisis of confidence. Only the return of Solidarity could provide the guarantee needed by the public. On its side, the 'Party–government' proposed the establishment of a new office of President, to be elected for four to seven years by the old Sejm. Unlike the existing ceremonial Presidency, it would have extensive powers: to dissolve the Sejm, introduce a state of emergency, call referenda, propose candidates for the Premiership, and control the armed forces and Committee of National Defence. After objections from Geremek, the issue was put on hold. He commented afterwards that the proposed new Presidency was clearly designed to replace the leadership role of the Party in the state. The legalisation of independent trade unions in 1980 had ended the leading role of the Party in social life. Through the Round Table, the Party hoped to transfer its leading role in the state to the communist Presidency: 'In that sense, it brought to culmination a decade-long process'.[19]

Deadlock on this issue was broken, in early March, by a suggestion from Kwaśniewski that the Senate be chosen in free and democratic elections: 100 senators would be chosen – 2 from each voivodship, with a third seat for Warsaw and Katowice. Though this meant abandoning its original idea that the President would nominate the Senate, there remained a clear understanding that the President would be Jaruzelski. Envisaged on the lines of the executive Presidency assumed by Gorbachev after his ouster of Gromyko in September 1988, it would reassure the Russians that its Polish interests remained in good hands. Since Solidarity delegates were likely to enter the new parliament, including those interned by General Jaruzelski under martial law, the possibility

[19] *Rok 1989*, pp. 93–4.

of their abstention in such a vote – or even absenteeism – was mooted privately: 'If it looks as if the President will not get the necessary majority, some of us will just have to get "flu".'[20]

The emerging package was debated at a stormy session of the Party's Central Committee on 31 March. There is no transcript, but we have Ciosek's concise summary to Round Table participants the next day: 'Fierce attacks on the line of [reaching an] agreement, distrust of the Round Table and prepared reforms. Populistic slogans and demagogy from the official unions.' He adds laconically, 'The Plenum had to take them into account.'[21] It would appear that the leadership listened to complaints and decided to ignore them.

Solidarity's National Executive (KKW) also approved the package on 5 April.[22] It was signed that afternoon. Wałęsa's address began: '"There is no freedom without Solidarity"' – that is the truth with which we approached the Round Table'; 'We came to the table from prisons, from under the truncheons of the ZOMO, with vivid memories of those who had spilled their blood for Solidarity.' Looking ahead, he feared for implementation. Postulates could remain mere paper. Yet, 'the liquidation of the *nomenklatura* and also fulfilment of all our other postulates in the area of political, social and economic pluralism, in law, the judiciary and territorial self-management, are indispensable conditions for the construction of a democratic order in Poland.' The Round Table could become 'the beginning of the road to democracy and a free Poland'.

The closing ceremony was put in jeopardy by a last-minute demand to speak from Miodowicz. After a very tense stand-off, and threatened walkouts – which in the opinion of Geremek could have led to the rupture (*zerwanie*) of the Round Table[23] – it was agreed that Miodowicz could speak. His remarks having been heard, the proceedings ended with Kiszczak and Wałęsa signing the final communiqué at 10.10 p.m.

June elections

The Round Table provided for partially free elections in the near future, to be followed by fully free elections in four years' time. The authorities, confident of winning, were determined to hold them promptly. New electoral laws were formulated within forty-eight hours and the Council

20 T. Garton Ash, *We the People* (Harmondsworth, 1999), p. 39.
21 Dubiński (ed.), *Okrągły Stół*, p. 435.
22 *AS* KO 87–88, KKW 98, pp. 186ff.
23 *Rok 1989*, p. 133; Raina (ed.), *Rozmowy*, pp. 442–5.

of State announced the timetable on 13 April. The first round would take place on Sunday 4 June, with any run-offs a fortnight later.

Faced with this deliberately tight schedule, Solidarity took crucial decisions. On 7 April, the National Executive decided to hand the electoral campaign to the Citizens' Committee and to extend its structure nationwide. They would draw up the list of candidates, select election commissioners – to register candidates, run polling stations and count the votes – and engage the public in the campaign. This was debated by the Citizens' Committee the next day. Extending the rubric to other opposition groupings, in order to achieve a shared platform, was advocated by the Gdańsk delegate Aleksander Hall. But the majority view of the Citizens' Committee was that the movement's unity was paramount: 66 members supported the motion, 19 were in favour of a wider 'coalition for democracy' and 13 abstained.

The US Embassy was following developments closely and had excellent connections within both the Party and the opposition. Its Ambassador John R. Davis Jr, who had been the US *chargé d'affaires* to Poland since 1983, had no doubt about the outcome. He reported to Washington: 'The elections in June are, for the regime, an unpredictable danger and, for the opposition, an enormous opportunity. The authorities, having staked a great deal, are hoping for some modest success. But they are more likely to meet total defeat and great embarrassment.' He thought the Party's much-vaunted 'superior organisation' would have little impact in persuading the electorate, since Solidarity had changed the rules of the game. For their part, he saw signs that 'Solidarity's inexperience and disorganisation are being overcome'.[24]

Citizens' Committees sprang up like mushrooms all over the country. Solidarity and Rural Solidarity activists were joined by many others, including the KIK, which often provided the chairmen. The names of candidates they proposed were sent to a central steering group, which included Geremek, Kuroń and Andrzej Wielowieyski. Where there were local disputes, Warsaw was asked to mediate. Geremek estimated that 10–15 per cent of candidates were centrally selected.[25]

The list was ready for approval by 23 April and was accepted with near-unanimity. However, a number of prominent figures declined to stand. Mazowiecki and Hall did so on grounds of inclusivity, noting that their proposal to extend the rubric had been rejected. Key activists from the Solidarity period and its later underground existence, including Bujak and Frasyniuk, continued to give priority to their trade union activity.

[24] NSA, 'Election '89: The Year of Solidarity' (19 April 1989), pp. 1–2.
[25] Geremek, *Rok 1989*, pp. 156–7.

Wałęsa himself did not stand, fearful of a general humiliation in the poll. But both his name and that of Solidarity itself performed a vital symbolic function during the election campaign. Each of the 262 candidates was photographed shaking hands with Wałęsa, with the familiar *Solidarność* logo in the background. A massive publicity campaign plastered this poster – together with the names of the local opposition candidate – across the towns and villages.

Vital support for Solidarity came from the Church. This disappointed Party officials who had expected it to remain neutral, as during the Round Table. Ciosek fulminated to its representatives that 'The Church has gone over to the opposition, abandoned its neutrality, taken sides. We were relying on the Church to be a neutral moral strength, a corrective for both sides.'[26] Despite none-too-subtle threats, the Church held firm.

An Episcopal Communiqué (2 May) called on Catholics to take part in the elections: 'The opportunity should be used by believers as an important step on the road to subjectivity (*upodmiotowienia*) and ending the monopoly of a "single leader".'[27] A secret Party document outlined the range of Church activity in favour of the opposition:

> Public information from the pulpit about dates and places of meetings organised by Solidarity and encouragement to attend; providing premises and open spaces for Solidarity activists; allowing Church buildings to display propaganda materials of the opposition; using Church services to distribute vouchers for the electoral fund of the opposition; agitation in favour of opposition candidates; instructing on the method and technique of voting.[28]

This last service helped to counteract Solidarity's fear that ordinary electors – faced with complex and multiple lists of candidates – would panic and simply drop the bundle untouched into the urns provided. In the case of the 'national list' of thirty-five prominent officials, the anxiety was that electors would simply drop the list unmarked into the urn. This was the officially favoured method of 'voting without crossing out' which had characterised all elections since 1947. Instead, Solidarity voters were provided with a 'crib sheet' containing the names of its candidates, recommending that other candidates should be crossed off.[29] They sometimes stated 'A good communist is a communist crossed out.'

There was now an explosion of unofficial information. Solidarity's weekly (*Tygodnik Solidarność*) reappeared. *Gazeta Wyborcza* was launched, largely by staff transferring from the underground *Tygodnik*

[26] Perzkowski (ed.), *Tajne dokumenty Biura Politycznego i Sekretariatu KC*, pp. 376–7 (31 May 1989).
[27] A. Dudek and R. Gryz, *Komuniści i Kościół* (Warsaw, 2005), p. 438.
[28] AAN 237/2142/72 (20 May 1989). [29] See Garton Ash, *We the People*, pp. 26–8.

Mazowsze. The print-run was 500,000. Its second issue carried an article by the editor-in-chief, Adam Michnik, entitled 'A Spectre is Haunting Europe':

> The Round Table was an act of consent to transforming the policy of police monologue to one of political dialogue; it was also an act of practical denouncement of the whole philosophy and practice of martial law which had allowed people to speak only from the underground, prison or dock. Such reorientation, which aroused great resistance within the power camp, was not easy since it was preceded by years of a propaganda campaign slandering Solidarity people. We had been offered capitulation, exit or re-socialisation in prison. We had been assured that political dialogue with Wałęsa and Solidarity would never be held.

Now was the chance to replace the totalitarian system with parliamentary democracy and sovereignty: 'However, we reject revolution and violence, aware that it is easy to replace one dictatorship with another. We believe that changes taking place in other countries, in particular the Soviet Union, are our natural ally. These changes have been opening up new prospects for Poland.'[30] It is interesting to note how this analysis differed from Western Sovietology. While they considered that the Soviet-type system had evolved from its totalitarian stage into new stages such as 'bureaucratic pluralism', Michnik took the activist's view that politics was either monopolistic or it was not.

A feature of the election campaign was access to television time for opposition parties, although its actual allocation (23 per cent on television, 32 per cent on radio) was abrogated by the authorities using many other programmes for electoral purposes. Given such control of the mass media, as well as the vast personnel at their disposal, the 'ruling coalition' approached the election with confidence. An important analysis by Antoni Dudek catalogues their misconceptions.[31]

The starting-point was the naive belief that the Round Table formulation of 'non-confrontational elections' would enable the Party to prevail under a different guise. This new-formula 'Party–government coalition' would be a similar fig-leaf to earlier electioneering bodies: the Front of National Unity or the Patriotic Movement for National Rebirth. Second, as we have seen, it was expected that the process of 'normalising Church–state relations', enshrined by decrees passed in mid-May, would suffice to neutralise the Church. Thirdly, the Party made a crucial blunder in its mode of selecting candidates. In an attempt to breathe life into the demoralised rank-and-file, the Politburo called for multiple

[30] *Gazeta Wyborcza* 9 May 1989.
[31] A. Dudek, 'Decydujące miesiące. Polska, kwiecień-sierpień 1989' in Machcewicz (ed.), *Polska 1986–1989*, vol. I, pp. 125–30.

candidates. An internal memo of 6 May reported 'vehement, spontaneous putting forward of candidates'. The outcome was a plethora of multiple candidacies, including many who had not been selected or had been de-selected by the centre. At the final ballot, there were on average 4.4 Party candidates for each Sejm seat.[32] This confusion put further strains on the 'Ruling Coalition', whose junior partners felt increasingly excluded. As Dudek notes, this decomposition of the ruling coalition, even prior to the election, made the formation of a post-communist government afterwards much easier.

A final miscalculation was one the opposition did not make. The Solidarity slate was simple – vote for the candidate of Solidarity and Wałęsa. The Party side attempted to promote celebrities from the world media or popular culture. They included a well-known TV presenter, an astronaut, a famous cardiologist and the Director of the Wrocław Zoo. But since most of the electorate saw the vote as a verdict on the entire communist era, rather than a current popularity contest, the ploy failed.

The campaign was not free from violence. Solidarity activists were beaten up in several localities. Most important were street protests demanding registration of the Independent Union of Students (NKZ), the main troubles taking place in Kraków.[33] But registration was refused. Intended to undermine support for independent Solidarity, the refusal backfired. Protests extended to forty-two places of higher education. They do not seem to have influenced the election result, except perhaps by making protestors more determined to vote.

Solidarity leaders were fearful of the result. Geremek stated on 3 April: 'Losing the elections means the loss of the country's chances, of Solidarity's chances. No-one will forgive us if in the first partly free election east of the Elbe the communist Party achieves legitimation.'[34] Kuroń was cautious too. Talking at Warsaw University (10 April), he put committed oppositionists at no more than 20 per cent of the population: larger than those supporting the authorities, but this left a silent majority, somewhat hostile to the authorities, but not enthusiastic about the opposition, long portrayed in the media as dangerous extremists.[35]

The US Ambassador had no such inhibitions. He cabled to Washington, two days before the poll, 'Solidarity has emerged as a genuine and capable political party, has defined the elections in terms of a plebiscite. The stakes are enormous. Anxieties and uncertainty dominate expectations, while

[32] M. Castle, *Triggering Communism's Collapse. Perceptions and Power in Poland's Transition* (Lanham, 2003), p. 164.
[33] Dudek and Marszałkowski, *Walki uliczne*, pp. 392–5.
[34] Cited by Castle, *Triggering Communism's Collapse*, p. 156. [35] *Ibid.*

the absence of either objective data or precedent makes confident predictions impossible. As a matter of faith, however, we assume nearly-total Solidarity victory.' He added that the Party had confirmed itself to be merely 'a political bureaucracy of a decaying power elite wholly incapable of performing the classical functions of a political party in electoral competition'.[36]

In a landslide, Solidarity won 160 of the 161 Sejm seats they were allowed to contest. They also won 92 seats in the 100-strong Senate. A single Solidarity candidate was defeated – by a wealthy farmer from Silesia. By contrast, the National List of 35 Party and coalition notables, including known reformers, was rejected in all but 2 cases. The second of these, named Zieliński, probably survived crossing out by being at the bottom of the page. This came despite Wałęsa's televised statement on the eve of the poll that he would be voting for the whole National List, bar 1. We may conjecture that he meant Rakowski. Solidarity's support came from all parts of the country. Subsequent research showed that there was no significant variation according to population density or level of industrialisation.[37]

When the still-ruling Party pondered this disaster, there was some discussion of invalidating the result. One possible pretext would be to argue that failure of the National List abrogated the Round Table at which it had been agreed. Dudek suggests one motive for prudence was the voting pattern in the military and militia where the 'ruling coalition' candidates had also done badly.[38] The Party leaders' first priority was to calm down the uproar from its own rank-and-file. But to accept that their case in January against the Round Table was now proven would destroy the remaining credibility of the Jaruzelski team. A second problem came from the 'coalition' itself. 'Allied parties' were further disoriented that Solidarity had endorsed their candidates in some constituencies and might do so again in the second round.[39]

The better option was to put a brave face on the results. Officials stressed that a 62.2 per cent turn-out was lower than Solidarity – or opinion polls – had expected. As Jaruzelski put it, 'Solidarity had encouraged people to vote and 40% had not turned out.'[40] The Politburo declared on 6 June that 'none of the decisions taken at the Round Table

[36] NSA, 'Election '89: Solidarity's Coming Victory: Big or Too Big?' (2 June 1989), pp. 1–5.
[37] NSA, 'Election '89', p. 198.
[38] Dudek, 'Decydujące miesiące' in Machcewicz (ed.), *Polska 1986–1989*, vol. I, p. 131.
[39] Perzkowski (ed.), *Tajne dokumenty Biura Politycznego i Sekretariatu KC*, p. 391 (Secretariat, 5 June 1989).
[40] Interview with the *Independent* (London) 8 June 1989.

have lost their relevance or political *raison d'être*. The Party has been and remains a loyal partner, committed to its obligations. It expects the same from the opposition.'[41] Kiszczak saw Solidarity as 'shocked, not knowing how to behave'. Kwaśniewski stated that Solidarity was fearful of spontaneous demonstrations and was thus adopting a 'peaceful tone, without triumphalism'.[42] But this did not translate into a calm approach to the opposition on the part of the Party.

Czyrek called in Ambassador Davis to state that any revision of the 4 June result should be seen as a 'natural correction' (*poprawa*) of the result, not manipulation. He appealed for US understanding of the situation and the government's efforts to resolve the crisis. He also confirmed the long-standing invitation for President Bush to visit Poland.[43]

Geremek and Mazowiecki met Party leaders (Kiszczak, Ciosek and Gdula) on 6 June: 'The government side was categorical, sharp and aggressive. They asked bluntly whether we wanted to take power, if a change of thinking [from the Round Table] had taken place on our side.' When Geremek denied this, 'they stated that the authorities were under strong pressure to invalidate the elections'. As he noted, 'the whole democratic process was still extremely fragile and one puff could have blown it away'.[44]

During a tense nine-hour meeting of the post-Round-Table Conciliation Commission (8 June) a solution to the thirty-five vacant seats from the National List was hammered out. It was agreed that the Council of State would resolve the issue by changing the electoral list in time for the second round.[45] It transferred the thirty-five seats from the National List to regional ones, which were not contested. Many in Solidarity and beyond took the view that changing the electoral law between the two rounds was inconsistent with democratic politics. But it resolved the crisis.

The second-round turnout was only 25 per cent. Solidarity won its only missing Sejm seat and seven out of eight remaining Senate places. Solidarity also endorsed a number of independent-minded Party candidates, including Tadeusz Fiszbach, still respected from the 1980 Gdańsk negotiations. When these deputies took their seats, the cohesion of the 'ruling coalition' was further weakened.

41 AAN 237/V/488, pp. 235–41.
42 Perzkowski (ed.), *Tajne dokumenty Biura Politycznego i Sekretariatu KC*, pp. 391–2 (Secretariat, 5 June 1989).
43 NSA, 'Czyrek Appeals for Understanding on National List Issue' (6 June 1989).
44 Geremek, *Rok 1989*, p. 200. 45 Dubiński (ed.), *Okrągły Stół*, p. 511.

Soviet policy

The most complete analysis of Soviet policy towards Eastern Europe in 1989 is by Jacques Levesque. He sees the 'very close relationship' between Jaruzelski and Gorbachev as vital to the success of peaceful change. Thus, in the stormy January Plenum, seen above, Jaruzelski's team survived by threatening resignation. This worked because Moscow did not wish to intervene on behalf of an alternative team. According to Reykowski, the opponents of democratic change in Poland boasted of their support in Moscow. When this 'bluff' was called, by asking them to name their Soviet backers, the Party *beton* (concrete) refused to do so. In fact, they had none and knew that intervention had been ruled out by renunciation of the 'Brezhnev Doctrine'.[46]

But this is not to say that Moscow's policy towards Eastern Europe had been fully reformulated. Contrary to the subsequent assumption in both Warsaw and the West, it seems that no boundaries for change had yet been agreed by Soviet leaders. Hence, when asked by a Solidarity intermediary, Stemachowski (later Marshal of the Sejm), 'What are the limits to the changes the Soviets are willing to accept in Poland?', Jaruzelski replied: 'I don't know myself. Let's discover them together.'[47] He gave a similar answer to Geremek at the height of a later crisis in August 1989. Asked then about Moscow's attitude towards the Party leaving power, he replied, 'I don't know what the Russian reaction will be.' He explained that in recent years Poland had taken decisions in the foreknowledge of what the Russians might accept. They had reached such a boundary again. He did not know how long they could remain there without crossing it.[48]

At the start of 1989, Gorbachev told his Politburo about a recent meeting with 'elder statesmen' of the Trilateral Commission. They wanted to know how the Soviet Union intended to integrate with the world economy. Kissinger had asked directly: 'How are you going to react if Eastern Europe wants to join the European Commission?' Gorbachev took the point that Western leaders realised 'our friends [the East Europeans] are already knocking on the door'.

Gorbachev took the case of Hungary, where an opposition party, led by market-refomer Miklós Nemeth, had emerged, to illustrate the point. It was likely to consider the EC option very seriously. Hungary needed new technologies. Gorbachev's view was: 'If we do not deal with that, there will be a split and they will run away.' Every country should 'have its own

[46] Levesque, *The Enigma of 1989*, p. 112. [47] *Ibid.* p. 113.
[48] Geremek, *Rok 1989*, pp. 249–50.

face. We will continue to be friends because the socialist basis will be preserved in all of them.' The answer lay in *perestroika*: 'We should try to involve our friends, to get them interested in our economic reforms. Let Aleksandr Yakovlev, with scholars, look at it.' Yet the other socialist countries were sure to ask: 'What about the CPSU – what kind of leash will they use to keep our countries in line?' His answer was disarming: 'They simply do not know that if they pulled this leash harder it would break.'[49]

His public language was more diplomatic. Gorbachev told an audience in Kiev on 23 February that the USSR was restructuring relations with socialist countries to stress 'unconditional independence, full equality, strict non-interference in internal affairs and rectification of the deformations and mistakes linked with the earlier period of the history of socialism'.[50] The history of Hungary was again a test case. Relatives of Imre Nagy and other executed martyrs of 1956, many of them still communists, had long called for their remains to be revealed and ceremonially reburied. They set up a Committee for Historical Justice on 6 June 1988, declaring 'the time has come for Hungarian society to demand the full moral, political and legal rehabilitation of the victims [of 1956] both dead and living'. As a precursor to such a ceremony in Budapest, a memorial to Imre Nagy was unveiled at Père Lachaise cemetery in Paris on the thirtieth anniversary of his execution. Amongst the international speakers at this event was an official of the Italian Communist Party, West Europe's largest, who stated: 'When in 1956 we accepted the official Soviet explanation for the bloody suppression of the Hungarian uprising we were misled. We now know what happened was the legitimate revolt of a nation against foreign intervention and dictatorship.'[51]

On 26 January 1989, the Hungarian government finally announced its consent to the exhumation and reburial of the executed leaders. Two days later, the reform politician and new Politburo member Imre Poszgay announced on the radio that 1956 should no longer be considered a 'counter-revolution'. It had been a 'popular uprising against an oligarchic regime that was humiliating the nation'. Hungarian leaders waited nervously for Moscow's riposte. When none came, they rang up and were told there would not be any reaction. It transpired that several had been prepared, rehearsing the traditional Soviet view that mob violence against

49 'A. Chernyaev's Notes from the Politburo Session', CWIHP Virtual Archive (21 January 1989).

50 Cited by Kramer, 'Beyond the Brezhnev Doctrine', pp. 40–1.

51 B. Lomax, 'Hungary: From Kadarism to Democracy' in Spring (ed.), *The Impact of Gorbachev*, p. 162.

Hungarian communists in 1956 had been a 'counter-revolution'. But Gorbachev forbade their dispatch.[52]

In conversation with Károly Grosz shortly afterwards, Gorbachev stated: 'The evaluation of the 1956 events is entirely up to you. You have to stand on firm ground; you have to examine what really happened there and then.' But this was followed by the statement that Soviet leaders had recently conducted the same exercise for Czechoslovakia in 1968. This concluded that it had become a 'counter-revolution' at least in its later stages. Grosz suggested a similiar process of degeneration for Hungary 1956: student protests, then popular uprising and finally counter-revolution. Gorbachev concurred, but added that 'today we have to preclude repeated foreign intervention in the internal affairs of socialist countries'.[53] Gorbachev kept to this precept.

The Hungarian authorities met the opposition Democratic Forum on 20 January, starting a process which led to the converging of eight dissident groups at their own 'Opposition Round Table' on 20 March.[54] That led in turn to the opening of a National Round Table on 13 June. Hungary's internal politics – exacerbated by economic instability – was sharply polarised. It seems that Grosz, having failed to gain Soviet economic support for a rescue package, considered its domestic imposition under 'a state of economic, not military, emergency'. But he realised that external constraints made the option of force unusable: 'Not only would we have been condemned by Western countries and subjected to sanctions, but, above all, such an action would have collided head on with the whole thrust of Soviet foreign policy, and we could have been isolated in our own camp as well.'[55] This last point seems unlikely.

There were already rumblings from Romania about the course of events in Hungary and Poland 'and their dangerous effects on socialism as a whole'. In time-honoured fashion, Ceauşescu called for an urgent meeting of General-Secretaries to construct 'a unified and active appearance of the Socialist countries, especially against the "avalanche-like" Western campaign on human rights'.[56]

Polish–Soviet relations were discussed by Gorbachev and Jaruzelski in Moscow on 28 April. Jaruzelski informed Gorbachev about the position in Poland since the Round Table and the 'prospects for an understanding of different social and political forces' it had opened up. Gorbachev kept

[52] Levesque, *The Enigma of 1989*, pp. 129–30.
[53] 'Memorandum of Conversation' (Moscow, 23–24 March 1989), *CWIHP Bulletin* (12/13).
[54] A. Bozóki, 'The Hungarian Road to Systemic Change'.
[55] Levesque, *The Enigma of 1989*, pp. 132–3.
[56] NSA, 'Ambassador Plasche to H. Axen' (30 March 1989).

to generalities. Common to the variety of forms of renewal in the socialist countries was a core principle: 'democratisation, aspirations to create conditions for real participation of working people in running the economy and solving political questions'. More concretely, he noted that in the recent Soviet elections (26 March) people had voted resolutely for *perestroika*. He added that the commission examining the officially ignored issues – 'white, or blank spots' – in bi-lateral relations (formed in April 1987) was reaching conclusions. There would soon be a statement on the the immediate origins of the Second World War, the secret clause of the Nazi–Soviet Pact to partition Poland, and the subsequent occupation and Sovietisation of eastern Poland. A statement on the Katyń massacre of Polish soldiers by the Soviet secret police (NKVD) was finally forthcoming.[57]

The most dramatic re-evaluation of Soviet foreign policy concerned the two Germanys. Bases for a new policy had been sketched out in April 1989. This memo, by Vyacheslav Dashichev, was entitled 'The Concept of the "Common European Home" and the German Question'. Whilst no longer espousing German neutralisation, let alone reunification, it raised hard questions about the long-term viability of the DDR. The state was seen as falling further behind the Federal Republic in standards of living, leading to the likelihood of popular discontent spilling onto the streets. Since Moscow had ruled out crushing such protests by force (as in 1953), the only alternative was to push East Germany into radical reforms. He suggested that reforms would receive financial backing from West Germany. Pan-German rapprochement would undermine the case for a permanently militarised Europe. Thus the Cold War could be ended, at least on the continent.[58]

Gorbachev's triumphant June visit to Bonn, where he was received as a peace-maker, appeared to give credence to this prospect, at least in the longer run. Talking to Chancellor Kohl (12 June), Gorbachev noted that the West should not be concerned by 'the serious shift in the socialist countries'. Each should be left to go their own way. It would be fatal if anyone tried to destabilise the situation: 'it would disrupt the process of building trust between West and East and destroy everything that has been achieved so far. We want a rapprochement, not a return to confrontation.'[59]

Shevardnadze visited the East German leaders just after the Polish election. The Soviet Foreign Minister called for a 'profound analysis' of the 'very difficult position' in which the Polish Party now was.

[57] *CWIHP Bulletin* (12/13). [58] Levesque, *The Enigma of 1989*, pp. 144–6.
[59] NSA, 'Notes of A. Chernyaev', Bonn (12 June 1989).

Honecker replied bluntly: 'Poland lies between the DDR and USSR. Socialism cannot be lost in Poland.' There was a similar difference of approach to Hungary. While Shevardnadze saw 'unsettling developments', Honecker was apocalyptic: 'Probably unstoppable processes' reminded him of 1956 and the role of Imre Nagy.[60]

Soviet aspirations for a 'common European house' were set out in Gorbachev's speech to the Strasbourg parliament on 6 July. After reiterating that the European states belonged to different social systems, and giving no indication that the gains of socialism were reversible, he then removed what remained of the Brezhnev Doctrine: 'Social and political orders of certain countries changed in the past and may change again in future.' That was exclusively the choice of the countries concerned: 'Any attempts to limit the sovereignty of states – including friends and *allies*, or anyone else – are impermissible.'[61]

Gorbachev elaborated his new scheme for international relations at a Warsaw Pact summit immediately afterwards (7–8 July). The planned economies' imperative was to reverse the lag of technology, lack of growth and mounting hard-currency debts, all of which signified to the West the 'sunset of socialism'. Socialist foreign policy renewal had four main elements:

1. *Super-power disarmament*. There should be a Soviet–American agreement to cut strategic offensive weapons by 50 per cent, and strict adherence to the 1972 ABM Treaty. It was Warsaw Pact policy to seek the elimination of all chemical weapons.
2. *A pan-European home*. There needed to be unity of Europe from the Atlantic to the Urals, with equal dialogue and contacts across the continent. There should be no attempt to destabilise any socialist country or undermine the East–West confidence-building measures already agreed.
3. *Troop withdrawals in Europe*. The USSR was ready to coordinate with allies the size of Soviet redeployments from Eastern Europe. Withdrawals should take into consideration political, military and geographical factors. The US proposal for equal ceilings on super-power deployments in Europe should be considered in a broader context.
4. *A second 'Helsinki-type meeting'*. This should review all three 'baskets' from 1975. It was time to speed up the process of building security in Europe. There should be joint programmes with Western Europe on transport, environment, technology, nuclear power safety and other common issues.

[60] NSA, 'Honecker–Shevardnadze' (9 June 1989).
[61] Kramer, 'Beyond the Brezhnev Doctrine', p. 41 (italics added).

According to Gorbachev this was a new 'political philosophy of international relations'. It combined 'active struggle for transition towards a new international order and a reliable defence of our [own] countries'. There were mixed responses from his audience. Ceauşescu took the most negative view, cast doubt on the concept of a 'pan-European home' and ridiculed the notion of 'renewal'.[62] The Hungarian leader Nemeth found this performance disturbing. He saw Ceauşescu as 'mentally ill' and supported this view with a wealth of detail about his conduct at the conference.[63] Some observers consider that this was the meeting that formally revoked the 'Brezhnev Doctrine'. They point to the final declaration that future relations would be based on 'equality, independence and the right of each country to arrive at its own political position, strategy, and tactics without interference from an outside party'.[64]

Day Two of the summit considered the member countries one by one. Jaruzelski underlined 'the role of Russian *perestroika* and our support for it'. Turning to domestic politics, he noted that the recent elections, 'although not useful for the Party', provided the chance for a non-confrontational development of the Polish situation. Poland was fully aware of its international responsibilities.[65] Its new-style parliament would not change the country's foreign-policy orientation: 'Poland will remain a member of the Warsaw Pact and of the socialist community.'[66] Overall, the meeting exposed sharp divisions. Only the Russians and Hungarians were convinced by the new Polish road. The remaining four leaders, of the DDR, Czechoslovakia, Romania and Bulgaria, expressed degrees of concern.[67] The position to be taken by Soviet leaders towards further change was therefore pivotal.

During a two-hour 'negotiation' with Gorbachev at the end of July, the Hungarians had summarised the agenda for their next Party Congress. The goals were 'democratic socialism, self-government, parliamentary democracy and economic democracy'. In response, Gorbachev expressed both interest and understanding of such developments 'on the road to democratic socialism'. He did have reservations about the re-introduction of private property and foreign capital, but on bi-lateral relations he was more accommodating. Withdrawal of Soviet troops stationed in

62 'Memorandum from Mladenov to the Bulgarian Politburo' (12 July 1989), CWIHP Vitual Archive.
63 NSA, 'Conversation of Chancellor Kohl' (25 August 1989).
64 T. Blanton, 'When did the Cold War end?' *CWIHP Bulletin* (10).
65 AAN 237/V/490 'Notatki Informacyjne' (10 July 1989).
66 His draft speech is 'Projekt wystąpienia' (4 July 1989) in Perzkowski (ed.), *Tajne dokumenty Biura Politycznego i Sekretariatu KC*, pp. 429–31.
67 Levesque, *The Enigma of 1989*, pp. 119–21.

Hungary, agreed in March, would be made public. Gorbachev agreed to lift this embargo on condition that it was stated to be taking place 'in accordance with the European disarmament process and with the progress of the Vienna [troop reduction] talks'.[68]

'Your President, our Prime Minister'

Though the Round Table agreements had not said so explicitly, the common assumption was that Jaruzelski would become President. Given this, the Solidarity side concentrated on limiting the prerogatives of the new incumbent, particularly towards domestic politics. Then its attention turned towards the Premiership. A new formulation started to emerge: 'Your President, our Prime Minister'.

Its originator appears to have been Professor Rejkowski in conversation with Adam Michnik in the corridors of the new Sejm[69]. Michnik saw the point immediately and informed Wałęsa. They became its strong proponents. Michnik sought further clarification from General Kiszczak about the Party's post-election idea of a 'Grand Coalition'. If Jaruzelski became President, then Michnik suggested Geremek should become Prime Minister. He said this had Wałęsa's endorsement, though Geremek himself had not been approached yet.[70] But this was not a notion of power-sharing the Party was ready to accept.

Kiszczak told Archbishop Dąbrowski that only Jaruzelski could command authority over the Party. If he were not elected President, 'we will be threatened with further destabilisation and the whole process of political change will have to end'. The security services and military would not accept any other President. Dąbrowski replied that Wałęsa's advisers were realists and sought only an evolutionary change of system.[71] At a second meeting, Dąbrowski asked whether a 'palace coup' could be staged. Kiszczak replied that it was a real possibility. It would only need to remove Generals Jaruzelski and Siwicki (co-author of martial law). If Jaruzelski was not President, soon 'a dramatic situation would arise'. In order 'to stabilise power swiftly after the elections', he wanted the Church to prompt Solidarity to accept Jaruzelski as President.[72]

Czyrek then called in the American Deputy Head of Mission.[73] He expressed concern about 'rumours' that the USA was supporting

[68] 'Memorandum of Conversation', CWIHP Virtual Archive (1 July 1989).
[69] Skórzyński, *Ugoda*, p. 274.
[70] Perzkowski (ed.), *Tajne dokumenty Biura Politycznego i Sekretariatu KC*, p. 400 (Secretariat, 9 July 1989).
[71] Raina (ed.), *Rozmowy*, p. 450 (10 June 1989). [72] *Ibid.* p. 452 (13 June 1989).
[73] Ambassador Davis was attending America Day at the Poznań International Trade Fair.

manoeuvres to block the Jaruzelski Presidency. A 'war' had flared up on the issue and the US side was being 'dragged in'. Challenged to name the source of 'rumours', Czyrek referred vaguely to 'hearsay and word of mouth' and 'extremists amongst the opposition'. According to Czyrek, 'Poland's fate is at stake. The process underway could lead either to chaos or rigid dictatorship. If the latter fate is Poland's future, then both Czyrek and Geremek will be at the Swedish Embassy asking for asylum.' Everyone would lose. He asked the USA 'to exert influence on Solidarity to provide enough votes to ensure [Jaruzelski's] election'.[74] Ambassador Davis had been told by one of Jaruzelski's military aides that soundings amongst both the military and militia officers indicated they would 'feel personally threatened if Jaruzelski were not President and would move to overturn the Round Table and election results'.[75] The Cold War was clearly melting when the USA was being enlisted to head off a *coup* in Polish politics.

Ambassador Davis noted that Czyrek was being held personally responsible for both the Round Table (as chief negotiator) and the ensuing disaster at the polls. He was under pressure to salvage the election of Jaruzelski to the Presidency. Jaruzelski would need more than 'begrudging acceptance of a silent opposition' to stabilise Poland through a very unstable period. Davis' next cable to Washington summarised the views of Solidarity leaders. One was: 'if Jaruzelski is not elected President, there is a danger of civil war ending, in most scenarios, with a reluctant but brutal Soviet intervention'. They were therefore considering strategems such as feigned illness or being 'otherwise unable to attend', to avoid having to vote.

The original intention was to hold the vote on 5 July, but this now looked unfeasible. Jaruzelski and Rakowski were due at the Warsaw Pact summit. Their non-attendance might be interpreted as showing events in Poland were out of control. Jaruzelski asked for a postponement but Gorbachev declined on the grounds of 'tensions within the Pact between Romania and Hungary'. This evidently concerned the treatment of the Hungarian minority in Tranyslvania. Grosz stated later: 'Having received nuclear [*sic*] threats from Ceauşescu, I had troops along the Austrian border transferred to the border with Romania.'[76] The other diary difficulty was the imminent arrival of President George Bush in Poland. If he

[74] NSA, 'Politburo member warns that US has been "dragged into the war" over election of Jaruzelski as President' (16 June 1989), pp. 1–3.
[75] NSA, 'Politburo member warns', pp. 5–9.
[76] For the threat, see Levesque, *The Enigma of 1989*, p. 133 note 18.

were not President by then, Jaruzelski would receive him in his old capacity as Chairman of the Council of State.[77]

When the Citizen's Parliamentary Club first met (23 June), it was decided not to run a candidate for the Presidency. Referring to Jaruzelski, Wałęsa explained: 'I know that none of us, myself included, have talked to Mr Gorbachev or Mr Honecker, and we don't know what such talks are like: how pacts, blocs and so on function. But we will now have our own group in the Sejm and Senate, which will look into these taboo subjects, so we will learn about it.'[78] However, the candidacy was soon in trouble from another quarter.

Jaruzelski abruptly informed a dismayed Politburo (29 June) that he had decided not to stand. He explained bluntly that sufficient votes of the 'coalition partners' could not be relied upon. There was the further risk that an opposition candidate would come forward, with support from some coalition deputies, and fatally defeat the coalition candidate. He therefore proposed a President 'who will not meet such strong opposition'. Through the recent Round Table, this person had established his role as an effective mediator and shown he was able to stabilise the state.[79] On television the next day, Jaruzelski recommended 'a soldier, politician and patriot who has been close to me for many years – Comrade Czesław Kiszczak'.

This may have been a ploy to challenge his opponents. Kiszczak admitted to the Party Secretariat (3 July) that there were 'disquieting signals from certain responsible comrades' who were raising awkward questions. Young officers of the Interior Ministry were being asked whether they favoured a continuation of the Party, or thought new socialist parties could be created from its remnants. They were asked: 'is the Interior Ministry for the General [Jaruzelski] or against?'[80]

When he met Wałęsa (4 July), General Kiszczak declared that the decision to stand was either his or Jaruzelski's. The choice would be discussed by the Warsaw Pact's political advisory committee in three days' time. They needed also to know whom George Bush would back as President. The Solidarity leader declared his support for the General's Presidency and stated that the Citizens' Parliamentary Club would endorse him also. Encouraged, Kiszczak asked whom Wałęsa would like to see as Premier. He replied that 'if the coalition forms the

[77] NSA, 'How to Elect Jaruzelski without voting for him, and will he run?' (23 June 1989).
[78] *Gazeta Wyborcza* 24 June 1989. [79] AAN 237/V/489 (Politburo, 29 June 1989).
[80] Perzkowski (ed.), *Tajne dokumenty Biura Politycznego i Sekretariatu KC*, p. 422 (Secretariat, 3 July 1989).

government, Solidarity would support the economist Professor Baka. If it was the opposition, Professor Geremek would be Premier.'[81]

In a famous article, Michnik made public his solution to power-sharing: 'Your President, our Premier'.[82] He proposed an alliance of the democratic opposition and the reform-minded wing of the Party. The opposition would provide the Premier, and the Party would have the Presidency. This caused a storm within the opposition. Only Kuroń supported the idea unequivocally. Others thought it prudent to wait until a parliamentary majority appeared. Without it, a Solidarity Premier would be blamed for all ills. Mazowiecki asked whether Solidarity had a coherent programme for overcoming the economic crisis that would be acceptable to Polish society. Without one, they should not stand.[83]

But Gorbachev's advisers expressed equanimity. Vadim Zagladin, asked in Paris about a possible Solidarity government, replied: 'We will maintain relations with whatever government is elected in Poland. We are pleased by the course of the democratic process in that country and that the situation in Poland cannot [any longer] be called critical.'[84] Gorbachev himself spoke similarly at a private dinner with the French President: 'The Poles want to avoid the repetition of the 1980 events above all. That is why Jaruzelski's course of dialogue with Solidarity, Lech Wałęsa and all of Poland's political forces, is gaining wide support amongst the people.'[85]

Ambassador Davis' briefing before the Bush visit assured him of the warmest welcome. Poles were delighted that his visit was not part of a visit to Moscow, but was linked instead to Budapest and Paris: 'Landing in Warsaw, the President will find himself in the center of the world's most pro-American country. Poles have always shared our love of individual freedom, they respect and admire the success of our revolution and remember that Kościuszko and Puławski fought for General Washington and helped us to success.'

Now Poland was embarked on another revolution, 'this time a peaceful and careful one. It was inspired by the moral and political leadership of Lech Wałęsa and John Paul II', who took 'a very active and personal interest in developments in his mother-land'; 'His influence here is beyond description.' The third key player was the 'enigmatic, unpopular, but indispensable General Jaruzelski'. He suggested the Presidential address to the Sejm be focussed on 'soaring themes': democracy,

[81] Raina (ed.), *Rozmowy*, pp. 461–3. [82] *Gazeta Wyborcza* 3 July 1989.
[83] *Tygodnik Solidarność* 14 July 1989. [84] Skórzyński, *Ugoda*, p. 278.
[85] NSA, 'Gorbachev and Mitterand' (5 July 1989).

human rights and the reintegration of Europe. Whilst Poles recognised that deterrence had kept the peace in Europe for forty-four years, it had distorted the national economy towards military spending and more dependence on the USSR: 'They are eager to move beyond confrontation and competition to broad cooperation and reintegration.'[86]

The visit itself was a low-key success for both sides. Bush kept his prior promise not to inflame the situation. Congressional funding was to be sought for economic enterprise – though much less than the Poles hoped – and there would be debt relief. He met the main political actors and found Jaruzelski convincing.[87] This was construed by Jaruzelski as endorsement.

A few days later, Jaruzelski made known his change of mind. As in every career move, he had to be pushed upwards reluctantly. He always did his duty. Having, as Tina Rosenberg remarks, 'vigorously objected his way to almost absolute power',[88] he now felt obliged to run for the Presidency. He gave three main reasons:

- A clear stand by the body of generals in the Ministry of Defence and Council for National Defence
- Some unambiguous external reactions: talks at the Warsaw Pact summit and some expressions used by visiting President Bush
- The position of the majority of colleagues at the Party Plenum

Such pressures had forced him to revise his opinion. One unfortunate obstacle was Solidarity's statements in favour of Kiszczak.

Through the Stelmachowski channel, Jaruzelski asked whether their stance might be reversed. He was willing to meet Solidarity half-way by visiting its Parliamentary Club 'by invitation'. Kiszczak would come too. No journalists would be present at their meeting.[89] It proved a stormy session, at which his responsibility for martial law was questioned by Solidarity deputies.[90]

When the National Assembly met to elect a President on 19 July, Jaruzelski was the only candidate. There were 270 votes in favour, 233 against, with 34 abstentions. In addition to a small number of cross-votes, 7 deputies, organised by Andrzej Wielowieyski, spoiled their ballots. Jaruzelski thus achieved the required 50 per cent majority of the 537 votes by a single vote. It was a humiliation and did not provide the anchor that Jaruzelski's backers craved.

[86] NSA, 'Poland looks to President Bush' (27 June 1989).
[87] M. Beschloss and S. Talbott, *At the Highest Levels* (Boston, 1993), pp. 85–9.
[88] Rosenberg, *The Haunted Land*, pp. 200–1. [89] *CWIHP Bulletin* (12/13).
[90] Archiwum Senatu OKP (17 July 1989), pp. 117–253.

Mazowiecki

At his meeting with Solidarity deputies, Jaruzelski had proposed a 'grand coalition' in which the opposition would hold the Ministries of Industry, Health, Environment and Construction, and also provide a Deputy-Premier. When he returned to the project after the Presidential election, Wałęsa declined, replying that 'the only sensible solution would be to transfer government to those forces which have the support of the majority of society'.[91] He also mentioned that a 'shadow government' was being formed at his request, by Geremek. The brief period of Wałęsa's accommodation with those in power was clearly ending.

It was abruptly terminated four days later, when the Party replaced Jaruzelski as First Secretary with the politician most distrusted by Solidarity: Rakowski. The move also increased opposition within the Central Committee. Though Rakowski had been the only candidate, forty-one members voted against him. Moreover, the Party's Parliamentary Club meeting on 1 August, to decide on Party-line voting, was boycotted by fifty Party deputies. The pattern was repeated amongst the junior 'coalition' partners, who met separately and stormily, throwing down challenges to their own leaders.

Political decomposition was accelerated by Jaruzelski's next decision: to nominate Kiszczak as Premier. Two generals would thus head the state. Jaruzelski probably counted on Wałęsa's consent, but was soon disillusioned. Wałęsa stated: 'I supported General Kiszczak for President, but I refuse to support him for Prime Minister',[92] and asked for this view to be conveyed to the Citizens' Parliamentary Club.

When the Citizens' Club met, later that day, to consider the options, Ziółkowski noted 'a great acceleration of the political process': 'The fact that Jaruzelski is President is good, and stabilising. But we see a huge weakness in the authorities, a rebellion within the Party. There is a contest within the coalition, the ZSL is bending over backwards and SD must be in a similar position.'[93]

There was no consensus between Solidarity and these junior 'coalition' partners. When the latters' representatives arrived they were denied the floor. Nor was there support for the view of Mazowiecki – who attended as an adviser – that the best position would be neutrality. He thought the Club should abstain rather than oppose the Kiszczak candidacy: 'If we are not reaching for power ourselves, we should allow the other side to do so.'[94]

[91] *Rok 1989*, p. 230. [92] Archiwum Senatu, OKP (1 August 1989), p. 1.
[93] Archiwum Senatu, OKP, pp. 6–7. [94] Archiwum Senatu, OKP, p. 4.

Senator Wielowieyski reminded deputies that 'Big Brother has other methods of conducting politics. Removing the Party from power would be a big blow to Gorbachev. The outcome – a fatal poisoning of our life, the impossibility of achieving anything.' Michnik, listening with increasing impatience to their 'academic discussion', commented that, if opposition deputies debated much longer, they would have to leave parliament, 'called off by people from the queues'.[95] Neither Kiszczak nor anyone else could change that. The system had received its death sentence: 'Do you know what will remain of the Party – the shit will be left ... We have an international constellation, an historic moment, at which something can be caught. We should not use the argument that we have no programme. Who in the world does? What, for example, would Russia or Yugoslavia do?'[96]

The Polish drama took a new turn on 7 August when Wałęsa announced that the Party was the main source of the country's crisis. He therefore proposed the formation of a new government 'without communists'. It would include the junior 'coalition partners'. Ignoring the Solidarity Parliamentary Club, he authorised two Gdańsk activists, the Kaczyński twins, both now Senators (and fifteen years later President and Prime Minister), to conduct the necessary negotiations.[97] This unilateral act caused a storm. The Polish Party called it an abrogation of the Round Table. This view was echoed in the hitherto-cautious Soviet press. *Izvestiya* and *Pravda* now accused Wałęsa of seeking a '*coup d'état*'.[98]

Kiszczak called in John Davis for what he said was his first private conversation with a NATO ambassador. In a lengthy exposé, he outlined an alarming position at home and abroad: '100 senior officials of the Interior Ministry and Ministry of Defence have been meeting and have expressed deep fears concerning future developments.' Political strikes in Poland could lead to a repetition of the 'Chinese events'. The massacre of Tiananmen Square took place on 4 July, the day of the Polish election. Abroad, 'Gorbachev is in trouble' and *perestroika* 'is increasingly perceived as a failure'. Complaints were being heard that under Stalin the country won the Second World War and became a respected super-power. Now they had *glasnost*' and nothing to eat.[99]

Wałęsa's statement marked the end of Kiszczak's efforts to form a government. He announced his resignation as Premier on 14 August. The initiative now lay with Wałęsa. In an astute move to reassure

[95] The Party announced swingeing price rises on 1 August.
[96] Archiwum Senatu, OKP (1 August 1989), p. 9. [97] *Rok 1989*, p. 240.
[98] Levesque, *The Enigma of 1989*, p. 124.
[99] NSA, 'Conversation with General Kiszczak' (11 August 1989).

Moscow, he reversed his position. Communists should now join the next government, and indeed hold the Ministries of Defence and the Interior. Wałęsa stated: 'Poland will fulfill its Warsaw Pact obligations.' He also decided to restore contacts with the Citizens' Parliamentary Club and announced he would attend its session at the Sejm the next day.

When this met, the Premiership was still unfilled. Wałęsa made clear he was not interested in the position for himself, but did not name an alternative. He simply stated, 'A new coalition has been set up. It will select the most suitable candidate for Prime Minister. For the time being, we don't say who that will be.' During questions, he conceded, 'I have my three candidates.'[100] These statements were disingenuous since he had just met Mazowiecki at the Hotel Europejski, and urged him to take the position. Mazowiecki had asked for twenty-four hours to consider.

Stark alternatives were presented by Rakowski to an emergency Plenum. Faced with this new context, the Party could:

1. Proclaim a state of emergency. In his view this would be a political defeat.
2. Withdraw into political opposition. This would make it harder to gain broad public support. They were still analysing the motives of the 38 per cent of electoral abstainers, with a view to winning them over.
3. Enter a Solidarity government. This would be on conditions agreed in writing. The Party would hold ministries beyond the 'geopolitical' ones.

A further concern was that former Party officials might be brought before a state tribunal. They would ask Mazowiecki for guarantees against 'persecuting communists' and warned that they would respond vigorously to any such attempts.[101] The unresolved question of communist responsibility for previous wrong-doings became a burning issue in the post-communist period.

Wałęsa met leaders of the junior 'coalition partners' on 17 August. They favoured Mazowiecki rather than his two other candidates, Geremek and Kuroń. It seems that Church leaders shared this preference, though the Vatican remained silent in public. At noon, former political prisoner Wałęsa told his gaoler Jaruzelski whom to make Prime Minister.

Rakowski tried one last card. In a forty-minute telephone conversation with Gorbachev (22 August), he declared that, whatever happened, Poland would not withdraw from the Warsaw Pact. But in domestic politics the Party was not in a position to impose its demands on Solidarity.

[100] Citizens' Parliamentary Club (16 August 1989, 11.30 p.m.), *CWIHP Bulletin* (12/13).
[101] *Polska 1986–1989: koniec systemu*, vol. III, pp. 314–15.

In response to this implied call for assistance, Gorbachev responded that the Polish Party 'had at its disposal all the instruments of power by which it had to enforce its authority'.[102] Rakowski wished to visit Moscow for immediate consultations. Gorbachev replied this would be inopportune because it would be widely seen as Soviet opposition to change in Poland, or at least as outside interference.[103] He thought that a coalition government would be the best way out of a complicated and difficult situation.[104] Such caution in part reflected Gorbachev's own domestic difficulties. There had been extensive miners' strikes since July.[105] He certainly did not need his own position threatened by further troubles in Eastern Europe.

Mazowiecki addressed the Sejm on 24 August. Afterwards, a total of 378 deputies voted for him, 4 against and 41 abstained. Thus, within seven weeks of the first partially free post-war election, Poland obtained the world's first post-communist Prime Minister. Communism fell in five more countries within the next four months.

Neighbours

There had always been East European anxieties about 'contamination' or transmission of the 'Polish disease'. Czechoslovak and East German leaders had often been vociferous about the Polish virus. There was now a new complainant: Ceauşescu.

Ambassadors of the Warsaw Pact countries were summoned to the Romanian Foreign Ministry on the night of 19–20 August to receive his *démarche* concerning Poland. They were told that long-term adverse developments had culminated in General Kiszczak's resignation as Prime Minister. He had handed over the task of forming a government to 'a leader of Solidarity, editor-in-chief of the *Solidarity* magazine'. Taken with Wałęsa's recent proposal to form a government without communists, this confirmed that the Polish Party had abandoned its leading role. That could not remain an internal matter. Allowing Solidarity to form a government 'opens the way to liquidating the achievements of socialism in Poland, is in direct contradiction to the scientific principles of revolutionary socialism and serves the interests of the most reactionary imperialist circles'. It was a concern of socialist states

[102] NSA, 'Notes on Conversation of Chancellor Kohl with Minister President Nemeth' (25 August 1989).
[103] Levesque, *The Enigma of 1989*, p. 125. [104] Rakowski, *Jak to się stało*, pp. 243–5.
[105] See V. Haynes and O. Semyonova, *Syndicalisme et liberté en Union Soviétique* (Paris, 1979).

worldwide to prevent power in Poland 'slipping from the hands of workers and peasants into reactionary hands'.

Ceauşescu's solution was to set aside the Polish elections 'in favour of the interests of the nation and the working class'. He took the bizarre case of Panama, where elections had been annulled after it was ascertained that American interference had influenced the result. This proved what 'a small nation can do when it wants to defend its independence and not accept the *diktat* of the USA'.[106] He added an appeal to Honecker to help 'delay the course aimed at removing socialism in Poland'.[107]

In a dignified reply (21 August), the Polish Politburo stated that 'the composition of the Polish government and the way it is formed are matters for the Polish people alone'. There was a basic international norm of non-interference in the internal matters of other states. They pointed out that Romanian leaders always staunchly upheld this principle in respect of their own country. It was also the reason given for their refusal to take part in the invasion of Czechoslovakia in 1968. By contrast, Poland's continued membership of the Warsaw Pact had never been in doubt. The stabilisation of Poland would strengthen the country's external position and thereby 'enhance our contribution to European security and to the increasing significance of the Warsaw Pact in international affairs'.[108]

Honecker's initial response (25 August) was non-committal. He said the DDR leadership shared Romania's great concern over developments in Poland, and were fully supporting the Polish Party in its 'complicated struggle'. During September 1989 they would jointly commemorate the start of the Second World War. This mutual event would 'decidedly rebuff revanchist attacks on the inviolability of all states in Europe'.[109] Later he objected that the proposed crisis summit would be counterproductive. Solidarity and other opposition circles were bound to claim it proved that the Polish Party was 'a force not in the interests of the state'. He was convinced that the Polish Party remained an influential force: 'The CPSU maintains constant contact with its leadership.'[110]

Such optimism seems surprising. It was maintained in public as late as December 1989, when Gorbachev invited Rakowski to a Warsaw Pact summit in Moscow. He still treated him as head of a political force capable of renovating communism in Poland.[111] In private though,

106 *Gazeta Wyborcza* 29 September 1989.
107 NSA, 'Cable from Ambassador Plasche to Berlin' (20 August 1989).
108 *Gazeta Wyborcza* 29 September 1989.
109 NSA, 'SED CC Internal memorandum' (25 August 1989).
110 NSA, 'Response of the DDR' (29 August 1989).
111 Levesque, *The Enigma of 1989*, pp. 126–7.

Soviet leaders acknowledged that communism had lost in Poland and Hungary. Polish comrades had failed to use the opportunities which had opened up in the early 1980s. And Kádár, at the end of his life, had regretted not acting in time. The lesson seemed clear: change now before it is too late.[112]

The Soviet side had favoured the post-Kádár reform programme. The Hungarian reform Congress (6–10 October) was seen as a by-product of *perestroika*. Its chances of success, which observers both East and West rated quite highly, gave Hungary particular importance as a laboratory for mooted changes in the Soviet Union itself.[113] Gorbachev thought the Hungarian renewal would hasten the Soviets' own. Instead, the Congress marked the end of Hungarian communism. A Hungarian Socialist Party was formed and Károly Grosz was forced out. He commented in retirement that 'It is not the collapse of the East European regimes that led to the collapse of the USSR, but the opposite. It is because, in essence, the Soviet regime had already collapsed that the East European regimes fell.'[114] But this had not happened yet. Was it possible to draw a line under the Polish and Hungarian cases and leave the transformation at that? The test case was now East Germany.

Gorbachev flew to East Germany (6 October), to celebrate its fortieth anniversary. He went with many reservations and was determined to say nothing to suppport Honecker.[115] But something had to be said about the East German refugees streaming to the West through the newly opened Hungarian–Austrian border. This mass exodus had started with the removal of barbed-wire along the border in May 1989. Over the summer, many East Germans, particularly young people, travelled to Hungary in the hope of crossing through Austria to the Federal Republic. They besieged West German embassies in Budapest and Prague demanding exit visas. In response, the SED leadership closed the border with Czechoslovakia (3 October) and prepared a show of strength against popular protests. But the Western media talked about German reunification and rumours that during Gorbachev's visit people would storm the Wall.

Gorbachev was indeed welcomed as a liberator by huge crowds in East Berlin. Jacques Levesque notes the symbolism implicit in his speech: 'the drawing together of East and West, through which *all the walls* of hostility, alienation and distrust between Europeans will fall'.[116] Instead of a show

112 NSA, 'Gorbachev-SED' (Berlin, 7 October 1989).
113 'Memorandum of Conversation', CWIHP Virtual Archive (1 July 1989).
114 Levesque, *The Enigma of 1989*, p. 137.
115 NSA, 'Notes of Anatoly Chernyaev' (5 October 1989).
116 Levesque, *The Enigma of 1989*, p. 155.

of strength, the authorities dissolved in the face of mass peaceful protests.[117] Gorbachev gave unmistakable advice to the 78-year-old Honecker (in power since 1971): 'One must not miss the time for change. A dialogue with society is necessary. There is no other way for a leading Party to act.'[118] The hint was ignored and Honecker was removed on 17 October. Gorbachev hoped the new leadership would 'direct events in the DDR towards the establishment of new relations between the two German states by introducing major domestic reforms'.[119]

The new leader Egon Krenz had a difficult meeting with Gorbachev in Moscow (1 November). He stated that the SED Politburo had just held its first session on the economy. All had been shocked to find how poor the country was. The external balance of payments deficit at the end of 1989 would run to $12.1 billion. Gorbachev was astonished by these figures. Krenz then asked Gorbachev 'to explain more clearly what role the USSR ascribed to the BRD and DDR in the all-European house'. He added that, unlike the other socialist states, the DDR was in some sense a Soviet creation: 'the child of the Soviet Union, and one has to acknowledge paternity with regard to one's children'.[120]

Gorbachev replied that talks with Western leaders had convinced him 'they all viewed the question of German unity as extremely explosive in the present situation'. None wanted existing alliances to dissolve. They favoured Poland and Hungary remaining within the Warsaw Pact. The consensus was that the balance of power in Europe should not be disturbed since nobody knew what repercussions this would have. If a 'tendency of rapprochement in Europe' were to continue for several decades, this might eventually be seen in a different light. But this was not a problem of actual policy today.[121] History, however, did not wait.

In an extraordinary show of 'people power', social protests took over the streets of East Berlin and other East German cities. Thousands of others voted with their feet: 130,000 East Germans emigrated in November alone. On 9 November, East German leaders formally renounced the Party's leading role and agreed to free elections. They also published a draft law on foreign travel, but only for the minority of citizens holding passports. This did not act as the intended safety valve. Instead, as vast crowds approached the Berlin Wall that night, the border guards raised the barriers, allowing East Germans to pass through. The pattern was

[117] In the week starting 30 October, 1.4 million East Germans marched in 210 demonstrations.

[118] *CWIHP Bulletin* (12/13).

[119] Cited by Levesque, *The Enigma of 1989*, p. 156 note 37.

[120] *CWIHP Bulletin* (12/13).

[121] *Ibid.*

repeated along the German–German border.[122] Scenes of jubilation appeared live on prime-time US television.

Gorbachev awoke to find the Wall had fallen. In conversation with Shevardnadze, he agreed that 'the events were the result of a mass movement that could not be held back by any government'. This meant keeping political control of the Soviet armed forces, whose leadership were immediately discussing ways in which to restore the *status quo ante*. The 350,000 Soviet soldiers in the DDR had to be confined to barracks and told that the fall of the Wall could not be reversed by military intervention. Beyond this, the options were limited. The Soviet Politburo decided to make a virtue of necessity. Telling their East German counterpart to avoid bloodshed, they informed the press that Krenz' decision on 'border and travel regulations' had been a 'correct, clever and wise decision'. The same line was taken with Western leaders.

Chancellor Kohl was on a state visit to Poland when the Wall fell. He was accompanied by eighty businessmen keen for openings to the East. During talks in Warsaw (9 November), Wałęsa expressed the anxiety that events in the DDR were moving too fast. For Poland, they came at the wrong time since 'the Federal Republic would be bound to redirect its attention to the DDR as a top priority, inevitably pushing Polish reforms into the background'. Wałęsa told the Chancellor that, if it were up to him to decide, he would 'announce that a complete opening of the border is being prepared, explain a political programme and introduce a clever and unambiguous solution'. Kohl's view was that Krenz' programme was far too late: 'Had Honecker implemented this two years earlier, it would perhaps have worked.'[123]

Gorbachev's message to Kohl (10 November) called for a calm response. There would be no repetition of the Soviet intervention of June 1953. But there also needed to be restraint on the Western side to avoid 'destabilisation of the situation not only in the centre of Europe but also beyond'. Similiar verbal messages were transmitted to Mitterand, Thatcher and George Bush.

President Bush was happy to concur. He explained later: 'I did not want to overplay the hand of the USA, I did not want at that critical moment for us to gloat, to stick my thumb in Mr Gorbachev's eyes, which would have been the worst thing you could possibly do. So, restraint was called for.'[124] Secretary of State James Baker sent Moscow a message that the USA, while welcoming the changes in East and Central Europe, was

[122] H.-H. Hertle, 'The Fall of the Wall', *Ibid.*
[123] NSA, 'Conversation between Chancellor Kohl and Lech Wałęsa' (9 November 1989).
[124] Bush interview with Hertle, *CWIHP Bulletin* (12/13).

not hoping for instability there, nor seeking to gain advantages at Soviet expense.

It was a decisive moment: East German society had spoken.[125] Politicians could only react. One of Gorbachev's closest advisers, and greatest admirers, noted:

> The main thing is the DDR, the Berlin Wall. For it has not only to do with 'socialism' but with a shift in the world balance of forces. This is the end of Yalta, of the Stalinist legacy and the 'defeat of Hitlerite Germany'. This is what Gorbachev has done. And he has indeed turned out to be a great leader. He has sensed the pace of history and helped history to find a natural channel.[126]

Chernyaev was present when Gorbachev met Kohl (28 October). He felt they were entering a new world. He made no claim for the originality of Gorbachev's 'new thinking', and saw it simply as acting according to common sense. But its provenance was truly remarkable. Gorbachev,

> who came out of Soviet Marxism–Leninism, Soviet society conditioned from top to bottom by Stalinism, began to carry out these ideas with all earnestness and sincerity when he became head of state. No wonder that the world is stunned and full of admiration. And our public still cannot appreciate that he has already transferred all of them from one state to another.[127]

The fall of the Wall is remembered as the symbolic end of the Cold War, soon followed by the end of the division of Germany and of Europe. On 28 November, Chancellor Kohl unveiled to the Bundestag his ten-point plan for German reunification. No date was set and several intermediary steps were envisaged. Even so, Soviet leaders responded with outrage to this 'ultimatum'. Yet there was no scope within the 'new thinking' to gainsay its conclusions. After all, Gorbachev was as committed as any, and probably more than most, to the 'common European home'. Yet he intended a more gradual movement towards reunification, during which the West, and the Federal Republic of Germany above all, would fund Eastern economic renewal and jointly evolve a new security framework for Europe.

US policy towards Eastern Europe in 1989 had two main phases. During the first six months of his Presidency, George Bush sought to act as a 'responsible catalyst'.[128] This meant cautious encouragement for political change, whilst not openly advocating any policy that could be

125 M. Fulbrook, *The People's State: East German Society from Hitler to the Holocaust* (New Haven: Yale University Press, 2004).
126 NSA, 'Notes of Anatoly Chernyaev' (10 November 1989).
127 NSA, 'Excerpt from Anatoly Chernyaev's Diary' (28 October 1989).
128 G. Bush and B. Scowcroft, *A World Transformed* (New York, 1988), p. 117.

construed as 'roll-back'. Such restraint led critics in Washington to accuse the White House of passivity. Yet, rather than change towards a more strident approach, the new Administration sought to calm East Europe down. As we saw over Poland in the summer months, the USA went to some lengths to support the forces of law and order, personified by General Jaruzelski, rather than the 'hotheads' amongst Solidarity. The 'responsible catalyst' became a 'reluctant inhibitor'.[129]

The 'Solidarity factor' impinged in two further respects. First, its ethos of non-violence found great resonance in Czechoslovakia. This is hardly surprising, given that country's pioneering reisistance to the Warsaw Pact invasion of 1968.[130] On 21 August, the twenty-first anniversary of the invasion, nearly 10,000 people, mostly students, took to the streets, chanting 'Long Live Dubček' and 'Long Live Poland and Hungary'. On 19 November twelve opposition groups created Civic Forum on Havel's initiative in Prague. One of its first acts was to call on Gorbachev and Bush to condemn the 1968 intervention. Daily demonstrations in Prague grew to gigantic proportions – as many as 750,000 protestors on 21 November. The Party leadership, bewildered and paralysed, sought Gorbachev's support to stay in government. It was withheld. Communism in Czechoslovakia ended peacefully.

The only exception to the pattern – soon followed in Bulgaria – was Romania, which underwent both a popular insurrection and an internal *coup d'état*. The Timişoara rebellion (16 December) took up the chant of East Berlin crowds: 'We Are the People.' The massacre of demonstrators did not contain opposition across the country.[131] The Ceauşescus fled from Bucharest on 22 December. They were captured and summarily executed.

The second impact of Solidarity was in the USSR itself. Its five-man delegation went to the Ukraine (8–10 September) to receive a heroes' welcome from the founding Congress of the Rukh movement. At a ceremony in central Kyiv, they unveiled a Polish flag emblazoned with the *Solidarność* logo. The huge crowd greeted this with cries of 'Long live independent Ukraine', 'Solidarność' and 'Long Live Poland'.[132] Some weeks later Michnik told a journalists' conference in Moscow that 'today the problem lies not so much in *glasnost'* between East and West but in *glasnost'* in East–East relations. I believe it is in our common interest to

129 NSA, Virtual Archive, G. Domber, 'Solidarity's Coming Victory', p. 2.

130 See A. Roberts in Windsor and Roberts, *Czechoslovakia 1968*, pp. 97–143.

131 J. Eyal, 'Why Romania Could not avoid Bloodshed' in G. Prins (ed.), *Spring in Winter: The 1989 Revolutions* (Manchester, 1990).

132 M. Kramer, 'The Collapse of East European Communism and the Repercussions within the Soviet Union' (Part 1), *Journal of Cold War Studies* Fall 2003 (5.4).

speak about Polish–Russian, Polish–Ukrainian or Polish–Latvian issues in a loud and honest manner, as two free and equal partners.'[133]

When Soviet leaders insisted that they could not accept the Lithuanian declaration of independence (March 1990), Solidarity again intervened. Wałęsa's Open Letter to Gorbachev stated that the country should have the same 'right of choice' as exercised by Eastern Europe in 1989: 'To violate Lithuania's sovereignty is a step directed against the process of constructing a new democratic order in Europe. The history of the USSR and Eastern Europe proves that force and threats used with a view to solving political problems are invalid. They have been condemned by the international community on numerous occasions.'[134]

[133] *Rzeczpospolita* 20 October 1989. [134] *Gazeta Wyborcza* 28 March 1990.

Bibliography

ARCHIVAL SOURCES

Archiwum Akt Nowych (Warsaw) (AAN) (Archive of Modern Acts), Polish United Workers' Party

Secretariat: 237/V

Organisational Department 237/VII

Department of Propaganda and Agitation 237/VIII

Department of Science 237/XVI

Department of Education 237/XVII

Department of Culture 237/XVIII

Archiwum Senatu (Warsaw) (Senate Archive)

Archiwum Solidarności (Warsaw) (Solidarity Archive)

Gosudarstvennyi Arkhiv Rossiiskoi Federatsii (Moscow) (State Archive of the Russian Federation)

National Security Archive (Washington) (NSA)

LBJ Presidential Library (Austin, Texas)

PUBLISHED PRIMARY SOURCES

PARTY/STATE DOCUMENTS

Andrzejewski, J. (A. Paczkowski) (ed.), *Gomułka i inni. Dokumenty z archiwum KC 1948–1982* (Warsaw, 1986, and London, 1987)

Documents on Polish–Soviet Relations, 1939–1945 (London, 1961)

Domański, P. (ed.), *Tajne dokumenty Biura Politycznego. Grudzień 1970* (London, 1991)

Dubiński, K. (ed.), *Okrągły Stół* (Warsaw, 1999)

Dudek, A., Kochański, A. and Persak, K. (eds.), *Centrum Władzy. Protokoły posiedzeń kierownictwa PZPR. Wybór z lat 1949–1970* (Warsaw, 2000)

Eisler, J. (ed.), *Grudzień 1970 w dokumentach MSW* (Warsaw, 2000)

Eisler, J. and Trepczyński, S. (eds.), *Grudzień 70 wewnątrz 'Białego Domu'* (Warsaw, 1991)

Friszke, A. and Zaremba, M., *Wizyta Jana Pawła II w Polsce 1979. Dokumenty KC PZPR i MSW* (Warsaw, 2005)

Garlicki, A. and Paczkowski, A. (eds.), *Zaciskanie pętli. Tajne dokumenty dotyczące Czechosłowacji 1968r* (Warsaw, 1995)

Jarosz, D. and Wolska, T., *Komisja specjalna do walki z nadużyciami i szkodnictwem gospodarczym 1945–1956. Wybór dokumentów* (Warsaw, 1995)
Kwiek, J. (ed.), *Marzec 1968 w Krakowie w dokumentach* (Kraków, 2005)
Nałęcz, D. (compiler), *Główny urząd kontroli prasy, 1945–1956* (Warsaw, 1994)
Paczkowski, A., *Aparat bezpieczeństwa w latach 1945–1956*, 2 vols. (Warsaw, 1994)
Paczkowski, A. (ed.), *Tajne dokumenty Biura Politycznego. PRL-ZSRR 1956–1970* (London, 1998)
Perzkowski, S. [A. Paczkowski] (ed.), *Tajne dokumenty Biura Politycznego i Sekretariatu KC. Ostatni rok władzy 1988–1989* (London, 1994)
Polońsky, A. and Drukier, B., *The Beginnings of Communist Rule in Poland* (London, 1980)
Volokitina, T. V. (chief ed.), *Sovetskii faktor v vostochnoi Evrope, 1944–1953*, 2 vols. (Moscow, 1999, 2002)
Włodek, Z. (ed.), *Tajne dokumenty Biura Politycznego. PZPR a 'Solidarność' 1980–1981* (London, 1992)
Zaremba, M. (ed.), *Marzec 1968. Trzydzieści lat później*, vol. XI: *Aneks źródłowy* (Warsaw, 1998)
Zinner, Paul E. (ed.), *National Communism and Popular Revolt in Eastern Europe. A Selection of Documents* (New York, 1956)

SOLIDARITY/OPPOSITION DOCUMENTS

Chmiel, B. and Kaczyńska, E., *Postulaty. Materiały do dziejów wystąpień pracowniczych w latach 1970–71 i 1980 (Gdańsk i Szczecin)* (Warsaw, 1988)
Postulaty 1970–71 i 1980 (Warsaw, 1998)
Drzycimski, A. and Skutnik, T., *Zapis Rokowań Gdańskich. Sierpień 1980* (Paris, 1986). Reissued as *Gdańsk Sierpień '80. Rozmowy* (Gdańsk, 1990)
Gdańsk-Sierpień 1980. Rozmowy Komisji Rządowej z Międzyzakładowym Komitetem Strajkowym w Stoczni Gdańskiej (23–31 sierpnia 1980 r.) (Warsaw, 1981)
Hemmerling, Z. and Nadolski, M. (eds.), *Opozycja antykomunistyczna w Polsce, 1944–1956. Wybór dokumentów* (Warsaw, 1990)
Opozycja wobec rządów komunistycznych w Polsce, 1956–1976. Wybór dokumentów (Warsaw, 1991)
Opozycja demokratyczna w Polsce 1976–1980. Wybór dokumentów (Warsaw, 1994)
Polski Sierpień 1980. Reedycja Almanachu Gdańskich Środowisk Twórczych 'Punkt' nr 12/80 (New York, 1981)
Sołtysiak, G. and Stępiań, J. (eds.), *Marzec '68. Między tragedią a podłością* (Warsaw, 1998)
Szejnert, M. and Zalewski, T., *Szczecin: Grudzień-Sierpień-Grudzień* (Warsaw, 1984)
Wacowska, E., *Rewolta Szczecińska i jej znaczenie* (Paris, 1971)

Krajowa Komisja Porozumiewawcza NSZZ Solidarność

Posiedzenie w dniach 2-3 IX 1981 r. (Warsaw, 1988)
Posiedzenie w dniach 9–10 kwietnia 1981 r. (Warsaw, 1996)
Posiedzenie w dniu 4 czerwca 1981 r. (Warsaw, 1995)
Posiedzenie w dniu 23 kwietnia 1981 r., ed. T. Tabako and M. Włostowski, (Warsaw, 1995)
Rozmowy z rządem PRL. Negocjacje pomiędzy NSZZ 'Solidarność' a rządem w dniach 15–18 października 1981 (Warsaw, 1998)

Komisja Krajowa NSZZ Solidarność

Posiedzenie 3–4 listopada 1981 r. (Warsaw, 1999)
Posiedzenie w dniach 11–12 grudnia 1981 r. (Warsaw, 1986)
Posiedzenie w dniach 22–23 X 1981 r. (Warsaw, 1987)
Komitet Obywatelski przy Lechu Wałęsie 1988–1989; Krajowa Komisja Wykonawcza NSZZ Solidarność 1989, ed. J. M. Owsiński (Warsaw, 1999)

CATHOLIC CHURCH DOCUMENTS

A Freedom Within. The Prison Notes of Stefan, Cardinal Wyszyński (London, 1985)
Jan Pawel II, Prymas i Episkopat Polski o stanie wojennym (London, 1982)
Laborem Exercens (London, 1981)
Raina, P. (ed.), *Stefan Kardynał Wyszyński*, vol. II (London, 1986)
Kościół w PRL. Kościół katolicki a państwo w świetle dokumentów 1945–1989, 3 vols. (Poznań, 1994–6)
Rozmowy z władzami PRL. Arcybiskup Dąbrowski w służbie Kościoła i narodu, vol. I: *1970–1981* (Warsaw, 1995); vol. II: *1982–1989*, (Warsaw, 1995)
Droga do 'Okrągłego Stołu'. Zakulisowe rozmowy przygotowawcze (Warsaw, 1999)
Tajne dokumenty Państwo-Kościół 1960–1980 (London, 1996)
Tajne dokumenty Państwo-Kościół 1980–1989 (London, 1993)
Troska o internowanych. Interwencje abpa Dąbrowskiego u gen. Kiszczaka 1982–1989 (Warsaw, 1999)
Wizyty Apostolskie Jana Pawla II w Polsce. Rozmowy przygotowawcze Watykan-PRL-Episkopat (Warsaw, 1997)

INTERNATIONAL CONFERENCES

Fifth World Congress of Central and East European Studies, Warsaw, 1995 A. Kemp-Welch (ed. and trans.), *Stalinism in Poland, 1944–1956. Selected Papers* (New York, 1999). Contributors: Sergei Kudryashov, Andrzej Paczkowski, Dariusz Jarosz, Krystyna Kersten, Paweł Machcewicz, János Tischler and Andrzej Friszke

Poland 1980–82: Internal Crisis, International Dimensions, Jachranka, 1997 *Wejdą nie Wejdą. Polska 1980–1982: wewnętrzny kryzys, międzynarodowe uwarunkowania. Konferencja w Jachrance, listopad 1997* (London, 1999)

Poland 1986–89: End of the System, Międzynorodowe, 1999 *Polska 1986–1989: koniec systemu. Materiały międzynarodowej konferencji: Miedzieszyn,*

21–23 października 1999, vol. I: *Referaty* (ed. Paweł Machcewicz); vol. II: *Dyskusja* (ed. Andrzej Paczkowski); vol. III: *Dokumenty* (ed. Antoni Dudek, Andrzej Friszke) (Warsaw, 2002)

Communism's Negotiated Collapse: The Polish Round Table Talks of 1989. Ten Years Later, University of Michigan, 1999 www.umich.eduiinet/PolishRoundTable

1956 and Its Legacy. Hungary and Poland, University of Glasgow, 1956 *Special Issue: Europe-Asia Studies* December 2006 (58.8)

SELECTED BIBLIOGRAPHY

Aczel, T. (ed.), *Ten Years After. A Commemoration of the Tenth Anniversary of the Hungarian Revolution* (London, 1966)

Alliluyeva, S., *Twenty Letters to a Friend* (New York, 1967)

Andrews, N., *Poland 1980–81. Solidarity versus the Party* (Washington, 1985)

Anusz, A., *Niezależne Zrzeszenie Studentów w latach 1980–1989* (Warsaw, 1991)

Ascherson, N., *The Polish August* (London, 1981)

Ash, T. Garton, *The Polish Revolution* (London, 1983)

We the People (Harmondsworth, 1999)

Aslund, A., *Gorbachev's Struggle for Economic Reform. The Soviet Reform Process, 1985–1988* (London, 1989)

Baka, W., *U źródeł wielkiej transformacji* (Warsaw, 1999)

Barber, J., *Soviet Historians in Crisis, 1928–1932* (London, 1981)

Bender, P., *East Europe in Search of Security* (London, 1972)

Bereś, W. and Skoczylas, J., *Generał Kiszczak mówi . . . prawie wszystko* (Warsaw, 1991)

Beschloss, M. and Talbott, S., *At the Highest Levels* (Boston, 1993)

Biagio, A. di, 'The Establishment of the Cominform' in G. Procacci (ed.), *The Cominform, Minutes of Three Conferences 1947/1948/1949* (Milan, 1994)

Bialer, S., *The Soviet Paradox: External Expansion, Internal Decline* (London, 1986)

Bierut, B., *0 upowszechnienie kultury* (Warsaw, 1948)

Biologia i Polityka. Materiały narad biologów (Warsaw, 1956)

Black, J. and Strong, J. (eds.), *Sisyphus and Poland. Reflections on Martial Law* (Winnipeg, 1986)

Blejwas, A., *Realism in Polish Politics: Warsaw Positivism and National Survival in Nineteenth Century Poland* (New Haven, Conn., 1984)

Blobaum, B. (ed.), *Anti-Semitism and its Opponents in Modern Poland* (Ithaca, 2005)

Błażyński, Z., *Mówi Józef Światło. Za kulisami bezpieki i partii 1940–1955*, 3rd edn (London, 1986)

Bobrowski, C., *Jugosławia socjalistyczna* (Warsaw, 1957)

Bozo, F., *La Politique étrangère de la France depuis 1945* (Paris, 1997)

Brandt, W., *People and Politics. The Years 1960–1975* (London, 1978)

Bratkowski, S. (ed.), *Październik 1956. Pierwszy wyłom w systemie* (Warsaw, 1996)

Bruce-Lockhart, R., *My Europe* (London, 1952)

Brus, W. and Jakubowicz, S., *System jugosłowiański z bliska* (Warsaw, 1957)

Brzeziński, Z., *Power and Principle. Memoirs of the National Security Adviser 1977–1981* (London, 1983)
Brzostek, B., *Robotnicy Warszawy. Konflikty codzienne (1950–1954)* (Warsaw, 2002)
Burlatskii, F., *Vozhdi i sovetniki. O Khrushcheve, Andropove i ne tol'ko o nikh* (Moscow, 1990)
Bush, G. and Scowcroft, B., *A World Transformed* (New York, 1988)
Butler, S. (ed.), *My Dear Mr. Stalin. The Complete Correspondence of Franklin D. Roosevelt and Joseph V. Stalin* (New Haven, 2005)
Castle, M., *Triggering Communism's Collapse. Perceptions and Power in Poland's Transition* (Lanham, 2003)
Charmley, J., *Churchill's Grand Alliance. The Anglo-American Special Relationship, 1940–1957* (London, 1995)
Chojecki, M. (ed.), *Gdańsk-Sierpień 1980* (Warsaw, 1981)
Churchill, W., *The Second World War*, vol VI (London, 1954)
Clarke, R. A. (ed.), *Poland: The Economy in the 1980s* (London, 1989)
Coleman, P., *The Liberal Conspiracy: The Congress for Cultural Freedom and the Struggle for the Mind of Post-war Europe* (New York, 1989)
Conference on Security and Cooperation in Europe. Final Act (London, 1975)
Cynkin, T., *Soviet and American Signalling in the Polish Crisis* (Basingstoke, 1988)
Czarna księga cenzury PRL, 2 vols. (London, 1977–8)
Danilov, V. P., *Rural Russia Under the New Regime* (Bloomington, Ind., 1988)
Deutscher, I., *Heretics and Renegades* (London, 1955)
Djilas, M., *Conversations with Stalin* (London, 1963)
Dobbs, M., *Down with Big Brother: The Fall of the Soviet Empire* (New York, 1997)
Dobieszewski, A., *Kolektywizacja wsi w Polsce, 1948–1956* (Warsaw, 1993)
Drozdowski, M. (ed.), *1956. Polska emigracja a Kraj* (Warsaw, 1998)
Dubiński, K., *Rewolta radomska. Czerwiec 76* (Warsaw, 1991)
Dudek, A., *Państwo i Kościół w Polsce, 1945–1970* (Kraków, 1995)
Dudek, A. (ed.), *Stan wojenny w Polsce, 1981–1983* (Warsaw, 2003)
Dudek, A. and Gryz, R., *Komuniści i Kościół* (Warsaw, 2005)
Dudek, A. and Madej, K., *Świadectwa stanu wojennego* (Warsaw, 2001)
Dudek, A. and Marszałkowski, T., *Walki uliczne w PRL, 1956–1989* (Krakow, 1999)
Dyskusja o prawie wartości ciąg dalszy (Warsaw, 1957)
Eisler, J., *Marzec 1968* (Warsaw, 1991)
List 34 (Warsaw, 1993)
Grudzień 1970. Geneza, przebieg, konsekwencje (Warsaw, 2000)
Eisler, J. (ed.), *Czerwiec 1976 w materiałach archiwalnych* (Warsaw, 2001)
Ekonomiści dyskutują o prawie wartości (Warsaw, 1956)
Elster, J. (ed.), *The Roundtable Talks and the Breakdown of Communism* (Chicago, 1996)
Eyal, J., 'Why Romania Could not Avoid Bloodshed' in G. Prins (ed.), *Spring in Winter: The 1989 Revolutions* (Manchester, 1990)
Fijalkowska, B., *Polityka i twórcy (1948–1959)* (Warsaw, 1985)
Fink, C., Gassert, P. and Junker, D. (eds.) *1968: The World Transformed* (Cambridge, 1998)
Fitzpatrick, S., (ed.), *Cultural Revolution in Russia, 1928–1931* (Bloomington, Ind., 1978)

Friszke, A., *Opozycja polityczna w PRL, 1945–1980* (London, 1994)
Oaza na Kopernika. Klub Inteligencji Katolickiej 1956–1989 (Warsaw, 1997)
Koło Posłów 'Znak' w Sejmie PRL, 1957–1976 (Warsaw, 2002)
Friszke, A. (ed.), *Solidarność Podziemna, 1981–1989* (Warsaw, 2006)
Fulbrook, M., *The People's State: East German Society from Hitler to the Holocaust* (New Haven, 2004)
Garlicki, A., *Karuzela. Rzecz o Okrągłym Stole* (Warsaw, 2003)
Rycerze Okrągłego Stołu (Warsaw, 2004)
Gates, R., *From the Shadows: The Ultimate Insider's Story of Five Presidents and How They Won the Cold War* (New York, 1996)
Gati, C., *Failed Illusions. Moscow, Washington, Budapest and the 1956 Hungarian Revolt* (Stanford and Washington, 2006)
Gebert, K., *Mebel* (London, 1990)
Gerrits, A., *The Failure of Authoritarian Change. Reform, Opposition and Geo-Politics in Poland in the 1980s* (Dartmouth, 1990)
Giełżyński, W., *Gdańsk, maj 88* (Warsaw, 1988). Reprinted in *Robotnicy '88* (London, 1989)
Giełżyński, W. and Stefański, L., *Gdańsk-Sierpień 80* (Warsaw, 1981)
Głuchowski, L. and Nalepa, E., *The Soviet–Polish Confrontation of October 1956: The Situation in the Polish Internal Security Corps*, CWIHP Working Paper No. 17 (Washington, 1997)
Gomori, G., *Polish and Hungarian Poetry. 1945–1956* (Oxford, 1964)
Gorbachev, M. S., *Perestroika: New Thinking for our Country and the World* (London, 1988)
Memoirs (London, 1996)
Gorlizki, Y. and Khlevniuk, O., *Cold Peace. Stalin and the Soviet Ruling Circle, 1945–1953* (Oxford, 2004)
Goudoever, Albert P. van, *The Limits of De-Stalinization in the Soviet Union: Political Rehabilitations in the Soviet Union since Stalin* (London, 1986)
Gross, Jan T., *Polish Society Under German Occupation: The Generalgouvernement, 1939–1944* (Princeton, N.J., 1979)
Revolution from Abroad. The Soviet Conquest of Poland's Western Ukraine and Western Byelorussia (Princeton, N.J., 1988)
Haig, A., *Caveat. Realism, Reagan and Foreign Policy* (London, 1984)
Halecki, O., *The Limits and Divisions of European History* (London, 1950)
Hanhimaki, J., *The Flawed Architect. Henry Kissinger and American Foreign Policy* (Oxford, 2004)
Haynes, V. and Semyonova, O., *Syndicalisme et liberté en Union Soviétique* (Paris, 1979)
Hill, R., *Soviet Politics, Political Science and Reform* (Oxford, 1980)
Hirszowicz, M., *The Bureaucratic Leviathan: A Study in the Sociology of Communism* (Oxford, 1980)
Holzer, J., *Solidarność 1980–1981. Geneza i Historia* (Warsaw, 1983)
Jakubowicz, S., *Bitwa o samorząd 1980–1981* (London, 1988)
James, R. R. (ed.), *Churchill Speaks. Winston S. Churchill in Peace and War. Collected Speeches, 1897–1963* (New York, 1981)
Jankowiak, S. and Rogulska A. (eds.), *Poznański Czerwiec 1956* (Warsaw, 2002)

Jarosz, D., *Polityka władz komunistycznych w Polsce w latach 1948–1956 a chłopi* (Warsaw, 1998)

Jarosz, D. and Pasztor, M., *W krzywym zwierciadle. Polityka władz komunistycznych w Polsce w świetle plotek i pogłosek z lat 1949–1956* (Warsaw, 1995)

Jaruzelski, W., *Stan wojenny . . . dlaczego* (Warsaw, 1992)

Jedlicki, W., *Klub Krzywego Koła* (Paris, 1963)

Jegliński, P. (ed.), *Grudzień 1970* (Paris, 1986)

Język Propagandy (Warsaw, 1979)

Jones, J. M., *The Fifteen Weeks (February 21 – June 5, 1947)* (New York, 1955)

Jordan, Z., *Philosophy and Ideology: The Development of Philosophy and Marxism–Leninism in Poland since the Second World War* (Dordrecht, 1963)

Jovanov, N., *Radnički Strajkowi u SFRJ, 1958–1969* (Belgrade, 1979)

Judt, T., *Postwar: A History of Europe Since 1945* (London, 2005)

Kądzielski, J., *0 problemie modelu rewolucji kulturalnej* (Łódź, 1964)

Kaliski, B., *'Antysocjalistyczne zbiorowisko?' I Krajowy Zjazd Delegatów NSZZ Solidarność* (Warsaw, 2003)

Kamiński, L., *Strajki robotnicze w Polsce w latach 1945–1948* (Wrocław, 1999)

Kania, S., *Zatrzymać konfrontacje* (Warsaw, 1991)

Karpiński, J., *Nie być w myśleniu posłusznym (Ossowscy, sociologia, filozofia)* (London, 1989)

Karski, Jan, *The Great Powers and Poland, 1919–1945: From Versailles to Yalta* (London, 1985)

Kaser, M. (ed.), *The Economic History of Eastern Europe 1919–1975*, vol. III: *Institutional Change within a Planned Economy* (Oxford, 1986)

Kemp-Welch, A., *The Birth of Solidarity* (London, 1983); 2nd edn (London, 1991)

Stalin and the Literary Intelligentsia, 1928–1939 (London, 1991)

Kenney, P., *Rebuilding Poland. Workers and Communists, 1945–1950* (Ithaca, 1997)

A Carnival of Revolution: Central Europe 1989 (Oxford, 2002)

Kersten, K., *The Establishment of Communist Rule in Poland, 1943–1948* (Berkeley, 1991)

Polacy, Żydzi, Komunizm: Anatomia półprawd, 1939–1968 (Warsaw, 1992)

Kersten, K. (ed.), *Polska 1956 – próba nowego spojrzenia*, Studia i materiały 3 (Warsaw, 1997)

Khrushchev Remembers (Boston, 1970)

Khrushchev Remembers: The Last Testament (Boston, 1974)

Kis, J., *Politics in Hungary: For a Democratic Alternative* (New Jersey, 1989)

Kissinger, H., *Nuclear Weapons and Foreign Policy* (New York, 1957)

White House Years (Boston, 1979)

Kollontai, A., *The Workers' Opposition*, Solidarity Pamphlet 7 (London, 1968)

Kołakowski, L., *Marxism and Beyond. On Historical Understanding and Individual Responsibility* (London, 1971)

Kopka, B., *Obozy pracy w Polsce 1944–1950* (Warsaw, 2002)

Korzoń, A., *Polsko-radzieckie kontakty kulturalne w latach 1944–1980* (Wrocław, 1982)

Kowalik, T., *Spory o ustrój społeczno-gospodarczy Polski 1944–48* (Warsaw, 1980)

Kowalski, L., *Generał ze skazą. Biografia wojskowa gen. armii Wojciecha Jaruzelskiego* (Warsaw, 2001)
Kozlov, V., *Massovye besporiadki v SSSR pri Khrushcheve i Brezhneve (1953–nachalo 1980-kh gg.)* (Novosibirsk, 1999)
Kramer, M., *Soviet Deliberations during the Polish Crisis, 1980–1981*, Cold War International History Project Special Working Paper No. 1 (Washington, April 1999)
Książka dla Jacka. W sześćdziesiątą rocznicę urodzin Jacka Kuronia (Warsaw, 1975)
Kubik, J., *The Power of Symbols Against the Symbols of Power* (University Park, Pa., 1994)
Kula, H., *Dwa Oblicza Grudnia '70. Oficjalne-Rzeczywiste* (Gdańsk, 2000)
Kula, M., Osęka, P. and Zaremba, M. *Paryż, Londyn i Waszyngton patrzą na Październik 1956 r. w Polsce* (Warsaw, 1992)
Kula, M., Oseka, P. and Zaremba, M. (eds.), *Marzec 1968. Trzydzieści lat później*, vol. I (Warsaw, 1998)
Kupiecki, R., *'Natchnienie milionów': kult Józefa Stalina w Polsce, 1945–1956* (Warsaw, 1993)
Kurczewski, J., *The Resurrection of Rights in Poland* (Oxford, 1993)
Kuroń, J., *Wiara i Wina. Do i od komunizmu* (Warsaw, 1990)
Gwiezdny czas (London, 1991)
Kuroń, J. and Modzelewski, K., *List otwarty do partii* (Paris, 1966)
Kwaśniewska, W., *Grudzień '70 w Gdyni* (Warsaw, 1986)
Laba, R., *The Roots of Solidarity. A Political Sociology of Poland's Working-class Democratization* (Princeton, 1991)
Lane, M. (ed.), *Poland: The State of the Republic. Reports by the Experience and the Future Discussion Group (DiP) Warsaw* (London, 1981)
Laqueur, W., *A Continent Astray. Europe, 1970–1978* (Oxford, 1979)
Leffler, M., *A Preponderance of Power: National Security, the Truman Administration and the Cold War* (Stanford, 1992)
Levesque, J., *The Enigma of 1989: The USSR and the Liberation of Eastern Europe* (Berkeley, 1997)
Lewin, M., *Lenin's Last Struggle* (London, 1975)
The Gorbachev Phenomenon. A Historical Interpretation (Calif., 1988)
Lipski, J. J., *KOR. A History of the Workers' Defense Committee in Poland, 1976–1981* (Berkeley, 1985)
Listy Pasterskie Episkopatu Polski (Paris, 1975)
Litvan, G. (ed.), *The Hungarian Revolution of 1956. Reform, Revolt and Repression 1953–1963* (London, 1996)
Lomax, B., *Hungary 1956* (London, 1976)
'Hungary: From Kadarism to Democracy' in D. Spring (ed.), *The Impact of Gorbachev. The First Phase, 1985–90* (London, 1991)
Lucas, S., *Freedom's War. The US Crusade Against the Soviet Union, 1945–1956* (Manchester, 1999)
Lundestad, G., *The American Non-Policy Towards Eastern Europe. Universalism in an Area Not of Essential Interest to the United States* (Oslo, 1978)
Łabędź, K., *Spory wokół zagadnień programowych w publikacjach opozycji politycznej w Polsce 1981–89* (Krakow, 1997)

Łabędź, L. and Hayward, M. (eds.), *On Trial. The Case of Sinyavsky (Tertz) and Daniel (Arzhak)* (London, 1967)
Łopieńska, B. and Szymańska, E., *Stare numery* (Warsaw, 1990)
Łopiński, M., Moskit, M. and Wilk, M., *Konspira. Solidarity Underground.* (Berkeley, 1990)
MacEachin, D., *US Intelligence and the Confrontation in Poland, 1980–1981* (University Park, Pa., 2002)
MacFarlane, L., *The Right to Strike* (Harmonsdworth, 1981)
Machcewicz, P., *Polski Rok 1956* (Warsaw, 1993)
Kampania wyborcza i wybory do Sejmu 20 stycznia 1957 (Warsaw, 2000)
Machowski, E., *Poznański Czerwiec 1956. Pierwszy bunt społeczeństwa w PRL* (Poznań, 2001)
Maclean, I., Montefiore, A. and Winsch, P. (eds.), *The Political Responsibility of Intellectuals* (Cambridge, 1990)
Malia, M., *The Soviet Tragedy: A History of Socialism in Russia, 1917–1991* (New York, 1994)
Marcuse, H., *An Essay on Liberation* (Boston, 1969)
Five Lectures (London, 1970)
Maresca, J., *To Helsinki: The Conference on Security and Cooperation in Europe, 1973–1975* (Durham, N.C., 1985)
Maritain, J., *The Rights of Man and Natural Law* (New York, 1947)
Mark, E., *Revolution by Degrees. Stalin's National-Front Strategy for Europe, 1941–1947*, CWIHP Working Paper no. 31 (Washington, 2001)
Marshall, B., *Willy Brandt: A Political Biography* (London, 1997)
Matthews, J., *Majales: The Abortive Student Revolt in Czechoslovakia in 1956*, CWIHP Working Paper no. 25 (Washington, 1998)
May, E. (ed.), *American Cold War Strategy: Interpreting NSC 68* (Boston, 1993)
Mazewski, L. and Turek, M. (eds.), *'Solidarność' i opozycja antykomunistyczna w Gdańsku 1980–1989* (Gdańsk, 1995)
Mazowiecki, T., *Rozdroża i Wartości* (Warsaw, 1970)
McDermott, K. and Stibbe, M., *Revolution and Resistance in Eastern Europe. Challenges to Communist Rule* (Oxford, 2006)
Medvedev, R., *K sudu istorii. Genezis i posledstviya stalinizma* (New York, 1974)
Khrushchev (Oxford, 1982)
Mett, Ida, *La Commune de Cronstadt* (Paris, 1938)
Micewski, A., *Współrządzić czy nie kłamać? Pax i Znak w Polsce 1945–1976* (Paris, 1978)
Michnik, A., *Letters from Prison and Other Essays* (Berkeley, 1985)
Takie czasy . . . Rzecz o kompromisie (Warsaw, 1986)
Kościół-Lewica-Dialog (Paris, 1977); trans. Ost, *The Church and the Left* (Chicago, 1993)
Letters from Freedom. Post-Cold War Realities and Perspectives (Berkeley, 1998)
Michta, A., *Red Eagle. The Army in Polish Politics, 1944–1988* (Stanford, 1990)
Micunovic, V., *Moscow Diary* (London, 1980)
Mikołajczyk, S., *The Pattern of Soviet Domination* (London, 1948)
Miłosz, C., *The Captive Mind* (1953; reprinted London, 1985)
Mitrany, D., *Marx Against the Peasant. A Study in Social Dogmatism* (London, 1951)

Mitter, R. and Major, P. (eds.), *Across the Blocs: Cold War Cultural and Social History* (London, 2004)
Mizerski, W. (ed.), *Radomski Czerwiec 1976*, vol. I, 2nd edn (Lublin, 1991)
Mlynář, Z., *Notions of Political Pluralism in the Policy of the Communist Party of Czechoslovakia in 1968*, 'Experiences of the Prague Spring 1968', Research Project Working Paper no. 3 (Vienna, 1979)
Morgenthau, H., *Politics Among Nations* (Chicago, 1948)
Mrożek, S., *Słoń* (Warsaw, 1957)
Murashko, G. P. (chief ed.), *Vostochnaia Evropa v dokumentakh rossiiskikh arkhivov, 1944–1953*, vol. I (Moscow, 1997)
Myant, M., *Poland: A Crisis for Socialism* (London, 1982)
Naimark, N., *The Russians in Germany. A History of the Soviet Zone of Occupation, 1945–1949* (Cambridge, Mass., 1995)
Naimark, N. and Gibianskii, L. (eds.), *The Establishment of Communist Regimes in Eastern Europe, 1944–1949* (Westview, 1997)
Nalepa, E., *Pacyfikacja zbuntowanego miasta. Wojsko Polskie w czerwcu 1956 r. w Poznaniu* (Warsaw, 1992)
Oficerowie armii radzieckiej w wojsku Polskim 1943–1948 (Warsaw, 1995)
Navrátil, J. (ed.), *The Prague Spring, 1968* (Budapest, 1998)
Nove, A. (ed.), *The East European Economies in the 1970s* (London, 1982)
Osgood, R., *Limited War. The Challenge to American Strategy* (Chicago, 1957)
Ośinski, Z., *Grotowski and His Laboratory* (New York, 1986)
Ossowski, S., *Marksizm i twórczość naukowa w społeczeństwie socjalistycznym* (Warsaw, 1957)
Class Structure in the Social Consciousness (London, 1963)
O stanie wojennym. W sejmowej komisji odpowiedzialności konstytucyjnej (Warsaw, 1997)
Ostermann, C., *The United States, the East German Uprising of 1953, and the Limits of Rollback*, CWIHP Working Paper no. 11 (Washington, 1994)
Paczkowski, A., *Stanisław Mikołajczyk czyli klęska realisty (zarys biografii politycznej)* (Warsaw, 1991)
Pół wieku dziejów Polski, 1939–1989 (Warsaw, 1995)
Centrum władzy w Polsce, 1948–1970 (Warsaw, 2003)
Paczkowski, A. (ed.), *Polska 1986–1989: od kooptacji do negocjacji* (Warsaw, 1997)
Parrish, S., *New Evidence on the Soviet Rejection of the Marshall Plan, 1947*, CWIHP Working Paper no. 9 (Washington, 1994)
Persak, K., *Sprawa Henryka Hollanda* (Warsaw, 2006)
Persky, S., *At the Lenin Shipyard. Poland and the Rise of the Solidarity Trade Union* (Vancouver, 1981)
Piechuch, H., *Spotkania z Fejginem (zza kulis bezpieki)* (Warsaw, 1990)
Polonsky, A., *Politics in Independent Poland 1921–1939. The Crisis of Constitutional Government* (Oxford, 1972)
Portes, R., *The Polish Crisis: Western Economic Policy Options* (London, 1981)
Potel, J.-Y., *The Summer before the Frost. Solidarity in Poland* (London, 1982)
Ptasiński, J., *Pierwszy z trzech zwrotów, czyli rzecz o Gomułce* (Warsaw, 1983)
Public Papers of the Presidents: Harry S. Truman, 1945 (Washington, 1961); *1947* (Washington, 1963); *1952–53* (Washington, 1965)

Rachwald, A., *In Search of Poland. The Superpowers' Response to Solidarity, 1980–1989* (Hoover, Calif., 1990)
Raina, P., *Political Opposition in Poland, 1954–1977* (London, 1978)
Independent Social Movements in Poland (London, 1981)
Poland 1981. Towards Social Renewal (London, 1985)
Rainer, J. *The New Course in Hungary in 1953,* CWIHP Working Paper no. 38 (Washington, 2002)
Rakovski, M., *Towards an East European Marxism* (London, 1978)
Rakowski, M., *Tajny referat Rakowskiego. Uwagi dotyczące niektórych aspektów politycznej i gospodarczej sytuacji PRL w drugiej połowie lat osiemdziesiątych* (Warsaw, 1988)
Jak to się stało (Warsaw, 1991)
Remington, R. (ed.), *Winter in Prague. Documents on Czechoslovak Communism in Crisis* (Cambridge, Mass., 1969)
Richter, J., *Re-examining Soviet Policy Towards Germany During the Beria Interregnum,* CWIHP Working Paper no. 3 (Washington, 1992)
Roberts, A. (ed.), *Civilian Resistance as a National Defence. Non-violent Action Against Aggression* (London, 1969)
Robinson, T. and Shambaugh, D. (eds.), *Chinese Foreign Policy: Theory and Practice* (Oxford, 1994)
Rok 1989. Geremek opowiada. Jacek Żakowski pyta (Warsaw, 1990)
Rolicki, J. (ed.), *Edward Gierek: Przerwana dekada* (Warsaw, 1990)
Roosevelt and Churchill. Their Secret Wartime Correspondence (New York, 1975)
Rosenberg, T., *The Haunted Land. Facing Europe's Ghosts After Communism* (London, 1995)
Rostow, W. W., *The Division of Europe after World War II 1946* (Austin, 1981)
Roszkowski, W., *Historia Polski, 1914–1991,* 2nd enlarged edn (Warsaw, 1992)
Ruane, K., *The Polish Challenge* (London, 1981)
Ruble, B., *Soviet Trade Unions* (Cambridge, 1981)
Rykowski, Z. and Władyka, W., *Polska próba. Październik '56* (Kraków, 1989)
Rządowy raport o stanie gospodarki (Warsaw, 1981)
Sarotte, M., *Dealing with the Devil. East Germany, Détente, and Ostpolitik 1969–1973* (Chapel Hill, 2001)
Schapiro, L. (ed.), *Political Opposition in One-Party States* (Basingstoke, 1972)
Shakhnazarov, G., *Tsena svobody: Reformatsiya Gorbacheva glazami ego pomoshchnika* (Moscow, 1993)
Sharp, G., *Walka bez stosowania przemocy* (Gdańsk, 1984)
Sheshukov, S., *Neistovye revniteli. Iz istorii literaturnoi borby 20-kh godov* (Moscow, 1970)
Shulman, M., *Beyond the Cold War* (New Haven, 1966)
Simonov, K., *Glazami cheloveka moego pokoleniia* (Moscow, 1988)
Singer, D., *The Road to Gdańsk* (London, 1981)
Skilling, H. Gordon, *Czechoslovakia's Interrupted Revolution* (Princeton, N. J., 1976)
Charter 77 and Human Rights in Czechoslovakia (London, 1981)
Skórzyński, J., *Ugoda i Rewolucja. Władza i Opozycja 1985–1989* (Warsaw, 1995)

Smoleński, P., *A na hucie strajk* ... (Warsaw, 1988); reprinted in *Robotnicy '88* (London, 1989)

Społeczeństwo i władza lat osiemdziesiątych w badaniach CBOS (Warsaw, 1994)

Stalin, J. V., *Sochineniya*, vol. XI (Moscow, 1949)

Stan wojenny w Polsce. Kalendarium wydarzeń 13 X11 1981 – 31 X11 1982 (Warsaw, 1999)

Stelmachowski, A., *Kształtowanie się ustroju 111 Rzeczypospolitej* (Warsaw, 1998)

Stoła, D., *Kampania antysyjonistyczna w Polsce 1967–1968* (Warsaw, 2000)

Sto sorok besed S Molotovym. Iz dnevnika F Chueva (Moscow, 1991)

Stromseth, J., *The Origins of Flexible Response. NATO's Debate over Strategy in the 1960s* (New York, 1988)

Suleja, W., *Dolnośląski Marzec '68. Anatomia protestu* (Warsaw, 2006)

Suraska, W., *How the Soviet Union Disappeared* (Durham, N.C., 1998)

Suri, J., *Power and Protest: Global Revolution and the Rise of Détente* (Cambridge, Mass., 2003)

Swayze, H., *Political Control of Literature in the USSR, 1946–1959* (Cambridge, Mass., 1962)

Swidlicki, A., *Political Trials in Poland, 1981–1986* (London, 1988)

Szajkowski, B., *Next to God ... Poland. Politics and Religion in Contemporary Poland* (London, 1983)

Taubman, W., *Khrushchev. The Man and his Era* (New York, 2003)

Taubman, W., *et al.* (eds.), *Nikita Khrushchev and the Creation of a Superpower* (University Park, Pa., 2000)

Thatcher, M., *The Downing Street Years* (London, 1993)

The Anti-Stalin Campaign and International Communism (New York, 1956)

The Book of Lech Wałęsa (London, 1982)

The Conferences at Cairo–Tehran, 1943, Foreign Relations of the United States (Washington, 1961)

The Soviet–Yugoslav Dispute. Text of the Published Correspondence (London, 1948)

The Trade Union Situation in the USSR (Geneva, 1960)

Thomas, D., *The Helsinki Effect: International Norms, Human Rights, and the Demise of Communism* (Princeton, N.J., 2001)

Tighe, C., *Gdańsk. National Identity in the Polish–German Borderlands* (London, 1990)

Tinguy, A. de, *US–Soviet Relations During the Détente* (New York, 1999)

Tischler, J., *Rewolucja węgierska 1956 w polskich dokumentach* (Warsaw, 1995)

Tischner, J., *Polski kształt dialogu* (Kraków, 1980)

Etyka Solidarności (Kraków, 1981; Paris, 1982)

Tismaneanu, V., *Gheorghiu-Dej and the Romanian Workers Party: From De-Sovietization to the Emergence of National Communism*, CWIHP Working Paper no. 7 (Washington, 2002)

Torańska, T., *Oni. Stalin's Polish Puppets* (London, 1987)

Truman, H., *Memoirs: Years of Trial and Hope* (New York, 1965)

Tucker, Robert C., *The Soviet Political Mind*, revised edn (New York, 1972)

Tucker, Robert C. (ed.), *Stalinism: Essays in Historical Interpretation* (New York, 1977)

Tymowski, A., *Próba określenia minimum spożycia* (Warsaw, 1971)

Ulam, A., *Dangerous Relations. The Soviet Union in World Politics, 1970–1982* (Oxford, 1983)
Vamos, P., *Evolution and Revolution: Sino-Hungarian Relations and the 1956 Revolution*, CWIHP Working Paper no. 54 (Washington, 2006)
Volkogonov, D., *Lenin: A New Biography* (New York, 1994)
Walicki, A., 'Three Traditions in Polish Patriotism' in S. Gomułka and A. Polonsky (eds.), *Polish Paradoxes* (London, 1990)
Waligóra, G., *Ruch Obrony Praw Człowieka i Obywatela, 1977–1981* (Warsaw, 2006)
Wałęsa, L., *A Path of Hope* (London, 1987)
Wedel, J. (ed.), *The Unplanned Society* (New York, 1992)
Westad, O. A., *The Global Cold War: Third World Interventions and the Making of our Times* (Cambridge, 2005)
Windsor, P., *City on Leave. A History of Berlin, 1948–1962* (London, 1963)
Windsor, P. and Roberts, A., *Czechoslovakia 1968. Reform, Repression and Resistance* (London, 1969)
Zaremba, M., 'Opinia publiczna w Polsce wobec choroby i śmierci Józefa Stalina' in A. Friszke (ed.), *Władza a społeczeństwo w PRL* (Warsaw, 2003)
Zawieyski, J., *Kartki z dziennika, 1955–1969* (Warsaw, 1983)
Zielonka, Z., *Political Ideas in Contemporary Poland* (Aldershot, 1989)
Znaniecki, F., *The Social Role of the Man of Knowledge* (New York, 1940)
Zubkova, E., *Russia After the War. Hopes, Illusions, and Disappointments, 1945–1957* (New York, 1998)
Zubok, V., *Soviet Intelligence and the Cold War: The 'Small' Committee of Information, 1952–53*, CWIHP Working Paper no. 4 (Washington, 1992)
Zubok, V. and Pleshakov, C., *Inside the Kremlin's Cold War: From Stalin to Khrushchev* (Cambridge, Mass., 1966)
Zuzowski, R., *The Workers' Defence Committee KOR* (New York, 1992)
Żabicki, Z., *'Kuźnica' i jej program literacki* (Kraków, 1966)

AUDIOVISUAL MATERIAL

Polska Kronika Filmowa (Warsaw) Weekly official newsreel
Struggles for Poland (Peterborough, UK) Channel 4 series
Tape 2. *Occupation, 1939–1945*; *Friends and neighbours, 1939–1945*; *Bright days of tomorrow, 1945–1956*
Tape 3. *The sweepers of squares, 1956–1970*; *The eagle and the cross, 1900–1981*; *The workers' state, 1970–1980.*

Index